THE REGULATION OF TOXIC SUBSTANCES AND HAZARDOUS WASTES

SECOND EDITION

by

JOHN S. APPLEGATE
Walter W. Foskett Professor of Law
Indiana University Maurer School of Law
Vice President for University Regional Affairs, Planning, and Policy
Indiana University

JAN G. LAITOS
John A. Carver, Jr., Professor of Law
University of Denver Sturm College of Law

JEFFREY M. GABA
Professor of Law
Southern Methodist University Dedman School of Law

NOAH M. SACHS
Associate Professor of Law
University of Richmond School of Law

FOUNDATION PRESS
2011

THOMSON REUTERS™

© 2000 FOUNDATION PRESS

© 2011 By THOMSON REUTERS/FOUNDATION PRESS

      1 New York Plaza, 34th Floor

      New York, NY 10004

      Phone Toll Free 1–877–888–1330

      Fax 646–424–5201

      foundation–press.com

Printed in the United States of America

ISBN 978–1–59941–233–7

Mat #40543596

For Amy
J.S.A.

For Carrie
J.G.L.

For Thelma and Morton
J.M.G.

*To Roberta, Adam, and Claudia, and to my great-
great-grandfather Louis Lewin (1850–1929), a
pioneer of modern toxicology*
N.M.S.

PREFACE

Environmental law has expanded dramatically since the early 1970s, from a few major federal statutes to a sprawling field involving local, state, federal, and international issues and complex scientific and economic debates. The Clean Air Act alone is said to be the second most complicated statute in American law (after the Internal Revenue Code). Students interested in careers in environmental law, or those who just want to learn more about it, therefore need materials that go into greater depth than is possible in an introductory environmental law course.

This casebook provides an in-depth look at one area of environmental law, toxic substances and hazardous wastes. The laws in this field are primarily designed to protect human health from toxic agents. The high stakes involved and the billions of dollars spent every year on implementation make this field highly controversial. A fundamental function of government is to protect citizens from harm, but there is widespread disagreement on how to measure risk, how to manage it, how much we should spend to address it, and which level of government should take the lead role. Scientists play a crucial role in the implementation of these laws. They also serve as expert witnesses in private litigation over toxic hazards. But there are major disagreements about how scientific advice should interact with the regulatory process and about the extent to which scientific opinion should be balanced or supplemented with input from community groups and laypeople.

Policymakers and legal scholars have been debating these issues in the decades since the statutes governing toxic chemicals were enacted in the 1970s. But regulation of toxic substances and hazardous wastes has also changed dramatically in recent years due to the rise of new technologies, whole new industries, and advances in toxicology and risk assessment. Additionally, this field has changed because of broader trends in regulation and administrative law, particularly the rise of cost-benefit analysis and the increasing litigiousness of American society.

Since the first edition of this casebook in 2000, there have been major developments in the courts, in Congress, and in the regulatory agencies. These developments call for a fresh look at this fast-evolving field. Congress has enacted a new statute to protect brownfields developers from liability, for example, and the Supreme Court has issued decisions regarding pesticide regulation and hazardous waste clean-up liability. This second edition highlights recent developments, traces the long history of this field, explores the major statutes, and provides perspective on how this field affects our daily lives. It crosses disciplinary boundaries and shows how politics, policy, science, and economics interact to shape this crucial component of American environmental law.

We have tried to be comprehensive in this book. All significant aspects of the subject are covered to some degree, and instructors will be able to use all or part of this casebook, depending on interest and available time. This casebook is intended to be useful as a first course in environmental law or for advanced, specialized study. We have shortened the casebook considerably since the first edition to make it possible to cover the entire book in a semester, if the instructor chooses.

Students should be able to use the book as a learning tool and as a jumping off point for further investigation. While there is much diversity in this area of environmental law, it is bound together by the common problem of managing risks from chemicals. In writing this book, we have sought to emphasize, therefore, both the common problems and the multiplicity of regulatory responses to toxics.

The casebook begins with a review of the foundations—scientific, political, and economic—on which the law of toxic substances and hazardous wastes has been built. It then proceeds statute by statute, stressing the major "life cycle" statutes that students will most often see in practice, but also covering a variety of other statutes that present different approaches to toxics regulation. While we recognize the interactions and overlap among the several statutes, we are also firmly committed to the view that each statute has its own internal structure and integrity. There are many cross-cutting issues, of course, but we have chosen not to organize the presentation around them. Rather, we encourage the reader to compare and contrast the different regulatory approaches to analogous issues. This casebook also explores major new directions in toxics regulation—primarily alternatives to traditional "end-of-pipe" standard setting—which, we believe, will become more important with each passing year.

Our aim is to provide a multifaceted look at the way that the law of toxic substances and hazardous waste has developed. Like most casebooks, the text contains both primary substantive materials and materials that comment or expand on the primary materials. The primary materials consist of text written by the authors and of cases, legislative and administrative materials, and excerpts of secondary sources. In some cases, we felt that subjects were better handled by direct exposition than by derivation from other sources. Following each primary source, we add notes and questions, long and short problems, summary materials, and case studies. It is our hope that this presentation will both improve comprehension of often complex material and provide the basis for lively classroom discussion. The questions we ask are not intended to be rhetorical; an effective class (and effective class preparation) can be based on them.

The longest chapters in this book address RCRA and CERCLA. We recognize that many instructors will choose to emphasize these statutes in their courses. We provide an overview of these statutes largely in our own words, and the chapters are comprehensive. The student is invited to engage with the material through the examples and problems provided, instead of the usual case analysis. In Chapters 3 and 4, we use FIFRA,

TSCA, FFDCA, OSHA, and other statutes to explore broader issues of regulatory policy, such as cost-benefit analysis and regulation in the face of scientific uncertainty. The notes identify key issues in the main readings, place them in the context of other materials in the book, and present discussable problems.

To make effective use of the text, instructors and students will need to refer regularly to a current version of the environmental statutes covered in the book, such as may be found in West's *Selected Environmental Law Statutes*. The text often requires students to read the statute itself and to answer questions about it, unaided by detailed summaries or explanations. We believe that this is an essential skill for environmental lawyers. For the same reason, we usually refer to statutes by their statutory section number rather than the U.S. Code section number. Most courts follow this convention, and it better expresses the relationship among parts of a statute. Since West's statutory compilation conveniently references both sets of numbers, students should experience little difficulty with this arrangement, once it has been brought to their attention.

*

Acknowledgments

We owe a large debt of gratitude to many people and institutions who have helped in many ways in the production of the second edition of this book. John Applegate thanks Dean Lauren Robel and the Indiana University Maurer School of Law for encouragement and support; President Michael McRobbie; and research assistants CR Davis, Byron Graw, Angela King, Wen–Hsiang Kung, Jennifer Mueller, Nancy Rachlis, Mick Pettersen, Matt Wallace, and Rochelle Warren. Jan Laitos thanks Theann Kennebeck, Jennifer Kingsbury, Amanda Becker, and, of course, Alyson Gould. Jeffrey Gaba thanks Dean John Attanasio and the SMU Dedman School of Law for their encouragement and support. Noah Sachs thanks Dean John Douglass, the University of Richmond School of Law faculty, and research assistant Carla Pool. And we all want to thank our editor, Mary Spohn, and the very patient and accommodating staff of Foundation Press. The Rocky Mountain Mineral Law Foundation through its Grants Committee provided generous financial support, for which we are very grateful.

Last, but not least, each of us would like to thank our families—Amy, Jesse, Jamey, and Gillian Applegate; Erik Laitos; Brenda, Matthew, and Jacob Gaba; and Roberta, Adam, and Claudia Sachs—for their support along the sometimes arduous trail toward completion of this project. They are the true foundation on which this book was built.

*

Editing Conventions

In editing the excerpts that are reprinted in this book, we have followed several general editing practices. We have tried to retain the substance and style of the original works, while presenting only that which is needed to convey the relevant point. To the extent that our editing has distorted or weakened the original work, we apologize in advance to the affected authors.

Specifically, we have eliminated without indication most footnotes, both substantive and citation, and most textual citation material. In some cases, we have reformatted citations to conform to the book's style or for brevity. Our additions to quoted materials are indicated by brackets in text and by "-EDS." in footnotes. Footnotes in quoted excerpts are renumbered to conform to the numbering in the chapter of this text. The form of headings in quoted excerpts has been standardized in some cases, and occasionally deleted where the organization was otherwise clear. Our deletions are indicated by starred ellipses (* * *); deletions in the original are indicated with periods (...).

COPYRIGHT PERMISSIONS

Rapid City Journal

> The Associated Press, North Dakota Gravel Sparks Cancer Fears, Rapid City Journal, April 6, 2008. Copyright © The Rapid City Journal, Reprinted with Permission from The Rapid City Journal, Rapid City, South Dakota.

American Bar Association Journal

> DNA Poised to Show its Civil Side, ABA Journal, March 2008. Copyright © The American Bar Association Journal, Reprinted with Permission from the American Bar Association, Chicago, Ill.

New Jersey Record

> Jan Barry, Families Sue Ford Over Waste Dumping, New Jersey Record, Jan. 19, 2006. Copyright © NorthJersey.com, Reprinted with Permission from NorthJersey.com, New Jersey.

Chapter 3

Environmental Law Institute

> David Roe, Toxic Chemical Control Policy: Three Unabsorbed Facts, 32 Envtl. L. Rep. 10232 (2002). Copyright © 2002 Environmental Law Institute®, Washington, DC. Reprinted with permission from ELR®.

Chapter 4

Elsevier Limited

> Jerry Cooper & Hans Dobson, The Benefits of Pesticides to Mankind and the Environment, 26 Crop Protection 1337 (2007).

Houghton Mifflin Harcourt

> Excerpts from SILENT SPRING by Rachel Carson. Copyright © 1962 by Rachel Carson. Copyright © renewed 1990 by Roger Christie. Reprinted by permission of Houghton Mifflin Harcourt Publishing Company. All Rights Reserved.

Vanderbilt Law Review

> Noah M. Sachs, Jumping the Pond: Transnational Law and the Future of Chemical Regulation, 62 Vanderbilt Law Review 1817, 1864–67 (2009).

Chapter 5

Fordham Environmental Law Review and Carlton Waterhouse

> Carlton Waterhouse, Abandon All Hope Ye that Enter? Equal Protection, Title VI, and the Divine Comedy of Environmental Justice, 20 Fordham Envtl. L. Rev. 51 (2009). Copyright © 2009. Reprinted with permission of the Fordham Environmental Law Review.

Chapter 6

Environmental Law Institute

> Jeffrey M. Gaba, United States v. Atlantic Research: The Supreme Court Almost Gets It Right, 37 ELR 10810 (2007). Copyright © The Environmental Law Institute®, Washington DC, Reprinted with permission from ELR®.

The San Francisco Chronicle

> Peter Fimrite, Inside the Belly of the Beast: Redding's Toxic Hellhole, San Francisco Chronicle, Aug. 29, 2010, page 1. Copyright © 2010, San Francisco Chronicle, San Francisco, California. Reprinted with permissions from the San Francisco Chronicle.

GLOSSARY OF ACRONYMS

ALARA	as low as is reasonably achievable
ALJ	Administrative Law Judge
APA	Administrative Procedure Act
ARAR	applicable or relevant and appropriate requirement
BAT	best available technology
BDAT	best demonstrated available technology
BIF	boiler and industrial furnace
CAA	Clean Air Act
CAB	citizens advisory board
CAMU	corrective action management unit
CBA	cost-benefit analysis
CDC	Centers for Disease Control
CEG	conditionally exempt generator
CEQ	Council on Environmental Quality
CERCLA	Comprehensive Environmental Response, Compensation, and Liability Act
CERCLIS	Comprehensive Environmental Response, Compensation, and Liability Information System
CFC	chlorofluorocarbon
CGL	comprehensive general liability
CRA	comparative risk assessment
CV	contingent valuation
CWA	Clean Water Act
DDT	dichloro-diphenyl-trichloro-ethane
DOI	Department of the Interior
DOJ	Department of Justice
DOT	Department of Transportation
EDF	Environmental Defense Fund
EPA	U.S. Environmental Protection Agency
EPCRA	Emergency Planning and Community Right-to-Know Act
ETS	emergency temporary standard
FDA	Food and Drug Administration
FFDCA	Federal Food, Drug, and Cosmetic Act (also FD & C Act)
FIFRA	Federal Insecticide, Fungicide, and Rodenticide Act
FQPA	Food Quality Protection Act
FWPCA	Federal Water Pollution Control Act (Clean Water Act)
GAO	Government Accountability Office (*formerly* General Accounting Office)
GCP	Generic Cancer Policy

HAP   hazardous air pollutant
HRS   Hazard Ranking System
HWIR   Hazardous Waste Identification Rule
HWSA   Hazardous and Solid Waste Amendments of 1984
IAG   interagency agreement
IARC   International Agency for Research on Cancer
IPM   integrated pest management
IRIS   Integrated Risk Information System
ITC   Interagency Testing Committee

LDR   land disposal restriction
LEPC   local emergency planning commission
LOAEL   lowest observed adverse effects level
LQG   large quantity generator

MACT   maximum achievable control technology
MCL   maximum contaminant level
MCLG   maximum contaminant level goal
μg   microgram
mg   milligram
MOA   memorandum of agreement
MSDS   material safety data sheet

NAAQS   national ambient air quality standard
NAS   National Academy of Sciences
NBAR   nonbinding preliminary allocation of responsibility
NCI   National Cancer Institute
NCP   National Contingency Plan
NEPA   National Environmental Policy Act
NESHAP   national emission standard for hazardous air pollutants
NIOSH   National Institute for Occupational Safety and Health
NOAEL   no observed adverse effects level
NPL   National Priorities List
NRD   natural resource damages
NRDC   Natural Resources Defense Council
NSPS   new source performance standard

OIRA   Office of Information and Regulatory Affairs
OMB   Office of Management and Budget
OSHA   Occupational Safety and Health Administration
OSHAct   Occupational Safety and Health Act

PA/SI   preliminary assessment/site investigation
PCB   polychlorinated biphenyl
PEL   permissible exposure limit
PIC   prior informed consent
PMN   pre-manufacture notification
POTW   publicly owned treatment works
PP   proposed plan
PPA   Pollution Prevention Act
ppb   parts per billion

ppm	parts per million
ppq	parts per quadrillion
PRP	potentially responsible party
PTSD	post-traumatic stress disorder
PVC	polyvinyl chloride
QRA	quantitative risk assessment
RCRA	Resource Conservation and Recovery Act
RD/RA	remedial design/remedial action
RFA	RCRA facility assessment
RfD	reference dose
RI/FS	remedial investigation/feasibility study
RME	reasonable maximum exposure
ROD	record of decision
RQ	reportable quantity
SARA	Superfund Amendments and Reauthorization Act
SDWA	Safe Drinking Water Act
SQG	small quantity generator
SWDA	Solid Waste Disposal Act
SWMU	solid waste management unit
TCE	tricholorethylene
TCLP	toxicity characteristic leaching procedure
TLV	threshold limit value
TMDL	total maximum daily load
TPQ	threshold planning quantity
TRI	Toxic Release Inventory
TSCA	Toxic Substances Control Act
TSDF	treatment, storage, and disposal facility
UCATA	Uniform Contribution Among Tortfeasors Act
UCC	Uniform Commercial Code
UCFA	Uniform Comparative Fault Act
UMTRCA	Uranium Mill Tailings Radiation Control Act
USDA	U.S. Department of Agriculture
USGS	United States Geological Survey
UST	underground storage tank
VOC	volatile organic compound

SUMMARY OF CONTENTS

TABLE OF CONTENTS

TABLE OF PRINCIPAL CASES

THE REGULATION OF TOXIC SUBSTANCES AND HAZARDOUS WASTES

CHAPTER 1

THE ANALYTICAL BASICS

A. Risk Assessment

    1. Introduction to Chemical Toxicity

        Rodricks, *Calculated Risks: The Toxicity and Human Health Risks of Chemicals in Our Environment*

    2. The Risk Assessment Process

        National Research Council, *Risk Assessment in the Federal Government: Managing the Process*

        a. Hazard Identification

        b. Dose–Response Assessment

        c. Exposure Assessment

        d. Risk Characterization

            Presidential/Congressional Commission, *Risk Assessment and Risk Management in Regulatory Decision–Making*

    3. The Risk Assessment Data Gap

        U.S. Government Accountability Office, *Chemical Assessments: Low Productivity and New Interagency Review Process Limit the Usefulness and Credibility of EPA's Integrated Risk Information System*

        Lyndon, *Information Economics and Chemical Toxicity: Designing Laws to Produce and Use Data*

B. Risk Management

    Presidential/Congressional Commission, *Risk Assessment and Risk Management in Regulatory Decision–Making*

    1. Risk Perception and Risk Management

        Slovic and Weber, *Perception of Risk Posed by Extreme Events*

    2. The Risk Management Toolbox

    3. The Precautionary Principle

        Schroeder, *Perspective on the Precautionary Principle*

Bailey, *A Precautionary Tale*

C.   Cost–Benefit Analysis

Office of Management and Budget, *Circular A–4*

Revesz and Livermore, *Retaking Rationality: How Cost–Benefit Analysis Can Better Protect the Environment and Our Health*

Ackerman and Heinzerling, *Priceless: On Knowing the Price of Everything and the Value of Nothing*

In 2005, the U.S. chemical industry produced or imported about 27 trillion pounds of chemicals, or over 73 billion pounds of chemicals per day. These chemicals are the raw materials that are used to make our cars, electronics, homes, medicines, plastics, clothing, packaging, and other goods. Chemicals are also routinely released into the environment as byproducts of manufacturing and electricity generation. In 2008, U.S. industries released 3.86 billion pounds of toxic chemicals into air, water, and land in the United States, according to the Environmental Protection Agency (EPA).

For the vast majority of chemicals, we lack basic data on their health and environmental impacts. Are we adrift in a sea of toxic chemicals that are harming human health and the ecosystems on which we depend, or is this just "chemophobia," a largely irrational fear of certain kinds of chemicals, especially those that may cause cancer? What are the real risks associated with toxic substances and hazardous wastes? How are risks measured and how does the law address these risks? Are bans and phase-outs the most effective and efficient tools for managing toxic and hazardous substances, or should we adopt more fine-tuned legal controls?

This casebook addresses these questions and more. In this initial chapter, we discuss how policymakers measure and manage the risks from toxic substances. In subsequent chapters, we consider the role of the judiciary in overseeing tort litigation over toxic risks and in reviewing the regulatory activities of the EPA and other federal agencies. We also proceed, statute by statute, to analyze the federal regulatory structures that govern toxic substances and hazardous wastes.

It is impossible to convey succinctly the breadth of the subject of toxic substance and hazardous waste regulation, or to describe all the concerns that inspired the regulatory regime (really, many regimes) that this book documents. This field ranges from the question of how to clean up industrial solvents discarded in the nineteenth century to the question of how to regulate the brand new field of nanotechnology (engineered microscopic substances used in sunscreens, fabrics, and industrial materials). Even an apple at your local supermarket is subject to federal toxics statutes (governing pesticide residues on food). We will examine the laws that govern introduction of new chemicals and pesticides, regulations that govern how hazardous wastes should be managed and stored, and the system of liability rules that governs clean-up of hazardous substances.

Almost all the statutes explored in this book address four central questions:

1. How do we measure the risks from toxic substances and hazardous wastes?

2. How should we proceed when science cannot provide definitive information about those risks?

3. What regulatory or technological tools are available to protect public health and the environment, assuming we choose to act?

4. How should we make trade-offs between the benefits of risk reduction and the costs we impose through regulation?

This chapter begins with sections on risk assessment and risk management, which are the subjects of the first three questions above. It then shifts to a section on cost-benefit analysis, which is the subject of question four above. Cost-benefit analysis is frequently used to decide whether a risk is worth regulating and which risk management approach to adopt. These are the analytical tools that scientists and regulators use in the field of toxic substances and hazardous wastes. By exploring these tools, this chapter will provide you with the foundation you will need to understand the statutes described in later chapters in this book.

A. RISK ASSESSMENT

The first steps in any regulatory program for toxic substances and hazardous wastes are identifying substances that may harm human health, the specific adverse effects that they cause, and the quantities in which they have such effects. This is the science of risk assessment.

Nearly all chemicals can be toxic, in the sense of producing adverse effects, if given in high enough doses. Therefore, there is no firm dividing line between "toxic" and "non-toxic" substances. When we use the term toxic substances in this book, we are referring to substances that can have adverse effects on human health in small doses, such as an ounce or less given to an adult of average weight.

Toxicity differs from risk. *Risk* is simply the probability that a harmful effect will occur. In this field of law, risk can be viewed as a function of both the intrinsic hazards of a substance and the likely exposure to that substance. It is the probability that a harmful effect will be produced under actual conditions of exposure. Risk assessment combines the study of toxicity information (the identification of chemical hazards and their potency) with the study of how humans are exposed to these hazards (exposure pathways and exposure amounts).

A formal risk assessment aims to generate a quantitative estimate of the severity of a risk to human health, to other species, or to ecosystems. For example, a risk assessment might aim to calculate the number of excess cancers that will occur in a population if it is exposed to a specified dose of a toxic chemical. A risk assessment might also aim to calculate whether there is a safe exposure level for a chemical below which there is no observable effect on human health. In hazardous waste remediation, risk assessors calculate the risk to human health and to wildlife from contaminated soils or sediments as well as the risk reduction that would occur through various clean-up options.

1. INTRODUCTION TO CHEMICAL TOXICITY

To begin to understand how regulators and scientists conduct risk assessment, it is important to understand how chemicals can adversely affect the health of humans and other species. One of the central precepts of toxicology is that "the dose makes the poison." That is, chemicals have different effects, including beneficial effects, in different amounts. Toxicologists distinguish among three types of harmful effects of chemicals: acute (or fast), chronic (slow), and carcinogenic (cancer-causing). The same chemical can have all three effects, depending on the dose. At relatively high doses, arsenic has its famous lethal effect; at lower doses (i.e., not immediately fatal doses) it affects eyesight, the peripheral nervous system, and the vascular system; and at lower doses still, where the exposure is not even noticed, it can cause cancer.

The acute effects of a chemical substance are the ones we most commonly associate with poisons. Because acute effects appear quickly after exposure, it is usually easy to identify both the causative substance and the physical effect: illness, death, or other dysfunction.

While acute toxicity is usually associated with obvious illnesses (including, but not limited to, death), chronic toxicity alters some aspect of an organism's metabolism or bodily system, which may go unnoticed or which might be quite harmful or painful. Chronic effects may include neurotoxicity, organ damage, and reproductive toxicity. Air pollution, for example, may be chronically toxic to the lungs, causing asthma or emphysema, after many years of exposure. Another chronic effect, emerging as a concern for regulators, is endocrine disruption. Endocrine disruption refers to the ability of chemicals to mimic human hormones and block, or sometimes over-activate, hormonal signals to the brain, glands, and reproductive organs.

Many chemicals have carcinogenic effects. For some regulatory programs, such as the Superfund program governing clean-up of hazardous waste sites, carcinogenic effects are the dominant concern of regulators. Carcinogenic chemicals often produce visible tumors, and carcinogenic effects are therefore usually easier to identify and measure compared to chronic effects such as neurotoxicity or endocrine disruption.

The generic term "cancer" covers over 100 diseases of different organs and systems of the human body. The principal characteristic of cancer is the abnormal, apparently unconstrained, proliferation of cells: "mitosis run amuck."[1] These cells invade neighboring tissues or, in the case of metastases, invade tissues in a wholly separate part of the body. Cancerous

---

1. SANDRA STEINGRABER, LIVING DOWNSTREAM: AN ECOLOGIST LOOKS AT CANCER AND THE ENVIRONMENT 241 (1997). This book is an excellent introduction to the scientific and human dimensions of cancer.

cells can be found in discrete tumors or in systems like the blood. Usually, cancerous structures and neighboring tissues can no longer function properly; if unchecked, this can lead to death.

While cancer has been known from the earliest times, it was only in 1775 that the idea of chemical induction of cancer was suggested by British physician Percival Potts, who noticed the association between soot and the high rates of scrotal cancer among London chimney sweeps. One question that Potts was unable to answer is how much soot would be required to induce cancer in a chimney sweep. Would exposure to a single particle of soot be sufficient, or would it take several years of working in chimneys to cause cancer?

Dose-response curves help scientists understand the relationship between the amount of a carcinogen (or other type of chemical) and adverse effects on humans or other species. One of the major debates in risk assessment is whether there is a *threshold* below which exposure to a substance will have no adverse effects. If there is no threshold, then *any* exposure to a toxic substance, even in minute amounts, could potentially cause some damage to the human body.

Calculated Risks: The Toxicity and Human Health Risks of Chemicals in Our Environment

Joseph V. Rodricks
pp. 151–153, 160–161 (2d ed. 2007)

It seems pretty clear that the initiating event [for cancer] is brought about when the chemical carcinogen . . . reaches a cell's nucleus and chemically reacts with DNA, the genetic material. This reaction constitutes DNA damage, an unwelcome event because this magnificent molecule controls the life of the cell and the integrity of its reproduction. Fortunately, cells have a tremendous capacity to repair DNA damage; these repair mechanisms have been at work probably since life began to evolve, because most types of cells are constantly being assaulted by DNA-damaging radiation and chemicals from many natural sources. If some of the damage is not repaired, and this happens because repair is not 100% efficient, and the cell undergoes replication when the damage is present, then the damage is passed on to the new cells, and can become permanent—a *mutation* has occurred. * * *

The ultimate neoplasm is thus a population of cells that arises from a single cell, what biologists refer to as a population of *clones*, which have expanded in numbers. The monoclonal origin of cancers is suggested by many studies of human and animal cancers.

This broad picture is considered pretty accurate by most cancer experts. Multiple stages are involved. They take place at different rates, and whether and at what rate they occur depends on many factors, including at least:

1) The concentration over time of the initiating carcinogenic chemical (typically a metabolite) at the cellular target.

2) The presence of chemicals, which might be the carcinogen itself, its metabolites or even some other chemical—including some normal dietary components—that may restrict or enhance conversion or development at several different points in the process.

3) The influence of host factors, including cellular genetics and factors such as the host's hormonal and immune systems, that may either restrict or enhance neoplastic conversion or development.

What emerges here is a picture in which the carcinogenic process is influenced by a fairly long list of factors, and is either aided or inhibited by those factors. When we administer a chemical to lab animals and count tumors at the end of their lives, we are observing only two points, and not particularly interesting points, connected by a long sequence of molecular and cellular events. * * *

Initiating events involve gene damage and this may result in the fixation in the cell's genetic material of a permanent abnormality. This feature of carcinogenesis perhaps makes it different in kind from most other forms of toxicity [such as skin irritation, liver damage, or respiratory damage, EDS.]. Here the chemical insult occurs and the damage it produces remains in cells even if exposure to the insulting chemical ceases. If doses of the genotoxic agent keep piling up, so do the numbers of those permanent changes. This rather frightening picture is made less so when we recall that cells have a tremendous capacity to repair DNA damage before it becomes fixed, so that not every damaging event, in fact perhaps only a tiny fraction of them, actually translates to a mutation, and only a small fraction of mutations will likely occur at sites that are critical for the development of cancer.

One implication of this view of initiation—and an exceedingly important one—is expressed in the "no-threshold" hypothesis for carcinogens. Any amount of a DNA damaging chemical that reaches its target (the DNA) can increase the probability of converting a cell to a neoplastic state.

This does not mean that every such event will *cause* a neoplastic conversion, but only that the *probability*, or *risk*, of that occurrence becomes greater than zero as soon as the effective target-site concentration of the gene-damaging chemical is reached, and that the risk increases with increasing target-site concentration. * * *

Actually, the notion that human cancers might result from exceedingly small doses arose first in connection with radiation-induced malignancies. In the 1950s E.B. Lewis of the California Institute of Technology proposed, based on studies of leukemia rates among Japanese atomic bomb survivors and cancer rates among radiologists, that cancer risks might exist at all doses greater than zero, and that a linear dose-response relation is to be expected.

NOTES AND QUESTIONS

1. *Thresholds.* As discussed by Rodricks, risk assessors usually adopt the so-called "Linear No Threshold" model for carcinogens. This model suggests, first, that the relationship between a dose of a carcinogen and the probability of cancer is a linear one, and second, that there is no dose threshold below which we should consider the risk of cancer to be zero. However, other forms of toxicity are assumed to have a threshold. For example, high consumption of alcohol over many years is needed to cause cirrhosis of the liver. Some scientists believe that thresholds do exist for carcinogens as well. Nevertheless, EPA and other agencies that conduct risk assessments generally assume that a threshold does *not* exist for carcinogens. Why would they make that assumption? Why is the no-threshold hypothesis sometimes called a "one-hit" theory?

2. *Setting regulatory standards.* Many regulations governing toxic substances and hazardous waste set a numeric standard for how much chemical exposure will be considered acceptable. For instance, EPA sets allowable pesticide residue levels for fruits and vegetables sold to consumers. The Occupational Safety and Health Administration (OSHA) sets permissible exposure limits for workers using hazardous substances. By setting a numeric standard, these agencies are asserting, implicitly, that any concentration or exposure below this level is "safe" (or at least legally permissible), and any concentration or exposure above this level is "unsafe" (or at least prohibited by law). Do such legal bright lines make sense when we are talking about the impacts of chemicals on diverse subpopulations of Americans? Given the difficulty of determining whether a threshold exists for cancer, how should such standards be set for potential carcinogens? Should the EPA and OSHA seek to prevent all human exposure to carcinogens, and if so, how?

3. *Cancer incidence and cancer death rates.* The incidence of cancer in the United States rose 49.3 percent between 1950 and 1991. Sandra Steingraber, Living Downstream 40 (1997). Since chemical production and use also grew dramatically after World War II, many people have linked high cancer rates with chemical exposures. But cancer incidence has been declining recently, at an average annual rate of 1.1% per year between 1999 and 2006. National Cancer Institute, Cancer Statistics Review, 1975–2006 (updated January 2010). Countering this good news, cancer incidence among children climbed slightly between 1975 and 2006. What might be causing these trends?

While scientists have confirmed that numerous chemicals are capable of causing cancer in the human body, it is much more difficult to determine the percentage of all cancers in the United States attributable to pollutants in the environment. In a 1996 study of death rates, epidemiologists concluded that about 2 percent of cancer deaths can be attributed to environmental pollution.[2] In 2010, however, the President's Cancer Panel released a major report that criticized the longstanding use of the 2 percent estimate as "woefully out of date." It concluded that the "true burden of environmentally induced cancer has been grossly underestimated."[3] The American Cancer Society takes the position that while environmental pollutants contribute to cancer, most cancers are caused by lifestyle factors—such as smoking, alcohol use, sun exposure, and obesity—and that prevention efforts should prioritize those areas.

It seems clear that focusing on cancers caused by air pollutants, occupational exposures to chemicals, food additives, and pesticides is only one piece of the overall picture of cancer in the United States. But even assuming that most cancers are caused by other factors, does it logically force the conclusion that environmental carcinogens are of little concern? Or does it suggest that we should act aggressively to control any cancer cause over which we have some influence?

————

Carcinogens share several characteristics that complicate both regulatory and judicial decision making. Some of the more important ones are summarized below:

> *Nontraceability.* * * * A few relatively unusual cancers are linked to specific substances. Mesothelioma, for example, is uniquely caused by asbestos, a fact that has simplified a number of actual cases. [Thus mesothelioma is called a *signature* effect of asbestos.] Unfortunately, the vast majority of cancers, and the most common cancers, may be caused by scores of different chemicals. When these cancers develop, it becomes virtually impossible to say with confidence which substance "caused" the cancer. It is even more difficult to determine that a certain substance played a given role at a specific stage of cancer development. Causes of cancer leave no "marker" in the body identifying the nature of their lethal role.

> * * *

> *Latency.* If cancer happened as suddenly as the Bhopal deaths from methyl isocyanate, it would be much easier to find the cause of certain cancers. Cancer, however, typically takes decades to develop from initiation to metastasis. Determining the source of any specific cancer therefore requires a historical search into exposures long past.

---

2. Dimitrios Trichopoulos *et al*, *What Causes Cancer?* SCIENTIFIC AMERICAN 81–87 (Sept. 1996) (concluding that smoking and high fat/low fiber diets cause a majority of cancer deaths in the United States). The 2 percent figure had been the accepted estimate of cancer death rates from pollutants since 1981, when that figure appeared in an influential study by Richard Doll and Richard Peto in the Journal of the National Cancer Institute. Doll & Peto, *The Causes of Cancer: Quantitative Estimates of Avoidable Risks of Cancer*, 66 J. OF THE NAT'L CANCER INST. 1191 (1981).

3. PRESIDENT'S CANCER PANEL, NATIONAL CANCER INSTITUTE, REDUCING ENVIRONMENTAL CANCER RISK: WHAT WE CAN DO NOW (April 2010).

* * *

Apparent Randomness. Science has revealed certain factors that contribute to cancer, ranging from environmental pollutants to genetic susceptibility. Yet it appears that none of these factors is certain to cause cancer, and it is very unusual that any factor even appears to make cancer more probable than not. Rather, exposure to current environmental cancer-inducing factors typically may create a 1 in 10,000 risk of cancer or less. Thus only about 1 out of 10,000 similarly situated persons will get cancer because of a given exposure. The very expression of this risk, in terms of odds, implies the seeming randomness of the cancer risk.

This is not to suggest that those individuals who actually contract cancer are simply unlucky. Cancer may one day prove to be entirely deterministic, with our present probabilities explained by the numerous biological interactions of the cancer development process or defined genetic characteristics of the cancer victim. Scientific knowledge, however, is decades away from establishing cancer causation with such deterministic precision. For now and the foreseeable future, the law must respond to a disease that strikes individuals with apparent randomness.

FRANK B. CROSS, ENVIRONMENTALLY INDUCED CANCER AND THE LAW: RISKS, REGULATION, AND VICTIM COMPENSATION 12–14 (1989).

Adding to the uncertainty of connecting any particular chemical exposure to cancer or other bodily harms is the problem of confounding factors. Confounding factors create a risk of the disease of interest and are also associated with the exposure of interest. For example, many workers who have a long history of exposure to asbestos through their jobs (in plumbing, ship building, auto repair etc.) are also heavy smokers. If they contract lung cancer, their smoking becomes a confounding factor in directly attributing the lung cancer to the asbestos inhalation.

The non-signature, latency, randomness, and relative rarity characteristics combine with the mechanism of carcinogenesis and potential confounding factors to make toxics regulation extraordinarily difficult. In tort law, courts generally require proof by a preponderance of the evidence that a defendant caused the harm alleged by the plaintiff. But in regulating toxic chemicals, we rarely can prove deterministically that a substance caused harm in a particular individual. The judgment regulators must make is instead *probabilistic*: they know only that there is a certain probability of cancer occurring when an individual (or a whole population) is exposed to a specified dose of a chemical.

Perhaps the single most important consequence of a probabilistic mechanism of chemical carcinogenesis is that it becomes difficult to label exposures as being "safe" or "unsafe." We can only label cancer danger in terms of risk probabilities. Complete safety, or "zero risk," is not regarded as a realistic goal for regulation. Therefore, the regulatory system must find a way to set the "acceptable" level of risk. These issues characterize toxics regulation, and, as we shall see, they pose its fundamental challenge.

2.   THE RISK ASSESSMENT PROCESS

A 1983 publication of the National Academy of Sciences (NAS), *Risk Assessment in the Federal Government: Managing the Process,* familiarly known as the Red Book, set out the form of risk assessment that has come to dominate environmental regulation today. In its present form, quantitative risk assessment is profoundly influenced by the problem of non-threshold carcinogens, and this in turn affects the ways in which we regulate such substances. After this excerpt, we will return to a more detailed discussion of each of the steps in the risk assessment process.

Risk Assessment in the Federal Government: Managing the Process

National Research Council[4]
pp. 18–28 (1983)

RISK ASSESSMENT AND RISK MANAGEMENT

We use *risk assessment* to mean the characterization of the potential adverse health effects of human exposures to environmental hazards. Risk assessments include several elements: description of the potential adverse health effects based on an evaluation of results of epidemiologic, clinical, toxicologic, and environmental research; extrapolation from those results to predict the type and estimate the extent of health effects in humans under given conditions of exposure; judgments as to the number and characteristics of persons exposed at various intensities and durations; and summary judgments on the existence and overall magnitude of the public-health problem. Risk assessment also includes characterization of the uncertainties inherent in the process of inferring risk. * * *

The Committee uses the term *risk management* to describe the process of evaluating alternative regulatory actions and selecting among them. Risk management, which is carried out by regulatory agencies under various legislative mandates, is an agency decision-making process that entails consideration of political, social, economic, and engineering information with risk-related information to develop, analyze, and compare regulatory options and to select the appropriate regulatory response to a potential chronic health hazard. The selection process necessarily requires the use of value judgments on such issues as the acceptability of risk and the reasonableness of the costs of control.

STEPS IN RISK ASSESSMENT

Risk assessment can be divided into four major steps: hazard identification, dose-response assessment, exposure assessment, and risk

---

4. The operating arm of the National Academy of Sciences is the National Research Council (NRC); consequently, the author of Academy reports is the Council.

characterization. A risk assessment might stop with the first step, hazard identification, if no adverse effect is found or if an agency elects to take regulatory action without further analysis, for reasons of policy or statutory mandate.

Of the four steps, *hazard identification* is the most easily recognized in the actions of regulatory agencies. It is defined here as the process of determining whether exposure to an agent can cause an increase in the incidence of a health condition (cancer, birth defect, etc.). * * *

Dose-response assessment is the process of characterizing the relation between the dose of an agent administered or received and the incidence of an adverse health effect in exposed populations and estimating the incidence of the effect as a function of human exposure to the agent. It takes account of intensity of exposure, age pattern of exposure, and possibly other variables that might affect response, such as sex, lifestyle, and other modifying factors. A dose-response assessment usually requires extrapolation from high to low dose and extrapolation from animals to humans. A dose-response assessment should describe and justify the methods of extrapolation used to predict incidence and should characterize the statistical and biologic uncertainties in these methods.

Exposure assessment is the process of measuring or estimating the intensity, frequency, and duration of human exposures to an agent currently present in the environment or of estimating hypothetical exposures that might arise from the release of new chemicals into the environment. In its most complete form, it describes the magnitude, duration, schedule, and route of exposure; the size, nature, and classes of the human populations exposed; and the uncertainties in all estimates. Exposure assessment is often used to identify feasible prospective control options and to predict the effects of available control technologies on exposure.

Risk characterization is the process of estimating the incidence of a health effect under the various conditions of human exposure described in exposure assessment. It is performed by combining the exposure and dose-response assessments. The summary effects of the uncertainties in the preceding steps are described in this step.

The relations among the four steps of risk assessment and between risk assessment and risk management are depicted in Figure 1.1. The type of research information needed for each step is also illustrated.

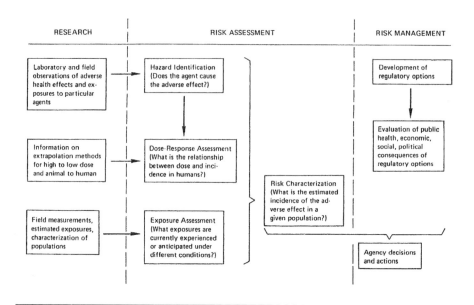

Figure 1.1–The Red Book Model

a.   HAZARD IDENTIFICATION

Hazard identification is the first step in the Red Book's risk assessment process. It answers the general causation question; Does Chemical X cause Effect Y? Without the causal finding, performing the remainder of the risk assessment would be pointless. Perhaps the best way to illustrate hazard identification, and to distinguish it from the related dose-response assessment, is to examine an actual study of the relationship between benzene and leukemia.[5]

Toxicology studies of various kinds (clinical observations, epidemiology, and animal bioassays) over several decades had suggested a causal association between benzene, a common industrial solvent, and certain cancers of the blood and lymphatic systems, notably leukemia. To clarify this relationship, a group of scientists at the National Institute for Occupational Safety and Health (NIOSH) undertook a retrospective epidemiological study of workers exposed to benzene. Their study was based on the recorded causes of death of workers at three Ohio plants that manufactured rubber film. The manufacturing process involved dissolving natural rubber in benzene, spreading it on a conveyor, and then evaporating and recovering the benzene, leaving a thin film of rubber. The workers at these plants were exposed to significant amounts of benzene (though usually within applicable legal limits), and their exposures had been closely followed by their

---

5.   Robert A. Rinsky *et al.*, *Benzene and Leukemia: An Epidemiologic Risk Assessment*, 316 NEW ENGLAND JOURNAL OF MEDICINE 1044 (1987).

The Rinsky study is a very important part of the regulation of toxic substances, because the data reported in it were part of the basis for the OSHA regulations that were overturned in the landmark Supreme Court case on toxics regulation, Industrial Union Department, AFL–CIO v. American Petroleum Institute, 448 U.S. 607 (1980) (it is reprinted in Chapter 3, *infra*), also known as the *Benzene* case.

employers for compliance purposes. As a result, these workers presented an unusually good opportunity to study the toxic effects of benzene on a human population.

In their initial pass through the data, Robert A. Rinsky and his colleagues compared the expected number and cause of deaths in the population as a whole, based on standard mortality patterns, with the number and cause of deaths in the worker population that was studied. Their results are summarized below:

Table 1. Observed and Expected Deaths from All Causes, All Malignant Neoplasms, and Lymphatic and Hematopoietic Cancers in Rubber Workers Exposed to Benzene		
CAUSE OF DEATH	NO. OF DEATHS	
	OBSERVED	EXPECTED
All causes	330	331.6
All malignant neoplasms	69	66.8
Lymphatic & hematopoietic cancers	15	6.6
Leukemia	9	2.7
Multiple myeloma	4	1.0

The researchers found a statistically significant increase in deaths from all lymphatic and blood system cancers, especially leukemia and multiple myeloma. There was no similar increase in mortality from all causes of death combined or from all cancers combined. OSHA regarded these findings as a strong demonstration of a causal link between benzene and leukemia. Can you see why? Today, benzene is classified as a "known human carcinogen," placing it in a very exclusive club.

The data in Table 1 (together with the other studies of benzene) fulfill the hazard identification function for a risk assessment of benzene. But notice what is left out of the analysis. The table classifies deaths only by disease, so there is no indication of the effects of benzene at different doses, nor is there any accounting for the latency period between exposure and health effect. Therefore, while the data in Table 1 identify a hazard, they do not establish the potency of the chemical at different levels of exposure. The latter, of course, is the province of dose-response assessment.

To fill this gap, Rinsky and his collaborators reanalyzed their data in a second study. The results are summarized below:

Table 2. Observed and Expected Deaths from Leukemia in 1,165 White Men with at Least One Day of Exposure to Benzene from January 1, 1940, through December 31, 1965, According to Cumulative Exposure and Years of Latency

LATENCY (YR)	EXPOSURE (PPM-YR)				
	0.001–40	40–200	200–400	400	TOTAL[*]
	observed/expected deaths				
<5	2/0.10	0/0.02	—	—	2/0.12
5–10	0/0.16	0/0.05	0/0.01	—	0/0.22
10–15	0/0.22	1/0.07	1/0.02	0/0.00	2/0.31
15–20	0/0.27	1/0.09	1/0.03[**]	2/0.01	3/0.39
20–25	0/0.32	0/0.10	0/0.03	1/0.01	1/0.46
25–30	0/0.37	0/0.12	0/0.04	0/0.01	0/0.54
>30	0/0.40	0/0.16	1/0.04	0/0.01	1/0.62
Total[*]	2/1.83	2/0.62	2/0.17	3/0.04	9/2.66

[*]The numbers of expected deaths has been rounded.
[**]Probably should read 0/0.03.–EDS.

The NIOSH researchers concluded that the data in Table 2 show "a marked, progressive increase [in leukemia] with increasing cumulative exposure to benzene." Compare Table 1 and Table 2. How are they different? How much data went into each? What does Table 2 show that Table 1 does not? Why is the additional information in Table 2 useful to regulators? That is, why not base regulatory action against benzene on the results in Table 1 alone?

The NIOSH investigators went on to extrapolate a dose-response curve applicable to the low exposures (1–10 ppm) anticipated by OSHA's regulation. They calculated that leukemia risk would be dramatically reduced by lowering exposures to 1 ppm, and that at 0.1 ppm the risk would be indistinguishable from background rates of leukemia. The current OSHA Permissible Exposure Limit is 1 ppm of benzene in air, averaged over an 8–hour period. 29 CFR § 1910.1028(c)(1).

b. DOSE–RESPONSE ASSESSMENT

As the Rinsky study demonstrates, the complexity of the dose-response assessment is much greater than the initial hazard identification. The level of uncertainty is much greater as well. "The uncertainties inherent in risk assessment can be grouped in two general categories: missing or ambiguous information on a particular substance and gaps in current scientific theory. When scientific uncertainty is encountered in the risk assessment process, inferential bridges are needed to allow the process to continue." Red Book, *supra*, at 28. These "inferential bridges" are usually called "default assumptions."

The two most important areas of dose-response assessment in which default assumptions are used are (1) the application of animal test results to human beings, and (2) estimation of the effects on humans at very low doses. Default assumptions are needed in these areas because, for obvious reasons, direct experimentation on humans is impossible and because scientists need to use high doses to stimulate observable effects in the laboratory.

As for the first issue, whether a substance that causes cancer in animals will also cause cancer in humans, risk assessors generally assume an affirmative answer.

> In these cancer guidelines, tumors observed in animals are gener-ally assumed to indicate that an agent may produce tumors in humans. Mode of action may help inform this assumption on a chemical-specific basis. Moreover, the absence of tumors in well-conducted, long-term animal studies in at least two species pro-vides reasonable assurance that an agent may not be a carcinogenic concern for humans. * * * Thus far, there is evidence that growth control mechanisms at the level of the cell are homologous among mammals, but there is no evidence that these mechanisms are site concordant. Moreover, agents observed to produce tumors in both humans and animals have produced tumors either at the same site (e.g., vinyl chloride) or different sites (e.g., benzene). Hence, site concordance is not always assumed between animals and humans.

U.S. EPA, *Guidelines for Carcinogen Risk Assessment*, 70 Fed. Reg. 17765, 17783 (April 7, 2005).

The default assumption that animal carcinogens are also human carcinogens is bolstered (though not conclusively confirmed) by the fact that all known human carcinogens have also been shown to be carcinogenic in at least one animal species.

As for the second issue, estimating human equivalent doses in extrapo-lating from animal studies, risk assessors usually rely on conversion factors. One common conversion factor relates to the difference in body weight between the test animal and a "typical" human. For oral exposures to a carcinogen, a human equivalent dose is often estimated from data on another species by adjusting the animal oral dose by a scaling factor of body weight to the 0.75 power.

Laboratory animals are usually given a high dose of a test chemical relative to the animal's body weight so that scientists can observe any health effects. EPA's 2005 Guidelines for Carcinogen Risk Assessment call for using at least three "dose groups" of laboratory rodents (each group with at least 50 male animals and 50 female animals), and one "control" group. The doses administered are a "high" dose established so that scientists can easily detect carcinogenic effects, a "middle" dose, and a "low" dose. *Id.* at 17781. The effects observed from these three doses can then be used to plot a rudimentary dose-response curve. However, further extrapolation is often needed to estimate the health effects on the animal (and subsequently on humans) that would be predicted to occur at doses far lower than the doses that were actually delivered to the animals. There is no guarantee that the curve that best fits the data from the administered doses is also the curve that best predicts effects at the very low doses to which humans may be exposed. Here, one common default assumption is the linear, no-threshold model discussed *supra*, which predicts straight-line reductions in the severity of the health effect under lower doses. This assumption provides an "upper-bound" estimate for very low dose carcinogenic effects, but should not be viewed as predicting the "exact" risk from low doses.

NOTES AND QUESTIONS

1.   Why are default assumptions necessary and important for dose-response analysis? What is the justification for adopting protective default assumptions? Is there a danger that use of protective default assumptions will lead to unnecessary expenditure of resources to reduce exposures to chemicals that actually pose little risk to humans?

2.   *Types of uncertainty.* Two types of uncertainty give rise to the need to use default assumptions:

> *Information uncertainty* and *knowledge uncertainty* * * *. [I]nformation uncertainty arises when relevant data is not collected, although it could be or when existing information is not made available to the decision maker who needs it. Knowledge uncertainty, in comparison, stems from a lack of adequate scientific understanding, or from situations where the collection of necessary information is infeasible.
>
> There is no clear demarcation between information uncertainty and knowledge uncertainty; the marginal point at which information becomes so difficult or expensive to collect that it is effectively unobtainable will often be indistinct. Nevertheless, the dichotomy is significant from a legal perspective because the consequences of allocating the burdens of production and proof may vary greatly depending on the nature of the uncertainty presented. Information uncertainty can be eliminated if the value of the missing data makes collection worthwhile. A doctrine designating one party responsible for resolution of information uncertainty presents that party with a realistic choice: either provide the information or surrender the point. Which alternative is selected depends on how the designated party perceives the relative costs and benefits of production. The picture is quite different when knowledge uncertainty is involved. Research may be directed toward a critical problem, but there is rarely any assurance that the desired knowledge can be acquired, especially within the time frame associated with a specific legal controversy. Thus, a rule assigning legal responsibility for knowledge uncertainty also determines the eventual result in most cases: whoever bears that burden generally loses.

Howard A. Latin, *The "Significance" of Toxic Health Risks: An Essay on Legal Decisionmaking Under Uncertainty*, 10 ECOLOGY L.Q. 339, 356–57 (1982). Where do the low-dose and animal-to-human assumptions fit into these categories? What difference do these two kinds of uncertainty make in risk assessment?

c.   EXPOSURE ASSESSMENT

Once scientists have identified the hazards that a chemical is capable of causing and the doses at which adverse effects can be predicted, the next step in risk assessment is to estimate typical human exposures to the chemical of concern.

Exposure assessment follows the chemical of concern from its external source to its target cells in the body. The physical properties of chemicals are important to exposure analysis in several ways. For example, solubility in water is crucial to understanding the movement of a toxic substance through the environment. Even weight is important—heavier elements travel less, so soil contamination near a smokestack is likely to be highly concentrated close to the source and limited at a distance. The route of exposure matters as well. For example, an NAS study of radon in drinking water determined that radon that is ingested is of little health concern, but when it is inhaled it is a serious problem: 20 out of 13,000 stomach cancers yearly can be attributed to radon, while 19,860 out of 160,000 lung cancers have some involvement with radon.[6]

How do we determine the dose humans receive in real-world situations? Exposure assessment methods include taking samples (from drinking water, indoor air etc.), surveys of workers or community members, and observations of how workers and members of the public interact with toxic substances. For instance, in assessing the risk from contaminated sediments in a river, investigators may observe the frequency of fishing that occurs near those sediments; they may take surveys of fishermen to determine how many fish from the area they eat each week; and they may test contamination levels in the tissues of those local fish. In many cases, however, direct observation and testing is not feasible, and regulators must make assumptions about the level of human exposure to a toxic substance.

Some minority populations are exposed to higher than usual levels of single or multiple toxic substances, due to cultural practices, location of residence, occupational exposures, dietary habits, and other behavior patterns. Children may have higher tissue exposures to toxic chemicals because they are slower than adults to metabolize and excrete many chemicals. And certain occupational groups, such as pest exterminators, may also be subject to unusually high exposure to toxic substances. Should exposure assumptions be based on the most exposed individuals? The most likely exposure scenario? The average or median level of exposure? We will return to the issue of disproportionate—and potentially discriminatory—exposure of low-income and minority populations to toxic chemicals throughout this book, and particularly in Chapter 5.

NOTES AND QUESTIONS

1.   *Exposure and uncertainty.* Exposure assessment clearly requires the exercise of judgment by risk assessors, just as dose-response assessment does. What kinds of uncertainty are present in exposure assessment? Do you

6.   Warren E. Levy, *Radon More Dangerous in Air than in Water*, New York Times, Sept. 16, 1998.

think most exposure uncertainties are resolvable through further research? Are they information uncertainties or knowledge uncertainties?

2. *Conservative assumptions.* Risk assessors often use protective ("conservative") assumptions in exposure assessments. For example, they may assume that the average worker the metal plating industry directly inhales carcinogens for 8 hours a day, 5 days a week, for a working lifetime of 40 years. Or, in assessing the risk from contaminated sediments at a hazardous waste site, they may assume that a child will play barefoot in those sediments for 100 days per year, leading to absorption of contaminants through the child's skin. Critics contend that conservative exposure assumptions can lead to over-regulation or overly stringent clean-up standards. What are the benefits and drawbacks of using conservative exposure assumptions?

3. *Gender and age.* For decades, nuclear regulators have used a 70 kg (154 pound), 20–30 year old male as the "Reference Man" for calculating maximum allowable radiation doses. The National Academy of Sciences concluded in 2006, however, that women and children generally have a higher risk of dying from cancer than a man who receives the same radiation dose.[7] The NAS also found that a female infant drinking milk contaminated with radioactive iodine has a 70 times greater risk of contracting thyroid cancer than an adult male for the same radiation exposure.[8] How should regulators take into account gender and age differences in assessing exposures? In setting regulatory standards?

d.   RISK CHARACTERIZATION

Risk characterization is technically simple: Risk = hazard × exposure. But the uncertainty and variability discussed above complicate matters considerably. A multiplication formula is simple if the values are certain and fixed, but what should be done with uncertain numbers and ranges of values?

Risk Assessment and Risk Management in Regulatory Decision–Making

The Presidential/Congressional Commission on Risk Assessment and Risk Management
vol. 2, pp. 85–88 (Final Report 1997)

Risk characterization is the primary vehicle for communicating health risk assessment findings. * * *

Risk assessment is an uncertain process that requires both scientific data and science-based judgment. Risk assessments are conducted to estimate risks below the range of observable events in people or in studies

---

7. NATIONAL RESEARCH COUNCIL, HEALTH RISKS FROM EXPOSURE TO LOW LEVELS OF IONIZING RADIATION: BEIR VII—PHASE 2 15 (2006).

8. *Id.* at 311. *See also* Arjun Makhijani, *The Use of Reference Man in Radiation Protection Standards and Guidance with Recommendations for Change*, INSTITUTE FOR ENERGY AND ENVIRON-MENTAL RESEARCH (2009).

of laboratory animals. For example, 10–100 percent of laboratory animals exposed to a relatively high dose of a carcinogen throughout their lives might develop cancers, but regulatory agencies are expected to protect populations from exposure to doses of chemicals that might pose a risk of up to one in a million, not one in ten. The impact of a one-in-a-million cancer risk on a population cannot be detected or measured, because one-fourth of that population is already expected to die of cancer, even in the absence of a particular chemical exposure. As a result, estimates of small risks are speculative; they cannot be verified. Expressing a small risk solely in numerical terms, especially in single numbers, is misleading and falsely conveys accuracy.

* * *

Often, qualitative information is more useful and understandable than quantitative estimates of risk. Qualitative assessments include a careful description of the nature of the potential health effects of concern, who might experience the effects under different exposure conditions, the strength and consistency of the evidence that supports an agency's classification of a chemical or other exposure as a health hazard, and any means to prevent or reverse the effects of exposure. Qualitative information should also include the range of informed views about a risk and its nature, likelihood, and strength of the supporting evidence. For example, if an agency considers a substance likely to be a human carcinogen on the basis of studies of laboratory animals, but there is some evidence that the classification is flawed, both views should be presented. A discussion of that uncertainty would note the several types of evidence that support the substance's classification as a likely human carcinogen and also the contradictory evidence. Based on this type of discussion, the risk manager might conclude that because the weight of the scientific evidence supports the substance's classification, the best option is to regulate it as a carcinogen in the interest of protecting public health (*i.e.*, invoking the precautionary principle). Alternatively, the risk manager might conclude that the evidence is so uncertain that it is best to focus on conducting additional research or to maintain the status quo.

NOTES AND QUESTIONS

1. What are the purposes of risk characterization, according to the above description? Who uses risk assessments? How do the purposes and audience(s) affect its content?

2. Should risk be characterized as individual risk (*e.g.*, 1×10^{-4} chance of an individual contracting cancer) or population risk (*i.e.*, expected number of deaths in a community over a given period of time)? Why does EPA—and Congress, when it has been this specific—tend to use individual risk characterizations?

3. *Why quantify?* To determine whether a given level of risk reduction is worth the cost, regulators are under increasing pressure to quantify the exact level of reduction in cancer risk, or the number of lives that will be saved, from a regulation. In light of what you have read so far, do you think

it very likely that EPA can produce precise data on risk reduction levels? Why or why not? Should we abandon quantitative risk assessment in favor of qualitative risk assessment?

4. *Multiple conservatism.* A frequent criticism of risk assessment is the practice of compounding conservative assumptions. For example, in addition to assuming that a child will play barefoot in contaminated sediments, risk assessors may also assume that the child will ingest some of the sediments by putting her fingers in her mouth during play near the sediments. Further, if the contamination involves carcinogens, risk assessors may assume that the risk of cancer from exposure to the carcinogens has no threshold. Critics argue that multiple conservatism results in "worst case scenarios" rather than risk assessments. Defenders of the practice point out that, since the true values are either unknown, unknowable, or variable (that is why assumptions are being used in the first place), we cannot be certain that the "worst case" is not in fact the actual case. Should EPA rethink its practice of using multiple conservative assumptions? If so, which assumptions should be revised? Is it feasible, for example, to replace assumptions with a single uncertainty factor?

3.   THE RISK ASSESSMENT DATA GAP

The science of chemical risk assessment has grown tremendously since the 1970s, and scientists have identified dozens of chemicals as known carcinogens. Yet there are still enormous gaps in our understanding of which chemicals can cause cancer, and even wider gaps in our understanding of the noncarcinogenic effects of chemicals.

As of 2010, about 84,000 different chemicals had been introduced into commerce in the United States, but formal risk assessments have been conducted for a small fraction of these—by some estimates less than 2 percent. Risk assessment, where it has been conducted, has focused primarily on the human health effects of chemicals and not on ecosystem effects. Moreover, risk assessment is almost always conducted to test the risk of a single chemical. The synergistic effects of chemicals (health and environmental effects of combinations of chemicals) have received little attention, despite the fact that we know that humans are exposed to a multitude of chemicals from multiple sources (air pollution, water pollution, indoor air, smoking, pharmaceuticals, pesticides, etc.).

One reason for this data gap is that risk assessments are expensive. The primary way to assess chemical hazards is through animal testing, but the costs are substantial. The standard rodent study for carcinogenicity costs up to $4 million and can take four years or more to complete. Given these costs, and the potential impact of regulations on industry, the U.S. government has proceeded glacially in performing risk assessments. A governmental risk assessment for dioxin, for example, has been underway for 25 years and still is not complete as of the summer of 2010.

Many scholars believe that the gaps in our knowledge of chemical risks result not just from the cost of testing or the uncertainties involved in risk assessment, but also from failures of law.[9] They contend that existing law provides insufficient incentives for the private sector to conduct research on the toxicity of chemicals and may actually encourage ignorance of chemical risks. The excerpts below describe the data gap and the hurdles to producing more information on risk.

Chemical Assessments: Low Productivity and New Interagency Review Process Limit the Usefulness and Credibility of EPA's Integrated Risk Information System

U.S. Government Accountability Office
March 2008

The Environmental Protection Agency's (EPA) Integrated Risk Information System (IRIS)—a database integral to the agency's mission of protecting human health and the environment—contains EPA's scientific position on the potential human health effects that may result from exposure to various chemicals in the environment. IRIS data provide the fundamental scientific components needed to develop human health risk assessments. These health risk assessments, in turn, provide the foundation for risk management decisions, such as whether EPA should establish air and water quality standards to protect the public from exposure to toxic chemicals or set cleanup standards for hazardous waste sites. In addition, state and local environmental programs, as well as some international regulatory bodies, rely on IRIS health effects information in managing their environmental protection programs. Although the information in IRIS is a critical primary component of EPA's capacity to support scientifically sound decisions, policies, and regulations, many IRIS assessments are outdated, and few assessments have been completed in recent years. This has resulted in a significant backlog of incomplete chemical assessments and a growing number of outdated assessments. Further, while EPA's IRIS database currently includes about 540 chemicals, every year approximately 700 new chemicals enter commerce, any number of which could pose significant human health risks.

Overall, the goal of the IRIS assessment process is to produce quantitative estimates of cancer and noncancer effects from chronic (long term) exposure to the chemicals assessed. One impact of not having current and complete IRIS assessments of many potentially harmful chemicals is that some chemicals that pose health risks to the public may not be regulated under, for example, air or drinking water statutes, or are regulated by standards that may not sufficiently take into account the best available science on human health effects. For example, trichloroethylene (TCE), a

---

9. *See, e.g.*, Noah M. Sachs, *Jumping the Pond, Transnational Law and the Future of Chemical Regulation*, 62 Vanderbilt L. Rev. 1817 (2009); Wendy Wagner, *Commons Ignorance: The Failure of Environmental Law to Produce Needed Information on Health and the Environment*, 53 Duke L. J. 1619 (2004).

solvent widely used as a degreasing agent in industrial and manufacturing settings, is the most frequently reported organic contaminant in groundwater and has been linked to cancer and other health hazards, according to the National Academies. Yet, because of questions raised by peer reviewers about the IRIS cancer assessment for TCE, EPA withdrew the assessment from IRIS in 1989, did not initiate a new TCE assessment until 1998, and likely will not complete that assessment until 2010 or later. This delay represents an information gap of at least 21 years. Without completed IRIS assessments reflecting current risk data, EPA lacks assurance that its regulatory decisions concerning this widespread chemical reflect the best available science on its potential health effects. * * *

Although the number of program staff has quadrupled from 8 to 37 between 2000 and 2007, EPA has, on average, completed about five IRIS assessments per year—and in fiscal years 2006 and 2007, completed only two each year. * * *

[W]hile it is difficult to overstate the importance of the IRIS program to EPA's ability to effectively conduct its mission of protecting human health and the environment, this program currently uses about 0.1 percent of EPA's annual appropriations—specifically, in fiscal year 2007, the program received about $9.6 million of EPA's $7.3 billion budget. EPA's current estimate that it will be able to complete 16 assessments a year by 2011 would represent a substantial increase over recent productivity; however, it is not clear that this level will be sufficient to maintain the viability of the IRIS database.

Information Economics and Chemical Toxicity: Designing Laws to Produce and Use Data

Mary L. Lyndon
87 MICH. L. REV. 1795, 1810–17 (1989)

The market for chemicals will not produce and distribute data on toxicity and exposure unless an incentive structure is developed and maintained. Several factors work to prevent the current system from providing such incentives.

The dearth of toxicity data is in part due to the "public good" nature of the information. The virtues of flexibility and ease of transfer that characterize public goods becomes liabilities in commerce, because public goods cannot easily be held for exclusive use. If only one person "buys" the information, others may still benefit; the costs of producing the data cannot be recouped by multiple individual sales. Because public goods are difficult to own and to control, the market produces them at lower levels than may be desirable.* * *

Cost-reducing inventions are one kind of information likely to be produced privately. But toxicological data has a less ready marketability than many cost-saving inventions. It has value only to those who bear the costs that it reduces. Since even the individual victims of chemical-related disease can rarely identify its specific cause, little demand has developed for assurance of safe or low-risk chemical products.

A further disincentive to private research is the fact that the information produced is often inexact. Toxicologists currently have three basic tools with which to gather data: laboratory cell analyses, bioassays, and epidemiology. Each has strengths and weaknesses that support different levels of confidence in their results.

* * *

Epidemiological studies and bioassays are both costly. Moreover, the cost of an individual bioassay has risen dramatically during the past decade. Firms will be reluctant to make substantial investments in research that produces uncertain health data, instead of new products.

Of course, the price of toxicological knowledge cannot be understood as a simple function of the expense of conducting individual studies. Toxicological research as a social enterprise has produced a substantial amount of health information in a relatively short span of time, and as the field matures, it is developing new methodologies. A developed and accessible database on chemical characteristics is itself a powerful research tool. Also, as toxicology identifies sources of disease, it fills out the cost-benefit equation: it identifies the externalities of chemical toxicity. In addition, it may allow for continued use of a chemical by making possible preventive medicine and by reducing the cost to society of using the chemical. Unfortunately, these benefits may not be recovered by individual firms, or their impact may not be easily identifiable as the results of one company's research. Thus, firms are unlikely to undertake costly testing, because the benefits are public and cumulative and not reflected in the corporate balance sheet. Toxicological data collection is beyond the reach of the individual and is a problematic investment for firms.

Another important influence on data production is the simple fact that toxicity and exposure are negative features of chemical products. As long as no way exists for buyers to identify the toxic effects of specific chemicals, there is no commercial incentive for chemical producers to identify and publicize them. Sellers will not willingly reveal negative characteristics of their products. Comprehensive and accessible toxicity rating systems would support affirmative advertising, but without a developed information context, there is no incentive to study a chemical: the long-term health effects remain invisible for one's own products and for those of one's competitors.

A series of market dysfunctions arises from these factors. The invisibility of chemical toxicity has destructive effects on the market for chemicals. If product quality cannot be guaged by consumers, the overall quality of products in the market will be affected. Buyers inability to screen products removes any incentive for manufacturers to differentiate between toxic and nontoxic products and to screen before production. * * * Indeed, as long as the information market remains undeveloped, ignorance of toxicity may be an advantage to a product. New or unstudied chemicals will do better in relation to chemicals that have been shown to have some indication of toxicity. Ignorance will tend to prevail.

NOTES AND QUESTIONS

1. *Chemical risk assessments and environmental statutes.* The discussion of TCE in the excerpt from the Government Accountability Office points to a fundamental challenge of environmental law: without abundant risk assessment data that can withstand regulatory and judicial scrutiny, it becomes difficult to regulate substances under a wide variety of statutes, such as the Clean Air Act, the Clean Water Act, and the Occupational Safety and Health Act. In what specific ways do you think the risk assessment data gap might affect implementation of environmental statutes? Does the data gap undermine the intent of Congress in enacting those statutes? Or does the data gap perhaps *reflect* the intent of Congress (note the minuscule annual appropriations for EPA's IRIS program)? What is the impact of the risk assessment data gap on private law, such as tort suits over chemical exposures?

2. *The data gap and the market.* Mary Lyndon argues that information on the risks of chemicals is a "public good." What does she mean? Why does she argue that research on chemical toxicity will be undersupplied by the private market?

3. *Roles and responsibilities.* After reading the two excerpts above, do you believe that risk assessment for toxic substances and hazardous wastes should primarily be conducted by the government (at taxpayer expense), chemical manufacturers, chemical emitters (such as oil refiners and paint manufacturers), or by some combination of all three? If you believe it should primarily be conducted by private industry, what legal changes would be needed to provide the necessary incentives?

B.   Risk Management

It is impossible to understand the debates over risk assessment without understanding the uses to which risk assessments are put. Risk *management* is the decision-making process for how society, or a particular regulatory agency, will respond to and mitigate risk. A wide range of factors go into risk management decisions, including not only the estimated scientific extent of risk, but also public perceptions of risk, available resources, distributional concerns, morals and ethics, and the interplay of political interest groups. The proper balancing of these factors is controversial, and risk management usually involves many political stakeholders in addition to toxicologists and other scientists.

Risk Assessment and Risk Management in Regulatory Decision–Making

The Presidential/Congressional Commission on Risk Assessment and Risk Management
vol. 1, pp. 1–46 (Final Report 1997)

Risk management is the process of identifying, evaluating, selecting, and implementing actions to reduce risk to human health and to ecosystems. The goal of risk management is scientifically sound, cost-effective, integrated actions that reduce or prevent risks while taking into account social, cultural, ethical, political, and legal considerations.

Our definition of risk management is broader than the traditional definition, which is restricted to the process of evaluating alternative regulatory actions and selecting among them.* * *

* * *

Creative, integrated strategies that address multiple environmental media and multiple sources of risk are needed if we are to sustain and strengthen the environmental improvements and risk reduction our nation has attained over the last 25 years. To help meet these needs, the Commission has developed a systematic, comprehensive Risk Management Framework.

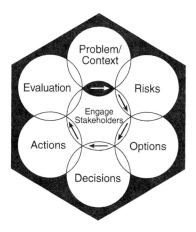

Figure 1.2–Risk Management Framework

* * *

Every stage of the Framework relies on three key principles:

Broader contexts. Instead of evaluating single risks associated with single chemicals in single environmental media, the Framework puts health and environmental media problems in their larger, real-world contexts. Evaluating problems in context involves evaluating different sources of a particular chemical or chemical exposure, considering other chemicals that could affect a particular risk or pose additional risks, assessing other similar risks, and evaluating the extent to which different exposures contribute to a particular health effect of concern. The goal of considering problems in their context is to clarify the impact that individual risk management actions are likely to have on public health or the environment and to help direct actions and resources where they will do the most good.

Stakeholder participation. Involvement of stakeholders—parties who are concerned about or affected by the risk management problem—is critical to making and successfully implementing sound, cost-effective, informed risk management decisions. For this reason, the Framework encourages stakeholder involvement to the extent appropriate and feasible during all stages of the risk management process. * * *

Iteration. Valuable information or perspective may emerge during any stage of the risk management process. This framework is designed so that parts of it may be repeated, giving risk managers and stakeholders the flexibility to revisit early stages of the process when new findings made during later stages shed sufficiently important light on earlier deliberations and decisions.

---

1.   RISK PERCEPTION AND RISK MANAGEMENT

One reason that risk management decisions often involve many stakeholders is that people have different views about how much risk is tolerable or acceptable, as well as different views about how to go about reducing risk. Think of all the forms of risk to human health, safety, and the environment that we face, including toxic substances, radiation, crime, auto accidents, contaminated food, contagious diseases, obesity, water pollution, and climate change. How should Congress and regulatory agencies choose which risks deserve priority attention? Risk assessment purports to be a technical, scientific procedure that could help us rank the risks that society faces. But clearly the choice about which risks to address, and to what extent, also involves value judgments about how to "weigh" risks to different populations. Should risks that we voluntarily accept, such as the risk of an accident from driving in a car, be given the same attention as risks that exist without people's consent or knowledge, such as most pesticide exposures?

One reason for involving the public in risk management decisions is that the public views risk differently from technical experts. The public often views new technologies with more fear or skepticism than existing technologies, for example, and also may be particularly fearful of substances or technologies that have received of adverse media coverage. What should policy makers do if the public is clamoring for regulatory action against risks that experts deem to be relatively insignificant? The following article addresses these issues.

Perception of Risk Posed by Extreme Events[10]
Paul Slovic and Elke U. Weber, April 2002

Perceptions of risk play a prominent role in the decisions people make, in the sense that differences in risk perception lie at the heart of disagree-

---

10.   Unpublished paper presented at the conference "Risk Management Strategies in an Uncertain World," Palisades, New York, April 12–13, 2002.

ments about the best course of action between technical experts and members of the general public, men vs. women, and people from different cultures. * * *

Before reviewing research on public perceptions of risk, it is instructive to examine the very nature of the risk concept itself. It contains elements of subjectivity that provide insight into the complexities of public perceptions. There are clearly multiple conceptions of risk. In fact, a paragraph written by an expert may use the word several times, each time with a different meaning not acknowledged by the writer. The most common uses are:

* Risk as a hazard. Example: "Which risks should we rank?"

* Risk as probability. Example: "What is the risk of getting AIDS from an infected needle?"

* Risk as consequence. Example: "What is the risk of letting your parking meter expire" (answer: "Getting a ticket")

* Risk as potential adversity or threat. Example: "How great is the risk of riding a motorcycle?"

The fact that the word "risk" has so many different meanings often causes problems in communication. Regardless of the definition, however, the probabilities and consequences of adverse events, and hence the "risks," are typically assumed to be <u>objectively</u> quantified by risk assessment.

Much social science analysis rejects this notion, arguing instead that such objective characterization of the distribution of possible outcomes is incomplete at best and misleading at worst. These approaches focus instead on the effects that risky outcome distributions have on the people who experience them. In this tradition, risk is seen as inherently subjective. It does not exist "out there," independent of our minds and cultures, waiting to be measured. Instead, risk is seen as a concept that human beings have invented to help them understand and cope with the dangers and uncertainties of life. Although these dangers are real, there is no such thing as "real risk" or "objective risk." The nuclear engineer's probabilistic risk estimate for a nuclear accident or the toxicologist's quantitative estimate of a chemical's carcinogenic risk are both based on theoretical models, whose structure is subjective and assumption-laden, and whose inputs are dependent on judgment. Nonscientists have their own models, assumptions, and subjective assessment techniques (intuitive risk assessments), which are sometimes very different from the scientists' models. * * *

[T]he concept "risk" means different things to different people. When experts judge risk, their responses correlate highly with technical estimates of annual fatalities. Lay people can assess annual fatalities if they are asked to (and produce estimates somewhat like the technical estimates). However, their judgments of risk are related more to other hazard characteristics (for example, catastrophic potential threat to future generations) and, as a result, tend to differ from their own (and experts') estimates of annual fatalities. * * *

Investigation of these interrelationships by means of factor analysis has indicated that the broader domain of characteristics can be condensed to a small set of higher-order characteristics or factors. The factor space presented in [Figure 1.3] has been replicated across groups of lay people and experts judging large and diverse sets of hazards. Factor 1, labeled "dread risk," is defined at its high (right hand) end of perceived lack of control, dread, catastrophic potential, fatal consequences, and the inequitable distribution of risks and benefits. Nuclear weapons and nuclear power score highest on the characteristics that make up this factor. Factor 2, labeled "unknown risk," is defined at its high end by hazards judged to be unobservable, unknown, new, and delayed in their manifestation of harm. Chemical and DNA technologies score particularly high on this factor. A third factor, reflecting the number of people exposed to the risk, has been obtained in several studies. Although we do not know of recent studies of risk perception regarding the terrorism of September 11 and the subsequent anthrax attacks, these incidents would most certainly fall in the extreme upper-right quadrant of Figure 3.

Research has shown that laypeople's risk perceptions and attitudes are closely related to the position of a hazard within the factor space. Most important is the factor "dread risk." The higher a hazard's score on this factor (i.e., the further to the right it appears in the space), the higher its perceived risk, the more people want to see its current risks reduced, and the more they want to see strict regulation employed to achieve the desired reduction in risk. In contrast, experts' perceptions of risk are not closely related to any of the various risk characteristics or factors derived from these characteristics. Instead, experts appear to see riskiness as synonymous with expected annual mortality. Many conflicts between experts and laypeople regarding the acceptability of particular risks are the result of different definitions of the concept of risk. * * *

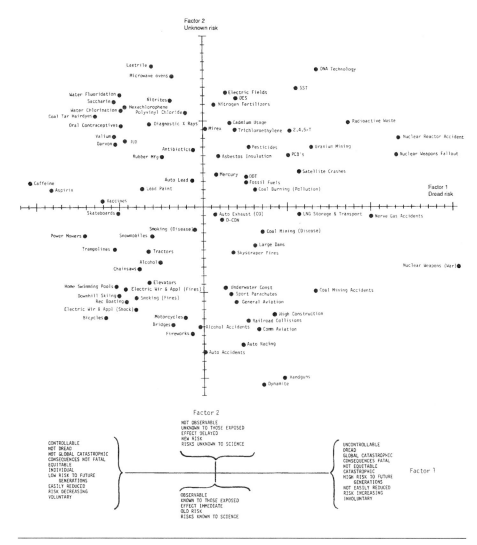

Figure 1.3—Factors in Risk Perception

Perceptions of risk and the location of hazard events within the factor space shown in [Figure 1.3] play a key role in a process labeled social amplification of risk. Social amplification is triggered by the occurrence of an adverse event, which could be a major or minor accident, a discovery of pollution, an outbreak of disease, an incident of sabotage, and so on that falls into the either risk-unknown or risk-previously-ignored category and has potential consequences for a wide range of people. Through the process of risk amplification, the adverse impacts of such an event sometimes extend far beyond the direct damages to victims and property and may result in massive indirect impacts such as litigation against a company or loss of sales, increased regulation of an industry, and so on. In some cases, all companies within an industry are affected, regardless of which company was responsible for the mishap. Thus, the event can be thought of as a stone dropped in a pond. The ripples spread outward, encompassing first the directly affected victims, then the responsible company or agency, and, in the extreme, reaching other companies, agencies, or industries. Examples of events resulting in extreme higher order impacts include the chemical manufacturing accident at Bhopal, India, the disastrous launch of the space shuttle Challenger, the nuclear-reactor accidents at Three Mile Island and Chernobyl, the adverse effects of the drug Thalidomide, the Exxon Valdez oil spill, the adulteration of Tylenol capsules with cyanide, and, most recently, the terrorist attack on the World Trade Center and the deaths of several individuals from anthrax. An important aspect of social amplification is that the direct impacts need not be too large to trigger major indirect impacts. The seven deaths due to the Tylenol tampering resulted in more than 125,000 stories in the print media alone and inflicted losses of more than one billion dollars upon the Johnson & Johnson Company, due to the damaged image of the product. The ripples resulting from several deaths due to anthrax have been even more costly than the Tylenol incident.

Multiple mechanisms contribute to the social amplification of risk. One such mechanism arises out of the interpretation of unfortunate events as clues or signals regarding the magnitude of the risk and the adequacy of the risk-management process. The informativeness or signal potential of a mishap, and thus its potential social impact, appears to be systematically related to the perceived characteristics of the hazard. An accident that takes many lives may produce relatively little social disturbance (beyond that caused to the victims' families and friends) if it occurs as part of a familiar and well-understood system (e.g., a train wreck). However, a small incident in an unfamiliar system (or one perceived as poorly understood), such as a nuclear waste repository or a recombinant DNA laboratory, may have immense social consequences if it is perceived as a harbinger of future and possibly catastrophic mishaps.

NOTES AND QUESTIONS

1. *A richer conception of risk.* Can you enumerate the qualities of risk that differentiate the expert and lay perspectives? Are some more important than others? Should risk management decisions be based on expert assessment of risk, public assessment of risk, or some combination of both?

2. *Perceptions of risk from toxic substances and hazardous waste.* Note that many toxic substances and hazardous wastes are listed in the upper-right quadrant of Figure 1.3. That is, there is a lot of scientific uncertainty about the risk, the effects are often unobservable, and the public views the risks as involuntary, with a high catastrophic potential. What is the impact of these public perceptions on law and regulation? Do you believe there is an inherent tendency to "over-regulate" in this area of law to respond to public demands?

3. *Risk ranking.* Should Congress or regulatory agencies attempt to rank the most serious health and safety risks that Americans face, and address them in some form of priority order? If so, what metric should govern our ranking decisions? Lives that might be saved? Health expenditures that might be avoided? Should risks that affect children be prioritized

higher than those that affect the elderly, on the grounds that children have more years to live?

4. *The vicious circle.* Justice Stephen Breyer, in a 1993 book written before his appointment to the Supreme Court,[11] argued that U.S. decisions on what to regulate, and how stringently, are often driven by public outcry. This results in what he called "regulatory tunnel vision" (overregulation of certain high-profile risks, such as PCBs), and in "random agenda selection," or lax regulation of some serious risks, such as noncarcinogenic effects of chemicals. His solution was to establish an expert group of elite civil servants—a kind of super-agency—which would rationalize risk management and prioritize which risks to address throughout the federal bureaucracy. More recently, Cass Sunstein has argued that if "the public demand for regulation is likely to be distorted by unjustified fear, a major role should be given to more insulated officials who are in a better position to judge whether risks are real."[12] Do you think that Congress and agencies would make better or worse risk management decisions if they were more insulated from public pressure?

2. The Risk Management Toolbox

As the above discussion suggests, risk management encompasses more than an agency's decision about how stringently to regulate a certain identified risk. It also involves important legislative decisions about: (1) which risks deserve attention and (2) what form of legislation should be enacted to address those risks.

In the 40-year history of modern environmental law, Congress has selected a number of common tools from its risk management "toolbox." This book explores more than a dozen statutes that employ one or more of these tools. Below is a brief introduction to the risk management tools that Congress has authorized in these statutes. We return to these tools of risk management in much more detail in chapter 3, including looking at some typical statutory examples.

Health-based goals. Many statutes identify chemicals and wastes that are harmful and then set standards limiting the quantity of these pollutants based solely or primarily on protecting human health and the environment. For such statutes, the costs of achieving the standard, as well as the technological feasibility of attaining the standard, are secondary or irrelevant considerations. If achievement of the prescribed levels of pollution is impossible or simply too expensive, so be it. Health-based standards are intended to be "technology forcing." That is, they create an incentive for affected industries to develop technologies that can achieve very low levels of pollution.

Technological feasibility. Unlike health-based standards, feasibility standards require that discharges of harmful pollutants be limited only to

---

11. Stephen Breyer, Breaking the Vicious Circle: Toward Effective Risk Regulation 10–20 (1993).

12. Cass Sunstein, Laws of Fear: Beyond the Precautionary Principle 126 (2005).

the extent that it technologically possible to do so, now or in the foreseeable future. Such standards may require that companies install "best available technology" to minimize releases of pollutants. A technological feasibility approach thus assumes the continued presence in the environment of toxic substances and hazardous wastes that may be quite harmful, because it is not feasible to abate them entirely using the best technology in the marketplace.

Cost-benefit balancing. Some statutes require agencies to balance the degree of protection from regulation against expected costs and to choose the most cost-effective regulatory option for managing risk. Other statutes require a looser consideration of costs, requiring agencies to consider the costs of regulatory action as one of many criteria in choosing a risk management method. For example, cost is usually one of the statutory criteria for determining which kinds of technology are "best available" or "feasible" to control pollution. Cost-benefit balancing is discussed in more detail later in this chapter.

Incentives. The type of regulation most favored by economists is a financial charge ("pollution tax") imposed on the discharge or production of toxic substances and hazardous wastes. This creates an economic disincentive to engage in practices that have a negative social cost, and the decision on precisely how much pollution to emit is left to the individual firm, based on the financial consequences of increased taxation. State and federal gas taxes are one example of incentive-based environmental law (gasoline combustion is a major source of toxic air pollution). Another example is the "tipping fees" charged by municipalities to dump waste at landfills. Beyond a few examples, however, pollution taxes are relatively rare as a risk management approach in the field of toxic substances and hazardous waste.

Command and control. Command and control regulation refers to risk management based on detailed regulatory standards, permits, and enforcement mechanisms. Rather than providing incentives for private firms to reduce pollution in any way they choose, command and control regulations spell out exactly how firms must manage their toxic substances and hazardous wastes. One example is the Resource Conservation and Recovery Act (RCRA), which establishes a "cradle to grave" regulatory system for hazardous waste through complex regulations governing labeling, storage, transport, and disposal.

Information production. Risks can also be managed through regulations designed to generate and disclose information. Toxics statutes often require record keeping and reporting by firms, allow monitoring and inspections by the government, and require information disclosure as a condition of obtaining a license to engage in certain activities. The "shame" factor from disclosing negative information to the government may prompt firms to change their internal practices, resulting in reduced discharges of toxic substances and hazardous wastes even without any direct government command to do so.

As you learn more about the statutes covered in this book, look at the mix of risk management approaches contained in each. Often, in a single statutory section, several of these approaches will be deployed. Consider why Congress chose a specific risk management tool to confront a specific problem in the area of toxic substances and hazardous waste. After each chapter, ask yourself: Could alternative approaches have been used? Would they have worked as well?

3. The Precautionary Principle

As should be clear from this chapter, uncertainty is a defining feature of toxics regulation. For risk managers, uncertainty poses the practical problem of whether to go forward on the basis of what is known, to delay action until more is known, or to take interim action pending further study. These are questions that the law influences strongly. In an area marked by pervasive uncertainty, the greater the proof required for agencies to take regulatory action, the less action can be taken. We will return to this problem again and again in this book.

Many scholars have suggested that the "precautionary principle" provides a path out of the dilemma of how to manage risk in contexts of scientific uncertainty. The precautionary principle stands for the proposition that lack of full scientific certainty about the nature or extent of a risk should not be used as an excuse to postpone regulatory measures to address the risk. It is one of the principles in the Rio Declaration on Environment and Development, adopted by the 175 nations (including the United States) at the Earth Summit in 1992. It is also an explicit foundation of European Union environmental policy, but it has been controversial in the United States. Few politicians or regulators have explicitly stated that risk management in the United States should be governed by the precautionary principle.

For advocates, the principle reflects the common sense notion that it is better to be safe than sorry. The principle aims to anticipate harm before it occurs, and it cuts off arguments that risk management must wait until an agency has "full" knowledge of the nature and extent of risk (which is a rare state of knowledge in most areas of environmental law). Critics say, however, that applying the precautionary principle may squelch promising new technologies and impose enormous costs on society to address speculative risks. They also contend that the principle does not tell us how to set priorities among many risks that may need addressing. The two excerpts below provide a flavor of this debate.

Perspective on the Precautionary Principle
Christopher H. Schroeder, Center for Progressive Reform, 2006

Living with risk and uncertainty is not optional. The actions society takes to address risk and uncertainty are. Until the 1970s, a reactive approach to the risks and uncertainty of industrial pollution and workplace safety predominated in the United States and other Western societies. Under this approach, risk creators are held responsible when their actions unreasonably cause harm to humans and their property, but not otherwise. Society accepts risky actions until solid evidence exists that those actions are causing harm. This approach gives risk creators two distinct advantages:

- People exposed to risky actions must bear the risks of such actions until they cause (or are nearly certain to cause) harm to health or the environment.

- The people exposed to risk bear the responsibility for demonstrating that actions caused harm.

In the last three decades, the reactive approach has been replaced by the precautionary approach in several key arenas. For example, when Congress wrote such statutes as the Clean Air Act, it included the mandate that EPA issue standards that protect health with an "adequate margin" of safety, recognizing that it is impossible to determine exactly how much pollution is "safe" or acceptable.

The full implications of the precautionary approach are still developing, and when people have tried to reduce the approach to a statement of principle, various versions have been created. The 1992 Rio Declaration on Environment and Development states the principle this way:

> Where there are threats of serious or irreversible damage, lack of full scientific certainty shall not be used as a reason for postponing cost-effective measures to prevent environmental degradation.

* * * All statements of the precautionary principle share a common feature: they authorize government to intervene with respect to risky actions while there is still uncertainty about whether those actions will cause harm.

The precautionary approach alters both of the advantages that risk creators enjoy under the reactive approach. Under the precautionary approach:

- People exposed to risk can ask for precautionary actions to be taken before risky actions cause harm.

- Once some preliminary basis for taking precautionary action exists, risk creators bear the responsibility of showing that actions are safe, or at least acceptably risky.

* * *

In American environmental policy circles, there is a general sense that greater recognition of the precautionary principle will mean more regulation and tighter controls. Accordingly, a concerted effort has been mounted to discredit the whole idea as an illogical principle that is self-contradictory, ignores the risks of regulation, demands the impossible, and is anti-scientific. These last two objections—"anti-scientific" and "demands the impossible"—go to the heart of the debate. * * *

Opponents of the precautionary principle claim that its supporters want to impose regulatory measures supported by nothing more than vague and baseless fears, regardless of whether there is evidence to support their fears. Insisting on more science before government can intervene is effectively an attempt to push us back to the reactive approach, forestalling action until science has proven a causal connection between a risky action and harm. In situations of scientific uncertainty of the kind found at the heart of most environmental, health and safety controversies, however, the reactive approach sets up perverse incentives. The risk-takers are often best positioned with respect both to knowledge and to resources to investigate the potential hazards of their actions. By saying it is acceptable for risk-takers to proceed unrestrained until harm has been proven, the reactive approach creates disincentives for them to undertake such investigation.

Far from being anti-science, the precautionary approach encourages the development of more scientific knowledge by switching those incentives, now making it worth the risk-takers' while to reduce scientific uncertainty, thereby relieving whatever restraints might be put in place in the name of precaution.

Precautionary Tale

Ronald Bailey
Reason Magazine, April 1999

The heart of the Principle, of course, is the admonition that "precautionary measures should be taken even if some cause-and-effect relationships are not fully established scientifically." * * * Anyone who merely raises "threats of harm" with no more evidence than their fearful imagination gets to invoke precautionary measures. Precautionists would not need to establish any empirical basis for their fears; they may simply posit that something might go wrong and thus stymie any proposed action.

Ah, so. Just what these activists had in mind all along, as we shall see.

But let's parse the Principle a bit more. One troublesome issue is that some activities that promote human health might "raise threats of harm to the environment," and some activities that might be thought of as promoting the environment might "raise threats of harm to human health."

Take the use of pesticides. Humanity has used them to better control disease-carrying insects like flies, mosquitoes, and cockroaches, and to protect crops. Clearly, pesticide use has significantly improved the health of scores of millions of people. But some pesticides have had side effects on the environment, such as harming nontargeted species. The Precautionary Principle gives no guidance on how to make this tradeoff between human health and the protection of nonpest species. * * *

Proponents of the Precautionary Principle are trying to smuggle in a default position: The environment trumps all other values. Yet the panelists all pretended that the Principle is a value-neutral scientific procedure for determining which policies humanity should pursue. The fact is that the Precautionary Principle incorporates the values of the most extreme versions of know-nothing environmentalism. * * *

[One corollary to the Precautionary Principle] is that "the proponent of an activity, rather than the public, should bear the burden of proof (reverse onus)." This means that "proponents would have to demonstrate through an open process that a technology is safe or necessary and that no better alternatives were available." * * * The result: Anything new is guilty until proven innocent. It's like demanding that a newborn baby prove that it will never grow up to be a serial killer, or even just a schoolyard bully, before the baby is allowed to leave the hospital. Under this corollary, inventors, scientists, and manufacturers would have to prove that their creations wouldn't cause harm—ever—to the environment or human health before they would be allowed to offer them to the public. This is asking them to prove a negative. How can someone prove that a new plastic will never, ever interact with any metabolic pathway in any plant, animal, microbe, or person? There is simply no way to test for all possible effects given the millions of different species living on the earth. * * *

The plain fact is that the introduction of thousands of synthetic chemicals has not resulted in increased levels of death and disease but *has* resulted in substantial health benefits and greater convenience and efficiency. Life expectancy has never been higher and, as just reported by the National Cancer Institute, even cancer incidence rates are going down. In addition, the Food and Drug Administration estimates that less than 2 percent of cancers are the result of exposure to man-made substances. Finally, the few bad actors, like some organochlorine compounds, have been replaced.

NOTES AND QUESTIONS

1. Who has the better argument on whether the precautionary principle provides a useful approach to risk management? If you agree with Bailey that the precautionary principle should be rejected, what alternative approaches should regulators use to manage risk in contexts of scientific uncertainty?

2. *The costs of precautionary risk management.* The Rio Declaration states that "lack of full scientific certainty shall not be used as a reason for postponing *cost-effective* measures to prevent environmental degradation." [Emphasis added]. Does the insertion of "cost-effective" undermine the overall goals of the precautionary principle? Or is there a way to implement the precautionary principle in risk management while being sensitive to the costs of regulation? How should policymakers handle situations where taking precautionary action to address one risk (such as health harm from pesticides) might create other risks (such as increased crop loss)? Cass Sunstein and other scholars have argued that the precautionary principle is paralyzing for decision making because there is no logical justification for advocating precautionary action against the "target risk," such as pesticides, while ignoring the countervailing risk. Stringent environmental

regulation could actually run afoul of the precautionary principle, Sunstein claims, because "such regulation might well deprive society of significant benefits, and hence produce serious harms that would otherwise not occur." CASS SUNSTEIN, LAWS OF FEAR: BEYOND THE PRECAUTIONARY PRINCIPLE 29 (2005). Do you agree?

3.   *The burden of proof.* Do you agree that the precautionary principle implements a guilty-until-proven-innocent approach, as Bailey suggests? What are the advantages and disadvantages of such an approach in the field of toxic substances and hazardous waste? Can you think of circumstances where guilty-until-proven-innocent (putting the burden of proof on the proponents of risky products or activities to prove that risks are acceptable) would be a sensible approach to managing health and environmental risks?[13]

4.   *Precaution, cell phones, and brain cancer.* Several scientific risk assessments have linked use of cell phones to brain cancer.[14] One such study, published in the World Journal of Surgical Oncology in 2006, found statistically-significant increases in brain tumors among users of digital and analog cell phones, as well as cordless phones.[15] The National Cancer Institute, the Federal Communications Commission, and the World Health Organization reject the link between cell phones and brain cancer, however. How, if at all, should the precautionary principle be applied in this context? If you have heard about this debate, have you personally taken any precautionary steps to change your cell phone use? What kinds of precautionary measures, if any, should government take in response to the conflicting risk assessments on cell phone dangers? In 2010, the City of San Francisco enacted a first-in-the-nation labeling law for cell phones, under which retailers must disclose the radiation levels from phones.[16] Do labeling and public disclosure provide a sensible "middle ground" between proponents and opponents of precautionary regulatory action? Or are there drawbacks to the labeling of risks that are not conclusively proven?

C.   COST–BENEFIT ANALYSIS

Risk management entails enormous information, administrative, and decision-making costs for government. Information must be gathered and organized; decision-making bodies (agencies, regulators, courts) must be created and staffed; decisions must be made about the type of government intervention that is appropriate, and enforcement staffs must be created to detect and respond to violations. And this list does not include the costs that

---

13.   For an extensive discussion of the role of the burden of proof in implementing the precautionary principle, see Noah M. Sachs, *Rescuing the Strong Precautionary Principle from Its Critics: The Case of Chemical Regulation*, 2011 U. OF ILL. L. REV.

14.   For an overview in the popular press of these studies, see Brian Walsh, *How Safe is Your Cell Phone?* TIME MAGAZINE, March 15, 2010.

15.   Lennart Hardell et al., *Tumour Risk Associated with Use of Cellular Telephones or Cordless Desktop Telephones*, 4 WORLD JOURNAL OF SURGICAL ONCOLOGY 74 (2006).

16.   Jesse McKinley, *San Francisco Passes Cellphone Radiation Law*, N.Y. TIMES, June 15, 2010.

the private sector must bear in complying with governmental regulations, which are usually far larger than the cost to taxpayers.

Cost–Benefit Analysis (CBA) attempts to rationalize decision making on risk by telling us whether risk reducing interventions are worth the cost. Once a risk assessment is conducted, CBA can also be used to *compare* risk management options to determine which one offers the most reduction in risk for a given dollar cost. According to proponents, CBA can also attune regulators to risk-risk tradeoffs—situations where intervening to manage one risk might cause different risks to arise. For example, stringent regulation of hazardous waste disposal may lead to illegal "midnight dumping" of hazardous waste, which can harm whole communities. Tough mandates to "scrub" smokestack emissions of toxic air pollutants might result in those same toxic pollutants ending up in ash that must be disposed of in landfills. Every regulatory intervention has some cost, and CBA can help regulators assess whether the regulatory cure is worse than the disease.[17]

The fundamental justification for CBA is economic efficiency: we should not spend more to reduce harm from an activity than the cost of the harm itself, and when we do regulate, it should be in a manner that garners the most benefits with the least cost.

CBA is firmly institutionalized in American environmental law and is required by numerous statutes. For example, the Toxic Substances Control Act requires that EPA implement a form of CBA in determining whether the risks posed by a chemical are "unreasonable." EPA must make explicit findings regarding the underlying chemical risks, the economic impact of restricting the chemical, and the benefits of the chemical. As we shall see, there are also some environmental statutes that have been interpreted to prohibit cost-benefit balancing, such as Section 109 of the Clean Air Act, regarding National Ambient Air Quality Standards, which we discuss in Chapter 3.

More broadly, since the Reagan Administration, CBA has been institutionalized through executive orders that affect every agency within the Executive Branch. Executive Order 12866, originally issued by President Clinton, provides the basis for this CBA requirement today. The Order requires agencies to perform a Regulatory Impact Analysis (grounded in CBA) for "significant regulatory actions," such as those with an expected annual impact on the U.S. economy of $100 million or more.[18] It also

---

17. Frank B. Cross, *When Environmental Regulations Kill: The Role of Health/Health Analysis*, 22 ECOLOGY L.Q. 729 (1995). Edward W. Warren & Gary E. Marchant, *"More Good than Harm": A First Principle for Environmental Agencies and Reviewing Courts*, 20 ECOLOGY L.Q. 379 (1993) (advocating judicial authority to impose a "more good than harm" standard on agency action, based on the court's own determination of good and harm).

18. E.O. 12866, 58 Fed.Reg. 51735 (Oct. 4, 1993). Specifically, a "significant regulatory action" is defined as a regulatory action that is likely to result in a rule that may: (1) Have an annual effect on the economy of $100 million or more or adversely affect in a material way the economy, a sector of the economy, productivity, competition, jobs, the environment, public health or safety, or state, local, or tribal governments or communities; (2) Create a serious inconsistency or otherwise interfere with an action taken or planned by another agency; (3) Materially alter the budgetary impact of entitlements, grants, user fees, or loan programs or

requires that each agency submit the RIA for review by the Office of Information and Regulatory Affairs (OIRA), a White House office, before the proposed rule can become final. In most cases, OIRA has 90 days in which to review the proposed regulation, review the agency's assessment of costs and benefits and regulatory alternatives, and determine whether the regulation is consistent with the President's priorities. OIRA may approve the rule or suggest changes by returning it to the agency for reconsideration.

The requirements of Executive Order 12866, which are often justified as bringing rationality to the federal government's risk management efforts, also increase the steps an agency must take before finalizing a regulation. If EPA wanted to modify its regulations governing how long hazardous waste could be stored at the site where it is being generated (a rule that would likely be considered "significant"), EPA would have to prepare a Regulatory Impact Analysis and comply with Executive Order 12866, in addition to the requirements for rulemaking under the Administrative Procedure Act.[19] The entire process often lasts two years or more.

The process established by Executive Order 12866 is designed to ensure that the benefits of proposed regulations exceed projected costs and to ensure that the White House can coordinate all the regulatory activity across the Executive Branch. Below is an excerpt from a document used by OIRA to guide agencies on how to conduct their Regulatory Impact Analyses.

Circular A–4

Office of Management and Budget
September 17, 2003

A good regulatory analysis should include the following three basic elements: (1) a statement of the need for the proposed action, (2) an examination of alternative approaches, and (3) an evaluation of the benefits and costs—quantitative and qualitative—of the proposed action and the main alternatives identified by the analysis.

To evaluate properly the benefits and costs of regulations and their alternatives, you will need to do the following:

- Explain how the actions required by the rule are linked to the expected benefits. For example, indicate how additional safety equipment will reduce safety risks. A similar analysis should be done for each of the alternatives.

- Identify a baseline. Benefits and costs are defined in comparison with a clearly stated alternative. This normally will be a "no action"

---

the rights and obligations of recipients thereof; or (4) Raise novel legal or policy issues arising out of legal mandates, the President's priorities, or the principles set forth in the Executive Order. Id. at § 3(f).

19. Notably, the Executive Order and its CBA requirements do not apply when the agency wants to *repeal* an existing regulation.

baseline: what the world will be like if the proposed rule is not adopted. Comparisons to a "next best" alternative are also especially useful.

- Identify the expected undesirable side-effects and ancillary benefits of the proposed regulatory action and the alternatives. These should be added to the direct benefits and costs as appropriate.

With this information, you should be able to assess quantitatively the benefits and costs of the proposed rule and its alternatives. A complete regulatory analysis includes a discussion of nonquantified as well as quantified benefits and costs. A nonquantified outcome is a benefit or cost that has not been quantified or monetized in the analysis. When there are important nonmonetary values at stake, you should also identify them in your analysis so policymakers can compare them with the monetary benefits and costs. When your analysis is complete, you should present a summary of the benefit and cost estimates for each alternative, including the qualitative and non-monetized factors affected by the rule, so that readers can evaluate them.

Because of the pervasiveness of CBA requirements in federal law and in toxic substances and hazardous waste regulation in particular, it is important to understand its benefits and limitations.

Table 3 summarizes the main categories of costs and benefits that would be relevant to policymakers charged with conducting CBA.

COSTS OF REGULATION	BENEFITS OF REGULATION
1. Opportunity Costs (the value of opportunities lost due to a regulation. This may include the cost of doing without the substance or activity affected by the regulation)	**1. Human Lives Saved** (economic value of a human life multiplied by the number of lives expected to be saved by the regulation)
2. Compliance Costs (the cost—typically borne by regulated entities—of technology, personnel, and process changes needed to comply with the regulation)	**2. Human Health Protected** (medical expenses avoided as a result of the regulation)

Costs of Regulation	Benefits of Regulation
3. Social Resource Cost	**3. Third Party Benefits**
(the regulation's effect on the markets for goods and services —manifested by changed prices or disruptions in supply chains)	(indirect benefits to people who would be willing to pay for a cleaner environment, or who would be willing to pay to protect the health of others)[22]

Table 3–Elements of costs and benefits

In the field of toxic substances and hazardous waste, as in most areas of environmental law, the "cost" column above is usually easier for agencies to calculate than the "benefit" column. The costs of regulations tend to be nearer-term, and industry is usually eager to present agencies with the relevant data about what a regulation is expected to cost. On the "benefit" side, however, agencies must make complex calculations about risk reduction and monetary savings over several decades. They must also value health outcomes and ecosystem protections for which no price is readily available.

As we have seen, there can be great uncertainty and scientific debate about the extent to which a regulation can reduce cancer risks and other health harms. There is also uncertainty about the benefits of a regulation for wildlife, plants, and aquatic organisms. Even where risk reduction can be accurately estimated, there are inherent difficulties in placing a monetary value on reductions in health and environmental risks. What is the dollar value of a reduction in pancreatic cancer risk in a certain community from 1 in 10,000 to 1 in 1 million? What is the monetary benefit of stringent hazardous waste storage and transport regulations in terms of accidents avoided or lives extended?

Given the difficulties of monetizing the benefits of regulation in many areas of environmental law, environmentalists often charge that CBA systematically devalues environmental and health protection in government decision making. Proponents, on the other hand, argue that CBA helps to set regulatory priorities and avoid costly regulatory mistakes. In envi-

---

22. Different methods may be used to calculate how much such third parties would pay for policies that do not directly affect them. The *contingent valuation method* uses surveys to measure how much potential users of an area might pay to enhance its environmental quality sufficiently to justify a visit there. *Option value* determines how much individuals are willing to pay to ensure future availability of a resource. *Existence value* seeks to calculate either the value that people place in an environmental improvement for its own sake, or the value that some people place on the fact that other people at another time may enjoy the improvement. *See, e.g.,* Binger, Copple, and Hoffman, *The Use of Contingent Valuation Methodology in Natural Resource Damage Assessments: Legal Fact and Economic Fiction*, 89 Nw. U. L. Rev. 1029 (1995).

ronmental law, they argue that CBA can help agencies with limited resources choose which set of regulations will result in the greatest net benefits to human health. The first excerpt below makes the case for using CBA in environmental law. The second excerpt argues against it.

Retaking Rationality: How Cost–Benefit Analysis Can Better Protect the Environment and Our Health

Richard L. Revesz and Michael A. Livermore (2008)
pp. 10–13

The goal of cost-benefit analysis is straightforward: It seeks to maximize the net benefits of regulation. Net benefits are calculated by subtracting the *costs* of regulation—such as compliance costs, job loss, and the reduced consumer well-being resulting from price increases—from the *benefits*—such as lives saved or protected from disease and disability, wilderness preservation, and the creation of jobs or recreational opportunities. In practice, of course, the question of counting costs and benefits gets very complicated very quickly. But the core idea is simple and intuitive. * * *

This book makes the case for cost-benefit analysis not only because such analysis is inevitable, but also because it is desirable. We live in a world of finite resources. Some social problems will resist being fully resolved, even if we spend every dollar we have to address them. Consider "no-threshold pollutants"—environmental contaminants that have adverse health effects even at very low concentrations. To eliminate the risk associated with a no-threshold pollutant, we would have to eliminate or capture every single molecule of the contaminant in the environment—clearly an impossible task. Yet although we cannot achieve zero risk, we can always reduce risk just a bit further. In the absence of an obvious endpoint, we need a mechanism that tells us when to stop spending money. Cost-benefit analysis is that mechanism; it allows us to spend money to the point at which the last dollar spent buys one dollar of risk reduction. If we spend beyond that point, we will pay more than we receive. But if we spend any less, we forego risk reductions that are socially desirable.

For certain kinds of government programs, the use of cost-benefit analysis is a requirement of basic rationality. When considering any regulation aimed at increasing economic efficiency, a responsible regulator must estimate the economic costs and benefits. Otherwise, it is impossible to know at what point to stop spending money to achieve one goal and start spending to achieve another. Even for regulation motivated by goals other than efficiency—protecting rights, redistributing wealth, or fulfilling moral obligations—the economic impacts are clearly a relevant consideration.

Cost-benefit analysis also makes decision makers more accountable by making their decisions more transparent. Cost-benefit analysis is here to stay, but in some sense it has always been with us. Most political decisions involve some form of cost-benefit analysis, however crude, with some costs not counted at all (such as those imposed on the politically weak) and some benefits given undue weight (such as those accruing to the politically powerful). By providing a more accurate assessment of the real costs and benefits of a decision, formalized cost-benefit analysis reveals the distortions of politics—the backroom deals and special-interest politics—for what they are. And when the bum deals are measured against an objective scale, it is easier for voters to act by "throwing the bums out." * * *

Another important justification for cost-benefit analysis is that it imposes structure on the vast discretion that is given to administrative agencies. In an ideal democracy, the people, or the elected representatives of the people, make the laws and determine their enforcement. That approach is impossible, however, in a complex society such as ours. In order to regulate the American economy, an army of bureaucrats, scientists, lawyers, and economists is needed to gather and process information, and make decisions. Because of the technical nature of many regulatory decisions, bureaucrats and experts deep in the bowels of the federal government wield substantial power over our lives. Cost-benefit analysis can be used to ensure that their decisions are based on reasoned analysis and not, for instance, on the unaccountable whim of an official or a bargain-hunting special interest.

Priceless: On Knowing the Price of Everything and the Value of Nothing

Frank Ackerman and Lisa Heinzerling (2004)
pp. 7–11

At the start of the twenty-first century, the clock is starting to run backward as laws and regulations protecting health, safety, and the natural environment—some of the proudest accomplishments of the past 30 years—are now under attack.

The attackers do not explicitly advocate pollution, illness, and natural degradation; instead, they call for more "economic analysis." * * *

The new trend toward economic critique of health and environmental protection has caught on in every branch of the federal government—within the White House, in Congress, and even in the courts. Environmental advocates, decision makers, and citizens concerned about the environment often find themselves on the defensive, without an effective response to the arcane arguments and imposing data offered to show why, when it comes to protective regulation, less is better.

The basic problem with narrow economic analysis of health and environmental protection is that human life, health, and nature cannot be described meaningfully in monetary terms; they are priceless. When the question is whether to allow one person to hurt another, or to destroy a natural resource; when a life or a landscape cannot be replaced; when harms stretch out over decades or even generations; when outcomes are uncertain; when risks are shared or resources are used in common; when the people "buying" harms have no relationship with the people actually harmed—then we are in the realm of the priceless, where market values tell us little about the social values at stake.

There are hard questions to be answered about protection of human health and the environment, and there are many useful insights about these questions from the field of economics. But there is no reason to think that the right answers will emerge from the strange process of assigning dollar values to human life, human health, and nature itself, and then crunching the numbers. Indeed, in pursuing this approach, formal cost-benefit analysis often hurts more than it helps: it muddies rather than clarifies fundamental clashes about values. By proceeding as if its assumptions are scientific and by speaking a language all its own, economic analysis too easily conceals the basic human questions that lie at its heart and excludes the voices of people untrained in the field. Again and again, economic theory gives us opaque and technical reasons to do the obviously wrong thing.
* * *

To say that life, health, and nature are priceless is not to say that we should spend an infinite amount of money to protect them. Rather, it is to say that translating life, health, and nature into dollars is not a fruitful way of deciding how much protection to give to them. A different way of thinking and deciding about them is required.

The most common justification for the new mode of economic screening of regulations is that even a rich society can't afford to do everything. There are tradeoffs between different policy options, the argument goes, so it is important to pick the most cost-effective ones. Our response is twofold. First, resources are of course ultimately limited, but there is no evidence that we have approached the limits of what is possible (or desirable) in health and environmental protection. For instance, the fuel efficiency of automobiles is ultimately limited by physical laws, and cannot keep improving forever. But we are so far from the ultimate constraint that it is irrelevant to the practical challenge of improving fuel efficiency today.

Also, widely quoted evidence of absurdly expensive regulations is, as we explain in Chapter 3, mistaken on numerous grounds, and does not deserve to be taken seriously. In fact, only a minority of the costs of regulation show up in the federal budget. For federal expenditures, the limiting factor is not our society's limited resources in any absolute sense, but rather the mania for tax cut after tax cut, especially for those at the top who are most able to pay. However, most of the costs of regulation are borne not by the government but by the regulated industries themselves. There is no evidence that these corporate burdens are, or are about to be, unaffordable. * * *

The second part of our response is that, even if some kind of screening of regulations is needed, the current methods are incoherent, as we will explain in the following chapters. Cost-benefit analysis of health and environmental protection rests on simplistic, implausible hypotheses about the prices that would prevail if priceless values were to show up next to the lettuce on the supermarket shelf. * * *

[W]e advocate a more holistic analysis, one that replaces the reductive approach of cost-benefit analysis with a broader and more integrative perspective. We also urge precaution in the face of scientific uncertainty and fairness in the treatment of the current and future generations. Above all, perhaps, we aim to restore a sense of moral urgency to the protection of life, health, and the environment—the kind of moral urgency today reserved mostly for questions concerning the military.

NOTES AND QUESTIONS

1.   Do you agree with Revesz and Livermore that some form of "crude" cost-benefit analysis is inevitable whenever we make decisions and that it is better to formalize the process by making calculations and assumptions explicit? If CBA were rejected, how would agencies decide what risks to regulate? How would they decide how stringent regulations should be?

2.   *The "affirmative" case for CBA.* Historically, advocacy of CBA has been closely aligned with advocacy of environmental deregulation. CBA proponents have long charged that environmental regulations cost too much per life saved. But Revesz and Livermore argue that CBA could be used to expose and reform areas of law where current regulation is too lax. Discussing dirty power plants built in the 1950s and 1960s that were "grandfathered" under the Clean Air Act, they argue that "[a]ny cost-benefit analysis would show that there are clear economic benefits to shutting down these plants and building newer, more efficient models." Revesz and Livermore, *supra*, at 18. Where CBA supports protecting the environment, they contend, there is no "tragic choice" between economic and environmental values. *Id.* Lisa Heinzerling counters, however, that CBA is a fundamentally flawed procedure that is unlikely to help an environmentalist agenda. "[T]he biases in cost-benefit analysis are not an oversight. They are the manifestations of an ingrained philosophy that is deeply hostile to environmentalists' arguments."[23] In what areas do you think the United States "overspends" or "underspends" to reduce health and environmental risk? Do you agree with Heinzerling that CBA necessarily undermines strong environmental protection?

3.   *Value of a human life.* In calculating the benefits of regulations, how should we calculate the monetary value of lives saved or diseases avoided? Federal agencies use widely varying estimates for the value of a human life saved. In 2008, the U.S. Consumer Product Safety Commission used a value of $5 million in a proposed regulation to reduce the risk of furniture fires. In 2007, in a proposed rule tightening air travel security, the Department of Homeland Security used two separate life values: $3 million and $6 million. EPA typically uses a value of $6 to $7 million per life saved in preparing its regulatory impact analyses for OIRA. So far, neither Congress nor the White House has stepped in to mandate use of a consistent value for a life saved across the federal government.

---

23.   *Lisa Heinzerling Responds to Richard Revesz on Cost–Benefit Analysis*, Grist, May 14, 2008, available at http://www.grist.org/article/cost-benefit-environmentalism-an-oxymoron. This post is part of a three-part dialogue between Heinzerling and Revesz on "cost-benefit environmentalism." The entire dialogue is worth reading if you are interested in the controversies surrounding CBA in environmental law.

The value-of-life calculations are often based on wage premium studies, in which economists examine the extra wages that workers demand to work in particularly risky occupations, such as mining or construction.[24] By comparing the wage premium to the extra mortality risk these workers face, economists determine the monetary value these workers are implicitly placing on their own life. These studies have been criticized on the grounds that workers in risky occupations may have few other career options and therefore may not bear the extra risk voluntarily. They have also been criticized on the grounds that the choice of some workers to accept a higher on-the-job mortality risk in exchange for higher wages should not become the basis for measuring the value of a life for the remainder of Americans who do not choose those jobs.[25] What do we gain from putting an explicit monetary value on lives saved? What are some other options regulators could use in "pricing" human life for the purposes of CBA? Is there a way to conduct CBA without putting an explicit value on a human life?

4. *Discount rate.* Another challenge for conducting CBA is the discount rate to be applied to costs and benefits. Under basic economic theory, future income or expenses must be "discounted" by presumed inflation, rates of return, and other factors to reflect the idea that money now is worth more to a person than future money. To put this in health terms, most people would pay far more money to avoid death from cancer next year than they would to avoid death from cancer 10 years from now. Therefore, in performing CBA on a proposed regulation, avoiding cancers that would have otherwise manifested 10 years from now is worth "less" in the equation than avoiding near-term cancers. But the question is, how much less? The choice of discount rate has an enormous impact on any calculation that includes costs and benefits that continue well into the future, and there is no "correct" discount rate. Different people adopt different rates, largely on the basis of political and social views, because technical economic arguments can support a large range of rates.[26] Why do you suppose that would be the case? Is there a general tendency in environmental law for the costs of regulation to be felt in the (undiscounted) present and the benefits of regulation to be felt in the (discounted) future?

---

24. For an overview of how the value of a statistical life is calculated, see W. Kip Viscusi and Joseph E. Aldy, *The Value of a Statistical Life: A Critical Review of Market Estimates throughout the World*, 27 JOURNAL OF RISK AND UNCERTAINTY 5 (2003).

25. *See* DOUGLAS A. KYSAR, REGULATING FROM NOWHERE: ENVIRONMENTAL LAW AND THE SEARCH FOR OBJECTIVITY 111–113 (2010); ACKERMAN & HEINZERLING, *supra*, at 75–81.

26. For detailed discussion of the propriety of using discounting and of appropriate rates, *see* DOUGLAS A. KYSAR, REGULATING FROM NOWHERE: ENVIRONMENTAL LAW AND THE SEARCH FOR OBJECTIVITY, 158–171 (2010); PAUL R. PORTNEY & JOHN P. WEYANT, EDS., DISCOUNTING AND INTERGENERATIONAL EQUITY (1999); Lisa Heinzerling, *Discounting Life*, 108 YALE L.J. 1911 (1999); Richard L. Revesz, *Environmental Regulation, Cost–Benefit Analysis, and the Discounting of Human Lives*, 99 COLUM. L. REV. 941 (1999).

TOXIC TORTS

c.   Government Immunity

4.   Products Liability Defenses

Although much of the law of hazardous waste and toxic substances revolves around statutes that are implemented and enforced by administrative agencies, private parties may seek relief from exposure to environmental poisons by resorting to common law and statutory tort doctrine. The body of law that has emerged as a result of private litigation against polluters is often called "toxic torts." This chapter explores the characteristics of a toxic tort and the unique problems that arise when private parties rely on courts, not agencies, to redress toxic harms.[1]

A toxic torts case presents difficult problems of proof at nearly every stage of the proceedings. The chapter is organized around the legal issues and litigation-related matters that are inevitably confronted by plaintiffs and defendants engaged in a toxic tort lawsuit. These include: (1) the nature of the harm that triggers the lawsuit and for which relief is sought; (2) causation, that is, tracing the plaintiff's harm to a substance or activity under the control of the defendant; (3) legal theories of recovery, such as nuisance, trespass, negligence, and strict liability; (4) case management techniques, like consolidating suits and class actions; (5) defenses, *e.g.,* assumption of risk, contributory negligence; and (6) the interpretation of defendant's liability insurance agreements. The first five of these issues are, in effect, hurdles that a plaintiff must overcome in order to find the defendant liable. Insurance is usually a topic of primary interest to defendants, who seek to construe their liability policies as broadly as possible to cover the activity that is the subject of the plaintiff's lawsuit.

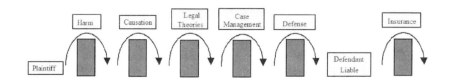

Figure 2.1–Proof Issues

A.   SPECIAL CHARACTERISTICS OF A TOXIC TORT CASE

Because toxic tort cases generally involve a claim of injury based on the actual or threatened release of and exposure to some type of toxic substance, a plaintiff bringing suit will encounter certain problems of proof at trial. The most common problem involves causation, and the majority of this subchapter is devoted to issues surrounding proof of causation. Other problems of proof at trial discussed below are: identifying the proper defendant; mustering reliable scientific and expert testimony; dealing with latent illness; and managing "mass" toxic torts.

---

1.   Two law school books that address the topic of toxic torts are GERALD W. BOSTON AND M. STUART MADDEN, LAW OF ENVIRONMENTAL AND TOXIC TORTS, 3RD ED. (2005); JEAN M. EGGEN, TOXIC TORTS IN A NUTSHELL, 4TH ED. (2010).

1. Proof of Causation

The most difficult problem a plaintiff will face in a toxic tort case is establishing a causal link between a toxic substance and the plaintiff's injury, as well as the specific connection between the defendant, the targeted toxic substance, and the plaintiff. Sometimes, causation difficulties are compounded when the plaintiff can identify a geographic source of the harm (*e.g.*, a local waste disposal site), but cannot determine who, among several entities that contributed to the site, is responsible for the specific harm suffered.

The centerpiece of a toxic tort case is the plaintiff's effort to draw a factual connection between some injury suffered by the plaintiff, and an activity, product, or substance traceable to some defendant. When the agent of harm is an allegedly toxic substance or hazardous activity, plaintiffs confront several complicating realities. If the injury is an illness or birth defect, the medical and scientific community may not be able to pinpoint the precise cause. This is particularly true when the injury is cancer, where hard clinical evidence linking chemical substances to that disease is often lacking. Sometimes, the plaintiff's disease appears throughout the general population and is not limited to persons who have been exposed to a substance that may be traced to a defendant. The plaintiff will have difficulty establishing that the disease is attributable only to the defendant, since others not exposed to the defendant's product or activity also have the disease. Proof of causation may also be thwarted by a long latency period between the time when the plaintiff encounters a potentially dangerous substance and the time when the injury first manifests itself. Other intervening events or actions may by then have caused or contributed to the harm.

Such difficulties have meant that a plaintiff in a toxic tort case must be prepared, as a practical matter, to face three different types of causation issues.[2] The chart in Figure 2.2 shows how causation is proved. First, the plaintiff must be able to rule out other factors that may have produced the injury and that are not connected to the defendant. For example, should the injury be cancer, it is possible that the disease has been caused by a plaintiff's smoking or exposure to second-hand smoke; genetic predisposition to cancer based on family history; exposure to chemicals other than those manufactured or discarded by the defendant; or earlier illness, not caused by the defendant, that made the plaintiff more susceptible to the cancer.

---

2. Two types of causation are legally required. *Cause-in-fact* or *but-for* causation entails presentation of evidence establishing the chain of specific factual events leading up to harm. *Proximate cause* involves the closeness of the relationship between the defendant's product or activity and the harm. The plaintiff must present evidence demonstrating that this relationship is not so remote or attenuated as to make the harm unforeseeable by the defendant. But-for causation is typically the issue in toxic torts, and that is the type discussed here.

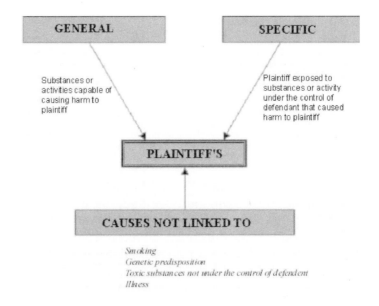

Figure 2.2–Causation Chart

Second, the plaintiff must establish *general* causation. This kind of causation requires proof that the particular substance be *capable* of causing the specific injury suffered by the plaintiff. *See Koehn v. Ayers*, 26 F. Supp. 2d 953, 955 (S.D. Tex. 1998); *Allen v. Pennsylvania Eng'g Corp.*, 102 F.3d 194, 199 (5th Cir. 1996) (scientific knowledge of the harmful level of exposure to a chemical is a fact necessary to sustain the plaintiff's burden in a toxic tort case). Put another way, the plaintiff must offer evidence that there is at least a *risk* that her particular injury is attributable to the toxic substance to which the plaintiff was exposed. *See* Margaret Berger, *Eliminating General Causation: Notes Toward a New Theory of Justice and Toxic Torts*, 97 Columbia L. Rev. 2117 (1997). Sometimes the fact of government regulation of the substance might affect the question of causation. *See* Richard J. Pierce, Jr., *Causation in Government Regulation and Toxic Torts*, 76 Wash. U. L.Q. 1307 (1998).

Third, specific causation must be proved. Specific causation establishes that *this* defendant's product or activity caused *this* plaintiff's injury.[3] In the ordinary torts case (say, an automobile accident) general and specific causation are, for all practical purposes, indistinguishable. However, where causation must be demonstrated by statistical, rather than mechanistic evidence (you will recall this distinction from Chapter 2), the difference between them becomes pronounced, as the following two cases demonstrate.

The requirements for specific and general causation are summarized in *Bonner v. ISP Techs.*, 259 F.3d 924 (8th Cir. 2001). In order to demonstrate

---

3. *See, e.g.,* Sterling v. Velsicol Chemical Corp., 647 F.Supp. 303 (W.D. Tenn. 1986), *aff'd in part and rev'd in part*, 855 F.2d 1188 (6th Cir. 1988).

specific causation, a plaintiff must prove that the alleged toxin caused the injury suffered; *general* causation is present when the substance in question is capable of causing the injury. Courts do not necessarily require statistical evidence. The general standard is that a reasonable person should have been able to find that a plaintiff's exposure to the toxin caused the plaintiff's injury.

Compare this standard to the following case, where the court analyzes *general* and *specific* causation issues in a toxic tort suit against a county for allowing mold spores to grow in a workplace where it adversely affected public employees.

Terry v. Caputo
875 N.E.2d 72 (Ohio 2007)

SYLLABUS OF THE COURT

1. To present a prima facie case involving an injury caused by exposure to mold or other toxic substance, a claimant must establish (1) that the toxin is capable of causing the medical condition or ailment (general causation) and (2) that the toxic substance in fact caused the claimant's medical condition (specific causation).

2. Establishing general causation and specific causation in cases involving exposure to mold or other toxic substances involves a scientific inquiry, and thus causation must be established by the testimony of a medical expert.

3. Without expert testimony to establish both general causation and specific causation, a claimant cannot establish a prima facie case of exposure to mold or other toxic substance.

■ O'Donnell, J.

Facts

In 1996, the Ottawa County Board of MRDD leased several suites in the Buckeye Building located in Port Clinton, Ohio, from W.W. Emerson, a company owned by John Caputo and Leonard Partin. At that time, Northcoast Property Management Company and Lake Investments had the responsibility of maintaining the building. After working in the building for some time, several board employees reported headaches and other physical ailments, which they attributed to damp conditions in the building. At the request of the employees, the Ottawa County MRDD Safety Committee conducted a building inspection; mold was visible in various areas, and a strong mildew odor permeated the premises. Following this inspection, the building was cleaned, and it appeared that the employees' symptoms eased.

Employees shortly discovered additional mold and claimed that their symptoms returned; as a result, the board vacated the building in August. Subsequent testing revealed five separate species of mold spores, including one fungus (stachybotrys chartarum) that could have explained the physical ailments described by the employees.

* * *

Claimants retained Jonathan Bernstein, M.D., as an expert, and although he never examined them individually, he did review their medical records and a microbial assessment survey compiled by Robert Clint Jones of Hygienetics Environmental Services, Inc. Using this information, Bernstein prepared a letter for claimants' counsel in which he connected the conditions at the Buckeye Building, specifically the presence of mold, with the symptoms alleged by the claimants. His letter states that the claimants "experienced clinical symptoms consistent with building-related illness that was the result of multiple problems including water incursion leading to mold and mildew growth, poor ventilation and poor filtration." Thereafter, appellants deposed Dr. Bernstein and jointly filed two motions: one for summary judgment and a second to exclude his testimony pursuant to Evid. R. 702 and *Daubert v. Merrell Dow Pharmaceuticals, Inc.* (1993), 509 U.S. 579, 113 S.Ct. 2786, 125 L.Ed.2d 469. The trial court, pursuant to Evid.R. 702, excluded Dr. Bernstein's testimony because (1) he did not base his report on sufficient facts or data, (2) his report was not the product of reliable principles and methods, and (3) he did not apply the principles and methods reliably to the facts of the case. Moreover, the trial court determined that Dr. Bernstein's testimony lacked a methodology satisfying *Daubert* as to the proximate cause of the claimants' injuries because (1) "he failed to adhere to an established methodology for differential diagnosis by not ruling in the suspected causes and by not ruling out any other possible causes," (2) "he failed to support his conclusions regarding a correlation between exposure to mold, irritants, and allergic reactions and the mold and irritants" present in the building as the proximate cause of the claimants' ailments, (3) "he relied solely on temporal causation to arrive at his conclusions," and (4) "he failed to present a review of the literature to support his conclusions." After excluding Dr. Bernstein's testimony, the trial court granted summary judgment because claimants had presented no other expert testimony in the case.

* * *

Appellants sought review in this court, and we accepted this discretionary appeal to consider the issue whether expert testimony is required to establish both general and specific causation in mold-exposure cases.

In conformity with our decision in *Darnell v. Eastman* (1970), 23 Ohio St.2d 13, 52 O.O.2d 76, 261 N.E.2d 114, appellants urge that claimants must present expert testimony to establish both that the substance at issue is capable of causing the condition ("general cause") and that the substance in fact caused the injury of which they complain ("specific cause").

Claimants maintain, in accord with the opinion of the court of appeals, that they have presented reliable expert testimony establishing general causation and, further, that they have provided reliable evidence as to specific causation sufficient to overcome summary judgment.

Causation Analysis

This court has not previously addressed this specific issue. We recognize, however, that the federal courts have frequently considered it. *Knight v. Kirby Inland Marine, Inc.* (C.A.5, 2007), 482 F.3d 347, 351; *Jazairi v. Royal Oaks Apt. Assoc., L.P.* (C.A.11, 2007), 217 Fed.Appx. 895, 898, 2007 WL 460843...

These courts have established "a two-step process in examining the admissibility of causation evidence in toxic tort cases." ... The first step requires a claimant to offer evidence establishing general causation—that is, " 'whether a substance is capable of causing a particular injury or condition in the general population.' " ...

The second step, which applies only after a court finds competent evidence establishing general causation, requires a claimant to offer specific causation evidence. This evidence relates to " 'whether a substance caused a particular individual's injury.' " ...

We find this two-step analysis to be reasonable and therefore adopt it in Ohio. To present a prima facie case involving an injury caused by exposure to mold or other toxic substance, a claimant must establish (1) that the toxin is capable of causing the medical condition or ailment (general causation), and (2) that the toxic substance in fact caused the claimant's medical condition (specific causation).

Daubert and *Darnell*

In *Darnell,* we stated, "[e]xcept [sic] as to questions of cause and effect which are so apparent as to be matters of common knowledge, the issue of causal connection between an injury and a specific subsequent physical disability involves a scientific inquiry and *must* be established by the opinion of medical witnesses competent to express such opinion." (Emphasis added.) 23 Ohio St.2d 13, 52 O.O.2d 76, 261 N.E.2d 114, syllabus. Establishing general causation and specific causation in cases involving exposure to mold or other toxic substances involves a scientific inquiry, and thus causation must be established by the testimony of a medical expert. Trial courts have broad discretion in determining the admissibility of expert testimony, subject to review for an abuse of discretion. See *Kumho Tire Co., Ltd. v. Carmichael* (1999), 526 U.S. 137, 119 S.Ct. 1167, 143 L.Ed.2d 238. In general, courts should admit such testimony when material and relevant, in accordance with Evid.R. 702, which permits a witness to testify as an expert in the following circumstances:

"(A) The witness' testimony either relates to matters beyond the knowledge or experience possessed by lay persons or dispels a misconception common among lay persons;

"(B) The witness is qualified as an expert by specialized knowledge, skill, experience, training, or education regarding the subject matter of the testimony;

"(C) The witness' testimony is based on reliable scientific, technical, or other specialized information. ...

* * *

As we noted in *State v. Nemeth* (1998), 82 Ohio St.3d 202, 207, 694 N.E.2d 1332, "[c]ourts [sic] should favor the admissibility of expert testimony whenever it is relevant and the criteria of Evid.R. 702 are met."

The United States Supreme Court in *Daubert,* 509 U.S. 579, 113 S.Ct. 2786, 125 L.Ed.2d 469, interpreted Fed.R.Evid. 702, the federal version of Evid.R. 702, as vesting the trial court with the role of gatekeeper. *See also Kumho,* 526 U.S. at 152, 119 S.Ct. 1167, 143 L.Ed.2d 238. This gatekeeping function imposes an obligation upon a trial court to assess both the reliability of an expert's methodology and the relevance of any testimony offered before permitting the expert to testify. ...

The test for reliability requires an assessment of the validity of the expert's methodology, by applying with flexibility several factors set forth in *Daubert.* ... The trial court should first assess whether the method or theory relied upon has been tested. ... Next, it should consider whether the theory has been the subject of peer review, and then whether the method has a known or potential error rate. *Id.* at 593–594, 113 S.Ct. 2786, 125 L.Ed.2d 469. Finally, *Daubert* instructs trial courts to look at whether the theory has gained general acceptance in the scientific community. ...

* * *

[The court of appeals] further concluded that Dr. Bernstein's invalid differential diagnosis rendered his testimony unreliable on the issue of whether the claimants' illnesses were caused by the exposure to mold, and thus the court determined that the trial court did not abuse its discretion in barring Bernstein's testimony on specific causation. That portion of the judgment is also affirmed.

* * *

... In accordance with our foregoing analysis, expert medical testimony is necessary to establish that particular types of mold found in the workplace were the specific cause of the claimants' ailments. Without expert testimony to establish both general causation and specific causation, a claimant cannot establish a prima facie case of exposure to mold or other toxic substance. ...

Judgment affirmed in part and reversed in part.

■ MOYER, C.J., and LUNDBERG, STRATTON, O'CONNOR, LANZINGER, and CUPP, JJ., concur.

■ PFEIFER, J., dissents.

NOTES AND QUESTIONS

1.   Courts vary in what they require plaintiffs to prove in terms of causation. The court in *Ferebee v. Chevron Chemical Co.,* 736 F.2d 1529 (D.C. Cir. 1984) admitted expert evidence and applied a *legal sufficiency* standard of causation, rather than a *scientific certainty* standard, in considering whether herbicide was responsible for pulmonary fibrosis. The

court asked the question, *could* a reasonable jury conclude from the expert testimony that the herbicide more likely than not caused the plaintiff's injury? It was irrelevant that a *scientific certainty* standard may have required more evidence to prove causation. Compare this with the court in *In Re "Agent Orange" Product Liability Litigation*, 611 F. Supp. 1223 (E.D.N.Y. 1985), which rejected expert evidence and applied a strict standard of causation in order to prove a statistical link existed between Agent Orange exposure and the resulting illness. This variation in requirements for causation may also extend to the pre-trial phase. Some courts require a plaintiff to produce a prima facie case for causation during this period, which may include filing affidavits demonstrating exposure to toxins, and submitting diagnostic physical statements. *See Adjemian v. American Smelting and Refining Co.*, 2002 WL 358829 (Tex.App. El Paso 2002).

2. The "strong" causation requirement is elaborated in one of the Bendectin cases, which involved the claim that an anti-morning-sickness drug caused birth defects. In *Richardson v. Richardson–Merrell*, 649 F.Supp. 799 (D.D.C. 1986), *aff'd*, 857 F.2d 823 (D.C. Cir. 1988), the court explained that the plaintiff needed to show *both* that Bendectin could cause the injuries complained of in *any*one, and that it caused them in the plaintiff *herself*. Richardson failed on both counts, the latter in large part because the vast majority of birth defects are of unknown origin, and there is no way to identify the precise cause in a particular case.

The California Supreme Court has adopted a different test for causation that requires only that the plaintiff allege that the defendant's product was a "substantial factor" in bringing about the plaintiff's harm. Specifically, a plaintiff must identify each product allegedly causing the injury, and then allege:

> (1) exposure to each of the toxic materials claimed to have caused a specific illness;

> (2) as a result of the exposure, the toxins entered the plaintiff's body;

> (3) illness, and that each toxic that entered plaintiff's body was a substantial factor in bringing about the illness;

> (4) each toxin absorbed was manufactured or supplied by a named defendant.

Bockrath v. Aldrich Chemical Co., 980 P.2d 398 (Cal. 1999). How is this test different from the "strong" causation requirement? *See Kennedy v. Southern Cal. Edison Co.*, 268 F.3d 763 (9th Cir. 2001) (proving causation under California law requires reasonable medical probability based upon expert testimony).

3. A distinct issue from the elements of causation is the *quality* of evidence that supports the expert's testimony. The United States Supreme Court addressed that question in the *Daubert* case, discussed below.

————

The causal connection between negligent conduct and resulting injury is examined below. The study concerns people who lived within one mile of the Pelham Bay Landfill, and subsequently developed leukemia and other diseases.

> The perplexing bruises that surfaced on Rita Sebastian's hands and feet at the age of 3 have long faded. But their meaning—leukemia—and memories of being among a dozen Bronx children who got cancer living in the shadow of a toxic city dump are so painful they still make her cry. "It made me think that I was going to die," Sebastian said tearfully as she recalled being held down for an excruciating spinal tap and enduring a decade of sickening chemotherapy and radiation to beat the disease. Sebastian, now 27, expects to testify at an upcoming trial ordered by the state's highest court after a 16-year legal battle that has pitted the victims, who lived near the Pelham Bay landfill, against the last 3 mayoral administrations.
>
> For Joan Kohn, whose daughter, Danielle Maglio, died of leukemia when she was 14, "the pain never goes away." Had Danielle lived, she would have just celebrated her 30th birthday. "What would she have looked like? She never had her first kiss. She never had a date," Kohn said, breaking down. "It subsides a little bit as time goes by, but she's always there."
>
> The Sanitation Department ran the landfill from 1963 until it was closed in 1979. But the toxic waste continued to be dumped there illegally, and the city entered into a consent decree in 1985 requiring it to remediate the site. Still, the 3 families whose children died and the 10 other kids who survived cancer say the city should take responsibility for letting benzene and other disease-causing chemicals be deposited at the 81–acre landfill, which borders Eastchester Bay, Pelham Bay Park, Co-op City and Country Club.
>
> Their combined lawsuits seek damages in the hundreds of millions of dollars. A Court of appeals ruling in June that the case could move forward was the final hurdle. Unless the city settles, a trial in Bronx Supreme Court is the next step, said Mitchel Ashley, the families' lawyer. "The city allowed companies to dump anything they wanted and didn't property monitor what was going in, didn't correctly maintain the dumps and put these things in residential neighborhoods," Ashley said. "We have to protect the citizens of those areas."
>
> Between 1988 and 1996, rates of childhood leukemia were more than 3 times higher on blocks closest to the dump than on those father away, according to an epidemiologist hired by the plaintiffs. They say 2 studies by city health officials that found no increases prevalence of acute lymphoid leukemia are biased. The city Law Department declined to comment on the case. But in court papers, it argued that, "[n]o matter how sympathetic a plaintiff may be, 'junk' or 'fuzzy' science to establish a causal connection to a disease is not acceptable in New York courts."

Pat Nonnon is convinced illegal dumping caused her daughter Kerri to die of leukemia when she was 10, 5 years after she was diagnosed. A third child, Justin Zeitlin, also died of the disease. "The landfill caused my daughter's death and other children to die and get sick of cancer," Nonnon said. "It was a horrible life for anyone, especially a child, who was innocent."

Hodgkin's disease survivor Brian Walsh, 32, also believes "there's an absolute connection there—the haze seen around it, the awful smell, stuff leaking into the bay." A neighborhood friend of Kerri's brother, Walsh was diagnosed at 16, 2 years after her death in 1989.

Side effects of Walsh's cancer treatment required him and his wife, Allison, to use in-vitro fertilization to conceive their son, who was born 2 months ago. And now, Walsh's brother has leukemia and his sister has multiple sclerosis. Both still live in the northeast Bronx. "You always have the thought in the back of your head that it will come back or lead to something else," Walsh said. He hasn't moved from the area for one reason: "[i]t's home."

Sebastian's mother, Terry, is sick now, too, fighting an unusual anal cancer that has spread to her bones. Racked with pain, she cannot help but question whether the landfill is responsible. "I certainly wonder about it because what I have is a rare cancer," Terry Sebastian, 54, said from her hospital room. "When I need strength, all I have to do is think about what she went through. Those children deserve their day in court." *Jordan Lite, Landfill's Ills*, NEW YORK DAILY NEWS, August 19, 2007.

At trial, the Court of Appeals of New York affirmed the denial of the defendant's motion to dismiss on procedural grounds. In ruling on a motion to dismiss, an appeals court only decides whether facts, including facts relevant to causation, could fit within a legally cognizable theory. *Nonnon v. City of New York*, NY Slip Op 05578 (N.Y. 2007).

Based on the reasoning in *Terry*, consider the following set of facts:

The Grasslands subdivision receives its drinking water from a well. The well water comes from an underground source that is hydrologically connected to the Blue River and approximately 100 families rely on this water supply. In 1998, several children became seriously ill and were diagnosed with leukemia. A group of parents began to investigate the cause of such an unusual number of children suffering from cancer. QTC Chemical Company is located 15 miles upstream of the subdivision along the Blue River, and the parents wondered whether the company was discharging its waste into the river. They requested the state environmental agency to investigate whether the well water was contaminated. The agency tested the well and concluded it was "somewhat contaminated" with trichloroethylene, an industrial solvent, and described the solvent as a "probable carcinogen." QTC manufacturers trichloroethylene. The parents would like to bring a claim against QTC and they come to you for legal representation. Build your case for both general and specific causation. What hurdles to causation do you face?

Terry cites *Daubert* and *Kumo Tire Co., Ltd.,* which are discussed in Subpart 3 below.

2. LATENT ILLNESS

The effects of exposure to a toxic substance or hazardous activity often do not manifest themselves until long after the initial exposure. The long latency period associated with toxic harms (*e.g.,* cancer, birth defects, genetic mutation) create several problems for plaintiffs whose injury may remain undetected for years, or even decades. One obvious problem involves causation. When many years (or generations) pass between an exposure and an injury, the collection of evidence and identification of responsible tortfeasors becomes difficult. *See Borel v. Fibreboard Paper Prods. Corp.,* 493 F.2d 1076 (5th Cir. 1973) (asbestos). Long latency periods also mean that plaintiffs who have been exposed to a toxic substance, but who have not yet developed any symptoms, may wish to seek recovery on the basis of increased *risk* of future illness. *See Ayers v. Township of Jackson,* 525 A.2d 287 (N.J. 1987); Note, *Latent Harms and Risk–Based Damages,* 111 HARV. L. REV. 1505 (1998).

LOUISIANA TOWN GOES TO TRIAL OVER WASTE PIT

KEVIN SACK

NEW YORK TIMES, July 13, 1998, p. A10

GRAND BOIS, La., July 10—The people of Grand Bois say their symptoms began almost immediately that day in March 1994 when eight tractor trailers loaded with oil field sludge rumbled past their tiny Acadian community and into an adjacent waste disposal site.

"When the trucks took the curve, the smell just took over the community," said Clarice M. Friloux, a 32-year-old mother of two. "The kids were getting off the school bus with their shirts over their faces. They stayed sick with diarrhea and dizziness for several days. Our noses were burning, sore throats. You'd wake up with swollen, puffy eyes."

For 10 days the convoys continued, 81 trucks in all, bringing waste laced with substances like benzene, xylene, hydrogen sulfide and arsenic from an Exxon petroleum treatment plant in Alabama. Men sheathed in white protective suits unloaded the waste into a giant open earthen pit, just 333 feet from the tin-roofed home of Lyes L. Verdin.

Mr. Verdin is a charcoal-haired bantam of a man whose Cajun accent is as impenetrable as the humidity along Bayou LaFourche. He maintains that his 8-year-old daughter, Angel, has suffered since that day from chronic headaches, rashes and diarrhea so severe that he must keep a bucket in his family car. As shipments have continued, residents across Grand Bois have blamed ailments from dizziness to chest pains on the chemicals.

On Monday, in a courtroom in nearby Thibodaux, Mr. Verdin and his neighbors in this settlement will seek their revenge. Led by a 33-year-old New Orleans lawyer who took the case two years out of law school, the first 11 of 301 plaintiffs–virtually the entire population of Grand Bois–will present their case against Exxon and the Campbell Wells Corporation, the former owners of the disposal site.

The trial pits the grandmamas and fishermen of Grand Bois against the most powerful industry in the state, an industry that won a Congressional exemption 18 years ago to allow it to dispose of oil field waste with virtually no regulation.

The residents are seeking at least $8 million in compensatory damages and unspecified punitive damages. Separate lawsuits have been filed in state and Federal courts seeking injunctions to shut down the waste disposal site.

The trial in Thibodaux, which is expected to last at least a month, will be watched closely by the oil industry, by Federal regulators and by the state government. Publicity about the problems in Grand Bois (pronounced Gran BWAH) has become an irritant for Gov. Mike Foster, who is distrusted by the residents and who, in turn, is deeply frustrated that the community has rejected the state's offers of medical and environmental testing.

Mr. Foster said that without the benefit of comprehensive testing, he remains unconvinced that the waste site is the source of the community's health problems. That is essentially the position taken by Exxon and Campbell Wells.

"We have not discovered a problem yet," said Mr. Foster, a first-term Republican who is considered friendly to business. "I mean, we can't identify a problem." Clearly exasperated, he said he empathized with the community but added: "I'm tired of it and I want to get it resolved. It is not good for the state of Louisiana to have these kinds of allegations floating around out there."

Here along the murky bayous of southern Louisiana, there has long been an uneasy coexistence between the oil industry and the vibrant, insular culture of the Cajuns and Houma Indians. It is a place where gleaming silver petrochemical plants rise out of vast stands of sugar cane like Oz out of the poppy fields. The gentle breezes that sway beards of Spanish moss in the oaks may also carry odors of sulphur and diesel across the porches of Acadian cottages.

But rarely have the tensions been as exposed as in Grand Bois, a community of 94 houses, too small for the maps, where residents see the neighboring waste pits as a threat to a beloved way of life. Folks here inevitably describe their hamlet as a single extended family, where people trust one another enough to leave keys in their car ignitions and where special occasions are celebrated around kettles of boiling crawfish.

The people fish and crab and work in the shipyards and hospitals. Even if they wanted to move away from the 18 waste cells, which are contained by low levees, few could afford to do so without selling their homes. For the time being, that is impossible. Residents have lined the main road with homemade signs warning of toxic chemicals and depicting the Grim Reaper. The real estate market is, to say the least, depressed.

The community's emotions swing from anger to sadness and fear. "I've had my life," said Joyceline M. Dominique, a 58-year-old grandmother of 12 who has filled five composition books with a chronicle of her family's ailments. "If I go, so be it. But with the children, these are the best years of their lives."

The trial is certain to become a battle of experts, thick with testimony about chemical compounds and medical histories. A central piece of evidence will be the blood and urine testing conducted by Dr. Patricia M. Williams, director of the Occupational Toxicology Outreach Program at the Louisiana state University Medical Center in Shreveport.

She found that 74 percent of the 99 women and children tested had stippled red blood cells, a deformity typically caused by heavy metal poisoning or chemical exposure.

"Normally you would find zero," Dr. Williams said. "So when you see such a spectrum with all these different children from different households, you have to say there's an outside environmental reason."

The residents' case will not be easy to prove, and not only because of the circumstantial nature of the evidence.

In 1980, when memories of the 1979 gas shortage were still stark, Congress granted petroleum exploration and production companies an exemption from the hazardous waste disposal regulations that apply to most other industries.

Those who question the exemption, including Carol M. Browner, the Administrator of the Environmental Protection Agency, call it a sweetheart deal for an industry protected by powerful politicians.

Industry spokesmen, like Mark Rubin, the senior manager for exploration and production of the American Petroleum Institute, say the exemption was granted because only small amounts of the waste produced by oil drilling are toxic and because stricter rules would cost the industry more than $1 billion a year.

The exemption left the regulation of oil field waste disposal to the states. And in Louisiana, where the petroleum industry employed 79,000 people last year, oil field waste has been defined as nonhazardous.

That leaves Gladstone Jones 3rd, the confident young lawyer for the Grand Bois residents, to prove that Exxon and Campbell Wells were negligent in their handling of the waste, and to convince a jury that his negligence claim outweighs the protection afforded by the oil industry's regulatory exemption.

In the end, the ambiguous evidence and the likely long latency period led to an unclear solution. Before the case went to the jury, Campbell Wells settled out of court for perhaps as high as $10 million, and agreed to close the four sludge pits nearest to the town. The jury eventually found in favor of four plaintiffs, but ordered Exxon to pay just $35,000 in damages.

A second issue arising from latent illness involves the statute of limitations. Under traditional statute of limitations doctrine, the period of time within which the plaintiff may bring the claim runs from the time of the "accrual" of the claim. If this concept were to apply to toxic torts characterized by latent illness, the action would have accrued at the time of the last exposure. Since the illness does not, because it is latent, become evident until many years after the last exposure, most plaintiffs' claims would be time-barred. Several jurisdictions have addressed this inherent problem with latent illnesses by ruling, through judicial decision or statute, that the cause of action accrues when the plaintiff knew or should have known of the injury, and of the potential cause. Several cases have concluded that a plaintiff suffering from a latent illness does not have a duty actively to investigate possible causes of the illness in order to satisfy the "knew or should have known" test and thereby preserve the cause of action. *Bano v. Union Carbide Corp.*, 361 F.3d 696 (2nd Cir. 2004) (holding that an injury manifesting itself a few weeks after the plaintiff's initial exposure should be treated the same as injuries with longer latency periods for purposes of New York's statute of limitations); *Evenson v. Osmose Wood Preserving Company of America*, 899 F.2d 701 (7th Cir. 1990); *Joseph v. Hess Oil*, 867 F.2d 179 (3d Cir. 1989). *See also Buttram v. Owens–Corning Fiberglas Corp.*, 941 P.2d 71, 80 (Cal. 1997) (diagnosis and discovery of actual injury should be the date on which a cause of action should be deemed to accrue).

A third legal issue associated with latent illness is whether an insurer of the plaintiff, under a comprehensive general liability policy, must indemnify the insured (usually a losing defendant in a toxic tort action) when a plaintiff is awarded compensation for an illness manifested long after exposure. This issue is answered according to what act causes the insurance policy to apply. If *exposure* to a toxic substance is that act, then the insurance policy provides coverage if the policy was in effect at the time of the plaintiff's exposure. If the *presence of the illness* is the critical act, then coverage must be supplied by the insurance carrier whose policy is applicable at the time of the discovery of the illness. *Eagle–Picher Industries, Inc. v. Liberty Mutual Insurance Co.*, 829 F.2d 227 (1st Cir. 1987). Some courts find coverage by any insurance policy in effect throughout the entire exposure-to-disease-manifestation period. The rationale here is that a toxic substance causes injury from the time of first exposure to the discovery of the illness. *Keene Corp. v. Insurance Company of North America*, 667 F.2d 1034 (D.C. Cir. 1981).

a. INDETERMINATE DEFENDANTS

Under traditional tort theory, the plaintiff must show that the defendant's product or conduct was responsible for the harm suffered by the plaintiff. In a toxic tort case, it may be impossible to identify who caused the injury. Even when the plaintiff can pinpoint a toxic substance that produced some medical ailment, it may not be possible to know who, among several manufacturers of the substance, was the one who actually made the substance that injured the plaintiff. Or, if the plaintiff has been injured from groundwater contaminated from a waste disposal site, it may be possible to identify the manufacturers of the toxic substances dumped into the site, but impossible to know which such substance, among several, caused the plaintiff's harm. When the plaintiff is unable to identify the defendant or defendants responsible for the harm suffered, the traditional rule is that the tort action must be dismissed.

However, some courts have adopted theories of liability to assist the beleaguered plaintiff. Under *market share liability*, manufacturers who produce a fungible and unidentifiable product that injures the plaintiff are held liable in proportion to their respective market shares. *See Sindell v. Abbott Laboratories*, 607 P.2d 924 (Cal. 1980); *Hymowitz v. Eli Lilly & Co.*, 539 N.E.2d 1069 (N.Y. 1989). While market-share liability, or a variant of it, has been adopted in several jurisdictions for DES cases, courts that have addressed the issue have rejected market share theory in toxic tort cases. *City of Philadelphia v. Lead Industries Assoc., Inc.*, 994 F.2d 112 (3d Cir. 1993) (market share liability not adopted in lead-based paint litigation because of unfairness to defendants); *Goldman v. Johns–Manville Sales Corp.*, 514 N.E.2d 691 (Ohio 1987) (asbestos litigation involving varying asbestos contents in the products of various manufacturers).

Market share liability beyond DES cases has been examined by some courts. Although the vast majority of market share liability cases involve DES, some courts have been willing to apply some form of market share liability to benefit plaintiffs in non-DES suits involving blood products, vaccines and asbestos lined break pads. *See e.g.,* Hamilton v. Beretta U.S.A. *Corp., 222 F.3d 36 (2d Cir. 2000) (detailing situations where market share liability applies to non-DES scenarios). The public policy behind market share liability seems to be to protect victims of toxic substances from facing the extraordinary hurdles that must be overcome when proving liability.*

Alternative liability holds that all tortfeasors who are unable to exculpate themselves are jointly and severally liable for the plaintiff's injury. *Summers v. Tice*, 199 P.2d 1 (Cal. 1948). The Restatement (Second) of Torts § 433B(3) adopts alternative liability:

> Where the conduct of two or more actors is tortious, and it is proved that harm has been caused to the plaintiff by only one of them, but there is uncertainty as to which one of them has caused it, the burden is upon each such actor to prove that he has not caused the harm.

The rationale behind alternative liability is that independently operating defendants may be in a better position to identify who was responsible for the plaintiff's injury. Alternative liability therefore makes no sense when manufacturers of a dangerous product are in no better position than the plaintiffs to determine the specific defendant who caused the alleged injury, as is frequently the case in toxic torts litigation, *see Collins v. Eli Lilly & Co.,* 342 N.W.2d 37 (Wis. 1984).

Enterprise liability permits liability to attach on the basis of an entire industry's culpable conduct. Each defendant who contributes to the development of an unreasonable industry-wide safety standard (*e.g.,* one established by a trade association) may be liable if the industry standard is found deficient. *Hall v. E.I. Du Pont Nemours & Co.,* 345 F.Supp. 353 (E.D.N.Y. 1972) (blasting caps). In the rare instances where enterprise liability has been found, the following facts are present: (1) a small number of manufacturers, virtually all of whom are named defendants, produced the injury-causing product; (2) the defendants had joint knowledge of the risks inherent in the risks, and possessed a joint capacity to reduce the risks; (3) each delegated responsibility to set safety standards to a third party representative of the defendants, which failed to reduce the risk.

Concerted action and *civil conspiracy* are similar theories of liability. *See McClure v. Owens Corning Fiberglas Corp.,* 720 N.E.2d 242 (Ill. 1999). Concerted action requires a plaintiff to prove the defendants acted in a common plan or design. For example, a plaintiff in a DES suit might argue that manufacturers collaborated to gain FDA approval to market the drug. Civil conspiracy requires a plaintiff to prove that defendants collectively marketed DES with knowledge that the product was unsafe. Courts have rejected both theories of liability with regards to DES. *See Smith v. Eli Lilly & Co.,* 527 N.E.2d 333 (Ill. 1988) (holding that parallel activity by drug manufacturers in producing and marketing DES does not establish civil conspiracy or concerted action), *rev'd on other grounds,* 560 N.E.2d 324 (Ill. 1990).

Courts have been reluctant to adopt these theories of liability in toxic tort cases. Why? Can you make the argument that they are particularly *appropriate* for toxic torts?

b. SPECIAL DEFENDANTS

Successor corporations traditionally do not assume the liability of their predecessors. However, there are four exceptions: (1) express or implied agreement for successor liability, *United States v. Iron Mountain Mines*, 987 F.Supp. 1233 (E.D. Cal.1997); (2) de facto consolidation or merger of the selling and purchasing corporation, *North Shore Gas Co. v. Salomon Inc.*, 152 F.3d 642 (7th Cir. 1998), overruled sub nom. Envision Healthcare, Inc. v. PreferredOne Ins. Co., 604 F.3d 983 (7th Cir. 2010); (3) the transaction is a mere continuation from the selling corporation to the purchasing corporation; *United States v. Carolina Transformer Co.*, 978 F.2d 832 (4th Cir. 1992); or (4) fraudulent action to avoid liability. *Simmons v. Mark Lift Indus., Inc.*, 622 S.E.2d 213 (S.C. 2005).

Predecessors in title are generally relieved of liability from claims by successors in title because the rule *caveat emptor* applies. One exception exists: the predecessor can be liable for affirmative concealment or passive failure to disclose a condition that poses an unreasonable risk. *See* Restatement (Second) of Torts § 353 (1965).

3.   Evidence and Expert Testimony

If causation is to be proved, it must be by the introduction of scientific and medical evidence through expert testimony. Judicial exclusion of some of this evidence is usually fatal to the case. The traditional approach to the admissibility of such evidence was deferential. Look back at *Ferebee*: What is the standard that the D.C. Circuit applied to the admissibility of the plaintiff's evidence in that case? What were the plaintiff's experts' qualifications to opine on causation issues? What was the basis for their conclusions?[4]

When determining the admissibility of scientific evidence, some courts still use the traditional *Frye* test. *Frye v. United States*, 293 F. 1013 (D.C. Cir. 1923). This test focuses on whether the scientific theory in question has achieved a level of general acceptance in its particular field. *See Goeb v. Tharaldson*, 615 N.W.2d 800 (Minn. 2000) (applying *Frye* test for evidence admissibility in Minnesota); *Slay v. Keller Industries, Inc.*, 823 So.2d 623 (Ala. 2001) (rejecting *Daubert* standard in favor of *Frye* test).

However, as deference began to lose favor in public regulation, courts in civil cases became increasingly concerned that juries were being allowed to reach multi-million-dollar verdicts on the basis of highly questionable scientific evidence.[5] Whatever the merits of this claim in general, it gathered support from the Bendectin litigation. Benedectin was an anti-nausea drug prescribed to combat morning sickness. Perhaps by analogy to Thalidomide and DES, other pregnancy drugs that proved to have disastrous adverse effects, concern arose regarding the teratogenic effects of Bendectin, and parents of children with birth defects began to file suit. Whereas the

---

4.   The Eleventh Circuit took a similar "battle of the experts" approach in *Wells v. Ortho*, 788 F.2d 741 (11th Cir.1986), *cert. denied*, 479 U.S. 950 (1986) (upholding jury verdict contrary to view of majority of medical community).

5.   Bendectin was a constant theme of the tort-reform movement of the 1980s. *See, e.g,* Peter W. Huber, Galileo's Revenge: Junk Science in the Courtroom (1991); Peter W. Huber *et al.*, Phantom Risk: Scientific Inference and the Law (1993). Apart from the outrageous anecdotes that Huber and others cite, however, the evidence of a widespread problem is extremely weak. *See* Marc Galanter, *Real World Torts: An Antidote to Anecdotes*, 55 Md.L.Rev. 1093 (1996).

evidence linking both Thalidomide and DES to subsequent harm was strong and the connection is today virtually uncontroverted, the evidence on Bendectin is far less clear. However, since the defendants were rarely in a position to offer an alternative explanation of the birth defect, the plaintiffs had notable success with juries, though almost none in keeping the verdicts after post-trial motions and appeal.[6] This seemed to point to the need for courts to step in to control juries and, in effect, to vindicate the judgment of the Food and Drug Administration that Bendectin is safe. (It remains an approved drug.) Indeed, the Fifth Circuit cited *Gulf South* in support of its view that, among other weaknesses, the plaintiffs could not rely on animal data. *Brock v. Merrell–Dow Pharmaceuticals*, 874 F.2d 307 (5th Cir. 1989), *revised*, 884 F.2d 166 (5th Cir.), *rehearing en banc denied*, 886 F.2d 1314, *cert. denied*, 494 U.S. 1046 (1990).[7]

Bendectin at last reached the Supreme Court in *Daubert v. Merrell Dow Pharmaceuticals*, 509 U.S. 579, 589–94 (1993), which set the standard for admissibility of scientific evidence in the federal courts today. Justice Blackmun departed strongly from the laissez-faire "battle of the experts" approach:

> [U]nder [Rule 702] the trial judge must ensure that any and all scientific testimony or evidence admitted is not only relevant, but reliable.

> The * * * subject of an expert's testimony must be "scientific … knowledge." * * * But, in order to qualify as "scientific knowledge," an inference or assertion must be derived by the scientific method. Proposed testimony must be supported by appropriate validation—*i.e.*, "good grounds," based on what is known. In short, the requirement that an expert's testimony pertain to "scientific knowledge" establishes a standard of evidentiary reliability.

> * * *

> * * * We are confident that federal judges possess the capacity to undertake this review. Many factors will bear on the inquiry, and we do not presume to set out a definitive checklist or test. But some general observations are appropriate.

> Ordinarily, a key question to be answered in determining whether a theory or technique is scientific knowledge that will assist the trier of fact will be whether it can be (and has been) tested. "Scientific methodology today is based on generating hypotheses and testing them to see if they can be falsified; indeed, this methodology is what distinguishes science from other fields of human inquiry." * * *

---

6. For excellent reviews of the Bendectin litigation, *see* Michael D. Green, *Expert Witnesses and Sufficiency of Evidence in Toxic Substances Litigation: The Legacy of the Agent Orange and Bendectin Litigation*, 86 Nw. U.L. Rev. 643 (1992); Joseph Sanders, *From Science to Evidence: The Testimony on Causation in the Bendectin Cases*, 46 Stan. L. Rev. 1 (1993).

7. There is a split among courts in accepting animal studies to demonstrate human effects. *See Sterling v. Velsicol Chemical Corp.*, 855 F.2d 1188 (6th Cir. 1988) (accepting); *but see In re Agent Orange Litigation*, 611 F.Supp. 1223, 1231 (E.D.N.Y. 1984), *aff'd*, 818 F.2d 187 (2d Cir. 1987), *cert. denied*, 487 U.S. 1234 (1988) (rejecting it).

Another pertinent consideration is whether the theory or technique has been subjected to peer review and publication. Publication (which is but one element of peer review) is not a *sine qua non* of admissibility; it does not necessarily correlate with reliability, * * * [b]ut submission to the scrutiny of the scientific community is a component of "good science," in part because it increases the likelihood that substantive flaws in methodology will be detected. * * *

* * *

Finally, "general acceptance" can yet have a bearing on the inquiry. * * * Widespread acceptance can be an important factor in ruling particular evidence admissible, and "a known technique that has been able to attract only minimal support within the community," may properly be viewed with skepticism.

The *Daubert* case, in other words, interprets the Federal Rules of Evidence to impose a test of "scientific validity" for admissibility.[8] This test requires the trial judge to ensure that any scientific testimony or evidence admitted is not only relevant, but also reliable. *Daubert* also serves as the standard for many state rulings on the admissibility of scientific evidence.[9]

Consequently, before ruling on evidence, trial courts may undertake a preliminary inquiry to ascertain whether the proffered evidence or testimony meets the *Daubert* standard. A number of courts have looked favorably on medical testimony that relies heavily on a temporal relationship between an illness and a causal event. These courts do not believe that *Daubert* requires a physician to rely on definitive published studies in such a situation to establish that a chemical is the most likely cause of a plaintiff's illness. For example, if a person was doused with chemical X and immediately thereafter developed symptom Y, the need for published literature showing a correlation between the two is lessened. *Heller v. Shaw Industries, Inc.*, 167 F.3d 146, 154–155 (3d Cir. 1999). (What does this suggest about the result in *Ferebee*?) *But see Moore v. Ashland, Chemical, Inc.*, 151 F.3d 269 (5th Cir. 1998) (rejecting a pulmonary specialist's testimony linking a former truck driver's respiratory illness to on-the-job exposure to hazardous chemicals, because the testimony—based on "speculative" clinical observations rather than peer-reviewed scientific studies— fell short of the *Daubert* standard for admissible expert testimony).

The Court has reaffirmed its adherence to *Daubert* in more recent cases. In *General Electric Co. v. Joiner*, 522 U.S. 136 (1997), the Court ruled that

---

8.   This test is derived by Federal Rule of Evidence 702, which governs the admissibility of expert testimony.

9.   *See generally* Daniel J. Capra, *The Daubert Puzzle*, 32 Ga. L. Rev. 699 (1998); Anthony Z. Roisman, *The Courts, Daubert, and Environmental Torts: Gatekeepers or Auditors?*, 14 Pace Envtl. L. Rev. 545 (1997); C. Cranor, John Fischer, and David Eastmond, *Judicial Boundary Drawing and the Need for Context–Sensitive Science in Toxic Torts After Daubert*, 16 Va. Envtl. L.J. 1 (1996).

If scientific, technical, or other specialized knowledge will assist the trier of fact to understand the evidence or to determine a fact in issue, a witness qualified as an expert by knowledge, skill, experience, training, or education, may testify thereto in the form of an opinion....

trial courts' decisions to exclude evidence should be reviewed under the very deferential "abuse of discretion" standard. In *Kumho Tire Company, Ltd. v. Carmichael*, 526 U.S. 137 (1999), the Court warned that judges should make certain that an expert, whether basing testimony upon professional studies or personal experience, employs in the courtroom the same level of rigor required in the expert's relevant field. However, judges retain great leeway in determining whether an expert's methods are sound. In sum, courts may reject theories that they find are unreliable, not backed by hard evidence, and that may cause delay and confusion. *In re TMI Litigation*, 193 F.3d 613 (3d Cir. 1999); *In re Paoli R.R. Yard PCB Litigation*, 113 F.3d 444 (3d Cir. 1997).

Novel scientific theories may be admissible under the *Daubert* standard if the scientific theory is connected to a valid method of investigation. *Smith v. General Elec. Co.*, 2004 WL 870832 (D. Mass. 2004) (finding plaintiff's scientific theories did not satisfy the *Daubert* standard because of a lack of scientific data demonstrating a connection between low-level radiation exposure and the plaintiff's type of leukemia). Evidence of causation will be excluded when based upon subjective opinion, instead of accepted scientific methodology. *O'Conner v. Commonwealth Edison Co.*, 13 F.3d 1090 (7th Cir. 1994). Courts are also skeptical of experts proposing to testify based on opinions developed expressly for purposes of litigation, as opposed to matters growing naturally out of research. *Freeport–McMoran Resource Partners v. B–B Paint*, 56 F.Supp. 2d 823 (E.D.Mich. 1999).

Consider this case study in light of the *Daubert* standard:

Case Study—Erionite

AP KILLDEER, N.D.—The sounds of children playing baseball have been silenced at one ball field in this western North Dakota city. Officials fear the ground water itself is simply too unsafe. The ballpark, one of two in this town of about 700 people, is covered with crushed gravel containing erionite, a mineral found in the chalky white rock mined from the nearby Killdeer Mountains.

The rock, used for decades on everything from gravel roads to flower beds, contains fibers that can collect in the lungs of people who breathe it, health officials say. Steve Way, a federal Environmental Protection Agency coordinator, said studies have shown that erionite causes cancer in lab rats, though the mineral is not regulated by his agency.

Erionite is found in at least a dozen states in the West, but Way said he did not know of another area in the U.S. that uses it "at the same magnitude" as Dunn County. The mineral also has been found in gravel mines in Stark and Slope counties, in southwestern North Dakota. Officials there also have been asked not to use the gravel.

"We definitely should be looking at this for health concerns," Way told a group of about 60 residents at a meeting Tuesday night in

---

Killdeer. Killdeer Mayor Dan Dolechek said the ballpark was shuttered as a precaution, and the county voluntarily quit using gravel from the Killdeer Mountains until studies are completed. But many residents are worried more about road maintenance than the risk of cancer from the gravel.

State Rep. Shirley Meyer told federal and state officials at the meeting that Dunn County now will have to look outside its borders for gravel, and potentially costly change. "It seems to me like you're making a mountain out of a molehill with what little data you have," Meyer told EPA and state officials. "The taxpayers in this country are having a tough time trying to swallow this." Federal and state officials have been testing rocks and airborne samples from Dunn County over the past two years. But they say more tests, including tests on humans, are needed.

Way said testing would continue through the spring, with results of the study completed in about 18 months. "I'm 80 years old, and it hasn't killed me yet," said Milton Johnson, who ranches in the Killdeer Mountains. "They can test my lungs if they want—I've been breathing it all my life." Gary Jepson, another rancher in the area, called the worries over erionite "one of those sky-is-falling kind of deals."

State geologist Ed Murphy, who notified the EPA of the erionite in the region two years ago, said the county officials are trying to balance one health concern against another. "We're looking at long-term health problems caused by erionite and somebody getting killed on the roads out there—you've got to keep something on the roads to keep them safe," Murphy said.

In the nation of Turkey, erionite has been linked to mesothelioma, an incurable form of lung cancer common only associated with asbestos exposure, health officials say. Erionite found in North Dakota differs slightly than the mineral found in Turkey, where it is a known carcinogen, Murphy said. Erionite in the state is more calcium based; the mineral in Turkey is sodium based, he said.

Western North Dakota could have "hundreds of miles" of roads paved with gravel containing erionite, Murphy said. Paving them with asphalt would be too costly, state officials say.

The bright white appearance of the rock mined from the Killdeer Mountains is the reason Deb Harsche puts it in her flower beds. "It looks nice. I haven't had any problems with it so far," she said. "Every white gravel road you see around here, that's what's on it. "If it is determined to be cancer-causing, then what?" she asked. Way, of the EPA, said the agency wasn't looking that far ahead. "I don't have an answer," he said. The Associated Press, *North Dakota Gravel Sparks Cancer Fears, Rapid City Journal, April 6, 2008.*

Epidemiological studies. In addition to experts, epidemiological studies are used in court to link exposure to a chemical agent and a disease. Epidemiology is the study of the distribution and determinants of disease frequency and occurrence in humans. It considers patterns of disease occurrence, and the factors that influence those occurrences. However, epidemiology cannot determine the impact on, or causes of, disease in any particular individual. *See* Fed. Jud. Ctr., *Reference Manual on Scientific Evidence* 125 (1st ed., West 1994).

When proper statistical and methodological techniques are used, epidemiological studies are generally recognized as the best method of analyzing and evaluating disease risks in human populations. For this reason, epidemiological studies are often used in toxic tort cases to show correlation between exposure to certain chemicals and commonly occurring diseases in that same geographic local.

Some courts impose standards on the admission of epidemiological studies. This standard is based on "relative risk." Relative risk measures the strength of the association between exposure to a toxic substance and disease. A relative risk of 1.0 indicates that there is no association between a substance and a disease. A relative risk of 1.0 occurs when the incidence of a disease is the same in a particular population that is exposed to a substance, and another group is that is not exposed to that substance. On the other hand, if a particular population shows that the exposed population's risk of contracting a disease is twice that of an unexposed population, the relative risk is a factor of 2.0. This standard is known as a "doubling of the risk" or "doubling dose" standard. Some courts may exclude epidemiological studies that do not meet the "double dose" standard. *See, e.g., In re Hanford Nuclear Reservation Litigation*, 292 F.3d 1124 (Wash. 2002).

4.   "MASS" TORT LITIGATION: WHO IS A PROPER PLAINTIFF?

Toxic tort litigation is unique because a combination of causal indeterminacy and the potential of large numbers of claimants (their numbers can be in the thousands) stretches the ability of the American judicial system to accommodate fairly the needs of multiple plaintiffs and defendants. Courts have struggled to manage problems that arise when (1) the identification of plaintiffs injured by a defendant is extremely difficult, and (2) there are large numbers of potential plaintiffs who may have been exposed to the harmful substance or activity. These issues often emerge in so-called mass tort cases, where many claimants have ingested a common substance, been exposed to a consumer product, or been poisoned by a toxic chemical.

In regard to identification of plaintiffs, it may be impossible to know precisely who has been injured by the defendant's product or activity because of long latency periods between exposure to a toxic substance and development of disease. Some who have been in contact with the harm-producing agent, and who develop an illness, may have become sick because of some other cause, like smoking. These individuals may never know whether their illness was attributable to the toxic substance or activity at issue, or to something else. Moreover, some exposed persons may not have manifested any symptoms at the time the litigation commences. These "future" claimants certainly deserve relief, even after the lawsuit is over.

For plaintiffs who are unsure whether their illness can be traced to the defendant or to some independent factor, courts may loosen the causation requirement. Such plaintiffs may be able to shift to the defendant the burden of *disproving* causation by showing, often with statistical data, that the defendant's actions increased the risk of harm, and that the plaintiff's personal history and lifestyle were inconsistent with the illness contracted. *See Allen v. United States*, 588 F.Supp. 247 (D. Utah 1984), *rev'd on other grounds*, 816 F.2d 1417 (10th Cir. 1987). Future victims may obtain relief if defendants agree, pursuant to some broad pre-trial settlement, to provide compensation to parties who (1) were exposed in the past to the toxic product, and (2) submit claims in the future when and if the injury occurs. *See Carlough v. Amchem Products, Inc.*, 834 F.Supp. 1437 (E.D. Pa. 1993).

In regard to managing mass tort cases effectively, it is often helpful to aggregate the plaintiffs. A class action, pursuant to Rule 23 of the Federal Rules of Civil Procedure, allows a few individuals to sue as representatives of a large group of claimants. A class action permits plaintiffs who might not otherwise pursue a claim to be represented as part of the class. A class action serves the twin goals of judicial economy and protection of those who cannot afford to press individual claims separately. *Ellington v. Philip Morris Incorporated*, 2003 WL 22319075 (D. Nev. 2003) (finding that choice of law problems may prevent the court from certifying a class action because choice of law issues make it difficult to satisfy the commonality and typicality requirements of Fed. R. Civ. Pro 23(a)); *Klein v. O'Neal, Inc.*, 222 F.R.D. 564 (N.D. Tex. 2004) (holding that in nationwide drug product liability class action suit, differences in applicable state laws do not preclude class certification); *In Re Simon II Litigation,* 407 F.3d 125 (2nd Cir. 2005) (de-certifying limited fund class action suit because plaintiffs failed to establish the fund's ascertainable limit). Courts accept class actions when the following conditions are present:

- The class is so large that joinder of all members is impractical;

- Claims of representative plaintiffs are typical of class members;

- Representatives of the class will fairly and adequately protect the interests of the class

- Common issues of law and fact predominate; and

- Class action will not be so unmanageable or confusing as to unduly prejudice defendants. *Sterling v. Velsicol Chemical Corp.*, 855 F.2d 1188 (6th Cir. 1988).

Before a class action can commence, the class must be defined so that the court knows who the plaintiffs are and whose interests are being represented. The class must have some kind of commonality, such as exposure to a toxic substance. A good example of this kind of class can be found in the Agent Orange litigation. The judge there defined the relevant class as those members of the United States, New Zealand, and Australian armed forces who had manifested some injury after being exposed to phenoxy herbicides in Vietnam. *In re Agent Orange Product Liability Litigation*, 100 F.R.D. 718 (D.N.Y. 1983). Standing problems may preclude defining a class as persons who were exposed to a toxic substance but have not yet become symptomatic. *McElhaney v. Eli Lilly & Co.*, 93 F.R.D. 875 (D.S.D. 1982).

PROBLEM

In a mass tort case involving a toxic substance (e.g., asbestos products), may the plaintiffs be required to resolve their claims through alternative dispute resolution (ADR) instead of in court? Or does the ADR process deny plaintiffs due process by depriving them of their day in court? *See, e.g., Amchem Products, Inc. v. Windsor, 521 U.S. 591 (1997).*

Another method for managing mass toxic torts is consolidation, governed by Federal Rule of Civil Procedure 42(a). Consolidation of individual actions against a defendant or group of defendants is appropriate when the plaintiffs' claims present a common question of law or fact. If the court in its discretion concludes that commonality exists, and consolidation furthers judicial economy while avoiding repetition, then the decision to consolidate may occur even without the consent of the parties. If, on the other hand, there are disparities among the various plaintiffs' claims, as well as factual differences (*e.g.*, exposure at different locations, for different times, manifesting different diseases), consolidation may be impermissible. *See, e.g., Malcolm v. National Gypsum Co.*, 995 F.2d 346 (2d Cir. 1993); *In re Fibreboard Corp. v. Pittsburgh Corning Corp.*, 893 F.2d 706 (5th Cir. 1990).

B.   The Plaintiff's Case

Causation is perhaps the salient feature of toxic tort litigation, but plaintiffs must also prove the other elements of a tort cause of action. A lawyer representing a plaintiff must ask: Under what legal theory should she bring suit? Should the claim be founded in common law tort or in statutory law? What kind of harm should be alleged? What kind of relief should be sought?

1.   Legal Theories of Recovery

Toxic tort plaintiffs most often base their claim on one of two legal theories—trespass or nuisance. This is because in most toxic tort cases, there has been some invasion of the plaintiff's property which has in some way interfered with its use.

a.   TRESPASS

The tort of trespass applies when some type of physical invasion interferes with another person's exclusive possession of real property. While trespass is traditionally classified as an intentional tort, the defendant need not have intended to enter onto the plaintiff's property. The tort of trespass is satisfied if the plaintiff can prove that the defendant intended the act that resulted in the trespass. In a toxic tort case, where the claim is based upon the movement of noxious liquids from one property to another, the defendant is liable for a neighbor's damage therefrom, when there is good reason to know or expect that there would be passage from defendant's to plaintiff's land. In *Scribner v. Summers*, 84 F.3d 554 (2d Cir. 1996), although the defendant did not intend waste water used in a cleaning process to enter plaintiff's land, the court determined that there had been a trespass because the defendant should have expected that barium particles would pass from its pavement into the waste water and onto plaintiff's property.

b. NUISANCE

A nuisance is an interference with the use and enjoyment of a person's property. There are two types of nuisance, public and private. The RESTATE-MENT (SECOND) OF TORTS § 821B defines a public nuisance as an "unreasonable interference with a right common to the general public." Such public rights are usually protected by a public body, such as a health department. *State of New York v. Schenectady Chemicals, Inc.*, 479 N.Y.S.2d 1010 (N.Y.A.D. 3 Dept. 1984). In toxic tort cases, private individuals are sometimes able to bring public nuisance claims, but they "must have suffered harm of a kind different from that suffered by other members of the public exercising the right common to the general public that was the subject of interference." REST. (2D) § 821C. This is referred to as the "special injury" rule, and has been applied strictly by courts. *See Briggs & Stratton Corp. v. Concrete Sales & Services*, 29 F. Supp. 2d 1372, 1376 (M.D. Ga. 1998) (release of hazardous substance was not public nuisance as it did not affect a common right of all members of the public); *Brown v. Petrolane, Inc.*, 102 Cal.App.3d 720 (Cal. App. 1980) (court refused to allow public nuisance action brought by private citizens who were fearful of the proximity of explosive substances handled by defendant). *See also Venuto v. Owens–Corning Fiberglas Corp.*, 22 Cal.App.3d 116 (Cal. App. 1971) (court held that individuals complaining of emissions from a plant polluting air and causing health complaints among neighboring residents could not maintain action for public nuisance because same injuries were suffered by all residents). Some courts, however, permit private parties to bring public nuisance actions when individual health problems constitute the special injury. *Anderson v. W.R. Grace & Co.*, 628 F.Supp. 1219 (Mass. 1986).[10] In certain states, polluting a body of water is a public nuisance. *State of California v. Campbell*, 138 F.3d 772, 782 (9th Cir. 1998).

A private nuisance claim does not have the special inquiry requirement. The essence of the cause of action is that the defendant's actions constituted an "unreasonable" interference with the plaintiff's use and enjoyment of the property. Diminution of market value alone, buttressed by no accompanying or personal property damage, does not constitute unreasonable interference. *National Telephone Co-op Assn. v. Exxon Corp.*, 38 F.Supp. 2d 1 (D.D.C. 1998). But a private nuisance claim is stated if the allegation is both diminution of property value *and* fear for the health of the plaintiff's

---

10. *See* David P. Hodas, *Private Actions for Public Nuisance: Common Law Citizen Suits for Relief From Environmental Harm*, 16 ECOLOGY L. Q. 837 (1989).

children resulting from the defendant's dumping activities. *Lewis v. General Electric Co.*, 37 F.Supp. 2d 55 (D.Mass. 1999).

Reasonableness is a subjective judgment that involves the weighing of several factors: the manner, the place, and the circumstances; the relative priority dates of plaintiff and defendant in location; the character of neighborhood; and nature of the alleged wrong. *Williams Pipeline Co. v. Bayer Corp.*, 964 F.Supp. 1300 (S.D. Iowa 1997). *See also Crowe v. Coleman*, 113 F.3d 1536 (11th Cir. 1997) (because of proximity and the nature of the hazardous substance, one landowner was liable in private nuisance to immediately adjacent landowner in connection with seepage of gasoline from his property to the other landowner's property). RESTATEMENT (SECOND) OF TORTS 821B lists as factors in determining "unreasonableness" whether the conduct is of a "continuing" nature and whether it has produced a "permanent" or "long-lasting" effect.

The tort of trespass is often confused with the tort of nuisance. The former is based on an interference with plaintiff's interest in possession of property; the latter with the plaintiff's use and enjoyment of it. *See Rudd v. Electrolux Corp.*, 982 F.Supp. 355, 369 (M.D. N.C. 1997) (continued migration of contaminants is a nuisance, while a trespass is when a contaminant crosses onto adjoining property). In some pollution cases the courts have emphasized the physical similarities of trespass and nuisance actions and have permitted the plaintiff to proceed on both theories simultaneously or on a merged version of the two. *See Martin v. Reynolds Metals Co.* 342 P.2d 790 (Or. 1959); *Bradley v. American Smelting and Refining Co.* 709 P.2d 782 (Wash. 1985).

The two cases below outline trespass and nuisance theories of recovery. The first case concerns a toxic plume of trichloroethylene that continued to migrate to the plaintiff's well, even after the defendant stopped disposing of the toxin.

Robert N. Hoery v. United States

64 P.3d 214 (Colo. 2003)

■ JUSTICE BENDER delivered the Opinion of the Court.

I. INTRODUCTION

In this case, we agreed to answer two certified questions from the United States Court of Appeals for the Tenth Circuit regarding continuing trespass and nuisance under Colorado law. Pursuant to C.A.R. 21.1, the Tenth Circuit certified the following state law questions pertinent to an appeal pending in that court:

> (1) Does the continued migration of toxic chemicals from defendant's property to plaintiff's property, allegedly caused by chemical releases by the defendant, constitute continuing trespass and/or nuisance under Colorado law?

(2) Does the ongoing presence of those toxic chemicals on plaintiff's property constitute continuing trespass and/or nuisance under Colorado law?

We answer both questions in the affirmative.

* * *

II. FACTS AND PROCEEDINGS

* * *

Robert Hoery and his wife bought a residence in the East Montclair neighborhood of Denver, Colorado in 1993. The property has a groundwater well in the backyard to irrigate the lawn and vegetable garden. ... The well is approximately 48 feet deep and pumps underground water in the alluvial material above the Denver Aquifer. Hoery's well is located seven blocks north of Lowry Air Force Base.

The United States operated Lowry as an active military base between the 1940s and September 1994. During that time period, the United States disposed of trichloroethylene ("TCE") and other toxic chemicals at Lowry. These releases created plumes of toxic pollution underneath property extending several miles north of Lowry, including the area underneath Hoery's property in the Montclair neighborhood. In 1997, the United States tested Hoery's irrigation well and found it was contaminated with TCE. TCE was detected in groundwater samples in Hoery's well at 20 micrograms per liter. The State of Colorado maximum contaminant level for TCE in drinking water is 5 micrograms per liter. *See* Memorandum from Versar Inc. to Lowry Air Force Base (Aug. 19, 1997).

Although the United States stopped all operations at Lowry related to the use of TCE in 1994, the toxic plume continues to migrate underneath the Montclair neighborhood. TCE remains on Hoery's property and enters his groundwater and soil on a daily basis, unabated by the United States.

Even though the United States retained an ownership interest in the property, we assume for our purposes here that the release of TCE from Lowry ceased in September 1994. Hoery's expert, a hydrogeologist, testified in his affidavit that based upon the information available in November 1999, the contamination was not permanent and there were remediation strategies that could restore Hoery's property. The United States did not address this factual issue.

Hoery brought suit under the Federal Tort Claims Act ("FTCA") in 1998 against the United States asserting claims for, among other things, continuing trespass and nuisance and sought unspecified damages. *See* 28 U.S.C. §§ 2671–80. Hoery alleged that the United States negligently released the TCE and caused contamination of his property, including groundwater, soil, and a well.

* * *

III. ANALYSIS

* * *

A.   Trespass and Nuisance

The elements for the tort of trespass are a physical intrusion upon the property of another without the proper permission from the person legally entitled to possession of that property. … The intrusion can occur when an actor intentionally enters land possessed by someone else, or when an actor causes something else to enter the land. For instance, an "actor, without himself entering the land, may invade another's interest in its exclusive possession by … placing a thing either on or beneath the surface of the land." RESTATEMENT (SECOND) OF TORTS §§ 158(a) cmt. i, 159(1) (1965). A landowner who sets in motion a force which, in the usual course of events, will damage property of another is guilty of a trespass on such property. …

Another type of property invasion is a nuisance. A claim for nuisance is predicated upon a substantial invasion of an individual's interest in the use and enjoyment of his property. … Liability for nuisance may rest upon any one of three types of conduct: an intentional invasion of a person's interest; a negligent invasion of a person's interest; or, conduct so dangerous to life or property and so abnormal or out-of-place in its surroundings as to fall within the principles of strict liability. … Like a trespass, conduct constituting a nuisance can include indirect or physical conditions created by defendant that cause harm. …

A private nuisance is distinguishable from a public nuisance. A private nuisance is a tort against land and the plaintiff's actions must always be founded upon his interest in the land. A public or common nuisance covers the invasion of public rights, that is, rights common to all members of the public. *See* RESTATEMENT (SECOND) OF TORTS §§ 821B, 821D. Here, we refer only to a private nuisance.

B.   Continuing and Permanent Tort

Having delineated the elements of the underlying torts of trespass and nuisance, we must determine what makes them "continuing" or "permanent." The typical trespass or nuisance is complete when it is committed; the cause of action accrues, and the statute of limitations beings to run at that time. But in cases, for example, when the defendant erects a structure or places something on or underneath the plaintiff's land, the defendant's invasion continues if he fails to stop the invasion and to remove the harmful condition. In such a case, there is a continuing tort so long as the offending object remains and continues to cause the plaintiff harm. …

In the context of trespass, an actor's failure to remove a thing tortiously placed on another's land is considered a "continuing trespass" for the entire time during which the thing is wrongfully on the land. RESTATEMENT (SECOND) OF TORTS § 161 cmt. b. Until the thing tortiously placed on the land, or underneath the land, is removed, then liability for trespass remains. *See* 75 AMER. JUR.2d Trespass § 26 (2002).

The same is true for nuisance. If the defendant causes the creation of a physical condition that is of itself harmful, even after the activity that created it has ceased, a person who carried on the activity that created the condition is subject to continuing liability for the physical condition. RESTATEMENT (SECOND) OF TORTS § 834 cmt. e.

For continuing intrusions—either by way of trespass or nuisance—each repetition or continuance amounts to another wrong, giving rise to a new cause of action. *See* Fowler V. Harper et al., *The Law of Torts* § 1.7 (3d ed. 1996). The practical significance of the continuing tort concept is that for statute of limitation purposes, the claim does not begin to accrue until the tortious conduct has ceased. *Id.*

We recognized claims for continuing torts in *Wright,* 40 Colo. 437, 91 P. 43. In *Wright,* the plaintiff's house was adjacent to the defendant's slaughterhouse. We held that the harmful noises and stenches emanating from the slaughterhouse to the plaintiff's property constituted a continuing nuisance. We reasoned that the defendant was liable until the "nuisance was abated and the cause of damage removed." 40 Colo. at 440, 91 P. at 44 (citing *Consol. Home Supply Ditch Co. v. Hamlin,* 6 Colo.App. 341, 40 P. 582 (1894)). The plaintiff's claim was not barred by the statute of limitations because "the continuing of a trespass or nuisance from day to day is considered in law a several trespass on each day." *Id.* In other words, for statute of limitations purposes, a claim would only accrue once the defendant abated the nuisance and removed the cause of damage.

* * *

In sum, Colorado law recognizes the concepts of continuing trespass and nuisance for those property invasions where a defendant fails to stop or remove continuing, harmful physical conditions that are wrongfully placed on a plaintiff's land. The only exception is a factual situation—such as an irrigation ditch or a railway line—where the property invasion will and should continue indefinitely because defendants, with lawful authority, constructed a socially beneficial structure intended to be permanent.

C.   Whether the Ongoing Presence and Continued Migration of Toxic Chemicals Each Constitutes a Continuing Trespass and Nuisance under Colorado Law

Having reviewed our cases regarding continuing and permanent torts, we turn to the certified questions before us. Specifically, we must determine whether the continuing migration and ongoing presence of toxic pollution on a plaintiff's property constitutes a continuing trespass and/or nuisance, even though the condition causing that pollution has ceased.

* * *

Technically speaking, this is an issue of first impression in Colorado. Although we have recognized the concepts of continuing and permanent torts, we have not addressed an environmental contamination case where the contamination remains and continues to migrate daily onto a plaintiff's property, but where the cause of the contamination has ceased.

While we have not addressed this issue, other jurisdictions have. A number of jurisdictions have determined that the cessation of the condition causing the contamination is not material. These jurisdictions have held that even if the condition causing the contamination has ceased, provided the contamination remains on the plaintiff's land, or continues to migrate onto the plaintiff's land, the defendant remains liable for a continuing tort. *See Nieman v. NLO Inc.,* 108 F.3d 1546, 1559 (6th Cir.1997)(nuclear processing facility stopped operating but uranium contamination remained on plaintiff's property); *Arcade Water Dist. v. United States,* 940 F.2d 1265, 1266 (9th Cir.1991) (laundry facility closed but contamination continued to leach into plaintiff's well)....

Arcade is particularly instructive because the facts are analogous to this case. In *Arcade,* the United States operated an army laundry facility from 1941 until 1973. During that time period, the laundry discharged waste residues into the ground. A domestic-use water well, operated by the Arcade Water District, was located approximately 2,000 feet from the laundry facility. *Arcade,* 940 F.2d at 1266. Although the United States closed the laundry facility in 1973, subsequent testing of Arcade's well revealed that it was contaminated and that ground contamination from the laundry continued to leach into Arcade's well. In 1984, Arcade filed a FTCA suit against the United States, alleging that the release of laundry wastes constituted a continuing nuisance. The District Court dismissed the complaint as time-barred.

On appeal the Ninth Circuit reversed, holding that it was not material that the laundry facility was no longer operational. In determining under California law whether the nuisance was continuing, the Ninth Circuit reasoned that the most salient allegation was that contamination continued to leach into Arcade's well. *Id.* at 1268. That court concluded that because Arcade presented an engineer's affidavit stating that he could not say the contamination was permanent, it could not hold as a matter of law that the nuisance was permanent. Thus, the court held that Arcade alleged a set of facts which constituted a continuing nuisance.

We find the analysis in *Arcade* and other cases that have considered this issue persuasive and consistent with *Wright* and our continuing tort concept. Therefore, we agree with Hoery that the ongoing presence and continued migration of toxic chemicals originally emanating from Lowry constitute a continuing trespass and nuisance and decline to extend the permanent tort concept of the irrigation ditch cases to the facts alleged here.

For purposes of answering the certified questions before us, no dispute exists about whether the United States released TCE into the ground and by doing so, invaded Hoery's property. The property invasion constituted a trespass because the toxic pollution released by the United States physically intruded upon Hoery's property without his permission. *See Public Serv. Co. of Colorado,* 27 P.3d at 389. It also constituted a nuisance because the toxic pollution released by the United States substantially invaded Hoery's interest in the use and enjoyment of his property. *See id.* at 391.

We also hold that these property invasions by way of trespass and nuisance are continuing. The allegations in this case support such a finding on two grounds. First, TCE pollution remains on Hoery's property. The failure of the United States to remove the pollution from Hoery's property which it wrongfully placed there constitutes a continuing property invasion for the entire time the contamination remains. ... Second, the toxic pollution continues to migrate onto his property on a daily basis. The failure of the United States to stop the toxic pollution plume that it created from entering Hoery's property also constitutes a continuing property invasion. ...

* * *

■ Justice Kourlis dissents, and Justice Coats joins in the dissent.

State v. Lead Industries, Ass'n, Inc.

951 A.2d 428 (R.I. 2008)

■ Present: Williams, C.J., Flaherty, Suttell, and Robinson, JJ.

OPINION

Addressing the issues *seriatim* for a unanimous Court, Chief Justice WILLIAMS authored Tracks I and II and Associate Justices SUTTELL, FLAHERTY, and ROBINSON authored Tracks III, IV, and V, respectively. In this landmark lawsuit, filed in 1999, the then Attorney General, on behalf of the State of Rhode Island (the state), filed suit against various former lead pigment manufacturers and the Lead Industries Association (LIA), a national trade association of lead producers formed in 1928.

After the first trial resulted in a mistrial, a second trial commenced; that second trial, spanning four months, became the longest civil jury trial in the state's history. This monumental lawsuit marked the first time in the United States that a trial resulted in a verdict that imposed liability on lead pigment manufacturers for creating a public nuisance.

* * *

Track I
Liability

■ Chief Justice Williams, for the Court.

On appeal from, *inter alia,* the trial justice's denial of their motion to dismiss, their renewed motion for judgment as a matter of law, and their alternative motion for a new trial, defendants, Millennium, NL, and Sherwin–Williams, argue that the trial justice erred by: (1) misapplying the law of public nuisance; (2) finding a causal connection between defendants' actions and lead poisoning in Rhode Island; and (3) failing to hold that this action is barred by the constitutional provision concerning separation of powers. ... For the reasons set forth herein, we reverse the judgment of the Superior Court as to the liability of defendants, Millennium, NL, and Sherwin–Williams, because we conclude that the trial justice erred by denying defendants' motion to dismiss. More specifically, we conclude that the state has not and cannot allege any set of facts to support its public nuisance claim that would establish that defendants interfered with a public right or that defendants were in control of the lead pigment they, or their predecessors, manufactured *at the time* it caused harm to Rhode Island children.

In reaching this conclusion, we do not mean to minimize the severity of the harm that thousands of children in Rhode Island have suffered as a result of lead poisoning. Our hearts go out to those children whose lives forever have been changed by the poisonous presence of lead. But, however grave the problem of lead poisoning is in Rhode Island, public nuisance law simply does not provide a remedy for this harm. The state has not and cannot allege facts that would fall within the parameters of what would constitute public nuisance under Rhode Island law. As set forth more thoroughly herein, defendants were not in control of any lead pigment at the time the lead caused harm to children in Rhode Island, making defendants unable to abate the alleged nuisance, the standard remedy in a public nuisance action. Furthermore, the General Assembly has recognized defendants' lack of control and inability to abate the alleged nuisance because it has placed the burden on landlords and property owners to make their properties lead-safe.

This Court is bound by the law and can provide justice only to the extent that the law allows. Law consists for the most part of enactments that the General Assembly provides to us, whereas justice extends farther. Justice is based on the relationship among people, but it must be based upon the rule of law. This Court is powerless to fashion independently a cause of action that would achieve the justice that these children deserve. United States Supreme Court Justice Benjamin N. Cardozo, a rightly revered student of the law, once summarized as follows the inherent limitations of the judicial role:

"The judge, even when he is free, is still not wholly free. He is not to innovate at pleasure. He is not a knight-errant roaming at will in pursuit of his own ideal of beauty or of goodness. He is to draw his inspiration from consecrated principles. He is not to yield to spasmodic sentiment, to vague and unregulated benevolence. He is to exercise a discretion informed by tradition, methodized by analogy, disciplined by system, and subordinated to 'the primordial necessity of order in the social life.' " ...

Likewise, in the words of United States Supreme Court Chief Justice John G. Roberts, Jr., "judges must be constantly aware that their role, while important, is limited. They do not have a commission to solve society's problems, as they see them, but simply to decide cases before them according to the rule of law." ....

Facts and Travel

It is undisputed that lead poisoning constitutes a public health crisis that has plagued and continues to plague this country, particularly its children. The General Assembly has declared that although "[c]hildhood lead poisoning is completely preventable," G.L. 1956 § 23–24.6–2(3), it is "the most severe environmental health problem in Rhode Island." Section 23–24.6–3. Indeed, Providence has received the unfavorable nickname "the lead paint capital" because of its disproportionately large number of children with elevated blood-lead levels. ...

* * *

D

Attorney General's Lawsuit

On October 12, 1999, the Attorney General, on behalf of the state filed a ten-count complaint against eight former lead pigment manufacturers, John Doe corporations, and the LIA. ...

* * *

The state alleged that the manufacturers or their predecessors-in-interest had manufactured, promoted, distributed, and sold lead pigment for use in residential paint, despite that they knew or should have known, since the early 1900s, that lead is hazardous to human health. ...

* * *

In January 2000, defendants moved to dismiss all counts of the state's complaint pursuant to Rule 12(b)(6) of the Superior Court Rules of Civil Procedure.

* * *

This Court has defined public nuisance as "an unreasonable interference with a right common to the general public." ... "[I]t is behavior that unreasonably interferes with the health, safety, peace, comfort or convenience of the general community." ... Put another way, "public nuisance is an act or omission which obstructs or causes inconvenience or damage to the public in the exercise of rights common to all." ...

Although this Court previously has not had the opportunity to address all the elements of public nuisance, to the extent that we have addressed this common law cause of action, our definition largely is consistent with that of many other jurisdictions, the RESTATEMENT (SECOND) OF TORTS, and several scholarly commentators.

The RESTATEMENT (SECOND) defines public nuisance, in relevant part, as follows:

"(1) A public nuisance is an unreasonable interference with a right common to the general public.

"(2) Circumstances that may sustain a holding that an interference with a public right is unreasonable include the following:

"(a) Whether the conduct involves a significant interference with the public health, the public safety, the public peace, the public comfort or the public convenience * * *." 4 RESTATEMENT (SECOND) TORTS § 821B at 87.

The Supreme Court of New Jersey, considering facts that were virtually identical to those in this case, elaborated on the necessary elements to maintain a public nuisance action. In that case, the New Jersey court held:

"First, a public nuisance, by definition, is related to conduct, performed in a location within the actor's control, which has an adverse effect on a common right. Second, a private party who has suffered special injury may seek to recover damages to the extent of the special injury and, by extension, may also seek to abate. Third, a public entity which proceeds against the one in control of the nuisance may only seek to abate, at the expense of the one in control of the nuisance. These time-honored elements of the tort of public nuisance must be our guide in our consideration of whether these complaints have stated such a claim." *In re Lead Paint Litigation,* 191 N.J. 405, 924 A.2d 484, 499 (2007).

This Court recognizes three principal elements that are essential to establish public nuisance: (1) an unreasonable interference; (2) with a right common to the general public; (3) by a person or people with control over the instrumentality alleged to have created the nuisance when the damage occurred. After establishing the presence of the three elements of public nuisance, one must then determine whether the defendant caused the public nuisance. We will address each element in turn.

i
Unreasonable Interference

Whether an interference with a public right is unreasonable will depend upon the activity in question and the magnitude of the interference it creates. Activities carried out in violation of state laws or local ordinances generally have been considered unreasonable if they interfere with a public right. ...The plaintiff bears the burden of showing that a legal activity is unreasonable. ...

* * *

ii
Public Right

... This Court also has emphasized the requirement that "the nuisance must affect an interest common to the general public, rather than peculiar to one individual, or several." ...

Indeed, the Connecticut Supreme Court has explained that "[t]he test is not the number of persons annoyed, but the possibility of annoyance to the public by the invasion of its rights. A public nuisance is one that injures the citizens generally who may be so circumstanced as to come within its influence." *Higgins v. Connecticut Light & Power Co.,* 129 Conn. 606, 30 A.2d 388, 391 (1943) (quoting *Nolan v. New Britain,* 69 Conn. 668, 38 A. 703, 706 (1897)). ... Unlike an interference with a public resource,

"[t]he manufacture and distribution of products rarely, if ever, causes a violation of a public right as that term has been understood in the law of public nuisance. Products generally are purchased and used by individual consumers, and any harm they cause—even if the use of the product is widespread and the manufacturer's or distributor's conduct is unreasonable—is not an actionable violation of a public right. * * * The sheer number of violations does not transform the harm from individual injury to communal injury." Gifford, 71 U. Cin. L. Rev. at 817.

iii
Control

As an additional prerequisite to the imposition of liability for public nuisance, a defendant must have *control* over the instrumentality causing the alleged nuisance *at the time the damage occurs.* Put simply, "[o]ne who controls a nuisance is liable for damages caused by that nuisance." *Friends of the Sakonnet v. Dutra,* 749 F.Supp. 381, 395 (D.R.I.1990). ...

* * *

Indeed, control at the time the damage occurs is critical in public nuisance cases, especially because the principal remedy for the harm caused by the nuisance is abatement. ...

* * *

iv
Causation

The party alleging the existence of a public nuisance not only must demonstrate the existence of the nuisance, but also must demonstrate "that injury has been caused by the nuisance complained of." *Citizens for Preservation of Waterman Lake,* 420 A.2d at 59 (citing *McClellan v. Thompson,* 114 R.I. 334, 344, 333 A.2d 424, 429 (1975)). Causation is a basic requirement in any public nuisance action; such a requirement is consistent with the law of torts generally. ...

* * *

In addition to proving that a defendant is the cause-in-fact of an injury, a plaintiff must demonstrate proximate causation. *See DiPetrillo v. The Dow Chemical Co.,* 729 A.2d 677, 692–93 (R.I.1999) (affirming that the jury be instructed on both "but for" and proximate causation in the products liability context); *Moretti v. C.S. Realty Co.,* 78 R.I. 341, 353, 82 A.2d 608, 615 (1951) (instructing on proximate cause in nuisance case). Proximate cause is a more exacting standard than simple "but for" causation. *Tavares v. Aramark Corp.,* 841 A.2d 1124, 1128 (R.I.2004). ...

* * *

3
Whether the Presence of Lead Paint
Constitutes a Public Nuisance

* * *

...The state's complaint alleges simply that "[d]efendants created an environmental hazard that continues and will continue to unreasonably interfere with the health, safety, peace, comfort or convenience of the residents of the [s]tate, thereby constituting a public nuisance." Absent from the state's complaint is any allegation that defendants have interfered with a public right as that term long has been understood in the law of public nuisance. Equally problematic is the absence of any allegation that defendants had control over the lead pigment at the time it caused harm to children.

At the motion to dismiss stage, defendants argued that "the [s]tate has not asserted a public nuisance claim because a public right has not been infringed and because the defendants' lead did not cause the alleged harm while within their control as product manufacturers or promoters." The defendants also argued that the state's complaint did not seek to enjoin those people who were responsible for maintaining the public nuisance. For its part, the state argued that the public's right to be free from the hazards of unabated lead had been infringed and that defendants were responsible for the presence of lead in public and private properties throughout Rhode Island. After considering both these arguments, the trial justice denied defendants' motion to dismiss, concluding that the state had sufficiently averred that defendants' conduct "unreasonably interfered with the health, safety, peace, comfort or convenience of the general community." We disagree.

A necessary element of public nuisance is an interference with a public right—those indivisible resources shared by the public at large, such as air, water, or public rights of way. The interference must deprive all members of the community of a right to some resource to which they otherwise are entitled. *See* 4 Restatement (Second) Torts § 821B, cmt. *g* at 92. The Restatement (Second) provides much guidance in ascertaining the fine distinction between a public right and an aggregation of private rights. "Conduct does not become a public nuisance merely because it interferes with the use and enjoyment of land by a large number of persons." …

Although the state asserts that the public's right to be free from the hazards of unabated lead had been infringed, this contention falls far short of alleging an interference with a public right as that term traditionally has been understood in the law of public nuisance. The state's allegation that defendants have interfered with the "health, safety, peace, comfort or convenience of the residents of the [s]tate" standing alone does not constitute an allegation of interference with a public right. *See Beretta U.S.A. Corp.*, 290 Ill.Dec. 525, 821 N.E.2d at 1114. The term public right is reserved more appropriately for those indivisible resources shared by the public at large, such as air, water, or public rights of way. … Expanding the definition of public right based on the allegations in the complaint would be antithetical to the common law and would lead to a widespread expansion of public nuisance law that never was intended, as we discuss *infra*. …

* * *

The enormous leap that the state urges us to take is wholly inconsistent with the widely recognized principle that the evolution of the common law should occur gradually, predictably, and incrementally. Were we to hold otherwise, we would change the meaning of public right to encompass all behavior that causes a widespread interference with the private rights of numerous individuals.

* * *

Even had the state adequately alleged an interference with a right common to the general public, which we conclude it did not, the state's complaint also fails to allege any facts that would support a conclusion that defendants were in control of the lead pigment at the time it harmed Rhode Island's children.

The state filed suit against defendants in their capacity "either as the manufacturer of* * * lead pigment * * * or as the successors in interest to such manufacturers" for "the cumulative presence of lead pigment in paints and coatings in or on buildings throughout the [s]tate of Rhode Island." For the alleged public nuisance to be actionable, the state would have had to assert that defendants not only manufactured the lead pigment but also controlled that pigment at the time it caused injury to children in Rhode Island—and there is no allegation of such control.

The New Jersey Supreme Court applied these same elements to the lead paint litigation in that jurisdiction and likewise held that public nuisance was an improper cause of action. The court emphasized that were it "to permit these complaints to proceed, [it] would stretch the concept of public nuisance far beyond recognition and would create a new and entirely unbounded tort antithetical to the meaning and inherent theoretical limitations of the tort of public nuisance." *In re Lead Paint Litigation,* 924 A.2d at 494. We agree.

We conclude, therefore, that there was no set of facts alleged in the state's complaint that, even if proven, could have demonstrated that defendants' conduct, however unreasonable, interfered with a public right or that defendants had control over the product causing the alleged nuisance at the time children were injured. Accordingly, we need not decide whether defendants' conduct was unreasonable or whether defendants caused an injury to children in Rhode Island.

* * *

Conclusion

For the foregoing reasons, we conclude that the trial justice erred in denying defendants' motion to dismiss.

* * *

NOTES AND QUESTIONS

1. In *Wood v. Picillo,* 443 A.2d 1244 (R.I. 1982), the court did not require the plaintiffs to prove negligence in order to establish a successful nuisance claim against defendants for maintaining a hazardous waste dump on their farm. A successful nuisance claim rests upon unreasonably injury, rather than a defendant's unreasonable conduct. Thus, a plaintiff could recover under nuisance liability despite the otherwise reasonable conduct that creates the injury.

2. The court in *Lead Industries* applies the law of public nuisance to the case, yet it then makes a public policy argument contrary to its ruling.

The court questions why the plaintiffs did not pursue their claim under the tort of products liability. Why did the plaintiffs not bring a private nuisance claim?

3. Consider the following facts in light of both *Hoery* and *Lead Industries Ass'n, Inc.*:

> The Taylor family enjoys recreating at Rock Bottom Lake during the summer months. Rock Bottom Lake is an artificial lake that was created by damming the Truman River. During the summer of 2004, the Taylor's two small children began complaining of dizziness and shortness of breath after spending time in the water at Rock Bottom Lake. ZIM Corporation operates a dump site five miles upstream along Truman River. According to health department records, ZIM Corporation's methods for maintaining their site comply with all federal and state regulations. If the Taylor family can prove that ZIM Corporation's waste has migrated to Rock Bottom Lake, do they have a successful trespass and/or nuisance claim?

4. Common law public nuisance is discussed in the Restatement (Second) of Torts § 821B, Comment b. Public nuisances may include activities that interfere with public health, such as maintaining diseased animals, or a pond where malarial mosquitoes breed. Most states have enacted statutes that criminalize public nuisances. Often the statutes provide either no definition of public nuisance or only a vague definition. However, these statutes have uniformly been interpreted to include the common law definition of nuisance. *See* Restatement (Second) of Torts § 821B cmt. c.

5. For a public nuisance claim, the conduct in question must amount to an interference with a public right. Conduct that merely interferes with the use and enjoyment of land by a large number of persons does not amount to interference with a public right. The notion of public right is collective in nature, rather than individual. It is common to all members of the general public. For example, it is not a public nuisance if 100 people are deprived of their riparian water right because of pollution in the stream abutting their land. However, the pollution becomes a public nuisance once it kills fish in the stream and prevents the public from fishing. Restatement (Second) of Torts § 821B cmt. g.

c. NEGLIGENCE

The basic elements of a common law negligence claim are (1) duty; (2) breach of duty; (3) actual loss or harm; and (4) causal connection between the breach of duty and the harm. As noted above, plaintiffs encounter difficulty proving the elements of a standard negligence claim because causation is sometimes impossible to establish in light of the long latency period between exposure to the toxic substance and manifestation of illness. Asserting a claim of negligence also requires the plaintiff to show that the defendant had knowledge of the dangers at the time of exposure, and further, that there was foreseeable harm to the plaintiff. For example, in

Redland Soccer Club v. Department of Army of U.S., 55 F.3d 827 (3rd Cir. 1995), plaintiffs asserted that exposure to toxic wastes deposited by the U.S. Army in a landfill that was later converted to a soccer field constituted negligence. The court stated that the plaintiffs "must establish that the Army's failure to exercise reasonable care towards them, and any breach of its duty, exposed them to an elevated risk of foreseeable harm, which resulted in injury." A plaintiff may also claim that the defendant violated a standard of care or conduct established by statute or regulation, and thus that the defendant is negligent "per se." In jurisdictions where negligence per se is recognized, the plaintiff must show that the relevant statute was enacted (1) to protect the class of persons of which the plaintiff is a member, and (2) to address the kind of harm that the plaintiff suffered. *See Anderson v. Minnesota*, 693 N.W.2d 181 (Minn. 2005) (discussing state pesticide regulations requiring that such products be properly labeled); *Nunez v. J.L. Sims Co., Inc.*, 2003 WL 21473328 (Ohio App. 1 Dist. 2003) (determining that for negligence per se standard to apply, regulatory standard must provide that defendant breach a specific duty). In toxic tort cases, many courts hesitate to apply a presumption of negligence, though some plaintiffs have been successful.[11]

Res Ipsa Loquitur allows a plaintiff to prove a defendant was negligent by showing that the accident does not occur in the absence of negligence. Essentially, this theory permits an inference of negligence. *O'Neal v. Department of the Army*, 852 F.Supp. 327 (M.D. Pa. 1994) (finding it is possible for well contamination by toxic chemicals to occur in the absence of negligence, so that contamination of wells by toxic chemicals which migrated from Army aircraft maintenance facility did not establish negligence on a theory of res ipsa loquitur).

d. STRICT LIABILITY

Under a theory of strict liability the plaintiff can recover for injury without showing fault on the part of the defendant, if she can show that the defendant is engaging in an "abnormally dangerous activity." The development of the abnormally dangerous activity doctrine began with the English case of *Rylands v. Fletcher*, L.R. 3 H.L. 330 (1868), which emphasized the inappropriateness of certain activities to their locations ("non-natural use"). The modern criteria is embodied in the RESTATEMENT OF TORTS:

In determining whether an activity is abnormally dangerous, the following factors are to be considered:

- existence of a high degree of risk of some harm to the person, land or chattels of others;
- likelihood that the harm that results from it will be great;
- inability to eliminate the risk by the exercise of reasonable care;

11. *See, e.g., Bagley v. Controlled Environment Corp.*, 503 A.2d 823 (N.H. 1986) (court allowed a negligence per se claim under state statute which required operators of hazardous waste facilities to obtain a permit.)

- extent to which the activity is not a matter of common usage;

- inappropriateness of the activity to the place where it is carried on and;

- extent to which its value to the community is outweighed by its dangerous attributes.

REST. (2D) TORTS § 520.

The policy behind holding a toxic tort defendant strictly liable is that, despite the social utility of the activity, the defendant is introducing an extraordinary risk of harm to the public. *See, e.g., Department of Environmental Protection v. Ventron Corp.*, 468 A.2d 150 (N.J. 1983) (court ruled that mercury and other toxic wastes are "abnormally dangerous" and disposal of them, past or present, is an abnormally dangerous activity); *T. & E Indus. Inc. v. Safety Light Corp.*, 587 A.2d 1249 (N.J. 1991) (court ruled that processing, handling and disposal of radium constituted an abnormally dangerous activity, where processor's successor was strictly liable for resulting harm after radium was dumped into vacant urban lot). *But see McDonald v. Timex Corp.*, 9 F. Supp. 2d 120, 122–23 (D. Conn. 1998) (actively dumping hazardous wastes on property not necessarily an abnormally dangerous activity if the wastes are not so inherently dangerous that the risk of probable injury may be eliminated by due care).

e. PRODUCTS LIABILITY

Products liability is an area of the law where parties who make products available to the public are held responsible for the injuries those products cause. In 1965, the RESTATEMENT (SECOND) OF TORTS contained a controversial provision that sellers should be strictly liable for product defects. However, the RESTATEMENT (THIRD) OF TORTS (1998) outlined several other theories of recovery in addition to strict liability for hazardous products.

Design defect claims contend that the entire design of the product is flawed and therefore creates an unreasonable hazard. These claims often arise with prescription drugs, asbestos products, and chemical compounds. Prior to the RESTATEMENT (THIRD), courts used the *consumer expectation* test to determine whether a design defect existed. The test examined whether the product was unreasonably dangerous to the ordinary consumer. However, the RESTATEMENT (THIRD) articulated a *risk utility* test, which weighs the dangerousness of the product against its utility. Jurisdictions use both tests. *See, e.g., Wright v. Brooke Group Ltd.*, 652 N.W.2d 159 (Iowa 2002) (adopting the RESTATEMENT (THIRD) test for design defect claims).

Manufacturing defect suits involve a product that has deviated from its intended design. A plaintiff may assert a manufacturing defect claim under negligence or strict liability. Under a negligence theory of recovery, *res ipsa loquitur* applies because a manufacturing defect is an aberration from the production line. The argument then is that its defect would not happen in the absence of negligence. Under a strict liability theory of recovery, the general rule is that a manufacturer of an item is strictly liable when it proves to have a defect after it is placed in the market, knowing it would be used without an inspection for defects. *Greenman v. Yuba Power Products, Inc.*, 377 P.2d 897 (Cal. 1963). Courts examine the condition of the product to determine whether there was a substantial change in the condition of the product from the time it was sold.

Warning defects are defects in the instructions or labeling of the product. Generally there are three types of warnings defects: no warning, inadequate warning, and inadequate placement of the warning. The majority of jurisdictions use the *state of the art* test to determine whether a warning defect exists. This test examines whether the manufacturer knew or should have known about the risk, and whether the manufacturer reasonably communicated the risk to the ultimate user of the product. A minority of jurisdictions use the test articulated in the RESTATEMENT (THIRD) OF TORTS. This test examines the foreseeable risks of a product, and whether those risks could have been avoided or reduced by reasonable warnings.

Does Federal Law Preempt State Products Liability Law?

The United States Supreme Court in *Wyeth v. Levine*, 129 S.Ct. 1187 (2009) held that state law failure-to-warn claims against manufacturers were not preempted by federal law because (1) the manufacturer could have modified the warning label placed on the drug once it was approved by the FDA, and (2) it was not impossible for the manufacturer to comply with both state law duties underlying failure-to-warn claims, and its federal labeling duties.

Post-sale duty to warn weighs the risk of harm that may be avoided if a seller conveys a remedial warning to a consumer, against the burden on manufacturer in providing this warning. The post-sale claim is separate from the warning claim asserted with respect to the point of sale because the knowledge that requires a seller to provide a post-sale warning does not arise until after the sale. RESTATEMENT (THIRD) OF TORTS: PRODUCTS LIABILITY ch. 2 (1998); *Patton v. Hutchinson Wil–Rich Mfg. Co.*, 861 P.2d 1299, 1310 (Kan. 1993). Since the publishing of the RESTATEMENT THIRD, over thirty states have adopted various versions post-sale duties to warn.

f.   WARRANTY

A purchaser of a product found to be harmful may wish to sue the seller if there have been any assurances made about the nature of the product. These lawsuits allege breach of warranty. The law governing claims arising from breach of warranty is found in Article Two of the Uniform Commercial Code (UCC). A warranty may be express, in which case it is subject to UCC § 2–313, which provides that a seller makes an express warranty by an (1) affirmation of fact or promise made, (2) description of the goods, or (3) sample or model. A plaintiff may also assert a claim based on breach of implied warranty, as established in UCC § 2–314. This provision is based on the idea that there is an implied warranty of merchantability in a contract of sale between buyer and seller.

In *Fleming Farms v. Dixie AG Supply*, Inc., 631 So.2d 922 (Ala. 1994), purchasers who bought a product to reduce the adverse effect of chemicals used on cotton brought claims for breach of express and implied warranty after the product allegedly damaged their cotton crops. The label on the product stated that it was a "safener," and would reduce damage to their cotton. The plaintiffs asserted that this declaration constituted an "affirmation of fact or promise and became part of the basis of the bargain," and was therefore an express warranty. Alternatively, plaintiffs asserted a breach of implied warranty of merchantability claim. The court rejected both arguments, primarily because a "warranty disclaimer" that had been printed in large, bold print in the center of a receipt form proved sufficient to limit defendant's liability. *See also B.C.F. Oil Refining, Inc. v. Consolidated Edison Co.*, 982 F.Supp. 302, 309 (S.D. N.Y. 1997) (oil refining company which hired carrier to transport waste oil could not reasonably have relied on carrier for information on composition of liquid waste, and thus could not maintain breach of warranty claim based on carrier's delivery of waste which contained hazardous materials).

g. FRAUD AND MISREPRESENTATION

Fraud and *misrepresentation* claims raise the issue of whether the disclosures made by a particular party were intentionally misleading or inadequate and whether those disclosures were relied upon by the claimant. Fraudulent misrepresentation claims require a plaintiff to prove the following five elements: (1) materially false representation by a defendant, (2) knowledge by a defendant that the representation was false, (3) intent to induce a plaintiff to act or refrain from acting, (4) justifiable reliance by a plaintiff, and (5) damage to a plaintiff. *Potts v. UAP–GA AG Chem., Inc.*, 567 S.E.2d 316 (Ga. Ct. App. 2002). *But see The City of New York v. Lead Industries Assoc., Inc.*, 660 N.Y.S.2d 422 (1st Dept. 1997) (finding that when a manufacturer intentionally misrepresents the safety of its product to the public, or withholds information regarding its hazards, with the intent that a class of people will buy the product, a fraud claim will lie even though the injured party was not aware of the misrepresentation).

Negligent misrepresentation exists when a defendant owes a duty of care to a plaintiff and then negligently asserts a false statement to a plaintiff. For an example of a statutory duty of care, *see Visconti v. Pepper Partners Ltd. Partnership*, 825 A.2d 210 (Conn. App. Ct. 2003) (law requiring seller of land to disclose property contamination prior to sale). The sellers' broad statement about the quality of the home did not constitute *fraudulent* misrepresentation in *Adams v. NVR Homes, Inc.*, 135 F. Supp. 2d 675 (D. Md. 2001), even though the seller did not inform the buyers that the homes were built on top of a solid waste dump. However, the buyers' *negligent* misrepresentation claim in *Adams* was a question for the jury, because the sellers had a legally recognized duty to disclose material facts.

h. STATUTORY CAUSES OF ACTION

A plaintiff may wish to supplement common law claims with ones based in statutory law. For example, where it has been adopted by a state legislature, the Model Toxics Control Act provides that a past or present property owner is liable for the cleanup and damages to the environment caused by the release of toxic substances. *Dash Point Village Assoc. v. Exxon Corp.*, 937 P.2d 1148 (Wash. App. 1997). Like most toxics statutes, the Comprehensive Environmental Response, Compensation and Liability Act (CERCLA) contains a citizen suit provision that allows "any person" to bring an action directly against a "person * * * who is alleged to be in violation of any standard, regulation, condition, requirement, or order" pursuant to CERCLA. CERCLA § 310(a)(1), 42 U.S.C. § 9659(a)(1). A defendant can be liable under both CERCLA and common law. *See, e.g., United States v. Burlington N. & Santa Fe Ry.*, 520 F.3d 918 (9th Cir. 2008) (discussing CERCLA and strict liability); *New Mexico v. GE*, 467 F.3d 1223 (10th Cir. 2006) (asserting claims of statutory and common law nuisance, negligence and trespass against defendant for ground water contamination); *GenCorp Inc. v. Olin Corp.*, 390 F.3d 433 (6th Cir. 2004) (finding that one does not need to actively participate in disposal to be held liable under CERCLA); *Morton Intern., Inc. v. A.E. Staley Mfg. Co.*, 343 F.3d 669 (3d Cir. 2003) (discussing requirement that party must demonstrate control or knowledge of the hazardous waste for liability to apply); *150 Acres of Land v. United States*, 204 F.3d 698 (6th Cir. 2000) (passive leaking of waste does not constitute disposal of a hazardous substance under CERCLA). This provision permits persons to act as private attorneys general to remedy violations of the Act.[12] Although CERCLA contains no private right of action for damages for persons who claim to have been injured by releases of hazardous wastes encompassed by the statute (the remedies available are injunctive relief and civil penalties), it does contain a savings clause that recognizes and preserves the rights of individuals to pursue their tort claims under state law. CERCLA § 310(h), 42 U.S.C. § 9659(h). As a result, a toxic tort defendant may find that it is both jointly and severally liable under CERCLA, and in common law. *United States v. Occidental Chemical Corp.*, 965 F.Supp. 408 (W.D. N.Y. 1997) (city liable under CERCLA and in public nuisance); *State of New York v. Shore Realty Corp.*, 759 F.2d 1032 (2d Cir. 1985) (same). CERCLA liability is the subject of Chapter 11. Anti-pollution statutes, such as the Clean Water Act, also contain citizen suit provisions permitting any individual to sue any party in violation of the statute. *American Canoe Ass'n Inc. v. District of Columbia Water and Sewer Authority*, 306 F. Supp. 2d 30 (D.D.C. 2004) (discussing citizen suit provision of Clean Water Act). *Parker v. Scrap Metal Processors, Inc.*, 468 F.3d 733 (11th Cir. 2006) (suit involving negligence, negligence per se, nuisance, trespass, and violations of the CWA); *United States v. Ortiz*, 427 F.3d 1278 (10th Cir. 2005) (discussing negligence in discharge a pollutant into the

---

12. The United States Supreme Court has limited the scope of citizen suits by requiring that the citizen plaintiff meet constitutional standing demands. *Lujan v. Defenders of Wildlife*, 504 U.S. 555 (1992). In the case of citizen suits under the Clean Water Act, 33 U.S.C. § 1251–1387, the Court has held that violations must be ongoing or repetitive for a citizens' suit to be proper. *Gwaltney of Smithfield v. Chesapeake Bay Foundation*, 484 U.S. 49 (1987). On the other hand, where a federal environmental statute does not explicitly provide for a citizen suit, a court may acknowledge the existence of an *implied* private right of action if there is evidence of congressional intent to allow such suits. *Middlesex County Sewarage Authority v. National Sea Clammers Assoc.*, 453 U.S. 1 (1981).

river and its violation of the CWA). Chemical manufacturers may have regulatory duties that create additional liability outside of common law strict liability for products. The Federal Register includes the Hazard Communication Standard that requires manufacturers, using all available scientific data, to evaluate chemicals used in the manufacturing process so as to determine their potential hazards. *See* 29 C.F.R. 1910.1200.

When federal statutory law exists in areas traditionally addressed by private causes of action, the federal statute may preempt a cause of action based on state statutory or common law. *Compare Cipollone v. Liggett Group, Inc.*, 505 U.S. 504 (1992) (the Federal Cigarette Labeling and Advertising Act requiring warnings on cigarette packages preempted common law claims based on failure of warn); *Roberts v. Florida Power & Light Co.*, 146 F.3d 1305 (11th Cir. 1998) (federal safety regulations under Atomic Energy Act of 1954 conclusively establish duty of care owed in liability action arising from exposure to nuclear radiation); *Papas v. Upjohn Co.*, 985 F.2d 516 (11th Cir. 1993) (labeling of pesticides pursuant to the Federal Insecticide, Fungicide, and Rodenticide Act (FIFRA) preempted state claims alleging manufacturer's failure to warn consumers of hazardous chemicals in the product); *with Wisconsin Public Intervenor v. Mortier*, 501 U.S. 597 (1991) (FIFRA did not preempt the regulation of pesticides by local governments). State statutes can also preempt common law toxic tort claims. *See San Diego Gas & Electric Co. v. Superior Court*, 920 P.2d 669 (Cal. 1996) (state Public Utilities Act preempted private nuisance action brought against utility owners of power lines).

i.   EMPLOYER LIABILITY

When employees bring common law causes of action against their employees because of exposure to a toxic substance in the work place, the existence of workers' compensation schemes may preclude the lawsuit. *See Cutlip v. Norfolk Southern Corp.*, 2003 WL 1861015 (Ohio App. 6 Dist. 2003) (discussing negligence tort action against employer). Most statutes require a worker's illness to be associated with the worker's specific occupation in order to be considered as an occupational disease. In other words, the disease cannot be one that ordinarily occurs. Many state statutes allow only workers' compensation claims as a remedy for on-the-job injuries, thus barring workers from bringing tort actions against their employers. However, most states recognize the following exceptions: (1) intentional misconduct of employer; (2) employer's conduct aggravates a worker's injury; and (3) an employer undertakes a duty of care outside of the employer—employee relationship, known as *dual capacity*. *Ashdown v. Ameron Int'l Corp.*, 100 Cal.Rptr.2d 20 (Cal. App. 1 Dist. 2000) (rejecting *dual capacity* argument that company had duty to warn as both employer and manufacturer of hazardous product). For examples employer discrimination claims, *see, e.g, Chevron U.S.A. v. Echazabal*, 536 U.S. 73 (2002) (finding that the Americans with Disabilities Act did not preclude employer from refusing employment to individual whose abnormal liver would be further impaired by exposure to workplace toxins); *J.A.M. Builders, Inc. v. Herman*, 233 F.3d

1350 (11th Cir. 2000) (discussing requirement that employer's violation of Occupational Safety and Health Requirements must be willful for criminal penalties).

The court in *Oros v. Hull*, 302 F. Supp. 2d 839 (N.D. Ohio 2004) addressed whether an employer committed an intentional tort when an employee was exposed to toxins while supervising a waste removal site. Because workers' compensation often limits the liability of employers in toxic tort suits, an employee must establish that an employer committed an intentional tort. In order to demonstrate an intentional tort, an employee must prove: (1) that the employer knew of the existence of a dangerous condition; (2) that the employer knew that if the employee was exposed to the dangerous condition, harm was substantially certain to occur; and (3) the employer required the employee to work in dangerous conditions. The court dismissed the employer's motion for summary judgment and held that a jury could find that the employer committed an intentional tort because the employer told the employee he did not need protective equipment, and because the employer failed to tell the employee that toxic chemicals had been discovered at the waste removal site.

DNA technology will likely impact workers' compensation claims because the new technology can accurately determine the toxic cause of an individual's injury.

The advent of DNA testing in the mid-1980's revolutionized the criminal justice system. Now a new type of DNA technology is ready to have a similar effect on civil litigation. Its creators say the technology can determine with near certainty whether an individual has been physically injured from exposure to a particular chemical, such as benzene. If that's the case, experts says, the technique could transform the quality of evidence in workers' compensation and toxic tort cases, which are now largely dependent on circumstantial and anecdotal evidence. It could also cut down on frivolous claims, streamline discovery, precipitate more out-of-court settlements and, barring privacy concerns, lead to improvements in workplace safety.

"Assuming they can actually do what they say they can do, this could be a revolutionary development, both in terms of civil litigation and for medical treatment purposes," says Julie Burger, a Chicago–Kent College of law professor who specializes in the social, legal and ethical implications of emerging technologies, including genetics. The method is an application of existing technology used in the medical field. It measures the release of proteins known as cytokines that are produced by DNA strands when cells are exposed to harmful substances, according to Dr. Bruce Gillis, a Los Angeles medical toxicologist who developed the technology, known as MSDS1 or cytokine testing.

Every chemical substance creates its own telltale "signature" of cytokine releases—or genetic fingerprints—in a person, Gillis says. Once a chemical's unique signature has been identified, the test can determine what chemical, if any, triggered the identical releases pattern in an individual's DNA. Gillis says the test will help identify individuals who have genuinely been injured by exposure to a particular substance. It also offers employers a tool for improving workplace safety and monitoring employee health.

The science behind the technology is sound, Gillis says. It is based on established principles of cell biology long used in the treatment of cancer and other diseases. And the underlying research on the cytokine test has been peer reviewed in two scientific publications. The tests, being conducted at the University of Illinois College of Medicine in Chicago, where Gillis went to medical school and with which he is now affiliated, are now being done for two known toxins, benzene and hexavalent chromium, the chemicals made famous in the 2000 film *Erin Brockovich*. But Gillis says the test can be performed for any toxic substance once its signature has been identified, for $12,500 per test.

Gillis doesn't foresee admissibility problems with the technology, either. He notes that the type of DNA testing used in criminal cases, which is now universally accepted in the courts, relies on 13 points of comparison—called parameters—to determine whether two DNA samples are a match. The cytokine test, by contrast, uses up to 36,000 parameters of an individual's DNA to determine whether the person has been injured from exposure to a particular chemical or its metbolites; the test boasts an accuracy rate of more than 99.9 percent.

Burger can't vouch for the scientific validity of the technology. And she says the admissibility of such evidence is sure to be challenged until it has proven to be reliable. She also suggests that such a test would be subject to some major limitations. It can't tell when or whether a particular exposure occurred, for instance. And it doesn't take into account such factors as an individual's susceptibility to certain diseases or the cumulative effects of repeated exposure to the same toxic substance over a prolonged period of time. "I wouldn't view it as having the kind of slam-dunk effect that DNA evidence has had in criminal cases. It's not going to end all toxic tort litigation overnight," she says. "But if the technology turns out to be reliable, it would have a big impact on the way these kinds of cases pay out."

The test has, in fact, already been used in more than two dozen workers' compensation cases in California by mutual agreement between the two sides, according to Gillis. And the results have gone both ways. Some cases have been dropped after the test showed that an applicant had not been injured by exposure to the chemicals from which he or she was alleging harm. Other cases have been settled after the test showed that the applicant was injured by exposure to a chemical present in the workplace.

Los Angeles-area insurance defense lawyer Neal Jardine says his firm has used the test twice, both times with favorable results. In one case, he says, the test saved his client more than $1 million in potential damages when it showed that a man who had worked around tires all his life didn't get cancer from exposure to benzene—used to make tires—commonly found there. In the other case, a different test used the same process showed that a nurse who claimed to be in chronic pain and permanently disabled from a back injury on the job exhibited none of the physical signs of the cellular inflammation associated with pain. "Now, finally, we have a test that can tell us, in an objective, up-or-down way, whether an individual has been harmed by exposure to a certain substance," he says.

Jardine says the test is proving to be valuable for insurers—one that not only saves time and money but could also eventually eliminate the need for the kinds of anecdotal and circumstantial evidence on which such cases have long relied. But he also detects resistance on both sides to using the technology. Some applicants' lawyers don't want to use the test because it could mean the end of their cause. But even some defense lawyers are reluctant to use the test because of its cost or because they don't understand its potential value.

Bedford, Mass., lawyer Leonard Nason, who represents both sides in workers' compensation cases, says the test would appear to have great potential, both as a litigation tool and as a way of making the workplace safer. But Nason, who chairs the Workers' Compensation and Employers' Liability Law Committee of the ABA's Tort Trial and Insurance Practice Section, says such technology also raises concerns about privacy and potential discrimination. That's why Nason's committee is sponsoring several programs on the topic at the section's scheduled conference in Chicago March 26–28. The conference, which focuses on the national trends, emerging issues and cutting-edge medical disability determinations affecting state workers' compensation laws, includes an introduction to the technology by Gillis, a tour of Cytokine Institute's laboratory facilities at the University of Illinois medical school, and a panel discussion of the potential privacy and discrimination issues raised by the use of such technology.

Although no current federal law prohibits genetic testing, Nason points out, pending legislation in Congress would bar employers from denying employees health insurance based on the use of such tests. More than 20 states have laws that either limit or prohibit employers from collecting genetic information from employees. The $2.2 million settlement of a 2001 discrimination suit against the Burlington Northern Santa Fe Corp. by the Equal Employment Opportunity Commission may also come into place, according to Nason. *EEOC v. Burlington Northern Santa Fe Railway Co., No. 02-C-0456, 2002 WL 32155386 (E.D. Wis. 2002).*

In that case, the government's first against alleged workplace DNA discrimination, the EEOC accused the railway of violating the Americans with Disabilities Act by requiring employees to submit to a physical that included a blood test that was used to look for predisposed medical conditions without the employee's knowledge or permission.

> While the company denied violating the law, the EEOC took the position that the mere gathering of an employee's DNA may constitute a violation of the ADA.
>
> Burger says a problem posed by the use of such technology is that there is no single comprehensive law covering the use of genetic information for employment and insurance purposes. And that problem is compounded by the fact that state laws dealing with the subject may or may not address the kind of technology such testing represents. "We're venturing into potentially uncharted legal waters," she says. *Mark Hansen, DNA Poised to Show Its Civil Side: After Changing Criminal Law, Tests are Ready for Workers' Comp Toxic Test Cases*, ABA JOURNAL, March 2008.

j. OTHER CLAIMS

Claimants can bring a variety of other toxic tort claims, including assault and battery, civil Racketeer Influenced and Corrupt Organizations Act (RICO) claims, concealment, and restitution and unjust enrichment claims. *Assault* and *battery* claims are often brought together as a type of intentional tort. A *battery* occurs when an act by a defendant intends to cause harm or offensive contact with a plaintiff. An *assault* is an act by a defendant that causes apprehension of harmful or offensive contact by a plaintiff. Both torts relate to toxic torts because in both a defendant must have intent to cause harm. *Bogner v. Airco*, Inc. 353 F. Supp. 2d 977 (C.D.Ill. 2005) (dismissing battery claim because knowledge of hazards did not satisfy the intent requirement). A *civil RICO* claim requires a showing of *racketeering*, which occurs when a party engages in an illegal business. While *civil RICO* cases in toxic tort are uncommon, a plaintiff may utilize this action because a successful claim allows for *treble damages*. *Philip Morris USA, Inc. v. United States*, 396 F.3d 1190 (D.C. Cir. 2005) (finding RICO Act authorizes only forward-looking remedies); *Service Employees Intern. Union Health and Welfare Fund v. Philip Morris Inc.*, 249 F.3d 1068 (D.C. Cir. 2001) (holding plaintiffs did not satisfy RICO claim because alleged damages were too remote).

The tort of *concealment* is similar to a claim of misrepresentation. The RESTATEMENT SECOND OF TORTS defines concealment as one party to a transaction intentionally preventing another party from acquiring material information, or misleading someone into thinking the information does not exist. The party committing concealment is liable for pecuniary damages. The concepts of *restitution* and *unjust enrichment* are equitable doctrines requiring a person who has been unjustly enriched at the expense of another to make restitution to the other party. These doctrines commonly occur in toxic tort suits when a landowner seeks restitution from a previous owner for the costs of cleaning up hazardous waste. *Santa Clara Valley Water Dist. v. Olin Corp.*, 2008 WL 3876166 (N.D. Cal. 2008) (discussing restitution and unjust enrichment in toxic tort cases).

k. TORT REFORM

Federal Tort Reform Efforts have attempted to establish negligence and warranty law as the legal basis for the liability of a seller. There has been a push to remove the doctrine of strict products liability. Additionally, there has been a move towards caps on punitive damages, and requiring clear and convincing evidence to establish such a claim. *State Tort Reform* has moved towards capping non-economic damages for non-catastrophic injuries, and limiting punitive damages to twice the amount of pain and suffering.

Joint and Several Liability Reform has moved towards removing joint liability in favor of several liability only. Exceptions to joint and several liability may apply directly to toxic tort cases in the following situations: (1) several liability does not apply with hazardous waste litigation and certain types of products liability suits; and (2) some states have suggested reforms based upon a defendant's percentage share of fault as determined by a jury. If the liability is greater than a particular percentage, joint and several liability applies. *The Closing of Punitive Damages' Iron Cage*, 38 Loy. L.A. L. Rev. 1297 (2005) (discussing punitive damages' reform).

There has also been tort reform easing the burden on plaintiffs. For example, several states have enacted legislation reviving previously extinguished toxic tort claims. In 1986, New York adopted a discovery statute for toxic tort claims, and also permitted parties asserting damage associated with five toxic substances an additional one-year to maintain actions based on latent effects from the exposure to the five substances. 1986 N.Y. Laws ch. 682 § 4; *Germantown Central School District v. Clark, Clark, Millis & Gilson,* 100 N.Y.2d 202 (N.Y. 2003) (applying the New York extended statute of limitations in case involving asbestos exposure in school building).

2. NATURE OF THE HARM AND REMEDIES

In most toxic tort cases, plaintiffs believe they have suffered some physical injury resulting from exposure to toxic substances or hazardous wastes. The injury is typically some physical illness or medical condition. In other cases, there may be no immediate personal harm, but the otherwise healthy plaintiff may have an enhanced risk of disease in future due to exposure to a toxic chemical. Or the injury is not physical, but economic. When the harm alleged is anything other than simple medical injury, a toxic tort plaintiff may have to overcome certain obstacles that arise with non-physical harms.

- *Enhanced risk.* Claims based upon the risk of developing some illness in the future as a result of exposure to a toxic substance fly in the face of traditional notions of injury. A plaintiff bringing an enhanced risk action is not only basing the claim on some future event—the illness or disease for which she is at risk—but the plaintiff also cannot guarantee that the event will occur at all. Courts have offered varying resolutions to the problems inherent in enhanced risk cases. Some jurisdictions require a present physical injury so that there is some evidence of extant harm that can form the basis of a higher probability of similar future injury. *See*

Brafford v. Susquehanna Corp., 586 F.Supp. 14 (D. Colo. 1984) (present injury exists when at the time of the lawsuit damage exists to cellular and subcellular structures). The leading case for claims alleging only increased risk is *Ayers v. Township of Jackson*, 525 A.2d 287 (N.J. 1987). In *Ayers*, none of the plaintiffs were, at the time of the lawsuit, suffering any physical injuries or illnesses stemming from the defendant's contamination of their drinking water supply. Ordinarily, this would be the end of the case. However, the court agreed that increased risk alone was actionable, but required that the plaintiffs demonstrate that the actual risk be quantified. When risk cannot be quantified, such as when science cannot assess whether other factors not under control of the defendant may contribute to the likelihood of future illness, the increased risk claim will be rejected. *See also Hagerty v. L & L Marine Services, Inc.*, 788 F.2d 315 (5th Cir. 1986) (enhanced risk recognized when the toxic exposure "more probably than not" will lead to cancer).

- *Emotional distress.* Although psychological harm can be raised alongside physical harm arising from exposure to a toxic substance, some plaintiffs who have not yet developed any symptoms may seek compensation based on their present fear of future illness.[13] Several jurisdictions permit recovery for emotional distress based on a fear of future cancer, even when the plaintiff is healthy, and can prove only there has been contact with a cancer-producing agent. *In re Methyl Tertiary Butyl Ether Prods. Liab. Litig.*, 528 F. Supp. 2d 303 (S.D.N.Y. 2007) (rejecting emotional distress claim against a gas station owner for oil leaking into the surrounding soil and contaminating ground water). *Bernbach v. Timex Corp.*, 989 F.Supp. 403, 408 (D. Conn. 1996); *Herber v. Johns–Manville Corp.*, 785 F.2d 79 (3d Cir. 1985); *Devlin v. Johns–Manville*, 495 A.2d 495 (N.J. Super. 1985). Some courts that permit recovery for emotional distress require the plaintiff to prove more than the fact of exposure. In California, the emotional distress must be based on a knowledge, grounded in reliable medical or scientific data, that the quantitative likelihood of developing cancer is more likely than not. *Potter v. Firestone Tire and Rubber Co.*, 863 P.2d 795 (Cal. 1993). *See also* E. Jean Johnson, *Environmental Stigma Damages: Speculative Damages in Environmental Tort Cases*, 15 UCLA J. OF ENVTL. L. & POLICY 185 (1997). In general, outrageous conduct is necessary to recover for emotional distress. *Contreras v. Thor Norfolk Hotel, L.L.C.*, 292 F. Supp. 2d 798 (E.D. Va. 2003) (rejecting claim for emotional distress when outrageous conduct was not directed towards plaintiff).

---

13. Fear of developing leukemia from power lines was one of the allegations made in the *San Diego Gas & Electric Co.* case noted above. Emotional distress for witnessing a family member die of a disease caused by defendant's alleged conduct was a claim raised in the Woburn, Massachusetts case, *Anderson v. W.R. Grace & Co.*, 628 F.Supp. 1219, 1228–1230 (D. Mass. 1986).

- *Fear of future injury.* The claim of damages for fear of future injuries is closely related to emotional distress. Such claims are based on exposures to toxic substances, which allegedly increase the possibility that the plaintiff will suffer particular injuries, such as disease, in the future. In order to be compensable, most courts require the fear of contracting such diseases to be identifiable, specific, and substantial. *Ayers v. Jackson Township*, 525 A.2d 287 (N.J. 1987) (allowing no recovery for alleged enhanced risk of contracting cancer after exposure to contaminants in water when the percentage increase in risk could not be quantified); *see also Potter v. Firestone Tire & Rubber Co.*, 863 P.2d 795, 800 (1993) ("Our analysis of existing case law and policy considerations relevant to the availability of damages from emotional distress leads us to conclude that, generally, in the absence of a present physical injury or illness, recovery of damages for fear of cancer in a negligence action should be allowed only if the plaintiff pleads and proves that the fear steams from the knowledge, corroborated by a reliable medical and scientific opinion, that it is more likely than not that the feared cancer will develop in the future due to the toxic exposure."). In addition, most courts require a physical injury prior to recovery for fear of future injury. *Eagle–Picher Indus. v. Cox*, 481 So.2d 517 (Fla. App. 3d Dist. 1985); *see Norfolk & Western Ry. Co. v. Ayers*, 538 U.S. 135 (2003).

- *Cancerphobia.* Cancerphobia is a type of fear of future injury claim, but instead of fear of contracting the full range of afflictions, it is concerned only with cancer. Such claims have been limited to situations where there is: a serious fear of cancer; the fear is caused by exposure to the substance; and the fear of contracting cancer because of such exposure is reasonable. *See Deleski v. Raymark Indus., Inc.*, 819 F.2d 377 (3d Cir. 1987). Some courts make a distinction between cancerphobia and fear of injury claims and impose special burdens upon parties seeking recovery for cancerphobia. This distinction is based on the idea that cancerphobia is a psychological disorder, requiring medical expertise to determine its presence, cause and extent. *Eagle–Picher Indus. v. Cox*, 481 So.2d 517, 526 n.13 (Fla.Dist.Ct.App. 1985); but see *Broussard v. Olin Corp.*, 546 So.2d 1301 (La. App. 1989) (refusing to distinguish between fear of cancer claim and increased risk of cancer claim).

- *Post-traumatic stress.* Post-traumatic stress claims are similar to generalized emotional distress allegations. However, the medical and legal professions recognize the disorder as a distinct mental disability and require proof that certain precise characteristics are present before recovery is permitted. *Sterling v. Velsicol Chemical Corp.*, 855 F.2d 1188, 1210 (6th Cir. 1988). The elements of post-traumatic stress are: 1) a recognizable trauma; 2) Some form of re-experiencing the trauma; 3) Change in normal expected behavior patterns of patient; 4) new behavior patterns in patient not existent before trauma and 5) the prior elements last a minimum of one month. AMERICAN PSYCHIATRIC ASSOCIATION, DIAGNOSTIC & STATISTICAL MANUAL OF MENTAL DISORDERS (3rd Ed. 1980).

- *Quality of life.* Quality of life claims are closely related to other more traditional toxic tort compensation claims such as emotional distress; however, they are often pursued as separate causes of action. Quality of life claims are based upon the daily loss of the normal amenities of life. *See Coffin v. Board of Supervisors of Louisiana St. Univ. Agric. and Mech. College, 620 So.2d 1354 (La. Ct. App. 1993) (awarding separate damages for loss of quality of life due to damage to patient's voice).*

- *Medical monitoring.* Claims for medical monitoring seek to reimburse the plaintiff for future costs associated with diagnostic tests and periodic medical examinations thought necessary because of the likelihood of disease after the termination of the lawsuit. Medical monitoring is needed only when there is an increased risk that such monitoring is reasonably anticipated to be incurred as a result of some earlier exposure to a toxic substance.[14] While most jurisdictions do not require the plaintiff to manifest any present symptoms of illness, the plaintiff must be able to prove exposure(s) to some toxic or hazardous substance under the control of the defendant, making medical monitoring necessary due to increased risk of future disease, where testing procedures exist that can detect the onset of disease at a early stage. *Hinton ex rel. Hinton v. Monsanto Co.,* 813 So.2d 827 (Ala. 2001) (court did not recognize a plaintiff's medical monitoring claim absent a present physical injury); *Leach v. E.I. Du Pont de Nemours & Co.,* 2002 WL 1270121 (W. Va. Cir. Ct. 2002) (approving class action suit for medical monitoring claim); *In re Tobacco Litig. (Med. Monitoring Cases),* 600 S.E.2d 188 (W. Va. 2004) (case dismissed for failure to show medical monitoring was reasonably necessary); *In re Paoli Yard PCP Litigation,* 916 F.2d 829 (3d Cir. 1990); *Merry v. Westinghouse Electric Corp.,* 684 F.Supp. 847 (M.D. Pa. 1988); Jamie A. Grodsky, *Genomics and Toxic Torts: Dismantling the Risk-Injury Divide,* 59 STAN. L. REV. 1671 (2007) (addressing detection of injury and medical monitoring).

- *Increased Risk of Future Injury.* Also known as "enhanced risk," this claim alleges that the plaintiff is more likely to suffer future injuries due to the exposure of a toxic substance than those not exposed. For the most part courts have been reluctant to permit the award of damages on this basis. *See e.g., Rainer v. Union Carbide Corp.,* 402 F.3d 608 (6th Cir. 2005). Court's reluctance to recognize this claim is based on the reasoning that, "award[ing] damages based on a mere mathematical probability would significantly undercompensate those who actually do develop cancer and would be a windfall to those who do not." *Arnett v. Dow Chemical Co., SF Master File No.*

---

14. Medical monitoring does not compensate for any damages associated with enhanced risk, as such, or for the plaintiff's emotional distress over becoming sick in the future.

729586, slip op. at 15 (Cal. Super. Ct. [S.F. cty] Mar. 21, 1983); see also Stites v. Sundstrand Heat Transfer, Inc., 660 F.Supp. 1516 (W.D. Mich. 1987) (dismissing increased risk of injury claims based upon exposure to trichloroethylene). Other courts deny recovery for this claim, fearing that recovery would extinguish plaintiff's right to future recovery if and when an injury actually manifested itself. Adams v. Johns–Manville Sales Corp., 727 F.2d 533 (5th Cir. 1984). Despite these concerns, some courts permit recovery if plaintiffs can show that they are more likely than not to suffer cancer or other future illness. Anderson v. W.R. Grace & Co., 628 F.Supp. 1219 (D. Mass. 1986). Still other courts permit recovery where the claimant's increased risk of contracting a particular affliction was substantially less than fifty percent. *Capital Holding Corp. v. Bailey, 873 S.W.2d 187 (Ky. 1994).*

- *Economic loss.* Where the nature of the plaintiff's injury is economic, unaccompanied by physical injury or injury to real property, courts have typically denied recovery under strict liability and negligence theories.[15] For example, in *Adams v. Star Enterprise*, 51 F.3d 417 (4th Cir. 1995), landowners argued that a Virginia statute imposing strict liability for discharges of oil onto private lands did not require actual physical damage to property, but allowed recovery for the diminution in the value of their properties resulting from their proximity to the defendant's oil spill. The Court denied recovery, primarily because the statute permitted liability only when there was "injury to property," but this phrase did not encompass purely economic losses.

When courts permit recovery for economic injury, they focus on the relative bargaining power of the parties, and the allocation of loss to the better risk-bearer. *Mainline Tractor & Equipment Co. v. Nutrite Corp.*, 937 F.Supp. 1095 (D. Vt. 1996). Even if parties can receive relief for purely economic losses resulting from the effects of the defendant's operation of a hazardous facility, plaintiffs must introduce evidence establishing their economic losses; it is not sufficient to merely present evidence that the defendant's actions were a potential cause of injury. *In re Hanford Nuclear Reservation Litigation*, 894 F.Supp. 1436 (E.D. Wash. 1995) (although plaintiffs proved a decline in fish runs during the years a nuclear facility discharged effluent into the Columbia River, the Court will not infer economic injury from the declines, or from the fact that the plaintiffs caught fewer fish during this time).

The *Isabel* case considers both the advantages and limitations of an emotional distress lawsuit.

---

15. Jurisdictions adopting Restatement (Second) of Torts § 40213 may allow recovery for economic losses based on fraudulent or negligent misrepresentation. The Restatement (Second) of Torts § 929 governs awards of damages for injury to property resulting from past invasions that do not amount to a total destruction of property. *See* Richard E. Speidel, *Warranty Theory, Economic Loss, and the Privity Requirement: Once More Into the Void*, 67 B.U. L. Rev. 9 (1987).

Isabel v. Velsicol Chemical Co.

327 F. Supp. 2d 915 (W.D. Tenn. 2004)

ORDER GRANTING IN PART AND DENYING IN PART DEFENDANT'S MOTION TO DISMISS

■ DONALD, DISTRICT JUDGE.

Before the Court is the motion of Velsicol Chemical Corporation ("Defendant") for partial dismissal of the class action complaint of Mildred Isabel, Charles and Evalina Black, and Elizabeth Gate ("Plaintiffs"). Specifically, Defendant requests dismissal of Plaintiffs' claims for (1) strict liability, (2) damages based on emotional distress, (3) attorney fees, and (4) punitive damages. The Court has jurisdiction over this matter based on 28 U.S.C. §§ 1332 and 1441. For the following reasons, the Court grants in part Defendant's motion to dismiss the claim for attorney fees and denies in part Defendant's motion to dismiss the claims for strict liability, emotional distress damages, and punitive damages.

I.   FACTUAL BACKGROUND

For purposes of this motion to dismiss, the Court takes the facts as alleged in Plaintiffs' complaint.

Plaintiffs are owners of real property located in Memphis, Tennessee. Defendant is an Illinois corporation. Plaintiffs bring this lawsuit on behalf of:

* * *

Defendant owns a manufacturing plant in Memphis, Tennessee. In the mid-to-late 1940s, Defendant discovered and began to produce a chemical called Aldrin. Aldrin turns into a chemical called Dieldrin after a certain time.

Defendant began discharging Aldrin/Dieldrin along with wastewater downstream into Cypress Creek, where the chemicals collected in the soils at the creek's bottom and along its banks. Aldrin and Dieldrin are hydrophobic, and both, but especially Dieldrin, do not dissolve easily in water. Therefore, Dieldrin remains in the soil for an extremely long period of time.

Dieldrin is known to pose serious long-term health risks and has been linked to cancer, Parkinson's disease, birth defects, and other health problems. Any amount of Dieldrin above normal levels in the soil can potentially cause long-term health problems to those exposed, and the detection of any above-normal level requires removal of the Dieldrin or evacuation of the premises.

In or about May 2002, Defendant tested various property owners' soils. From those tests, Defendant learned that the properties along the banks of the Cypress Creek contained elevated levels of Dieldrin. Plaintiffs and the other class members own residential property located along the banks of Cypress Creek downstream from Defendant's manufacturing plant.

On or about March 24, 2004, Defendant began informing certain class members that their property contained heightened levels of Dieldrin in the soil. In those letters, Defendant admitted that the compounds got into the creek sediments from wastewater discharges from its manufacturing plant.

The real property of Plaintiffs and the class members has been rendered worthless in its present form as a result of Defendant's discharge of the dangerous chemicals, and Plaintiffs allege that they and the class members have suffered monetary damages. Plaintiffs and the class members now fear for their personal health and well-being, and for the health and well-being of their family members and those who come in contact with their property. Plaintiffs and the class members also fear that the value of their property will be diminished.

* * *

IV. ANALYSIS

* * *

B. EMOTIONAL DISTRESS DAMAGES

Defendant argues that Plaintiffs have not stated a claim for emotional distress damages based on their alleged concerns for their health because they did not allege actual exposure to the chemicals. Plaintiffs respond that they alleged that the soil of their and the class members' property is contaminated with the chemicals, and that it is a logical inference that they came into contact with the soil on their property, thus putting them into contact with the chemicals.

What Plaintiffs must show to receive emotional distress damages on this basis is shown by the Tennessee Supreme Court's decision in *Laxton v. Orkin Exterminating Company, Incorporated,* 639 S.W.2d 431 (Tenn.1982). In *Laxton,* the defendant negligently contaminated the plaintiffs' water supply with chlordane, a dangerous, potentially carcinogenic chemical, while spraying for insects. *Id.* at 432–33. The evidence at trial indicated that the plaintiffs drank the contaminated water, but medical examinations revealed that no physical damage had been done to them. *Id.* at 434. Also, the mental anxiety of the plaintiffs did not manifest itself in any physical way. *Id.* at 433. After a jury verdict for the plaintiffs, the Court of Appeals affirmed the judgment for property damages and out-of-pocket expenses, but reversed the judgment for damages based on mental anguish. *Id.* at 431–32. On appeal, the Tennessee Supreme Court concluded that the plaintiffs could still recover for their emotional distress damages based on their fear for the health and welfare of themselves and their children, despite the fact that the traditional requirements of the physical injury or manifestation rule had not been met. *Id.* at 434.

In our opinion, in addition to cases where it has previously been allowed, recovery for the negligent infliction of mental anguish should be allowed in cases where, as a result of a defendant's negligence, a plaintiff has ingested an indefinite amount of a harmful substance. In such cases the finder of fact may conclude that the plaintiff has sustained sufficient physical injury to support an award for mental anguish even if subsequent medical diagnosis fails to reveal any other physical injury. The period of mental anguish, of course, would be confined to the time between discovery of the ingestion and the negative medical diagnosis or other information that puts to rest the fear of injury.

Id.; cf. Carroll v. Sisters of Saint Francis Health Servs., Inc., 868 S.W.2d 585 (Tenn.1993) (holding that, to recover damages for negligent infliction of emotional distress based on fear of contracting AIDS, plaintiff must allege actual exposure to HIV). In other words, the de minimus "physical injury" of ingesting the contaminated water sufficiently satisfied the physical injury or manifestation rule so as to justify the award of emotional distress damages.

The Court later reaffirmed the basis of *Laxton* for general negligence claims that allege emotional distress damages as part of multiple types of claimed damages. *See Estate of Amos v. Vanderbilt Univ.,* 62 S.W.3d 133, 136–37 (Tenn.2001). The Court differentiated such general negligence claims with emotional distress damages from those for damages based solely on negligent infliction of emotional distress. Negligent infliction of emotional distress claims no longer require proof of a physical injury or manifestation in Tennessee, but they do have other heightened proof requirements. *See Camper v. Minor,* 915 S.W.2d 437, 446 (Tenn.1996). On the other hand, negligence actions that claim damages for emotional distress in addition to other types of damages do not involve the same heightened proof. *See Amos,* 62 S.W.3d at 137. *Camper* did not affect the longstanding rule that emotional injuries are compensable if accompanied by additional claims for damages. *Id.*

Plaintiffs in this case specifically allege damages based on the diminished value of their real property and on their emotional distress based on fears over their health. Notwithstanding the general language of *Amos,* under *Laxton,* it appears that emotional distress damages may not be "parasitic" upon property damages alone, because the plaintiffs in *Laxton* suffered property damage based on diminished value, but the Court still required them to prove some de minimus "physical injury," specifically, ingestion. *Laxton,* 639 S.W.2d at 431, 434. Thus, it appears that Plaintiffs here must also prove some sort of "physical injury," even though they also alleged property damage.

It is taken as true for this motion that the soil on Plaintiffs' and the other class members' property was contaminated with Aldrin/Dieldrin. Plaintiffs argue that, since the contaminated soil was on their real property, they necessarily came into contact with it, thus providing the required allegation of actual exposure. The Court finds this to be a logical inference. Plaintiffs obviously need not allege that they ingested the contaminated soil; unlike in a contaminated drinking water case, the Court could not realistically require ingestion. Contact appears to satisfy the exposure requirement under the circumstances, and logic dictates that Plaintiffs came into contact with the soil on their property. Plaintiffs, of course, will have to prove exposure should this case proceed to trial, but, for the purposes of this Rule 12(b)(6) motion, the Court holds that the allegations in the complaint sufficiently state a claim for emotional distress damages based on fear over health problems. Accordingly, the Court denies Defendant's motion to dismiss Plaintiffs' claim for such emotional distress damages.

NOTES AND QUESTIONS

1. Examine this incident involving the Ford Motor Company in light of the previous case.

> In what could be the largest environmental lawsuit ever in New Jersey, Upper Ringwood residents sued the Ford Motor Co. on Wednesday, alleging personal injury and property damage from industrial waste dumped a generation ago. More than 700 former and current residents claim that toxic castoffs from Ford's former Mahwah factor caused a multitude of illnesses in the community and even now have essentially left their neighborhood a Superfund site.
>
> The mass tort claim says Ford and its agents dumped an ocean of contaminants, concealed the health hazards the waste created and deliberately conducted only a partial cleanup. The 13-count suit filed in the state Superior Court in Paterson alleges fraud and negligence and seeks medial monitoring and unspecified financial compensation. In a separate filing last month, attorneys put the borough of Ringwood on notice that it also may be sued. The attorneys said they would seek $3 million per resident, a total that could exceed $2 billion.
>
> "We are seeking just and fair compensation for the complainants," attorney Joseph S. Rosato, who works in the New York office for The Cochran Firm, said after delivering the suit. "There's a lot to be done for this community." Rosato is part of the A–Team of attorneys behind Wednesday's suit, which pits Native Americans against an icon of American business. The residents are represented by marquee firms, including one founded by Robert Kennedy Jr.
>
> Among the residents are hundreds of members of the state-recognized Ramapough Mountain Indian tribe, who have lived in the remote community for more than 200 years. They blame Ford for a multitude of illnesses: pervasive asthma, unexplained skin rashes and many cancers. In the suit, the residents seek compensation for personal injuries, emotional distress, "fear of cancer," cost of medical care, and the expense of medical monitoring. "This is a nightmare that has turned into a dream," said Vivian Milligan, a neighborhood leader. "All the waiting and waiting, it became unbearable, and it's finally turning around."
>
> Ford spokesman Jon Holt declined comment pending review of the litigation. Ford acknowledges that contractors it hired dumped millions of gallons of paint sludge and other industrial waste in this mountain community from 1967 to 1971, when a Ford subsidiary owned the land.

Tons of waste remain on the onetime Superfund site, despite four federally supervised cleanups.

In the ongoing cleanup, Ford reports it has removed more waste this time than in all the previous projects combined. Last week, the federal Environmental Protection Agency announced plans to relist the Ringwood site to guarantee a thorough and federally backed cleanup.

"Ford's choice to perform four inadequate investigations and cleanups has devastated this community," said Kevin Madonna, a law partner of Robert F. Kennedy Jr. In preparing its defense, Ford is not expected to deny that a company contractor dumped industrial waste at the site 30 years ago. However, the company is likely to seek to shift liability onto others it also considers responsible.

Besides Ford, the suit names a company that carted waste for Ford, ISA in New Jersey, and others including an environmental consultant and local manufacturer, Arrow Group Industries of Haskell. An executive with that company declined comment pending review of the suit. Many of the suit's contentions mirror the findings of The Record's "Toxic Legacy" series last fall. The series found that Ford's consultants had conducted only a limited Superfund cleanup 10 years ago while assuring the EPA the job was thoroughly done. Tests by the paper found dangerous levels of contaminants in soil and water.

The lawsuit accuses Ford and the other companies of negligence and fraud in failing to warn residents of the extent of the dumping and the potential danger it posed. It claims Ford and other companies profited from "virtually free disposal and storage of toxic waste for decades." The complaint accuses the companies of trespass and battery, because waste ended up in some of the residents' properties.

The residents, many of them descendants of the Van Dunks, the Manns and the DeGroats who have lived in the ridges and hollows of this mountain since the Revolutionary War era, will ask a jury to decide one of the most difficult legal and scientific issues: Is there a cause-and-effect relationship between Ford's pollution and the illness in the population? Lawyers will be able to note New Jersey's own findings announced last July of elevated rate of some cancers in this low-income minority community.

The case for the residents will include myriad medical records, environmental test results and volumes of Ford's documents. Families, the case alleges, were continually exposed to a variety of toxic substances including volatile organic compounds, heavy metals including lead, arsenic and chromium, and PCB's, which caused widespread illness. Since so many people hunt and hike in this rural enclave, the exposure was widespread: through inhalation of toxic vapors from burning contaminants at the dumpsite, skin contact with contaminated soil and ingestion of contaminated well water, the suit maintains.

> However, environmental experts warn that the plaintiffs will have difficulty proving that toxic substances caused illness or death. Often environmental studies are inconclusive in linking exposure of industrial waste to illness, experts say.
>
> The massive tort claim joins the ranks of major New Jersey environmental civil cases in a state that is home to 135 Superfund sites, the most in the country. Among the notorious are the Toms River case, in which nearly 70 families whose children were stricken with cancer who won a settlement of at least $13 million, paid by two chemical companies and a water company in 2001. In Pompton Lakes, more than 1,000 property owners sued DuPont in 2002, arguing that the chemical giant was responsible for multiple illnesses in the community. The case was settled for an undisclosed amount and a guarantee of health monitoring paid for by DuPont. Jan Barry, *Families Sue Ford Over Waste Dumping*, NEW JERSEY RECORD, Jan. 19, 2006.

2. *Harms and remedies.* The harms that a court is willing to redress and the remedies that it is willing to grant are two sides of the same coin. Put another way, the permissible remedies tell us what kinds of harm are cognizable in tort. For example, in *Anderson v. W.R. Grace and Co.*, 628 F.Supp. 1219 (D. Mass. 1986) the plaintiffs' claim for emotional distress of a bystander—for witnessing the slow death of a family member due to leukemia—failed because there was no short term traumatic event followed by immediate emotional distress. Rather the plaintiffs' distress occurred during the prolonged illnesses of their children. Courts have held that a plaintiff's claim for enhanced risk of a disease fails when the risk was uncertain in the present, despite the fact it was reasonably probable in the future. The disease must be medically reasonably certain to award damages. *See Ayers v. Township of Jackson*, 525 A.2d 287 (N.J. 1987) and *Sterling v. Velsicol Chemical Corp.*, 855 F.2d 1188 (6th Cir. 1988).

3. *The "present value" of risk.* You can think of some of the remedies discussed in the cases as providing a surrogate measure of risk or as something that gives risk a present value. Which remedies fit this description? Which do not? Can you see a pattern in terms of the willingness of courts to grant such relief?

4. *Compensatory damages.* Where a plaintiff suffers a physical injury resulting from exposure to a toxic substance, a court will typically award money damages intended to compensate the plaintiff for the harm. However, the nature and extent of injury and illness to a plaintiff is often unknown at the time a suit is filed. This is particularly true in toxic tort cases, where the lengthy latency periods may result in illnesses many years after the initial exposure, sometimes long after the lawsuit is filed. A plaintiff seeking compensatory damages must, at the time of trial, prove damages for any present injury or illness, as well as any future losses likely to result either from the present injury, or from exposure to the toxic substance. This principle, known as the "single recovery rule," is intended to award damages to a plaintiff for all losses resulting from an injury at one time, to avoid

further suits if the toxic substance produces more harm after the trial is over.[16]

5. *Permanent damages in lieu of injunctive relief.* Injunctive relief depends in part on the plausibility of abating the nuisance, or taking affirmative action to restore damaged property to its previous condition. Where one or both of these are improbable or impossible, courts may award permanent damages as compensation, instead of an injunction. A good example of this type of situation is found in *Boomer v. Atlantic Cement Co.*, 257 N.E.2d 870 (1970), where plaintiff landowners sought an injunction restraining the operator of a cement plant from emitting dust and raw materials, and conducting excessive blasting which created a public nuisance. The court determined that it appeared unlikely that techniques to eliminate the nuisance would be developed within any short period of time, and chose to award permanent damages to compensate the plaintiffs for the servitude that the defendants had placed on the land. The downside of a permanent damages remedy is that the defendant is able to continue engaging in activities which harm the environment. *See* A. Mitchell Polinsky, *Resolving Nuisance Disputes: The Simple Economics of Injunctive and Damage Remedies,* 32 STAN. L. REV. 1075 (1980). The *Ayers* court, *supra*, confronted a similar issue in approving medical monitoring damages—whether to require a lump sum payment up front or to permit the court to impose an as-needed, insurance-like scheme. *Ayers* permitted the trial court to choose between them: what factors do you think should be considered in making this decision?

6. *Injunctive relief.* One element of relief demanded, but not considered by the court in *Sterling,* is an injunction. Injunctive relief can take two forms. A "prohibitory" injunction stops a defendant from engaging in a certain activity, while a "mandatory" injunction requires a defendant to take steps to remedy an existing or potential harm. Since it is an equitable remedy, courts possess a great deal of discretion in granting and shaping injunctive relief. The RESTATEMENT (SECOND) provides a list of factors to be considered in granting an injunction, including:

- the nature of the interest to be protected,
- the relative adequacy to the plaintiff of injunction and of other remedies,
- any unreasonable delay by the plaintiff in bringing suit,
- any related misconduct on the part of the plaintiff,
- the relative hardship likely to result to defendant if an injunction is granted and to plaintiff if it is denied,
- the interests of third persons and of the public, and
- the practicability of framing and enforcing the order or judgment.

---

16. The types of losses that are typically associated with an injury include medical expenses, lost wages and/or earning capacity, medical complications, and pain and suffering. *See Capelouto v. Kaiser Found. Hosp.*, 500 P.2d 880 (Cal. 1972) (the concept of "pain and suffering" includes recovery for physical pain, as well as fright, nervousness, grief, anxiety, worry, mortification, shock, humiliation, indignity, embarrassment, apprehension, terror or ordeal).

Rest. (2d) of Torts § 936(1). *See also Village of Wilsonville, et al. v. SCA Services, Inc.*, 426 N.E.2d 824 (Ill. 1981) (court balanced the relative hardship to be caused to the plaintiffs and the operator of the site before granting a permanent injunction enjoining the operation of the chemical waste disposal site that presented a public nuisance, and requiring the defendant to restore the property to its previous condition).

7. *Punitive damages.* Punitive damages differ from compensatory damages in that they are intended to punish the defendant and in so doing to deter others from engaging in similar conduct. The Restatement (Second) of Torts § 908 permits punitive damages when the defendant's conduct is "outrageous," because of the "defendant's evil motive or his reckless indifference to the rights of others." Factors that are relevant in judging whether a toxic tort defendant is sufficiently "evil" to warrant punitive damages include whether the defendant intentionally violated state pollution standards, manipulated the discharges in an attempt to escape detection, disregarded neighbors' complaints, and withheld information from state health officials. *Orjias v. Louisiana–Pacific Corp.*, 31 F.3d 995 (10th Cir. 1994). If the standard for punitive damages has been met,[17] the jury sets the actual amount of the damages. The dollars awarded in a punitive damages verdict vary according to the plaintiff's litigation expenses, the degree of hazard to the public posed by the defendant's product or conduct, the financial worth of the defendant, the extent to which the defendant profited from its misconduct, and the amount deemed necessary to deter other potential defendants. *Johns–Manville Sales Corp. v. Janssens*, 463 So.2d 242 (Fla. App. 1984). As punitive damages become larger and more frequent, particularly with toxic torts, there have been calls for both legislative reform[18] and judicial review[19] of the reasonableness of enormous awards.

8. *Attorney's Fees* can be statutorily defined and may be awarded to prevailing plaintiffs. *Stigma Damages* involve property value that is adversely affected by previous contamination. Courts have rejected property monitoring and inspection as a remedy to determine future contamination. *See Carter v. Monsanto Co.*, 575 S.E.2d 342 (W.Va. 2002).

C. The Defendant's Response

After a plaintiff files a toxic tort case, the defendant is likely to respond in one of three ways. First, the defendant may seek to reject a specific cause

---

17. In some jurisdictions, the burden of proof has been changed by statute to a "clear and convincing" standard, which is higher than the traditional tort standard of a "preponderance of the evidence." Cal. Civ. Code § 294 (West 1970, Supp. 1995).

18. *See, e.g.*, Colo. Rev. Stat. § 13–21–102(1) (1989) (limiting the amount a plaintiff can recover in punitive damages to the amount received in compensatory damages). *See Cooper Industries, Inc. v. Leatherman Tool Group, Inc.*, 532 U.S. 424 (2001) (appellate review of punitive damages is de novo); *Boerner v. Brown & Williamson Tobacco Co.*, 394 F.3d 594 (8th Cir. 2005) (reducing punitive damages award to estate of a smoker); *Romo v. Ford Motor Co.*, 6 Cal.Rptr.3d 793 (Cal. App. 5th Dist. 2003) (calculation of punitive damages award should focus on defendant's conduct directed toward plaintiff).

19. *See, e.g.*, *BMW of North America, Inc. v. Gore*, 517 U.S. 559 (1996) (a punitive damages award may be grossly excessive if there is great disparity in the harm suffered by the plaintiff and the punitive damages).

of action by arguing that the plaintiff has failed to state a claim that satisfies the substantive elements of that particular tort. Second, the defendant may raise a common law affirmative defense, typically grounded in the plaintiff's misconduct. Third, statutory defenses may be asserted.

1.   FAILURE TO STATE A CAUSE OF ACTION IN TORT LAW

The defendant can seek to show that the defendant's conduct does not fit the legal requirements of the tort or torts alleged by the plaintiff. For example, if a plaintiff brings a negligent trespass claim against a manufacturing plant alleging that the plant's discharge of PCBs had caused damage to the plaintiff's property, the claim will be dismissed if the plaintiff cannot prove the actual harm caused by the claimed presence of PCBs on her property. *See e.g., Mercer v. Rockwell Int'l Corp.*, 24 F. Supp. 2d 735 (W.D. Ky. 1998). Or, if the plaintiff is a purchaser of contaminated property who seeks recovery from the seller for cleanup expenses under a negligence theory, the plaintiff typically must establish that the defendant had a duty to plaintiffs to maintain the property in a safe condition. If the defendant can show that there is no such duty under the common law, then the plaintiff has failed to state a cause of action negligence against the defendant. *See, e.g., Cross Oil Co. v. Phillips Petroleum Co.*, 944 F.Supp. 787 (E.D. Mo., 1996); *Dartron Corp. v. Uniroyal Chemical Co.*, 893 F.Supp. 730 (N.D. Ohio 1995). Or, if the plaintiff brings a toxic tort action against a tire factory alleging nuisance as a result of the factory's release of petroleum naptha into the soil near the plaintiff's property, the court will conclude that that complaint has failed to state a claim in nuisance if the plaintiff has not alleged how the naptha plume under its property interferes with the use and enjoyment of the land. *Bradley v. Armstrong Rubber Company*, 130 F.3d 168 (5th Cir. 1997).

Another way for the defendant to argue that the plaintiff has failed to state a toxic tort cause of action is to show the court that the plaintiff's remedy does not lie in tort law at all. For example, the "economic loss" doctrine holds that a party bringing a tort claim cannot recover damages if the claim arises out of a commercial transaction. *Stoughton Trailers, Inc. v. Henkel Corp.*, 965 F.Supp. 1227 (W.D. Wis. 1997). The doctrine rests upon the general distinction between contract and tort law: when contractual expectations are frustrated because of a defect in the subject matter of a contract, the remedy lies in contract; when the subject matter of a contract causes physical harm to persons or property other than the contract's subject matter, a remedy lies in tort. *Compare Northridge Co. v. W.R. Grace and Co.*, 471 N.W.2d 179 (Wis. 1991) (court agreed plaintiff had stated claim in tort—negligence—when plaintiff's suit against the seller of an asbestos-based fireproofing material did not allege damages because of injury to the product itself, but rather the claim was that the product released toxic substances into the environment and caused damage to the building, and a health hazard to the occupants), *with Raytheon Co. v. McGraw–Edison Co.*, 979 F.Supp. 858 (E.D. Wis. 1997) (action in tort is *not* stated by purchaser of contaminated land, who in effect is asserting that the product itself—the land—is defective because it is contaminated, and therefore any damages incurred are because of injury to the product itself).[20]

Consider the ruling in *Humble Sand & Gravel Inc.*—there is no duty to warn of the commonly known dangers of a byproduct of construction.

Humble Sand & Gravel Inc. v. Gomez
146 S.W.3d 170 (Tex. 2004)

■ Justice Hecht delivered the opinion of the Court, in which Justice Owen, Justice Jefferson, Justice Smith, Justice Wainwright, and Justice Brister joined.

Generally, a product supplier must warn expected users of foreseeable risks that make the product unreasonably dangerous, but a supplier need not warn of risks that are common knowledge, and when the product is supplied through an intermediary, a supplier may sometimes rely on the intermediary to warn the actual product users. We must apply these basic principles to the circumstances presented in this case. ...

If the flint supplier in this case had such a duty, it is only because all similarly situated flint suppliers have the same duty, not because of some peculiar aspect of this one defendant's situation. Therefore, to determine whether a general legal duty exists, we must look beyond the particular circumstances of the injury here complained of, just as the parties themselves have done, to the broader industrial setting in which that injury occurred. The record before us establishes that by the 1980s, the dangers of using flint in abrasive blasting had been well known throughout the abrasive blasting industry as well as to health and safety professionals and government regulators for most of the twentieth century, but that blasting workers themselves remained largely ignorant of those dangers, and their employers were careless in enforcing workplace conditions that would protect workers' safety. The record also reflects that federal regulations have been imposed on employers to improve working conditions but not on flint manufacturers to warn of dangers involved in the use of their product. While the parties here no longer dispute that such a warning by the defendant supplier would have prevented the plaintiff's injury, missing from this record is any evidence that, in general, warnings by flint suppliers could effectively reach their customers' employees actually engaged in abrasive blasting. Without such evidence, we are unable to determine whether a duty to warn should be imposed on flint suppliers. Consequently, we reverse the judgment of the court of appeals and, in the interest of justice, remand the case to the trial court for a new trial.

I

Raymond Gomez contracted silicosis while working at and around abrasive blasting (often but less accurately called sandblasting) for about 6

---

20. Some jurisdictions recognize an exception to the economic loss doctrine for a select group of intentional torts, such as negligent misrepresentation and fraud in the inducement of a contract. *Huron Tool and Engineering Co. v. Precision Consulting Serv., Inc.*, 532 N.W.2d 541 (Mich. App. 1995); *HTP, Ltd. v. Lineas Aereas Costaricenses, S.A.*, 685 So.2d 1238 (Fla. 1996).

1/2 years, from 1984–1987 and again from 1991–1994, at plants in Odessa, where he was born and raised, and in Corpus Christi, where his wife was from. In 1995, Gomez filed suit in Jefferson County against more than twenty defendants, including four suppliers of flint used as the abrasive in the blasting work, two suppliers of blasting equipment, thirteen suppliers of protective gear worn by workers, and several jobsite owners. Gomez settled with all of the defendants except Humble Sand & Gravel Company, one of the flint suppliers, for a total of $389,200, and then following a jury trial obtained a judgment against Humble for about $2 million. Much of the evidence relevant to the issues now before us was undisputed at trial, but where it was conflicting, we of course recite that which was most favorable to Gomez.

Gomez left school after the ninth grade because his wife was pregnant with their first child. Within the year, at age 18, he started work for Spincote Plastic Coating Co. in Odessa, where he stayed six months before moving to Corpus Christi to work at Spincote's plant there for three years. Spincote was in the business of using abrasive blasting to clean and condition oilfield tubing. This involved spraying steel tubing with particles of flint shot through a nozzle with compressed air under pressures around 100 p.s.i. Flint is very hard stone composed mostly of crystalline silica (silica dioxide (SiO_2), commonly called quartz), which in its natural, undisturbed state is not at all dangerous. But when flint particles are blasted against metal at high pressure, they not only scour and abrade the surface, they shatter into an airborne dust of smaller particles. Some of this dust is coarse enough to rebound against workers, injuring exposed skin, and to hang in the air, obscuring visibility. But some particles of free silica are so fine–5 microns (or about 200 millionths of an inch) in diameter, something like 1/20th the diameter of a human hair—as to be invisible to the naked eye. The visible dust can clog the nose and mouth but is too coarse to be inhaled into the lungs and is relatively harmless. But the microscopic particles of free silica are both respirable and toxic. Inhaled over months or years, free silica particles cause silicosis, an incurable disease involving a fibrosis and scarring of the lungs and other complications that can eventually result in disability and death. Silicosis is caused only by inhaling free silica. Inhalation of free silica particles cannot be prevented by ordinary, loose-fitting, disposable paper masks; the particles are too small. People working around silica dust must wear air-fed hoods or respirators covering their heads or faces to protect themselves.

The parties here agree, and the record establishes, that the health risks from inhaling silica dust have been well known for a very long time. ...

* * *

Studies of the health hazards of abrasive blasting with flint also determined that such work could be done relatively safely if workers were required to use suitable airline respirators—devices that fit over the face or head with a clean air supply for workers to breathe. Dr. Bingham and Dr. Rose testified that the American National Standards Institute, a consensus group made up of various industry participants including manufacturers, suppliers, employers, unions, and customers, first adopted safety standards calling for the use of respirators in abrasive blasting in 1938. OSHA regulations for abrasive blasting originally promulgated in the early 1970s also require the use of respirators, or air-fed hoods, "constructed [to] cover the wearer's head, neck, and shoulders to protect him from rebounding abrasive." These regulations also require employers to develop written procedures for selecting respirators, to instruct employees in their use, to keep respirators clean and well-maintained, and to conduct frequent random inspections to ensure employee compliance. Given these safety standards and regulations and the long-held concerns that led to their adoption, Dr. Rose testified that one "would expect a professional in ... the abrasive blasting industry to know about the hazards of abrasive blasting" and "the requirements to provide air-supplied respiratory equipment to the workers." Frank Bogran, a witness called by Gomez, who had run a major abrasive blasting business since 1962, agreed that "[b]y 1975 the people that were in that sandblasting industry, they knew about the hazards" and "knew about the need to wear proper air-fed equipment."

But their employees usually did not. The widespread knowledge of the dangers of silica dust produced by abrasive blasting and the necessity of wearing proper protective equipment was not often shared by the ordinary workers themselves or their supervisors and did not translate into safety in the workplace. It is undisputed on the record before us that the dangers of silicosis frequently went unheeded in practice. In 1974, the National Institute for Occupational Safety and Health sponsored a survey conducted by Boeing Aerospace Co. of some 400 businesses across the country "to determine the degree of respiratory protection currently afforded workers in industries which employ abrasive blasting techniques". The survey found the condition of respiratory equipment "generally deplorable". In many workplaces, respirators were ill-fitting, not cleaned or maintained, not supplied with clean air, or not regularly used by employees, and management was often "unaware of the inadequacy of their equipment." ...

* * *

Humble, a relatively small, family-owned and-operated business with eight employees located in Picher, Oklahoma, began packaging and selling flint for abrasive blasting in 1982. ... From the beginning, Ron Humble, who ran the business with his father, knew that breathing the silica dust generated by abrasive blasting could cause silicosis and that the disease could be fatal. He also knew that he should put some sort of warning label on the bags, and after making inquiries of OSHA and a trade organization that yielded him no useful information, he decided to copy the following label used by a competitor, Independent Gravel, who he understood had been in business for more than fifty years:

WARNING!
MAY BE INJURIOUS TO HEALTH IF PROPER
PROTECTIVE EQUIPMENT IS NOT USED.

* * *

Abrasive blasting at Spincote's plants was done inside a building in an area called the blast house. Gomez was hired to work as an "end grinder", a job that did not involve blasting but was performed in the dusty environment of the building. Gomez was given only a disposable paper mask that was held against his face with rubber bands. After his first month, Gomez was moved to "end cutter", a job that did involve blasting. At that point, he was provided an air-fed hood in addition to the paper mask and was shown how to use the hood properly. ...

* * *

... Gomez testified that the first time he saw Humble's bags, he noticed the warning label and asked his foreman about it. His foreman replied that as long as he wore his hood and mask he would be all right. Gomez thought the phrase on the label, "injurious to health," meant that dust rebounding off blasted surfaces could hurt when it struck the skin and was bad to breathe. The hood, he thought, was for protection from the flying dust and the paper mask was to prevent inhalation. Still, he thought, the dust was ordinary dust, like what he might sweep out of his garage. He did not know that the dust contained invisible free silica particles too fine to be screened by a paper mask.

* * *

In November 1994, Gomez sought medical treatment for shortness of breath, and within a few days he was diagnosed as having subacute silicosis. A biopsy of his lung tissue confirmed that he had had a high exposure to silica dust. ...

* * *

We granted Humble's petition for review. Two months later Gomez's counsel filed a suggestion of his death, the date and cause unstated. We proceed as if Gomez remained a party to the appeal.

II

Humble argues here, as it did in the court of appeals, that a product supplier has no duty to warn its customers' employees of the risks of using the product if the customers should already know of those risks and are themselves obliged by law to warn their own employees. Awareness of risks, Humble contends, must be determined objectively in the context of the industry or business involved—what an ordinary person in that situation *should* know, not what one person or another actually *does* know. ...

Gomez argues that regardless of anything Spincote should have done, Humble had a duty to warn him of two things: that inhaling silica dust could lead to disability and death, and that an air-fed hood should be worn around silica dust at all times. Employers like Spincote, Gomez contends, could not be relied on to provide these warnings. ...

* * *

In deciding whether to impose a commonlaw duty, this Court has applied the familiar factors identified in *Graff v. Beard,* 858 S.W.2d 918, 920 (Tex.1993), *Greater Houston Transportation Co. v. Phillips,* 801 S.W.2d 523,

525 (Tex.1990), and *Otis Engineering Corp. v. Clark,* 668 S.W.2d 307, 309 (Tex.1983). The considerations include social, economic, and political questions and their application to the facts at hand. We have weighed the risk, foreseeability, and likelihood of injury against the social utility of the actor's conduct, the magnitude of the burden of guarding against the injury, and the consequences of placing the burden on the defendant. Also among the considerations are whether one party would generally have superior knowledge of the risk or a right to control the actor who caused the harm.

* * *

Humble's argument has two components: one, it had no duty to warn its customers of the risks of working around silica dust because those risks were common knowledge in the abrasive blasting industry long before 1984; and two, it had no duty to warn its customers' employees of those risks because its customers were in a better position to warn their own employees. If the risks of silica dust were not commonly known in the industry, then Humble had at least a duty to warn its customers, which Gomez argues Humble did not do. Even if the risks were commonly known, the question remains whether Humble still had a duty to warn its customers' employees. We consider each component of Humble's argument in turn.

III

A supplier has no duty to warn of risks involved in a product's use that are commonly known to foreseeable users, even if some users are not aware of them. "Commonly" does not mean universally. "Commonly known" means "beyond dispute." As we have said, "the inquiry whether a recognition of risk 'is within the ordinary knowledge common to the community' is an objective standard." ... For example, in *Sauder Custom Fabrication, Inc. v. Boyd,* we held that a scaffolding supplier had no duty to warn a boilermaker of the risk of falling because "[n]o ordinary person trained to do the work [he] and his crew were doing could have failed to appreciate the obvious risk." What level of appreciation amounts to common knowledge is to be determined by the court as a matter of law unless there are factual issues that must be resolved.

With these principles in mind, we turn to the present case. Over fifty years ago, the United States Supreme Court observed: "It is a matter of common knowledge that it is injurious to the lungs and dangerous to health to work in silica dust, a fact which defendant [a railroad, the injured worker's employer] was bound to know." Over 10 years ago this Court noted: "Inhaling silica dust may cause respiratory disease, a risk that has been recognized for more than a century." Consistent with these general observations, the record before us in this case establishes, and the parties do not disagree, that as a matter of objective fact, the general dangers of inhaling silica dust, including disability and death, and of not wearing air-fed hoods to protect against inhalation, have been common knowledge among flint suppliers and abrasive blasting operators for decades and were certainly so in 1984 when Gomez went to work for Spincote. Humble admittedly knew of these dangers in 1982 when it began selling flint, and there is evidence that

Spincote's Odessa plant foreman, Workman, knew of them as well, having worked for many years in the abrasive blasting industry.

The evidence that operators like Spincote were often careless in conducting abrasive blasting and insufficiently motivated to provide for the safety of their workers does not ascribe their indifference to inadequate warnings by flint suppliers. On the contrary, the evidence is that operators neglected safety *despite* their knowledge of the seriousness of silicosis and the standards, industrial and legal, for abrasive blasting. ... Gomez does not contend that flint suppliers should or could have instructed operators or workers in the proper use of protective equipment. The two warnings Gomez does contend Humble should have given were of dangers well known, though largely unheeded, in the abrasive blasting industry.

At the same time, it is equally well established on this record that the dangers of silica dust were not generally known to workers like Gomez employed in abrasive blasting operations. ...

From this record we conclude that flint suppliers like Humble had no duty to warn its customers like Spincote and Sivalls, abrasive blasting operators, that inhaling silica dust can be disabling and fatal and that workers must wear air-fed hoods, because that information had long been commonly known throughout the industry. Blasting operators' disregard of the risks to their employees of inhaling silica dust was not for want of additional information that flint suppliers should have furnished, but for want of care. We turn, then, to the question whether Humble had a duty to warn its customers' employees, who were not generally aware of the risks.

■ Justice O'Neill, joined by Justice Schneider, dissenting.

* * *

Conflating duty and causation, and combining select elements of different exceptions to a product supplier's general duty to warn, the Court concludes that this case should be retried to allow Humble to prove that it owed no duty to workers like Raymond Gomez. If I were Humble, I would surely appreciate the second chance—but I wouldn't have a clue what to do. *See Golden Eagle Archery, Inc. v. Jackson,* 116 S.W.3d 757, 776 (Tex.2003) (O'Neill, J., concurring). For example, is proof that two out of four employees working around silica flint would disregard an adequate warning sufficient to negate the general duty to warn? Does the relevant inquiry concern only abrasive blasters, or all employees who work in blasting facilities and are exposed to silica dust? If only thirty-five percent of blasting businesses provide safe working conditions, is the duty to warn discharged? If only twenty percent of the silica flint used in the industry is supplied in bags, are bag-suppliers relieved of a duty to warn? Is the "industry" to which the Court refers national, state or regional? Not to mention the inherent difficulty of obtaining and presenting the type of fact-intensive proof that the Court describes, the Court's analysis raises these and myriad other question that will likely prove to be problematic, at best, if not unanswerable.

NOTES AND QUESTIONS

1. The threshold question for a negligence claim is whether the defendant owed a duty to the plaintiff. The court in *Humble Sand & Gravel Inc.* mentions the social, economic, and political factors of a imposing such a duty. An omitted portion of the opinion holds that the defendant supplier did not owe a duty to its customers' employees. The court's conclusion rests on whether the plaintiff had experiential knowledge of the dangers of working with a common construction substance. Do you agree with the court's analysis?

2. Compare *American Tobacco v. Grinnell*, 951 S.W.2d 420 (Tex. 1997) to the previous case. The court in *American Tobacco* concluded that the general health risks associated with smoking were common knowledge, but the risk of addiction was not common knowledge. At the time of the litigation the tobacco industry had not reached a consensus about the risk of addiction. Can this ruling be reconciled with *Humble Sand & Gravel Inc.*?

3. The court in *Joseph E. Seagram & Sons, Inc. v. McGuire*, 814 S.W.2d 385 (Tex.1991) concluded that the danger of consuming excessive amounts of alcohol was common knowledge. Since the general public had known of alcoholism since "ancient times," despite the plaintiffs' assertion that they were personally unaware of any risk, there was no duty.

2. COMMON LAW AFFIRMATIVE DEFENSES

The common law affirmative defenses most frequently asserted in toxic tort cases are: (1) assumption of risk; (2) contributory negligence; and (3) "coming to the nuisance." In order to raise the assumption of risk defense in a toxic torts case, the defendant must prove that the plaintiff knew that the exposure was dangerous, appreciated the nature or extent of the danger, and voluntarily exposed himself to the danger. RESTATEMENT (SECOND) OF TORTS § 840C. In *Cornell v. Exxon Corp.*, 162 A.D.2d 892, 558 N.Y.S.2d 647 (1990), the defendant raised the assumption of risk defense in response to plaintiff's nuisance, trespass, and negligence claims arising from drinking contaminated well water. Since the plaintiffs were advised not to drink the water, but continued using it for bathing, cooking, and cleaning purposes, the court determined there was a factual question for the jury whether the plaintiffs had knowledge of the risk and still voluntarily chose to encounter it. The *Cornell* case illustrates the difficulties facing defendants who must present evidence that the plaintiff had knowledge of the risk. Because of long latency periods with most toxic substances, the exposure to the substance could have occurred many years before the toxic tort claim is filed, making it nearly impossible for defendants to collect evidence regarding the plaintiff's knowledge dating back to the time of the exposure.

Contributory negligence is addressed in the RESTATEMENT (SECOND) OF TORTS § 840B. The availability of the defense varies according to the nature of the defendant's conduct. If the defendant's negligent conduct causes a nuisance, contributory negligence is a defense. If the defendant's conduct has produced an abnormally dangerous condition, contributory negligence is a defense only if the plaintiff has voluntarily assumed the risk of harm. If the defendant knows that its conduct is causing a nuisance and intentionally continues, then contributory negligence is not a defense.

The "coming to the nuisance" defense can be raised only when plaintiffs have acquired property after the creation of the nuisance. Most jurisdictions have rejected this defense when the plaintiff alleges a toxic tort. *See Patrick v. Sharon Steel Corp.*, 549 F.Supp. 1259 (N.D. W. Va. 1982). The RESTATEMENT (SECOND) OF TORTS § 840D characterizes coming to the nuisance not as an absolute defense, but as one factor to consider in determining whether a claim has been stated. Some early decisions still accept the defense when the plaintiffs knowingly placed themselves in harm's way, and when the coming to the nuisance defense protects reasonable expectations of existing industry. *Fischer v. Atlantic Richfield*, 774 F.Supp. 616 (W.D. Okl. 1989); *East St. Johns Shingle Co. v. City of Portland*, 246 P.2d 554 (Or. 1952).

3.   STATUTORY DEFENSES

In addition to traditional common law defenses, statutes of limitations and repose can defeat a toxic tort action. Both act to prevent plaintiffs from bringing a lawsuit that is too late. Conversely, statutes waiving sovereign immunity permit plaintiffs to sue government defendants otherwise protected from such litigation.

a.   STATUTE OF LIMITATIONS

A statute of limitations defense prevents a plaintiff from commencing a claim after a certain period of time. In the case of a recurrent or continuing trespass, a statute of limitations also creates the window of time for assessing damages, that is, damages may not be collected for the period of time before the limitations period.[21]

The application of a statute of limitations in a toxic tort case is complicated by the long latency periods of toxic and hazardous materials. When there is a long period of time between a plaintiff's initial exposure to the harm-producing agent and manifestation of an injury or illness, the question is: at what point does the claim accrue? The injury giving rise to the claim can be said to occur at the time of exposure or, much later, at the time an illness manifests itself.

> Historically, tort actions were thought to accrue at the time of initial exposure. This meant that a plaintiff whose illness did not become known, or was not discovered, until many years after the exposure would usually find the tort claim time-barred, since the statute of limitations would have begun to run on the date of exposure. *See, e.g., Bassham v. Owens–Corning Fiber Glass Corp.*, 327 F.Supp. 1007 (D.N.M. 1971). This "exposure rule" seemed unfair for toxic substances, because it precluded claims before plaintiffs would have reason to know of harm resulting from

---

21.   Where pollution is recurrent, such that a new cause of action arises day by day, or injury by injury, a nuisance action can be brought for damages incurred within the applicable statute of limitations period. *Nieman v. NLO, Inc.*, 108 F.3d 1546 (6th Cir. 1997); *Brown v. County Commissioners*, 622 N.E.2d 1153 (Ohio App. 1993).

exposure—or even, in many cases, to suspect that exposure had occurred. Both legislatures and courts responded to the unfairness inherent in the exposure rule by adopting a "discovery rule" that an action accrues when a plaintiff knew, or should have known, of an injury or illness. *See, e.g.*, N.Y. Civ. Prac. L. & R. 214–c(2) (McKinney 1990) (statute of limitations begins to run at the time a reasonable person would have discovered the injury); *Urie v. Thompson*, 337 U.S. 163 (1949) (statute of limitations should be triggered at time of discovery of latent illness).

Three issues have arisen with respect to the discovery rule. First, how should courts decide whether a plaintiff "should have known" that an actionable tort claim has arisen? *See Kullman v. Owens–Corning Fiberglas Corp.*, 943 F.2d 613 (6th Cir. 1991) (plaintiff's action time-barred because he should have known that the dust breathed in the workplace might have been responsible for his breathing problems that eventually was diagnosed as asbestosis). Second, to what extent must the plaintiff be aware not only of an illness, but also of its cause? *See Seneca Meadows Inc. v. ECI Liquidating, Inc.*, 983 F.Supp. 360, 363 (W.D. N.Y. 1997) (claim accrues when plaintiff "had actual knowledge of both the injury and its cause"); *Evenson v. Osmose Wood Preserving Company of America*, 899 F.2d 701 (7th Cir. 1990) (statute of limitations began to run when the plaintiff had knowledge of a "reasonable possibility" that a workplace chemical was the cause of his symptoms). Third, should the discovery rule apply to damage to property? *See Dombrowski v. Gould Electronics, Inc.*, 954 F.Supp. 1006 (M.D. Pa. 1996) (discovery rule applies, and statute of limitations begins to run, when plaintiff-homeowners became aware of the fact that they had suffered diminution in value of their residences because of neighboring battery crushing plant); *contra, Corporation of Mercer University v. National Gypsum Co.*, 877 F.2d 35 (11th Cir. 1989) (property damage claim not subject to discovery rule).

What was the basis for distinguishing among the plaintiffs in *Anderson*? Does it seem fair to you? If not, how would you revise the discovery rule—remembering that statutes of limitation still have an important role to play in protecting defendants from stale claims?

b. STATUTES OF REPOSE

Statutes of limitations bar claims brought beyond a certain period of time after the accrual of the claim; statutes of repose bar claims brought by a plaintiff beyond a designated period of time after the happening of a certain event, such as the date of sale of a product. Where the running of a statute of limitations may depend on the plaintiff's discovery of the claim or manifestation of illness, statutes of repose bar any claim made beyond a designated amount of time after a specific event, whether or not the elements of a claim have accrued. Statutes of repose operate as an "absolute time limit beyond which liability no longer exists and is not tolled for any reason because to do so would upset the economic balance struck by the legislative body." *Baughn v. Eli Lilly and Co.*, 356 F. Supp. 2d 1166 (D. Kan. 2005) (statute of repose terminates at the end of a product's safe life). *First*

United Methodist Church v. U.S. Gypsum Co., 882 F.2d 862, 866 (4th Cir. 1989). *See, e.g., United Proteins, Inc. v. Farmland Indus. Inc.*, 915 P.2d 80 (Kan. 1996) (plaintiff's suit in trespass and nuisance against a fertilizer manufacturing plant whose release of toxic chemicals had contaminated the aquifer beneath the plaintiff's pet food plant was barred by a statute of repose). The discovery rule, in other words, is of no help in avoiding a statute of repose.

c. GOVERNMENT IMMUNITY

Generally speaking, governmental entities enjoy sovereign immunity from most kinds of lawsuits, including toxic tort actions, by private parties. The policy behind sovereign immunity is to protect government decision-makers from involvement in private litigation so that they may function effectively without fear of liability. Governments may waive their sovereign immunity by statute. Both federal and state statutes give to private parties a limited cause of action in tort against federal and state governments, subject to a myriad of exceptions.[22]

The Federal Tort Claims Act, 28 U.S.C. § 1346(b), is waiver of sovereign immunity from tort claims against the United States for injury, wrongful death, or property damage as a result of a negligent act or omission by a Government employee within the scope of employment. The Federal Tort Claims Act would otherwise give private parties a cause of action against the federal government for toxic torts, but for the sweeping "discretionary function" exception. Pursuant to this exception, the United States may not be held liable for any claim "based upon the exercise or performance or the failure to exercise or perform a discretionary function or duty * * *, whether or not the discretion involved be abused." 28 U.S.C. § 2680(a).

There are usually two inquiries that address whether the discretionary function exception applies. The initial inquiry is whether the plaintiff's injury was the result of a discretionary function or duty. The United States Supreme Court in *Berkovitz v. United States*, 486 U.S. 531 (1988) established that this prong of the exception does not apply "when a federal statute, regulation, or policy specifically prescribes a course of action for an employee to follow." If this first inquiry is satisfied, then a court must determine whether the challenged conduct was of a kind that the discretionary function exception was designed to shield. Since the exception was intended to prevent lawsuits against officials making non-mandatory policy judgments, especially where those judgments are meant to further the public interest, federal officials making or implementing discretionary policy will typically be immune from a tort action. *See, e.g., Angle v. United States*, 931 F.Supp. 1386 (W.D. Mich. 1994) (exception applicable to negligence action brought on behalf of an infant child who allegedly suffered lead poisoning from lead-based paint found in military family housing, because the federal government's decision not to remediate the hazard or warn residents of it was based upon a policy judgment about the substantial

---

22. The extent to which the federal government may be sued for violating federal environmental statutes is usually specified in the relevant statute. *See* chapters 5 (RCRA) and 6 (CERCLA).

commitment of resources that would have been required to alleviate the toxic risks of lead-based paint in military housing).[23] *See also Whisnant v. United States*, 400 F.3d 1177 (9th Cir. 2005) (the government is not immune from negligence claims resulting from implementation of its own procedures); Jean Macchiaroli Eggen, *Toxic Torts at Ground Zero*, 39 ARIZ. ST. L.J. 383 (2007) (discussing federal government immunity in toxic torts from claims arising from 9/11 damages).

Government contractors. Immunity is generally extended to government contractors for policy reasons. To establish a defense, a government contractor must show that (1) the government established the relevant specifications; (2) the government contractor met the government's specifications in all material aspects; and (3) the government contractor warned the government of all relevant hazards. *Miller v. Diamond Shamrock Co.*, 275 F.3d 414 (5th Cir. 2001) (government contractors only have a duty to warn the government of hazards that the contractor has actual knowledge about).

4. PRODUCTS LIABILITY DEFENSES

State-of-the-Art is traditionally a defense used with strict products liability claims where the defendant has failed to warn of the product's hazards. This defense contends that at the time of the plaintiff's exposure to the product, the defendant did not know, and could not have reasonably known, of the dangerousness of the product.

Unavoidably Unsafe Products is a defense used when the product's dangerousness is outweighed by its utility. These are products that are inherently dangerous; therefore, the product is not defective or unreasonably dangerous when it is manufactured properly and possesses an adequate warning. *United States Court of Appeals for the Ninth Circuit in Ricardo Ruiz–Guzman v. Amvac Chemical Corp.*, 7 P.3d 795 (Wash. 2000) (a pesticide can be considered unavoidably unsafe).

Sophisticated User Defense applies in commercial use situations, when the user of the product has superior or equal knowledge to that of the seller of the product's hazards. This defense is often used in an industrial context when a supplier sells the product to an intermediary. The intermediary then assumes liability if the ultimate user of the product is harmed. *Hoffman v. Houghton Chemical Corp.*, 751 N.E.2d 848 (Mass. 2001) (suppliers are relieved of liability from bulk products because it is usually too difficult to warn the ultimate users of the product).

Learned Intermediary Doctrine is used in medical malpractice suits to protect suppliers of medical products. The intermediary with superior knowledge has the duty to warn the ultimate user of the product, not the

---

23. State and local governments also enjoy sovereign immunity. This immunity from toxic tort claims can be waived by a state statute, which, like the Federal Torts Claims Act, often contains a variety of exceptions to liability. *See, e.g., Kenney v. Scientific, Inc.*, 497 A.2d 1310 (N.J. Super. 1985) (New Jersey Tort Claims Act not applicable to toxic tort action brought against State for licensing landfills and failing to properly inspect them, when Act provided that no public entity may be liable for licensing or improperly supervising a landfill).

supplier. *Larkin v. Pfizer, Inc.*, 153 S.W.3d 758 (Ky. 2004) (adopting the learned intermediary doctrine as a defense). Additionally, *blood shield statutes* protect suppliers of blood, blood products and other bodily fluids from strict products liability. *Weishorn v. Miles–Cutter*, 746 A.2d 1117 (Pa. 2000) (upholding the validity of blood shield statutes). The court in *Walls v. Alpharma USPD, Inc.* 887 So.2d 881 (Ala. 2004) extended the *Learned Intermediary Doctrine* to protect pharmacists from liability. The court reasoned that the patient's doctor acts as a learned intermediary between the manufacturer of the prescription drug and the ultimate user. A pharmacist does not have a duty to warn the ultimate user of the foreseeable risks of the prescribed mediation unless required to do so by statute.

A NOTE ON INSURANCE

When toxic tort litigation ensues, regardless of whether the suit involves a toxic product, disposal of hazardous wastes, or a CERCLA action, issues regarding insurance coverage become critical to the defendant. Claims against defendants are often in the millions of dollars—not to mention the costs of the litigation itself—and in rare cases billions of dollars. Defendants facing these kinds of costs (the insured) hope that their liability insurance agreements will be construed broadly so as to cover the activities that engendered the lawsuit. Insurance companies (the insurers) seek to limit their exposure, both by arguing for a narrow interpretation of the relevant policy, and by including within insurance agreements exclusions for toxic tort claims. *See* Kenneth Abraham, *The Maze of Mega–Coverage Litigation*, 97 COLUMBIA L. REV. 2102 (1997). As a result, a great deal of toxic tort litigation revolves around the scope of the defendant's insurance, rather than the validity of the plaintiff's claims. Limits of insurance coverage often determine settlement amounts.

Insurance indemnifies insureds for both the costs of defending litigation (regardless of outcome) and of judgments, settlements, and other elements of the insured's liability. *See, e.g., Chemical Leaman Tank Lines v. Aetna Cas. and Surety Co.*, 177 F.3d 210 (3rd Cir. 1999) (a duty to indemnify requires an insurer to pay on behalf of the policyholder all sums that the insurer is contractually obligated to pay as damages because of harms or losses—including costs incurred in connection with remedial investigation and feasibility study mandated under CERCLA—covered by the policy); *Aetna Cas. and Surety Co. v. Dow Chemical Co.*, 44 F. Supp. 2d 847 (E.D. Mich. 1997) (duty to defend may exist when it is ultimately determined there is no duty to indemnify under policy). The latter aspect, coverage of liability, is typically governed by a "comprehensive general liability" (CGL) policy, the terms of which are standard throughout the insurance industry. *Johnson v. Orleans Parish Sch. Bd.*, 975 So.2d 698 (La.App. 2008) (*cert. denied*) (insurers of city housing authority's CGL were liable for all sums owed to class of homeowners who were exposed to toxic chemicals from a landfill formerly located on the site where their homes were built). By 1966, most CGL policies used this language to establish the insuring agreement:

[The insurer] hereby agrees to pay on behalf of the insured all sums which the insured shall be legally obligated to pay *as damages* because of *bodily injury* or *property damage* to which this insurance applies caused by an *occurrence.* * * *[24]

An insurance policy includes both terms of coverage and of exclusion. Around 1970, the insurance industry added a pollution exclusion to the standard CGL policy in 1970. The original pollution exclusion clause was known as the "sudden and accidental" exclusion, and it provided that the policy did not apply to bodily injury or property damage arising out of:

the discharge, dispersal, release, or escape of * * * toxic chemicals, * * * waste materials, * * * contaminants or *pollutants* into or upon the land, the atmosphere or any water course * * *; but this exclusion does not apply if such * * * release * * * is *sudden and accidental.* * * * This insurance does not apply to property damage to property *owned or occupied* by or rented to the insured.

this exclusion—in particular the "sudden and accidental" and "property damage" phrases—engendered much litigation. *see, e.g., Lakeside Non-Ferrous Metals v. Hanover Ins. Co.*, 172 F.3d 702 (9th Cir. 1999) (trespass and nuisance claims arising out of insured's contamination of land involved "property damage" subject to pollution exclusion, and could not be recast as personal injury claim). As a result, insurers changed the language of the pollution exclusion clause in the 1980s by deleting the "sudden and accidental" exception and simplifying the conditions that would trigger the exclusion's applicability. This more insurer-friendly provision is known as the "absolute" pollution exclusion, and it dominates the insurance market today. *See Gencorp, Inc. v. American Intern. Underwriters*, 178 F.3d 804 (6th Cir. 1999) (absolute pollution exclusion does not violate public policy). Although the sudden and accidental exclusion has largely been replaced by the absolute pollution exclusion, it still has relevance for toxic tort litigation because a court may decide that an older policy applies.

---

24. Most CGL policies also contain language requiring the insurance company to defend any "suit" against the insured. The duty to defend often arises from the allegations in the complaint against the insured. Susan Randall, *Redefining the Insurer's Duty to Defend*, 2 Conn. Ins. L. J. 221,222 (1997). The legal question that has arisen is what constitutes a "suit" within this language. *Compare Northern Security Ins. Co. v. Mitec Telecom*, 38 F. Supp. 2d 345 (D.Vt. 1999) (demand letter sent to insured by counsel for homeowners notifying insured that groundwater beneath house was contaminated with TCE from insured's lot was not a "suit"), *with Compass Ins. Co. v. City of Littleton*, 984 P.2d 606 (Colo. 1999) (coercive EPA actions initiated under CERCLA were "suites."

Under pre-1996 policies the insurer agreed to pay damages because of bodily injury or property damage "caused by an accident." *See, e.g., St. Paul Fire v. McCormick & Baxter*, 923 P.2d 1200 (Or. 1996) (an "accident" in a CGL policy is not necessarily only an unintended event that results from unintentional acts, but also an incident or occurrence that happens by chance, without design and contrary to intention and expectation).

When there are multiple CGL insurers, there are two approaches that can be used. Under the "pro rata" approach, liability for continuing injury is allocated among all triggered liability policies according to the insurer's proportion of time on risk; under "joint and several" liability approach, each insured is jointly and severally liable for continuing injury. *U.S. Fidelity & Guaranty Co. v. Treadwell Corp.*, 58 F.Supp 2d 77 (S.D.N.Y. 1999).

Based on the materials on toxic torts, what other problems would you expect to find in determining the coverage for alleged injury from toxic and hazardous materials?

CHAPTER 3
APPROACHES TO SETTING REGULATORY STANDARDS

123

Whitman v. American Trucking Associations, Inc.

Entergy Corp. v. Riverkeeper, Inc.

F. Toward "Unreasonable Risk"

_____

As we saw in Chapter 1, toxic substances (as exemplified by carcinogens) pose a unique challenge to environmental, health, and safety regulation, because their non-threshold, latency, statistical, and ultimately uncertain harms challenge our intuitive, common-sense ideas of harm and causation.[1] In Chapter 2, we saw how the nature of toxic harm and causation plays out in the context of the tort system. Proof in such cases is complex and challenging for both plaintiffs and defendants. Even if proof in toxic torts cases were simple and definitive, however, tort law is limited in its ability to address the societal problem of toxic substances and hazardous wastes. While *ex post* tort judgments should in theory have an *ex ante* deterrent effect on future potential tortfeasors, the tort system is not fundamentally preventive. For this reason, government has stepped in to create regulatory regimes for toxic substances and hazardous wastes.

From the beginning of the Environmental Decade, and before, Congress clearly recognized the special problem of toxic substances and so accorded them a special status in statutes whose main objects were public health (in the traditional sense) and pollution control. Much regulation of toxic substances occurs, therefore, under the rubric of these statutes, and together they regulate many important carcinogens. More importantly for our purposes, these statutes represent a veritable menu of approaches to toxics regulation. In this chapter, we explore five different approaches to development of regulatory limitations on toxic substances:

- Hazard

- Feasibility

- Best available technology (BAT)

- Information disclosure

- Cost of regulating.

Each approach is capable of numerous variations, some of which we will see in each subchapter. The remaining chapters of the casebook examine statutes that by and large rely on a sixth basic approach: "unreasonable risk," which considers many of the factors in the above five approaches, but in a more comprehensive and less structured way. We emphasize the

_____

1. *Lead Industries Association, Inc. v. EPA*, 647 F.2d 1130 (D.C. Cir. 1980), *cert. denied*, 449 U.S. 1042 (1980), illustrates the traditional regulatory paradigm. The agency's and court's analyses were technical and complex, but underlying them was a relatively simple, mechanistic model of disease: at certain determinable levels of exposure to a given chemical, well defined adverse biological effects can be predicted with great certainty (allowing for truly idiosyncratic individual reactions).

comparative aspect of these statutes in the present chapter because, in a constantly evolving area of law, there are always opportunities to learn from experience.

A. Hazard

The Hazard-based approach to regulation means that specified consequences flow from the identification of a chemical with a given effect, notably carcinogens. Further inquiry into the strength or weakness of the effect is not, at least in theory, required.

1. The Delaney Clause

This chapter begins with the Delaney Clause of the Federal Food, Drug, and Cosmetic Act (FFDCA), because it is Congress' earliest effort, still in effect, to regulate carcinogens. The FFDCA invests the Secretary of Health and Human Services, who acts through the Commissioner of the Food and Drug Administration (FDA), with responsibility for the safety of many aspects of the nation's food supply, for the approval of human and animal drugs and medical devices, and for the safety of cosmetics. Carcinogens are the particular subject of the 1958 Delaney Clause, which was named for its sponsor, Congressman James Delaney of New York.[2]

Under section 408 of the FFDCA, pesticide residues on raw agricultural commodities are regulated for safety, but safety is balanced against the interest in an "adequate, wholesome, and economical food supply."[3] 21 U.S.C. § 346a. Section 409, which contains the Delaney Clause, replaces that balancing standard with a much more stringent one for carcinogens:

(a) Unsafe food additives; exception for conformity with exemption or regulation

A food additive shall, with respect to any particular use or intended use of such additives, be deemed to be unsafe ... unless ... (2) there is in effect, and it and its use or intended use are in conformity with, a regulation issued under this section prescribing the conditions under which such additive may be safely used; * * *.

(b) Petition for regulation prescribing conditions of safe use; contents; description of production methods and controls; samples; notice of regulation

(1) Any person may, with respect to any intended use of a food additive, file with the Secretary a petition proposing the issuance of a regulation prescribing the conditions under which such additive may be safely used.

---

2. The Delaney Clause proper can be found at 21 U.S.C. § 348, and the subsequently added color additives language at 21 U.S.C. § 376. Related provisions regarding animal drug residues can be found at 21 U.S.C. § 360b.

3. Section 408 was amended by the Food Quality Protection Act of 1996, Pub. L. No. 104–170, 110 Stat. 1489, but the central proviso of the Delaney Clause, reprinted here, was unchanged. *See* James S. Turner, *Delaney Lives! Reports of Delaney's Death are Greatly Exaggerated*, 28 Envtl. L. Rep. (Envtl. L. Inst.) 10003 (1998).

* * *

(c) Approval or denial of petition; time for issuance of orders; evaluation of data; factors

* * *

(3) No such regulation shall issue if a fair evaluation of the data before the Secretary—

(A) fails to establish that the proposed use of the food additive, under the conditions of use to be specified in the regulation, will be safe: *Provided*, That no additive shall be deemed to be safe if it is found to induce cancer when ingested by man or animal, or if it is found, after tests which are appropriate for the evaluation of the safety of food additives, to induce cancer in man or animal....

21 U.S.C. § 348. Despite being for many years the object of a concerted and broad-based effort for reform, the key proviso of the Delaney Clause remains unchanged from 1958.

The strictness of the Delaney Clause created serious difficulties for the FDA over the years. The former Chief Counsel of FDA, Richard Merrill, described the problem:

> The coverage of the Delaney Clause, and thus the problems encountered in administering it, are largely a function of two circumstances: (1) the number of substances that fall within the definition of "food additive," and (2) the number of substances within this universe that are found to "induce cancer." Through the 1970s, scientific advances in two arenas enlarged dramatically the universe of substances to which the Delaney Clause might apply. At the same time, a consensus began to emerge among public health experts that while a substantial portion of human cancer was linked with diet, little could be attributed to synthetic chemicals in food.
>
> FDA officials were not oblivious to these developments. Agency spokespersons remarked on the dramatic advances in analytical chemistry which were revealing "additives" in food whose occurrence had not previously been expected. They also recognized that more comprehensive and sensitive testing of chemicals was expanding the list of proven animal carcinogens. And they became less hesitant about pointing out that the food supply contains hundreds of trace chemicals, most present "naturally," that have been associated with tumor formation in experimental animals. Furthermore, Agency officials were reminded of the growing concern about the links between dietary patterns and human cancer when food producers began promoting products as high in fibre or rich in Vitamin C while invoking the findings of the National Cancer Institute. These developments eroded both of the assumptions of the framers of the Delaney Clause: few chemical "additives" caused cancer, but those few presented a serious threat to public health.

Richard A. Merrill, *FDA's Implementation of the Delaney Clause: Repudiation of Congressional Choice or Reasoned Adaptation to Scientific Progress?*, 5 YALE J. ON REG. 1, 12–13 (1988).[4]

By the mid–1980s, FDA was fed up with the many legal devices (one might even say subterfuges) that had developed for avoiding application of the Delaney Clause in cases in which the actual risk was very low. The agency decided to meet the problem head on, and adopted a *de minimis* exception for color additives. This sparked a challenge from a public interest group.

Public Citizen v. Young

831 F.2d 1108 (D.C. Cir. 1987)

■ WILLIAMS, CIRCUIT JUDGE:

The Color Additive Amendments of 1960 (codified at 21 U.S.C. § 376 (1982)), part of the Food, Drug and Cosmetic Act (the "Act"), establish an elaborate system for regulation of color additives in the interests of safety. A color additive may be used only after the Food and Drug Administration ("FDA") has published a regulation listing the additive for such uses as are safe. Such listing may occur only if the color additive in question satisfies (among other things) the requirements of the applicable "Delaney Clause," one of three such clauses in the total system for regulation of color additives, food and animal food and drugs. The Clause prohibits the listing of any color additive "found ... to induce cancer in man or animal."

In No. 86–1548, Public Citizen and certain individuals challenge the decision of the FDA to list two color additives, Orange No. 17 and Red No. 19, based on quantitative risk assessments indicating that the cancer risks presented by these dyes were trivial. This case thus requires us to determine whether the Delaney Clause for color additives is subject to an implicit *"de minimis"* exception. We conclude, with some reluctance, that the Clause lacks such an exception.

* * *

I. THE DELANEY CLAUSE AND "DE MINIMIS" EXCEPTIONS

A. Factual Background

The FDA listed Orange No. 17 and Red No. 19 for use in externally applied cosmetics on August 7, 1986. In the listing notices, it carefully explained the testing processes for both dyes and praised the processes as "current state-of-the-art toxicological testing." In both notices it specifically rejected industry arguments that the Delaney Clause did not apply because the tests were inappropriate for evaluation of the dyes. It thus concluded that the studies established that the substances caused cancer in the test animals.

---

4. For detailed descriptions of the Delaney Clause's passage and implementation, *see id.*; Richard A. Merrill, *Regulating Carcinogens in Food: A Legislator's Guide to the Food Safety Provisions of the Federal Food, Drug, and Cosmetic Act*, 77 MICH. L. REV. 171 (1978).

* * *

* * * The scientific review panel found the lifetime cancer risks of the substances extremely small: for Orange No. 17, it calculated them as one in 19 billion at worst, and for Red No. 19 one in nine million at worst. The FDA explained that the panel had used conservative assumptions in deriving these figures, and it characterized the risks as "so trivial as to be effectively no risk." It concluded that the two dyes were safe.

The FDA candidly acknowledged that its safety findings represented a departure from past agency practice: "In the past, because the data and information show that D & C Orange No. 17 is a carcinogen when ingested by laboratory animals, FDA in all likelihood would have terminated the provisional listing and denied CTFA's petition for the externally applied uses ... without any further discussion." It also acknowledged that "[a] strictly literal application of the Delaney Clause would prohibit FDA from finding [both dyes] safe, and therefore, prohibit FDA from permanently listing [them]...." Because the risks presented by these dyes were so small, however, the agency declared that it had "inherent authority" under the *de minimis* doctrine to list them for use in spite of this language. It indicated that as a general matter any risk lower than a one-in-one-million lifetime risk would meet the requirements for a *de minimis* exception to the Delaney Clause.

Assuming that the quantitative risk assessments are accurate, as we do for these purposes, it seems altogether correct to characterize these risks as trivial. * * *

* * *

B.   Plain Language and the De Minimis Doctrine

The Delaney Clause of the Color Additive Amendments provides as follows:

> a color additive ... (ii) shall be deemed unsafe, and shall not be listed, for any use which will not result in ingestion of any part of such additive, if, after tests which are appropriate for the evaluation of the safety of additives for such use, or after other relevant exposure of man or animal to such additive, it is found by the Secretary to induce cancer in man or animal....

21 U.S.C. § 376(b)(5)(B).

The natural—almost inescapable—reading of this language is that if the Secretary finds the additive to "induce" cancer in animals, he must deny listing. Here, of course, the agency made precisely the finding that Orange No. 17 and Red No. 19 "induce[ ] cancer when tested in laboratory animals." * * *

The setting of the clause supports this strict reading. Adjacent to it is a section governing safety generally and directing the FDA to consider a variety of factors, including probable exposure, cumulative effects, and detection difficulties. 21 U.S.C. § 376(b)(5)(A). The contrast in approach seems to us significant. For all safety hazards other than carcinogens,

Congress made safety the issue, and authorized the agency to pursue a multifaceted inquiry in arriving at an evaluation. For carcinogens, however, it framed the issue in the simple form, "If A [finding that cancer is induced in man or animals], then B [no listing]." There is language inviting administrative discretion, but it relates only to the process leading to the finding of carcinogenicity: "appropriate" tests or "other relevant exposure," and the agency's "evaluation" of such data. Once the finding is made, the dye "shall be deemed unsafe, and shall not be listed." 21 U.S.C. § 367(b)(5)(B).

Courts (and agencies) are not, of course, helpless slaves to literalism. One escape hatch, invoked by the government and CTFA here, is the *de minimis* doctrine, shorthand for *de minimis non curat lex* ("the law does not concern itself with trifles"). The doctrine—articulated in recent times in a series of decisions by Judge Leventhal—serves a number of purposes. One is to spare agency resources for more important matters. But that is a goal of dubious relevance here. The finding of trivial risk necessarily followed not only the elaborate animal testing, but also the quantitative risk assessment process itself; indeed, application of the doctrine required additional expenditure of agency resources.

More relevant is the concept that "notwithstanding the 'plain meaning' of a statute, a court must look beyond the words to the purpose of the act where its literal terms lead to 'absurd or futile results.' " *Alabama Power Co. v. Costle*, 636 F.2d 323, 360 n.89. Imposition of pointless burdens on regulated entities is obviously to be avoided if possible, especially as burdens on them almost invariably entail losses for their customers: here, obviously, loss of access to the colors made possible by a broad range of dyes.

We have employed the concept in construing the Clean Air Act's mandate to the Environmental Protection Agency to set standards providing "an ample margin of safety to protect the public health," 42 U.S.C. § 7412(b)(1) (1982). That does not, we said, require limits assuring a "risk-free" environment. Rather, the agency must decide "what risks are acceptable in the world in which we live" and set limits accordingly [citing the *Benzene* case, *infra*]. Assuming as always the validity of the risk assessments, we believe that the risks posed by the two dyes would have to be characterized as "acceptable." Accordingly, if the statute were to permit a *de minimis* exception, this would appear to be a case for its application.[5]

Moreover, failure to employ a *de minimis* doctrine may lead to regulation that not only is "absurd or futile" in some general cost-benefit sense but also is directly contrary to the primary legislative goal. In a certain sense, precisely that may be the effect here. The primary goal of the Act is human safety, but literal application of the Delaney Clause may in some instances increase risk. No one contends that the Color Additive Amendments impose a zero-risk standard for non-carcinogenic substances; if they did, the number of dyes passing muster might prove minuscule. As a result, makers

---

5. We do not, of course, purport to decide the appropriate dividing point between *de minimis* and other risks. FDA's proposed one-in-one-million dividing point has been used by EPA to distinguish acceptable and unacceptable risks. FDA has used the same break point to determine whether the general safety clause of the Act applies.

of drugs and cosmetics who are barred from using a carcinogenic dye carrying a one-in–20–million lifetime risk may use instead a noncarcinogenic, but toxic, dye carrying, say, a one-in–10–million lifetime risk. The substitution appears to be a clear loss for safety.

Judge Leventhal articulated the standard for application of *de minimis* as virtually a presumption in its favor: "Unless Congress has been extraordinarily rigid, there is likely a basis for an implication of *de minimis* authority to provide [an] exemption when the burdens of regulation yield a gain of trivial or no value." But the doctrine obviously is not available to thwart a statutory command; it must be interpreted with a view to "implementing the legislative design." Nor is an agency to apply it on a finding merely that regulatory costs exceed regulatory benefits.

Here, we cannot find that exemption of exceedingly small (but measurable) risks tends to implement the legislative design of the color additive Delaney Clause. The language itself is rigid; the context—an alternative design admitting administrative discretion for all risks other than carcinogens—tends to confirm that rigidity. Below we consider first the legislative history; rather than offering any hint of softening, this only strengthens the inference. Second, we consider a number of factors that make Congress's apparent decision at least a comprehensible policy choice.

1. Legislative History

* * * Taken as a whole, the remarks do not seem strong enough to undermine the inference we have drawn that the clause was to operate automatically once the FDA squeezed the scientific trigger. * * *

2. Possible Explanations for an Absolute Rule

Like all legislative history, this is hardly conclusive. But short of an explicit declaration in the statute barring use of a *de minimis* exception, this is perhaps as strong as it is likely to get. Facing the explicit claim that the Clause was "extraordinarily rigid," a claim well supported by the Clause's language in contrast with the bill's grants of discretion elsewhere, Congress persevered.

Moreover, our reading of the legislative history suggests some possible explanations for Congress's apparent rigidity. One is that Congress, and the nation in general (at least as perceived by Congress), appear to have been truly alarmed about the risks of cancer. This concern resulted in a close focus on substances increasing cancer threats and a willingness to take extreme steps to lessen even small risks. Congress hoped to reduce the incidence of cancer by banning carcinogenic dyes, and may also have hoped to lessen public fears by demonstrating strong resolve.

A second possible explanation for Congress's failure to authorize greater administrative discretion is that it perceived color additives as lacking any great value. For example, Congressman Delaney remarked, "Some food additives serve a useful purpose…. However, color additives provide no nutrient value. They have no value at all, except so-called eye appeal." Representative Sullivan said, "we like the bright and light [lipstick] shades but if they cannot safely be produced, then we prefer to do without these particular shades." And Representative King: "The colors which go into our foods and cosmetics are in no way essential to the public interest or the national security.... [C]onsumers will easily get along without [carcinogenic colors]."

It is true that the legislation as a whole implicitly recognizes that color additives are of value, since one of its purposes was to allow tolerances for certain dyes—harmful but not carcinogenic—that would have been banned under the former law. There was also testimony pointing out that in some uses color additives advance health: they can help identify medications and prevent misapplications where a patient must take several. Nevertheless, there is evidence that Congress thought the public could get along without carcinogenic colors, especially in view of the existence of safer substitutes. Thus the legislators may have estimated the costs of an overly protective rule as trivial.

So far as we can determine, no one drew the legislators' attention to the way in which the Delaney Clause, interacting with the flexible standard for determining safety of non-carcinogens, might cause manufacturers to substitute more dangerous toxic chemicals for less dangerous carcinogens. But the obviously more stringent standard for carcinogens may rest on a view that cancer deaths are in some way more to be feared than others.

Finally, as we have already noted, the House committee (or its amanuenses) considered the possibility that its no-threshold assumption might prove false and contemplated a solution: renewed consideration by Congress.

Considering these circumstances—great concern over a specific health risk, the apparently low cost of protection, and the possibility of remedying any mistakes—Congress's enactment of an absolute rule seems less surprising.

* * *

D. The Meaning of "[I]nduce Cancer"

After Public Citizen initiated [this] litigation, the FDA published a notice embellishing the preamble to its initial safety determinations. These notices effectively apply quantitative risk assessment at the stage of determining whether a substance "induce[s] cancer in man or animal." They assert that even where a substance does cause cancer in animals in the conventional sense of the term, the FDA may find that it does not "induce cancer in man or animal" within the meaning of 21 U.S.C. § 376(b)(5)(B). * * * [T]he notices argued:

> The words "induce cancer in man or animal" as used in the Delaney Clause are terms of art intended to convey a regulatory judgment that is something more than a scientific observation that an additive is carcinogenic in laboratory animals. To limit this judgment to such a simple observation would be to arbitrarily exclude from FDA's consideration developing sophisticated testing and

analytical methodologies, leaving FDA with only the most primitive techniques for its use in this important endeavor to protect public health. Certainly the language of the Delaney Clause itself cannot be read to mandate such a counterproductive limit on FDA's discharge of its responsibilities.

The notices acknowledged that the words "to induce cancer" had not been "rigorously and unambiguously" so limited in the previous notices. This is a considerable understatement. The original determinations were quite unambiguous in concluding that the colors induced cancer in animals in valid tests; the explanations went to some trouble to rebut industry arguments to the contrary. Despite these arguments, FDA concluded that the tests demonstrated that the dyes were responsible for increases in animal tumors.

The plain language of the Delaney Clause covers all animals exposed to color additives, including laboratory animals exposed to high doses. It would be surprising if it did not. High-dose exposures are standard testing procedure, today just as in 1960; such high doses are justified to offset practical limitations on such tests: compared to expected exposure of millions of humans over long periods, the time periods are short and the animals few. Many references in the legislative history reflect awareness of reliance on animal testing, and at least the more sophisticated participants must have been aware that this meant high-dose testing. A few so specified.

All this indicates to us that Congress did not intend the FDA to be able to take a finding that a substance causes only trivial risk in humans and work back from that to a finding that the substance does not "induce cancer in ... animals." This is simply the basic question—is the operation of the clause automatic once the FDA makes a finding of carcinogenicity in animals?—in a new guise. The only new argument offered in the notices is that, without the new interpretation, only "primitive techniques" could be used. In fact, of course, the agency is clearly free to incorporate the latest breakthroughs in animal testing; indeed, here it touted the most recent animal tests as "state of the art." The limitation on techniques is only that the agency may not, once a color additive is found to induce cancer in test animals in the conventional sense of the term, undercut the statutory consequence. As we find the FDA's construction "contrary to clear congressional intent," *Chevron U.S.A. v. Natural Resources Defense Council, Inc.,* 467 U.S. 837 (1984), we need not defer to it.

* * *

NOTES AND QUESTIONS

1. *The statutory text.* (a) Where is the Delaney *Clause*? What is the substantive standard that it imposes? To what does the clause apply? To what does it *not* apply?

(b) The standard seems to be absolute, as the court concludes. Is there any room for FDA to exercise discretion *not* to apply it? For example, we have previously seen that there are many areas in which the risk assessment process involves policy decisions. Could any of the following choices be used by FDA to avoid application of the Delaney Clause:

- animal *versus* human carcinogens
- possible *versus* probable *versus* known carcinogens
- potent *versus* weak carcinogens
- negligible cancer risk?

(c) Where is the burden of proof under the Delaney Clause? How can you tell? Why is the burden placed where it is?

2. Merrill asserts that the principal problem with the Delaney Clause is the erosion of the assumptions upon which it was based. What are the assumptions behind the Delaney standard? How have they eroded and what has been the effect on the clause?

To take a contrary position, haven't the developments in science that Merrill describes simply shown that the problem is even worse than Rep. Delaney imagined? Why does the expanded scope of the problem cast *doubt* on its significance?

3. The court suggests that the Delaney ban may actually be perverse in terms of overall safety. How could that come about? Is the solution to weaken the Delaney Clause or to close its loopholes?

4. *Saccharin, Act I.* FDA's proposal to ban saccharin as a sweetener in most foods and drinks focused national attention on the potential consequences of implementing the Delaney Clause. Professor Merrill describes the situation:[6]

> In April, 1977, FDA proposed to withdraw approval for the use of saccharin in all foods, including artificially sweetened soft drinks, and in ingested cosmetics and drugs as well. * * *
>
> FDA's proposal triggered protests from consumers, legislators, clinicians who treated juvenile diabetics, and manufacturers of saccharin sweetened foods. Congress acted quickly to prevent implementation of the ban, directing FDA to commission studies by NAS and amending the FD & C Act to foreclose for two years any FDA action based on the existing animal test to ban or restrict use of saccharin. The Saccharin Ban Moratorium provisions have been reenacted four times.
>
> * * *
>
> In short, by 1977 FDA officials believed that they had exhausted every available excuse for not enforcing the Delaney Clause, including the claim that more time was needed to complete and analyze studies of saccharin's effects, a claim which had sustained the ingredient for nearly a decade. FDA's proposed ban of saccharin

---

6. Merrill, *FDA's Implementation, supra,* at 29–32. For more detailed discussions of the saccharine case, *see* KATHRYN HARRISON & GEORGE HOBERG, RISK, SCIENCE, AND POLITICS: REGULATING TOXIC SUBSTANCES IN CANADA AND THE UNITED STATES 77–98 (1994); Richard A. Merrill & Michael R. Taylor, *Saccharine: A Case Study of Government Regulation of Environmental Carcinogens,* 5 VA. J. NAT. RES. L. 1 (1985).

can therefore be viewed as the reluctant action of an agency that had already come to question the wisdom of the Delaney Clause and in other contexts had exploited legal devices to avoid it.

* * *

The repudiation of its saccharin proposal taught FDA officials that some food ingredients enjoy a distinct status. Congress's rejection of the very premises that inspired enactment of the Delaney Clause sent a clear message: some ingredients are too important to ban. A second, more important lesson was that legislative revision of the law was improbable. Congress was prepared to create exceptions to the FD & C Act's general requirements—including ingredient-specific exceptions to the Delaney Clause—but it seemed unwilling to entertain seriously any categorical revisions of this icon. Almost none of the food safety bills subsequently introduced risked frontal repeal of the anticancer language that Congress almost casually, perhaps even reluctantly, had included in 1958. * * *

As Merrill describes, Congress did not agree with FDA's decision to ban saccharin. Instead, it enacted the Saccharin Study and Labeling Act, Pub.L. 95–203, § 3, Nov. 23, 1977, 91 Stat. 1452 (as amended):

> During the period ending May 1, 2002, the Secretary * * *
>
> (2) may * * * not take any other action under the Federal Food, Drug, and Cosmetic Act to prohibit or restrict the sale or distribution of saccharin, any food permitted by such interim food additive regulation to contain saccharin, or any drug or cosmetic containing saccharin, solely on the basis of the carcinogenic or other toxic effect of saccharin as determined by any study made available to the Secretary before the date of the enactment of this Act [Nov. 23, 1977] which involved human studies or animal testing, or both.

It further provided that products containing saccharin will be considered misbranded unless its label bears the following statement: USE OF THIS PRODUCT MAY BE HAZARDOUS TO YOUR HEALTH. THIS PRODUCT CONTAINS SACCHARIN WHICH HAS BEEN DETERMINED TO CAUSE CANCER IN LABORATORY ANIMALS. 21 U.S.C. § 343(o)(1).

Is it a rational risk decision to exempt saccharin from the usual rule for carcinogens? Congress in fact responded to the saccharin ban quickly and with only spotty information about its benefits.

5. *Saccharin, Act II.* On May 15, 2000, the National Toxicology Program announced that it was proposing to "delist" saccharin as a human carcinogen because nearly two decades of further testing had indicated that saccharin's carcinogenic effect on rats is not applicable to humans. Does this change in saccharin's status (if approved) mean that the original decision to ban saccharin was wrong? Does it make a legal difference under the Delaney Clause?

Following the publication of the new National Toxicology Program position on saccharin, Congress repealed the saccharin labeling and study requirements at 21 U.S.C. §§ 343(o) and 343a. The name of the new legislation is a mouthful—Saccharin Warning Elimination via Environmental Testing Employing Science and Technology Act—but its acronym is positively saccharine: the SWEETEST Act (Pub. L. No. 106–554, § 518 (2000)).

The Food Quality Protection Act of 1996

The Delaney Clause distinguishes between carcinogens and all other food hazards, and it bans the former when they are food additives. But what about pesticide residues (the reason your mother told you to wash fruits and vegetables)? Aren't they added to foods? Under the pre-1996 FFDCA, the answer was yes and no. First, the federal pesticide statute (FIFRA, which we examine in Chapter 4) permitted pesticide residues on raw agricultural commodities as long as they were below a "tolerance level" established through a risk-benefit calculation (unlike the Delaney Clause). 7 U.S.C. § 136a(c)(5). Moreover, such residues could legally "flow through" to processed agricultural commodities as long as they did not concentrate further during the manufacturing process. 21 U.S.C. §§ 342(a)(2)(B)–(C), 346a. This was the Delaney Paradox: some foods containing pesticide residues were subject to a *de minimis* risk standard, and some to a *zero risk* standard.[7]

FDA sought to use this inconsistency in treatment to leverage reconsideration of the *Public Citizen* case, but in *Les v. Reilly*, 968 F.2d 985 (9th Cir. 1992), the Ninth Circuit refused to permit a *de minimis* standard to be applied to pesticides covered by the Delaney Clause. Convinced that the distinction was irrational and faced with a court order to begin canceling the registrations of several important pesticides, Congress passed the Food Quality Protection Act of 1996.[8] The revised statute provides a single standard for all pesticide residues. As you read the excerpted section below, consider: What is the safety standard that the FQPA imposes? How is it different from the Delaney Clause standard? What other changes do you see? What are the advantages and disadvantages of the new approach?

Sec. 346a. Tolerances and exemptions for pesticide chemical residues

(a) Requirement for tolerance or exemption

---

7. *See* NATIONAL RESEARCH COUNCIL, REGULATING PESTICIDES IN FOOD: THE DELANEY PARADOX (1987); EPA, Regulation of Pesticides in Food: Addressing the Delaney Paradox Policy Statement, 53 Fed. Reg. 41104 (1988).

8. *See generally* Lynn Bergeson & Carla N. Hutton, *The Food Quality Protection Act—Implementation and Legal Challenges*, 34 Envtl. L. Rep. (Envtl. L. Inst.) 10733 (2004). The FQPA and its background are helpfully described in Dominic P. Madigan, Note, *Setting an Anti-Cancer Policy: Risk, Politics, and the Food Quality Protection Act of 1996*, 17 VA. ENVTL. L.J. 187 (1998), and James S. Turner, *Delaney Lives! Reports of Delaney's Death Are Greatly Exaggerated*, 28 Envtl. L. Rep. (Envtl. L. Inst.) 10003 (1998). For the view that the FQPA still overregulates pesticide residues, *see* Frank B. Cross, *The Consequences of Consensus: Dangerous Compromises of the Food Quality Protection Act*, 75 WASH. U. L.Q. 1155 (1997).

General rule

Except as provided in paragraph (2) or (3), any pesticide chemical residue in or on a food shall be deemed unsafe for the purpose of section 342(a)(2)(B) of this title unless—

(A) a tolerance for such pesticide chemical residue in or on such food is in effect under this section and the quantity of the residue is within the limits of the tolerance; * * *.

(b) *Authority and standard for tolerance * * ***

(2) *Standard*

    (A) *General rule*

        (i) *Standard*

The Administrator may establish or leave in effect a tolerance for a pesticide chemical residue in or on a food only if the Administrator determines that the tolerance is safe. The Administrator shall modify or revoke a tolerance if the Administrator determines it is not safe.

        (ii) *Determination of safety*

As used in this section, the term "safe," with respect to a tolerance for a pesticide chemical residue, means that the Administrator has determined that there is a reasonable certainty that no harm will result from aggregate exposure to the pesticide chemical residue, including all anticipated dietary exposures and all other exposures for which there is reliable information.

        (iii) *Rule of construction*

With respect to a tolerance, a pesticide chemical residue meeting the standard under clause (i) is not an eligible pesticide chemical residue for purposes of subparagraph (B).

    (B) *Tolerances for eligible pesticide chemical residues*

        (i) *Definition*

As used in this subparagraph, the term "eligible pesticide chemical residue'" means a pesticide chemical residue as to which

        (I) the Administrator is not able to identify a level of exposure to the residue at which the residue will not cause or contribute to a known or anticipated harm to human health (referred to in this section as a nonthreshold effect);

        (II) the lifetime risk of experiencing the nonthreshold effect is appropriately assessed by quantitative risk assessment; and

(III) with regard to any known or anticipated harm to human health for which the Administrator is able to identify a level at which the residue will not cause such harm (referred to in this section as a "threshold effect' "), the Administrator determines that the level of aggregate exposure is safe.

(ii) *Determination of tolerance*

Notwithstanding subparagraph (A)(i), a tolerance for an eligible pesticide chemical residue may be left in effect or modified under this subparagraph if—

(I) at least one of the conditions described in clause (iii) is met; and

(II) both of the conditions described in clause (iv) are met.

(iii) *Conditions regarding use*

For purposes of clause (ii), the conditions described in this clause with respect to a tolerance for an eligible pesticide chemical residue are the following:

(I) Use of the pesticide chemical that produces the residue protects consumers from adverse effects on health that would pose a greater risk than the dietary risk from the residue.

(II) Use of the pesticide chemical that produces the residue is necessary to avoid a significant disruption in domestic production of an adequate, wholesome, and economical food supply.

(iv) *Conditions regarding risk*

For purposes of clause (ii), the conditions described in this clause with respect to a tolerance for an eligible pesticide chemical residue are the following:

(I) The yearly risk associated with the nonthreshold effect from aggregate exposure to the residue does not exceed 10 times the yearly risk that would be allowed under subparagraph (A) for such effect.

(II) The tolerance is limited so as to ensure that the risk over a lifetime associated with the nonthreshold effect from aggregate exposure to the residue is not greater than twice the lifetime risk that would be allowed under subparagraph (A) for such effect. * * *

(vi) *Infants and children*

Any tolerance under this subparagraph shall meet the requirements of subparagraph (C).

(C) *Exposure of infants and children*

In establishing, modifying, leaving in effect, or revoking a tolerance or exemption for a pesticide chemical residue, the Administrator

(i) shall assess the risk of the pesticide chemical residue based on—

(I) available information about consumption patterns among infants and children that are likely to result in disproportionately high consumption of foods containing or bearing such residue among infants and children in comparison to the general population;

(II) available information concerning the special susceptibility of infants and children to the pesticide chemical residues, including neurological differences between infants and children and adults, and effects of in utero exposure to pesticide chemicals; and

(III) available information concerning the cumulative effects on infants and children of such residues and other substances that have a common mechanism of toxicity; and

(ii) shall—

(I) ensure that there is a reasonable certainty that no harm will result to infants and children from aggregate exposure to the pesticide chemical residue; and

(II) publish a specific determination regarding the safety of the pesticide chemical residue for infants and children. * * *

(D) *Factors*

In establishing, modifying, leaving in effect, or revoking a tolerance or exemption for a pesticide chemical residue, the Administrator shall consider, among other relevant factors—

(i) the validity, completeness, and reliability of the available data from studies of the pesticide chemical and pesticide chemical residue;

(ii) the nature of any toxic effect shown to be caused by the pesticide chemical or pesticide chemical residue in such studies;

(iii) available information concerning the relationship of the results of such studies to human risk;

(iv) available information concerning the dietary consumption patterns of consumers (and major identifiable subgroups of consumers);

(v) available information concerning the cumulative effects of such residues and other substances that have a common mechanism of toxicity;

(vi) available information concerning the aggregate exposure levels of consumers (and major identifiable subgroups of consumers) to the pesticide chemical residue and to other related substances, including dietary exposure under the tolerance and all other tolerances in effect for the pesticide chemical residue, and exposure from other nonoccupational sources;

(vii) available information concerning the variability of the sensitivities of major identifiable subgroups of consumers;

(viii) such information as the Administrator may require on whether the pesticide chemical may have an effect in humans that is similar to an effect produced by a naturally occurring estrogen or other endocrine effects; and

(ix) safety factors which in the opinion of experts qualified by scientific training and experience to evaluate the safety of food additives are generally recognized as appropriate for the use of animal experimentation data.

* * *

2. *RESERVE MINING CO. v. EPA*

While *Public Citizen* describes the Congress' first major substantive encounter with the regulation of carcinogens, the landmark *Reserve Mining* case was the first major judicial encounter with the problem of toxic risk, and without the benefit of specific direction from Congress. The case marks the point at which a *pollution* paradigm of environmental law (dumping asbestos-bearing mining waste into Lake Superior) was supplanted by a *toxics* paradigm (asbestos as a threat to human health). On the night of May 20, 1973, an EPA toxicologist dreamt that asbestos fibers from Reserve Mining's tailings would find their way into the drinking water of Duluth, Minnesota, which used Lake Superior for this purpose. John S. Applegate, *The Story of* Reserve Mining, ENVIRONMENTAL LAW STORIES (Lazarus & Houck, eds. 2005); THOMAS F. BASTOW, "THIS VAST POLLUTION": *UNITED STATES OF AMERICA v. RESERVE MINING CO.* 96–100 (1986). As the following case relates, the dream was true.

Reserve Mining Co. v. EPA

514 F.2d 492 (8th Cir. 1975) (*en banc*)

■ BRIGHT, CIRCUIT JUDGE:

The United States, the States of Michigan, Wisconsin, and Minnesota, and several environmental groups seek an injunction ordering Reserve Mining Company to cease discharging wastes from its iron ore processing plant in Silver Bay, Minnesota, into the ambient air of Silver Bay and the waters of Lake Superior. [The plaintiffs alleged violations of, *inter alia*, the pre-1972 Federal Water Pollution Control Act (FWPCA).] * * *

* * *

In 1947, Reserve Mining Company (Reserve), then contemplating a venture in which it would mine low-grade iron ore ("taconite") present in Minnesota's Mesabi Iron Range and process the ore into iron-rich pellets at facilities bordering on Lake Superior, received a permit from the State of Minnesota to discharge the wastes (called "tailings") from its processing operations into the lake.

Reserve commenced the processing of taconite ore in Silver Bay, Minnesota, in 1955, and that operation continues today. Taconite mined near Babbitt, Minnesota, is shipped by rail some 47 miles to the Silver Bay "beneficiating" plant where it is concentrated into pellets containing some 65 percent iron ore. The process involves crushing the taconite into fine granules, separating out the metallic iron with huge magnets, and flushing the residual tailings into Lake Superior. The tailings enter the lake as a slurry of approximately 1.5 percent solids. The slurry acts as a heavy density current bearing the bulk of the suspended particles to the lake bottom. In this manner, approximately 67,000 tons of tailings are discharged daily.[9]

* * *

Until June 8, 1973, the case was essentially a water pollution abatement case, but on that date the focus of the controversy shifted to the public health impact of the tailings discharge.... [The plaintiffs alleged that the material discharged by Reserve was identical or substantially identical to amosite asbestos. Reserve disputed this characterization of the tailings, but the district court and court of appeals found that tailings fibers were found in Duluth drinking water, and that they could be fairly characterized as asbestos.] * * *

* * *

On April 20, 1974, the district court entered an order closing Reserve's Silver Bay facility. [Reserve sought and obtained a stay from the Eighth Circuit, pending the present decision from the full court.] * * *

* * *

---

9. The Silver Bay processing operation employs about 3,000 workers and is central to the economic livelihood of Silver Bay and surrounding communities.

The claim that Reserve's discharge of tailings into Lake Superior causes a hazard to public health raises many of the same uncertainties present with respect to the discharge into air. Thus, the previous discussion of fiber identity and fiber size is also applicable to the water discharge. In two respects, however, the discharge into water raises added uncertainties: first, whether the ingestion of fibers, as compared with their inhalation, poses any danger whatsoever; and second, should ingestion pose a danger, whether the exposure resulting from Reserve's discharge may be said to present a legally cognizable risk to health.

1. *Ingestion of Fibers as a Danger to Health.*

All epidemiological studies which associate asbestos fibers with harm to health are based upon inhalation of these fibers by humans. Thus, although medical opinion agrees that fibers entering the respiratory tract can interact with body tissues and produce disease, it is unknown whether the same can be said of fibers entering the digestive tract. If asbestos fibers do not interact with digestive tissue, they are presumably eliminated as waste without harmful effect upon the body.

The evidence bearing upon possible harm from ingestion of fibers falls into three areas: first, the court-sponsored tissue study, designed to measure whether asbestos fibers are present in the tissues of long-time Duluth residents; second, animal experiments designed to measure whether, as a biological phenomenon, fibers can penetrate the gastrointestinal mucosa and thus interact with body tissues; third, the increased incidence of gastrointestinal cancer among workers occupationally exposed to asbestos, and the hypothesis that this increase may be due to the ingestion of fibers initially inhaled.

a. *The Tissue Study.*

Recognizing the complete lack of any direct evidence (epidemiological or otherwise) on the issue of whether the ingestion of fibers poses a risk, the trial court directed that a tissue study be conducted to determine whether the tissues of long-time Duluth residents contain any residue of asbestos-like fibers.

The study sought to analyze by electron microscope the tissues of recently deceased Duluth residents who had ingested Duluth water for at least 15 years; that is, approximately since the beginning of Reserve's operations. As a "control" check on results, tissue samples were obtained from the deceased residents of Houston, Texas, where the water is free of asbestos fibers. Although this study was necessarily expedited, plaintiffs' principal medical witness, Dr. Selikoff, testified to the sound design of the study and expressed his belief that it would yield significant information.

One of the court-appointed experts, Dr. Frederick Pooley, in explaining the results of the study, stated that he found that the tissues of the Duluth residents were virtually free of any fibers which could be attributed to the Reserve discharge. * * *

As we noted in the stay opinion, the parties dispute the significance to be attributed to the results of this study. Dr. Selikoff, prior to the conclusion of the study, expressed this view:

Now, our feeling was that no matter what air samples show or water samples show or anything else, unless it is found that asbestos is in the tissues of people who have drunk this water * * * if we do not find it in the tissues in appreciable quantities, then I would risk a professional opinion that there is no danger, at least up to this point, to the population no matter what our samples show or water samples.

After negative results had been actually obtained, however, plaintiffs argued, and the district court agreed, that because the specimens of tissue represented only a microscopically minute body area, the actual presence of fibers may have been overlooked.

* * *

The district court decided, and we agree, that the study cannot be deemed conclusive in exonerating the ingestion of fibers in Lake Superior water as a hazard. The negative results must, however, be given some weight in assessing the probabilities of harm from Reserve's discharge into water. The results also weigh heavily in indicating that no emergency or imminent hazard to health exists. Thus, while this study crucially bears on the determination of whether it is necessary to close Reserve down immediately, the negative results do not dispose of the broader issue of whether the ingestion of fibers poses some danger to public health justifying abatement on less immediate terms.

b. *Animal Studies and Penetration of the Gastrointestinal Mucosa.*

At a somewhat more theoretical level, the determination of whether ingested fibers can penetrate the gastrointestinal mucosa bears on the issue of harm through ingestion. If penetration is biologically impossible, then presumably the interaction of the fibers with body tissues will not occur.

This medical issue has been investigated through experiments with animals, which, unfortunately, have produced conflicting results. * * *

On this conflicting scientific evidence, Dr. Brown[10] testified that the [conflicting] studies provide some support for the hypothesis that asbestos fibers can penetrate the gastrointestinal mucosa.[11]

c. *Excess Gastrointestinal Cancer Among the Occupationally Exposed.*

The affirmative evidence supporting the proposition that the ingestion of fibers poses a danger to health focuses on the increased rate of gastrointestinal cancer among workers occupationally exposed to asbestos dust. Plaintiffs' experts attribute this excess incidence of gastrointestinal cancer

___

10. Dr. Arnold Brown, a distinguished physician, served as both a technical advisor and impartial witness for the district court.—EDS.

11. We note from the record that while attempts to induce tumors in experimental animals through the inhalation of fibers have succeeded, attempts to induce tumors by ingestion have generally failed. * * *

to a theory that the asbestos workers first inhaled the asbestos dust and thereafter coughed up and swallowed the asbestos particles.

The attribution of health harm from ingestion rests upon a theoretical basis. As Dr. Selikoff explained, there are several possible explanations for the increased evidence of gastrointestinal cancer, some of which do not involve ingestion. Moreover, as noted previously, the excess rates of gastrointestinal cancer are generally "modest," and substantially lower than the excess rates of mesothelioma and lung cancer associated with inhalation of asbestos dust. Also, the experts advised that an analysis of a small exposed population may produce statistically "unstable" results.

The existence of an excess rate of gastrointestinal cancer among asbestos workers is a matter of concern. The theory that excess cancers may be attributed to the ingestion of asbestos fibers rests on a tenable medical hypothesis. Indeed, Dr. Selikoff testified that ingestion is the "probable" route accounting for the excess in gastrointestinal cancer. The occupational studies support the proposition that the ingestion of asbestos fibers can result in harm to health.

2. *Level of Exposure Via Ingestion.*

The second primary uncertainty with respect to ingestion involves the attempt to assess whether the level of exposure from drinking water is hazardous. Of course, this inquiry is handicapped by the great variation in fiber counts, and Dr. Brown's admonition that only a qualitative, and not a quantitative, statement can be made about the presence of fibers.

In spite of these difficulties, the district court found that the level of exposure resulting from the drinking of Duluth water was "comparable" to that found to cause gastrointestinal cancer in asbestos workers. The court drew this finding from an elaborate calculation by Dr. Nicholson in which he attempted to make a statistical comparison between the fibers probably ingested by an asbestos worker subject to an excess risk of gastrointestinal cancer with the probable number of amphibole fibers ingested by a Duluth resident over a period of 18 years. * * * Reserve witness Dr. Gross performed a calculation similar to Dr. Nicholson's, but using somewhat different assumptions, and concluded that Duluth water would have to contain several hundred million fibers/liter and be ingested for 60 years before an exposure comparable with occupational levels would be reached.

The comparison has other weaknesses, for without regard to the comparability of the gross exposure levels, the dynamics of the exposure process are markedly different. The vagaries attendant to the use of assumptions rather than facts result in comparisons which are of dubious accuracy. Thus, Dr. Brown testified that, if Nicholson's calculations were correct, he would conclude only that the risk was non-negligible.

The Nicholson comparison, although evidentially weak, must be considered with other evidence. The record does show that the ingestion of asbestos fibers poses some risk to health, but to an undetermined degree. Given these circumstances, Dr. Brown testified that the possibility of a future excess incidence of cancer attributable to the discharge cannot be ignored:

* * *

After some degree of exposure to the literature and to the testimony given in this trial I would say that the scientific evidence that I have seen is not complete in terms of allowing me to draw a conclusion one way or another concerning the problem of a public health hazard in the water in Lake Superior.

* * *

As a medical person, sir, I think that I have to err, if err I do, on the side of what is best for the greatest number. And having concluded or having come to the conclusions that I have given you, the carcinogenicity of asbestos, I can come to no conclusion, sir, other than that the fibers should not be present in the drinking water of the people of the North Shore.

* * *

C.   Conclusion.

The preceding extensive discussion of the evidence demonstrates that the medical and scientific conclusions here in dispute clearly lie "on the frontiers of scientific knowledge." *Industrial Union Department, AFL–CIO v. Hodgson*, 499 F.2d 467, 474 (1974). The trial court, not having any proof of actual harm, was faced with a consideration of (1) the probabilities of any health harm and (2) the consequences, if any, should the harm actually occur.

* * *

In assessing probabilities in this case, it cannot be said that the probability of harm is more likely than not. Moreover, the level of probability does not readily convert into a prediction of consequences. On this record it cannot be forecast that the rates of cancer will increase from drinking Lake Superior water or breathing Silver Bay air. The best that can be said is that the existence of this asbestos contaminant in air and water gives rise to a reasonable medical concern for the public health. The public's exposure to asbestos fibers in air and water creates some health risk. Such a contaminant should be removed.

As we demonstrate in the following sections of the opinion, the existence of this risk to the public justifies an injunction decree requiring abatement of the health hazard on reasonable terms as a precautionary and preventive measure to protect the public health.

IV.   *FEDERAL WATER POLLUTION CONTROL ACT*

The district court found that Reserve's discharge into Lake Superior violated §§ 1160(c)(5) and (g)(1) of the Federal Water Pollution Control Act (FWPCA). These two provisions authorize an action by the United States to secure abatement of water discharges in interstate waters where the discharges violate state water quality standards and "endanger * * * the health or welfare of persons." § 1160(g)(1).

* * *

In this review, we must determine whether "endangering" within the meaning of the FWPCA encompasses the potential of harm to public health in the degree shown here. * * * The term "endangering," as used by Congress in § 1160(g)(1), connotes a lesser risk of harm than the phrase "imminent and substantial endangerment to the health of persons" as used by Congress in the 1972 amendments to the FWPCA. 33 U.S.C. § 1364.

In the context of this environmental legislation, we believe that Congress used the term "endangering" in a precautionary or preventive sense, and, therefore, evidence of potential harm as well as actual harm comes within the purview of that term. We are fortified in this view by the flexible provisions for injunctive relief which permit a court "to enter such judgment and orders enforcing such judgment as the public interest and the equities of the case may require." 33 U.S.C. § 1160(c)(5).

* * *

The record shows that Reserve is discharging a substance into Lake Superior waters which under an acceptable but unproved medical theory may be considered as carcinogenic. As previously discussed, this discharge gives rise to a reasonable medical concern over the public health. We sustain the district court's determination that Reserve's discharge into Lake Superior constitutes pollution of waters "endangering the health or welfare of persons" within the terms of §§ 1160(c)(5) and (g)(1) of the Federal Water Pollution Control Act and is subject to abatement.

* * *

VII.   REMEDY

* * *

* * * In the absence of proof of a reasonable risk of imminent or actual harm, a legal standard requiring immediate cessation of industrial operations will cause unnecessary economic loss, including unemployment, and, in a case such as this, jeopardize a continuing domestic source of critical metals without conferring adequate countervailing benefits.

We believe that on this record the district court abused its discretion by immediately closing this major industrial plant. * * *

Reserve shall be given a reasonable time to stop discharging its wastes into Lake Superior. * * * Assuming agreement and designation of an appropriate land disposal site, Reserve is entitled to a reasonable turn-around time to construct the necessary facilities and accomplish a changeover in the means of disposing of its taconite wastes.

* * *

NOTES AND QUESTIONS

1. What is the legal standard applied in *Reserve Mining*, and how is it similar to the standard of the Delaney Clause? Is there a reason that they are both "firsts" in their respective areas?

2. *The scientific problem.* What was EPA's theory of the mechanism of harm? What evidence did EPA assemble in support of its request for an injunction? What gaps remained in its evidence? Why weren't the gaps fatal to EPA's case?

3. *Scientific uncertainty.* You have no doubt noticed that the procedural setting of *Reserve Mining* is not quite the same as ordinary review of agency decisionmaking. How is it different? What effect would you expect it to have on the level of judicial scrutiny of agency action? Note the district court's use of specially appointed experts and specially ordered studies. Is this an appropriate judicial role? Where does EPA's expertise fit in?

4. The *Reserve Mining* approach was followed and elaborated upon in *Ethyl Corp. v. EPA*,[12] which affirmed EPA's lead phase-out rule for gasoline:

> * * * The court thus allowed regulation of the effluent on only a "reasonable" or "potential" showing of danger, hardly the "probable" finding urged by Ethyl as the proper reading of the "endanger" language in Section 211 [of the Clean Air Act, 42 U.S.C. § 7545]. The reason this relatively slight showing of probability of risk justified regulation is clear: the harm to be avoided, cancer, was particularly great. * * *

> * * * Where a statute is precautionary in nature, the evidence difficult to come by, uncertain, or conflicting because it is on the frontiers of scientific knowledge, the regulations designed to protect the public health, and the decision that of an expert administrator, we will not demand rigorous step-by-step proof of cause and effect. Such proof may be impossible to obtain if the precautionary purpose of the statute is to be served. Of course, we are not suggesting that the Administrator has the power to act on hunches or wild guesses. * * * However, we do hold that in such cases the Administrator may assess risks. He must take account of available facts, of course, but his inquiry does not end there. The Administrator may apply his expertise to draw conclusions from suspected, but not completely substantiated, relationships between facts, from trends among facts, from theoretical projections from imperfect data, from probative preliminary data not yet certifiable as "fact," and the like. We believe that a conclusion so drawn [from] a risk assessment may, if rational, form the basis for health-related regulations under the "will endanger" language of Section 211.

541 F.2d 1, 19, 28 (D.C. Cir. 1976) (*en banc*), *cert. denied*, 426 U.S. 941 (1976). Why does it follow from the "endanger" standard that EPA "may assess risks"? What does it mean that the "statute is precautionary in

---

12. Actually, *Reserve Mining* itself relied on the panel opinion in *Ethyl*, which was superseded by the *en banc* opinion, which in turn relied on *Reserve Mining*.

nature"? *See also Hodgson, supra*, 499 F.2d at 474–75.

5. *Cost and procedure.* The "endanger" standard is silent on the role of cost in the agency's or court's deliberations. How did *Reserve* handle the cost issue? What was the impact of the procedural setting of the case? How should cost be handled where equitable flexibility is unavailable?

6. *Lead time and competitiveness.* The effect of asbestos in drinking water remains uncertain. In a study of the regulation of dioxin under the Clean Water Act, Professor Oliver Houck concluded[13]:

> Viewing the issue more broadly, no issue more than dioxin demonstrates that the science of even the best studied toxins is inadequate to produce anything but near-arbitrary decisions on numerical, health, and environmental standards. As one dioxin researcher has concluded:
>
>> This series of events shows many of the problems with quantitative risk assessment. There is uncertainty about even the most basic questions such as the classification of tumors in laboratory animals. A large number of assumptions are required, each of which must be independently justified. Because of the uncertainty and the number of assumptions, it may be possible, in the absence of checks and balances, to construct nearly any result.
>
> * * *
>
> Unfortunately, rather than address the obvious, we are about to engage in yet another expenditure of money, effort, and time reexamining the risks of dioxin. * * * The industry is poised, with its experts, to show the current standards "too stringent." Environmental organizations are readying themselves to prove the standards "too weak." In all likelihood, neither will emerge content, or convinced. For certain, neither will be proven wrong. We continue to pursue a will-o-the-wisp.
>
> On the other hand, the saga of dioxin offers at least a glimpse of a silver lining. The near-routine predictions of layoffs, plant closings, and economic ruin notwithstanding, when the paper industry has had, at last, to convert to a less polluting process, it has done so. At bottom, the struggle is not over the ability not to pollute, but over lead time and competitiveness. Any solution to toxic pollution will have to accommodate these legitimate industry needs. A solution, on the other hand, that fosters differing state standards and differing state applications of these standards breeds uncertainty, contention, unfairness, and endless opposition.

---

13. Oliver A. Houck, *The Regulation of Toxic Products Under the Clean Water Act*, 21 ENVTL. L. REP. (ENVTL. L. INST.) 10528, 10549–54 (1991).

Houck suggests that the real problem to be addressed is "lead time and competitiveness." What does he mean? What sort of legal standard does that suggest?

B.   FEASIBILITY

Like the hazard-based approach, feasibility-based standards involve a narrow range of considerations. However, in addition to the identification of a chemical with a harmful effect, feasibility calibrates the regulatory response to the practical ability to reduce the harm. In this sense, feasibility is a clearer example of the two parts that any regulatory standard must include: the regulatory trigger and the regulatory standard. As described by Professors Shapiro and Glicksman:

> The "regulatory trigger" establishes the evidence burden that an agency has to meet in order to regulate a toxic substance or other hazard. Agencies operate under one of four triggers: no threshold, a threshold based on the existence of a "risk" or "significant risk," or a cost-benefit balancing threshold.

> * * *

> The second structural element consists of the "regulatory standard" or the standard that specifies the level or stringency of regulation. The standards vary in terms of what factors an agency is to take into account in setting the level of regulation.

SIDNEY A. SHAPIRO & ROBERT L. GLICKSMAN, RISK REGULATION AT RISK: RESTORING A PRAGMATIC APPROACH 34–35 (Stan. Univ. Press 2003); *see also* John S. Applegate, *Worst Things First: Risk, Information, and Regulatory Structure in Toxic Substances Control,* 9 YALE J. ON REG. 277, 305–306 (1992). The approach we are about to examine clearly distinguishes the trigger—identification as a hazardous substance—from the regulatory standard—feasibility—which is described in the materials below.

THE OCCUPATIONAL SAFETY AND HEALTH ACT

Enacted in 1970, the Occupational Safety and Health Act (OSH Act) established within the Department of Labor a new agency, the Occupational Safety and Health Administration (OSHA), to be responsible for promulgating and enforcing workplace safety and health standards to protect American workers. The act's substantive regulatory structure is straightforward. Section 5 establishes a general duty on the part of employers to provide safe workplaces and of employees to follow safety rules.[14] Section 6 creates three classes of health and safety standards that OSHA may promulgate: start-

---

14. The decision to assure safety in the workplace through governmental regulation instead of bargaining between employers and unions or individual workers was highly contested at the time of OSHA's enactment, and since. For a spirited discussion of wage premiums, assumption of risk, and other unique workplace issues, *compare* W. Kip Viscusi, *Structuring an Effective Occupational Disease Policy: Victim Compensation and Risk Regulation,* 2 YALE J. ON REG. 53, 56–57 (1984); W. KIP VISCUSI, RISK BY CHOICE: REGULATING HEALTH AND SAFETY IN THE WORKPLACE 38–45, 96–106 (1983), *with* Thomas O. McGarity & Sidney A. Shapiro, *OSHA's Critics and Regulatory Reform,* 31 WAKE FOREST L. REV. 587, 605–07 (1996).

up, readily promulgated standards based on existing governmental or industry "national consensus" standards (§ 6(a)); regular health and safety standards, which may be updates or revisions of the national consensus standards (§ 6(b)); and "emergency temporary standards" for risks that need to be addressed before the rulemaking process would normally be completed (§ 6(c)). Section 6 also establishes special procedures for the promulgation and judicial review of standards, including adoption of the "substantial evidence" test (§ 6(f)). Inspection and enforcement powers, recordkeeping and medical monitoring, penalties for violations, and judicial and administrative review of enforcement actions are provided in the remainder of the statute.

The OSH Act contains a special provision for "toxic materials or harmful physical agents." § 6(b)(5). While the nature, severity, and number of injuries varies widely among workplaces, the workplace has a special importance in the toxics area, because the effects of some of the most notorious toxic substances (*e.g.*, asbestos and benzene) first came to light in the occupational setting. We now turn to two Supreme Court decisions interpreting the toxics provisions of the OSH Act, sections 3(8) and 6(b)(5), in the *Benzene* and *Cotton Dust* cases.[15] *Benzene* in particular has become a foundation of toxics regulation and jurisprudence.

Industrial Union Dep't, AFL–CIO v. American Petroleum Inst.
(The *Benzene* Case)
448 U.S. 607 (1980)

■ Mr. Justice Stevens announced the judgment of the Court and delivered an opinion, in which The Chief Justice and Mr. Justice Stewart joined and in Parts I, II, III–A, III–B, III–C and III–E of which Mr. Justice Powell joined.

The Occupational Safety and Health Act of 1970 (Act) was enacted for the purpose of ensuring safe and healthful working conditions for every working man and woman in the Nation. This litigation concerns a standard promulgated by the Secretary of Labor to regulate occupational exposure to benzene, a substance which has been shown to cause cancer at high exposure levels. The principal question is whether such a showing is a sufficient basis for a standard that places the most stringent limitation on exposure to benzene that is technologically and economically possible.

The Act delegates broad authority to the Secretary to promulgate different kinds of standards. The basic definition of an "occupational safety and health standard" is found in § 3(8), which provides:

> The term "occupational safety and health standard" means a standard which requires conditions, or the adoption or use of

---

15. *See* Thomas O. McGarity, *The Story of the Benzene Case: Judicially Imposed Regulatory Reform Through Risk Assessment, in* Environmental Law Stories 141 (Richard J. Lazarus & Oliver A. Houck, eds., Foundation Press 2005).

one or more practices, means, methods, operations, or processes, reasonably necessary or appropriate to provide safe or healthful employment and places of employment. 29 U.S.C. § 652(8).

Where toxic materials or harmful physical agents are concerned, a standard must also comply with 6(b)(5), which provides:

> The Secretary, in promulgating standards dealing with toxic materials or harmful physical agents under this subsection, shall set the standard which most adequately assures, to the extent feasible, on the basis of the best available evidence, that no employee will suffer material impairment of health or functional capacity even if such employee has regular exposure to the hazard dealt with by such standard for the period of his working life. Development of standards under this subsection shall be based upon research, demonstrations, experiments, and such other information as may be appropriate. In addition to the attainment of the highest degree of health and safety protection for the employee, other considerations shall be the latest available scientific data in the field, the feasibility of the standards, and experience gained under this and other health and safety laws. 29 U.S.C. § 655(b)(5).

Wherever the toxic material to be regulated is a carcinogen, the Secretary has taken the position that no safe exposure level can be determined and that § 6(b)(5) requires him to set an exposure limit at the lowest technologically feasible level that will not impair the viability of the industries regulated. In this case, after having determined that there is a causal connection between benzene and leukemia (a cancer of the white blood cells), the Secretary set an exposure limit on airborne concentrations of benzene of one part benzene per million parts of air (1 ppm), regulated dermal and eye contact with solutions containing benzene, and imposed complex monitoring and medical testing requirements on employers whose workplaces contain 0.5 ppm or more of benzene.

* * *

I

Benzene is a familiar and important commodity. It is a colorless, aromatic liquid that evaporates rapidly under ordinary atmospheric conditions. Approximately 11 billion pounds of benzene were produced in the United States in 1976. Ninety-four percent of that total was produced by the petroleum and petrochemical industries, with the remainder produced by the steel industry as a byproduct of coking operations. Benzene is used in manufacturing a variety of products including motor fuels (which may contain as much as 2% benzene), solvents, detergents, pesticides, and other organic chemicals.

The entire population of the United States is exposed to small quantities of benzene, ranging from a few parts per billion to 0.5 ppm, in the ambient air. Over one million workers are subject to additional low-level exposures as a consequence of their employment. The majority of these employees work in gasoline service stations, benzene production (petroleum refineries and coking operations), chemical processing, benzene transportation, rubber manufacturing, and laboratory operations.

Benzene is a toxic substance. Although it could conceivably cause harm to a person who swallowed or touched it, the principal risk of harm comes from inhalation of benzene vapors. When these vapors are inhaled, the benzene diffuses through the lungs and is quickly absorbed into the blood. Exposure to high concentrations produces an almost immediate effect on the central nervous system. * * *

Industrial health experts have long been aware that exposure to benzene may lead to various types of nonmalignant diseases[, including serious and potentially fatal blood disorders].

* * *

As early as 1928, some health experts theorized that there might also be a connection between benzene in the workplace and leukemia. In the late 1960's and early 1970's a number of epidemiological studies were published indicating that workers exposed to high concentrations of benzene were subject to significantly increased risk of leukemia. [In 1976, the National Institute for Occupational Safety and Health (NIOSH), OSHA's research arm, reported its belief that recent] studies provided "conclusive" proof of a causal connection between benzene and leukemia. * * *

* * *

In its published statement giving notice of the proposed permanent standard, OSHA did not ask for comments as to whether or not benzene presented a significant health risk at exposures of 10 ppm or less. Rather, it asked for comments as to whether 1 ppm was the minimum feasible exposure limit. As OSHA's Deputy Director of Health Standards, Grover Wrenn, testified at the hearing, this formulation of the issue to be considered by the Agency was consistent with OSHA's general policy with respect to carcinogens. Whenever a carcinogen is involved, OSHA will presume [in accordance with its Generic Cancer Policy] that no safe level of exposure exists in the absence of clear proof establishing such a level and will accordingly set the exposure limit at the lowest level feasible. The proposed 1 ppm exposure limit in this case thus was established not on the basis of a proven hazard at 10 ppm, but rather on the basis of "OSHA's best judgment at the time of the proposal of the feasibility of compliance with the proposed standard by the [a]ffected industries." Given OSHA's cancer policy, it was in fact irrelevant whether there was any evidence at all of a leukemia risk at 10 ppm.* * *

As presently formulated, the benzene standard is an expensive way of providing some additional protection for a relatively small number of employees. * * *

Although OSHA did not quantify the benefits to each category of worker in terms of decreased exposure to benzene, it appears from the economic impact study done at OSHA's direction that those benefits may be relatively small. * * *

II

* * *

In the end OSHA's rationale for lowering the permissible exposure limit to 1 ppm was based, not on any finding that leukemia has ever [in fact] been caused by exposure to 10 ppm of benzene and that it will *not* be caused by exposure to 1 ppm, but rather on a series of assumptions indicating that some leukemias might result from exposure to 10 ppm and that the number of cases might be reduced by reducing the exposure level to 1 ppm. In reaching that result, the Agency first unequivocally concluded that benzene is a human carcinogen. Second, it concluded that industry had failed to prove that there is a safe threshold level of exposure to benzene below which no excess leukemia cases would occur. In reaching this conclusion OSHA rejected industry contentions that certain epidemiological studies indicating no excess risk of leukemia among workers exposed at levels below 10 ppm were sufficient to establish that the threshold level of safe exposure was at or above 10 ppm. It also rejected an industry witness' testimony that a dose-response curve could be constructed on the basis of the reported epidemiological studies and that this curve indicated that reducing the permissible exposure limit from 10 to 1 ppm would prevent at most one leukemia and one other cancer death every six years.

Third, the Agency applied its standard policy with respect to carcinogens, concluding that, in the absence of definitive proof of a safe level, it must be assumed that any level above zero presents *some* increased risk of cancer. As the federal parties point out in their brief, there are a number of scientists and public health specialists who subscribe to this view, theorizing that a susceptible person may contract cancer from the absorption of even one molecule of a carcinogen like benzene.

Fourth, the Agency reiterated its view of the Act, stating that it was required by § 6(b)(5) to set the standard either at the level that has been demonstrated to be safe or at the lowest level feasible, whichever is higher. If no safe level is established, as in this case, the Secretary's interpretation of the statute automatically leads to the selection of an exposure limit that is the lowest feasible. Because of benzene's importance to the economy, no one has ever suggested that it would be feasible to eliminate its use entirely, or to try to limit exposures to the small amounts that are omnipresent. Rather, the Agency selected 1 ppm as a workable exposure level, and then determined that compliance with that level was technologically feasible and that "the economic impact of * * * [compliance] will not be such as to threaten the financial welfare of the affected firms or the general economy." It therefore held that 1 ppm was the minimum feasible exposure level within the meaning of § 6(b)(5) of the Act.

* * *

It is noteworthy that at no point in its lengthy explanation did the Agency quote or even cite § 3(8) of the Act. It made no finding that any of the provisions of the new standard were "reasonably necessary or appropriate to provide safe or healthful employment and places of employment." Nor did it allude to the possibility that any such finding might have been appropriate.

III

Our resolution of the issues in these cases turns, to a large extent, on the meaning of and the relationship between § 3(8), which defines a health and safety standard as a standard that is "reasonably necessary and appropriate to provide safe or healthful employment," and § 6(b)(5), which directs the Secretary in promulgating a health and safety standard for toxic materials to "set the standard which most adequately assures, to the extent feasible, on the basis of the best available evidence, that no employee will suffer material impairment of health or functional capacity...."

* * *

A

Under the Government's view, § 3(8), if it has any substantive content at all, merely requires OSHA to issue standards that are reasonably calculated to produce a safer or more healthy work environment. Apart from this minimal requirement of rationality, the Government argues that § 3(8) imposes no limits on the Agency's power, and thus would not prevent it from requiring employers to do whatever would be "reasonably necessary" to eliminate all risks of any harm from their workplaces. With respect to toxic substances and harmful physical agents, the Government takes an even more extreme position. Relying on § 6(b)(5)'s direction to set a standard "which most adequately assures * * * that no employee will suffer material impairment of health or functional capacity," the Government contends that the Secretary is required to impose standards that either guarantee workplaces that are free from any risk of material health impairment, however small, or that come as close as possible to doing so without ruining entire industries.

If the purpose of the statute were to eliminate completely and with absolute certainty any risk of serious harm, we would agree that it would be proper for the Secretary to interpret §§ 3(8) and 6(b)(5) in this fashion. But we think it is clear that the statute was not designed to require employers to provide absolutely risk-free workplaces whenever it is technologically feasible to do so, so long as the cost is not great enough to destroy an entire industry. Rather, both the language and structure of the Act, as well as its legislative history, indicate that it was intended to require the elimination, as far as feasible, of significant risks of harm.

B

By empowering the Secretary to promulgate standards that are "reasonably necessary or appropriate to provide safe or healthful employment and places of employment," the Act implies that, before promulgating any standard, the Secretary must make a finding that the workplaces in question are not safe. But "safe" is not the equivalent of "risk-free." There are many activities that we engage in every day—such as driving a car or even breathing city air—that entail some risk of accident or material health impairment; nevertheless, few people would consider these activities "unsafe." Similarly, a workplace can hardly be considered "unsafe" unless it threatens the workers with a significant risk of harm.

Therefore, before he can promulgate *any* permanent health or safety standard, the Secretary is required to make a threshold finding that a place of employment is unsafe—in the sense that significant risks are present and can be eliminated or lessened by a change in practices. This requirement applies to permanent standards promulgated pursuant to § 6(b)(5), as well as to other types of permanent standards. * * *

* * *

In the absence of a clear mandate in the Act, it is unreasonable to assume that Congress intended to give the Secretary the unprecedented power over American industry that would result from the Government's view of §§ 3(8) and 6(b)(5), coupled with OSHA's cancer policy. Expert testimony that a substance is probably a human carcinogen—either because it has caused cancer in animals or because individuals have contracted cancer following extremely high exposures—would justify the conclusion that the substance poses some risk of serious harm no matter how minute the exposure and no matter how many experts testified that they regarded the risk as insignificant. That conclusion would in turn justify pervasive regulation limited only by the constraint of feasibility. In light of the fact that there are literally thousands of substances used in the workplace that have been identified as carcinogens or suspect carcinogens, the Government's theory would give OSHA power to impose enormous costs that might produce little, if any, discernible benefit.

If the Government was correct in arguing that neither § 3(8) nor § 6(b)(5) requires that the risk from a toxic substance be quantified sufficiently to enable the Secretary to characterize it as significant in an understandable way, the statute would make such a "sweeping delegation of legislative power" that it might be unconstitutional under the Court's reasoning in *A.L.A. Schechter Poultry Corp. v. United States*, 295 U.S. 495, 539 [(1935)], and *Panama Refining Co. v. Ryan*, 293 U.S. 388 [(1935)]. A construction of the statute that avoids this kind of open-ended grant should certainly be favored.

C

The legislative history also supports the conclusion that Congress was concerned, not with absolute safety, but with the elimination of significant harm. The examples of industrial hazards referred to in the Committee hearings and debates all involved situations in which the risk was unquestionably significant[, for example, byssinosis ("brown lung," caused by cotton dust) and asbestosis]. * * *

Moreover, Congress specifically amended § 6(b)(5) to make it perfectly clear that it does not require the Secretary to promulgate standards that would assure an absolutely risk-free workplace. * * *

* * *

D

Given the conclusion that the Act empowers the Secretary to promulgate health and safety standards only where a significant risk of harm exists, the critical issue becomes how to define and allocate the burden of proving the significance of the risk in a case such as this, where scientific knowledge is imperfect and the precise quantification of risks is therefore impossible. The Agency's position is that there is substantial evidence in the record to support its conclusion that there is no absolutely safe level for a carcinogen and that, therefore, the burden is properly on industry to prove, apparently beyond a shadow of a doubt, that there is a safe level for benzene exposure. The Agency argues that, because of the uncertainties in this area, any other approach would render it helpless, forcing it to wait for the leukemia deaths that it believes are likely to occur before taking any regulatory action.

We disagree. As we read the statute, the burden was on the Agency to show, on the basis of substantial evidence, that it is at least more likely than not that long-term exposure to 10 ppm of benzene presents a significant risk of material health impairment. Ordinarily, it is the proponent of a rule or order who has the burden of proof in administrative proceedings. *See* 5 U.S.C. § 556(d). In some cases involving toxic substances, Congress has shifted the burden of proving that a particular substance is safe onto the party opposing the proposed rule. The fact that Congress did not follow this course in enacting the Occupational Safety and Health Act indicates that it intended the Agency to bear the normal burden of establishing the need for a proposed standard.

In this case OSHA did not even attempt to carry its burden of proof. The closest it came to making a finding that benzene presented a significant risk of harm in the workplace was its statement that the benefits to be derived from lowering the permissible exposure level from 10 to 1 ppm were "likely" to be "appreciable." The Court of Appeals held that this finding was not supported by substantial evidence. Of greater importance, even if it were supported by substantial evidence, such a finding would not be sufficient to satisfy the Agency's obligations under the Act.

* * *

Contrary to the Government's contentions, imposing a burden on the Agency of demonstrating a significant risk of harm will not strip it of its ability to regulate carcinogens, nor will it require the Agency to wait for deaths to occur before taking any action. First, the requirement that a "significant" risk be identified is not a mathematical straitjacket. It is the Agency's responsibility to determine, in the first instance, what it considers to be a "significant" risk. Some risks are plainly acceptable and others are plainly unacceptable. If, for example, the odds are one in a billion that a person will die from cancer by taking a drink of chlorinated water, the risk clearly could not be considered significant. On the other hand, if the odds are one in a thousand that regular inhalation of gasoline vapors that are 2% benzene will be fatal, a reasonable person might well consider the risk significant and take appropriate steps to decrease or eliminate it. Although the Agency has no duty to calculate the exact probability of harm, it does have an obligation to find that a significant risk is present before it can characterize a place of employment as "unsafe."[16]

Second, OSHA is not required to support its finding that a significant risk exists with anything approaching scientific certainty. Although the Agency's findings must be supported by substantial evidence, 29 U.S.C. § 655(f), § 6(b)(5) specifically allows the Secretary to regulate on the basis of the "best available evidence." As several Courts of Appeals have held, this provision requires a reviewing court to give OSHA some leeway where its findings must be made on the frontiers of scientific knowledge. *See Industrial Union Dept., AFL–CIO v. Hodgson.* Thus, so long as they are supported by a body of reputable scientific thought, the Agency is free to use conservative assumptions in interpreting the data with respect to carcinogens, risking error on the side of overprotection rather than underprotection.

Finally, the record in this case and OSHA's own rulings on other carcinogens indicate that there are a number of ways in which the Agency can make a rational judgment about the relative significance of the risks associated with exposure to a particular carcinogen.

* * *

E

* * *

In this case the record makes it perfectly clear that the Secretary relied squarely on a special policy for carcinogens that imposed the burden on industry of proving the existence of a safe level of exposure, thereby avoiding the Secretary's threshold responsibility of establishing the need for more stringent standards. In so interpreting his statutory authority, the Secretary exceeded his power.

* * *

■ MR. CHIEF JUSTICE BURGER, concurring.

* * * When discharging his duties under the statute, the Secretary is well admonished to remember that a heavy responsibility burdens his

---

16. In his dissenting opinion, Mr. Justice MARSHALL states: "[W]hen the question involves determination of the acceptable level of risk, the ultimate decision must necessarily be based on considerations of policy as well as empirically verifiable facts. Factual determinations can at most define the risk in some statistical way; the judgment whether that risk is tolerable cannot be based solely on a resolution of the facts." We agree. Thus, while the Agency must support its finding that a certain level of risk exists by substantial evidence, we recognize that its determination that a particular level of risk is "significant" will be based largely on policy considerations. At this point we have no need to reach the issue of what level of scrutiny a reviewing court should apply to the latter type of determination.

authority. Inherent in this statutory scheme is authority to refrain from regulation of insignificant or *de minimis* risks. *See Alabama Power Co. v. Costle*, 636 F.2d 323, 360–361 (1979) (opinion of Leventhal, J.) [(interpreting the Clean Air Act)]. When the administrative record reveals only scant or minimal risk of material health impairment, responsible administration calls for avoidance of extravagant, comprehensive regulation. Perfect safety is a chimera; regulation must not strangle human activity in the search for the impossible.

■ MR. JUSTICE POWELL, concurring in part and concurring in the judgment.

* * * I conclude that the statute also requires the agency to determine that the economic effects of its standard bear a reasonable relationship to the expected benefits[, as the Fifth Circuit did.[17]] An occupational health standard is neither "reasonably necessary" nor "feasible," as required by statute, if it calls for expenditures wholly disproportionate to the expected health and safety benefits.

* * *

* * * OSHA's interpretation of § 6(b)(5) would force it to regulate in a manner inconsistent with the important health and safety purposes of the legislation we construe today. Thousands of toxic substances present risks that fairly could be characterized as "significant." Even if OSHA succeeded in selecting the gravest risks for earliest regulation, a standard-setting process that ignored economic considerations would result in a serious misallocation of resources and a lower effective level of safety than could be achieved under standards set with reference to the comparative benefits available at a lower cost. I would not attribute such an irrational intention to Congress.

* * *

■ MR. JUSTICE REHNQUIST, concurring in the judgment.

* * * [Justice Rehnquist invoked the constitutional nondelegation doctrine, in that Congress failed to provide an "intelligible standard" for OSHA to follow when it delegated decisionmaking power to the agency in § 6(b)(5).] Read literally, the relevant portion of § 6(b)(5) is completely precatory, admonishing the Secretary to adopt the most protective standard if he can, but excusing him from that duty if he cannot. In the case of a hazardous substance for which a "safe" level is either unknown or impractical, the language of § 6(b)(5) gives the Secretary absolutely no indication where on the continuum of relative safety he should draw his line. Especially in light of the importance of the interests at stake, I have no doubt that the provision at issue, standing alone, would violate the doctrine against uncanalized delegations of legislative power.

---

17. The Fifth Circuit stated: "Although the agency does not have to conduct an elaborate cost-benefit analysis, it does have to determine whether the benefits expected from the standard bear a reasonable relationship to the costs imposed by the standard. The only way to tell whether the relationship between the benefits and costs of the benzene standard is reasonable is to estimate the extent of the expected benefits and costs." American Petroleum Inst. v. OSHA, 581 F.2d 493, 503 (5th Cir. 1978).—EDS.

* * *

If we are ever to reshoulder the burden of ensuring that Congress itself make the critical policy decisions, these are surely the cases in which to do it. It is difficult to imagine a more obvious example of Congress simply avoiding a choice which was both fundamental for purposes of the statute and yet politically so divisive that the necessary decision or compromise was difficult, if not impossible, to hammer out in the legislative forge. Far from detracting from the substantive authority of Congress, a declaration that the first sentence of § 6(b)(5) of the Occupational Safety and Health Act constitutes an invalid delegation to the Secretary of Labor would preserve the authority of Congress. If Congress wishes to legislate in an area which it has not previously sought to enter, it will in today's political world undoubtedly run into opposition no matter how the legislation is formulated. But that is the very essence of legislative authority under our system. It is the hard choices, and not the filling in of the blanks, which must be made by the elected representatives of the people. When fundamental policy decisions underlying important legislation about to be enacted are to be made, the buck stops with Congress and the President insofar as he exercises his constitutional role in the legislative process.

* * *

■ MR. JUSTICE MARSHALL, with whom MR. JUSTICE BRENNAN, MR. JUSTICE WHITE, and MR. JUSTICE BLACKMUN join, dissenting.

* * *

II

The plurality's discussion of the record in this case is both extraordinarily arrogant and extraordinarily unfair. * * * Contrary to the plurality's suggestion, the Secretary did not rely blindly on some Draconian carcinogen "policy." If he had, it would have been sufficient for him to have observed that benzene is a carcinogen, a proposition that respondents do not dispute. Instead, the Secretary gathered over 50 volumes of exhibits and testimony and offered a detailed and evenhanded discussion of the relationship between exposure to benzene at all recorded exposure levels and chromosomal damage, aplastic anemia, and leukemia. In that discussion he evaluated, and took seriously, respondents' evidence of a safe exposure level.

* * *

III

A

* * *

The decision to take action in conditions of uncertainty bears little resemblance to the sort of empirically verifiable factual conclusions to which the substantial evidence test is normally applied. Such decisions were not intended to be unreviewable; they too must be scrutinized to ensure that the Secretary has acted reasonably and within the boundaries set by Congress.

But a reviewing court must be mindful of the limited nature of its role. It must recognize that the ultimate decision cannot be based solely on determinations of fact, and that those factual conclusions that have been reached are ones which the courts are ill-equipped to resolve on their own.

* * *

B

The plurality avoids this conclusion through reasoning that may charitably be described as obscure. According to the plurality, the definition of occupational safety and health standards as those "reasonably necessary or appropriate to provide safe or healthful * * * working conditions" requires the Secretary to show that it is "more likely than not" that the risk he seeks to regulate is a "significant" one. The plurality does not show how this requirement can be plausibly derived from the "reasonably necessary or appropriate" clause. Indeed, the plurality's reasoning is refuted by the Act's language, structure, and legislative history, and it is foreclosed by every applicable guide to statutory construction. In short, the plurality's standard is a fabrication bearing no connection with the acts or intentions of Congress.

* * *

C

The plurality is obviously more interested in the consequences of its decision than in discerning the intention of Congress. But since the language and legislative history of the Act are plain, there is no need for conjecture about the effects of today's decision. "It is not for us to speculate, much less act, on whether Congress would have altered its stance had the specific events of this case been anticipated." *TVA v. Hill*, 437 U.S. [153, 185 (1978), the Endangered Species Act "snail darter" case]. I do not pretend to know whether the test the plurality erects today is, as a matter of policy, preferable to that created by Congress and its delegates: the area is too fraught with scientific uncertainty, and too dependent on considerations of policy, for a court to be able to determine whether it is desirable to require identification of a "significant" risk before allowing an administrative agency to take regulatory action. But in light of the tenor of the plurality opinion, it is necessary to point out that the question is not one-sided, and that Congress' decision to authorize the Secretary to promulgate the regulation at issue here was a reasonable one. In this case the Secretary found that exposure to benzene at levels above 1 ppm posed a definite albeit unquantifiable risk of chromosomal damage, nonmalignant blood disorders, and leukemia. The existing evidence was sufficient to justify the conclusion that such a risk was presented, but it did not permit even rough quantification of that risk. Discounting for the various scientific uncertainties, the Secretary gave "careful consideration to the question of whether the[ ] substantial costs" of the standard "are justified in light of the hazards of exposure to benzene," and concluded that "these costs are necessary in order to effectuate the statutory purpose * * * and to adequately protect employees from the hazards of exposure to benzene."

* * *

In these circumstances it seems clear that the Secretary found a risk that is "significant" in the sense that the word is normally used. There was some direct evidence of chromosomal damage, nonmalignant blood disorders, and leukemia at exposures at or near 10 ppm and below. In addition, expert after expert testified that the recorded effects of benzene exposure at higher levels justified an inference that an exposure level above 1 ppm was dangerous. The plurality's extraordinarily searching scrutiny of this factual record reveals no basis for a conclusion that quantification is, on the basis of "the best available evidence," possible at the present time. If the Secretary decided to wait until definitive information was available, American workers would be subjected for the indefinite future to a possibly substantial risk of benzene-induced leukemia and other illnesses. It is unsurprising, at least to me, that he concluded that the statute authorized him to take regulatory action now.

Under these circumstances, the plurality's requirement of identification of a "significant" risk will have one of two consequences. If the plurality means to require the Secretary realistically to "quantify" the risk in order to satisfy a court that it is "significant," the record shows that the plurality means to require him to do the impossible. But the regulatory inaction has very significant costs of its own. The adoption of such a test would subject American workers to a continuing risk of cancer and other serious diseases; it would disable the Secretary from regulating a wide variety of carcinogens for which quantification simply cannot be undertaken at the present time.

There are encouraging signs that today's decision does not extend that far. My Brother POWELL concludes that the Secretary is not prevented from taking regulatory action "when reasonable quantification cannot be accomplished by any known methods." The plurality also indicates that it would not prohibit the Secretary from promulgating safety standards when quantification of the benefits is impossible. * * *

* * * [T]he record amply demonstrates that in light of existing scientific knowledge, no purpose would be served by requiring the Secretary to take steps to quantify the risk of exposure to benzene at low levels. Any such quantification would be based not on scientific "knowledge" as that term is normally understood, but on considerations of policy. For carcinogens like benzene, the assumptions on which a dose-response curve must be based are necessarily arbitrary. To require a quantitative showing of a "significant" risk, therefore, would either paralyze the Secretary into inaction or force him to deceive the public by acting on the basis of assumptions that must be considered too speculative to support any realistic assessment of the relevant risk. *See* McGarity, *Substantive and Procedural Discretion in Administrative Resolution of Science Policy Questions: Regulating Carcinogens in EPA and OSHA*, 67 GEO.L.J. 729, 806 (1979). It is encouraging that the Court appears willing not to require quantification when it is not fairly possible.

* * *

NOTES AND QUESTIONS

1. What is the Court's holding—on what grounds did the plurality overturn the benzene standard? Did the justices find that OSHA lacked evidence of carcinogenicity? Why is burden of proof such a critical issue here?

The plurality opinion also includes some important dicta, including comments on the acceptable levels of risk and quantification of risk estimates. What guidance does the plurality give for subsequent cases?

2. *The Generic Cancer Policy.* The plurality and dissent refer several times to OSHA's cancer policy. What was the gist of the policy? Does it strike you as out of line with your understanding of carcinogenesis? If not, what is the plurality's objection to it? At the time of the *Benzene* decision, the so-called Generic Cancer Policy (GCP) had been proposed as a rule,[18] and the *Benzene* case was its death knell.

3. Explain the analysis that the plurality requires of OSHA. How is this derived from the relevant statutory language? Why does the GCP fail to meet this test? How does the plurality's approach differ from the concurrence and the dissent?

4. *Burden of proof.* One of the central features of the *Benzene* case is its emphasis on the allocation of the burden of proof. Who has the burden of proof, and what is the evidentiary standard that must be met? Specifically, how do the "substantial evidence," "more likely than not," and "significant risk" standards interact? Are they separate questions, and if so, does the plurality confuse them?

Why does the plurality allocate the burden as it does? Professor Latin strongly criticized the plurality's allocation of the burden of proof, urging courts to examine the relevant statutory interests, the particular factual situation, the respective abilities of the parties to resolve uncertainty, and the desirable result (*i.e.*, action or inaction) in the face of uncertainty. Howard A. Latin, *The "Significance" of Toxic Health Risks: An Essay on Legal Decisionmaking Under Uncertainty*, 10 Ecology L.Q. 339 (1982).(*See also* Howard A. Latin, *The Feasibility of Occupational Health Standards: An Essay on Legal Decisionmaking Under Uncertainty*, 78 Nw. U.L. Rev. 583, 600–08 (1983).) How do these factors weigh in the regulation of benzene?

5. *Quantification and risk assessment. Benzene* has generally been understood to require agencies to quantify (or attempt to quantify) the risks of the substance at issue. OSHA subsequently concluded that *Benzene* requires the agency to "attempt to quantify risk, if possible, and determine whether the risk is significant." OSHA, Occupational Exposure to Benzene, 52 Fed. Reg. 34,460, 34,461 (1987). What does the plurality *in fact* require? Is the requirement to quantify a fair implication from the opinion's language? Does Chief Justice Burger's concurrence help to clarify the matter?

6. *Costs and benefits.* The plurality states early in the opinion that OSHA's regulation "is an expensive way of providing some additional

---

18. *See* OSHA, Proposed Rule on the Identification, Classification, and Regulation of Toxic Substances Posing a Potential Carcinogenic Risk, 42 Fed. Reg. 54148 (1977).

protection for a relatively small number of employees." How is this relevant to judicial review? Why does the plurality say it?

What were the options open to the Court in dealing with regulation it deemed unwise? Clearly, it could not simply overturn the regulation because it disagreed (why not?). What is Justice Powell's solution? Why doesn't the plurality adopt it? What does Chief Justice Burger suggest in his concurrence?

7. *The nondelegation doctrine.* Where does Justice Rehnquist place the blame? Accepting the view that the OSH Act represents a kind of congressional failure, why did Congress draft the legislation that way to begin with? Would the dissenters' position be a better solution to the delegation problem?[19]

8. *Asbestos.* The plurality suggested that asbestos was different from benzene and that the regulation of asbestos is more easily justified. How are they different? How does the Court know this? Is the reasoning of *Reserve Mining* consistent with *Benzene*?

9. *Subsequent regulation of benzene.* The benzene standard was eventually repromulgated, in essentially its original form, after seven years of steady work on the standard and more litigation. The preamble to the final PEL is in many ways the gold standard of justification of risk regulation. It explores cost issues (technological feasibility, economic feasibility, percentage of industry revenue), alternative regulatory techniques (averaging, short-and long-term exposure levels, action levels for monitoring, differentiation among industries, flexible mechanisms (engineering controls and personal protective devices), signs and labels, training, and hazard communication—and it brings to bear an enormous range of risk data, including multiple epidemiology studies, human dose-response data, multiple animal studies, and risk assessments by outside agencies, other neutral bodies, and even industry. The agency concluded that the reduction from 10 ppm to 1 ppm—

> will result in substantial reduction in the workers' risk of developing leukemia and other diseases of the blood and blood-forming organs. According to OSHA's best estimates, a working lifetime of exposure to benzene at 10 ppm would cause an excess leukemia risk of 95 leukemia deaths per 1000 exposed workers. * * * These are clearly significant risks, greatly exceeding the excess risks of occupationally related accident deaths in high and average risk industries which are 30 and 3 per 1000 workers, respectively.
>
> The new standard will create a minimum reduction in excess risk of 90 percent, a very substantial reduction based on comparing exposures at 10 ppm and 1 ppm. On the basis of the current

---

19. After the *Benzene* decision, the nondelegation doctrine quickly returned to near-oblivion and remained there until a 1999 decision of the D.C. Circuit, *American Trucking Ass'ns v. EPA*, 175 F.3d 1027 (D.C. Cir. 1999), sought to revive it. The court of appeals was definitively overruled in a unanimous Supreme Court decision, *Whitman v. American Trucking Ass'ns*, 531 U.S. 457 (2001) (excerpted in Section D.2, *infra*). Only Justice Thomas, in a concurring opinion, left open any serious likelihood of successful nondelegation challenges in the future.

distribution of exposures, OSHA estimates that the new standard will prevent a minimum of 326 deaths from leukemia and disease of the blood and blood-forming organs over a working lifetime of 45 years.

OSHA, Occupational Exposure to Benzene, 52 Fed. Reg. 34460, 34460–61 (1987). Does the new rationale meet the requirements of *Benzene*?

On the broader policy question, one has to ask what was gained (and who gained it) by the delay. As an observer has noted, "if OSHA's risk assessments are accurate, delaying promulgation of the stricter PEL judicial intervention has resulted in the exposure of thousands of workers to risks that will result in scores of additional deaths." Percival et al., Environmental Regulation: Law, Science, and Policy 513 (2d ed. 1996). Is this a fair criticism of the *Benzene* case?

American Textile Mnfrs. Inst. v. Donovan (The *Cotton Dust* Case)
452 U.S. 490 (1981)

■ Justice Brennan delivered the opinion of the Court.

* * *

I

Byssinosis, known in its more severe manifestations as "brown lung" disease, is a serious and potentially disabling respiratory disease primarily caused by the inhalation of cotton dust. Byssinosis is a "continuum ... disease" that has been categorized into four grades. In its least serious form, byssinosis produces both subjective symptoms, such as chest tightness, shortness of breath, coughing, and wheezing, and objective indications of loss of pulmonary functions. In its most serious form, byssinosis is a chronic and irreversible obstructive pulmonary disease, clinically similar to chronic bronchitis or emphysema, and can be severely disabling. At worst, as is true of other respiratory diseases including bronchitis, emphysema, and asthma, byssinosis can create an additional strain on cardiovascular functions and can contribute to death from heart failure. One authority has described the increasing seriousness of byssinosis as follows:

> In the first few years of exposure [to cotton dust], symptoms occur on Monday, or other days after absence from the work environment; later, symptoms occur on other days of the week; and eventually, symptoms are continuous, even in the absence of dust exposure.

* * *

The Cotton Dust Standard promulgated by OSHA mandatory PELs over an 8–hour period of 200 µg/m³ for yarn manufacturing, 750 µg/m³ for slashing and weaving operations, and 500 µg/m³ for all other processes in the cotton industry. These levels represent a relaxation of the proposed PEL of 200 µg/m³ for all segments of the cotton industry.

* * *

On the basis of the evidence in the record as a whole, the Secretary determined that exposure to cotton dust represents a "significant health hazard to employees." and that "the prevalence of byssinosis should be significantly reduced" by the adoption of the Standard's PELs. In assessing the health risks from cotton dust and the risk reduction obtained from lowered exposure, OSHA relied particularly on data showing a strong linear relationship between the prevalence of byssinosis and the concentration of lint-free respirable cotton dust. Even at the 200 µg/m³ PEL, OSHA found that the prevalence of at least Grade ½ byssinosis would be 13% of all employees in the yarn manufacturing sector.

In promulgating the Cotton Dust Standard, OSHA interpreted the Act to require adoption of the most stringent standard to protect against material health impairment, bounded only by technological and economic feasibility. * * * The agency expressly found the Standard to be both technologically and economically feasible based on the evidence in the record as a whole. Although recognizing that permitted levels of exposure to cotton dust would still cause some byssinosis, OSHA nevertheless rejected the union proposal for a 100 µg/m³ PEL because it was not within the "technological capabilities of the industry." * * *

The Court of Appeals upheld the Standard in all major respects. * * *

II

The principal question presented in these cases is whether the Occupational Safety and Health Act requires the Secretary, in promulgating a standard pursuant to § 6(b)(5) of the Act, 29 U.S.C. § 655(b)(5), to determine that the costs of the standard bear a reasonable relationship to its benefits. Relying on §§ 6(b)(5) and 3(8) of the Act, 29 U.S.C. §§ 655(b)(5) and 652(8), petitioners urge not only that OSHA must show that a standard addresses a significant risk of material health impairment, but also that OSHA must demonstrate that the reduction in risk of material health impairment is significant in light of the costs of attaining that reduction. Respondents on the other hand contend that the Act requires OSHA to promulgate standards that eliminate or reduce such risks "to the extent such protection is technologically and economically feasible."[20] To resolve this debate, we must turn to the language, structure, and legislative history of the Act.

A

* * * Although their interpretations differ, all parties agree that the phrase "to the extent feasible" contains the critical language in § 6(b)(5) for purposes of these cases.

20. As described by the union respondents, the test for determining whether a standard promulgated to regulate a "toxic material or harmful physical agent" satisfies the Act has three parts:

> "First, whether the 'place of employment is unsafe—in the sense that significant risks are present and can be eliminated or lessened by a change in practices.' Second, whether of the possible available correctives the Secretary has selected 'the standard . . . that is most protective.' Third, whether that standard is 'feasible.' We will sometimes refer to this test as 'feasibility analysis.' "

The plain meaning of the word "feasible" supports respondents' interpretation of the statute. According to Webster's Third New International Dictionary of the English Language 831 (1976), "feasible" means "capable of being done, executed, or effected." Thus, § 6(b)(5) directs the Secretary to issue the standard that "most adequately assures ... that no employee will suffer material impairment of health," limited only by the extent to which this is "capable of being done." In effect then, as the Court of Appeals held, Congress itself defined the basic relationship between costs and benefits, by placing the "benefit" of worker health above all other considerations save those making attainment of this "benefit" unachievable. Any standard based on a balancing of costs and benefits by the Secretary that strikes a different balance than that struck by Congress would be inconsistent with the command set forth in § 6(b)(5). Thus, cost-benefit analysis by OSHA is not required by the statute because feasibility analysis is.

When Congress has intended that an agency engage in cost-benefit analysis, it has clearly indicated such intent on the face of the statute[, giving examples]. * * *

B

Even though the plain language of § 6(b)(5) supports this construction, we must still decide whether § 3(8), the general definition of an occupational safety and health standard, either alone or in tandem with § 6(b)(5), incorporates a cost-benefit requirement for standards dealing with toxic materials or harmful physical agents. * * * We need not decide whether § 3(8), standing alone, would contemplate some form of cost-benefit analysis. For even if it does, Congress specifically chose in § 6(b)(5) to impose separate and additional requirements for issuance of a subcategory of occupational safety and health standards dealing with toxic materials and harmful physical agents: it required that those standards be issued to prevent material impairment of health *to the extent feasible*. Congress could reasonably have concluded that *health* standards should be subject to different criteria than *safety* standards because of the special problems presented in regulating them.

Agreement with petitioners' argument that § 3(8) imposes an additional and overriding requirement of cost-benefit analysis on the issuance of § 6(b)(5) standards would eviscerate the "to the extent feasible" requirement. Standards would inevitably be set at the level indicated by cost-benefit analysis, and not at the level specified by § 6(b)(5). For example, if cost-benefit analysis indicated a protective standard of 1,000 µg/m³ PEL, while feasibility analysis indicated a 500 µg/m³ PEL, the agency would be forced by the cost-benefit requirement to choose the less stringent point. We cannot believe that Congress intended the general terms of § 3(8) to countermand the specific feasibility requirement of § 6(b)(5). Adoption of petitioners' interpretation would effectively write § 6(b)(5) out of the Act. We decline to render Congress' decision to include a feasibility requirement nugatory, thereby offending the well-settled rule that all parts of a statute, if possible, are to be given effect. Congress did not contemplate any further balancing by the agency for toxic material and harmful physical agents standards, and we should not " 'impute to Congress a purpose to paralyze with one hand what it sought to promote with the other.' "

C

The legislative history of the Act, while concededly not crystal clear, provides general support for respondents' interpretation of the Act. The congressional Reports and debates certainly confirm that Congress meant "feasible" and nothing else in using that term. Congress was concerned that the Act might be thought to require achievement of absolute safety, an impossible standard, and therefore insisted that health and safety goals be capable of economic and technological accomplishment. Perhaps most telling is the absence of any indication whatsoever that Congress intended OSHA to conduct its own cost-benefit analysis before promulgating a toxic material or harmful physical agent standard. The legislative history demonstrates conclusively that Congress was fully aware that the Act would impose real and substantial costs of compliance on industry, and believed that such costs were part of the cost of doing business. * * *

* * *

Accordingly, the judgment of the Court of Appeals is affirmed * * *.

[Justice Powell did not participate in the decision; Justice Stewart dissented on the ground that OSHA had not demonstrated the feasibility of the PELs by substantial evidence; and Justice Rehnquist and Chief Justice Burger renewed Rehnquist's objection in *Benzene* that the OSHA standard violated the nondelegation doctrine.]

NOTES AND QUESTIONS

1. What does *Cotton Dust* add to *Benzene*? Is the Court correct in asserting that *Benzene* left the cost-benefit question open, or has the Court changed its mind? Note, for example, the treatment of section 3(8) in *Cotton Dust*—in what ways is it consistent with *Benzene*? In what ways is it inconsistent?

2. What does "feasible" mean? What are the elements of a feasibility determination, as described by the Court?

What is "feasibility analysis" and how is it different from "cost-benefit analysis"? What is the relationship between feasibility and cost in *Cotton Dust*?

3. *Technology-based regulation.* Professor McGarity has suggested that, given the law of diminishing returns, "feasibility" means looking for the "knee of the curve" in the graph of the escalating marginal costs of control: "In practice the regulatory entity examines the costs of the various available technologies, compares their efficacy, and looks for the point at which costs begin to escalate much more rapidly than efficacy." Thomas O. McGarity, *Media–Quality, Technology, and Cost–Benefit Balancing Strategies for Health and Environmental Regulation*, 46(3) L. & Contemp. Probs. 159, 205 (Summer 1983). Is this a sensible interpretation of "feasible"? Does it avoid some the complexity otherwise imposed by the *Benzene* case, or does it pose its own problems?

Less quantitatively, McGarity argues that the fundamental meaning of feasibility and other technology-based standards is that we should do "the best we can" to reduce identified risks.

> * * * The statutory language, however, rarely prescribes a finely tuned balancing of environmental considerations against feasibility considerations for setting technology-based standards. The language, rather, is aspirational. The agency is told to require the implementation of the "best available technology economically achievable," or the "best technological system of continuous emission reduction which * * * has been adequately demonstrated," or the technology capable of producing the "lowest achievable emission rate." Economic considerations are relevant to the standard-setting process, but they are not meant to dominate it. The economic impact of achieving technology-based standards is to be considered along with a host of other factors that may legitimately affect the regulatory entity's decision. * * * Congress has, in other words, announced to the world: "If we cannot have a perfectly clean workplace and environment, then we shall do the best that we can."[21]

> While neither of these goals meets the policy-oriented economist's efficiency criterion, they are both rational *political* end points. Society may rationally decide to make costs a relevant consideration to a media-quality approach only at the extremes and err on the side of overprotection. Similarly, a rational society might pledge itself to do the best that it can in pursuit of safe workplaces and a healthy environment even though it recognizes that even those efforts will not make those places safe or healthy in any absolute sense and even though they may, in the policy-oriented economist's opinion, cost too much.

McGarity, *supra*, at 199. Does this help to understand the statute and its application to benzene and cotton dust?

4. *ALARA.* The military use of nuclear materials poses radiological risks to the health of workers and the public, to the environment, and to peace and national security; the peaceful use of atomic energy also presents unavoidable risks from catastrophe (*e.g.*, a meltdown), releases into the environment, and occupational exposure. In view of the national commitment to maintain a nuclear arsenal and to support nuclear energy, a zero-exposure regulatory standard for these risks is obviously out of the question. Instead, NRC promulgated numerical exposure values that amount to a ceiling on acceptable doses. These ceiling numbers are supposed to be relatively unimportant in practice, however, because of the overriding ALARA standard.

---

21. Addressing the rationale for the technology-based effluent limitations of the 1972 amendments to the Clean Water Act, Senator Bayh explained: "The whole thrust of the bill is to force industry to do the best job it can do to clean up the nation's water and to keep making progress without incurring such massive costs that economic chaos would result."

ALARA (acronym for "as low as is reasonably achievable") means making every reasonable effort to maintain exposures to radiation as far below the dose limits in this part as is practical consistent with the purpose for which the licensed activity is undertaken, taking into account the state of technology, the economics of improvements in relation to state of technology, the economics of improvements in relation to benefits to the public health and safety, and other societal and socioeconomic considerations, and in relation to utilization of nuclear energy and licensed materials in the public interest.

10 C.F.R. § 20.1003. NRC has elaborated:

The radiation exposure limits referenced in 10 CFR Part 20 are considered safe; but to ensure additional margin of safety the NRC has adopted the concept of ALARA. * * * An underlying principle of ALARA is that radiological protection should be pursued to reduce exposures to a point where any further reduction in risk would not justify the effort required to accomplish it. It must be noted that the application of the ALARA goal involves highly subjective value judgments, which may also include economic and other sociological factors.

In the matter of General Electric, 24 N.R.C. 325, 340–341 (1986). ALARA, therefore, has three key elements. First radiation exposure must be limited to only those exposures that are necessary. For the general public, NRC regulations limit exposure to that which is absolutely necessary. Second, the NRC-established numerical values are the ceiling for occupational and public exposure. These limits are subdivided by persons exposed (workers, pregnant or minor workers, and the public) and to targets of exposure (general bodily or sensitive tissues). Workers at an NRC-licensed facility may receive up to an annual dose of 5 rem. For the general public, the facility's operator must limit the annual exposure to 0.1 rem. Third, the facility must strive to reduce exposure as far below the ceiling as practical. This determination is inherently subjective and involves some cost-benefit analysis,[22] but ALARA is intended to ascribe considerable weight to the risk side of the balance. *See York Committee for a Safe Environment v. United States Nuclear Regulatory Comm'n*, 527 F.2d 812 (D.C.Cir. 1975).

In fact, the acceptable level has plummeted over the years. *See* D.E. LEWIS & D.A. HAGEMEYER, OFFICE OF NUCLEAR REGULATORY RESEARCH, OCCUPATIONAL RADIATION EXPOSURE AT COMMERCIAL NUCLEAR POWER REACTORS AND OTHER FACILITIES 27 (2008) http://www.reirs.com/nureg2008/nureg2008.pdf). Should ALARA get the credit for these reductions? Might other factors be at work?

---

22. Neal Smith & Michael Baram, *The Nuclear Commission's Regulation of Radiation Hazards in the Workplace: Present Problems and New Approaches to Reproductive Health*, 13 ECOLOGY. L.Q. 879, 908 (1987).

C.   Best Available Technology

Best available technology (BAT) is a general approach to regulation that goes by several names in several variations.[23] (The Clean Water Act alone includes three or more variants.) Unlike the fairly unconstrained "best we can" of the feasibility standard, BAT involves a comparative analysis of similar pollution sources to determine "best." It is a sophisticated technique with several complexities (for example, similarity of sources is itself a contested threshold issue), but it is often relied on as a relatively speedy method for regulating toxic substances.

1.   The Clean Air Act Before 1990

The Clean Air Act (CAA) took its present form at the beginning of the Environmental Decade. As with the Clean Water Act, the existing state-based regulatory system had been unsuccessful in addressing the severe pollution problems that Congress perceived, and so the 1970 amendments in effect created a new legal structure for dealing with air pollution. The 1970 CAA received major overhauls in 1977 and again in 1990.[24]

The Clean Air Act divided air pollutants into stationary and mobile sources, and it further divided stationary sources into conventional ("criteria") air pollutants, new sources of conventional pollutants, and toxic ("hazardous") air pollutants. The 1970/1977 statutory standard for establishing national emission standards for hazardous air pollutants (NESHAPs), set out in section 112, follows[25]:

(a) Definitions. For the purposes of this section—

(1) The term "hazardous air pollutant" means an air pollutant to which no ambient air quality standard is applicable and which in the judgment of the Administrator causes, or contributes to, air pollution which may reasonably be anticipated to result in an increase in mortality or an increase in serious irreversible, or incapacitating reversible, illness.

* * *

(b) List of hazardous air pollutants; emission standards; pollution control techniques

---

23.   *See* Wendy E. Wagner, *The Triumph of Technology–Based Standards*, 2000 U. Ill. L. Rev. 83; Thomas O. McGarity, *Media–Quality, Technology, and Cost–Benefit Balancing Strategies for Health and Environmental Regulation*, 46 L. & Contemp. Probs. 159, 205, 203–224 (Summer 1983); Howard Latin, *Ideal Versus Real Regulatory Efficiency: Implementation of Uniform Standards and "Fine–Tuning" Regulatory Reforms*, 37 Stan. L. Rev. 1267 (1985); Sidney A. Shapiro & Thomas O. McGarity, *Not So Paradoxical: The Rationale for Technology–Based Regulation*, 1991 Duke L.J. 729, 731–39.

24.   For a useful overview of the development of the Clean Air Act, *see* Arnold W. Reitze, Jr., *The Legislative History of U.S. Air Pollution Control,* 36 Hous. L. Rev. 679 (1999).

25.   Accounts of the origins and passage of the 1970 and 1977 toxics provisions can be found in John P. Dwyer, *The Pathology of Symbolic Legislation*, 17 Ecology L.Q. 233 (1990); John D. Graham, *The Failure of Agency–Forcing: The Regulation of Airborne Carcinogens Under Section 112 of the Clean Air Act*, 1985 Duke L.J. 100; and David Schoenbrod, *Goals Statutes or Rules Statutes: The Case of the Clean Air Act*, 30 UCLA L. Rev. 740 (1983).

(1)(A) The Administrator shall, within 90 days after December 31, 1970, publish (and shall from time to time thereafter revise) a list which includes each hazardous air pollutant for which he intends to establish an emission standard under this section.

(B) Within 180 days after the inclusion of any air pollutant in such list, the Administrator shall publish proposed regulations establishing emission standards for such pollutant together with a notice of a public hearing within thirty days. Not later than 180 days after such publication, the Administrator shall prescribe an emission standard for such pollutant, unless he finds, on the basis of information presented at such hearings, that such pollutant clearly is not a hazardous air pollutant. The Administrator shall establish any such standard at the level which in his judgment provides an ample margin of safety to protect the public health from such hazardous air pollutant.

Analyze the statutory language. What steps was EPA to take in promulgating NESHAPs? What are the legal standards that apply to each step? Where does EPA have discretion, and where are its actions mandatory?

For a variety of reasons, EPA accumulated an impressive record of inaction under the 1970/1977 version of section 112. Between 1970 and 1990, EPA managed to list and regulate only seven hazardous air pollutants: arsenic, asbestos, benzene, beryllium, mercury, radionuclides, and vinyl chloride. Not only is this a low level of regulatory production (by comparison, Congress identified 189 toxic air pollutants in the 1990 Amendments), but the chemicals in question were hardly tough calls. Vinyl chloride, for example, the chemical at issue in the following case, is a known (not probable, not possible) human carcinogen.[26]

Natural Resources Defense Council v. EPA (The *Vinyl Chloride* Case)

824 F.2d 1146 (D.C. Cir. 1987) (*en banc*)

■ BORK, CIRCUIT JUDGE:

Current scientific knowledge does not permit a finding that there is a completely safe level of human exposure to carcinogenic agents. The Administrator of the Environmental Protection Agency, however, is charged with regulating hazardous pollutants, including carcinogens, under section 112 of the Clean Air Act by setting emission standards "at the level which in his judgment provides an ample margin of safety to protect the public health." We address here the question of the extent of the Administrator's authority under this delegation in setting emission standards for carcinogenic pollutants.

---

26. For an influential discussion of toxic substances regulation based on the pre-judicial phase of the vinyl chloride NESHAP, *see* David Doniger, *Federal Regulation of Vinyl Chloride: A Short Course on the Law and Policy of Toxic Substances Control*, 7 ECOLOGY L.Q. 497 (1978).

Petitioner Natural Resources Defense Council ("NRDC") contends that the Administrator must base a decision under section 112 exclusively on health-related factors and, therefore, that the uncertainty about the effects of carcinogenic agents requires the Administrator to prohibit all emissions. The Administrator argues that in the face of this uncertainty he is authorized to set standards that require emission reduction to the lowest level attainable by best available control technology whenever that level is below that at which harm to humans has been demonstrated. We find no support for either position in the language or legislative history of the Clean Air Act. We therefore grant the petition for review and remand to the Administrator for reconsideration in light of this opinion.

I

* * *

This case concerns vinyl chloride regulations. Vinyl chloride is a gaseous synthetic chemical used in the manufacture of plastics and is a strong carcinogen. In late 1975, the Administrator issued a notice of proposed rulemaking to establish an emission standard for vinyl chloride. In the notice, the EPA asserted that available data linked vinyl chloride to carcinogenic, as well as some noncarcinogenic, disorders and that "[r]easonable extrapolations" from this data suggested "that present ambient levels of vinyl chloride may cause or contribute to ... [such] disorders." The EPA also noted that vinyl chloride is "an apparent non-threshold pollutant," which means that it appears to create a risk to health at all non-zero levels of emission. Scientific uncertainty, due to the unavailability of dose-response data and the twenty-year latency period between initial exposure to vinyl chloride and the occurrence of disease, makes it impossible to establish any definite threshold level below which there are no adverse effects to human health. The notice also stated the "EPA's position that for a carcinogen it should be assumed, in the absence of strong evidence to the contrary, that there is no atmospheric concentration that poses absolutely no public health risk."

Because of this assumption, the EPA concluded that it was faced with two alternative interpretations of its duty under section 112. First, the EPA determined that section 112 might require a complete prohibition of emissions of non-threshold pollutants because a "zero emission limitation would be the only emission standard which would offer absolute safety from ambient exposure." The EPA found this alternative "neither desirable nor necessary" because "[c]omplete prohibition of all emissions could require closure of an entire industry," a cost the EPA found "extremely high for elimination of a risk to health that is of unknown dimensions."

The EPA stated the second alternative as follows:

An alternative interpretation of section 112 is that it authorizes setting emission standards that require emission reduction to the lowest level achievable by use of the best available control technology in cases involving apparent non-threshold pollutants, where complete emission prohibition would result in widespread industry closure and EPA has determined that the cost of such closure would be grossly disproportionate to the benefits of removing the risk that would remain after imposition of the best available control technology.

The EPA adopted this alternative on the belief that it would "produce the most stringent regulation of hazardous air pollutants short of requiring a complete prohibition in all cases."

On October 21, 1976, the EPA promulgated final emission standards for vinyl chloride which were based solely on the level attainable by the best available control technology. The EPA determined that this standard would reduce unregulated emissions by 95 percent. With respect to the effect of the standard on health, the EPA stated that it had assessed the risk to health at ambient levels of exposure by extrapolating from dose-response data at higher levels of exposure and then made the following findings:

> * * * Vinyl chloride is also estimated to produce * * * a total of somewhere between less than one and twenty cases of cancer per year of exposure among residents around plants. The number of these effects is expected to be reduced at least in proportion to the reduction in the ambient annual average vinyl chloride concentration, which is expected to be 5 percent of the uncontrolled levels after the standard is implemented.

The EPA did not state whether this risk to health is significant or not. Nor did the EPA explain the relationship between this risk to health and its duty to set an emission standard which will provide an "ample margin of safety."

* * *

III

The NRDC's challenge to the EPA's [vinyl chloride standard] is simple: because the statute adopts an exclusive focus on considerations of health, the Administrator must set a zero level of emissions when he cannot determine that there is a level below which no harm will occur.

* * * We find no support in the text or legislative history for the proposition that Congress intended to require a complete prohibition of emissions whenever the EPA cannot determine a threshold level for a hazardous pollutant. Instead, there is strong evidence that Congress considered such a requirement and rejected it.

Section 112 commands the Administrator to set an "emission standard" for a particular "hazardous air pollutant" which in his "judgment" will provide an "ample margin of safety." Congress' use of the term "ample margin of safety" is inconsistent with the NRDC's position that the Administrator has no discretion in the face of uncertainty. The statute nowhere defines "ample margin of safety." The Senate Report, however, in discussing a similar requirement in the context of setting ambient air standards under section 109 of the Act, explained the purpose of the "margin of safety" standard as one of affording "a reasonable degree of protection ... against hazards which research has not yet identified" (emphasis added). This view comports with the historical use of the term in engineering as "a safety factor ... meant to compensate for uncertainties and variabilities." * * * And while Congress used the modifier "ample" to exhort the Administrator not to allow "the public [or] the environment ... to be exposed to anything resembling the maximum risk" and, therefore, to set a margin "greater than 'normal' or 'adequate,' " Congress still left the EPA "great latitude in meeting its responsibility."

Congress' use of the word "safety," moreover, is significant evidence that it did not intend to require the Administrator to prohibit all emissions of non-threshold pollutants. As the Supreme Court has recently held, "safe" does not mean "risk-free." *Industrial Union Dep't, AFL–CIO v. American Petroleum Inst.*, 448 U.S. 607, 642 (1980). Instead, something is "unsafe" only when it threatens humans with "a significant risk of harm."

Thus, the terms of section 112 provide little support for the NRDC's position. The uncertainty about the effects of a particular carcinogenic pollutant invokes the Administrator's discretion under section 112. In contrast, the NRDC's position would eliminate any discretion and would render the standard "ample margin of safety" meaningless as applied to carcinogenic pollutants.[27] Whenever *any* scientific uncertainty existed about the ill effects of a nonzero level of hazardous air pollutants—and we think it unlikely that science will ever yield *absolute* certainty of safety in an area so complicated and rife with problems of measurement, modeling, long latency, and the like—the Administrator would have no discretion but would be required to prohibit all emissions. Had Congress intended that result, it could very easily have said so by writing a statute that states that no level of emissions shall be allowed as to which there is any uncertainty. But Congress chose instead to deal with the pervasive nature of scientific uncertainty and the inherent limitations of scientific knowledge by vesting in the Administrator the discretion to deal with uncertainty in each case.

* * *

IV

We turn now to the question whether the Administrator's chosen method for setting emission levels above zero is consistent with congressional intent. * * *

V

Since we cannot discern clear congressional intent to preclude consideration of cost and technological feasibility in setting emission standards under section 112, we necessarily find that the Administrator may consider these factors. * * * [Nevertheless, d]espite a deferential standard [of review], we find that the Administrator has ventured into a zone of impermissible action. The Administrator has not exercised his expertise to determine an acceptable risk to health. To the contrary, in the face of uncertainty about risks to health, he has simply substituted technological

---

27. With the exception of mercury, every pollutant the Administrator has listed or intends to list under § 112 is a non-threshold carcinogen. * * *

feasibility for health as the primary consideration under Section 112. Because this action is contrary to clearly discernible congressional intent, we grant the petition for review.

* * *

We find that the congressional mandate to provide "an ample margin of safety" "to protect the public health" requires the Administrator to make an initial determination of what is "safe." This determination must be based exclusively upon the Administrator's determination of the risk to health at a particular emission level. Because the Administrator in this case did not make any finding of the risk to health, the question of how that determination is to be made is not before us. We do wish to note, however, that the Administrator's decision does not require a finding that "safe" means "risk-free," *see Industrial Union Dep't*, or a finding that the determination is free from uncertainty. Instead, we find only that the Administrator's decision must be based upon an expert judgment with regard to the level of emission that will result in an "acceptable" risk to health. In this regard, the Administrator must determine what inferences should be drawn from available scientific data and decide what risks are acceptable in the world in which we live. *See Industrial Union Dep't* ("There are many activities that we engage in every day—such as driving a car or even breathing city air—that entail some risk of accident or material health impairment; nevertheless, few people would consider those activities 'unsafe.' "). This determination must be based solely upon the risk to health. The Administrator cannot under any circumstances consider cost and technological feasibility at this stage of the analysis. The latter factors have no relevance to the preliminary determination of what is safe. Of course, if the Administrator cannot find that there is an acceptable risk at any level, then the Administrator must set the level at zero.

Congress, however, recognized in section 112 that the determination of what is "safe" will always be marked by scientific uncertainty and thus exhorted the Administrator to set emission standards that will provide an "ample margin" of safety. This language permits the Administrator to take into account scientific uncertainty and to use expert discretion to determine what action should be taken in light of that uncertainty. In determining what is an "ample margin" the Administrator may, and perhaps must, take into account the inherent limitations of risk assessment and the limited scientific knowledge of the effects of exposure to carcinogens at various levels, and may therefore decide to set the level below that previously determined to be "safe." * * * It is only at this point of the regulatory process that the Administrator may set the emission standard at the lowest level that is technologically feasible. In fact, this is, we believe, precisely the type of policy choice that Congress envisioned when it directed the Administrator to provide an "ample margin of safety." Once "safety" is assured, the Administrator should be free to diminish as much of the statistically determined risk as possible by setting the standard at the lowest feasible level. Because consideration of these factors at this stage is clearly intended "to protect the public health," it is fully consistent with the Administrator's mandate under section 112.

We wish to reiterate the limited nature of our holding in this case because it is not the court's intention to bind the Administrator to any specific method of determining what is "safe" or what constitutes an "ample margin." We hold only that the Administrator cannot consider cost and technological feasibility in determining what is "safe." This determination must be based solely upon the risk to health. The issues of whether the Administrator can proceed on a case-by-case basis, what support the Administrator must provide for the determination of what is "safe," or what other factors may be considered, are issues that must be resolved after the Administrator has reached a decision upon reconsideration of the decision withdrawing the proposed 1977 amendments.

NOTES AND QUESTIONS

1.   *The* Vinyl Chloride *two-step.* What is the analytical procedure that the *Vinyl Chloride* case imposes? How does it compare to the two-step process set out in the statute? Do you detect the influence of the *Benzene* decision?

2.   How does section 112 use the term "margin of safety" as an element of its argument and as part of the agency's required analysis? Are section 112 and the opinion consistent? Is the opinion internally consistent on this point?

3.   *Acceptable risk.* What does the court say about the level of risk that is "acceptable"? How is EPA to go about setting that level?

4.   EPA did not appreciate the rebuff it received in *Vinyl Chloride*, and it was particularly unhappy with the *Benzene*-like analysis that the court mandated:

> Although not reflected in the *Vinyl Chloride* decision reviewed by the D.C. Circuit, the EPA's recent judgments under section 112 were made in integrated approaches that considered a range of health and risk factors, as well as cost and feasibility in certain cases. These approaches were followed in NESHAP for the source categories of radionuclides, arsenic, and the prior decisions on benzene source categories. However, the *Vinyl Chloride* decision eliminates those approaches to section 112, since the integrated approaches did not partition consideration of health factors into a first step separate from consideration of the other relevant factors.
>
> Thus, the *Vinyl Chloride* decision forces EPA to consider whether a risk is acceptable without at the same time considering benefits of the activity causing risk, feasibility of control, or other factors that EPA (or anyone) would normally consider in deciding whether a risk was "acceptable." This problem is particularly acute in the case of many carcinogens, for which the Agency has stated that it is unable to identify a threshold no-effect level.
>
> The very examples cited by the court bring home the unusual

nature of the court's "acceptable risk" decision step. The court (quoting the Supreme Court's decision in the OSHA *Benzene* Case) cited "driving a car or even breathing city air" as activities that "few people would consider * * * 'unsafe.' " But driving a car entails risks that most people would consider high; the annual incidence approximates 50,000 fatal accidents, and the average individual risk (not the maximum, but the actuarial average risk) approximates a 1 in 100 chance of automobile-related death over a 70–year lifetime. Yet the court was correct to say that our society accepts (or tolerates) risk from driving cars. As a society we continue to try to reduce the level of risk, but we value the benefits in increased mobility that the automobile affords. The same is true of "breathing city air"—leaving aside the circularity (city air may contain some of the contaminants that EPA is considering regulating), individuals live in cities to be close to the workplace, for the recreational and cultural advantages associated with cities, and for a variety of reasons extrinsic to the risk itself.

If decisions on the acceptability of risks are inherently balancing judgments, how is EPA to make those judgments on acceptability?

EPA, Proposed Rule, National Emission Standards for Hazardous Air Pollutants: Benzene Emissions, 53 Fed. Reg. 28496 (1988). What does EPA mean by "integrated" standards? Why does EPA so clearly prefer them? Do integrated standards really eliminate the difficulties created by *Vinyl Chloride*?

2.   THE 1990 CLEAN AIR ACT AMENDMENTS

Frustrated by the glacial pace of regulation under the original section 112, having received little assistance from the judiciary in moving the program along, and reacting to the first Toxic Release Inventory data (which revealed releases of over 2.7 billion pounds of hazardous air pollutants per year, to which EPA attributed 1,000–3,000 deaths), Congress devoted much attention to air toxics in the wide-ranging revision of the Clean Air Act in 1990. The new section 112 is in keeping with the rest of the legislation: it is very long (practically its own, freestanding regulatory structure), very detailed, and very different from the old provision.

Read the current section 112(a)–(h). Start with the table of contents of section 112 to get a sense of what it contains and how it is organized, then consider the following questions:

Listing: How does the new statute differ from the old? Why did Congress draft its own list? Are any of the definitions (§ 112(a)) important to understanding what a HAP is?

What is the standard for *de*listing HAPs? How is this different from the listing standard, and why?

Source Categories: Why is this step important? How does it differentiate the old and new sections 112? Why did Congress adopt a statutory list of pollutants, and yet order regulation to proceed by industry categories?

Should EPA be permitted to create subcategories within a general source category, which separate the low-risk and high-risk sources of HAPs? Why might EPA or a source want to create such subcategories?[28]

Maximum Achievable Control Technology (MACT): How is MACT determined? How does the new standard differ from the *Vinyl Chloride/Benzene* analysis?

Why did Congress (and industry, environmentalists, and EPA) think that MACT is a better, or at least faster, approach?[29] What are its drawbacks?[30]

Residual Risk: What is the relationship, in terms of schedule and stringency, between the "standard to protect health and the environment" and the MACT standards? The subsection goes to some length to preserve the "ample margin of safety" language from the pre-1990 statute—how does it differ from the pre-1990 standard and from the *Vinyl Chloride* analysis?

Why did Congress adopt the two-step process?

The 1990 Clean Air Act Amendments are extremely unusual among federal environmental statutes in using a quantitative risk standard in legislation, instead of solely a narrative standard. What advantages and disadvantages might such "bright-line" standards have? Does it solve EPA's "acceptable risk" problem?[31]

Schedule: What is the so-called "hammer" provision in section 112? What is its purpose, and why is it important?[32]

The following two cases address the calculations, respectively, of the MACT and residual risk standards.

---

28. *See* NRDC v. EPA, 489 F.3d 1364 (D.C. Cir. 2007); Bradford C. Mank, *A Scrivener's Error or Greater Protection of the Public: Does EPA Have the Authority to Delist "Low–Risk" Sources of Carcinogens from Section 112's Maximum Achievable Control Technology Requirements?*, 24 Va. Envtl. L.J. 75 (2005).

29. *See* articles on technology-based regulation, *supra*, note 23.

30. *See* Cass Sunstein, *Paradoxes of the Regulatory State*, 57 U. Chi. L. Rev. 407 (1990); John M. Mendeloff, The Dilemma of Toxic Substance Regulation (1988); John P. Dwyer, *Overregulation*, 15 Ecology L.Q. 719 (1988) (reviewing Mendeloff).

31. *See* Alon Rosenthal *et al.*, *Legislating Acceptable Cancer Risk from Exposure to Toxic Chemicals*, 19 Ecology L.Q. 269, 339, 360–61 (1992) (criticizing bright-line standards). There was, in fact, a strong push in early CAA amendment bills to make quantitative standards more prominent. For example, the original Senate bill would have required closure of plants that posed a 10^{-4} risk to highly exposed individuals, with that threshold lowering to 10^{-6} over time. The Conference compromise was to abandon quantitative standards as a primary measure, but to keep it as a screening tool (§ 112(c)(9)(B)(i)), as a priority-setting device (§ 112(f)(2)(A)), and as a fallback risk standard (§ 112(f)(2)(A)). Rosenthal *et al.* argue that these latter are appropriate uses of bright-line standards. *Id.*

32. The hammer has, in theory, long since fallen. For insight into the controversies in the area, *see* Sierra Club v. EPA, 551 F.3d 1019 (2008), and EPA's hammer rules, 67 Fed. Reg. 16582 (2002), 68 Fed. Reg. 32586 (2003).

Sierra Club v. EPA
479 F.3d 875 (D.C. Cir. 2007)

■ Per Curiam:

In this case, the Sierra Club challenges the Environmental Protection Agency's air pollution standards for brick and ceramics kilns. Because most of the standards violate the Clean Air Act as interpreted by this Court in *Cement Kiln Recycling Coalition v. EPA,* 255 F.3d 855 (D.C.Cir.2001) (per curiam), and *National Lime Ass'n v. EPA,* 233 F.3d 625 (D.C.Cir.2000), and because the remaining standards violate the Act's requirements for "work practice standards," we vacate the standards in their entirety and remand for further proceedings consistent with this opinion.

I

The Clean Air Act directs the Environmental Protection Agency to establish emission standards for "major sources" of hazardous air pollutants listed in the statute. 42 U.S.C. § 7412(d)(1). In *Cement Kiln,* we described the Act as follows:

> Until 1990, the Clean Air Act ... required the Environmental Protection Agency to set risk-based air pollution standards that would provide an "ample margin of safety to protect the public health." § 7412(b)(1)(B); *see also* H.R. Rep. No. 101-490, at 151, 322 (1990). To address problems with the implementation of risk-based regulation, Congress amended the Act in 1990 to require EPA to set the most stringent standards achievable, 42 U.S.C. § 7412(d)(2), that is, standards "based on the maximum reduction in emissions which can be achieved by application of [the] best available control technology." S. Rep. No. 101–228, at 133 (1989).

> The 1990 amendments included ... 42 U.S.C. § 7412(d)— which directs EPA to set standards limiting emissions of listed hazardous air pollutants ("HAPs"), §§ 7412(b), (c)(1)–(2), from major stationary sources. Section 7412(d)(2) provides that:

>> Emission standards ... shall require the maximum degree of reduction in emissions of the hazardous air pollutants subject to this section ... that the Administrator, taking into consideration the cost of achieving such emission reduction, and any non-air quality health and environmental impacts and energy requirements, determines is achievable for new or existing sources....

> Supplementing this general guidance, Congress imposed minimum stringency requirements—EPA calls them "emission floors"— which "apply without regard to either costs or the other factors and methods listed in section 7412(d)(2)." *Nat'l Lime Ass'n v. EPA,* 233 F.3d 625, 629 (D.C.Cir.2000) ("*National Lime II*"). For "new sources"—... sources on which construction begins after EPA publishes emission standards, 42 U.S.C. § 7411(a)(2)—"[t]he maximum degree of reduction in emissions that is deemed achievable ...

shall not be less stringent than the emission control that is achieved in practice by the best controlled similar source...." *Id.* § 7412(d)(3). For existing sources, what EPA deems achievable "shall not be less stringent than [ ] the average emission limitation achieved by the best performing 12 percent of the existing sources (for which the Administrator has emissions information)...." *Id.* As we explained in *National Lime II,* EPA implements these requirements through a two-step process: the Agency first sets emission floors for each pollutant and source category and then determines whether stricter standards, known as "beyond-the-floor" limits, are achievable in light of the factors listed in section 7412(d)(2).

In *Cement Kiln* we considered the Sierra Club's argument that EPA's emission floors for hazardous waste combustors violated section 7412(d)(3) of the Act, the provision at issue in this case. For existing sources, EPA had identified the best-performing 12 percent of sources for which it had information. Among these sources, EPA then identified the median source's emission control technology, which it called the "maximum achievable control technology"—or "MACT control"—as the "average" emission limitation of the best performers. EPA next identified the worst-performing source using the MACT control and set the floor at the emission level of that source. For new sources, EPA followed the same approach, except that instead of using the technology of the median source as the MACT control, it used the technology of the single best-performing source.

The Sierra Club argued that this technology-based approach violated section 7412(d)(3)'s requirement that floors reflect emissions actually "achieved" or "achieved in practice" by the best-performing sources. In response, EPA argued that section 7412(d)(3)'s floor provision "is a gloss" on section 7412(d)(2), which requires that beyond-the-floor emission standards be "achievable" by all sources, based on costs and other factors. According to EPA, section 7412(d)(3) incorporates section 7412(d)(2)'s achievability requirement, meaning that emission floors must also be achievable by all sources. We rejected EPA's interpretation, finding it to be an impermissible reading of the statute's unambiguous language:

> Section 7412(d)(3) ... limits the scope of the word "achievable" in section 7412(d)(2). While standards achievable by all sources using the MACT control might also ultimately reflect what the statutorily relevant sources achieve in practice, EPA may not deviate from section 7412(d)(3)'s requirement that floors reflect what the best performers actually achieve by claiming that floors must be achievable by all sources using MACT technology.

EPA chose not to file a petition for rehearing en banc or to seek Supreme Court review.

Cement Kiln was not the first time this court invalidated an EPA interpretation of section 7412(d)(3). Six months earlier, in *National Lime II,* we considered the Sierra Club's challenge to EPA's setting of "no control" floors—that is, no emission floors at all—forcertain HAPs emitted by cement plants. * * * We found EPA's interpretation of the statute untenable:

Nothing in the statute even suggests that EPA may set emission levels only for those listed HAPs controlled with technology. To the contrary, the statute ... requires EPA to "promulgate regulations establishing emission standards for each category or subcategory of major sources ... of hazardous air pollutants listed for regulation." [42 U.S.C.] § 7412(d)(1)....

Contrary to EPA's argument, nothing in *Sierra* relieves it of the clear statutory obligation to set emission standards for each listed HAP. Although *Sierra* permits the Agency to look at technological controls to set emission standards, it does not say that EPA may avoid setting standards for HAPs not controlled with technology.

Following the panel decision, EPA filed an unsuccessful petition for rehearing, but again sought neither en banc nor Supreme Court review.

With this background in mind, we turn to the facts of this case. At issue are EPA's emission standards for brick and structural clay products (BSCP) kilns and clay ceramics kilns. Over 500 brick kilns and more than 50 ceramics kilns operate throughout the United States. BSCPs include brick, clay pipe, and clay roof tile; ceramics include tile and sanitaryware, such as toilets and sinks. Production of BSCPs and ceramics involves processing common clays and shales and forming and firing shapes. Because transporting clays and shales over long distances is infeasible, kilns are located close to the mines supplying the clays and shales used in their products. BSCPs and ceramics are fired in one of two types of kilns: those that operate continuously, which include "tunnel" and "roller" kilns; and those that operate in batch cycles, known as "periodic" kilns. EPA divided brick kilns into three subcategories: large tunnel brick kilns, small tunnel brick kilns, and periodic brick kilns. It divided ceramics kilns into four subcategories: large tunnel ceramics kilns, small tunnel ceramics kilns, roller ceramics kilns, and periodic ceramics kilns. Reflecting the different standards set forth in sections 7412(d)(3) and 7412(d)(3)(A), EPA further divided each subcategory into new and existing kilns.

Each year, brick and ceramics kilns emit over 6,440 tons of HAPs, including hydrofluoric acid, hydrochloric acid, and particulate matter containing toxic metals, such as antimony, arsenic, beryllium, cadmium, chromium, cobalt, lead, manganese, nickel, and selenium. These HAPs can cause severe respiratory problems, cancer, neurological and organ damage, and adverse reproductive effects.

In 2002, EPA issued a proposed rule setting floors to limit HAP emissions from new and existing brick and ceramics kilns. For the subcategories in which few or no kilns use air pollution control devices, EPA proposed floors of "no emissions reductions"—in other words, no floors at all. For all remaining subcategories, EPA proposed floors based on the pollution control devices used by the best-performing kilns, i.e., those with the lowest emissions. In their comments on the proposed regulations, industry members insisted that installing the devices used by the best-performing sources would be technologically and economically infeasible. For its part, the Sierra Club complained that EPA had failed to consider non-technology factors—

e.g., fuel type, raw materials, additives and surface coatings, kiln design, and operator training—that contribute to emissions.

In response to these comments, EPA's final emission standards set floors for several subcategories based on the pollution control devices used by the second-best performers—not, as EPA had proposed, the best performers—and replaced "no emissions reductions" floors in other subcategories with a so-called "work practice standard" of using clean-burning fuels. *See* 42 U.S.C. § 7412(h) (explaining requirements for setting work practice standards in lieu of emission standards). * * * The Sierra Club now petitions for review. * * *

II

The Sierra Club argues that EPA's methodology in setting floors for brick and ceramics kilns violates the Clean Air Act's plain language as interpreted by *Cement Kiln* and *National Lime II*. We agree.

"Achieved," not "Achievable"

As discussed above, we held in *Cement Kiln* that "EPA may not deviate from section 7412(d)(3)'s requirement that floors reflect what the best performers actually achieve by claiming that floors must be achievable by all sources using MACT technology." In setting the floor for existing large tunnel brick kilns, however, EPA did just that.

Most large tunnel brick kilns that have installed air pollution control devices use dry lime adsorbers (DLA). Others use non-DLA technology, including dry lime injection fabric filters (DIFF), dry lime scrubber/fabric filters (DLS/FF), and wet scrubbers (WS). In its notice of proposed rulemaking, EPA concluded that these non-DLA pollution control devices "represent[ed] the best control[ ]." Because the 94th percentile (the median of the top 12 percent) of the best-performing large tunnel brick kilns used non-DLA technology, EPA—as required by *Cement Kiln*—proposed a floor based on this technology. But after receiving "numerous comments from industry representatives" saying that kilns were unable to retrofit with WS because of a lack of sewer access to treat wastewater from the device, or with DIFF or DLS/FF without affecting production, EPA changed course in its final rule. Finding that non-DLA technology would have "potentially significant impacts on the production process," and contrary to *Cement Kiln's* requirement that floors reflect emission levels of the best-performing sources, EPA excluded non-DLA technology from its ranking of best-performing kilns. It then set the floor for existing large tunnel brick kilns based on DLA.

EPA argues that it has "reasonably construe[d] the term 'best performing' ... to allow it to consider whether retrofitting kilns with a particular pollution control technology is technically feasible." But EPA cannot circumvent *Cement Kiln's* holding that section 7412(d)(3) requires floors based on the emission level actually *achieved* by the best performers (those with the lowest emission levels), not the emission level achievable by all sources, simply by redefining "best performing" to mean those sources with emission levels *achievable* by all sources. Moreover, EPA's rationales for excluding kilns equipped with non-DLA technology from its ranking of the best-performing large tunnel kilns (the infeasibility of retrofitting all kilns with certain non-DLA technology and the negative impact other non-DLA technology would have on productivity) amount to nothing more than a concern about ensuring that its floor is achievable by all kilns in the subcategory-precisely the position we rejected in *Cement Kiln.*

III

EPA's emission standards run counter to *Cement Kiln* and *National Lime II* in several other respects—all variations on the Agency's fundamental failure to set floors at the emission levels actually achieved by the best-performing sources.

Variability

In *Cement Kiln* we declared unlawful EPA's method of estimating variability among the best performers by lowering floors to the level of the worst performer using the same technology. We explained:

> [W]e are unpersuaded by EPA's claim that to account for the best-performing sources' operational variability, it had to base the floors on the worst performers' emissions. While we have recognized that a given control can experience operational variability, the relevant question here is not whether control technologies experience variability at all, but whether the variability experienced by the best-performing sources can be estimated by relying on emissions data from the worst-performing sources using the MACT control. In this case, the evidence EPA cites to support the MACT approach as a means of accounting for operational variability fails to demonstrate the relevant relationship. Some of the Agency's citations to the record merely contain assertions that "[the] approach ... fully accounts for normal process variability." The actual variability data EPA cites suggest only that emissions from sources using a given control vary over a wide range, not that the high emission levels achieved by sources at one end of that range reflect levels achieved by sources at the other end, nor that the best-performing sources ever experience a wide range of variability at all.

Here, EPA used the same flawed process to set floors for new large and small tunnel brick and ceramics kilns, as well as for existing large tunnel brick kilns. In its rulemaking, EPA explained that it "used the highest emission level associated with the[ ] best performers [*i.e.,* all DLA-controlled kilns] to set the emission standard because it was [EPA's] intent to set emission limits that reflect the performance that the best-controlled sources continually achieve considering variability." Citing a range of emission datapoints from a single DLA-equipped kiln, EPA explained that "[a]ll sources, including the best-controlled sources, have variability in emissions." Because these reasons for using the emission level achieved by the worst-performing kilns to predict the variability of the best performers differ little from the reasons EPA gave in *Cement Kiln,* this element of the Agency's floor-setting methodology is similarly unlawful.

Defending its approach, EPA points to *Mossville Environmental Action Now v. EPA,* 370 F.3d 1232 (D.C.Cir.2004), in which we held that floors may legitimately account for variability because "each [source] must meet the [specified] standard every day and under all operating conditions." In *Mossville,* however, record evidence demonstrated that the floor reasonably estimated the actual variability of the best-performing source. Here, by contrast, although EPA has some evidence that the best performers experience variability, it has failed to show that the emission levels achieved by the worst performers using a given pollution control device actually predict the range of emission levels achieved by the best performers using that device. Given *Cement Kiln's* holding that EPA may not use emission levels of the worst performers to estimate variability of the best performers without a demonstrated relationship between the two, we conclude that the emission floors for new large and small tunnel brick and ceramics kilns, as well as for existing large tunnel brick kilns, violate the Act.

Non–Technology Factors

In *Cement Kiln,* we rejected EPA's MACT approach to setting floors given record evidence that factors other than technology affected emissions. In doing so, we noted our conclusion in *National Lime II* that the MACT methodology, a purely technology-based approach, would satisfy the Clean Air Act "if pollution control technology were the *only* factor determining emission levels of that HAP." We were unpersuaded by EPA's twin justifications for refusing to consider the effect of other factors on emissions, namely that the effect proved "impossible to reliably quantify," and that "floors must be achievable by all sources using MACT technology." We explained:

> [I]f factors other than MACT technology do indeed influence a source's performance, it is not sufficient that EPA considered sources using only ... MACT controls....
>
> Even accepting the proposition that factors affecting source performance ... are difficult to quantify *when defining the MACT control,* nothing in the statute requires EPA to use the MACT approach. Section 7412(d)(3) requires only that EPA set floors at the emission level achieved by the best-performing sources. If EPA cannot meet this requirement using the MACT methodology, it must devise a different approach capable of producing floors that satisfy the Clean Air Act.

EPA's emission standards for existing large tunnel brick kilns and new large and small tunnel brick and ceramics kilns suffer from the same defect (in addition to the defects noted above). In its rulemaking, EPA noted that it had reviewed non-technology pollution prevention techniques-in particular the substitution of fuels and clays with lower amounts of hazardous constituents. It found that fuel type had no appreciable effect on emissions, that transporting clays over long distances was impractical, and that changes in either could affect kilns' ability to duplicate their existing product lines. Given these findings, EPA set floors based only on pollution control technology, explaining that "[w]hile we agree that factors other than [technology] type can affect emissions, we do not have the data to determine the specific degree of the effect of factors other than [technology] on emissions, and we believe that, for the BSCP industry, factors other than [technology] use are not viable MACT floor ... control options." Though acknowledging that at least one non-technology factor, clay type, had an appreciable effect on emissions, EPA has articulated the same justifications it offered in *Cement Kiln* for using technology-based floors, i.e., a lack of data to quantify the effects of non-technology factors and a concern that floors based on clean clay would be unachievable because of the inability of kilns to switch clays. These justifications are no more valid here than they were in *Cement Kiln.*

EPA argues that the Clean Air Act's command that it assess the emission "control" or "limitation" "achieved" refers to the deliberate steps kiln operators take to reduce emissions rather than to the "happenstance" of being located near cleaner clay. Yet we squarely held in *National Lime II* that the Clean Air Act requires neither an intentional action nor a deliberate strategy to reduce emissions. As we explained, "[t]he Clean Air Act requires the EPA to set MACT floors based upon the 'average emission limitation[s] achieved'; it nowhere suggests that this achievement must be the product of a specific intent." EPA's decision to base floors exclusively on technology even though non-technology factors affect emission levels thus violates the Act.

"No Control" Floors

As noted above, in *National Lime II* we found unlawful EPA's "no control" emission floors for categories in which the best performers used no emission control technology. As we explained, EPA has a "clear statutory obligation to set emission standards for each listed HAP," which does not allow it to "avoid setting standards for HAPs not controlled with technology."

EPA's failure to set floors for existing small tunnel brick kilns and existing and new periodic brick kilns violates section 7412(d)(3) for precisely the same reason. EPA set "no emissions reductions" floors for existing small tunnel brick kilns because the 94th percentile kiln used no air pollution control technology and because changes in non-technology factors were not "appropriate" or "viable." EPA also set "no emissions reductions" floors for all periodic brick kilns, explaining that they too use no pollution control technology. Other than again claiming that it has no obligation to set floors unless sources take some deliberate action to control emissions, EPA has failed to offer any reason for distinguishing what it did here from what we invalidated in *National Lime II.*

IV

This brings us to the one issue in this case controlled by neither *Cement Kiln* nor *National Lime II,* namely EPA's use of so-called work practice standards instead of emission floors for the remaining subcategories of kilns. Section 7412(h) of the Clean Air Act provides that "if it is not feasible in the judgment of the Administrator to prescribe or enforce an emission standard ..., the Administrator may, in lieu thereof, promulgate a design, equipment, work practice, or operational standard." 42 U.S.C. § 7412(h)(1). That section further explains that it is "not feasible" to set an emission standard when "the application of measurement methodology to a particular class of sources is not practicable due to technological and economic limitations." § 7412(h)(2)(B).

Invoking section 7412(h), EPA adopted the work practice standard of using clean-burning fuels for existing ceramics kilns and new periodic and roller ceramics kilns. To justify its use of work practice standards, EPA pointed out that ceramics kilns, like periodic brick kilns, use no pollution control devices and cannot feasibly substitute clays. Rather than setting "no control" floors, however, EPA imposed a clean-burning fuels standard. According to EPA, setting a more precise floor based on the emission levels achieved by the use of clean-burning fuels was not feasible given the absence of data necessary to make this calculation.

We agree with the Sierra Club that EPA's use of work practice standards instead of emission floors violates section 7412(h). That provision allows EPA to substitute work practice standards for emission floors only if measuring emission levels is technologically or economically impracticable. Here, EPA never determined that measuring emissions from ceramics kilns was impracticable; it determined only that it lacked emissions data from ceramics kilns. EPA thus had no basis under section 7412(h) for using work practice standards. To be sure, as EPA points out, because ceramics kilns already use clean-burning fuels, the work practice standard would have no impact on their products. For the same reason, of course, it would have no impact on emissions.

V

For the foregoing reasons, we vacate the emission standards for both brick and ceramics kilns and remand for further proceedings consistent with this opinion. If the Environmental Protection Agency disagrees with the Clean Air Act's requirements for setting emissions standards, it should take its concerns to Congress. If EPA disagrees with this court's interpretation of the Clean Air Act, it should seek rehearing en banc or file a petition for a writ of certiorari. In the meantime, it must obey the Clean Air Act as written by Congress and interpreted by this court.

NOTES AND QUESTIONS

1. *Setting MACT standards.* Trace the step-by-step process for setting MACT standards, as reflected in the *Sierra Club* case. What choices does EPA have to make at each step?[33] Are they scientific/technical, policy, or legal choices?

2. *"Achieved" vs. "achievable."* What is the difference between these two concepts, and why is it important?

---

33.   *See* Patricia Ross McCubbin, *The Risk in Technology–Based Standards*, 16 DUKE ENVTL. L. & POLICY FORUM 1 (2005) (showing that in practice risk and cost are both part of EPA's analysis of best available technology).

3. *Categorization.* On what basis did EPA divide the brick and ceramic kiln industry into subcategories? How did its subcategorization affect the content of the eventual standards?

How do categorization choices interact with what is "achieved" *versus* what is "achievable"? In a concurrence to the above opinion, Judge Williams observed:

> Section 112(d)(1) authorizes the Administrator to "distinguish among classes, types and sizes of sources within a category or subcategory," and the language of subsections 112(d)(2) and (3) pervasively refers to standards for sources in each *"category or subcategory."* The authority to generate subcategories is obviously not unqualified; at the least it must be limited by the usual ideas of reasonableness. And there is not necessarily any guarantee that, even with suitable subcategorization, every source will be able to achieve standards that meet a lawful application of § 112(d)(3) to reasonably defined subcategories. Nonetheless, one legitimate basis for creating additional subcategories must be the interest in keeping the relation between "achieved" and "achievable" in accord with common sense and the reasonable meaning of the statute.

Does the "reasonable meanings" approach open the door to abuse of subcategorization? How can courts ensure that EPA is demanding the stringent controls that Congress sought?

4. *No-control floors.* What is the problem with "no-control floors"? Are they always impermissible, or are there circumstances under which they might be allowed?

5. *Work practices.* The Clean Air Act permits EPA to consider work practices in setting MACT standards. What are the benefits of such an approach? What are the dangers?

6. EPA has considerably more discretion in setting the stricter "beyond-the-floor" standards, and indeed is not required to set them at all. *Sierra Club v. EPA*, 353 F.3d 976, 988–990 (D.C. Cir. 2004). Do you see a structural analogy to *Vinyl Chloride*? Can you identify other examples of the pattern of more flexible, more discretionary, or even optional second steps? Why do you think that this pattern exists?

Natural Resources Defense Council v. EPA

529 F.3d 1077 (D.C. Cir. 2008)

■ Silberman, Senior Circuit Judge.

Synthetic organic chemicals have few direct consumer uses, but they often serve as raw materials in the production of plastics, rubbers, fibers, protective coatings, and detergents. Petitioners, the Natural Resources Defense Council and the Louisiana Environmental Action Network, challenge EPA's residual risk rulemaking under subsection 112(f) of the Clean

Air Act for facilities that use or produce synthetic organic chemicals ("the industry"). Petitioners also challenge EPA's technology review under subsection 112(d)(6). In a rather unusual bit of rulemaking, the agency determined *by rule* not to change its previous rule, which gave rise to petitioners' challenge. We deny the petition.

I

* * * EPA initially promulgated technology-based [*i.e.,* MACT] emission standards for the industry in 1994 (there are 238 facilities in the United States that produce or use synthetic organic chemicals). Those standards required the use of control technologies such as recovery devices, thermal oxidizers, carbon absorbers, and steam strippers. After submitting the required report to Congress in 1999, the agency commenced residual risk rulemaking, apparently because—as we discuss below—it read the statute as requiring a rulemaking proceeding to consider whether to revise the technology-based standards, since the industry's emissions pose lifetime excess cancer risks of greater than one-in-one million.

II

A

Petitioners contend that subsection 112(f)(2)(A) obliged EPA to revise industry standards to reduce lifetime excess cancer risk to one-in-one million. Petitioners rely primarily on the last sentence of that subsection, whereas EPA looks to the whole subsection. [The court quotes 42 U.S.C. § 7412(f)(2)(A).]

It is undisputed that facilities that produce or use synthetic organic chemicals emit carcinogens and are, therefore, within the reach of the last sentence. It is also undisputed that, in light of the fact that existing technology-based standards do not reduce the risk to less than one-in-one million, EPA was obliged to "promulgate standards" under subsection 112(f). Petitioners contend that the third sentence obviously means that residual risk standards must meet the threshold test—*i.e.,* EPA must reduce such risks to one-in-one million. That may well be a possible interpretation, but the sentence contains a glaring omission; it does not say what petitioners would like us to infer. Rather, that sentence instructs the Administrator to "promulgate standards," but it says nothing about the substantive content of those standards. If Congress had wished to set a "bright line" standard, it would have been rather easy for the draftsmen to say just that. The failure to do so could not have been accidental. In light of the rest of the subsection's language (and other provisions), it seems to us that the subsection was drafted as a deliberately ambiguous compromise.

We reach that conclusion because the second sentence, which sets forth the substantive standard to be applied, simply calls for standards that "provide an ample margin of safety to protect public health" (unless the Administrator wishes to go further to avoid adverse environmental effects). No distinction is drawn between carcinogens and non-carcinogens. The third sentence, on which petitioners rely, not only lacks the language that petitioners ask us to infer; it also specifically states that if the one-in-one million trigger is met, the Administrator must promulgate standards "under this subsection," which, perforce, takes us back to the second sentence.[34]

EPA's construction of the subsection is bolstered by another paragraph, 112(f)(2)(B), which states:

> Nothing in subparagraph (A) or in any other provision of this section shall be construed as affecting, or applying to the Administrator's interpretation of this section, as in effect before November 15, 1990, and set forth in the Federal Register of September 14, 1989 (54 Federal Register 38044).

42 U.S.C. § 7412(f)(2)(B). The cited item in the Federal Register is EPA's emission standard for benzene, which is a carcinogenic hazardous air pollutant. In the *Benzene* rulemaking, EPA set forth its interpretation of "ample margin of safety," as that term was used in the 1970 version of the Clean Air Act. It said that the "ample margin" was met if as many people as possible faced excess lifetime cancer risks no greater than one-in-one million, and that no person faced a risk greater than 100-in-one million (one-in-ten thousand). In other words, the *Benzene* standard established a maximum excess risk of 100-in-one million, while adopting the one-in-one million standard as an aspirational goal. This standard, incorporated into the amended version of the Clean Air Act, undermines petitioners' assertion that EPA *must* reduce residual risks to one-in-one million for all sources that emit carcinogenic hazardous air pollutants.

* * *

The parenthetical clause in the second sentence of subsection 112(f)(2)(A) lends further support to EPA's position. That sentence states "[e]missions standards promulgated under this subsection shall provide an ample margin of safety to protect public health in accordance with this section (as in effect before November 15, 1990)...." EPA interprets the parenthetical as a "shorthand reference" to the *Benzene* standard, given that subsection (B) uses almost identical language, incorporating "the Administrator's interpretation of this section, as in effect before November 15, 1990, and set forth in the Federal Register...." The phrase "this section (as in effect before November 15, 1990)" is certainly broad enough to encompass EPA's prior *interpretations* of "this section" as well as the text itself. In fact, the operative provision of the pre–1990 version of section 112 uses the exact same "ample margin of safety" language as subsection 112(f)(2)(A) currently uses. Thus, the parenthetical must refer to something more than the bare text of "this section," or else it would be surplusage.

---

34. As one commentator has noted, subsection 112(f)(2) "does not require that the residual risk standard for a category be set at a level that would force the highest risk source in that category to achieve the one-in-one-million benchmark, but merely mandates an additional round of regulation." Bradford C. Mank, *What Comes After Technology: Using an "Exceptions Process" to Improve Residual Risk Regulation of Hazardous Air Pollutants*, 13 Stan. Envtl. L.J. 263, 276 (1994). The author continues: "By not requiring a one-in-a-million or any other residual risk standard in section 112(f), Congress essentially left the difficult task of defining an 'ample margin of safety' to the EPA's discretion."

Petitioners insist that EPA's interpretation renders the third sentence effectively meaningless. To be sure, the third sentence, as EPA interprets it, seems relatively anodyne; it lacks substantive force. But, at least as EPA reads it, the word "promulgate" means the agency is obliged to conduct a rulemaking to consider residual risks for sources that emit carcinogens. That extra procedural step is not a trivial obligation. Congress often imposes procedural requirements without dictating substantive outcomes, [for example, in] the National Environmental Policy Act [NEPA]. We also disagree with petitioners' argument that EPA did not "promulgate standards" under subsection 112(f)(2) because it simply readopted the initial standards. This position finds no support in the text of the statute. Subsection 112(f)(2) only mandates that residual risk standards "provide an ample margin of safety to protect public health." If EPA determines that the existing technology-based standards already provide an "ample margin of safety," then the agency is free to readopt those standards during a residual risk rulemaking.

Finally, petitioners argue that EPA unlawfully considered cost while setting the "ample margin of safety" in the residual risk standards. Petitioners are correct that the Supreme Court has "refused to find implicit in ambiguous sections of the [Clean Air Act] an authorization to consider costs that has elsewhere, and so often, been expressly granted."*Whitman v. Am. Trucking Ass'ns* [*infra*]. In this case, however, we believe the clear statement rule has been satisfied. As explained above, subsection 112(f)(2)(B) expressly incorporates EPA's interpretation of the Clean Air Act from the *Benzene* standard, complete with a citation to the Federal Register. In that rulemaking, EPA set its standard for benzene "at a level that provides 'an ample margin of safety' in consideration of all health information ... as well as other relevant factors *including costs and economic impacts,* technological feasibility, and other factors relevant to each particular decision." EPA considered cost in *Benzene,* and subsection 112(f)(2)(B) makes clear that nothing in the amended version of the Clean Air Act shall "affect[ ]" the agency's interpretation of the statute from that rulemaking.

In sum, we conclude that EPA's interpretation of subsection 112(f)(2), although not an inevitable one, certainly is, at least, a reasonable construction of the statute. *See Chevron*.

* * *

IV

For the aforementioned reasons, the petition for review is denied.

NOTES AND QUESTIONS

1. *Residual risk.* How does the court interpret the residual risk requirement? Does this interpretation surprise you?

2. The court suggests that the interpretation is best understood as a legislative compromise—how so? Can it be justified as making sense in its own right? Are you persuaded by the court's NEPA argument? Does *Vinyl Chloride* help to make sense of the interpretation?

3. *Voluntary reduction program.* The voluntary reduction program set out in section 112(i) allows polluters who reduce HAPs by 90% to defer

compliance with their MACT obligations by six years.[35] Why might an early reductions program be attractive to polluters? To regulators? Is this program consistent with the overall two-step (MACT plus residual risk) policy?

4. *Summing up.* In what ways do the 1990 amendments to section 112 of the Clean Air Act represent lessons learned from previous regulatory strategies for toxic substances?

D.   Information Disclosure

Instead of the traditional form of regulation, in which a governmental entity prescribes certain limitations on the production, use, or disposal of a hazardous material, some statutes encourage individual (private) decision-making based on information provided by a governmental entity or required by law. There are potential efficiencies in a market-mimicking approach like this—an analogy would be the market-perfecting disclosure requirements of securities regulation—but also some significant limitations.

1.   EPCRA and the Toxics Release Inventory

On the night of December 2–3, 1984, during routine maintenance operations at a Union Carbide plant in the city of Bhopal, India, an accident released several tons of the highly toxic chemical methyl isocyanate into the communities that surrounded the plant. The poisonous cloud killed over 2,000 residents of Bhopal and injured over 200,000 more. Less than a year later, in August 1985, a Union Carbide plant in Institute, West Virginia, released a different pesticide into the air. Nearly 150 people needed medical attention. Investigators determined that plant administrators did not adequately notify emergency response personnel, and that emergency response officials did not know what the substance that had escaped from the facility was or its characteristics.

The toxic releases in Bhopal and Institute occurred while Congress was considering the reauthorization of CERCLA. As a result, a separate bill, the Emergency Planning and Community Right-to-Know Act (EPCRA),[36] became Title III of the Superfund Amendments and Reauthorization Act of 1986 (SARA). EPCRA directly responded to Bhopal and Institute with emergency planning, emergency release reporting, and community right-to-know.

Emergency Planning (§§ 301–303). EPCRA requires the governor of each state to create a State Emergency Response Commission (SERC), and the SERC then divides the state into regions and appoints members to serve on the Local Emergency Planning Commissions (LEPCs). EPCRA requires an owner or operator of a facility that uses or stores extremely hazardous substances at or above a stated "threshold planning quantity (TPQ)" to identify themselves and submit detailed emergency planning information to SERCs and LEPCs, which must in turn respond to requests for information from the public.

---

35.   For a helpful guide to the early emissions program, *see* David P. Novello & Robert J. Martineau, Jr., *Better Earlier than Later: EPA's Air Toxics "Early Reduction" Program*, 24 Envt. Rep. (BNA) 401 (July 2, 1993).

36.   42 U.S.C. §§ 11001 *et seq.*

Emergency Release (§ 304). EPCRA requires facilities to report immediately to the LEPC or SERC a release that is above the reportable quantity (RQ, *not* TPQ). The notice must include the chemical name or identity of the substance released, whether the substance is extremely hazardous, the quantity of the release, the medium to which the release occurred, known and anticipated health risks from the substance, precautions to take because of the release, and the numbers and names of individuals to contact for further information.[37] A follow-up emergency notice containing an update on the information provided in the original notice and any procedures taken to contain or ameliorate the effects of the release must be filed as soon as practical after the release.[38]

Community Right-To-Know (§§ 311–313). For our purposes, the right-to-know provisions are of greatest interest because, in addition to requiring emergency preparedness, EPCRA uses information as a tool to promote environmental quality improvement. EPCRA seeks to empower local communities by telling them what chemicals are being stored and released by neighboring industries. Any facility that produces, uses, or stores a "hazardous chemical" above the required threshold must also comply with the reporting requirements of EPCRA. The term "hazardous chemical" is defined by reference to OSHA regulations,[39] and facilities that have hazardous chemicals on their premises must file a Material Safety Data Sheet (MSDS). OSHA regulations require that an MSDS contain the following information:

- identity of the hazardous chemical;
- its physical and chemical characteristics;
- physical hazards;
- health hazards, including symptoms of exposure;
- routes of entry into the body;
- applicable exposure limits;
- carcinogenicity (if any);
- precautions for use and handling;
- control measures;
- emergency and first aid procedures; and
- name, address, and phone number of preparor of MSDS.[40]

The MSDS in effect becomes the basis for reporting under EPCRA, and EPCRA requires two kinds of non-emergency reporting. First, it requires

---

37.   *See* 40 C.F.R. § 355.40(a) (2008).

38.   *See* 40 C.F.R. § 355.40(b) (2008).

39.   *See* 29 C.F.R. § 1910.1200(c) (1999). A "physical hazard" is defined as any chemical "for which there is scientifically valid evidence that it is a combustible liquid, a compressed gas, explosive, flammable, an organic peroxide, an oxidizer, pyrophoric, unstable (reactive) or water reactive." "Health hazard" is defined as "a chemical for which there is statistically significant evidence based on at least one study conducted in accordance with established scientific principles that acute or chronic health effects may occur in exposed employees." *Id.*

40.   29 C.F.R. § 1910.1200(g)(2)(i)–(xii) (1999).

reporting of hazardous chemicals that *are present at a facility* at any one time in the amount of 10,000 pounds or more, less for the most hazardous substances. A facility must at least submit a list of the hazardous substances that require an MSDS, and provide the MSDS itself to the LEPC, SERC, and local fire department. The annual "Tier I Form" includes an estimate of the maximum amount of hazardous chemicals present at the facility during the previous year, the average amount of hazardous chemicals present during the previous year, and the present approximate placement of the hazardous chemicals at the facility. Tier I information is to be submitted by the owner of the facility to the designated community planning committee, the SERC, and the local fire department.[41] The "Tier II Form," which is voluntary, contains the same information as a Tier I Form but in more detail.

Second, section 313 of EPCRA requires facilities to inform the public of *all releases* of hazardous chemicals that cumulatively exceed threshold quantities. Covered releases include accidents and also routine releases into streams and water bodies, fugitive or non-point air emissions, stack or point emissions, and other transfers of waste to public sewers or treatment facilities. Releases are reported to EPA annually on "Form R," the Toxic Chemical Release Form.[42] Form R includes the name, location, and the type of business of the facility; whether the toxic chemical at the facility is manufactured, processed, or otherwise used; the *estimate* of the type of releases that occurred from the facility in the previous year; the methods of disposal for each waste stream and the treatment efficiency for each waste stream; and the annual quantity of toxic chemicals that enter the environment each year.[43] EPA assembles the information acquired from Form R into a database called the Toxic Release Inventory (TRI). TRI data are now available on the Web in both tabular and geographic forms.[44]

The TRI provision is quite different from the emergency provisions of EPCRA, and unlike environmental statutes that regulate the disposal of chemicals and wastes at certain point sources, the right-to-know provisions of EPCRA attempt to use information to limit production and disposal of toxic chemicals and hazardous waste. One commentator has observed:

> Both utilitarian and entitlement rationales have been advanced to support these provisions. The Hazard Communication Standard [the OSHA regulation which requires MSDSs,] emphasizes utilitarian reasons: additional information encourages workers to take available precautionary measures and to develop new ones, and also assists them in seeking compensation for toxic injuries through the tort system. EPCRA's main utilitarian aim is local emergency planning. Its data also can be used to establish and revise laws and regulations, to influence lawmakers and regula-

41.   42 U.S.C. § 11022(a)(1)(A)–(C).

42.   42 U.S.C. § 11023(a).

43.   42 U.S.C. § 11023(g)(1)(A)–(C).

44.   These data can be accessed at http://www.epa.gov/tri/tridata/current_data/index.html.

tors, and to negotiate or litigate with emitters. The predominant rhetoric of EPCRA, however, is not utilitarian but, as its name suggests, "a fundamental right to know about what chemicals, toxic chemicals, are being released into [the American people's] environment hour after hour, day after day, year after year."

What the public is to do with the information to which it has a right is less clear. The knowledge of the presence of hazardous substances in the community seldom brings with it the ability to do anything about them. Supporters of EPCRA suggested that it provides communities with "the quantitative information necessary to use this data effectively" and would "allow communities to gauge the potential long-term chronic health effects of toxic chemical releases." At least in theory, workers can take precautions, bargain with their employers for safety, suggest safer procedures, refuse certain work, or even change jobs. Citizens generally, on the other hand, are in a much poorer position to reduce risk themselves. Moreover, it is questionable whether consumers or workers are in a position to make intelligent use of the information. Nevertheless, by providing toxicity and exposure information paralleling quantitative risk assessment, the data requirements of the right-to-know laws encourage individuals to undertake their own, informal risk assessments.

Once the public appetite for risk information is whetted by a sense of entitlement to it, and once data gaps are publicly identified, it is hard to see how government and industry can avoid additional demands for more specific information regarding the chemicals. If, as some advocate, risk assessments are routinely to be made available to the public, and if these risk assessments appropriately disclose their data gaps and assumptions, the public would be acutely aware of just how little is known about the chemicals to which it is exposed. Having opened the door to public scrutiny and comment on the risks associated with chemicals, the government will be called upon, with or without the unreasonable risk standard, to develop large amounts of the kind of information used in quantitative risk assessment. And when that happens, the gap between existing and desired information will widen rather than close.

John S. Applegate, *The Perils of Unreasonable Risk: Information, Regulatory Policy, and Toxic Substances Control*, 91 Colum. L. Rev. 261, 295–98 (1991).

The political impact of the TRI data was felt immediately upon the release of the very first TRI report in 1989. Citizens were shocked by the amounts of waste reported. Even the EPA stated that the volume of releases was "far higher than we thought was going to occur."[45] Not only did this

---

45. Sidney M. Wolf, *Fear and Loathing About the Public Right to Know: The Surprising Success of the Emergency Planning and Community Right-to-Know Act*, 11 J. Land Use & Envtl. L. 217, 282 (1996).

influence the ongoing consideration of the 1990 Amendments to the Clean Air Act, but it also embarrassed many businesses who did not want the reputation of a toxic polluter. Following the lead of Monsanto, one of the largest emitters,[46] many businesses promised to reduce releases.

NOTES AND QUESTIONS

1.   If knowledge is power, then EPCRA is intended to empower states and municipalities by providing them with information on the identities, amounts, and characteristics of hazardous substances at EPCRA-covered facilities. EPCRA also empowers citizens by requiring facilities to publish the amounts and types of releases from them. In what ways can states and municipalities exercise this power? How can they use EPCRA-generated data? How can citizens use TRI data?

2.   The TRI database contains only the name of the substance, the media to which the substance was released, the location of the release, and the amount of the substance released. This is fairly raw data. Does this limit its utility for states and municipalities? For citizens? How?

3.   EPA does not have the resources to monitor businesses regularly to ensure that the information businesses report are accurate,[47] and EPCRA does not require direct monitoring of releases. Instead, it permits a facility to use "reasonable estimates" when determining the amounts released from the facility.[48] Is this a concern, and if so, why? How does the use of estimates affect the uses that states, municipalities, and citizens make of EPCRA and TRI data? Why not require direct monitoring?

4.   Are information statutes a substitute for, or improvement upon, traditional "command and control" regulation? Should we decrease reliance on centralized agencies and increase reliance on the private market to control pollution through greater reliance on information as a legal tool? *See* Katherine Renshaw, Student Note, *Sounding Alarms: Does Environmental Regulation Help or Hinder Environmentalism?*, N.Y.U.ENVTL. L. J. 654 (2006) (outlining the strengths and weaknesses of information regulation systems).

2.   CALIFORNIA PROPOSITION 65

In 1986, the voters of California adopted Proposition 65, the Safe Drinking Water and Toxic Enforcement Act of 1986. It prohibits the discharge into drinking water or any exposure of individuals to chemicals "known to the state to cause cancer or reproductive toxicity." Importantly, it also permits exemptions for discharges or exposures that are below a "significant" level.

Safe Drinking Water and Toxic Enforcement Act of 1986

Cal. Health & Safety Code §§ 25249.5–25249.13

---

46.   David J. Abell, Comment, *Emergency Planning and Community Right to Know: The Toxics Release Inventory*, 47 SMU L. REV. 581, 588 (1994).

47.   *See* Eric M. Falkenberry, *The Emergency Planning and Community Right–To–Know Act: A Tool for Toxic Release Reduction in the 90s*, 3 BUFF. ENVTL.L.J. 1, 30–31 (1995).

48.   42 U.S.C. § 11023(g)(2).

25249.5. *Prohibition on Contaminating Drinking Water with Chemicals Known to Cause Cancer or Reproductive Toxicity.*

No person in the course of doing business shall knowingly discharge or release a chemical known to the state to cause cancer or reproductive toxicity into water or onto or into land where such chemical passes or probably will pass into any source of drinking water, notwithstanding any other provision or authorization of law except as provided in Section 25249.9.

25249.6. *Required Warning Before Exposure to Chemicals Known to Cause Cancer or Reproductive Toxicity.*

No person in the course of doing business shall knowingly and intentionally expose any individual to a chemical known to the state to cause cancer or reproductive toxicity without first giving clear and reasonable warning to such individual, except as provided in Section 25249.10.

25249.7. *Enforcement.*

(a) Any person that violates or threatens to violate Section 25249.5 or 25249.6 may be enjoined in any court of competent jurisdiction.

(b) (1) Any person who has violated Section 25249.5 or 25249.6 shall be liable for a civil penalty not to exceed two thousand five hundred dollars ($2500) per day for each violation in addition to any other penalty established by law. * * *

[Actions may be brought by the state attorney general, district attorneys, certain other public officials, and "any person in the public interest" if the individual has given prior notice to a public official and the alleged violator and no public official has "commenced and is diligently prosecuting an action against the violation."]

* * *

25249.8. *List of Chemicals Known to Cause Cancer or Reproductive Toxicity.*

(a) On or before March 1, 1987, the Governor shall cause to be published a list of those chemicals known to the state to cause cancer or reproductive toxicity within the meaning of this chapter, and he shall cause such list to be revised and republished in light of additional knowledge at least once per year thereafter. Such list shall include at a minimum those substances identified by reference in Labor Code Section 6382(b)(1) and those substances identified additionally by reference in Labor Code Section 6382(d).

(b) A chemical is known to the state to cause cancer or reproductive toxicity within the meaning of this chapter if in the opinion of the state's qualified experts it has been clearly shown through scientifically valid testing according to generally accepted principles to cause cancer or reproductive toxicity, or if a body considered to be authoritative by such experts has formally identified it as causing cancer or reproductive toxicity, or if an agency of the state or federal government has formally required it to be labeled or identified as causing cancer or reproductive toxicity.

* * *

25249.9. *Exemptions from Discharge Prohibition.** * *

(b) Section 25249.5 shall not apply to any discharge or release that meets both of the following criteria:

(1) The discharge or release will not cause any significant amount of the discharged or released chemical to enter any source of drinking water.

(2) The discharge or release is in conformity with all other laws and with every applicable regulation, permit, requirement, and order. In any action brought to enforce Section 25249.5, the burden of showing that a discharge or release meets the criteria of this subdivision shall be on the defendant.

25249.10. *Exemptions from Warning Requirement.*

Section 25249.6 shall not apply to any of the following:* * *

(c) An exposure for which the person responsible can show that the exposure poses no significant risk assuming lifetime exposure at the level in question for substances known to the state to cause cancer, and that the exposure will have no observable effect assuming exposure atone thousand (1,000) times the level in question for substances known to the state to cause reproductive toxicity, based on evidence and standards of comparable scientific validity to the evidence and standards which form the scientific basis for the listing of such chemical pursuant to subdivision (a) of Section 25249.8. In any action brought to enforce Section 25249.6, the burden of showing that an exposure meets the criteria of this subdivision shall be on the defendant.

25249.11. *Definitions.*

For purposes of this chapter:* * *

(c) "Significant amount" means any detectable amount except an amount which would meet the exemption test in subdivision (c) of Section 25249.10 if an individual were exposed to such an amount in drinking water.

* * *

(f) "Warning" within the meaning of Section 25249.6 need not be provided separately to each exposed individual and may be provided by general methods such as labels on consumer products, inclusion of notices in mailings to water customers, posting of notices, placing notices in public news media, and the like, provided that the warning accomplished is clear and reasonable. * * *[Note: The required warning is the statutory language: the contents or discharge is "known to the state of California to cause cancer."]

* * *

NOTES AND QUESTIONS

1. *The statutory text.* How does Proposition 65 work—what does it prohibit, and what does it permit? How are the discharge and notification requirements different and how are they related to each other? What is the

role of exemptions in the overall statutory structure?

2.   Who are the designated decisionmakers under Proposition 65? What criteria are given for their decisions?

3.   How is compliance with Proposition 65 enforced? What are the strengths and weaknesses of these mechanisms?

David Roe
Toxic Chemical Control Policy: Three Unabsorbed Facts
32 Envtl. L. Rep. (Envtl. L. Inst.) 10232 (2002)

This Dialogue offers three quantitative facts, drawn from long-term experience in toxic chemical control in the United States. Each one documents failure, on a large scale, of conventional federal policy to protect human health against toxic chemical hazards in the environment. Each also disproves some of the core assumptions of that policy. Individually and together, these three facts pose a deep challenge to the policymaking community, not only for toxic chemical control but for environmental regulation broadly.

At the risk of oversimplifying in advance of detailed discussion, the three facts lead to the following conclusions:

- Command-and-control restrictions on chemicals known to be specific health hazards and known to be emitted into ambient air fail to capture five-sixths of the easy potential reductions—those already known to the emitting facilities in question, and already technically, economically, and politically feasible from the facilities' own perspective.

- Federal laws dependent for their success on standard setting fail to generate one-tenth, or even one-hundredth, of the standards that are feasible within current scientific and political constraints, and that are necessary to carry out the laws' purposes.

- Even perfect success in the application and enforcement of all federal chemical control regimes combined, including successful generation and enforcement of 100% of all standards authorized under those regimes, would protect against less than one-tenth of the potentially hazardous chemicals now in U.S. commerce.

For a policy assessment of U.S. chemical regulation, the facts behind these conclusions would seem to be primary data. They suggest that successes in chemical control—and there have been numerous, highly creditable successes—have come more by luck than by design and cannot be assumed to be representative of success overall.

* * *

The Effect of Disclosure on Innovation and Voluntary Pollution Reduction

   Fact: An 85% Drop in Targeted Air Toxic Emissions

As reported to the toxic release inventory (TRI) under federal law, air emissions of known carcinogens and reproductive toxins from all TRI facilities have been reduced in quantity by approximately 85% in the state of California during the 10-year period of 1988 to 1997. * * * [T]he results for the rest of the country [are] an approximate 50% reduction in emissions of the same chemicals, in the same time period, from the same category of sources, *i.e.,* all facilities required to report.

* * *

POLICY IMPLICATIONS

• *Conventional Regulation of Toxic Chemicals Achieves Only a Small Fraction of Readily Available, Fully Acceptable, Low–Cost Reductions.* All the reductions [discussed here] are reductions below the supposedly minimum practicable levels achieved as of 1988 by direct regulatory controls on hazardous air pollutants, under both federal and California state law.

In 1988, the hazardous air pollutant section of CAA § 112 was fully in effect, as were corresponding provisions in the California CAA, and the prevailing assumption was that emissions of at least top-priority hazardous air pollutants—such as known carcinogens—were at or near their minimum practical levels. In other words, it was assumed that major reductions below those levels would not be possible without major economic disruption, or else major technical breakthroughs that would make reductions much cheaper to achieve. However, * * * 85% of those supposedly minimum quantities of air emissions (as of 1988) could be readily eliminated in a relatively short time period. No change in conventional federal or state air law in the period 1988 to 1997 explains a change of such magnitude and scope, covering more than 250 chemicals collectively.

In hindsight, it is obvious that the measures used to achieve those extra reductions were readily available. They were also usable by a very large range of polluting facilities with no guidance from mandates, government-sponsored research, or government technical assistance programs. The failure of best available control technology (BACT) regulations to capture such measures, representing so large an improvement on conventional norms, is astonishing in retrospect.

• *Pollution–Reducing Improvements Can Occur on a Large Scale, Quickly, and Without Significant Controversy or Resistance in the Presence of a Disclosure Incentive.* The improvements documented [here] have come without any significant complaint or resistance from the regulated community. Experience with political resistance to conventional regulation for hazardous air pollutants is strikingly different, and the contrast offers an important lesson for policymakers.

• *Technical Feasibility Need Not Be a Point of Contention.* There has been essentially no debate or complaint, at any time or from any quarter, about whether the measures used to accomplish the results * * * were or would be technically feasible. Undoubtedly this is because the measures were not mandatory. In every case, every participant had the option of simply making disclosures rather than implementing reductions. This meant that lack of feasibility was not a useful argument in political terms. When it is politically useful, by contrast, the lack of feasibility argument looms large.

• *Cost Need Not Be a Point of Contention.* Equally, there has been essentially no complaint about the cost of the large-scale reductions * * *. In fact, there is not even a serious estimate of what the costs have been from the affected industrial community itself. This is true even in California, where the requirements of Proposition 65 were highly controversial when they were passed and where they have been under consistent political attack from various industrial quarters ever since. Certainly California's economy in the 1988 to 1997 time period shows no discernable injury compared to the rest of the country due to deeper reductions in reported toxic air emissions.

It is unclear whether the absence of cost complaint occurred because costs were in fact small, or because industry would have been reluctant to disclose costs even if those costs were substantial. In either case, the political consequence is the same: cost debate has been nonexistent. In a disclosure-based system, of course, reduction costs are incurred voluntarily rather than mandatorily, with the alternative of simply reporting emissions at the unimproved level always available to every participant. In an important sense, all costs incurred to improve performance in this context are, by definition, less than the costs of reporting high emissions, in the judgment of each participating entity itself. If exactly the same level of improvement had been mandated, the issue of cost might not be so inconspicuous—even assuming exactly the same actual costs.

* * *

The Effect of Incentives on the Regulatory Process

Fact: Hundreds of Risk–Based Standards Set in Record Time

California state regulators succeeded in determining and publishing quantitative, risk-based standards for 282 individual chemicals in less than five years, without any legal mandate but with strong incentives for the regulated community to cooperate. Although those standards have been effectively governing private industry behavior throughout the giant California economy (one-sixth of the U.S. economy) and beyond for most of a decade, not one of the standards has yet been challenged by any affected entity, in any court, on any ground.

Context

California's Proposition 65 began to be enforceable in February 1988. Proposition 65 requires businesses that intentionally expose individuals to chemicals with known toxic properties to provide warning to those individuals. However, the law also provides for a risk-based exemption, i.e., that if the business responsible for the exposure can show that the level of exposure in question is below a scientifically based, statutorily defined threshold of risk, then no warning is required and no legal obligation attaches. State regulators are authorized, but not mandated, to enact regulations determining the relevant threshold level in quantitative terms on a chemical-by-chemical basis.

Unlike federal statutes that rely on risk-based, chemical-specific standards, Proposition 65 as a practical matter puts the onus on private industry, rather than government, to resolve scientific and technical uncertainties in the standard-setting process. It does so by putting the burden of proof on the private-industry defendant in any potential enforcement action to establish the elements of the "no significant risk" defense. In practice, this means that an affected industry must have all the necessary elements of risk assessment science already in hand, for the particular chemical and exposure situation in question, or else forfeit any defense based on lack of risk. Scientific uncertainty results in legal uncertainty for private industry.

Presumably as a result of this unusual incentive, affected private industries and industry associations cooperated closely with California regulators and supported the prompt issuance of so-called safe harbor numbers (SHNs) for the chemicals of significant concern to each industry. A list of 282 SHNs, officially published in January 1994, was in fact largely complete, in circulation, and guiding behavior by early 1992. Without any legal challenge whatsoever, regulators applied standardized rather than case-by-case risk assessment methodologies to generate these numbers. To set standards for 140 carcinogens, they used an "expedited" procedure that frankly "differs from [the] usual practice...."

The total budget in California government for this effort during the relevant period, approximately fiscal year 1989 through fiscal year 1992, was on the order of $5 million per year. The comparable expenditure by the U.S. Environmental Protection Agency (EPA) for chemical risk assessment activities during the same period was approximately $81 million per year. Yet EPA's regulatory output of chemical-specific, risk-based standards during that period was at least an order of magnitude smaller than California's, and on average during any comparable period of the modern regulatory era was closer to two orders of magnitude smaller, i.e., one-hundredth of California's.

Data Quality

One might speculate that California regulators received unusual leadership and support from the highest levels of government to implement "Proposition 65," allowing them to move much more quickly than usual. However, most of this period of regulatory productivity occurred during [periods of gubernatorial hostility or agency reorganization. Moreover, California regulation is subject to the same or greater level of potential judicial review as federal regulation.]

* * *

Finally, it is possible that California regulators had access to much greater scientific resources than, for example, their counterparts at EPA.

However, most of the scientific research and analysis on which the California regulators relied came directly from EPA file cabinets.

Policy Implications

• *Science–Based Regulatory Determinations Can Be Made Much Faster Than Commonly Assumed, Within Existing Scientific and Budgetary Constraints.* The scientific issues involved in setting SHNs under Proposition 65 are virtually identical to the issues underlying risk-based standards under the pre-1990 hazardous air pollutant section of CAA § 112 (which produced 7 standards in 20 years), and very similar to the issues involved in setting standards under other federal statutes. California regulators had no unique or unusual scientific expertise at their disposal during the 1988 to 1992 or 1988 to 1994 period, yet achieved "100 years of progress [by federal standards] in the areas of hazard identification, risk assessment, and exposure assessment" within the law's first five years. In other words, "the science is too difficult" is not a valid excuse. Neither is budgetary constraint. California budget expenditures for chemical risk assessment were a small fraction of EPA's during the relevant period.

• *The Regulated Community Is Capable of a High Degree of Cooperation With and Acceptance of Risk–Based Regulatory Determinations.* The regulated community in California (including nearly every industry in the U.S. economy) was as politically strong and as well funded in California as elsewhere, and saw its interests as highly threatened by Proposition 65's requirements. The change in the incentives felt by the regulated community appears to be the only plausible explanation for the change in regulatory productivity. Yet it did not challenge a single SHN and cooperated actively in the standard-setting process.

• *Regulatory Science Need Not Be Ironclad or Conventional in Order to Avoid Industry Challenge.* California's experimental "expedited" risk-assessment procedure had never been legally tested and would almost certainly have been vulnerable to legal challenge in an analogous federal context. Yet it was used in California to determine 140 quantitative safe harbor numbers in less than one year. Early litigation threats from industry, delivered behind closed doors to the state's top regulatory official for Proposition 65 matters, were ignored and were never acted on.

• *Lawmakers Could Greatly Improve Regulatory Productivity by Changing the Incentive Structure of Relevant Statutes.* Proposition 65 illustrates only one of many possible approaches. Of course, legislative action depends on two insights, neither of which is likely to be welcomed by legislators: (1) that their predecessors' statutory design was inherently self-defeating; and (2) that they themselves bear primary responsibility for current regulatory failures in standard setting because the primary causes are under their own control and not the control of regulatory officials.

• *Recognizing Whose Interests Are Jeopardized by Inaction Is a Key Factor in Identifying Regulatory Incentives.* The fact that the regulated community's interests would be jeopardized if SHNs were not determined appears to have been of decisive importance in producing the California results. From the perspective offered by this experience, it is easy to see that the incentives at work under comparable laws at the federal level are exactly the reverse: federal regulatory inaction on standard setting does not jeopardize any interest of, or create any legal vulnerability for, any member of the regulated community. Instead, the only interests jeopardized by federal inaction are those of the public (in being effectively protected against chemical risk), and perhaps of the regulators to the extent they share the public's goals.

NOTES AND QUESTIONS

1. David Roe was one of the authors of Proposition 65, and he offers a highly optimistic account of the initiative's success. Yet it does not appear that his account is unfair, either. Carl Cranor, *Information Generation and Use Under Proposition 65: Model Provisions for Other Postmarket Laws?*, 83 Ind. L.J. 609 (2008).[49] What are the factors to which Roe attributes this success? What role does the ever-present "option to disclose" have?

2. *Content of reporting.* Roe insists that the adopted standards were not toothless (giving the example of lead). At the same time, one might suspect that the standards are set at levels that industry found manageable, even if they were not comfortable. Is this necessarily a bad thing? *See* Stephen G. Breyer, Breaking the Vicious Circle: Toward Effective Risk Regulation 11 (1993) (criticizing the tendency to expend huge sums to achieve the "last 10%" of an environmental problem). Can you point ot any toxics statutes that heed Breyer's advice?

Does this suggest a de facto feasibility or BAT standard in Proposition 65? Does its success support the expanded use of such standards?

3. Note the huge difference in resources invested in making risk determinations and in regulatory productivity between California and U.S. EPA. What role should these considerations play in choosing a regulatory system?

4. Roe states that the process for setting exemption levels differed from the usual practice, in that it was highly expedited. Professor Cranor, who has been directly involved in the process, describes it as "a social division of responsibility for a full risk assessment." Cranor, *supra,* at 616–617. Why do you think it worked in California, and does not seem to have worked for federal regulation?

5. Massachusetts took the idea behind Proposition 65 in a different direction. The Massachusetts Toxics Use Reduction Act (TURA), Mass. Gen. Laws ch.21I (2004 & Supp. 2006), requires the creation of actual reduction

---

49. *See also* Bradley C. Karkkainen, *Bottlenecks and Baselines: Tackling Information Deficits in Environmental Regulation*, 86 Tex. L. Rev. 1409, 1427–1432 (2008); Clifford Rechtschaffen & Patrick Williams, *The Continued Success of Proposition 65 in Reducing Toxic Exposures*, 35 Envtl. L. Rep. (Envtl. L. Inst.) 10850 (2005); Renshaw, *supra*, at 671–673 (citing proponents and opponents). For a spirited colloquy on the success of Proposition 65, *compare* Carol Rene Brophy, *Proposition 65 at 20 Years*, 38(3) ABA Trends 4 (Jan./Feb. 2007) (arguing that it has spawned many frivolous lawsuits), *with* Roger Lane Carrick, *California's Proposition 65—A Blunt But Powerful Tool*, 38(5) ABA Trends 4 (May/June 2007) (responding that it has effected many positive changes).

and substitution *plans*, which are not required to be actually implemented, nor are they necessarily available to the public. Their purpose is to encourage internally motivated action by firms (for example, the investment in developing the plan may encourage implementation), rather than to generate public pressure.[50]

6. *The Food Quality Protection Act of 1996,* 21 U.S.C. § 346a, which we saw in Section A of this chapter, included the following provision:

(o) *Consumer right to know*

Not later than 2 years after August 3, 1996, and annually thereafter, the Administrator shall, in consultation with the Secretary of Agriculture and the Secretary of Health and Human Services, publish in a format understandable to a lay person, and distribute to large retail grocers for public display (in a manner determined by the grocer), the following information, at a minimum:

(1) A discussion of the risks and benefits of pesticide chemical residues in or on food purchased by consumers.

(2) A listing of actions taken under subparagraph (B) of subsection (b)(2) of this section that may result in pesticide chemical residues in or on food that present a yearly or lifetime risk above the risk allowed under subparagraph (A) of such subsection, and the food on which the pesticide chemicals producing the residues are used.

(3) Recommendations to consumers for reducing dietary exposure to pesticide chemical residues in a manner consistent with maintaining a healthy diet, including a list of food that may reasonably substitute for food listed under paragraph (2).

Nothing in this subsection shall prevent retail grocers from providing additional information.

How does this provision respond to criticisms of the TRI and Proposition 65? What are the drawbacks of the FQPA approach? Which do you recommend?

E. The Cost of Regulating

The final approach to toxics regulation that we consider in this chapter is cost as the critical limiting factor on regulatory controls that are otherwise determined by hazard or risk. The exact role of cost varies according to the statute, but the following statutes and judicial interpretations represent the most recent thinking on regulatory standards. It is plain

---

50. *See* Cary Coglianese & David Lazer, *Management–Based Regulation: Prescribing Private Management to Achieve Public Goals,* 37 Law & Soc'y Rev. 691, 700 (2003) (describing TURA as a management-based regulation that encourages firms to make gains in the prevention of pollution by requiring them to develop systems for reducing the use and emissions of toxins); Bradley C. Karkkainen, *Information as Environmental Regulation: TRI and Performance Benchmarking, Precursor to a New Paradigm?,* 89 Geo. L.J. 257, 354–56 (2001) (describing the structured self-monitoring program as an ambitious plan that encourages cost-effective innovation, but at the expense of public transparency and participation).

that the cost of regulation—and, we might infer, the presumption that it is a *high* cost—has become a dominant concern.

1. The Safe Drinking Water Act

The Safe Drinking Water Act (SDWA) was originally enacted in 1974, in the midst of the intense period of environmental lawmaking in the early 1970s. It required EPA to promulgate two kinds of standards: national primary drinking water regulations, which are legally binding standards addressed to health effects, and national secondary drinking water regulations, which are not enforceable by the federal government and are addressed to welfare effects such as the appearance and odor of water.[51] The primary regulations were to be in the form of performance standards, though they could instead require the adoption of particular treatment standards if measurement of a particular contaminant was too difficult. The primary standards (which have attracted the lion's share of EPA's attention) are each divided into two parts—recommended maximum contaminant levels goals (MCLGs) and maximum contaminant levels (MCLs)—a feature that has remained central to the statutory structure. Since most Americans obtain their drinking water from groundwater, which is protected only indirectly by the Clean Water Act, the 1974 SDWA also provided for regulation of underground injection wells (a method of waste disposal) and for a program of protection of drinking water aquifers. The states were to be the main enforcers of the program, pursuant to federal standards.

EPA's progress in issuing drinking water regulations was extremely slow, not unlike its pre-1990 Clean Air Act performance. By 1986, it had regulated about twenty of over two hundred contaminants of concern, so Congress amended the SDWA to impose an aggressive schedule of rulemakings, to mandate certain treatment techniques, and to address specific issues, such as a ban on lead-containing materials in plumbing. Progress nevertheless remained slow and the 1996 amendments to the SDWA sought to loosen what had become the stranglehold of the 1986 schedule, so that EPA could spend more time developing a scientific basis for its regulations and could do a better job of setting priorities based on risk. The 1996 amendments coincided with a major, but ultimately unsuccessful, push in the 104th Congress to require additional risk, cost, and benefit analyses before promulgating any environmental regulation. Consequently, the current statute includes a detailed section on risk assessment and cost analysis. *See* 42 U.S.C. § 300g–1(b)(3).[52]

The following case discusses the relationship between MCLGs and MCLs, between the pre- and post-1996 Act, and between both and the science of toxic pollutants.

---

51. There is a direct analogy, of course, to the primary and secondary national ambient air quality standards under the Clean Air Act, 42 U.S.C. § 7409(b), which are based on health and welfare effects, respectively.

52. For a thorough history of the Safe Drinking Water Act through the 1996 amendments, *see* William E. Cox, *Evolution of the Safe Drinking Water Act: A Search for Effective Quality Assurance Strategies and Workable Concepts of Federalism*, 21 Wm. & Mary Envtl. L. & Pol'y Rev. 69 (1997), on which the foregoing account is primarily based.

City of Waukesha v. EPA
320 F.3d 228 (D.C. Cir. 2003)

■ Per Curiam:

The petitioners—the City of Waukesha and its water utility customer Bruce Zivney, trade associations Nuclear Energy Institute and National Mining Association, and advocacy group Radiation, Science & Health ("RSH")—seekreview of regulations promulgated by the Environmental Protection Agency ("EPA") pursuant to the Safe Drinking Water Act of 1970 ("SDWA" or "Act"). The challenged regulations establish standards governing radionuclide levels in public water systems. Specifically, they set the maximum contaminant level goal ("MCLG") and the maximum contaminant level ("MCL") for radium-226 and radium-228, naturally occurring uranium, and various beta/photon emitters. Petitioners contend the regulations violate the SDWA * * * because in setting the radionuclides standards EPA did not (1) properly conduct required cost-benefit analyses; [or] (2) use the "best available science" to determine the appropriate MCLGs and MCLs * * *. We conclude that * * * EPA complied with the requirements of the SDWA * * *.

I. BACKGROUND

The SDWA generally applies to "each public water system in each State," 42 U.S.C. § 300g, and authorizes EPA to set standards for drinking water contaminants therein, 42 U.S.C. § 300g–1(b). For a given contaminant the Act directs that EPA first establish an MCLG which is "the level at which no known or anticipated adverse effects on the health of persons occur and which allows an adequate margin of safety." § 300g–1(b)(4)(A). EPA is then to set an MCL "as close to the [MCLG] as is feasible." § 300g–1(b)(4)(B).

* * *

III. THE APPLICABILITY OF THE COST–BENEFIT REQUIREMENTS TO THE RADIUM AND BETA/PHOTON MCLs

Petitioners attack EPA's final radium and beta/photon MCLs on the ground that § 1412(b)(3)(C)(i) of the SDWA, 42 U.S.C. § 300g–1(b)(3)(C)(i), allegedly required EPA to conduct a cost-benefit analysis for each MCL, which EPA failed to do. EPA responds that no cost-benefit analysis was required for these MCLs because the SDWA exempts pre-1986 MCLs from its cost-benefit requirements, and the agency left the pre-existing MCLs for radium and beta/photon emitters unchanged. Unless "Congress has directly spoken to the precise question at issue," we must uphold the agency's interpretation of the SDWA as long as it is "based on a permissible construction of the statute." *Chevron.*

In 1996, Congress amended § 1412 of the SDWA. As amended, § 1412(b)(3)(C)(i) provides that, "[w]hen proposing any national primary drinking water regulation that includes a maximum contaminant level," EPA must publish and seek public comment on an analysis of the health risk reduction benefits and costs associated with the proposed MCL. EPA is to use that analysis "for the purposes of paragraph [](4)," subparagraph (C) of which states:

> At the time the Administrator proposes a national primary drinking water regulation under this paragraph, the Administrator shall publish a determination as to whether the benefits of the maximum contaminant level justify, or do not justify, the costs based on the analysis conducted under paragraph (3)(C).

§ 300g–1(b)(4)(C). However, amended § 1412(a)(1) also includes a grandfather clause:

> Effective on June 19, 1986, each national interim or revised primary drinking water regulation promulgated under this section before June 19, 1986, shall be deemed to be a national primary drinking water regulation under subsection (b) of this section. *No such regulation shall be required to comply with the standards set forth in subsection (b)(4) of this section unless such regulation is amended to establish a different maximum contaminant level after June 19, 1986.*

§ 300g–1(a)(1) (emphasis added).

EPA argues that § 1412(a)(1) exempts the radium and beta/photon MCLs from the cost-benefit determination required by § 1412(b)(4)(C), because they do not establish different contaminant levels from those first promulgated in 1976. EPA further reasons that because the purpose of the cost-benefit analysis required by § 1412(b)(3)(C)(i) is to inform the cost-benefit determination required by § (b)(4)(C), and because that determination is not required for the preexisting MCLs, no cost-benefit analysis was required for those MCLs. In Part III.A we consider petitioners' attack on EPA's view that cost-benefit analyses are not required when the agency decides to retain pre-existing MCLs. In Part III.B we consider petitioners' claim that EPA did not in fact retain the pre-existing MCLs for radium and beta/photon radionuclides, but instead issued new standards. [The court found in EPA's favor on both points, based on a detailed analysis of the statutory language and deference to the agency's interpretation of ambiguous provisions.]

* * *

IV.   THE ADEQUACY OF THE COST–BENEFIT ANALYSES PERFORMED FOR THE URANIUM MCL

By contrast to the 2000 radium and beta/photon regulations, the uranium MCL issued in that year represented a "new" standard, as there was no pre-existing MCL for uranium. Section 1412(b)(3)(C)(i) therefore required EPA to prepare and publish a cost-benefit analysis, and it did so. Petitioners contend that EPA's analysis failed to satisfy the requirements of that section and the APA.

A.

Petitioners' first argument is that EPA failed to comply with § (b)(3)(C)(i) because it did not analyze the costs and benefits associated with compliance with the uranium MCL in contexts other than the SDWA. In particular, petitioners assert that EPA failed to evaluate the costs and benefits arising from compliance with the MCLs at hazardous waste sites governed by CERCLA. EPA counters that the SDWA does not require it to analyze such costs.

EPA again has the better of the argument. Section (b)(3)(C)(i)(III) requires EPA to analyze:

> Quantifiable and nonquantifiable costs for which there is a factual basis in the rulemaking record to conclude that such costs are likely to occur *solely as a result of compliance with the maximum contaminant level,* including monitoring, treatment, and other costs *and excluding costs resulting from compliance with other proposed or promulgated regulations.*

42 U.S.C. § 300g-1(b)(3)(C)(i)(III) (emphasis added). EPA reasonably reads the italicized words, particularly the phrase "excluding costs resulting from compliance with other ... regulations," as excluding costs associated with compliance with regulatory regimes other than the SDWA itself. As EPA argues, the purpose of the MCLs is to protect the public, as much as feasible, from the adverse health effects of drinking contaminated water. *See* § 300g-1(b)(4)(A), (B). That purpose would be undermined if the cost-benefit balance were skewed by consideration of the additional costs imposed by other uses of the MCLs, unrelated to protecting consumers of drinking water.

* * *

* * * [W]e reject petitioners' contention that EPA's cost-benefit analysis failed to analyze costs and benefits as required by § 1412(b)(3)(C)(i).

* * *

VI. *THE MERITS OF THE URANIUM MCLs*

Petitioners also challenge EPA's determination of both the MCLG at 0 µg/L and the MCL at 30 µg/L for uranium on the merits of the science used by EPA. They make three challenges to the MCLG and assert that EPA's reliance on an improper MCLG tainted its MCL determination, as did EPA's reliance on kidney toxicity data. Regarding the MCLG, petitioners contend that (1) "the best available peer-reviewed science," 42 U.S.C. § 300g-1(b)(3)(A)(i), does not support a 0 µg/L MCLG because the LNT [*i.e.*, linear non-threshold] model used by EPA is not supported by the science; [and] (2) under EPA's classification system for carcinogens, a 0 µg/L MCLG is inappropriate * * *. Finally, petitioners also argue that EPA's cost-benefit decision, which determined the final level for the MCL, was substantively flawed.

In setting the uranium standard, EPA first set the MCLG for uranium based on the risks of carcinogenicity. EPA reasoned that because natural uranium is a radionuclide, and all radionuclides emit ionizing radiation that can cause cancer, there was no threshold level of safety for uranium. EPA then concluded that the lowest feasible level for controlling the risks of cancer from natural uranium in drinking water was 20 µg/L. Next, EPA addressed the effects of uranium on the human kidney, deciding that the best available science showed that uranium did have toxic effects on the human kidney, and that the level of uranium in drinking water that could be expected to protect human health was 20 µg/L. EPA added that 30 µg/L would be expected to protect against the effects of kidney toxicity, but that any higher level might result in serious adverse effects on human kidneys. Finally, EPA relied on its cost-benefit analysis to conclude that at 30 µg/L essentially the same health benefits could be achieved at much lower cost compared to the 20 µg/L level. EPA therefore set the uranium MCL at 30 µg/L.

EPA relied on the LNT model in setting the MCLG for uranium at zero. According to petitioners, "there is no evidence in the record to support linearity and no evidence which detracts from the weight of the scientific evidence that supports the application of a non-linear model." There was evidence in the record, primarily provided by RSH, that radionuclides in general only cause harm above a certain threshold level. There were also specific critiques of the linearity model as applied to uranium. However, the bomb studies in the record provide ample support for the linearity model, and there is also evidence in the record that uranium may be a carcinogen without a threshold level of safety. EPA noted that there is clear evidence that uranium (as with all radionuclides in general) emits ionizing radiation, that ionizing radiation causes genetic defects, and that genetic defects may lead to cancer. Although this evidence is based on enriched uranium, that does not exclude the possibility that natural uranium may have the same impact. EPA noted that the impacts of natural uranium may be difficult to detect because of the small doses of radiation involved and the comparatively small changes in cancer risk that would result; moreover, the pathway for causation would be the same for both enriched and natural uranium.

The resolution of this contradictory data lies well within EPA's expertise. *Chlorine Chemistry Council*, [206 F.3d 1286 (D.C. Cir. 2000)], on which petitioners rely, is not to the contrary. In that case, the court concluded that EPA's reliance on the LNT model was inappropriate because EPA *itself* concluded that the chemical in question (chloroform) only caused harm above a threshold level. * * * In the instant case, by contrast, EPA maintains that the best available evidence still shows that uranium is a non-threshold carcinogen. Given the contradictory evidence in the record, there is no basis for the court to override EPA's decision for this is not a situation where "there is simply no rational relationship between the model chosen and the situation to which it is applied."

Petitioners' next contention is that EPA did not follow its own procedures for classifying carcinogens when it set the MCLG for uranium at zero. According to petitioners, EPA classifies substances as having an MCL of zero when the substance falls into one of three groups:

> Group A, human carcinogens based on strong evidence of carcinogenicity from drinking water ingestion or sufficient evidence from epidemiological studies; Group B–1, probable human carcinogen based on at least limited evidence of carcinogenicity based on epidemiological studies in humans; Group B–2, probable human

carcinogen based on sufficient evidence in animals and inadequate evidence or no data from epidemiological studies in humans.

EPA does not contest petitioners' characterization of its classification process, but denies that it misapplied it in this case.

Apparently EPA classifies all radionuclides as Group A carcinogens based on the fact that they emit ionizing radiation that can cause cancer. Again, this is a reasonable conclusion by EPA based on the evidence in the record. EPA is not relying on data from natural uranium, any effect of which EPA has concluded might be very difficult to detect through epidemiological or laboratory studies, but instead is relying on an extrapolation from other radionuclides and the laboratory and epidemiological data associated with those compounds. Although studies to date may not have detected any impacts of natural uranium on cancer rates when it is ingested in drinking water in humans, EPA could reasonably conclude that based on the known carcinogenic potential of similar substances, natural uranium should also be considered a Group A carcinogen.

* * *

Petitioners further maintain that EPA should be forced to treat radionuclides in the same manner that it treated asbestos, where EPA concluded that despite asbestos' status as a Group A or B chemical, it would not automatically be treated as a non-threshold carcinogen because the agency believed that the "additional evidence indicates that the overall evidence of carcinogenicity via ingestion is limited or inadequate." However, as EPA points out, asbestos is a completely different chemical from natural uranium. Given the evidence for similar radionuclides, EPA could reasonably conclude that the minimal direct evidence for natural uranium's carcinogenicity should be treated differently from the slightly more substantial direct evidence for asbestos.

* * *

Because EPA's MCLG is proper, petitioners' challenge to the MCL based on the MCLG fails. To the extent petitioners also challenge EPA's reliance on kidney toxicity data, data which it relied upon in setting the MCL at 30 μg/L, the thrust of petitioners' challenge is that EPA relied on studies that "showed risks so small that EPA could not determine whether exposure resulted in an adverse impact," that EPA admitted that human studies were uncertain as to the actual impacts on kidneys from uranium consumption, and that EPA's conclusions were primarily based on data from experiments on rats using uranyl nitrate, a compound of uranium, rather than natural uranium itself. However, in the face of uncertain laboratory and epidemiological data, it was reasonable for EPA to take the risk-averse approach of relying on the animal laboratory data to develop a lower standard.

Regarding petitioners' challenge to EPA's decision to set the final MCL at 30 μg/L based on its cost-benefit analysis, the court's review is limited to determining whether EPA's analysis and final cost-benefit decision is arbitrary and capricious. 42 U.S.C. § 300g–1(b)(6)(D). Petitioners contend that EPA "should have compared the cost per cancer case avoided":

When EPA selected from the acceptable uranium levels, EPA should have compared the cost per cancer case avoided for each proposed uranium MCL. EPA did not do that. Had the agency done so, it would have found that the incremental cost savings associated with raising the standard from 30 µg/L to 40 µg/L ($64.1 million) was even higher than the incremental cost savings that prompted EPA to raise the standard from 20 µg/L to 30µg/L ($45.2 million) while still achieving an acceptable cancer risk. Thus if EPA applied the same analysis to the cost differences between 30 µg/L and 40 µg/L, as it did to the costs between 20 µg/L to 30 µg/L, it would have concluded that an increase to 40 µg/L was appropriate.

The figures that petitioners cite in their brief are the aggregate amounts of money saved by relaxing the standards; at no point did petitioners discuss the increase in the number of cancer deaths or cases that would occur if the standards were relaxed. By definition, however, that increase must be considered in order to compare "the cost per cancer case avoided," as petitioners request. In other words, petitioners' contention is internally inconsistent. Furthermore, a review of EPA's cost-benefit analysis shows that the cost per cancer case avoided is lower, between 30 and 40 µg/L, compared to between 20 and 30 µg/L, contrary to petitioners' assertions. Most importantly, EPA concluded that kidney risks increased substantially above 30 µg/L, sharply increasing the benefits foregone by raising the standard above that point. EPA's decision therefore was not arbitrary and capricious.

* * *

NOTES AND QUESTIONS

1.   Under the statute, what is the process for promulgating an MCL? What triggers the process? What is the relationship between the MCL and MCLG? What are the applicable regulatory standards or targets of the two tiers? Why did Congress separate the MCLG and MCL?

2.   *The 1996 SDWA Amendments.* Before the SDWA was amended in 1996, section 1412(b) read as follows:

(4) Each maximum contaminant level goal established under this subsection shall be set at the level at which no known or anticipated adverse effects on health of persons occur and which allows an adequate margin of safety. Each national primary drinking water regulation for a contaminant for which a maximum contaminant level goal is established under this subsection shall specify a maximum level for such contaminant which is as close to the maximum contaminant level goal as is feasible.

(5) For the purposes of this subsection, the term "feasible" means feasible with the use of the best technology, treatment techniques and other means which the Administrator finds, after examination for efficacy under field conditions and not solely under laboratory conditions, are available (taking cost into consideration). * * *

How does this compare to the current language? How did Congress change EPA's decisionmaking under the SDWA in the 1996 amendments?

Pay particular attention to section 1412(b)(6)(A)—how does this provision change the standards in the statute as it read before 1996?

Now focus on section 1412(b)(3). What does it add? How does it affect the *City of Waukesha* case?

3. How does the court rule with respect to the radium standard, and why? In *City of Portland v. EPA*, 507 F.3d 706, 710–713 (D.C. Cir. 2007), the court considered a similar exemption specifically for the pathogenic microbe Cryptosporidium, which can contaminate public drinking water supplies and cause serious illness. Why do think Congress established special exemptions for pre-existing standards and specifically for Cryptosporidium?

4. How does the court justify upholding EPA's zero MCLG policy for Group A carcinogens? (Nearly 15 years earlier, the court had upheld the same policy as it applied to a chemical carcinogen in *Natural Resources Defense Council v. EPA*, 824 F.2d 1211 (D.C. Cir. 1987).) Is this analysis appropriate in light of *Benzene*?

5. What guidance does the statute give to EPA in carrying out its cost-benefit analysis? Why did Congress exclude the costs (and benefits) of compliance with other regulatory regimes?

6. Can you find the Precautionary Principle at work in *City of Waukesha*? How does it affect the result in the case?

7. *Problem.* The Safe Drinking Water Act Amendments and the Food Quality Protection Act, which is extensively excerpted in Section A, *supra*, were passed by Congress within *three days* of each other,[53] and yet they adopt significantly different approaches to regulation of toxic substances. How do the two approaches differ? Are the different approaches appropriate to the difference in subject matter? Can you explain why Congress took different approaches in these statutes?

2. The Supreme Court and Cost

You will recall that in *Benzene* the plurality opinion more or less gratuitously observed that OSHA's regulation was "an expensive way of providing some additional protection for a relatively small number of employees." A concern for the cost of regulation has been a recurrent theme in judicial treatment of toxics statutes, and two recent Supreme Court cases close this chapter with detailed discussions of the role of cost in regulatory structures that do not necessarily mandate it. The opinions of Justice Breyer are of particular interest, because he wrote extensively about risk regulation before his appointment to the Supreme Court,[54] and because he appears to occupy a kind of middle ground between the approaches of the other members of the Court.

---

53. Indeed, they also cover many of the same contaminants, since the SDWA requires EPA to consider all pesticides registered under FIFRA (§ 300g–1(b)(1)(B)(i)(II)), which is also the universe of the pesticide tolerances controlled by the FQPA.

54. Breyer, Breaking the Vicious Circle, *supra*.

Whitman v. American Trucking Associations, Inc.

531 U.S. 457 (2001)

■ Justice Scalia delivered the opinion of the Court.

These cases present the following questions: (1) Whether § 109(b)(1) of the Clean Air Act (CAA) delegates legislative power to the Administrator of the Environmental Protection Agency (EPA). (2) Whether the Administrator may consider the costs of implementation in setting national ambient air quality standards (NAAQS) under § 109(b)(1). * * *

I

Section 109(a) of the CAA, 42 U.S.C. § 7409(a), requires the Administrator of the EPA to promulgate NAAQS for each air pollutant for which "air quality criteria" have been issued under § 108. Once a NAAQS has been promulgated, the Administrator must review the standard (and the criteria on which it is based) "at five-year intervals" and make "such revisions ... as may be appropriate." These cases arose when, on July 18, 1997, the Administrator revised the NAAQS for particulate matter and ozone. American Trucking Associations, Inc., and its co-respondents—which include, in addition to other private companies, the States of Michigan, Ohio, and West Virginia—challenged the new standards in the Court of Appeals for the District of Columbia Circuit, pursuant to 42 U.S.C. § 7607(b)(1).

The District of Columbia Circuit accepted some of the challenges and rejected others. It agreed with respondents that § 109(b)(1) delegated legislative power to the Administrator in contravention of the United States Constitution, Art. I, § 1, because it found that the EPA had interpreted the statute to provide no "intelligible principle" to guide the agency's exercise of authority. The court thought, however, that the EPA could perhaps avoid the unconstitutional delegation by adopting a restrictive construction of § 109(b)(1), so instead of declaring the section unconstitutional the court remanded the NAAQS to the agency. (On this delegation point, Judge Tatel dissented, finding the statute constitutional as written.) On the second issue that the Court of Appeals addressed, it unanimously rejected respondents' argument that the court should depart from the rule of *Lead Industries Assn., Inc. v. EPA* [647 F.2d 1130 (D.C. Cir. 1979), *cert. denied*, 449 U.S. 1042 (1980)], that the EPA may not consider the cost of implementing a NAAQS in setting the initial standard. * * *

* * *

II

In *Lead Industries Assn., Inc. v. EPA*, the District of Columbia Circuit held that "economic considerations [may] play no part in the promulgation of ambient air quality standards under Section 109" of the CAA. In the present cases, the court adhered to that holding, as it had done on many other occasions. Respondents argue that these decisions are incorrect. We disagree; and since the first step in assessing whether a statute delegates legislative power is to determine what authority the statute confers, we address that issue of interpretation first and reach respondents' constitutional arguments in Part III, *infra*.

Section 109(b)(1) instructs the EPA to set primary ambient air quality standards "the attainment and maintenance of which ... are requisite to protect the public health" with "an adequate margin of safety." 42 U.S.C. § 7409(b)(1). Were it not for the hundreds of pages of briefing respondents have submitted on the issue, one would have thought it fairly clear that this text does not permit the EPA to consider costs in setting the standards. The language, as one scholar has noted, "is absolute." The EPA, "based on" the information about health effects contained in the technical "criteria" documents compiled under § 108(a)(2), is to identify the maximum airborne concentration of a pollutant that the public health can tolerate, decrease the concentration to provide an "adequate" margin of safety, and set the standard at that level. Nowhere are the costs of achieving such a standard made part of that initial calculation.

Against this most natural of readings, respondents make a lengthy, spirited, but ultimately unsuccessful attack. * * *

* * *

* * * The text of § 109(b), interpreted in its statutory and historical context and with appreciation for its importance to the CAA as a whole, unambiguously bars cost considerations from the NAAQS-setting process, and thus ends the matter for us as well as the EPA.[55] We therefore affirm the judgment of the Court of Appeals on this point.

III

[Turning to the non-delegation challenge, we] agree with the Solicitor General that the text of § 109(b)(1) of the CAA at a minimum requires that "[f]or a discrete set of pollutants and based on published air quality criteria that reflect the latest scientific knowledge, [the] EPA must establish uniform national standards at a level that is requisite to protect public health from the adverse effects of the pollutant in the ambient air." Requisite, in turn, "mean[s] sufficient, but not more than necessary." These limits on the EPA's discretion are strikingly similar to the ones we approved in *Touby v. United States,* 500 U.S. 160 (1991), which permitted the Attorney General to designate a drug as a controlled substance for purposes of criminal drug enforcement if doing so was " 'necessary to avoid an imminent hazard to the public safety.' " They also resemble the Occupational Safety and Health Act provision requiring the agency to "set the standard which most adequately assures, to the extent feasible, on the basis of the best available evidence, that no employee will suffer any impairment of health"—which the Court upheld in *Industrial Union Dept., AFL–CIO v. American Petroleum Institute [Benzene, supra]*, and which even then-Justice REHNQUIST, who alone in that case thought the statute violated the nondelegation doctrine, would have upheld if, like the statute here, it did not permit economic costs to be considered. See *American Textile Mfrs. Institute, Inc. v. Donovan [Cotton Dust, supra]*.

55. Respondents' speculation that the EPA is secretly considering the costs of attainment without telling anyone is irrelevant to our interpretive inquiry. If such an allegation could be proved, it would be grounds for vacating the NAAQS, because the Administrator had not followed the law. It would not, however, be grounds for this Court's changing the law.

The scope of discretion § 109(b)(1) allows is in fact well within the outer limits of our nondelegation precedents. * * *

It is true enough that the degree of agency discretion that is acceptable varies according to the scope of the power congressionally conferred. * * * But even in sweeping regulatory schemes we have never demanded, as the Court of Appeals did here, that statutes provide a "determinate criterion" for saying "how much [of the regulated harm] is too much." In *Touby,* for example, we did not require the statute to decree how "imminent" was too imminent, or how "necessary" was necessary enough, or even—most relevant here—how "hazardous" was too hazardous. * * * It is therefore not conclusive for delegation purposes that, as respondents argue, ozone and particulate matter are "nonthreshold" pollutants that inflict a continuum of adverse health effects at any airborne concentration greater than zero, and hence require the EPA to make judgments of degree. "[A] certain degree of discretion, and thus of lawmaking, inheres in most executive or judicial action." Section 109(b)(1) of the CAA, which to repeat we interpret as requiring the EPA to set air quality standards at the level that is "requisite"—that is, not lower or higher than is necessary—to protect the public health with an adequate margin of safety, fits comfortably within the scope of discretion permitted by our precedent.

We therefore reverse the judgment of the Court of Appeals remanding for reinterpretation that would avoid a supposed delegation of legislative power. * * *

* * *

[Justice THOMAS concurred in the nondelegation holding, but left open a greater possibility of future consideration of a stronger nondelegation doctrine. Justices STEVENS and SOUTER concurred in the judgment on the nondelegation question. They argued that Congress in fact did delegate legislative power to EPA, but that such delegations are perfectly constitutional as long as Congress has provided a sufficiently intelligible principle to guide the agency.]

■ JUSTICE BREYER, concurring in part and concurring in the judgment.

I join Parts I [and] III of the Court's opinion. I also agree with the Court's determination in Part II that the Clean Air Act does not permit the Environmental Protection Agency to consider the economic costs of implementation when setting national ambient air quality standards under § 109(b)(1) of the Act. But I would not rest this conclusion solely upon § 109's language * * *. [Instead,] I believe that, other things being equal, we should read silences or ambiguities in the language of regulatory statutes as permitting, not forbidding, this type of rational regulation.

In this case, however, other things are not equal. Here, legislative history, along with the statute's structure, indicates that § 109's language reflects a congressional decision not to delegate to the agency the legal authority to consider economic costs of compliance. [Justice Breyer here reviews the legislative history of section 109 of the Clean Air Act, emphasizing its intended "technology-forcing" effects—to the point that, quoting the Senate Report, "existing sources of pollutants either should meet the standard of the law or be closed down."]

To read this legislative history as meaning what it says does not impute to Congress an irrational intent. Technology-forcing hopes can prove realistic. Those persons, for example, who opposed the 1970 Act's insistence on a 90% reduction in auto emission pollutants, on the ground of excessive cost, saw the development of catalytic converter technology that helped achieve substantial reductions without the economic catastrophe that some had feared.

At the same time, the statute's technology-forcing objective makes regulatory efforts to determine the costs of implementation both less important and more difficult. It means that the relevant economic costs are speculative, for they include the cost of unknown future technologies. It also means that efforts to take costs into account can breed time-consuming and potentially unresolvable arguments about the accuracy and significance of cost estimates. Congress could have thought such efforts not worth the delays and uncertainties that would accompany them. In any event, that is what the statute's history seems to say. And the matter is one for Congress to decide.

Moreover, the Act does not, on this reading, wholly ignore cost and feasibility. As the majority points out, the Act allows regulators to take those concerns into account when they determine how to implement ambient air quality standards. Thus, States may consider economic costs when they select the particular control devices used to meet the standards, and industries experiencing difficulty in reducing their emissions can seek an exemption or variance from the state implementation plan.

The Act also permits the EPA, within certain limits, to consider costs when it sets deadlines by which areas must attain the ambient air quality standards. * * *

Finally, contrary to the suggestion of the Court of Appeals and of some parties, this interpretation of § 109 does not require the EPA to eliminate every health risk, however slight, at any economic cost, however great, to the point of "hurtling" industry over "the brink of ruin," or even forcing "deindustrialization." The statute, by its express terms, does not compel the elimination of *all* risk; and it grants the Administrator sufficient flexibility to avoid setting ambient air quality standards ruinous to industry.

Section 109(b)(1) directs the Administrator to set standards that are "requisite to protect the public health" with "an adequate margin of safety." But these words do not describe a world that is free of all risk—an impossible and undesirable objective. See *[Benzene, supra]* (the word "safe" does not mean "risk-free"). Nor are the words "requisite" and "public health" to be understood independent of context. We consider football equipment "safe" even if its use entails a level of risk that would make drinking water "unsafe" for consumption. And what counts as "requisite" to protecting the public health will similarly vary with background circumstances, such as the public's ordinary tolerance of the particular health risk in the particular context at issue. The Administrator can consider such background circumstances when "decid[ing] what risks are acceptable in the world in which we live."[*Vinyl Chloride, supra.*]

The statute also permits the Administrator to take account of comparative health risks. That is to say, she may consider whether a proposed rule promotes safety overall. A rule likely to cause more harm to health than it prevents is not a rule that is "requisite to protect the public health." For example, as the Court of Appeals held and the parties do not contest, the Administrator has the authority to determine to what extent possible health risks stemming from reductions in tropospheric ozone (which, it is claimed, helps prevent cataracts and skin cancer) should be taken into account in setting the ambient air quality standard for ozone.

The statute ultimately specifies that the standard set must be "requisite to protect the public health" *"in the judgment of the Administrator"* (emphasis added), a phrase that grants the Administrator considerable discretionary standard-setting authority.

The statute's words, then, authorize the Administrator to consider the severity of a pollutant's potential adverse health effects, the number of those likely to be affected, the distribution of the adverse effects, and the uncertainties surrounding each estimate. They permit the Administrator to take account of comparative health consequences. They allow her to take account of context when determining the acceptability of small risks to health. And they give her considerable discretion when she does so.

This discretion would seem sufficient to avoid the extreme results that some of the industry parties fear. After all, the EPA, in setting standards that "protect the public health" with "an adequate margin of safety," retains discretionary authority to avoid regulating risks that it reasonably concludes are trivial in context. Nor need regulation lead to deindustrialization. Preindustrial society was not a very healthy society; hence a standard demanding the return of the Stone Age would not prove "requisite to protect the public health."

Although I rely more heavily than does the Court upon legislative history and alternative sources of statutory flexibility, I reach the same ultimate conclusion. Section 109 does not delegate to the EPA authority to base the national ambient air quality standards, in whole or in part, upon the economic costs of compliance.

NOTES AND QUESTIONS

1. How do nonthreshold pollutants, in the D.C. Circuit panel's view, give rise to the nondelegation problem? Are they problematic for section 109, even if they do not raise constitutional difficulties?

2. The D.C. Circuit suggested that, were it not precluded from doing so by the court's consistent interpretation of section 109 to exclude cost, EPA might have solved the problem by using cost-benefit analysis to set the NAAQS. The Supreme Court said that adding cost would only make the nondelegation problem *worse*. Why did the D.C. Circuit think that cost-

benefit analysis would help? Why did the Supreme Court think it would hurt?

3. The Court's approach to determining whether the statute permits EPA to consider cost differs from that of the *Vinyl Chloride* case (and the *Michigan* case, cited in the majority's opinion) and of Justice Breyer's concurrence. Who has the better argument as a matter of law? Of environmental policy?

4. Without considering cost, how should EPA go about setting NAAQS levels for nonthreshold pollutants? Does this resemble the problem created by the *Vinyl Chloride* decision?

5. How does the Court's interpretation of the nondelegation doctrine differ from that of Justices Stevens and Souter? While EPA clearly won the day in this case, is there a way in which the Court's interpretation might constrain it in other ways? How, for example, would an "unreasonable risk" standard fare?

6. Would Justice Breyer's approach make it easier or harder for EPA to promulgate health-based regulations?

Entergy Corp. v. Riverkeeper, Inc.
___ U.S. ___, 129 S.Ct. 1498 (2009)

■ Justice Scalia delivered the opinion of the Court.

These cases concern a set of regulations adopted by the Environmental Protection Agency (EPA or agency) under § 316(b) of the Clean Water Act, 33 U.S.C. § 1326(b). Respondents—environmental groups and various States—challenged those regulations, and the Second Circuit set them aside. The issue for our decision is whether, as the Second Circuit held, the EPA is not permitted to use cost-benefit analysis in determining the content of regulations promulgated under § 1326(b).

I

Petitioners operate—or represent those who operate—large power plants. In the course of generating power, those plants also generate large amounts of heat. To cool their facilities, petitioners employ "cooling water intake structures" that extract water from nearby water sources. These structures pose various threats to the environment, chief among them the squashing against intake screens (elegantly called "impingement") or suction into the cooling system ("entrainment") of aquatic organisms that live in the affected water sources. Accordingly, the facilities are subject to regulation under the Clean Water Act, which mandates:

> "Any standard established pursuant to section 1311 of this title or section 1316 of this title and applicable to a point source shall require that the location, design, construction, and capacity of cooling water intake structures reflect the best technology available for minimizing adverse environmental impact." § 1326(b).

Sections 1311 and 1316, in turn, employ a variety of "best technology" standards to regulate the discharge of effluents into the Nation's waters.

* * *

To address those environmental impacts, the EPA set "national performance standards," requiring Phase II facilities [*i.e.*, existing, large power plants] (with some exceptions) to reduce "impingement mortality for all life stages of fish and shellfish by 80 to 95 percent from the calculation baseline"; a subset of facilities must also reduce entrainment of such aquatic organisms by "60 to 90 percent from the calculation baseline." Those targets are based on the environmental improvements achievable through deployment of a mix of remedial technologies, which the EPA determined were "commercially available and economically practicable."

In its Phase II rules, however, the EPA expressly declined to mandate adoption of closed-cycle cooling systems or equivalent reductions in impingement and entrainment, as it had done for new facilities subject to the Phase I [*i.e.*, new facilities] rules. It refused to take that step in part because of the "generally high costs" of converting existing facilities to closed-cycle operation, and because "other technologies approach the performance of this option." Thus, while closed-cycle cooling systems could reduce impingement and entrainment mortality by up to 98 percent (compared to the Phase II targets of 80 to 95 percent impingement reduction), the cost of rendering all Phase II facilities closed-cycle-compliant would be approximately \$3.5 billion per year, nine times the estimated cost of compliance with the Phase II performance standards. Moreover, Phase II facilities compelled to convert to closed-cycle cooling systems "would produce 2.4 percent to 4.0 percent less electricity even while burning the same amount of coal," possibly requiring the construction of "20 additional 400–MW plants ... to replace the generating capacity lost." The EPA thus concluded that "[a]lthough not identical, the ranges of impingement and entrainment reduction are similar under both options.... [Benefits of compliance with the Phase II rules] can approach those of closed-cycle recirculating at less cost with fewer implementation problems."

* * *

* * * We then granted certiorari limited to the following question: "Whether [§ 1326(b)] ... authorizes the [EPA] to compare costs with benefits in determining 'the best technology available for minimizing adverse environmental impact' at cooling water intake structures."

II

In setting the Phase II national performance standards and providing for site-specific cost-benefit variances, the EPA relied on its view that § 1326(b)'s "best technology available" standard permits consideration of the technology's costs and of the relationship between those costs and the environmental benefits produced. That view governs if it is a reasonable interpretation of the statute—not necessarily the only possible interpretation, nor even the interpretation deemed *most* reasonable by the courts. *Chevron.*

As we have described, § 1326(b) instructs the EPA to set standards for cooling water intake structures that reflect "the best technology available for minimizing adverse environmental impact." The Second Circuit took that language to mean the technology that achieves the greatest reduction in adverse environmental impacts at a cost that can reasonably be borne by the industry. That is certainly a plausible interpretation of the statute. The "best" technology—that which is "most advantageous," WEBSTER'S NEW INTERNATIONAL DICTIONARY 258 (2d ed.1953)—may well be the one that produces the most of some good, here a reduction in adverse environmental impact. But "best technology" may also describe the technology that most *efficiently* produces some good. In common parlance one could certainly use the phrase "best technology" to refer to that which produces a good at the lowest per-unit cost, even if it produces a lesser quantity of that good than other available technologies.

Respondents contend that this latter reading is precluded by the statute's use of the phrase "for minimizing adverse environmental impact." Minimizing, they argue, means reducing to the smallest amount possible, and the "best technology available for minimizing adverse environmental impacts," must be the economically feasible technology that achieves the greatest possible reduction in environmental harm. But "minimize" is a term that admits of degree and is not necessarily used to refer exclusively to the "greatest possible reduction." * * *

Other provisions in the Clean Water Act also suggest the agency's interpretation. When Congress wished to mandate the greatest feasible reduction in water pollution, it did so in plain language: The provision governing the discharge of toxic pollutants into the Nation's waters requires the EPA to set "effluent limitations [which] shall require the *elimination* of discharges of all pollutants if the Administrator finds ... that such elimination is technologically and economically achievable," § 1311(b)(2)(A) (emphasis added). See also § 1316(a)(1) (mandating "where practicable, a standard [for new point sources] permitting *no discharge* of pollutants" (emphasis added)). Section 1326(b)'s use of the less ambitious goal of "minimizing adverse environmental impact" suggests, we think, that the agency retains some discretion to determine the extent of reduction that is warranted under the circumstances. That determination could plausibly involve a consideration of the benefits derived from reductions and the costs of achieving them.

Respondents' alternative (and, alas, also more complex) argument rests upon the structure of the Clean Water Act. [The act adopts four different versions of best technology for different purposes under the statute, including "BTA," the version at issue here.] * * *

Respondents and the dissent argue that the mere fact that § 1326(b) does not expressly authorize cost-benefit analysis for the BTA test, though it does so for two of the other tests, displays an intent to forbid its use. This surely proves too much. For while it is true that two of the other tests authorize cost-benefit analysis, it is also true that *all four* of the other tests expressly authorize *some* consideration of costs. Thus, if respondents' and the dissent's conclusion regarding the import of § 1326(b)'s silence is correct, it is *a fortiori* true that the BTA test permits *no consideration of cost whatsoever*, not even the "cost-effectiveness" and "feasibility" analysis that the Second Circuit approved, that the dissent would approve, and that respondents acknowledge. The inference that respondents and the dissent would draw from the silence is, in any event, implausible, as § 1326(b) is silent not only with respect to cost-benefit analysis but with respect to all potentially relevant factors. If silence here implies prohibition, then the EPA could not consider *any* factors in implementing § 1326(b)—an obvious logical impossibility. It is eminently reasonable to conclude that § 1326(b)'s silence is meant to convey nothing more than a refusal to tie the agency's hands as to whether cost-benefit analysis should be used, and if so to what degree.

Contrary to the dissent's suggestion, our decisions in *Whitman v. American Trucking Assns.* and [*Cotton Dust*] do not undermine this conclusion. In *American Trucking*, we held that the text of § 109 of the Clean Air Act, "interpreted in its statutory and historical context ... unambiguously bars cost considerations" in setting air quality standards under that provision. The relevant "statutory context" included other provisions in the Clean Air Act that expressly authorized consideration of costs, whereas § 109 did not. *American Trucking* thus stands for the rather unremarkable proposition that sometimes statutory silence, when viewed in context, is best interpreted as limiting agency discretion. For the reasons discussed earlier, § 1326(b)'s silence cannot bear that interpretation.

In [*Cotton Dust*], the Court relied in part on a statute's failure to mention cost-benefit analysis in holding that the relevant agency was not required to engage in cost-benefit analysis in setting certain health and safety standards. But under *Chevron*, that an agency is not *required* to do so does not mean that an agency is not *permitted* to do so.

This extended consideration of the text of § 1326(b), and comparison of that with the text and statutory factors applicable to four parallel provisions of the Clean Water Act, lead us to the conclusion that it was well within the bounds of reasonable interpretation for the EPA to conclude that cost-benefit analysis is not categorically forbidden. Other arguments may be available to preclude such a rigorous form of cost-benefit analysis as that which was prescribed under the statute's former BPT standard, which required weighing "the total cost of application of technology" against "the ... benefits to be achieved." But that question is not before us.

In the Phase II requirements challenged here the EPA sought only to avoid extreme disparities between costs and benefits. * * * In the last analysis, even respondents ultimately recognize that some form of cost-benefit analysis is permissible. They acknowledge that the statute's language is "plainly not so constricted as to require EPA to require industry petitioners to spend billions to save one more fish or plankton." This concedes the principle—the permissibility of at least some cost-benefit analysis—and we see no statutory basis for limiting its use to situations where the benefits are de minimis rather than significantly disproportionate.

* * *

■ JUSTICE BREYER, concurring in part and dissenting in part.

I agree with the Court that the relevant statutory language authorizes the Environmental Protection Agency (EPA) to compare costs and benefits. Nonetheless the drafting history and legislative history of related provisions makes clear that those who sponsored the legislation intended the law's text to be read as restricting, though not forbidding, the use of cost-benefit comparisons. And I would apply that text accordingly.

I

* * *

As [the legislative history] suggests, the Act's sponsors had reasons for minimizing the EPA's investigation of, and reliance upon, cost-benefit comparisons. The preparation of formal cost-benefit analyses can take too much time, thereby delaying regulation. And the sponsors feared that such analyses would emphasize easily quantifiable factors over more qualitative factors (particularly environmental factors, for example, the value of pre-serving non-marketable species of fish). Above all, they hoped that minimizing the use of cost-benefit comparisons would force the development of cheaper control technologies; and doing so, whatever the initial inefficiencies, would eventually mean cheaper, more effective cleanup.

Nonetheless, neither the sponsors' language nor the underlying rationale requires the Act to be read in a way that would forbid cost-benefit comparisons. Any such total prohibition would be difficult to enforce, for every real choice requires a decisionmaker to weigh advantages against disadvantages, and disadvantages can be seen in terms of (often quantifiable) costs. Moreover, an absolute prohibition would bring about irrational results. As the respondents themselves say, it would make no sense to require plants to "spend billions to save one more fish or plankton." * * *

I believe, as I said, that [the legislative history's] language is deliberately nuanced. The statement says that where the statute uses the term *"best practicable,"* the statute *requires* comparisons of costs and benefits; but where the statute uses the term *"best available,"* such comparisons are not *"required"* (emphasis added). Senator Muskie [the primary sponsor of the bill] does not say that all efforts to compare costs and benefits are *forbidden*.

Moreover, the statement points out that where the statute uses the term *"best available,"* the Administrator "will be bound by a test of *reasonableness"*(emphasis added). It adds that the Administrator should apply this test in a way that *reflects* its ideal objective, moving as closely as is technologically possible to the elimination of pollution. It thereby says the Administrator should consider, *i.e.*, take into account, how much pollution would still remain if the *best available* technology were to be applied everywhere—"without regard to cost." It does not say that the Administrator *must* set the standard based solely on the result of that determination. (It would be difficult to reconcile the alternative, more absolute reading of this language with the Senator's earlier "test of reasonableness.")

* * *

The EPA's reading of the statute would seem to permit it to describe environmental benefits in non-monetized terms and to evaluate both costs and benefits in accordance with its expert judgment and scientific knowledge. The Agency can thereby avoid lengthy formal cost-benefit proceedings and futile attempts at comprehensive monetization; take account of Congress' technology-forcing objectives; and still prevent results that are absurd or unreasonable in light of extreme disparities between costs and benefits. This approach, in my view, rests upon a "reasonable interpretation" of the statute—legislative history included. Hence it is lawful. *Chevron.* Most of what the majority says is consistent with this view, and to that extent I agree with its opinion.

* * *

■ Justice Stevens, with whom Justice Souter and Justice Ginsburg join, dissenting.

Section 316(b) of the Clean Water Act (CWA), which governs industrial powerplant water intake structures, provides that the Environmental Protection Agency (EPA or Agency) "shall require" that such structures "reflect the best technology available for minimizing adverse environmental impact." The EPA has interpreted that mandate to authorize the use of cost-benefit analysis in promulgating regulations under § 316(b). For instance, under the Agency's interpretation, technology that would otherwise qualify as the best available need not be used if its costs are "significantly greater than the benefits" of compliance.

Like the Court of Appeals, I am convinced that the EPA has misinterpreted the plain text of § 316(b). Unless costs are so high that the best technology is not "available," Congress has decided that they are outweighed by the benefits of minimizing adverse environmental impact. Section 316(b) neither expressly nor implicitly authorizes the EPA to use cost-benefit analysis when setting regulatory standards; fairly read, it prohibits such use.

I

As typically performed by the EPA, cost-benefit analysis requires the Agency to first monetize the costs and benefits of a regulation, balance the results, and then choose the regulation with the greatest net benefits. The process is particularly controversial in the environmental context in which a regulation's financial costs are often more obvious and easier to quantify than its environmental benefits. And cost-benefit analysis often, if not always, yields a result that does not maximize environmental protection.

* * *

Because benefits can be more accurately monetized in some industries than in others, Congress typically decides whether it is appropriate for an agency to use cost-benefit analysis in crafting regulations. Indeed, this Court has recognized that "[w]hen Congress has intended that an agency engage in cost-benefit analysis, it has clearly indicated such intent on the face of the statute." [*Cotton Dust*]. Accordingly, we should not treat a provision's silence as an implicit source of cost-benefit authority, particularly when such authority is elsewhere expressly granted and it has the potential to fundamentally alter an agency's approach to regulation. Congress, we have noted, "does not alter the fundamental details of a regulatory scheme in vague terms or ancillary provisions—it does not, one might say, hide elephants in mouseholes." *American Trucking*.

* * *

Further motivating the Court in *American Trucking* was the fact that incorporating implementation costs into the Agency's calculus risked countermanding Congress' decision to protect public health. The cost of implementation, we said, "is both so indirectly related to public health and so full of potential for canceling the conclusions drawn from direct health effects that it would surely have been expressly mentioned in [the text] had Congress meant it to be considered."

American Trucking's approach should have guided the Court's reading of § 316(b). Nowhere in the text of § 316(b) does Congress explicitly authorize the use of cost-benefit analysis as it does elsewhere in the CWA. And the use of cost-benefit analysis, like the consideration of implementation costs in *American Trucking*, "pad[s]" § 316(b)'s environmental mandate with tangential economic efficiency concerns. Yet the majority fails to follow *American Trucking* despite that case's obvious relevance to our inquiry.

II

* * *

Section § 316(b) was an integral part of the statutory scheme [when Congress drafted the statute]. The provision instructs that "[a]ny standard established pursuant to section 1311 of this title or section 1316 of this title and applicable to a point source shall require that the location, design, construction, and capacity of cooling water intake structures reflect the *best technology available for minimizing adverse environmental impact*" (emphasis added). The "best technology available," or "BTA," standard delivers a clear command: To minimize the adverse environmental impact of water intake structures, the EPA must require industry to adopt the best technology available.

* * *

It is in [the light of the other best technology standards] that the BTA standard regulating water intake structures must be viewed. The use of cost-benefit analysis was a critical component of the CWA's structure and a key concern in the legislative process. We should therefore conclude that Congress intended to forbid cost-benefit analysis in one provision of the Act in which it was silent on the matter when it expressly authorized its use in another.[56] This is particularly true given Congress' decision that cost-benefit

---

56. The Court argues that, if silence in § 316(b) signals the prohibition of cost-benefit analysis, it must also foreclose the consideration of *all* other potentially relevant discretionary

analysis would play a temporary and exceptional role in the CWA to help existing plants transition to the Act's ambitious environmental standards. Allowing cost-benefit analysis in the BTA standard, a permanent mandate applicable to all powerplants, serves no such purpose and instead fundamentally weakens the provision's mandate.

Accordingly, I would hold that the EPA is without authority to perform cost-benefit analysis in setting BTA standards. * * *

NOTES AND QUESTIONS

1. The three opinions in *Entergy* explore the differences between a BAT and a cost-benefit standard. How are they different, according to the opinions? The dissent implies that BAT is indeed a version of cost-benefit analysis—in what way?

2. Is *Entergy* the logical extension of Justice Breyer's concurrence in *American Trucking*? If so, why does Breyer dissent (in part) in *Entergy*?

3. After *Entergy*, what must Congress say in legislation to exclude cost-benefit analysis from an agency's consideration in setting a regulatory standard? Put another way, how can Congress signal that it means "best we can do," rather than "most efficient"?

Or, should *Entergy* be regarded as a welcome corrective that tests virtually all regulation by its costs and benefits—in that sense reinforcing Executive Order 12,866, *supra*? How would *Entergy* affect *Public Citizen v. Young*, if at all? *Vinyl Chloride*?

Now re-examine *City of Waukesha*: "the purpose of the MCLs is to protect the public, as much as feasible.... That purpose would be undermined if the cost-benefit balance were skewed by consideration of ... additional costs...." Is that conclusion still good law? Does it remain a valid approach to interpretation of environmental statutes?

F. Toward "Unreasonable Risk"

You have now examined a veritable menu of approaches to regulating toxic substances, with an additional approach—"unreasonable risk"—to be introduced in the next chapter. Before turning the page on this menu of approaches, you might observe some commonalities. For example, you have probably noticed that *many* statutes employ the two-step analysis, trigger and standard, which is described at the beginning of Section B, *supra*.

In addition, Professors Shapiro and Glicksman analyzed the incidence of the approaches in this chapter in federal environmental, health, and

---

factors in setting BTA standards. This all-or-nothing reasoning rests on the deeply flawed assumption that Congress treated cost-benefit analysis as just one among many factors upon which the EPA could potentially rely to establish BTA. Yet, as explained above, the structure and legislative history of the CWA demonstrate that Congress viewed cost-benefit analysis with special skepticism and controlled its use accordingly. The Court's assumption of equivalence is thus plainly incorrect. Properly read, Congress' silence in § 316(b) forbids reliance on the cost-benefit tool but does not foreclose reliance on all other considerations, such as a determination whether a technology is so costly that it is not "available" for industry to adopt.

safety statutes. Their conclusions are expressed in the following table, which is adapted from their book, *Risk Regulation at Risk, supra,* at 32:

		Statutory Standards				
		Risk- or Ambient Quality–Based	*Phaseout*	*Constrained Balancing*	*Open–Ended Balancing*	*Cost–Benefit Balancing*
Triggers — *Statutory*	*No Threshold*	**FFDCA** Delaney Clause (1958) **FQPA** Pesticide Residues (1996)		**CWA** Existing Sources (1972, 1977) New Sources (1972)	**CWA** Ambient Quality Standards (1972)	
	Risk Threshold		**CAA** Ozone Depletion (1990)	**CAA** Nonattainment (1977, 1990); PSD (1977); NESHAPs (1990); Mobile Sources (1970); New Sources (1970, 1990)	**CAA** NAAQS/ SIPs (1970)	
	Significant Risk Threshold			**OSH Act** (1970) **SDWA** (1996) **RCRA** LDRs (1984)	**CERCLA** (1980, 1986)	
	Unreasonable Risk		**TSCA** PCBs (1976)	**TSCA** general (1976)	**FIFRA** (1972)	**CPSA** (1972, 1981)

Which regulatory standards are most common? Why do you think that is the case? Does your reading of this chapter suggest trends for the future?

Reflecting on the various approaches, which do you find most useful or appropriate for environmental protection?

———

We now turn to the four major statutes whose principal concern is toxic substances and hazardous wastes: the Federal Insecticide, Fungicide, and Rodenticide Act (FIFRA), the Toxic Substances Control Act (TSCA), the Resource Conservation and Recovery Amendments (RCRA) to the Solid Waste Disposal Act, and the Comprehensive Environmental Response, Compensation, and Liability Act (CERCLA, or Superfund). Collectively these statutes empower EPA to regulate the "life cycle" of toxic chemicals— from production to use, disposal, and finally to clean-up of failed disposal— and they all deploy a similar substantive standard for regulatory action.

- FIFRA requires the registration and approval by EPA of all pesticides and their intended uses, based on an evaluation of their
benefits and the risks they pose to human health and the
environment. The lodestar of approval and cancellation decisions is
whether the pesticide will have "unreasonable adverse effects on the

environment," a standard that is defined as an "unreasonable risk ... taking into account the economic, social, and environmental costs and benefits of [the pesticide's] use." 7 U.S.C. §§ 136(bb), 136a(c)(5).

- TSCA focuses on the production and use of industrial and commercial chemicals, though its potential range is much greater. EPA may take regulatory action against a chemical if it finds "an unreasonable risk of injury to [human] health or the environment." 15 U.S.C. § 2605(a). Congress chose not to define "unreasonable risk," but the legislative history makes it clear that it involves a case-by-case consideration of the severity and likelihood of harm as against the benefits of the chemical.

- RCRA requires EPA to identify and to regulate the disposal methods for "hazardous waste." Listing is a prerequisite for substantive regulation of waste generation, transportation, storage, and disposal under the standard "as may be necessary to protect human health and the environment." 42 U.S.C. § 6922(a). Again, the legislative history clearly contemplates a greater-than-zero level of post-regulation risk, determined by multiple factors.

- Under CERCLA, EPA or private parties may identify locations contaminated with hazardous chemicals, clean them up, and be compensated for their efforts by the generators of the waste and/or the owner of the site. In selecting the method and stringency of clean-up, EPA is to "select a remedial action that is protective of human health and the environment, that is cost effective, and that utilizes permanent solutions * * * to the maximum extent practicable." 42 U.S.C. § 9621(b), (d). EPA interprets this language to indicate a *range* of potential post-regulation risk levels, the final decision being based on many factors including cost and public acceptance. 40 C.F.R. § 300.430(e)–(f).

The substantive standard chosen by Congress in each of these statutes, although phrased in different ways, can generically be called the *unreasonable risk* approach.[57] The unreasonable risk standard exhibits four characteristics whose importance to risk regulation will become apparent as we examine each statute in detail: regulation of the risk of harm instead of actually realized harm; a quantitatively undefined regulatory goal of a greater-than-zero risk (*i.e.*, less than complete safety); facilitation, and indeed a requirement, of cost-risk-benefit balancing, to include both health considerations and non-health concerns such as technology, feasibility, and cost; and implementation of this balancing through *ad hoc* or case-by-case determinations. These characteristics directly respond to the scientific, economic, and political difficulties of regulating toxic substances, which have been developed in the foregoing chapters; they also determine to a great extent the shape of the resulting regulatory actions.

As you consider the unreasonable risk statutes in the following chapters, ask yourself whether one of the approaches in this chapter would be

---

57. Applegate, *Perils of Unreasonable Riski, supra*, at 267–271.

preferable—or whether the unreasonable risk approach would have been a better way to address the occupational health, drinking water, and other concerns in this chapter.

CHAPTER 4

PESTICIDE AND CHEMICAL REGULATION

A. Pesticide Regulation

    1. The Pesticides Dilemma

        Cooper and Dobson, *The Benefits of Pesticides to Mankind and the Environment*

        Carson, *Silent Spring*

    2. Overview of FIFRA

        Environmental Defense Fund v. EPA

        National Coalition Against the Misuse of Pesticides v. EPA

    3. Five Problems for Pesticide Regulation

        a. The Delaney Paradox and the Food Quality Protection Act of 1996

        b. Endocrine Disruption

        c. Farmworkers

        d. Preemption of State and Local Law

        e. Pesticide Exports

B. Chemical Regulation

    1. TSCA's Promise: An Overview of the Statute

        Council on Environmental Quality, *Toxic Substances*

    2. Information Gathering

    3. A Closer Look at "Unreasonable Risk" in Information Gathering

    4. Authority to Restrict Chemicals Under TSCA

        Environmental Protection Agency, *Asbestos: Manufacture, Importation, Processing, and Distribution in Commerce Prohibitions*

        Corrosion Proof Fittings v. EPA

    5. International Developments in Chemical Regulation

Should law reach an accommodation or balance between the human health and environmental risks of chemicals and their benefits for human welfare? Or should law restrict use of toxic chemicals to the maximum extent, given uncertainties in calculating both the harms and the benefits? What incentives can law provide to develop information on the risks of chemicals?

This chapter focuses on these questions in the context of pesticide regulation under the Federal Insecticide, Fungicide, and Rodenticide Act (FIFRA) and in the context of regulation of other useful chemicals under the Toxic Substances Control Act (TSCA). Pesticides are a subset of the total annual production of the chemical industry, and they are carved out for separate regulatory treatment in U.S. law because of assumed higher risk. Pesticides' purpose, after all, is to disrupt biological processes of living organisms, and they are intentionally applied to crops used for food. As we shall see, in FIFRA and TSCA, the United States has adopted very different regulatory regimes for pesticides and non-pesticide chemicals.

Despite their differences, both FIFRA and TSCA can be viewed as regulating the "front end" of the chemical life-cycle (introduction and use of chemicals for commercial applications). They are distinguishable from statutes we will cover in later chapters, which govern the "back end" of the chemical life-cycle (storage, transport, disposal, and recycling of hazardous wastes). This chapter examines FIFRA and TSCA and also discusses international developments in chemical regulation. Through these statutes, it explores some of the larger themes of risk regulation first introduced in Chapter 1, such as cost-benefit balancing and decision making in the face of scientific uncertainty.

A. PESTICIDE REGULATION

For centuries, humans have used various chemical agents to protect themselves, their buildings, and their crops from the enormous number of insects, weeds, and funguses that threaten disease, damage, and blight. The federal government has actively regulated pesticides since 1947, when FIFRA was enacted. FIFRA has since received numerous updates and overhauls, the most important of which were the 1972 amendments, which gave the statute its current structure. Today pesticide regulation in the United States has two principal components: regulation of the introduction, application, and labeling of pesticides under FIFRA, and regulation of pesticide residues on food, under the Federal Food, Drug, and Cosmetic Act (FFDCA). EPA's program under the FFDCA to set "tolerances," or maximum residue levels for pesticides on food, was discussed in Chapter 3. The discussion below, therefore, focuses primarily on FIFRA.

1.   THE PESTICIDES DILEMMA

Earlier versions of FIFRA called pesticides "economic poisons." 7 U.S.C. § 135(a) (repealed). As the term suggests, pesticides are both hazardous and economically valuable. In reading the following materials, focus on the arguments for and against their use. Do the arguments make sense? Is there a sensible method for "weighing" economic benefits and health risks? Is there any common ground between proponents and opponents?

The Benefits of Pesticides to Mankind and the Environment

Jerry Cooper and Hans Dobson
26 CROP PROTECTION 1337–48 (2007)

4.1.   The benefits of effect 1—controlling pests and plant disease vectors

Over the last 60 years, farmers and growers have changed the way they produce food in order to meet the expectations of consumers, governments and more recently, food processors and retailers. In doing so, they have made many changes to the way they farm, including the extensive use of pesticides. They have done this principally to prevent or reduce agricultural losses to pests, resulting in improved yield and greater availability of food, at a reasonable price, all year round. * * * [For example, U.S. corn yields] went from 30 bushels per acre to over 100 per acre over the period from 1920 to 1980. * * * While a significant proportion of the gains are due to better soil and water management, improved plant varieties and application of fertiliser, the use of pesticides has undoubtedly played a very significant role. * * *

Herbicides are the most widely used type of pesticide since weeds are the major constraint that limit yield in many crops. Herbicides represent around 50% of all crop protection chemicals used throughout the world, compared with insecticides and fungicides that are around 17% each. Without herbicides there would be an estimated US $13.3 billion loss in farm income in the U.S. [One 2005 study] put the figure for benefits of herbicide use even higher at $21 billion annually, against a cost of $6.6 billion for the product and application that reduced losses to weeds by 23% and avoided a loss of farm income valued at $8 billion. * * *

If marketable yields and quality are increasing, farm revenues are also likely to increase. This results in wealthier farmers with more disposable income to stimulate the local economy. Higher yields mean less pressure to cultivate un-cropped land—a wider benefit to biodiversity and the environment. * * *

More food in communities also allows better nutrition, which carries over into healthier lives. Healthier people are by and large also happier people, who are more productive and able to contribute better to their society. This contrasts with the situation where poor nutrition resulting from limited food supplies increases the susceptibility to diseases, reducing people's energy and productivity in a vicious circle of deprivation. Pesticides can help break this cycle that threatens security of personal livelihoods and quality of life.

Effective control of pests can have consequences beyond the geographic or chronological range of the initial intervention. If pest levels are suppressed by many farmers at once, it can have an area-wide effect—in other words, the source population for infection or infestation of future crops is reduced. In many cases, the threat to subsequent crops is therefore much lower, even without future interventions. For more mobile pests such as locusts, if populations can be controlled before they become too numerous in one country, it can prevent massive population expansion and migration to other countries. Non-pesticidal approaches such as egg bed destruction, digging trenches and burying the nymphs or beating them with branches are all too slow and act on too small a scale to have any significant impact on the overall locust populations in the area. The early interventions over large areas that are possible with aerially applied insecticides can be more cost effective and environmentally safe than the later "fire brigade" treatments over much larger areas and longer time periods that would otherwise be required. * * *

4.2.   Benefits of effect 2—controlling human/livestock disease vectors and nuisance organisms

In warmer climates especially, insects can spread devastating human diseases such as malaria, sleeping sickness, river blindness, and a range of serious fevers and disfiguring or debilitating illnesses. * * * [A 2001 study] showed that bed nets treated with deltamethrin significantly reduced indoor resting density, biting, light trap catches, human sourced engorgement rate and parous rate of malaria infection in Anopheles mosquitoes. Malaria incidence was reduced 59% in the treated net village, 35% in the untreated net village, and 9% in the no-net village. [A 2003 study] reported that use of treated bed nets reduced the number of infective bites per person per year by 75%. Half of this effect is attributable to an area-wide effect of reducing mosquito populations due to the nets killing those attracted to the human "bait." The other half of the effect is due to the personal protection afforded by the treated nets.* * *

The World Health Organization claims that without access to chemical control methods, life will continue to be unacceptably dangerous for a large proportion of mankind. Recognising this, nearly 30 years after phasing out the widespread use of indoor spraying with DDT and other insecticides to control malaria, the World Health Organization (WHO) announced that this intervention will once again play a major role in its efforts to fight the disease. WHO is now recommending the use of indoor residual spraying (IRS) not only in epidemic areas but also in areas with constant and high malaria transmission, including throughout Africa.

Insects such as cockroaches and houseflies are mechanical vectors for various micro-organisms that cause diarrhoeal diseases, which are rated by UNICEF as the number one killer of children under 5. * * *

There are also substantial benefits to reducing the number of people suffering sub-lethal effects of vectorborne diseases. The misery caused by frequent bouts of malaria or the insidious effects of river blindness on eyesight has a debilitating effect on the morale and productivity of communities, not to mention the cash cost of medicines to treat these diseases. * * *

A less obvious, but still significant benefit is the prevention of misery and disturbance caused by various biting insects, whether they transmit disease or not. This group includes mosquitoes, blackflies, midges, other biting flies, fleas, lice, and bedbugs. Studies in Cameroon have found people in some areas being bitten up to 2,000 times per day by Simuliid blackflies, effectively preventing them doing any useful agricultural or other outdoor work due to the nuisance and constant irritation. * * *

4.3.   Benefits of effect 3—preventing or controlling organisms that harm other activities or damage structures

In the same way that pests in agriculture and public health cause undesirable effects such as losses, spoilage, and damage, various organisms have a negative impact on human activities, infrastructure, and the materials of everyday life unless controlled. Pesticides play an important, if often unseen role in preventing this negative impact. The transport sector makes extensive use of pesticides, particularly herbicides, to ensure that roads, railways, and waterways are kept free of vegetation that might otherwise cause a hazard or nuisance. For example, if vegetation is allowed to grow too tall on roadsides, it reduces the drivers' view at junctions, and deposits branches or vegetation onto the road that might be an obstruction or make it very slippery. * * *

The destructive power of vegetation is also enormous; above ground growth around metal structures harbours moisture and can accelerate corrosion, and below ground, the roots of growing plants can crack pipes, open up potholes in the road or dislodge railway lines. Most people living in towns take for granted that roads, gutters, and pavements stay clear and weed-free, and are not aware that it is due to the regular use of herbicides. Thus, pesticides bring primary benefits associated with preventing these problems, leading to secondary benefits of reduced maintenance costs and increased transport safety. * * *

Insecticides protect buildings and other wooden structures from damage by termites and wood boring insects, thus decreasing maintenance costs and increasing longevity of buildings and their safety. This use also has wider environmental benefits in that timber—a renewable resource that can be produced in an environmentally beneficial way—becomes a more viable construction material. * * *

Rachel Carson's *Silent Spring* was the first mass-market book to call attention to the health and environmental dangers of pesticides. The book received widespread coverage in the media, and Carson is often credited with helping to launch the modern environmental movement, which gained steam in the late 1960s. DDT (dichloro-diphenyl-trichloro-ethane), a powerful insecticide, was gradually phased out by the U.S. Department of Agriculture, following publication of *Silent Spring*. In June 1972, the EPA Administrator banned all remaining crop uses of DDT. However, as the previous excerpt explained, the World Health Organization, while seeking a transition away from DDT, opposes a global ban on DDT in view of its effectiveness in malaria control in developing countries.

Silent Spring

Rachel Carson
pp. 15–23, 105–08 (1962)

Elixirs of Death

For the first time in the history of the world, every human being is now subjected to contact with dangerous chemicals, from the moment of conception until death. In the less than two decades of their use, the synthetic pesticides have been so thoroughly distributed throughout the animate and inanimate world that they occur virtually everywhere. They have been recovered from most of the major river systems and even from streams of groundwater flowing unseen through the earth. Residues of these chemicals linger in soil to which they may have been applied a dozen years before. They have entered and lodged in the bodies of fish, birds, reptiles, and domestic and wild animals so universally that scientists carrying on animal experiments find it almost impossible to locate subjects free from such contamination. They have been found in fish in remote mountain lakes, in earthworms burrowing in soil, in the eggs of birds—and in man himself. For these chemicals are now stored in the bodies of the vast majority of human beings, regardless of age. They occur in the mother's milk, and probably in the tissues of the unborn child.

All this has come about because of the sudden rise and prodigious growth of an industry for the production of man-made or synthetic chemicals with insecticidal properties. This industry is a child of the Second World War. In the course of developing agents of chemical warfare, some of the chemicals created in the laboratory were found to be lethal to insects. The discovery did not come by chance: insects were widely used to test chemicals as agents of death for man.

The result has been a seemingly endless stream of synthetic insecticides. In being man-made—by ingenious laboratory manipulation of the molecules, substituting atoms, altering their arrangement—they differ sharply from the simpler inorganic insecticides of prewar days. These were derived from naturally occurring minerals and plant products—compounds of arsenic, copper, lead, manganese, zinc, and other minerals, pyrethrum from the dried flowers of chrysanthemums, nicotine sulphate from some of the relatives of tobacco, and rotenone from leguminous plants of the East Indies.

What sets the new synthetic insecticides apart is their enormous biological potency. They have immense power not merely to poison but to enter into the most vital processes of the body and change them in sinister and often deadly ways. Thus, as we shall see, they destroy the very enzymes whose function is to protect the body from harm, they block the oxidation processes from which the body receives its energy, they prevent the normal functioning of various organs, and they may initiate in certain cells the slow and irreversible change that leads to malignancy.

Yet new and more deadly chemicals are added to the list each year and new uses are devised so that contact with these materials has become practically worldwide. * * *

* * *

Modern insecticides are still more deadly. The vast majority fall into one of two large groups of chemicals. One, represented by DDT, is known as the "chlorinated hydrocarbons." The other group consists of the organic phosphorus insecticides, and is represented by the reasonably familiar malathion and parathion. All have one thing in common. As mentioned above, they are built on a basis of carbon atoms, which are also the indispensable building blocks of the living world, and thus classed as "organic." To understand them, we must see of what they are made, and how, although linked with the basic chemistry of all life, they lend themselves to the modifications which make them agents of death.

* * *

DDT (short for dichloro-diphenyl-trichloro-ethane) was first synthesized by a German chemist in 1874, but its properties as an insecticide were not discovered until 1939. Almost immediately DDT was hailed as a means of stamping out insect-borne disease and winning the farmers' war against crop destroyers overnight. The discoverer, Paul Müller of Switzerland, won the Nobel Prize.

DDT is now so universally used that in most minds the product takes on the harmless aspect of the familiar. Perhaps the myth of the harmlessness of DDT rests on the fact that one of its first uses was the wartime dusting of many thousands of soldiers, refugees, and prisoners, to combat lice. It is widely believed that since so many people came into extremely intimate contact with DDT and suffered no immediate ill effects the chemical must certainly be innocent of harm. This understandable misconception arises from the fact that—unlike other chlorinated hydrocarbons—DDT in powder form is not readily absorbed through the skin. Dissolved in oil, as it usually is, DDT is definitely toxic. If swallowed, it is absorbed slowly through the digestive tract; it may also be absorbed through the lungs. Once it has entered the body it is stored largely in organs rich in fatty substances (because DDT itself is fat-soluble) such as the adrenals, testes, or thyroid.

Relatively large amounts are deposited in the liver, kidneys, and the fat of the large, protective mesenteries that enfold the intestines.

This storage of DDT begins with the smallest conceivable intake of the chemical (which is present as residues on most foodstuffs) and continues until quite high levels are reached. The fatty storage depots act as biological magnifiers, so that an intake of as little of 1/10 of 1 part per million in the diet results in storage of about 10 to 15 parts per million, an increase of one hundredfold or more. These terms of reference, so commonplace to the chemist or the pharmacologist, are unfamiliar to most of us. One part in a million sounds like a very small amount—and so it is. But such substances are so potent that a minute quantity can bring about vast changes in the body. In animal experiments, 3 parts per million has been found to inhibit an essential enzyme in heart muscle; only 5 parts per million has brought about necrosis or disintegration of liver cells; only 2.5 parts per million of the closely related chemicals dieldrin and chlordane did the same.

This is really not surprising. In the normal chemistry of the human body there is just such a disparity between cause and effect. For example, a quantity of iodine as small as two ten-thousandths of a gram spells the difference between health and disease. Because these small amounts of pesticides are cumulatively stored and only slowly excreted, the threat of chronic poisoning and degenerative changes of the liver and other organs is very real. * * *

One of the most sinister features of DDT and related chemicals is the way they are passed on from one organism to another through all the links of the food chains. For example, fields of alfalfa are dusted with DDT; meal is later prepared from the alfalfa and fed to hens; the hens lay eggs which contain DDT. Or the hay, containing residues of 7 to 8 parts per million, may be fed to cows. The DDT will turn up in the milk in the amount of about 3 parts per million, but in butter made from this milk the concentration may run to 65 parts per million. Through such a process of transfer, what started out as a very small amount of DDT may end as a heavy concentration. Farmers nowadays find it difficult to obtain uncontaminated fodder for their milk cows, though the Food and Drug Administration forbids the presence of insecticide residues in milk shipped in interstate commerce.

The poison may also be passed on from mother to offspring. Insecticide residues have been recovered from human milk in samples tested by Food and Drug Administration scientists. This means that the breast-fed human infant is receiving small but regular additions to the load of toxic chemicals building up in his body. It is by no means his first exposure, however: there is good reason to believe this begins while he is still in the womb. In experimental animals the chlorinated hydrocarbon insecticides freely cross the barrier of the placenta, the traditional protective shield between the embryo and harmful substances in the mother's body. While the quantities so received by human infants would normally be small, they are not unimportant because children are more susceptible to poisoning than adults. This situation also means that today the average individual almost certainly starts life with the first deposit of the growing load of chemicals his body will be required to carry thenceforth.

All these facts—storage at even low levels, subsequent accumulation, and occurrence of liver damage at levels that may easily occur in normal diets, caused Food and Drug Administration scientists to declare as early as 1950 that it is "extremely likely the potential hazard of DDT has been underestimated." There has been no such parallel situation in medical history. No one yet knows what the ultimate consequences may be.

Figure 4.1–DDT Spraying at Jones Beach, NY, 1945[1]

NOTES AND QUESTIONS

1.   *Pros and cons.* What makes pesticides so dangerous? Why are they useful? Do their dangers overlap with their benefits? What problem does that create for regulating pesticides?

2.   How do humans come into contact with pesticides? What are the routes of exposure, and who is exposed? What are the characteristics of pesticides that make exposure more or less likely?

3.   According to EPA, about 1.2 billion pounds of pesticides were used in the U.S. in 2001 (excluding microbial disinfectants, which alone account for about 2.6 billion pounds), which is about 24 percent of world-wide usage. U.S. expenditures on pesticides exceeded $11 billion in 2001, 67 percent of which was spent on agricultural pesticides. EPA, PESTICIDES INDUSTRY SALES AND USAGE: 2000 AND 2001 MARKET ESTIMATES (2004). Nearly 1400 pesticides

1.   Source: Corbis/Bettmann–UPI © 1945.

have been registered with EPA, and on average, about 18 new pesticides are introduced each year. National Cancer Institute, President's Cancer Panel, Reducing Environmental Cancer Risk: What We Can Do Now 45 (2010). Many pesticides contain active ingredients that are carcinogenic. Approximately 40 chemicals classified by the International Agency for Research on Cancer as known, probable, or possible human carcinogens are used in EPA-registered pesticides now on the market. *Id.*

4. *Pesticides and Food Productivity.* Several studies have attempted to calculate the impact of restricting pesticide use on crop production. Studies by researchers at Texas A & M University and at Auburn University found that "a 50 percent reduction in pesticide use on crops of nine fruits and vegetables (apples, grapes, lettuce, onions, oranges, peaches, potatoes, sweet corn, and tomatoes) would reduce average yields by 37 percent." A 1995 study by Robert C. Taylor of Auburn University estimated that eliminating the application of pesticides to U.S. fruits and vegetables would increase production costs 75 percent, wholesale prices 45 percent, and retail prices 27 percent." Stephen Huebner and Kenneth Chilton, *Environmental Alarmism: The Children's Crusade*, 15 Issues in Science & Technology 35, 37 (1998). These kinds of claims are a powerful counterweight to calls for the elimination of pesticides.

2.   Overview of FIFRA

The heart of FIFRA is the registration process in Section 3 of the Act. All pesticides must be registered with EPA prior to sale, and the Act imposes severe penalties (including criminal penalties) for marketing a pesticide without prior registration. FIFRA § 14. Enforcement of FIFRA lies solely with the federal government. FIFRA provides no private right of action for personal injury, wrongful product registration, or pesticide mislabeling.

To register a pesticide, the applicant must submit data to EPA on the physical and chemical properties of the pesticide, the environmental fate of the pesticide, hazards to humans, animals, and nontarget organisms, and potential exposure routes.[2] Much of the data on health effects is obtained through rodent studies, as explained in Chapter 1. As part of the registration process, the applicant must also submit a proposed label for the pesticide, which includes information on physical and chemical properties, directions for safe use, and health and safety warnings. 40 C.F.R. §§ 152.-50(e), 156.10. You can see these FIFRA labels on typical household pesticides, such as ant and roach killers.

Labeling is a critical component of FIFRA. Hundreds of hours are spent on development of pesticide labels and on negotiations between agency

---

2. Many new pesticide formulations are based on already-registered active ingredients. To minimize the burden of "follow-on" registrations and to avoid duplication of effort, FIFRA permits applicants for registration to rely on data previously submitted by others. § 3(c)(1)(F). To address the perceived unfairness of allowing subsequent registrants to profit from prior registrants' investment in research, Congress developed a process in which subsequent data users compensate the original data producers for part of the development costs. *Id.* The Supreme Court upheld the data compensation system against a taking challenge in *Ruckelshaus v. Monsanto*, 467 U.S. 986 (1984). A year later, in *Thomas v. Union Carbide*, 473 U.S. 568 (1985), the Court rejected a constitutional challenge to FIFRA's use of binding arbitration to determine the amount of compensation.

officials and pesticide manufacturers over the content of pesticide labels. The labeling strategy reflects that all pesticides have some risks that cannot be eliminated and that users should be warned of those risks. Would you support a strategy that relied solely on labeling and disclosure to manage pesticide risks?

After the application for registration is submitted to EPA, EPA must register the pesticide if it finds that:

- The pesticide's composition is such as to warrant the proposed claims for it;

- its labeling and other material required to be submitted comply with the requirements of the Act;

- it will perform its intended function without unreasonable adverse effects on the environment; and

- when used in accordance with widespread and commonly recognized practice, it will not generally cause unreasonable adverse effects on the environment.

FIFRA § 3(c)(5).

FIFRA defines an "unreasonable adverse effect on the environment" as "any unreasonable risk to man or the environment, taking into account the economic, social, and environmental costs and benefits of the use of the pesticide." FIFRA § 2(bb). This is a key definition that strongly reflects that FIFRA is a risk-benefit balancing statute. Note that while EPA must consider whether a proposed pesticide will cause an "unreasonable adverse effect on the environment," it cannot consider whether a proposed pesticide is needed (given other available pest control options). In other words, it must register both environmentally inferior and superior pesticides, as well as pesticides that duplicate the purposes of other pesticides on the market, as long as the pesticide meets the licensing criteria.

Once a pesticide is registered, Section 6 of FIFRA provides authority for EPA to "cancel," or revoke, a registration, after notice and opportunity for hearing, if it appears that there are violations of the Act or that the pesticide, when used as intended, "generally causes unreasonable adverse effects on the environment." The statute also authorizes EPA to order immediate "suspension" of a registration "if necessary to prevent an imminent hazard during the time required for cancellation ... proceedings." FIFRA § 6. Take some time to read FIFRA § 6(a)–(c). Cancellation and suspension procedures will become important in the two cases excerpted below, though these cases interpret an older version of FIFRA with slightly different language governing cancellation and suspension.

This brief overview highlights three of the major characteristics of FIFRA:

First, FIFRA is a licensing statute. It imposes a default prohibition on pesticide sales until the manufacturer has applied for and received a government registration. The decision on whether to register a pesticide involves an individualized, pre-market determination of risk, and the burden of proof is on the applicant. This has many similarities with the U.S. approach to reviewing new drug applications under the FFDCA.

Second, FIFRA is an information disclosure statute. A dominant approach of the statute is risk management through disclosure of pesticide risks and through provision of instructions for safe application.

Third, FIFRA is a risk-benefit balancing statute. The statute does more than just require warnings. It also aims to prevent the sale and use of any pesticide that poses "unreasonable adverse effects on the environment." The registration process explicitly calls on EPA to balance health and environmental risks of a pesticide with the economic, social, and environmental benefits of the pesticide.

FIFRA reflects both consumer protection goals (the pesticide should perform as promised) and environmental protection goals (it should be reasonably safe to use). The consumer protection and environmental protection functions are not necessarily inconsistent. Before 1970, however, the U.S. Department of Agriculture both promoted and regulated pesticides. Promotion and regulation are two very different goals, and their conflict led Congress to move FIFRA under the jurisdiction of the EPA when the agency was created in 1970.

The Supreme Court has described the evolution of FIFRA as a consumer protection and environmental regulation statute:

> As first enacted, FIFRA was primarily a licensing and labeling statute. It required that all pesticides be registered with the Secretary of Agriculture prior to their sale in interstate or foreign commerce. The 1947 legislation also contained general standards setting forth the types of information necessary for proper labeling of a registered pesticide, including directions for use; warnings to prevent harm to people, animals, and plants; and claims made about the efficacy of the product.

> * * *

> Because of mounting public concern about the safety of pesticides and their effect on the environment and because of a growing perception that the existing legislation was not equal to the task of safeguarding the public interest, Congress undertook a comprehensive revision of FIFRA through the adoption of the Federal Environmental Pesticide Control Act of 1972. The amendments transformed FIFRA from a labeling law into a comprehensive regulatory statute. As amended, FIFRA regulated the use, as well as the sale and labeling, of pesticides; regulated pesticides produced and sold in both intrastate and interstate commerce; provided for review, cancellation, and suspension of registration; and gave EPA greater enforcement authority. Congress also added a new criterion for registration: that EPA determine that the pesticide will not cause "unreasonable adverse effects on the environment." §§ 3(c)(5)(c) and (D).

Ruckelshaus v. Monsanto Co., 467 U.S. 986, 990–92 (1984).

The problem below explores the similarities between pesticide and drug registration. It is designed to provide further exposure to FIFRA's premarket licensing strategy.

**PROBLEM
THE PRESCRIPTION DRUG ANALOGY**

As the Supreme Court recounts, FIFRA originated as a consumer protection statute. As such, it was modeled on the Federal Food, Drug, and Cosmetic Act (FFDCA), and it was designed to ensure that pesticides are, like prescription drugs, both safe and effective when properly used. The FFDCA prohibits the sale of drugs that are "adulterated" or "misbranded." Adulteration covers a variety of sins, but its main thrust is what you would expect: products that contain unwholesome contaminants or that have been prepared under substandard conditions. 21 U.S.C. § 351(a). This is largely a matter of inspections and manufacturing practices. The substantive core of the statute is misbranding, and misbranding focuses attention on the drug's labeling. A drug is misbranded if, among other things, its labeling is false or misleading or it has inadequate directions or warnings. § 352(a), (f).

While misbranding is a general statutory prohibition, in fact, the principal arbiter of accuracy and adequacy in labeling is the Food and Drug Administration (FDA). A drug must obtain FDA's approval before it can be sold, § 355(a), and the statute creates an elaborate application and approval process. § 355(b)–(d). The manufacturer's application must include samples of all proposed labeling (most importantly, directions and warnings), § 355(b)(1)(F), and FDA must disapprove the application if there is insufficient information to support the claims of safety and effectiveness, or if FDA concludes that the labeling is inadequate. § 355(d)(4), (5), (7). As a practical matter, assuming that a drug can be shown to be effective for some uses and can be reasonably safely prescribed for those uses, much of the approval process involves negotiation over the contents of the warnings and directions on the label. Manufacturers tend to want to expand the number of uses for which a drug is approved and limit the nature and severity of the warnings; FDA officials tend to approach the label from the opposite direction. The label, then, becomes the principal way for the agency to mediate between the medicinal and harmful effects of prescription drugs.

FIFRA is, to a remarkable extent, still structured in the same way. Examine Sections 2, 3, and 12 of FIFRA. Section 12 prohibits misbranding and adulteration. What is "adulteration" under FIFRA? How does it protect the public? What is "misbranding?" What is the substantive standard for determining adequacy of labeling, directions, and warnings? Where is it found? What is the process by which EPA makes these determinations? Criminal penalties are provided for the use of pesticides contrary to their labeling,[3] as they are for prescription drugs. Is that an effective means of control?

Procedurally, you will notice in both Sections 3 and 6 that approval occurs on a case-by-case basis. Is this a necessary corollary to the FFDCA-based regulatory scheme? Could you imagine approvals of whole classes of pesticides, rather than individualized determination of risk? Substantively, what is the reason that Congress adopted a pre-market licensing strategy for both pesticides and drugs? What assumptions about pesticides does a licensing strategy imply? Are those assumptions correct? Why don't we apply a pre-market licensing strategy for other kinds of risky products, such as power tools or sporting goods?

FIFRA is unique among the toxics statutes in being based on a licensing system. Licensing provides an opportunity for governmental review of risks before a product hits the market and also provides incentives for industry to develop data on the nature and extent of risk. Licensing statutes place the burden of proof on the applicant, bringing "the full profit motive to bear in developing adequate [risk] data in an expeditious manner." John S. Applegate, *The Perils of Unreasonable Risk: Information, Regulatory Policy, and Toxic Substances Control*, 91 Colum. L. Rev. 261, 309 (1991). Because of the registration procedures of FIFRA, we have far more information about the toxicity of pesticides than we do about the toxicity of other, non-pesticide chemicals. However, a licensing strategy has drawbacks. These include delays in getting useful products to market, a cumbersome process of chemical-by-chemical review, and a reliance on industry to produce its own risk data, which provides opportunities for bias or "slanting" of data submissions. *Id.*

The cases that follow explore the relationship between FIFRA's licensing strategy and its substantive regulatory standards. They also consider the balance among the many conflicting interests in pesticide manufacture and use that EPA is expected to achieve. As you will see, the cases adopt very different approaches.

Environmental Defense Fund v. EPA (The *Heptachlor/Chlordane* Case)

548 F.2d 998 (D.C. Cir. 1976)

■ Leventhal, Circuit Judge:

This case involves the pesticides heptachlor and chlordane. Consolidated petitions seek review of an order of the Environmental Protection

---

3. *See, e.g., United States v. Saul*, 955 F.Supp. 1073 (E.D. Ark. 1996) (prosecuting a registered private applicator for using a pesticide to turn minnows into poison bait for blackbirds and white egrets, a use which is not authorized; he killed a possum, raccoons, a great horned owl, and blackbirds).

Agency (EPA) suspending the registration of those pesticides under the Federal Insecticide, Fungicide and Rodenticide Act (FIFRA) for certain uses. The Administrator of EPA issued an order on December 24, 1975. The order prohibited further production of these pesticides for the suspended uses, but permitted the pesticides' continued production and sale for limited minor uses. Even as to the suspended uses, the Order tempered its impact in certain respects: It delayed until August 1, 1976, the effective date of the prohibition of production for use on corn pests; and it permitted the continued sale and use of existing stocks of registered products formulated prior to July 29, 1975.

One petition to review was filed by Earl L. Butz, Secretary of Agriculture of the United States (U.S.D.A.). Secretary Butz and intervenor Velsicol Chemical Corporation, the sole manufacturer of heptachlor and chlordane, urge that the EPA order as to chlordane be set aside on both substantive and procedural grounds.[4] They contend that substantial evidence does not support the Administrator's conclusion that continued use of chlordane poses an "imminent hazard" to human health, and that the Administrator made critical errors in assessing the burden of proof and in weighing the benefits against the risks of continued use of chlordane.

The other petition, filed by Environmental Defense Fund, urges that the Order did not go far enough to protect against the hazards of heptachlor and chlordane use. EDF sought an injunction against the provisions permitting continued production and use of the pesticides on corn pests until August 1, 1976. EDF also challenges the Administrator's decision to allow continued use of the stocks of the two pesticides existing as of July 29, contending that EPA should have provided for retrieval and controlled disposal of such stocks. EDF also contends that the Administrator erred in failing to suspend certain "minor uses" of chlordane and heptachlor.

* * *

I. *STATUTORY FRAMEWORK AND STANDARD OF REVIEW*

The issues posed by administrative action pursuant to FIFRA are not new to this court, and we have previously extensively described the statutory framework for such actions. What is involved here is a suspension of registration of two pesticides during the pendency of the more elaborate cancellation of registration proceeding, initiated in this case by a November 18, 1974, notice of intent to cancel. This 1974 notice stated that there existed "substantial questions of safety amounting to an unreasonable risk to man and the environment" from continued use of heptachlor and chlordane. Public cancellation hearings pursuant to that notice were not expected to commence for some time. On July 29, 1975, the Administrator issued a Notice of Intent to Suspend the registrations of most uses of the two pesticides. The Administrator then commented on that expected delay in completing the cancellation hearings, and cited "new evidence * * * which

---

4. Velsicol has voluntarily ceased production of heptachlor for the uses suspended by the Administrator, and has not really attacked the Administrator's decision suspending those uses. * * *

confirms and heightens the human cancer hazard posed by these pesticides." On August 4, 1975, registrant Velsicol Chemical Corporation requested an expedited adversary hearing on the suspension question pursuant to § 6 of FIFRA. Administrative Law Judge Herbert L. Perlman presided over the cancellation hearings beginning August 12. Evidence was limited to human health issues and the benefits of continued use of heptachlor and chlordane. The record was closed December 4, 1975, and on December 12, the ALJ recommended against suspension, stating that he was unable to find that "heptachlor and chlordane are conclusively carcinogens in laboratory animals." The Administrator reversed that decision on December 24, 1975, and suspended most uses of chlordane and heptachlor.

The Administrator is authorized to suspend the registration of a pesticide where he determines that an "imminent hazard" is posed by continued use during the time required for cancellation. Section 6(c) of FIFRA. An "imminent hazard" exists where continued use during the time required for the cancellation proceeding would be likely to result in "unreasonable adverse effects on the environment." Section 2(l) of FIFRA. The term "unreasonable adverse effects on the environment" is, in turn, defined as "any unreasonable risk to man or the environment, taking into account the economic, social, and environmental costs and benefits of the use of any pesticide." Section 2(bb) of FIFRA.

As in our previous suspension case involving aldrin/dieldrin, the primary challenge raised by Velsicol and USDA goes to the adequacy of the evidentiary basis of EPA's finding that the suspended pesticides present an imminent hazard during the time required for cancellation. The standard against which we test that challenge is defined in Section 16(b) of FIFRA:

> The court shall consider all evidence of record. The order of the Administrator shall be sustained if it is supported by substantial evidence when considered on the record as a whole.

The standard of substantial evidence has been defined as:

> something less than the weight of the evidence * * * (T)he possibility of drawing two inconsistent conclusions from the evidence does not prevent an administrative agency's finding from being supported by substantial evidence.

In applying this principle of review[5] in the specific context of a suspension of pesticides, this court has reiterated that "the function of the suspension decision is to make a preliminary assessment of evidence, and probabilities, not an ultimate resolution of difficult issues. We cannot accept the proposition * * * that the Administrator's findings * * * (are) insufficient because controverted by respectable scientific authority. It (is) enough at this stage that the administrative record contain(s) respectable scientific authority supporting the Administrator."

---

5. The problem of applying the substantial evidence standard to decisions made at the frontiers of scientific knowledge was commented on in *Industrial Union v. Hodgson*, 499 F.2d 467 (1974) [discussed, *supra*, in Chapter 3 (Judicial Role)]. Similar problems are presented in review under the arbitrary and capricious standard.

These decisions of our court also point out that the Administrator is not required to establish that the product is unsafe in order to suspend registration, since FIFRA places "(t)he burden of establishing the safety of a product requisite for compliance with the labeling requirements * * * at all times on the applicant and registrant." Velsicol and USDA urge that this allocation of burden of proof relied on by the Administrator is inconsistent with the explicit terms of FIFRA. They rely on FIFRA's specific incorporation of subchapter II of the Administrative Procedure Act, which provides in relevant part that "Except as otherwise provided by statute, the proponent of a rule or order shall have the burden of proof." 5 U.S.C. § 556(d).

The EPA regulation governing the burden of proof in suspension proceedings provides:

> At the hearing, the proponent of suspension shall have the burden of going forward to present an affirmative case for the suspension. However, the ultimate burden of persuasion shall rest with the proponent of the registration.

Assuming that the Administrator is the "proponent" of a suspension order and is governed by § 556(d), the [1946] legislative history of that provision indicates that it allocates the burden of going forward rather than the burden of ultimate persuasion and is consistent with the EPA's apportionment of burden:

> That the proponent of a rule or order has the burden of proof means not only that the party initiating the proceeding has the general burden of coming forward with a prima facie case but that other parties, who are proponents of some different result, also for that purpose have a burden to maintain.

This allocation of the burden of going forward structures evaluation of the factual evidence adduced for both the Administrator and the reviewing court, and is consistent with the traditional approach that this burden normally falls on the party having knowledge of the facts involved.

In urging that the ultimate burden of proof in a suspension proceeding rests on the Administrator, Velsicol and USDA assert that the suspension decision is a drastic step differing fundamentally from both the registration and cancellation decisions made under FIFRA. But we have already cautioned that the "imminent hazard" requisite for suspension is not limited to a concept of crisis: "It is enough if there is *substantial likelihood* that serious harm will be experienced during the year or two required in any realistic projection of the administrative process." "FIFRA confers broad discretion" on the Administrator to find facts and "to set policy in the public interest." *Wellford v. Ruckelshaus,* 439 F.2d 598, 601 (1971). This broad discretion was conferred on the implicit assumption that interim action may be necessary to protect against the risk of harm to the environment and public health while a fuller factual record is developed in the cancellation proceeding. This avenue of protective relief would be effectively foreclosed if we accepted Velsicol's argument that the Administrator must prove imminent hazard apparently in some sense of weight of the evidence, going beyond substantial likelihood. But as we have already pointed out, the basic statutory directive requires affirmation of the Administrator's decision if supported by substantial evidence, and this requires "something less than the weight of the evidence." We reject that renewed invitation to exercise increased substantive control over the agency decision process, and turn to a consideration of whether the Administrator's decision to suspend most uses of heptachlor and chlordane is supported by substantial evidence.

II. SUBSTANTIAL EVIDENCE SUPPORT FOR THE ADMINISTRATOR'S DECISION

To evaluate whether use of a pesticide poses an "unreasonable risk to man or the environment," the Administrator engages in a cost-benefit analysis that takes "into account the economic, social, and environmental costs and benefits of the use of any pesticide." 7 U.S.C. § 136(bb). We have previously recognized that in the "preliminary assessment of probabilities" involved in a suspension proceeding, "it is not necessary to have evidence on * * * a specific use or area in order to be able to conclude on the basis of substantial evidence that the use of (a pesticide) in general is hazardous." *EDF v. EPA*, 489 F.2d at 1254, *quoted in EDF v. EPA (Shell Chemical Co.)*, 510 F.2d at 1301. "Reliance on general data, consideration of laboratory experiments on animals, etc." has been held a sufficient basis for an order canceling or suspending the registration of a pesticide. Once risk is shown, the responsibility to demonstrate that the benefits outweigh the risks is upon the proponents of continued registration. Conversely, the statute places a "heavy burden" of explanation on an Administrator who decides to permit the continued use of a chemical known to produce cancer in experimental animals. Applying these principles to the evidence adduced in this case, we conclude that the Administrator's decision to suspend most uses of heptachlor and chlordane and not to suspend others is supported by substantial evidence and is a rational exercise of his authority under FIFRA.

A. Risk Analysis of Carcinogenicity of Heptachlor and Chlordane

Velsicol and USDA contend that the laboratory tests on mice and rats do not "conclusively" demonstrate that chlordane is carcinogenic to those animals; that mice are too prone to tumors to be used in carcinogenicity testing in any case; and that human exposure to chlordane is insufficient to create a cancer risk. They place strong reliance on the Administrative Law Judge's refusal to recommend suspension because he was *"hesitantly unwilling at this time* to find that heptachlor and chlordane are conclusively carcinogens in laboratory animals." [emphasis in original]. The ALJ recognized however, that on the basis of the record made the Administrator "could determine that the pesticides involved pose potential or possible carcinogenic risk to man" and that he could "find that heptachlor and chlordane are conclusively carcinogenic in laboratory animals." While adopting the ALJ's factual findings, the Administrator concluded that the ALJ had applied an erroneous legal standard in requiring a conclusive rather than probable showing that the pesticides were animal carcinogens, and concluded in any case that the evidence showed heptachlor and chlordane to be animal carcinogens. We affirm.

1. Mice and Rat Studies

An ultimate finding in a suspension proceeding that continued use of challenged pesticides poses a "substantial likelihood of serious harm" must be supported by substantial, but not conclusive, evidence. In evaluating laboratory animal studies on heptachlor and chlordane there was sufficient "respectable scientific authority" upon which the Administrator could rely in determining that heptachlor and chlordane were carcinogenic in laboratory animals. * * * Velsicol was properly given an opportunity to put in evidence contesting [EPA principles accepting use of animal test data to evaluate human cancer risks], but failed to demonstrate anything more than some scientific disagreement with respect to them. Velsicol's principal complaint that mice are inappropriate test animals was specifically rejected by the Administrator * * *.

* * *

2. Extrapolation of Animal Data to Man

Human epidemiology studies so far attempted on chlordane and heptachlor gave no basis for concluding that the two pesticides are safe with respect to the issue of cancer. To conclude that they pose a carcinogenic risk to humans on the basis of such a finding of risk to laboratory animals, the Administrator must show a causal connection between the uses of the pesticides challenged and resultant exposure of humans to those pesticides. He made that link by showing that widespread residues of heptachlor and chlordane are present in the human diet and in human tissues. Their widespread occurrence in the environment and accumulation in the food chain is explained by their chemical properties of persistence, mobility and high solubility in lipids (the fats contained in all organic substances). Residues of chlordane and heptachlor remain in soils and in air and aquatic ecosystems for long periods of time. They are readily transported by means of vaporization, aerial drift, and runoff of eroding soil particles. The residues have been consistently found in meat, fish, poultry, and dairy products monitored in the FDA Market Basket Survey and are also frequent in components of animal feeds. This evidence supports a finding that a major route of human exposure is ingestion of contaminated foodstuffs. EPA's National Human Monitoring Survey data shows that heptachlor epoxide and oxychlordane, the principal metabolites of heptachlor and chlordane respectively, are present in the adipose tissue of over 90% of the U.S. population.

* * *

Velsicol urges that the dietary exposure resulting from agricultural uses of the pesticides is insignificant, and that current exposure is well below "safe" dose levels as calculated by the Mantel–Bryan formula, or by the World Health Organization's Acceptable Daily Intake figures. Mantel himself criticized the use of the formula for a persistent pesticide, and the Administrator rejected the concept of a "safe" dose level defined by mathematical modeling because of "the incomplete assumptions made by the registrant's witnesses about the sources of human exposure in the environment, the natural variation in human susceptibility to cancer, the lack of any evidence relating the level of human susceptibility to cancer from heptachlor and chlordane as opposed to that of the mouse, and the absence of precise knowledge as to the minimum exposure to a carcinogen necessary to cause cancer." That explanation is within the reasonable bounds of the agency's expertise in evaluating evidence. And it is confirmed by the common sense recognition that reliance on average "safe" dietary levels fail to protect people with dietary patterns based on high proportional consumption of residue-contaminated foods (*e.g.*, children who ingest greater quantities of milk than the general population).

There are several non-agricultural uses which involve a large volume of heptachlor and chlordane as well as significant human exposures. For example, the record shows that approximately six million pounds of chlordane are used annually on home lawns and gardens. The Administrator found that these uses involve high risks of human intake "due to the many avenues which exist for direct exposure, through improper handling and misuse, inhalation, and absorption through the skin from direct contact." * * * We have previously held that it is not necessary to have evidence on a specific use to be able to conclude that the use of a pesticide in general is hazardous. Once the initial showing of hazard is made for one mode of exposure in a suspension proceeding, and the pesticide is shown to be present in human tissues, the burden shifts to the registrant to rebut the inference that other modes of exposure may also pose a carcinogenic hazard for humans. Velsicol has totally failed to meet that burden here. * * *

B. Benefits

Velsicol and USDA challenge the Administrator's finding that the benefits derived from the suspended uses of chlordane do not outweigh the harms done. EDF urges that the Administrator's decision to continue some uses was not justified by evidence that the risk of harm was outweighed by benefits from the continued uses.

1. Use on Corn

Heptachlor and chlordane were used on an estimated 3.5% of the total corn acreage in the United States in 1975, largely in an effort to control black cutworm. Cutworms sporadically infest 2 to 8% of total U.S. corn farms, and occur most often in lowland, river bottom areas. Chlordane and heptachlor are used as preplant treatments to insure against possible infestations. The Administrator found, with record support, that no macroeconomic impact will occur as a result of suspending those pesticides. He also found that crop surveillance or "scouting" for infestations during the early weeks of plant growth, together with application of post-emergence baits or sprays where necessary, provide an effective alternative to the more indiscriminate prophylactic use of chlordane and heptachlor. Velsicol urges that this approach is not as effective as the persistent protection provided by chlordane. Especially in the absence of proof of a serious threat to the nation's corn, there is no requirement that a pesticide can be suspended only if alternatives to its use are absolutely equivalent in effectiveness. * * *

* * *

3. Non–Agricultural Uses Suspended by the Administrator

Chlordane is a common household, lawn, garden, and ornamental turf insecticide, with over 7.5 million pounds (36% of total use) so employed in 1974. The ALJ and Administrator found on the basis of substantial evidence that the "efficaciousness of the substitutes for control of household and lawn insects is not really at issue" and that when lack of evidence of substantial benefits from continued use is weighed against the special hazards of exposure presented by the possibilities of inhalation, dermal absorption, and the increased dangers associated with improper handling, suspension of those uses was justified. Similarly, on the basis of evidence in the record, the Administrator could reasonably find that the residual capacity of chlordane was not necessary to control either structural pests or ticks and chiggers, given the existence of effective alternatives to each of those uses.

4. The Administrator's Refusal to Suspend Certain Uses

EDF challenges the Administrator's refusal to suspend use of chlordane or heptachlor on strawberries, for seed treatment, pineapples, the white fringed beetle, Florida citrus, white grubs in Michigan, narcissi bulbs, harvester ants, imported fire ant, Japanese beetle quarantine, and black vine weevil quarantine in Michigan. Following the recommendations of the ALJ, the Administrator found that for each use the benefits outweighed the risks for the limited time under consideration, effective alternatives were generally not available, and that the exposure risk arising from the use was minimal. EDF counters that the total exposure resulting from these "minor" uses is in fact significant, and that the Administrator continued these uses whenever a "colorable" case of benefits had been made out.

Once the Administrator has found that a risk inheres in the use of a pesticide, he has an obligation to explain how the benefits of continued use outweigh that risk. We are satisfied that he has met that obligation here, and that substantial evidence supports his decision. We note, however, that we come to this conclusion in the context of a suspension proceeding where perforce the Administrator is engaged in making a "preliminary assessment" of the evidence; a more careful exploration of economic impact and available alternatives would be required to support continued registration in a cancellation proceeding.

C. Continued Sale and Use of Existing Stocks of Chlordane and Heptachlor for Suspended Uses

Although we have no doubt that the Administrator has the power under FIFRA to exempt from a suspension order the use of existing stocks (in this case stocks existing as of July 29, 1975), the Administrator acted arbitrarily when he failed to even inquire into the amount of stocks left, and the problem of returning and disposing of them. Some evidence must be adduced before an exemption decision is made, and it is the responsibility of the registrant to provide it. It may be that the lapse of time has lessened the current significance of this issue but we are in no position to do other than remand for further consideration.

We affirm the Agency's suspension order of December 24, 1975, as clarified by the order of January 19, 1976, except for the exemption of the sale and use of existing stocks. The record is remanded for further consideration of that issue.

SUPPLEMENTAL OPINION ON PETITION FOR REHEARING

Velsicol argues in its petition for rehearing that in upholding the Administrator's allocation of the burden of proof to the registrant this Court misinterpreted § 7(c) of the Administrative Procedure Act. Velsicol points out that the interpretation adopted by this Court was not advanced by any of the parties and that, in fact, the problem of interpreting the APA as opposed to Section 6(c)(2) of FIFRA was not briefed or argued in this proceeding.

* * *

This court has repeatedly held that the 1964 amendments to FIFRA were specifically intended to shift the burden of proof from the Secretary (now the Administrator) to the registrant. In *EDF v. Ruckelshaus, supra*, the court explained:

> Prior to 1964, the FIFRA required the Secretary to register "under protest" any pesticide or other item that failed to meet the statutory requirements. The product remained on the market, and the Secretary reported the violation to the United States Attorney for possible prosecution. In 1964 the statute was amended to eliminate the system of protest registration, and substitute the present administrative mechanism for canceling registrations. The stated purpose of the amendment was to protect the public by removing from the market any product whose safety or effectiveness was doubted by the Secretary. * * *

> Thus, we found that "(t)he legislative history supports the conclusion that Congress intended any substantial question of safety to trigger the issuance of cancellation notices, shifting to the manufacturer the burden of proving the safety of his product."

> Subsequent decisions reaffirmed this interpretation. * * *

* * *

Lastly, we do not discern in the statute an allocation of burden of proof that is different for suspension hearings than for registration or cancellation proceedings. While the suspension proceeding is in progress, the public is subject to the same risks of injury that are present in the cancellation context, the very risks which caused Congress to shift the burden of proof to the registrant in the original registration. Information relevant to the safety issues is or should be in the possession of the manufacturer. * * *

National Coalition Against the Misuse of Pesticides v. EPA

867 F.2d 636 (D.C. Cir. 1989)

■ SILBERMAN, CIRCUIT JUDGE:

The Administrator of the Environmental Protection Agency appeals from an order of the district court permanently enjoining EPA from permitting "sales, commercial use and commercial application of existing stocks" of the termiticides chlordane and heptachlor pursuant to a settlement agreement under which the producers of the chemicals agreed to voluntary cancellation of the chemicals' registrations under the Federal Insecticide, Fungicide and Rodenticide Act ("FIFRA"). We think the district court misconstrued the relevant provisions of FIFRA by holding unlawful EPA's determination to permit continued sale and use of existing stocks of the canceled termiticides. Accordingly, we reverse the district court and remand with instructions to vacate the injunction and thereby allow EPA to fulfill its commitments under the original settlements.

I

FIFRA provides a comprehensive framework for regulating the sale and distribution of pesticides within the United States. Under the statute, EPA may not approve a pesticide's introduction into commerce unless the Administrator finds that the pesticide "will not generally cause unreasonable adverse effects on the environment" when used in accordance with any EPA-imposed restrictions and "with widespread and commonly recognized practice." 7 U.S.C. § 136a(c)(5)(D) (1982). "Unreasonable adverse effects on the environment" are defined to include "any unreasonable risk to man or the environment, taking into account the economic, social, and environmental costs and benefits of the use of any pesticide." § 136(bb). With few exceptions, FIFRA prohibits the sale, distribution, and professional use of unregistered pesticides. §§ 136a(a) & 136j(a)(1).

Once registered, pesticides are still subject to continuing scrutiny by EPA. Indeed, Section 6 of FIFRA requires EPA to cancel a pesticide's registration after the first five years in which the registration has been effective (and at the conclusion of subsequent five year periods if the registration is renewed) "unless the registrant, or other interested person with the concurrence of the registrant, ... requests ... that the registration be continued in effect." § 136d(a). And at any time, EPA may propose cancellation of a registration and initiate elaborate cancellation proceedings if "it appears to the Administrator that a pesticide ... does not comply with [FIFRA] or ... generally causes unreasonable adverse effects on the environment...." § 136d(b).

During the pendency of cancellation proceedings, the registration remains in effect unless the Administrator "suspend[s] the registration of the pesticide immediately." § 136d(c). But before suspending, the Administrator must determine that an "imminent hazard" exists—that "continued use of the pesticide during the time required for cancellation proceeding[s] would be likely to result in unreasonable adverse effects on the environment...." § 136(*l*). Even then, FIFRA guarantees registrants the right to an expedited administrative hearing on that issue, and the pesticide's registration remains effective during this latter proceeding. § 136d(c)(2). Only if "the Administrator determines that an emergency exists that does not permit him to hold a hearing before suspending" may he prohibit commerce in the pesticide in advance of administrative proceedings. § 136d(c)(3).

While commerce in unregistered pesticides is generally prohibited, the Administrator may permit continued sale and use of existing stocks of pesticides whose registrations have been canceled provided "he determines that such sale or use is not inconsistent with the purposes of this subchapter and will not have unreasonable adverse effects on the environment." § 136d(a)(1). It is this last provision—Section 6(a)(1), concerning the disposition of existing stocks—that we are called upon to interpret today.

Chlordane and heptachlor (to which we refer simply as "chlordane") are part of a class of chlorinated hydrocarbon insecticides known generally as "cyclodienes," introduced into the marketplace for general use in the late 1940s and early 1950s. In recent years, the chemical has been sold and distributed both by chlordane's sole manufacturer, Velsicol Chemical Company, and a number of so-called "reformulator" companies who acquire chlordane from Velsicol and manufacture derivative products. Until 1987, Velsicol and the reformulators maintained various registrations for these products with EPA.

The regulatory action challenged here—concerning the termiticide uses of chlordane—follows an earlier, fiercely disputed controversy regarding the more general uses of the chemical. * * *

The termiticide uses of chlordane were not subject to the 1978 settlement, but the risks and benefits of such uses have been under more or less continuous study by EPA since the late 1970s. * * *

* * * [By 1987, EPA was prepared to conclude] that "the risks of continued use [of chlordane] outweigh the benefits"[, and it] prepared a draft notice of intent to cancel the termiticide registrations of chlordane.

In the meantime, NCAMP and the other plaintiffs brought this action in district court seeking cancellation and emergency suspension. Unbeknownst to them, at some point either shortly before or after the institution of litigation, EPA became engaged in settlement discussions with Velsicol concerning Velsicol's termiticide registrations. These negotiations led to an agreement whereby Velsicol consented to cancellation of certain registered termiticide uses, to suspension of certain others pending the completion of outstanding "data call-ins," and to a cessation of all manufacture, distribution, and sale of chlordane. In exchange, EPA agreed to permit indefinitely the sale and use of existing stocks of chlordane outside the control of Velsicol, which EPA estimated to amount to a two-months' supply at normal application rates.[6]

Upon publication of the settlement terms, plaintiffs amended their complaint and moved to restrain EPA from permitting any use of the existing stocks exempted from the EPA–Velsicol agreement, claiming that EPA had arbitrarily and capriciously failed to make the required FIFRA

---

6. Contemporaneously, EPA apparently executed similar voluntary cancellation agreements with certain of the reformulator registrants of chlordane. These settlements were not made public until the fall of 1987. Other reformulators had their product registrations suspended for failure to respond to EPA's December 1986 "data call-in," see 7 U.S.C. § 136a(c)(2)(B)(iv) (1982); the existing stocks outside the control of this latter group were subject to no restrictions as well. * * *

Section 6(a)(1) determination that "continued sale and use of [those] existing stocks ... [would] not have unreasonable adverse effects on the environment." 7 U.S.C. § 136d(a)(1) (1982). * * *

The Assistant Administrator's statement [in support of EPA's position] began by asserting that the evidentiary standards for a cancellation, suspension, and emergency suspension of a pesticide are different, with the latter two of the three being especially rigorous. He then recounted the scientific evidence (which he claimed was both disputed and incomplete) concerning the health risks of chlordane exposure, and, as required by the statute, weighed those risks against the "substantial" economic benefits of continued use of chlordane. In view of this risk-benefit analysis, and in light of EPA's conclusion that such analysis did not "warrant [ ] an emergency suspension, or even an ordinary suspension," Dr. Moore stated that EPA had preliminarily decided to issue only a notice of intent to cancel chlordane's termiticide registrations. Under these circumstances, according to Dr. Moore, the subsequent settlement with Velsicol, and its existing stocks provision:

> effected a dramatic reduction in the amount of chlordane compared to what would have been sold and used if there had been no settlement. Of course, if the cancellation proceeding did not result in cancellation, substantially greater amounts of chlordane would continue to have been used. Even if there had been a suspension hearing ..., the six months of hearings would have produced substantially more chlordane than is currently in the hands of applicators and distributors. Thus, the existing stocks provision in the settlement agreement did not constitute a true concession on the Agency's part; it did not permit any additional use that would not have occurred had the Agency declined to adopt the settlement.

Thus, EPA's Section 6(a)(1) determination in support of the existing stocks settlement provision rested principally on the notion that formal cancellation (and suspension) proceedings would allow much larger quantities of chlordane to be introduced into the environment.

On cross motions for summary judgment, the district court found EPA's final Section 6(a)(1) determination inadequate. * * * The district court thus construed Section 6(a)(1) of FIFRA, in the context of cancellation settlements, to require that the Administrator focus his analysis solely on the risks and benefits of continued use of the quantity of *then*-existing stocks, without consideration of what quantities of product might be *added* to pesticide stocks during agency proceedings *sans* a settlement agreement.[7] Accordingly, the district court held that EPA had failed to comply with Section 6(a)(1) and issued an order requiring EPA to prohibit by April 15, 1988, "sales, commercial use and commercial application of existing stocks of chlordane ... which have been the subject of voluntary cancellations...."

II

---

7. The court therefore found it unnecessary to inquire into the reasonableness of EPA's determination that suspension or emergency suspension of chlordane's registrations was inappropriate.

The district court implicitly interpreted Section 6(a)(1) to require the Administrator, when he negotiates a voluntary cancellation agreement, to assume hypothetically that he has already issued a cancellation order before he considers the existing stocks question. If a cancellation order formally issued—if cancellation proceedings had concluded—then the Administrator, when he turned to the issue of existing stocks, would have no reason to consider stock sales made during the pendency of litigation. Those sales or uses would have been accomplished and therefore beyond the regulatory power of the Administrator. So, according to appellees and the district court, it is illegitimate for the Administrator to take into account sales or uses that would otherwise be made during the period of litigation when negotiating an agreed-upon cancellation. In other words, the phrase "such sale or use" in Section 6(a)(1) refers only to sales or uses separately contemplated after a registration is actually canceled, and therefore the Administrator's interpretation of Section 6(a)(1) allowing consideration of sales or uses that would take place absent the settlement is impermissible.

* * *

Keeping in mind that it is common ground that the statute contemplates settlements, * * * the Administrator's interpretation facilitates such voluntary cancellations and the district court and appellees' interpretation does not. If the Administrator were not authorized to enter into settlement agreements containing existing stocks exemptions, registrants would have every incentive to contest cancellation proceedings, both for the prospect of prevailing and to use litigation time to dispose, at minimum, of existing stocks. In construing statutes that authorize enforcement proceedings, we look with disfavor upon interpretations offered by parties, in opposition to the administering agency, that induce litigation by making settlement impracticable.

Appellees contend that this litigation risk, which the Administrator avoids through settlement, is illusory. They emphasize that the proponent of continued registration bears the burden of persuasion as to whether a given chemical "generally causes unreasonable adverse effects on the environment." *See, e.g.*, 40 C.F.R. §§ 164.121(g), 164.80(b) (1987). But this procedural rule—as important as it may be—hardly eliminates the litigation risk for the Administrator, when acting in his prosecutorial role. Nor do our cases holding that the Administrator satisfies his burden of production by proffering "substantial evidence" of harm from respected scientific sources, *see Environmental Defense Fund, Inc. v. EPA*, 548 F.2d 998, 1005 (D.C.Cir.1976). *Environmental Defense Fund, Inc. v. EPA*, 510 F.2d 1292, 1297 (D.C.Cir.1975); *Environmental Defense Fund, Inc. v. EPA*, 465 F.2d 528, 537 (D.C.Cir.1972), mean that the Administrator is guaranteed victory if the proceedings are contested by the registrant and the ultimate order challenged subsequently in federal court. In any event, the Administrator *himself*, wearing his adjudicatory hat, might determine after an administrative hearing (involving the expenditure of substantial administrative resources) that scientific uncertainty as to the danger of a particular pesticide (combined perhaps with the economic impact of cancellation on "agricultural commodities, retail food prices and [ ] the agricultural economy," 7 U.S.C. § 136d(b) (1982)), indicates that the registration should not be canceled.

We cannot see how the statutory purpose is enhanced by interpreting FIFRA's ambiguous language to force the Administrator to litigate aggressively, even where a settlement might avoid administrative costs, litigation imponderables and, perhaps most important, continued sales of the product during administrative proceedings. After all, the Administrator's charge under Section 6(a)(1) is to determine whether permission to continue to sell or use existing stocks will have an *unreasonable* adverse effect" on the environment. § 136d(a)(1) (emphasis added). If entering into a settlement provides for less use than would be the case if the Administrator initiated formal cancellation proceedings, it seems rather obvious that the settlement, at minimum, meets the statutory test of reasonableness.

Appellees argue that the Administrator's primary rationale for agreeing to the settlement terms—that more chlordane would have been sold and used during litigation than the small amount that the Administrator allowed to be disposed of as part of the settlement—is a red herring. The Administrator, it is contended, could have issued a notice of intent to cancel *and* proceeded immediately to a suspension order or an emergency order, either of which would have avoided the existing stocks problem. One obvious difficulty with the appellees' argument in this case, however, is that even a suspension order could not have been issued before a hearing was conducted (assuming one was requested), which we are told would likely have lasted six months. Only by use of a draconian emergency order would the Administrator have avoided a hearing delay. This argument, moreover, is a good deal broader than simply a challenge to the Administrator's settlement policy. Appellees assert that a determination on the part of the Administrator to issue a notice of intent to cancel a pesticide necessarily implies a determination—except in rare cases—that the basis for seeking a suspension or emergency order has been acknowledged. So, goes the argument, it is a violation of the statute—in the normal case[8]—for the Administrator not to seek interim expedited relief when he issues his notice of intent to cancel.

In this case, it will be recalled, the Administrator had not yet issued a notice of intent to cancel. A draft notice had been prepared, but settlement discussions commenced and concluded before the Administrator decided to issue the notice. This is not without significance, for FIFRA generally requires the Administrator to consult with the Secretary of Agriculture (on economic questions) and a seven-member Scientific Advisory Panel (on environmental health questions) prior to making public any notice of intent to cancel. We are informed that the Administrator had not yet engaged in the required consultation by the time the instant litigation began. Nevertheless, we do not think this point is decisive. Had the notice issued, we do

---

8. Under appellees' narrow construction of the statute, the Administrator could refuse to seek suspension or emergency suspension upon noticing a cancellation only if he demonstrated either that short-term exposure to the pesticide does not present the same environmental hazards as long-term exposure, or that economic gains from certain immediate pesticide applications (for which alternative chemicals are not reasonably available) augment the benefit side of the short-term equation.

not believe the case would require different analysis. Appellees' logic fails on this account: the EPA reasonably reads the statute to provide different evidentiary thresholds for the three procedures the Administrator is authorized to pursue in defeating an existing registration. Accordingly, we think appellees incorrect in assuming that grounds which may support a cancellation notice automatically warrant the Administrator's recourse to FIFRA's summary procedures.

The language of the statute and the case law amply demonstrate that EPA's reading, even if arguably not compelled by the legislative text, is at least consistent with it. A notice of intent to cancel is called for if it *"appears to the Administrator that a pesticide ... generally causes unreasonable adverse effects on the environment."* 7 U.S.C. § 136d(b) (1982) (emphasis added). We have interpreted this standard as obliging the Administrator to issue such a notice "and thereby initiate the administrative process whenever there is a substantial question about the safety of a registered pesticide." *Environmental Defense Fund, Inc. v. Ruckelshaus*, 439 F.2d 584, 594 (D.C.Cir.1971). That standard is perhaps even less rigorous than the typical "reason to believe" with which many agencies begin enforcement proceedings. Analytically, a notice of intent to cancel is little more than "a determination ... that adjudicatory proceedings will commence."

By comparison, the Administrator may issue a notice of suspension only if he determines it "is necessary to prevent an imminent hazard" to human health or the environment. 7 U.S.C. § 136d(c)(1) (1982). If the notice is contested, the Administrator must conduct an "expedited" hearing before the suspension can take effect. § 136d(c)(2). We have described that standard as calling for more than a mere "substantial question of safety"; it requires an appraisal that harm to humans or the environment "would be likely to result" during the period required for interagency consultation and cancellation hearings. § 136(l); *see also Environmental Defense Fund, Inc.*, 548 F.2d at 1005 ("It is enough [to justify suspension] if there is substantial likelihood that serious harm will be experienced during the ... administrative process." (*quoting Environmental Defense Fund, Inc.*, 465 F.2d at 540)). The extraordinary step of emergency suspension is available only if the requisite unreasonable harm would be likely to materialize during the pendency of ordinary suspension proceedings. The Administrator therefore reasonably requires a showing of even more immediate harm before he may halt commerce in a pesticide prior to conducting often lengthy administrative proceedings.

From these different statutory standards it follows that the quality and quantity of evidence of harm to the environment that the Administrator properly requires before choosing one of these three procedural routes will vary along a continuum. The statute authorizes the Administrator to reserve expedited procedures for cases in which the available data reliably demonstrate some sort of immediate threat or where the information before him suggests greater certainty concerning the pesticide's danger to humans than would warrant merely initiating cancellation proceedings. It is true that we have held that the Administrator bears a heavy burden of explaining his decision not to seek suspension when he has issued a notice of cancellation under circumstances where there are "no offsetting claim[s] of any benefit to the public" in using the pesticide. However, our prior decisions in no way purport to conflate the varying standards for issuing a cancellation notice, noticing a suspension, and imposing an emergency suspension.

Under EPA's reasonable reading of the statute, then, the facts placed before the Administrator that might justify issuing a notice of intent to cancel may not necessarily justify suspension or emergency suspension procedures. Perhaps the most important variable in the Administrator's decision, one discounted by appellees, is the degree of certainty the scientific data provide as to the pesticide's danger. In cases such as ours, where the scientific data are uncertain and scientific opinion divided, we do not think Congress intended FIFRA to compel the Administrator to initiate expedited procedures. With that understanding we think appellees' argument concerning the proper construction of Section 6(a)(1) fails. It is not necessary for us to decide whether, if the Administrator had sought an interim prohibition of commerce in chlordane in this case and been challenged in court, we would have sustained his action. Suffice it for us to recognize that EPA reasonably distinguishes the standards for initiating these procedures. Given the difference in these discrete standards, it follows that there is no statutory bar to the Administrator's permitting sale or use of existing stocks in return for a registrant's consent to cancel an active pesticide registration.

III

The district court did not reach the question—which it had no need to do given its statutory construction—whether EPA's decision in this case not to pursue interim relief in favor of settling for a voluntary cancellation was arbitrary and capricious. We do so, rather than remand, since the issue is one of law and the record is complete. We believe the Administrator's determination was within the bounds of reasonableness. Assistant Administrator Moore's declaration explained that "many scientists do not think that chlordane poses a major risk to humans" and that "this divergence of viewpoints is one of the reasons [he] believed it important to have the Scientific Advisory Panel review and comment on the cancer issue." Nor did the agency, according to Moore, have reliable data as to the precise impact on fish and wildlife of termiticide uses of chlordane. Appellees do not dispute these contentions, although they do advance the premise that chlordane's risk to humans—whatever the degree of scientific certainty—obliged the Administrator to use expedited procedures in this case. We do not agree. We think the fundamental scientific question concerning the environmental effects of chlordane's termiticide uses was sufficiently unsettled to justify the Administrator's putative determination to seek only an ordinary cancellation. Under these circumstances, we believe it was reasonable for the Administrator to conclude that the settlement he reached, providing as it did for continued sale and use of existing stocks of chlordane, would involve the introduction of more moderate quantities of the chemical into the environment than would have been so if contested proceedings had ensued. Only an emergency suspension order would have resulted in less distribution than the settlement; the Administrator's determination that no emergency existed seems unassailable.

* * *

For the reasons stated, we reverse and remand with instructions to the district court to vacate its injunction so that EPA may fulfill the obligations it undertook in eliciting the cancellation settlements.

NOTES AND QUESTIONS

1. *Process.* Trace the procedures that EPA followed to cancel these registrations. Under the current statute, what is the range of actions that EPA is authorized to take if information comes to light that a pesticide already in use poses unreasonable risks? What are the substantive standards to be applied in each step of registration-cancellation-suspension procedures?

2. *Burden of proof.* The *Heptachlor/Chlordane* case centers on the allocation of the burden of proof, which it divides into a burden of going forward and a burden of persuasion. What is the difference between the two burdens, and how are they allocated by the court?

What is the legal source of the burden of proof holding of the court? Note that it is customary to place the burden of pleading on the party with the best access to information. Edward W. Cleary, *Presuming and Pleading: An Essay on Juristic Immaturity*, 12 Stan. L. Rev. 5, 11–14 (1959). And recall from Chapter 1 that some interpretations of the precautionary principle suggest that risk-creators should bear the burden of proof on acceptable risk. The allocation of the burden of proof can be outcome-determinative in many kinds of cases, and that is surely the case for toxic substances. Why? How did EPA meet its burden in *Heptachlor/Chlordane*?

3. In the early 1970s, as the *Heptachlor/Chlordane* case suggests, EPA had developed a specific litigation strategy for pesticide cancellations. It instituted cancellation proceedings that emphasized animal testing showing carcinogenicity, documented human exposure, and provided evidence of increasing pesticide resistance (which suggested limited benefits). An environmentally activist D.C. Circuit cooperated and produced a remarkable line of cases which almost seem to outdo each other in finding stringency in the statute. The foundation of these cases, detailed in *Heptachlor/Chlordane*, is the insistence that pesticide registrants prove that their products are reasonably safe, rather than the usual requirement that EPA prove unreasonable risk. *See Environmental Defense Fund v. Ruckelshaus*, 439 F.2d 584, 593–94 (D.C. Cir. 1971) ("[A]ny substantial question of safety ... trigger[s] the issuance of cancellation notices, shifting to the manufacturer the burden of proving the safety of his product."). In subsequent cases, the court held that the burden of proof on the applicant meant that the *agency* had to justify any decision *not* to impose its most powerful controls: once it had issued a notice of intent to cancel, the court suggested, the presumption was that suspension ought to follow, *Environmental Defense Fund v. EPA*, 465 F.2d 528 (D.C. Cir. 1972), and that sale of the product would be stopped in the interim. *Environmental Defense Fund v. EPA*, 510 F.2d 1292 (D.C. Cir. 1975). *Heptachlor/Chlordane* was the culmination of this line of cases.

4. *A shift in judicial review?* The procedural setting of the *NCAMP* case is complex, and the importance of the legal issue is a bit difficult to see. What, precisely, is the question before the court, and why is it important?

The *NCAMP* case was decided by a very different Court of Appeals than *Heptachlor/Chlordane*. Eight years of Reagan appointees to the D.C. Circuit had fundamentally altered its ideological point of view. Where do the two cases differ? Are they legally inconsistent, or simply inconsistent in approach or "mood"?

NCAMP is similar in tone to a decision a year earlier in the Ninth Circuit, which concerned EPA's suspension of the pesticide dinoseb, at least as the suspension applied to farmers in the Pacific Northwest. *Love v. Thomas*, 858 F.2d 1347 (9th Cir. 1988). There, the court found fault with EPA's risk-benefit balancing. It remanded for reconsideration of the suspension because EPA had based its suspension on "only a cursory evaluation of the availability of alternative pesticides and the consequent economic impact of suspension" and because "EPA was aware that the Pacific Northwest was subject to unusual conditions that made reliance on national [benefits] figures tenuous, if not completely arbitrary." *Id.* at 1360. The court admonished the agency: "[w]ith all due respect to the EPA and its overworked staff, such insensitivity to the local economic problems caused by its decision is unbecoming and inappropriate." *Id.* at 1362. This can only be characterized as a striking departure from the D.C. Circuit's approach in the 1970s.

Read the current version of Section 6(a)(1) of FIFRA, which was added in 1996. Does it confirm or overrule *NCAMP*?

5. *Pesticide uses.* Both *Heptachlor/Chlordane* and *NCAMP* refer to specific "uses" of pesticides, some of which were canceled, some left alone or modified, and some voluntarily abandoned. Why does EPA regulate particular uses separately, instead of a single standard for all uses of a pesticide? Where in FIFRA is EPA's authority to regulate different uses differently? Is the differentiation among uses related to FIFRA's use of an "unreasonable risk" approach for pesticides?

6. *Risk–Benefit Balancing.* Both *Heptachlor/Chlordane* and *NCAMP* illustrate how FIFRA functions as a risk-benefit balancing statute. Recall that in *Heptachlor/Chlordane*, EPA refused to suspend heptachlor and chlordane for certain uses—such as strawberries, seed treatment, pineapples, Florida citrus, and several others—on the grounds that the benefits of continued use outweighed the projected risks from minimal exposures. How should the agency balance risks and benefits in the context of pesticides? Does the statute require the agency to quantify risks and benefits in monetary terms? If not, how can risks and benefits be compared? Do you believe the D.C. Circuit acted properly in granting a large degree of deference to EPA conclusions on risk-benefit balancing in *Heptachlor/Chlordane*?

3. FIVE PROBLEMS FOR PESTICIDE REGULATION

a. THE DELANEY PARADOX AND THE FOOD QUALITY PROTECTION ACT OF 1996

For many years, a major source of contention in pesticide regulation was the so-called Delaney Paradox. The intersection of the Delaney Clause with FIFRA for pesticide residues on food had resulted in a double standard. For pesticide residues on raw agricultural products or in processed food products in which the processing did not cause the pesticide to concentrate, a pesticide tolerance could be issued on the basis of cost-benefit balancing. For pesticides in other processed foods, on the other hand, the Delaney zero-risk standard applied, meaning that no detectable residues were permitted. By the 1990s, there was general agreement that the differential treatment of residues in processed and raw foods was logically indefensible.

As noted in Chapter 3, the Food Quality Protection Act of 1996 (FQPA) repealed the Delaney Clause for pesticide residues but left it in effect for other carcinogenic food addatives. It also amended the pesticide tolerance provisions of the Food, Drug, and Cosmetic Act to apply a single health-based standard to pesticide residues: EPA could establish, or leave in effect, a pesticide tolerance only if it found there was "a reasonable certainty that no harm will result from aggregate exposure to the pesticide chemical residue." 21 U.S.C. § 346a(b)(2). In making this determination, EPA is required to consider all nonoccupational sources of exposure in its determination (including drinking water and exposure to other pesticides with similar toxic mechanisms). It must also make an explicit determination that the tolerance is safe for children, using an additional safety factor of 10 where necessary to account for uncertainty (the FQPA is one of the only U.S. environmental laws that explicitly calls for building in margins of safety in risk assessment to protect children). Moreover, the FQPA has special provisions for setting tolerances for non-threshold pesticides. Theoretically, a non-threshold pesticide could cause adverse health effects at any level of ingestion by humans. Nevertheless, the FQPA permits EPA to set a tolerance for a non-threshold pesticide if it makes specific findings that the benefits of that pesticide outweigh the risks.[9]

This and other compromises assured overwhelming passage of the FQPA by a Republican Congress and approval by a Democratic president, but the new analyses required by the FQPA have been criticized as impractical.[10] EPA is still struggling with the elaborate analytical tasks it must perform to make the findings required by the statute. John Wargo, an

---

9. Specifically, the EPA must find either that "(I) Use of the pesticide chemical that produces the residue protects consumers from adverse effects on health that would pose a greater risk than the dietary risk from the residue" or that "(II) Use of the pesticide chemical that produces the residue is necessary to avoid a significant disruption in domestic production of an adequate, wholesome, and economical food supply." 21 USC § 346a(b)(2)(B)(iii).

10. *See* Frank B. Cross, *The Consequences of Consensus: Dangerous Compromises of the Food Quality Protection Act*, 75 WASH. U.L.Q. 1155 (1997); Dominic P. Madigan, *Note, Setting an Anti–Cancer Policy: Risk, Politics, and the Food Quality Protection Act of 1996*, 17 VA. ENVTL. L.J. 187 (1998); James S. Turner, *Delaney Lives! Reports of Delaney's Death Are Greatly Exaggerated*, 28 ENVTL. L. REP. 10003 (1998).

advocate of strict pesticide regulation, has explained that the Delaney Clause had an important advantage in that it "avoided exposure assessment. It relied instead on toxicity tests to determine if cancer was "induced" in animals and on food processing tests to find if residues concentrated." But under the FQPA standard, "agency scientists must not only conduct these tests but also combine the results with estimates of pesticide exposure in diverse environments to judge the scale of risk. An enormous window of uncertainty has thus been added to the risk calculation." JOHN WARGO, OUR CHILDREN'S TOXIC LEGACY: HOW SCIENCE AND LAW FAIL TO PROTECT US FROM PESTICIDES 303 (2d ed. 1998).

The new FQPA standard is broadly worded. What does "reasonable certainty of no harm" mean? As in most of the toxics statutes we will examine in this book, Congress did not provide a definition for the core risk standard that is at the center of the statutory scheme. However, legislative history indicates that Congress intended this to mean a one-in-a-million risk level.[11] In other words, EPA should find "reasonable certainty of no harm" if the pesticide tolerance it sets will not cause more than a one-in-a-million increase in the lifetime risk of cancer for someone exposed to that pesticide on food. But why not just spell out that definition in the statute itself? Congress may have wanted the statutory standard to remain some-what vague to accommodate different interests. Read 21 U.S.C. § 346a(b)(2), which is reprinted in chapter 3. How did Congress accommodate the agriculture industry? Environmentalists? Other identifiable groups? Does § 346a(b)(2) make sense as risk assessment policy?

b.   ENDOCRINE DISRUPTION

In the early 1990s, scientists began to report that some common classes of pesticides, including organochlorines and organophosphates, are capable of disrupting the human endocrine (hormonal) system. For instance, the insecticide beta-benzene hexachloride has been identified as an estrogen agonist (mimic), which may overstimulate estrogen receptors in the brain, glands, and reproductive organs. Other pesticides, such as vinclozolin, are believed to be hormonal antagonists (blockers), which prevent normal operation of hormonal signals. The effects of endocrine disruption may include infertility, birth defects (especially abnormal reproductive organs), and learning disorders. According to some studies, pesticides and other chemicals may be responsible for declining sperm counts in men and for increasing rates of early-onset puberty in girls as young as six years old.[12]

---

11. *See* H.R. REP. NO. 104–669, pt. 2, at 41 (1996). That report states: "In the case of a nonthreshold effect which can be assessed through quantitative risk assessment, such as a cancer effect, the Committee expects, based on its understanding of current EPA practice, that a tolerance will be considered to provide a 'reasonable certainty of no harm' if any increase in lifetime risk, based on quantitative risk assessment using conservative assumptions, will be no greater than 'negligible.' It is the Committee's understanding that, under current EPA practice, … EPA interprets a negligible risk to be a one-in-a-million lifetime risk. The Committee expects the Administrator to continue to follow this interpretation."

12. *See, e.g.,* Stefan Lovgren, *Low Sperm Counts Blamed on Pesticides in U.S. Water,* NATIONAL GEOGRAPHIC NEWS, April 27, 2005; Kuriyama et al. *Developmental Exposure to Low–Dose PBDE–99: Effects on Male Fertility and Neurobehavior in Rat Offspring,* 113 ENVTL. HEALTH PERSPECTIVES 149 (2005); J.D. Meeker & H.M. Stapleton, *House Dust Concentrations of*

Our Stolen Future,[13] a 1996 book on endocrine disruption often compared to *Silent Spring*, attracted media and congressional attention to the issue, and research in the past decade has confirmed many of the initial conclusions about the hormonal effects of pesticides.[14]

The increasing evidence that pesticides and other chemicals can disrupt the human endocrine system poses special challenges for risk assessment. For one thing, endocrine disruption is a subtle effect, usually harder to detect than carcinogenic risks from chemicals. Also, many studies have shown that the *timing* of a dose of an endocrine-disrupting chemical, particularly during fetal development, may be far more important than the amount of the dose in triggering adverse effects. For example, exposure of a male fetus to a certain *in utero* dose of a pesticide during the first trimester of a pregnancy may affect its testicular development, while exposure of a male fetus to the same dose later in a pregnancy may have no effect. Endocrine-disrupting chemicals therefore challenge the longstanding risk assessment maxim that "the dose makes the poison." This makes regulatory standard-setting to limit exposure extraordinarily difficult. *See* Noah M. Sachs, *Blocked Pathways: Potential Legal Responses to Endocrine Disrupting Chemicals*, 24 COLUM J. ENVTL. L. 289 (1999).

Endocrine-disrupting chemicals also illustrate how the U.S. government responds to new kinds of toxic risks. Even with just a few years of prior scientific study, Congress was sufficiently concerned about endocrine disruption to include special provisions for it in the 1996 FQPA. In particular, Congress required EPA to create a special Endocrine Disruptor Screening Program, focusing on pesticides, to determine which substances are capable of endocrine disruption. *See* 21 U.S.C. § 346a(p). The FQPA required EPA to develop screening tests within two years and to begin to implement the screening program within three years. *Id.* The screening program was part

Organophosphate Flame Retardants in Relation to Hormone Levels and Semen Quality Parameters, 118 ENVTL. HEALTH PERSPECTIVES 318 (2010). For an overview of the debate over the causes of early-onset puberty, *see* SANDRA STEINGRABER, THE FALLING AGE OF PUBERTY IN U.S. GIRLS: WHAT WE KNOW, WHAT WE NEED TO KNOW (2007). *See also* M.S. Wolff et al., *Investigation of Relationships between Urinary Biomarkers of Phytoestrogens, Phthalates, and Phenols and Pubertal Stages in Girls*. 118 ENVTL. HEALTH PERSPECTIVES 1039 (2010).

13. THEO COLBURN, DIANE DUMANOSKI, & JOHN PETER MYERS, OUR STOLEN FUTURE: ARE WE THREATENING OUR FERTILITY, INTELLIGENCE, AND SURVIVAL? (2006).

14. *See, e.g.*, NATIONAL ACADEMY OF SCIENCES, COMMISSION ON LIFE SCIENCES, HORMONALLY ACTIVE AGENTS IN THE ENVIRONMENT 3 (1999) ("Adverse reproductive and developmental effects have been observed in human populations, wildlife, and laboratory animals as a consequence of exposures to HAAs [Hormonally Active Agents]"); Helle R. Andersen et al., *Impaired Reproductive Development in Sons of Women Occupationally Exposed to Pesticides during Pregnancy*, 116 ENVTL. HEALTH PERSPECTIVES 566, 569 (2008) ("Female greenhouse workers with confirmed pesticide exposure during pregnancy gave birth to boys with smaller penises and testicles, lower serum concentrations of testosterone and inhibin B, [and] higher serum concentrations [of other hormones] than unexposed workers."); WuQiang Fan et al., *Atrazine-Induced Aromatase Expression Is SF–1 Dependent: Implications for Endocrine Disruption in Wildlife and Reproductive Cancers in Humans*, 115 ENVTL. HEALTH PERSPECTIVES 720, 720 (2007) (concluding that atrazine is a risk factor for endocrine disruption in wildlife and for reproductive organ cancers in laboratory rodents and humans); Vance L. Trudeau et al., *Assessment of Estrogenic Endocrine–Disrupting Chemical Actions in the Brain Using* in Vivo *Somatic Gene Transfer*, 113 ENVTL. HEALTH PERSPECTIVES 329 (2005) ("A host of developmental and reproductive abnormalities in many species, including humans, result from exposure to estrogenic endocrine-disrupting chemicals.").

of a larger mandate in the FQPA for EPA to reassess, within a decade, all existing pesticide tolerances under the FQPA's new "reasonable certainty of no harm standard."[15]

This statutorily-mandated endocrine screening program was delayed for a decade, however, because of funding problems, the disbanding of a scientific advisory panel, and disputes within EPA and within the scientific community over how to validate testing to make sure tests accurately assessed hormonal effects and produced consistent results in different laboratories. There were also disputes over priority setting and minimization of animal testing. In 2000, EPA provided a status report to Congress on the screening program and predicted that testing would commence in 2003.[16] But the agency did not actually issue its first testing orders until 2009, about a decade after the deadline in the FQPA.[17] These orders were for "Tier 1" preliminary screening for 67 different pesticides and chemicals, and manufacturers were given two years to submit the requested data. The orders may be followed, ultimately, by orders for "Tier 2" testing, which will be designed to confirm endocrine-disrupting properties and establish dose-response relationships.

In sum, it will likely be two decades after the enactment of the FQPA before EPA gathers significant data on endocrine disrupting properties for a wide variety of pesticides and chemicals, and it will likely be longer before EPA implements a regulatory response. What does this process tell you about the ability of law and regulation to protect citizens from toxic risks? What would a more protective, or precautionary, approach to endocrine disruption look like? If there is no validated testing, how can we be sure which substances we should take precautions against?

c. FARMWORKERS

Pesticides pose elevated risks for certain groups and individuals. Employees of pesticide manufacturers are one group with heightened exposure risk. The pollution of the James River in Virginia by the pesticide Kepone, produced by the Allied Corporation near the banks of the James, was largely responsible for the strengthening of the toxics provisions of the Clean Water Act. The earliest signs that Kepone was dangerous were neurological problems (including uncontrollable "shakes") in Allied's employees.

Farmworkers are another group at risk of serious health problems from pesticides. Children of farmworkers are also at risk, as they often live in close proximity to the fields where pesticides are sprayed.

Although research on the effects of pesticides on humans is

15. EPA's reassessment of all pesticide tolerances was plagued by delays and inadequate resources, and EPA missed the 2006 deadline to complete the work. By 2010, EPA had reassessed 9,637 tolerances, or over 99% of the 9,721 tolerances required to be reassessed under the FQPA. This program resulted in the revocation or modification of almost 4,000 food tolerances. *See* U.S. EPA, Implementation of Requirements under the Food Quality Protection Act (FQPA), www.epa.gov/pesticides/regulating/laws/fqpa/fqpa_ implementation.htm.

16. U.S. EPA, Endocrine Disruption Screening Program, Report to Congress 15 (August 2000).

17. 74 Fed. Reg. 54222 (October 21, 2009).

inadequate, the limited data available suggest a link between pesticide exposure and the extraordinary number of farmworkers who suffer from chronic diseases. With farmworkers experiencing the highest rate of chemical-related occupational illnesses in the country, it is little wonder that farm work is considered among the three most dangerous jobs in the United States. The occupational death rate for farmworkers is five times greater than the national average for all industries. The American farmworker is almost 25 times more likely to develop a pesticide-related illness than the general population. * * *

Compared to the general population, migrant populations suffer disproportionately high rates of pesticide-related acute harm [such as nausea, vomiting, skin irritation, dizziness, and upper respiratory irritation]. Chronic, long-term harm includes cancer, birth defects, reproductive and developmental problems, and nervous system damage. Pesticide exposure has been linked to elevated rates of leukemia, non-Hodgkin's lymphoma, and sterility, as well as hypertension and diabetes. Birth defects and still births are more common among farm area residents, and exposure to pesticides during the first trimester of pregnancy increases the risk of neonatal death by over five times. Farmworkers also suffer from higher-than-normal rates of cancers of the prostate, testis, mouth, lung, liver, and stomach.

A recent 10–year study of California farmworkers found that Hispanic field laborers developed stomach cancer at rates 70 percent greater than the comparable non-agricultural Hispanic population. The study also indicated that male farmworkers faced an elevated risk of developing brain cancer, and female farmworkers were more likely to develop uterine cancer. Although drawing no definitive conclusions, the study suggested that exposure to pesticides may explain the elevated risk levels.

* * *

No one knows exactly how many of the nation's four million migrant and seasonal agricultural laborers are poisoned each year. Local studies suggest that the number must be large. For example, a recent survey of farmworkers in Colorado found that half had suffered acute injuries related to pesticide exposure, including skin rashes, inflamed eyes, headaches, and irritation of the nose and throat. An EPA-sponsored study in Oregon found that nearly two-thirds of the state's farmworkers had been directly exposed to pesticides by breathing toxic fumes and that over one-third had experienced symptoms related to acute pesticide exposure, including headaches and joint pain.

Epidemiologists and policymakers have tried to estimate the scope of the problem nationwide. One study, extrapolating from state data, suggested that doctors probably identify between 10,000 and 40,000 cases per year. The EPA and other observers have placed the actual number of poisonings (including unreported and misdiagnosed cases) at 300,000 per year. The World Heath Organization estimates that three million people are poisoned by pesticides annually, resulting in 220,000 deaths and 735,000 chronic injuries. But estimates of actual numbers vary widely, and they necessarily involve much guesswork. In 1993 the U.S. General Accounting Office concluded that there was no reliable national estimate of the extent of occupational injuries resulting from pesticide exposures.

* * *

Even if record-keeping procedures were in place, farmworkers would still be reluctant to go to doctors and inform them of their injuries because of workplace structures designed to discourage such reporting. Neither labor contractors nor farmworkers receive adequate training to recognize the symptoms of pesticide exposure. Whether out of malice or ignorance, growers have been known to tell poisoned workers that they must "be hung over" or have "eaten bad tacos" when in fact they are suffering from the ill effects of a pesticide exposure. In one recent poisoning incident in Colorado, 20 migrant workers were doused by a crop duster with a pesticide used to kill mites and worms. The workers gasped for breath, vomited, and experienced swollen eyes and numbness in their tongues. A foreman ordered them to continue working, stating that the crop duster had sprayed them only with soap and water.

Keith Cunningham–Parmeter, *A Poisoned Field: Farmworkers, Pesticide Exposure, and Tort Recovery in An Era Of Regulatory Failure*, 28 N.Y.U. REV. L. & SOC. CHANGE 431, 442–46 (2004).

Pesticide labels are designed to warn farmworkers and other end-users of health risks, but what if the end-users cannot read the labels? Many of the ultimate users of pesticides are migrant farmworkers who may not be able to read labels in English and may not be literate in Spanish or another native language. Pesticide labeling has therefore become a flashpoint for the Environmental Justice movement, which claims that environmental laws often neglect hazards to low-income and minority populations. *See* R. Geoffrey Dillard, *Multilingual Warning Labels: Product Liability, "Official English," and Consumer Safety*, 29 GA. L. REV. 197 (1994). Pesticide labels may be made more accessible to non-English speakers by printing warnings in different languages or using symbols to warn pesticide users of hazards. However, translations are ineffective for illiterate workers, and symbols may be too simplistic to completely convey desired information. *Id.* at 237–39.

EPA's efforts to protect farmworkers from pesticide exposures have met a great deal of resistance from agricultural interests.[18] EPA promulgated

---

18. For an interesting case study of the roles of Congress, USDA, the Office of Management and Budget, and the large and small agriculture lobbies in EPA's pesticide rulemaking, see Louis P. True, Jr., "Agricultural Pesticides and Worker Protection," *in* ECONOMIC ANALYSIS AT EPA:

265

worker protection standards in 1992,[19] with a few subsequent revisions. The regulations prohibit pesticide handlers from applying pesticides while agricultural workers are in the area being treated (and from applying them in such a way that the workers are exposed elsewhere). They also prohibit handlers from allowing agricultural workers to re-enter a treated area within specified periods after a pesticide has been applied. These standards are obviously essential to the protection of farmworkers, but they are also costly in terms of reduced productivity, and EPA has been under considerable pressure to shorten re-entry times and to permit exemptions to them. In addition, the regulations require personal protective equipment for handlers and early-entry workers, marking or other notification of treated areas, disclosure of label information, decontamination equipment, training, and emergency assistance.

What are the strengths and weaknesses of the regulatory strategies deployed in the Worker Protection Standards? What are the hurdles to enforcing the standards? Are there better ways to protect farmworkers?

d. PREEMPTION OF STATE AND LOCAL LAW

Because FIFRA designates a federally-approved label containing the uses, directions, and warnings for pesticides, much of American law about pesticides has been worked out in cases involving preemption—the interaction of federal standards with state and local law. Under the Constitution's Supremacy Clause, of course, Congress is empowered to preempt state and local regulation in any area of authorized federal activity. In most environmental regulation, however, Congress reserves an important state role as part of the enforcement system, the allocation of controls, or even standard setting. In this respect, FIFRA is typical. The states are recruited to participate in the enforcement of federal pesticide regulation, and they are permitted to impose sale and use restrictions on pesticides that are equally or more protective than federal requirements. FIFRA § 24(a). In *Wisconsin Public Intervenor v. Mortier*, 501 U.S. 597 (1991), the Supreme Court sustained the validity of local pesticide regulations, such as permit requirements for aerial application of pesticides and for application to public or quasi-public lands.

In the area of labeling, however, FIFRA (unlike the FFDCA) forbids states from imposing any labeling or packaging requirements that are in addition to or different from those imposed by EPA. FIFRA § 24(b). "The states have joint control with the federal government in regulating the use of pesticides, for the safety of its citizens and their environment, with the exception of EPA's exclusive supervision of labeling." *New York State Pesticide Coalition, Inc. v. Jorling*, 874 F.2d 115, 118 (2d Cir. 1989). According to many environmentalists and plaintiffs alleging pesticide injuries, the preemptive effect of pesticide labeling standards has a perverse effect. It means that federal labeling requirements designed to help con-

---

Assessing Regulatory Impact 303–32 (Richard D. Morgenstern, ed.; Resources for the Future 1997).

19. 57 Fed. Reg. 38102 (1992), codified at 40 C.F.R. part 170.

sumers can be used as a shield by pesticide manufacturers to ward off common law claims of personal injury and other damage.

The preemption cases on pesticide labeling come in two varieties. In the first variety, a pesticide manufacturer or applicator challenges a state statute that requires some form of disclosure about pesticide risks. Courts have generally held that states cannot require product warnings or disclosures that are more comprehensive than the FIFRA label, but they can require disclosures that are different-in-kind from the contents of the label, such as yard signs alerting neighbors when pesticides have been applied to a lawn. *See id.* at 119 (upholding New York law requiring certain disclosures by pesticide applicators, including yard signs and a "cover sheet" for the consumer summarizing warnings and safety information, because these do not "impair the integrity of the FIFRA label").

The second variety of FIFRA preemption cases are those in which a plaintiff claims personal injuries from a pesticide and sues the manufacturer or applicator on a failure-to-warn claim. The question here is whether an EPA-approved warning label preempts the state tort claim. Some early cases found no preemption in this context. *See Ferebee v. Chevron Chemical Co.*, 736 F.2d 1529 (D.C. Cir. 1984), *cert. denied*, 469 U.S. 1062 (1984) (holding that state tort damage actions for failure to warn "do not stand as an obstacle to the accomplishment of FIFRA's purposes"). Since the early 1990s, however, courts have almost uniformly held that such failure-to-warn claims are preempted by FIFRA. *See Papas v. Upjohn Co.*, 985 F.2d 516, 519 (11th Cir. 1993), *cert denied* 510 U.S. 913 (1993) ("If a pesticide manufacturer places EPA-approved warnings on the label and packaging of its product, its duty to warn is satisfied, and the adequate warning issue ends."). Decisions finding preemption under FIFRA increased following a 1992 Supreme Court case finding preemption of some state tort claims by federal cigarette labeling standards. *Cipollone v. Liggett Group, Inc.*, 505 U.S. 504 (1992). By 1997, at least seven circuits had rejected common law failure-to-warn claims related to pesticides as preempted by FIFRA. *See Kuiper v. American Cyanamid Co.*, 131 F.3d 656, 662 (7th Cir. 1997) (summarizing the cases).

Courts continue to recognize, however, the validity of state personal injury claims based on defective manufacture or design, such as toxic impurities in the pesticide. *See, e.g., Mortellite v. Novartis Crop Prot., Inc.*, 460 F.3d 483 (3d Cir. 2006) (holding that state law strict liability, negligent testing, and breach of express warranty claims do not impose "labeling requirements" and are not preempted by FIFRA); *National Bank of Commerce of El Dorado, Arkansas v. Dow Chemical Co.*, 165 F.3d 602, 609 (8th Cir. 1999) ("A claim of defective manufacture or design of this kind [alleging impurities] does not directly attack the EPA-approved label or packaging.").

What if a plaintiff's claim of defective design or breach of warranty, if successful, would likely induce a defendant to alter its pesticide label to protect against a subsequent suit? Would such claims be preempted by FIFRA? That question was raised in a widely watched U.S. Supreme Court case, *Bates v. Dow Agrosciences LLC*, 544 U.S. 431 (2005). In *Bates*, the

Court held that FIFRA did not preempt state common law claims for defective design, defective manufacture, negligent testing, and breach of express warranty. The Court overruled the preemption finding of the Fifth Circuit, which had reasoned that a judgment against the defendant on these state law claims would induce the defendant to alter its product labels. Instead, the Court held that the proper inquiry was whether the plaintiff was challenging the adequacy of the label itself, not whether a jury verdict for the plaintiff on other kinds of claims might encourage the defendant to change its labeling. The Court also preserved some room for state legislatures and courts to impose their own requirements for pesticide labels, as long as they are "equivalent to, and fully consistent with" federal requirements. *Id.* at 447. For example, a fraud claim challenging a pesticide label might not be preempted because FIFRA itself prohibits false or misleading statements in pesticide labels. *Bates* is widely viewed as a pro-plaintiff case, narrowing the scope of federal preemption of common law claims against pesticide manufacturers. *See* Alexandra Klass, *Pesticides, Children's Health Policy, and Common Law Tort Claims*, 7 Minn. J. L. Sci. & Tech. 89 (2005).

e. PESTICIDE EXPORTS

The United States exports enormous quantities of pesticides, including pesticides whose use is banned or tightly restricted by EPA. For developing countries, pesticides pose an intense dilemma: they are at once more urgently needed and more dangerous than in industrialized countries like the United States (in part because worker protections tend to be more lax). The international regulatory system, however, is far looser for pesticides exported to less developed countries than are the internal regulatory structures of industrialized countries.

Exported pesticides not only pose health risks to residents of developing countries, but also to U.S. residents. This is because many of the exported pesticides, banned in the United States, are applied to agricultural products in foreign countries that are then exported back to the United States. This is the so-called "Circle of Poison," through which unregistered pesticides can end up on U.S. dinner tables.

In response to concerns over the international chemical and pesticide trade, countries gathered in Rotterdam in 1998 adopted the Convention for the Application of Prior Informed Consent Procedure for Certain Hazardous Chemicals and Pesticides in International Trade.[20] The Rotterdam Convention establishes a prior informed consent procedure in which countries can consent to or prohibit importation of certain "severely hazardous pesticide formulations" and other industrial chemicals listed in Annex III of the Convention. The Convention was designed to promote sharing of information on chemical risks and to facilitate national decision making on which pesticides and chemicals will be allowed to be imported. As of 2010, there were only 29 pesticides covered by the Convention. The Convention is not currently being implemented in the United States because although the United States is a signatory to the Convention, it has never ratified it.

---

20. 38 I.L.M. 1 (1999).

FIFRA contains its own provisions on export of pesticides, including labeling requirements and a requirement that foreign purchasers of unregistered or severely restricted pesticides sign statements indicating that the purchaser understands that the pesticide is unregistered and cannot be legally sold in the United States. *See* FIFRA § 17(a), (b).

Why does FIFRA allow export of unregistered pesticides? If EPA itself has concluded that that a pesticide causes an "unreasonable adverse effect on the environment," should the law permit export, particularly given the possibility that the pesticide may be applied to food that is shipped back to the United States? One scholar summarized Congress's and EPA's rationale for allowing export of unregistered pesticides:

> As a matter of policy, the agency opposes the institution of a general ban on the exports of unregistered pesticides. First, the EPA believes that banning exports will not solve the pesticide problems of developing nations, since most if not all of the banned pesticides would be available from other pesticide-exporting countries. Second, concentrating on controlling the use and management of all pesticides will be more effective than concentrating upon a few. Third, the agency's regulatory decisions are based upon risk-benefit evaluations specific to the United States. The risk-benefit balance in other countries may differ due to different growing conditions, pest control problems, and environmental and public health considerations. Fourth, pesticide manufacturers may choose not to register a pesticide in the United States simply because there is no market for it. Another concern is that a complete ban might violate the open market provisions of the General Agreement on Trade and Tariffs (GATT).

James H. Colopy, *Poisoning the Developing World: The Exportation of Unregistered and Severely Restricted Pesticides from the United States,* 13 UCLA J. ENVTL. L. & POL'Y 167 (1994/95).[21]

Are these satisfactory justifications for permitting export of unregistered pesticides? Do you agree that the risk-benefit calculations inherent in pesticide regulation are "specific to the United States"? Given that U.S. law permits export of pesticides that cannot be sold domestically, does this implicitly mean that the law is weighing health risks to Americans more heavily than health risks to citizens of Mexico, Malaysia, or Morocco?

B.   CHEMICAL REGULATION

The Toxic Substances Control Act of 1976 authorizes EPA to investigate and regulate virtually all aspects of the creation, manufacture, distribution, use, and disposal of chemical substances. Its primary focus, however, is economic (i.e., industrial) chemicals rather than waste, and use rather than disposal. From its earliest incarnations, the essential elements of the statute included some form of screening of new chemicals for health risks,

---

21. For a full statement of EPA's rationale for allowing exports, see U.S. EPA, PESTICIDE EXPORT POLICY, 58 Fed. Reg. 9062 (1993).

information development concerning existing chemicals, and administrative authority to control distribution and use of chemicals. Unlike FIFRA, the burden of proof on whether the risks of a chemical are "unreasonable" lies with the government. This creates very different incentives and regulatory structures.

Below, we provide an overview of the legislative history of TSCA and explore an early problem in regulation under TSCA: control of chlorofluorocarbons that are damaging to the ozone layer. We then discuss the information gathering provisions of TSCA and EPA's authority to restrict chemicals under TSCA. Regulating the introduction and use of chemicals is a key leverage point for environmental regulation. It determines which chemicals may eventually end up in waste streams, landfills, and waterways. And the knowledge about chemical toxity gained through this process can assist in standard setting under many other environmental statutes, such as the Clean Air Act and the Clean Water Act. One question we consider in this section is whether TSCA is living up to this promise. Is it an effective statutory regime for chemical risk assessment? For chemical risk management?

1.   TSCA's Promise: An Overview of the Statute

Pressure for enactment of a chemical control law began when the White House Council on Environmental Quality (CEQ), barely a year old, issued a report, *Toxic Substances*, in support of President Nixon's proposed Toxic Substances Control Act of 1971. Many of the concerns in this report were also expressed by Congress, five years later, in the statute's findings and policy. *See* TSCA § 2.

Toxic Substances

Council on Environmental Quality
pp. 20–21 (1971)[22]

It is clear that current laws are inadequate to control the actual and potential dangers of toxic substances comprehensively or systematically. The controls over manufacture and distribution pertain to only a small percentage of the chemical substances which find their way into the environment. [Many serious environmental harms] relate to substances not covered by present controls over manufacture and distribution.

Both controls over production and controls over effluents suffer from the limited focus of their authority. For example, the Food and Drug Administration carefully examines food containers for their effect on food but does not address the environmental and health effects of incinerating the containers. With the exception of radioactive materials, disposal is not a consideration in any program controlling manufacture.

---

22. *Reprinted in* House Comm. on Interstate and Foreign Commerce, Committee Print, Legislative History of the Toxic Substances Control Act (1976) at 783–784.

But the problems of focus are broader than specific examples. Setting rational standards for many pollutants under existing legislation is almost impossible. The key factors involved in setting standards are the *total* human exposure to a substance and its *total* effect on the environment. The focus must be on a particular pollutant and all the pathways by which it travels through the ecosystem. Controls over distribution approach this perspective, but most fail to consider important environmental factors adequately.

The obvious limitation of controls over effluents is that they generally deal with a problem only *after* it is manifest. They do not provide for obtaining information on potential pollutants before widespread damage has occurred.

More subtle but more serious limitations of effluent controls arise from their focusing on the media—air or water—in which the pollution occurs. This approach has several consequences: First, it leads to concern with those substances found in air or water in the greatest quantities. For example, the Air Pollution Control Office uses the gross weight of air pollution. Gross weight is a valid indicator, but it disregards the degree of danger of the various pollutants. * * * [C]omparatively small amounts of some substances can cause severe damage, but media-oriented programs tend to overlook the importance of such substances. Another consequence of the media approach is that it cannot deal effectively with the fact that many, perhaps most, toxic substances find their way into the environment through several media. They cannot be characterized strictly as water pollutants or as air pollutants, for they are found in air, in water, and often in soil. The characteristic pervasiveness of toxic substances makes it difficult for the media-oriented programs to engage in adequate and efficient research, monitoring, and control activities for such substances. The need for such a comprehensive approach was a major rationale for the creation of the Environmental Protection Agency (EPA). * * *

The shortcomings of the legal authorities described above, the [health hazards] of toxic substances * * *, their increasing number and amounts * * *, and the inadequate attention paid to such substances all support the need for a new legal and institutional system to deal with toxic substances.

Our awareness of environmental threats, our ability to screen and test substances for adverse effects, and our capabilities for monitoring and predicting, although inadequate, are now sufficiently developed that we need to no longer remain in a purely reactive posture with respect to chemical hazards. We need no longer be limited to repairing damage after it has been done; nor should we allow the general population to be used as a laboratory for discovering adverse health effects. There is no longer any valid reason for continued failure to develop and exercise reasonable controls over toxic substances in the environment.

———

As the CEQ excerpt indicates, TSCA was intended to be a gap-filling statute. While other statutes (notably the Clean Air Act and Clean Water

Act) relate to pollution in particular media, TSCA was designed to identify harmful chemicals early, before their introduction into commerce and before they ever become effluent from manufacturing.[23] "Gap-filling" also means relying on a prevention, rather than just a control, strategy. Consider the Senate justification for the new statute:

> While air and water laws authorize limitations on discharges and emissions, the Occupational Safety and Health Act authorizes the establishment of ambient air standards for the workplace, and the Consumer Product Safety Act authorizes standards with respect to consumer products, there are no existing statutes which authorize the direct control of industrial chemicals themselves for their health or environmental effects. * * *

> While these other authorities will in many cases be sufficient to adequately protect health and the environment, the alternative of preventing or regulating the use of the chemical in the first instance may be a far more effective way of dealing with the hazards. If expensive sewage treatment facilities can be avoided, for example, through removing dangerous materials from household and industrial wastes, the authority to do so ought to be provided.

S. REP. NO. 698, 94TH CONG., 2D SESS. 1–2 (1976).

In the legislative debates over TSCA, the main dispute was whether a pre-market licensing system should be established for chemicals, similar to FIFRA. The Senate supported such a pre-market licensing system, but the House opposed it, and the chemical industry lobbied strongly to avoid a licensing structure for TSCA. This is a fundamental philosophical issue, because it signals where the "burden of proof" will lie for industrial chemicals. In a licensing system, the manufacturer usually bears the burden of proof to show that chemical risks are acceptable (the exact risk standard would need to be determined in the legislation, such as a lack of unreasonable adverse effects on the environment). In contrast, in a post-market review regime, a government agency could be empowered to restrict dangerous chemicals already on the market, but the agency would bear the burden of proof in that context. If a licensing system had been adopted in TSCA, it would have increased the costs of the statute from the standpoint of private testing costs and government oversight costs, but far more information would be generated over time about chemical risks.

In the closing days of the 94th Congress, a compromise, tolerated if not supported by industry, was reached. Instead of a pre-market approval process similar to FIFRA, Congress enacted a pre-manufacture *notice* requirement, in TSCA § 5. Manufacturers have to provide notice to EPA of

---

23.   TSCA has been amended three times to address gaps with respect to particular chemicals. In 1986, Congress added provisions for regulation of asbestos in schools; in 1988, to address radon gas in homes; and in 1992, to address lead-based paint. Each of these amendments deals with a problem that otherwise fell between the cracks: airborne asbestos exposure of schoolchildren, residential radon gas, and lead paint are not ambient (*i.e.*, outside) air or water problems, nor are the principally affected persons employees under the jurisdiction of OSHA.

new chemicals, including their physical and chemical properties, but there is no obligation to conduct toxicity testing, unless EPA specifically orders it. EPA can also act on a post-market basis to restrict chemicals, and the agency bears the burden of proof. Moreover, EPA's authority in the Act was carefully hedged with numerous procedural and substantive requirements. Across-the-board regulation was consistently rejected in favor of individualized risk determinations.[24] When he signed it into law on October 11, 1976, President Ford hailed TSCA as "one of the most important pieces of environmental legislation that has been enacted by the Congress."

Today, however, TSCA is widely conceded to be a disappointment. In 2009, the Government Accountability Office listed EPA's toxics regulatory program as a "high risk" government program, needing "broad based transformation" and priority attention from the Obama administration and Congress.[25] EPA Administrator Lisa Jackson testified in 2009 that TSCA is "outdated" and "does not provide the tools to adequately protect human health and the environment as the American people expect, demand and deserve."[26] And the American Chemistry Council, the principal chemical industry trade association, has stated that Congress should "begin the effort to modernize TSCA."[27]

Why do so many interest groups believe that TSCA is inadequately protective? One reason is that we know much more about chemical risks than we did in the 1970s. In the 1970s, it was widely assumed that human exposure to non-pesticide chemicals posed significantly lower risks than human exposure to pesticides. Because pesticides can be directly ingested along with food and are intended to disrupt biological systems, Congress sought to restrict them more carefully and to impose mandatory pre-market review of their health and environmental risks.

But that premise has turned out to be flawed. Scientists have now documented human uptake of chemicals used in common consumer products such as fabrics, cookware, plastics, and electronics, in addition to uptake of toxic air and water pollutants. The Centers for Disease Control and Prevention has shown in a series of "biomonitoring" studies that dozens of industrial chemicals (some carcinogenic) are present in the blood and urine of representative samples of the U.S. population.[28] And flame retar-

---

24. The passage and purposes of TSCA are described in detail in David Markell, *An Overview of TSCA, Its History and Key Underlying Assumptions, and Its Place in Environmental Regulation*, 32 WASH.U.J.L. & POL'Y 333 (2010); and Joel Reynolds, Note, *The Toxic Substances Control Act of 1976: An Introductory Background and Analysis*, 4 COL. J. ENVT'L L. 35, 35–60 (1977).

25. U.S. GOVERNMENT ACCOUNTABILITY OFFICE, REPORT TO THE CONGRESS, HIGH RISK SERIES: AN UPDATE 22 (2009) ("Without greater attention to EPA's efforts to assess toxic chemicals, the nation lacks assurance that human health and the environment are adequately protected.").

26. SENATE COMM. ON ENVT. AND PUB. WORKS, 111TH CONG. (December 2, 2009) (Statement of Lisa Jackson, Administrator, U.S. EPA).

27. REVISITING THE TOXIC SUBSTANCES CONTROL ACT OF 1976: HEARING BEFORE THE SUBCOMM. ON COMMERCE, TRADE AND CONSUMER PROT. OF THE HOUSE COMM. ON ENERGY AND COMMERCE, 111TH CONG. 2 (2009) (Statement of Cal Dooley, President, American Chemistry Council).

28. *See* CENTERS FOR DISEASE CONTROL AND PREVENTION, FOURTH NATIONAL REPORT ON HUMAN EXPOSURE TO ENVIRONMENTAL CHEMICALS (2009). In a 2003 study, the Environmental Working Group found that of 210 synthetic chemicals tested in a population of volunteers, 167 chemicals were present in at least one person, and some chemicals, such as flame retardants, were

dants used on fabrics, electronics, and furniture are concentrating in the breast tissue of American women, and in their breast milk.[29]

Because of the risk assessment data gap, discussed in Chapter 1, connecting the presence of industrial chemicals in the human body to specific health harms in the American population is complex and controversial. In 2010, the President's Cancer Panel called for a major expansion of federal research "to clarify the nature and magnitude of cancer risk attributable to environmental contaminants."[30] This call for more research echoes the same call by Rachel Carson in *Silent Spring*, nearly 50 years earlier. Yet while the United States spends close to $300 billion dollars per year on cancer (for treatment, lost productivity due to cancer, and cancer research), it spends less than $100 million dollars annually on research on occupational and environmental carcinogenesis.

One of the principal purposes of TSCA was to generate "adequate data . . . with respect to the effect of chemical substances and mixtures on health and the environment." TSCA § 2. Today, however, only a few thousand of the 84,000 chemicals that have been introduced in commerce have been extensively tested for health and environmental risks. As you study the materials in this chapter, ask yourself why TSCA has not lived up to its initial expectations. Is it because of weaknesses in the statute? Weaknesses in implementation? Or problems with judicial review? Can the statute be reinterpreted or reinvigorated through adding more personnel or funding, or does it need more fundamental reform?

To introduce how the statute operates, we use the following problem:

PROBLEM
THE REGULATION OF CHLOROFLUOROCARBONS

At the time of TSCA's passage, there was a growing awareness in the scientific and environmental communities that chlorofluorocarbons (CFCs) pose a risk to the global environment. In an early rulemaking under TSCA, EPA described the problem:

Ultraviolet radiation is thought to cause or to be a contributory factor to two different types of skin cancer in people. One, nonmelanoma skin cancer, is relatively common, occurring at the rate of about 150 cases per 100,000 population each year in the United States. However, it is very rarely fatal. The other, melanoma skin cancer, is much rarer, occurring at the rate of about four cases per 100,000 population each year in the United States. Melanoma is

---

present in nearly all the volunteers. *See* Jane Houlihan et al., Environmental Working Group, Body Burden: The Pollution in People 3 (2003).

29. National Center for Environmental Assessment, U.S. EPA, An Exposure Assessment for Polybrominated Diphenyl Ethers 5–37 (May 2010) (noting that the data suggest that average breast milk concentrations of flame retardants in American women are ten times higher than concentrations of women tested outside the United States); K.M. Main et al, *Flame Retardants in Placenta and Breast Milk and Cryptorchidism in Newborn Boys.* 115 Envtl. Health Perspectives 1519 (2007) (finding an association between levels of flame retardants in mother's breast milk and testicular maldescent in their infant sons).

30. President's Cancer Panel, National Cancer Institute, Reducing Environmental Cancer Risk: What We Can Do Now vii (April 2010).

fatal to about 30 percent of the people who contract it. The incidence of both types of skin cancer is rising rapidly. * * *

Most of the ultraviolet radiation produced by the sun is absorbed in the atmosphere before reaching the earth's surface. The screening takes place in the stratosphere—the portion of the atmosphere that extends from about 5 to 30 miles about the earth's surface. The ultraviolet radiation is absorbed by oxygen in two separate reactions. First, an oxygen molecule (O_2) absorbs ultraviolet light and is split into its component oxygen atoms (O). These oxygen atoms then combine with oxygen molecules to form ozone (O_3). Second, the ozone molecules themselves absorb ultraviolet radiation and are broken down again to oxygen molecules and free oxygen atoms.

* * *

A more substantial problem for the present involves the introduction of chlorine into the stratosphere from chlorine-containing chemical substances introduced into the atmosphere by man. In the stratosphere, chlorine atoms will enter into a reaction sequence resulting in the destruction of ozone molecules.

* * *

* * * No decrease in stratospheric ozone from this source has yet been observed. However, the calculated effect from the amount of these compounds so far released would not be distinguishable from natural variations in ozone levels.

In all respects in which it has been possible to check the theory described above against real-world observations, the theory has been confirmed. [Chlorofluoroalkanes, a particularly damaging CFC,] are found in the lower atmosphere and in the stratosphere at levels consistent with the theory. Their ozone destroying potential under stratospheric conditions has been demonstrated in laboratory experiments.

Accordingly, scientific controversy has increasingly centered not on whether continued use of these compounds will result in a depletion of the ozone layer, but on how much of a depletion would result.

* * *

At present, fully halogenated chlorofluoroalkanes are used in aerosol products, in refrigerators and air conditioners, as foam blowing agents, and as solvents. The major use in the United States, approximately 50 percent, is as aerosol propellants. * * *

Aerosol products release the propellant during normal use. In contrast, except for unintentional leakage, a refrigerator will keep the fully halogenated chlorofluoroalkane sealed within the unit during use. While disposal controls for refrigerators may be possible, this approach is not feasible for aerosols. In addition, substitute propellants or alternatives exist for most aerosol uses, whereas less is known about acceptable alternatives for the other uses. Finally, refrigerant and other nonpropellant uses are more integral to the functioning of society and the economy than aerosol uses, and hence are more difficult to evaluate in considering an appropriate regulatory course.* * *

With respect to aerosol propellant uses, technically feasible and economically acceptable alternatives exist for most uses of fully halogenated chlorofluoroalkane propellants. They fall into two categories: alternative propellants and alternative delivery systems.

EPA, Toxic Substances Control: Fully Halogenated Chlorofluoroalkanes, 42 Fed. Reg. 24542, 24543–44 (1977) (proposed rule) (The final rule may be found at 43 Fed. Reg. 11301 (1978)).

1. Suppose that you are the EPA official in charge of TSCA. You have been apprised of the above information by your staff, and you are inclined to take some sort of regulatory action. Consider how the TSCA process would work. Are CFCs even covered by the statute? How can you use the statute to gather information about them? What do you need to find out about them for regulatory purposes? If what you learn concerns you, what authority do you have to take regulatory action? What kind of action can you take and what standards must you meet to take action? Are there procedural hurdles? What kind of judicial review can you expect?

2. Assume instead that you are the general counsel of Acme Chemicals, a major manufacturer of chlorofluoroalkanes. Acme's scientists have been working on replacements for some time. Their solution, an existing chemical developed in Europe that replaces chlorine with bromine, seems to work as well as CFCs in most applications. Acme scientists have imported the new substance, and have synthesized small quantities for testing in some of Acme's air conditioning units. Acme has collected all the information it can on the characteristics and effects of the bromine-based chemicals, but EPA has not been notified of this discovery because the company considers it highly secret commercial information. Has Acme violated TSCA with respect to the bromine-based chemicals? What penalties are available? How can it bring itself into compliance and are there financial risks in doing so?

3. Finally, consider CFCs from the point of view of a staff attorney with the Environmental Defense Fund. EDF believes that EPA should take immediate steps to ban CFCs. What opportunities do you have to persuade EPA to ban them? To take other regulatory action? Can you *force* EPA to act? Can you recover attorneys' fees for your efforts?

NOTES

1. *Regulation of CFCs.* The final CFC regulations, which were codified at 40 C.F.R. part 762, had two main parts: the first phased out most aerosol uses of CFCs pursuant to Section 6, and the second required detailed reporting of aerosol uses under Section 8. The TSCA regulation did not, however, apply to uses of CFCs as a refrigerant. Those uses were not regulated until the Clean Air Act Amendments of 1990, in response to international treaty commitments under the Montreal Protocol on Substances that Deplete the Ozone Layer, Sept. 16, 1987, 26 I.L.M. 1550 (entered into force Jan. 1, 1989). The Clean Air Act Amendments, in fact, have superseded the TSCA regulations, because the Clean Air Act Amendments provide comprehensive regulation of CFCs, including the reduction and phase-out of all nonessential uses. 42 U.S.C. §§ 7671–7671p.

2. *CFCs and the purposes of TSCA.* As noted at the beginning of this chapter, the proponents of the bill identified two basic reasons for enacting TSCA: lack of information concerning toxic substances, and fragmentation and incompleteness in existing legislation. On the gap-filling point, two early commentators observed:

> That there were still loopholes in the law was amply demonstrated by the chlorofluorocarbon controversy. * * * [W]here should the regulation occur? Chlorofluorocarbons are not air pollutants in the usual sense; they are not poisonous; and they pose no hazard in the workplace. Even if regulated as consumer products, under [1977] law there would be no means of regulating them in industrial uses.

RAY M. DRULEY & GERALD L. ORDWAY, THE TOXIC SUBSTANCES CONTROL ACT 5–6 (1981). Were CFCs an appropriate subject of regulation under TSCA given the state of the scientific knowledge about their risks in the mid–1970s? Should EPA have waited for direct empirical confirmation that CFCs were damaging the ozone layer? Was it legally required to?

3. *Unreasonable risk.* Look again at the legal standard for applying the various regulatory tools authorized by TSCA. The touchstone of the statute, clearly, is the term "unreasonable risk." How does "unreasonable risk" differ from FIFRA's touchstone for registering a pesticide, "unreasonable adverse effects on the environment"? The term "unreasonable risk" appears more than 35 times in the text of TSCA. Note that it is used in several different ways—"may present an unreasonable risk" (§ 4(a)), "presents an unreasonable risk" (§ 6(a)), "imminent and unreasonable risk" (§ 7(f))—and for several different purposes—testing, priority-setting, regulating, notification, etc.

Now see if you can find a definition of unreasonable risk. You can't: Congress very deliberately declined to provide one. *See* H.R. REP. NO. 1341, 94TH CONG., 2D SESS. 13–15 (1976). While there is no statutory definition for "unreasonable risk" in TSCA, the legislative history makes it clear that the term is intended for EPA to balance the full range of human health and environmental risks of a chemical with the economic costs of regulation and the economic benefits of the chemical. The statute does not provide guidance for how EPA should distinguish between "unreasonable risks" of a chemical and reasonable risks. This is left to administrative discretion, but as we shall see, the courts also play a strong role in reviewing EPA's determination of "unreasonable risk."

4. *Comprehensive rationality.* TSCA can be seen as exemplifying an approach to regulation known as "comprehensive rationality." Under this model of administrative action, the agency resolves a problem as a whole by gathering all available scientific and economic data, not piecemeal or incrementally. To do so, the agency goes through a well-defined process of specifying goals, setting priorities, identifying alternatives, analyzing their consequences, and optimizing choices among the alternatives, often by quantifying risks and benefits in dollar terms. The comprehensive rationality paradigm has two very important consequences for the way that TSCA functions. First, quantitative risk assessment and required analysis of many regulatory alternatives for each chemical impose huge information demands on the agency. Congress recognized this by making information gathering a centerpiece of the statute and by providing a step-by-step process for obtaining information when needed. Second, a rationalist scheme is usually quantitative. It will try to measure and compare risks, costs, and benefits. This often means assigning a dollar value to the lives that might be saved by a regulation, or to avoided disease or cancers. Some of the challenges in doing this were discussed at the end of Chapter 1. How quantitative was the CFC rulemaking? Compare it to the court's approach in *Corrosion Proof Fittings*, which we excerpt later in this chapter.

In the subsections that follow, we discuss TSCA in terms of its two principal functions: promoting information gathering and providing authority to EPA to impose restrictions to protect human health and the environment. The first issue can be viewed as a data supply issue (i.e., how much information on chemical risks is available to the agency). The second issue can be viewed as a data demand issue (i.e., the amount of evidence on risk that the agency needs to impose restrictions). As we shall see, a significant gap has emerged between the statutory demand for data and the available supply.

2. Information Gathering

TSCA has three major data gathering provisions: premanufacture notification (§ 5), general data collection (§ 8), and test rules (§ 4).

New Chemicals: Pre–Manufacture Notification

Simply put, pre-manufacture notification (PMN) requires that anyone who proposes to manufacture (or to import) a new chemical must notify EPA of its intention to do so 90 days in advance, § 5(a), (d)(2). A "new" chemical is defined as a chemical that is not on the TSCA Inventory of "existing" chemicals, first prepared in 1979 and updated many times since then. As of 2010, there were more than 84,000 "existing" chemicals in the Inventory. About 21,000 of these have gone through the PMN process, because they were introduced since 1979. The remaining 63,000 "grandfathered" existing chemicals were first introduced before 1979.

In a PMN, the chemical manufacturer must provide EPA with "data which the person submitting the data believes show that * * * the manufacture, processing, distribution in commerce, use, and disposal of the chemical substance will not present an unreasonable risk." § 5(b)(2)(B), (d)(1). The requirements for the contents of a PMN are laid out in 40 C.F.R. parts 720, 721, and 723. PMNs must also be filed before manufacturing or processing existing chemicals for "significant new uses." § 5(a)(2).

The purpose of the PMN submissions, of course, is to give EPA an opportunity to screen the chemical for health and environmental risks before it is placed on the market. But it is an *opportunity* only—EPA may do nothing within the 90 day period, in which case the production may go forward, or it may seek to delay production if it finds that additional data are needed to evaluate the chemical's risks, § 5(e); or, if the PMN information reveals an unreasonable risk, EPA may issue a proposed restriction rule under Section 6 which becomes effective immediately. § 5(f). EPA must go to court to prevent production if it finds that the chemical "may present" an unreasonable risk, § 5(e)(1)(A), but the agency may act on its own if the chemical "presents or will present" an unreasonable risk. § 5(f). In each of these options, EPA bears the burden of proof to show unreasonable risk. Finally, EPA is authorized to grant exemptions from PMN reporting for categories of chemicals that it finds generally do not present an unreasonable risk and for small-volume chemicals for experimentation or test marketing. § 5(h).

One difference between TSCA and FIFRA is that the PMN provisions of TSCA do not require manufacturers to conduct any toxicity testing. Rather, manufacturers must disclose toxicity information about a new chemical only if it is in the manufacturer's "possession or control" or if it is "known to or reasonably ascertainable by" the submitter. 40 C.F.R. §§ 720.50(a)–(b) (2009). Some commentators have suggested that this "disclose it if you have it" regulatory model provides incentives *not* to conduct safety testing for new chemicals. *See, e.g.,* Noah M. Sachs, *Jumping the Pond: Transnational Law and the Future of Chemical Regulation*, 62 Vand. L. Rev. 1817, 1828 (2009).

The U.S. Government Accountability Office has reported that only 15 percent of PMNs contain any health and safety information.[31] The EPA receives over 700 PMNs annually, but only about 20 percent of PMNs receive a detailed review by agency staff (recall that there is only a 90–day window for agency review).[32] In the absence of chemical-specific test data, EPA uses computer models to compare new chemicals with chemicals of similar molecular structure on which toxicity data is available.[33] Use of

31. U.S. Gov't Accountability Office, Chemical Regulation: Options Exist To Improve EPA's Ability To Assess Health Risks and Manage its Chemical Review Program 12 (2005).

32. *Id.*

33. According to the GAO, EPA believes that the models "are useful as basic screening tools where actual test data on health and environmental effects information is not available from chemical companies" and that the models supply "a reasonable basis for either dropping the

modeling to estimate risk has been controversial, but EPA defends the practice, and in 2005, it reported that it had taken some action to reduce the risks of over 3,500 chemicals for which PMNs had been submitted.[34]

Existing Chemicals: Reporting and Recordkeeping

TSCA Section 8 provides broad authority for EPA to obtain chemical records, such as production volumes and studies of the risks of existing chemicals.

Section 8(a) is TSCA's broadest and most general information provision. It allows EPA by rule to require that a regulated entity maintain and report a wide range of information relevant to the "unreasonable risk" determination, including chemical identity, uses, amounts manufactured or processed (including projections), byproducts from manufacturing or use, existing health and environmental effects data, human exposure, and manner of disposal. § 8(a)(2).

Three other subsections require reporting and recordkeeping of particular types of information. Manufacturers and processors must maintain records of "significant adverse reactions to health or the environment * * * alleged to have been caused by the substance or mixture," § 8(c), and must *immediately* report "information which reasonably supports the conclusion that such substance or mixture presents a substantial risk of injury to health or the environment." § 8(e). Both subsections seem to require the reporter to decide in the first place whether a health effect was caused by a chemical and whether the effect is "significant" or "substantial."

Subsection 8(d) requires the submission of a list or copies of "health and safety studies" conducted by—or simply known to—the manufacturers or processors of specified chemicals. A threshold issue with Section 8(d) is defining what constitutes a "study." Is a preliminary report covered? How much analysis of data is required before it becomes a "study"? EPA's regulations deem exposure monitoring data a study "when they have been aggregated and analyzed to measure the exposure of humans." 40 C.F.R. § 716.3. This suggests that a "study" must involve some interpretation of raw data. But an EPA guidance document suggests that "incident information, exposure studies, *and their underlying data* should be considered covered under the term 'health and safety study.' "[35]

Existing Chemicals: Test Rules

Section 4 of TSCA authorizes EPA to require that manufacturers and processors of chemical substances generate and disclose data on any of the

chemical from further review or subjecting it to more detailed review and possible controls." *Id.* at 10.

34. *Id.* at 16. Note that the number of PMNs submitted since 1979 exceeds the number of chemicals added to the TSCA Inventory since 1979. This is because, in many cases, the submitter chooses not to proceed to full-scale manufacture and commercialization of the chemical.

35. U.S. EPA, TOXIC SUBSTANCES CONTROL ACT (TSCA) SECTION 8(E) NOTICES, FREQUENT QUESTIONS, *available at* http://www.epa.gov/oppt/tsca8e/pubs/frequently asked questions faqs.html. (emphasis added).

health or environmental issues relating to the underlying "unreasonable risk" determination, including toxicity, chemical characteristics, and exposure. Unlike Section 5, test rules are not a screening device; unlike Section 8, they generate truly new data, rather than just data from existing studies. A test rule may be predicated on information obtained under Sections 5 or 8, however, and a test rule is designed to provide the basis for further action under Sections 6 or 7. EPA is specifically required to initiate "appropriate action" under Section 5, 6, or 7 if it receives information that "indicates to the Administrator that there may be a reasonable basis to conclude that a chemical substance or mixture presents or will present a significant risk of serious or widespread harm to human beings from cancer, gene mutation, or birth defects." § 4(f).

Chemical testing is expensive. A single test on laboratory rodents of a chemical's cancer-causing or endocrine-disrupting effects may cost several hundred thousand dollars. And a full risk assessment usually involves multiple kinds of tests, with a potential price tag of $4 million or more. In 2010, EPA estimated that the cost of private sector compliance with a proposed test rule for 29 different high production volume chemicals was $10.21 million.[36] These costs are high, but on the other hand, industry revenues from a single high-volume chemical can sometimes exceed $1 billion per year. The test rules have the largest impact on industry when they are aimed at lower volume chemicals that provide marginal revenue.

In enacting Section 4, Congress expressed "one of the basic policy objectives of the bill: to require manufacturers and processors to bear the responsibility for adequately testing potentially dangerous chemical substances."[37] But given the costs of testing, the chemical industry has often litigated Section 4 test rules. Are there sound economic reasons for requiring chemical manufacturers to bear ("internalize") testing costs? If so, why not require chemical manufacturers to test all (or the vast majority of) chemical substances on the market? If you are in favor of more testing, consider whether it would be fair to industry for a government agency to impose millions of dollars of testing costs on a mere suspicion of potential harm? More broadly, how should the United States go about closing the "Data Gap" on toxic chemical risks discussed in Chapter 1?

From EPA's perspective, promulgation of test rules is an involved process that can take anywhere from two to ten years. First, the test rule process commences, not with EPA itself, but with a list of chemicals produced by an Interagency Testing Committee (ITC) made up of representatives from most federal health agencies. The ITC, based on standard risk assessment criteria, periodically lists chemicals for testing on a priority basis. The list may not exceed 50 chemicals at one time, and EPA may revise the reports, but it must respond to ITC recommendations either by issuing a test rule or by publicly deciding within one year not to do so. Second, the proposed rule is subject to the elaborate "hybrid rulemaking" procedures

---

36. *Testing of Certain High Production Volume Chemicals; Third Group of Chemicals*, 75 Fed. Reg. 8575, 8588 (Feb. 25, 2010).

37. H.R. REP. NO. 1341, *supra*, at 17; *accord*, TSCA § 2(b)(1).

specified by Section 19(a). Third, any test rule must be based on three express findings: (i) that either the chemical "may present an unreasonable risk of injury to health or the environment," or that the chemical is manufactured in "substantial quantities" to which "significant or substantial human exposure" is likely; (ii) that there exists "insufficient data and experience upon which the effects of [the chemical] can reasonably be determined or predicted"; and (iii) that "testing * * * is necessary to develop such data." Fourth, any test rule is subject to the special judicial review provisions of Section 19(c).

Under this process, EPA has issued Section 4 test rules for only about 200 "existing" chemicals out of the 84,000 total chemicals in the TSCA inventory. This number highlights one of the defining features of TSCA: the PMN process requires disclosures to EPA for every new chemical manufactured (though it does not require toxicity test data). But the far larger class of existing chemicals was "grandfathered" under TSCA. There is no routine or default disclosure or research requirement. EPA must instead rely on the Section 4 test rule process, or, in some cases, Section 8 data submissions. The data "supply" for new chemicals is therefore more robust than the data "supply" for existing chemicals, even though existing chemicals first introduced before 1979 (those on the original TSCA Inventory) comprise more than 95% of the volume of chemicals produced each year. Moreover, testing under TSCA Section 4 usually occurs on a chemical-by-chemical basis. The synergistic effects of chemicals—the health effects of combinations of different chemicals—are rarely tested under the statute.

NOTES AND QUESTIONS

1. *Screening.* The PMN process is a kind of screening device. It ensures a flow of data to EPA upon which EPA can act, or not act, but there is no affirmative burden on the chemical manufacturer to prove that a new chemical is "safe," or does not pose "unreasonable risk." How is this different from FIFRA? Are the data gathering provisions (and resulting agency judgments) under FIFRA and the PMN process equally reliable? We have discussed the early assumption that non-pesticide chemicals pose fewer risks than pesticides. Why else do you think Congress settled for a partial screening system for new chemicals under TSCA, rather than establishing a formal licensing system?

2. *Section 4 findings.* What is the purpose of requiring predicate findings for test rules under Section 4? Why did Congress choose these particular prerequisites? Why might EPA have difficulty meeting them? What is the rationale for the ITC's role in deciding which chemicals should be subject to test rules?

3. *New chemicals, existing chemicals, and innovation.* One of the arguments of TSCA's opponents was that the statute would stifle innovation in the chemical industry. Two scholars who reviewed the evidence reached these conclusions:

> The adverse effects [of pre-market approval] appear to be felt most
> by the small and newer firms, particularly those that produce

specialty chemicals for limited, dynamic markets. These effects derive principally from the following factors: the ability of large firms to monitor or influence the political and legal climate; the economies of scale in compliance that large firms may enjoy; and the disproportionate emphasis these regulations place on new as opposed to existing products. * * * The situation under TSCA is exacerbated by the disproportionate emphasis regulatory action has placed on new chemical substances, [which tend to be produced by new, small, and specialty firms,] as opposed to problems associated with existing products. Were strong regulatory actions under TSCA directed at existing products, this would create an incentive for the introduction of new, safer substitutes. * * *

Nicholas Ashford & George Heaton, *Regulation and Technological Innovation in the Chemical Industry*, 46 L. & CONTEMP. PROBS. 109, 146–57 (1983).

Exempting "existing" chemicals from routine screening is an example of grandfathering in environmental law—differential treatment of products or manufacturing facilities based on when they were placed into service. If you have had exposure to the Clean Air Act in an introductory environmental law class, you may recall the Act's New Source Review provisions, which impose stringent pollution controls on new sources but leave older sources with relatively lax controls. Grandfathering is often justified on the grounds that it would be too expensive to make existing plants conform to the latest pollution control standards. But these provisions of the Clean Air Act clearly provide incentives to keep inefficient manufacturing plants and electric generating stations (some built in the 1940s and 1950s) in operation.

What are the benefits and drawbacks of grandfathering in the context of chemical regulation? Is there a justification for the grandfathering of all "existing" chemicals introduced before 1979 by exempting them from routine screening or data reporting? Why did Congress write special PMN provisions for "new" chemicals? Is the differential treatment the result of the expense of testing chemicals already on the market, or some other reason? More generally, do you believe that chemical testing requirements are in tension with innovation in the chemical industry?

4. *Self-monitoring.* Obviously, Section 8 leaves a lot up to the discretion of the manufacturer in choosing what to report to the EPA. And under a Section 4 test rule, the actual risk assessment process is conducted by the manufacturer, not the government. The reliance on private sector test data reflects Congressional intent. See TSCA § 2 ("[T]he development of such [toxicity] data should be the responsibility of those who manufacture and those who process ... chemical substances and mixtures."). Given what you know about the process of risk assessment, what opportunities might chemical manufacturers have to slant test data in their favor? How can this be policed by the government? Does the command of Sections 8(d) and (e), encompassing the submission of information that the manufacturers or processors did not themselves create, but only know of, alleviate any concerns you may have about the reliability of data?

5. *Nanotechnology.* Nanotechnology—the science of engineering structures and controlling matter on a molecular scale—is a rapidly growing

industry in the United States. The worldwide market for products that contain nanoscale substances, which are around one billionth of a meter in size, is projected to exceed $2 trillion by 2015. Nanoscale substances are used widely in electronics, fabrics, paints, cosmetics, sunscreens, and hundreds of other product categories. They are also widely used in medical applications and in biotechnology, including as systems to deliver drugs within the human body. Many nanoscale materials are chemical analogues of their macro cousins. For instance, carbon nanotubes, used in industrial materials and consumer products because of their strength and electrical conductivity, are made entirely of elemental carbon, considered nontoxic to humans.

Yet nanomaterials may also pose serious health and environmental risks. Because of their size, they can be easily inhaled, ingested, and absorbed through the skin. They can enter the bloodstream, brain tissues, and developing fetuses. Therefore, even if their macroscale analogues are considered "safe" (not posing unreasonable risk), there is no assurance that nanomaterials are also safe. A widely publicized 2008 study, for example, found that carbon nanotubes injected into mice caused mesothelioma, the same kind of damage to the lungs caused by asbestos.[38] Scientists and environmentalists are calling for more federal money to study the health effects of nanoscale substances. Given the diversity of substances and the diversity of applications, health studies will need to focus on specific products and uses. It makes little sense to talk about the health effects of nanotechnology in general.

Nanoscale substances raise some urgent questions for regulators under TSCA. If a nanoscale substance has the exact same chemical composition as a chemical already on the Inventory, should it be treated as a "new" chemical subject to PMN requirements under Section 5, or as an "existing" chemical? In 2010, EPA was preparing some complicated rulemakings to sort out this question. For carbon nanotubes in particular, the agency has adopted the position that they are "new" chemicals, since they represent a different allotrope (structurally different form) of carbon than other forms of carbon, such as graphite. Other nanosubstances will likely be considered "existing" chemicals if they are chemically identical to substances already on the Inventory, but they may fall under a § 5(a)(2) Significant New Use Rule (SNUR) that EPA was preparing as this book went to press. The SNUR would subject these "existing" nanoscale substances to reporting when they are applied in new commercial uses. One potential gap in this strategy is that it does not seem to cover uses of nanoscale substances that existed by 2010, because ongoing uses cannot legally be addressed in a SNUR.

EPA is also beginning to use the information-gathering tools of TSCA to obtain more data from nanotech manufacturers, including a potential Section 8(a) rule (requiring submission of data such as production volume, methods of manufacture and processing, exposure and release information, and available health and safety data) and a Section 4 rule for certain

---

38. Craig A. Poland et al., *Carbon Nanotubes Introduced into the Abdominal Cavity of Mice Show Asbestos-like Pathogenicity in a Pilot Study*, 3 NATURE NANOTECHNOLOGY 423 (2008).

nanoscale materials that are already in commerce and that are not being tested by other federal and international organizations.[39]

Are the regulatory challenges for nanotechnology essentially the same as the regulatory challenges for CFCs in the 1970s? Some critics have argued that the debate over whether nanoscale substances are "existing" or "new" misses the more fundamental question: how can their true risks be assessed and managed? Does TSCA provide adequate regulatory tools for these tasks?

3. A Closer Look at "Unreasonable Risk" in Information Gathering

As noted above, the basic standard for data gathering under Sections 5, 8, and 4 is unreasonable risk, "a balancing of risks and benefits." S. Rep. No. 698, *supra*, at 12. In this subsection, we take a closer look at the "unreasonable risk" standard in the context of information gathering. Think about whether risk-benefit balancing is appropriate at the stage of information gathering. Is it feasible to engage in risk-benefit balancing before EPA has obtained the information it is seeking? Under Section 4, how sure does the agency need to be about the extent of risk before deciding that a chemical "may present" an "unreasonable risk"?

These issues were discussed at length in *Chemical Manufacturers Association v. EPA*, 859 F.2d 977 (D.C. Cir. 1988) (CMA I), a challenge to EPA's 1985 Section 4 test rule for 2–ethylhexanoic acid (EHA). We will use this case to explore the meaning of "unreasonable risk" and "may present" in TSCA. The case also highlights some of the practical challenges EPA faces in obtaining information about chemical risks.

EHA is used exclusively as a chemical intermediate. That is, it is completely consumed in the manufacturer of other products and compounds, so there can be no consumer exposure to EHA. Nevertheless, EPA was concerned principally about occupational dermal exposures to EHA during manufacturing. EPA did not collect actual data on worker exposures, but in its Section 4 test rule,[40] it explained that 400 workers were engaged in the manufacture, transfer, storage, and processing of 20 to 25 million pounds of EHA per year and that industrial hygiene procedures "can vary widely throughout the industry." In particular, the agency asserted, not all workers wore protective gloves (recall from Chapter 1 that risk is a product of hazard and exposure, so the issue of whether workers were actually being exposed to EHA loomed large in this case). As for showing hazard, EPA relied on prior studies showing toxicity of EHA in laboratory animals and also noted the recommendation of the ITC that further testing should be

---

39. For more information on nanotechnology regulation under TSCA, see EPA's website on nanotechnology, www.epa.gov/oppt/nano. *See also* Linda Breggin et al., Securing the Promise of Nanotechnology: Toward Transatlantic Cooperation (Environmental Law Institute, September 2009); Douglas A. Kysar, *Ecologic: Nanotechnology, Environmental Assurance Bonding, and Symmetric Humility*, 28 UCLA J. Envtl L. & Pol'y (2010); Scott Bomkamp, *Beyond Chemicals: The Lessons that Toxic Substances Regulatory Reform Can Learn from Nanotechnology*, 85 Indiana L. J. Supp. 24 (2010).

40. 2–Ethylhexanoic Acid Proposed Test Rule, 50 Fed. Reg. 20,678, 20,680–81 (1985).

conducted. In its final test rule—ordering a chronic toxicity test, a developmental toxicity test, and a pharmacokinetics test—EPA concluded that the "weight of evidence" supported its findings of potential toxicity and its order for further testing. The Chemical Manufacturers Association and four chemical companies sued to challenge the test rule.

In grappling with the meaning of "may present" an "unreasonable risk" in Section 4 of TSCA, the DC Circuit concluded that "may" means something less than more-probable-than-not. On the other hand, "may" means something more than a mere conjecture or supposition. This part of the decision is excerpted below:

> Consequently, we uphold the Agency's construction of TSCA as authorizing a test rule where EPA's basis for suspecting the existence of an "unreasonable risk of injury to health" is substantial—*i.e.*, when there is a more-than-theoretical basis for suspecting that some amount of exposure takes place and that the substance is sufficiently toxic at that level of exposure to present an "unreasonable risk of injury to health."

1. Text and Structure of the Statute

Both the wording and structure of TSCA reveal that Congress did not expect that EPA would have to document to a certainty the existence of an "unreasonable risk" before it could require testing. This is evident from the two-tier structure of the Act. In order for EPA to be empowered to regulate a chemical substance, the Agency must find that the substance "presents or will present an unreasonable risk of injury to health or the environment." TSCA § 6, 15 U.S.C. § 2605(a). The *testing* provision at issue here, by contrast, empowers EPA to act at a lower threshold of certainty than that required for regulation. Specifically, testing is warranted if the substance "*may* present an unreasonable risk of injury to health or the environment." TSCA § 4, 15 U.S.C. § 2603(a)(1)(A)(i) (emphasis added). Thus, the language of Section 4 signals that EPA is to make a probabilistic determination of the presence of "unreasonable risk."

2. Legislative History

The legislative history of TSCA compels a further conclusion. It not only shows that "unreasonable risk" need not be a matter of absolute certainty; it shows the reasonableness of EPA's conclusion that "unreasonable risk" need not be established to a more-probable-than-not degree.

A House Report on the version of the bill that eventually became TSCA underscores the distinction between the Section 6 standard and the Section 4 standard. To issue a test rule, EPA need not find that a substance actually does cause or present an "unreasonable risk."

> Such a finding requirement would defeat the purpose of the section, for if the Administrator is able to make such a determination, regulatory action to protect against the risk, not additional testing, is called for.

H.R.REP. No. 1341, 94TH CONG., 2D SESS. 17–18 (1976).

* * *

Of course, it is also evident from the legislative history that Congress did not intend to authorize EPA to issue test rules on the basis of mere hunches. The House Report states:

> [T]he term "may" ... does not permit the Administrator to make a finding respecting probability of a risk on the basis of mere conjecture or speculation, i.e., it may or may not cause a risk.

H.R.REP. No. 1341, *supra*, at 18. Congress obviously intended Section 4 to empower EPA to issue a test rule only after it had found a solid "basis for concern" by accumulating enough information to demonstrate a more-than-theoretical basis for suspecting that an "unreasonable risk" was involved in the use of the chemical.

859 F.2d at 984–86.

The D.C. Circuit then moved on to the issue of the judicial standard of review—the level of deference that a reviewing court should give to EPA's conclusion that a chemical "may present" an unreasonable risk. Courts normally defer to an agency's decisions and orders as long as the agency's action is not deemed "arbitrary and capricious" under the Administrative Procedure Act. *See, e.g., National Association of Home Builders v. Defenders of Wildlife*, 551 U.S. 644, 658 (2007). But TSCA specifically states (15 U.S.C. § 2618(c)(1)(B)(i)) that Section 4 test rules should instead be reviewed under the APA's "substantial evidence" standard, 5 U.S.C. § 706(2)(E). As we will see soon, TSCA also commands use of the same "substantial evidence" standard for judicial review of EPA decisions to restrict chemicals under Section 6 of TSCA. Therefore, it is important to understand what "substantial evidence" means, and how it differs from an "arbitrary and capricious" standard.

As the D.C. Circuit explained:

> The legislative history of TSCA further indicates that Congress perceived some difference between the standard it chose for TSCA and the APA's arbitrary-and-capricious standard. The House Report explained:

> > [I]t is the intent that the traditional presumption of validity of an agency rule would remain in effect, [but] ... [t]he

Committee has chosen to adopt the "substantial evidence test," for the Committee intends that the reviewing court engage in a *searching review* of the Administrator's reasons and explanations for the Administrator's conclusions.

* * *

This fairly rigorous standard of record review should not, however, be confused with the substantive statutory standard previously discussed at length. EPA's permissible interpretation of "may present an unreasonable risk" works in tandem with the "substantial evidence" standard of record review to effectuate a statutory scheme that empowers the Agency to require testing where the existence of an "unreasonable risk of injury to health" is not yet more-probable-than-not, but at the same time the Agency is required to identify the facts that underlie its determination that there is a more-than-theoretical basis to suspect the presence of such a risk.

859 F.2d at 991–92.

The court ultimately ruled in favor of EPA. It concluded that EPA had presented "substantial evidence"—both affirmative evidence and rebuttal of the Chemical Manufacturers Association evidence and arguments—to support its claims of exposure and toxicity and its determination that EHA "may present" unreasonable risk.

NOTES AND QUESTIONS

1. *Litigating Test Rules. CMA I* is typical of the Section 4 test cases that have been litigated. In these cases, the "substantial evidence" standard for judicial review, involving a searching inquiry into the decisions of the agency, has invited aggressive challenges to EPA's rules. Each of the test rule cases requires a large investment of agency time to produce a record to support the agency's action and then to defend its actions. Indeed, one reason that it takes between two and ten years to promulgate a test rule is that EPA aims to develop solid evidence of "unreasonable risk," before issuing the rule, to withstand a possible lawsuit.

Notice in *CMA I* that the parties and the court steered clear of the problem of defining what *level* of risk is unreasonable. Given the preliminary nature of the testing decision, this may well be justified. What, then, does the court say about the components of "unreasonable risk"? EPA announced in its test rule for EHA that it would approach the unreasonable risk analysis by first examining hazard (toxicity), then risk (toxicity X exposure), then unreasonableness (estimated risk compared to the cost of testing).[41] Is this policy required by TSCA? Does it commit the Agency to a virtual quantitative risk assessment before issuing a test rule to gather

---

41. For an explanation of this process for determining unreasonable risk in the context of testing, see Chloromethane Test Rule, 45 Fed. Reg. 48524, 48528–29 (1980).

information? Are the feasibility and cost issues appropriate for this stage of the regulatory process?

2. The addition of the term "may present" to unreasonable risk was obviously designed to distinguish Section 4 from the "presents or will present" standard for regulation in Section 6, and hence to relieve the agency of the burden of proving the actual existence of an unreasonable risk at the testing stage. But as *CMA I* indicates, it is not easy to define "may present" with any precision. Is it sensible to require EPA to prove, by "substantial evidence," that a chemical "may" present an unreasonable risk?

3. *TSCA's compromises.* If we step back from this particular case, we can now see why EPA has required testing for only about 200 existing chemicals since 1976: the statutory procedures are extraordinarily complex to obtain information on chemical risks, particularly for existing chemicals.

> Much of the confusion results from the proliferation of probabilistic criteria under Section 4. * * * EPA must promulgate a test rule when it finds a probability (substantial evidence) of a probability (may present) of a probability (risk). Moreover, each probability is a very different type of calculation: risk is a statement of frequency of effect; "may present" is a statement of the confidence of the induction from known data to frequency; and substantial evidence is a statement of the overall certainty with which the foregoing statements are made. Risk and "may present" take an *ex ante* perspective; substantial evidence is an *ex post* evaluation. The "may present" prong of the first Section 4 finding, in sum, cannot be made simple, and it constitutes a major obstacle to the smooth functioning of the TSCA requirement to test.

Applegate, *The Perils of Unreasonable Risk, supra*, at 322.

The complex procedural requirements for information gathering under TSCA reflect political compromise. Congress was willing to cede broad substantive powers to control industrial chemicals to EPA, but it wished to constrain EPA's actions within strict procedural limits.

> [TSCA] was a statute that had been debated for five years before passage, as the opposing forces around the bill had produced a legislative stalemate. The bill contains potentially powerful regulatory tools, but they have never been vigorously employed by the EPA, in large part because the statute is so procedurally complex. These procedural sections were drafted strategically, so that once the substantive and procedural provisions are read together, the net result is a bill that does not tilt strongly either in the direction of environmental protection or in the direction of permissively sanctioning industrial manufacture of toxic substances. Instead, it mirrors the closely divided political environment present when the statute was enacted, in which environmental sentiment was substantially offset by the opposition to new regulations on business of President Ford and his supporters in Congress.

James T. Hamilton & Christopher H. Schroeder, *Strategic Regulators and the Choice of Rulemaking Procedures: The Selection of Formal vs. Informal*

Rules in Regulating Hazardous Waste, 57(2) L. & CONTEMP. PROBS. 111, 122 n.33 (1994).

The result is that EPA is given considerable authority under TSCA, but industry is also given strong grounds for opposing or delaying its exercise. Is this a principled compromise or pusillanimous lawmaking?

4. *Alternatives for information gathering.* Are there any good alternatives to the "may present an unreasonable risk" standard for testing and the "substantial evidence" standard of judicial review of test rules? Take a look at FIFRA § 3(c)(2)(B), the data "call-in" provision that provides authority for the EPA Administrator to request additional data for pesticides already registered. What differences do you see between this provision and TSCA Section 4? Given widespread concern that only a small fraction of chemicals on the market have ever been tested, should EPA be able to issue test rules on the basis of a finding of *any* level of risk to human health? Should it be able to issue test rules on the basis of exposure or toxicity alone? Congress might even go further and simply legislate that all chemicals produced above a certain volume per year should be tested for toxicity and environmental effects. Would you support that legislative change to TSCA?

5. TSCA does, in fact, allow EPA to order testing without making formal risk findings where the chemical will be "produced in substantial quantities" *and* will either enter the environment in "substantial quantities" or result in "significant or substantial human exposure." § 4(a)(1)(B).[42] This is the main alternative in Section 4 to ordering testing based on "unreasonable risk." Under this statutory authority, EPA has developed a formal policy setting numerical thresholds for "substantial" production, environmental release, and human exposure.[43] It relied on the new policy in a number of test rules in the 1990s.[44]

4. AUTHORITY TO RESTRICT CHEMICALS UNDER TSCA

While the information gathering provisions of TSCA are relevant to risk *assessment*, the heart of TSCA's approach to risk *management* is Section 6.

---

42. This prong of TSCA was considered in *Chemical Manufacturers Association v. EPA*, 899 F.2d 344 (5th Cir. 1990) (*"CMA II"*). EPA ordered testing of the chemical cumene on the basis of occupational exposure of 700–800 workers and environmental releases of 3 million pounds per year of air emissions, concentrated in a few major metropolitan areas. Despite a challenge from CMA, the court found that EPA's findings were supported by substantial evidence, noting that the statutory term "substantial" "suggests that rough approximation suffices." The court rejected a series of elaborate textual challenges to EPA's interpretation of the statute, all of which would have required the agency to come forward with very specific evidence of risk (not just exposure) posed by the chemical. Nevertheless, the judges remanded the cumene test rule because "EPA has not articulated any understandable basis—either in the form of a general definition of or a set of criteria respecting the statutory term 'substantial' or in its analysis of the specific evidence respecting cumene—for its ultimate determinations" that the exposure was substantial. EPA was directed to develop such explanation or criteria. EPA's 4(a)(1)(b) Final Statement of Policy, issued in 1993, was a reaction to the CMA II decision.

43. U.S. EPA, TSCA § 4(a)(1)(b) Final Statement of Policy; Criteria for Evaluating Substantial Production, Substantial Release, and Substantial or Significant Human Exposure, 58 Fed. Reg. 28736, 28746 (May 14, 1993).

44. *E.g.*, U.S. EPA Endocrine Disrupter Screening Program; Proposed Statement of Policy, 63 Fed. Reg. 71542 (Dec. 28, 1998); U.S. EPA, Proposed Test Rules for Hazardous Air Pollutants, 61 Fed. Reg. 33178 (June 26, 1996).

Section 6 authorizes EPA to prohibit the manufacture, processing, or distribution of a chemical; to limit production to certain amounts, uses, or concentrations; or to require warnings or directions, record retention, tests, or quality control procedures. § 6(a), (b). As a package, this is very broad authority to address chemical risks. However, the exercise of this power is carefully cabined:

- EPA must have a "reasonable basis" for concluding that the chemical presents or will present "an unreasonable risk of injury to health or the environment";

- Any regulation must "protect adequately against such risk using the least burdensome requirements"; and

- EPA must consider not only the health and environmental effects of the substance, but also the benefits associated with it, the availability of substitutes for it, the alternatives to a ban, the costs of any proposal action, and "the reasonably ascertainable economic consequences" of regulation.

- EPA's proposed restrictions are reviewed by a court under the searching "substantial evidence" standard.

TSCA § 6(a), (c)(1), § 19(c)(1)(B)(i))

Note that the procedures and required findings under Sections 6(a) and 6(c) are the same whether EPA intends to enact a product ban or less aggressive measures, such as a warning requirement. Does this make sense as an approach to risk management?

When it comes to chemical restrictions, TSCA, like FIFRA, is a classic risk-benefit balancing statute. In determining whether a chemical meets this unreasonable risk standard, EPA should address the following, according to the TSCA Conference Report:

> the effects of the substance or mixture on health and the magnitude of human exposure to such substance or mixture; the effects of the substance or mixture on the environment and the magnitude of environmental exposure to such substance or mixture; the benefits of such substance or mixture for various uses and the availability of substitutes for such uses; and the reasonably ascertainable economic consequences of the rule, after consideration of the effects on the national economy, small business, innovation, the environment, and the public health.

H.R. REP. NO. 1679, *supra*, at 75–76. The House Report added: "The Committee has limited the Administrator to taking action only against unreasonable risks because to do otherwise assumes that a risk-free society is attainable, an assumption that the Committee does not make." H.R. REP. No. 1341, *supra*, at 15.

TSCA in fact calls for two related kinds of balancing—risk-benefit and cost-benefit—which are intended to reveal the situations in which regulation is "worth it." Risk-benefit balancing asks EPA to compare the harms to society that are likely to result from *not* regulating the substance against the benefits that society receives from the substance that will be foregone or diminished if the substance is regulated. A cost-benefit analysis asks the regulator to compare the costs associated with regulation—usually the economic costs of compliance by regulated firms and the social costs of doing without a banned substance—against the benefits of the regulation—reduced risks to human health and the environment.

Both the House and Senate reports emphasized, however, that the balancing should not necessarily entail a formal quantitative comparison of costs and benefits in which monetary values are assigned to risks, costs, and benefits. Such a mathematically precise balancing would be neither "useful" nor "feasible." H.R. REP. No. 1341, *supra*, at 14. If the balancing is not to be performed through conversions to dollar values, however, by what metric should EPA balance, say, a potential 1% reduction in the national incidence of liver cancer (as a result of a proposed ban on a chemical) with assurances from that chemical's manufacturer that it will close a Louisiana production facility if the chemical is restricted, resulting in loss of 300 jobs? How should future expected health benefits and near-term direct economic costs be weighed?

The agency's decision in 1989 to ban almost all uses of asbestos provides an excellent example of cost-risk-benefit balancing under TSCA. The decision was preceded by a data collection rule promulgated under Section 8(a), 10 years of data analysis, 22 days of public hearings, 13,000 pages of comments from more than 250 parties, and a 45,000 page record. EPA summarized its justification for the ban in the following excerpt. This excerpt is followed by the Fifth Circuit opinion ruling on industry's challenge to EPA's rule.

Asbestos: Manufacture, Importation, Processing, and Distribution in Commerce Prohibitions

Environmental Protection Agency
54 Fed. Reg. 29460 (July 12, 1989)

EPA is issuing this final rule under Section 6 of the Toxic Substance Control Act (TSCA) to prohibit, at staged intervals, the future manufacture, importation, processing, and distribution in commerce of asbestos in almost all products, as identified in this rule. EPA is issuing this rule to reduce the unreasonable risks presented to human health by exposure to asbestos during activities involving these products. * * *

To determine whether a risk from activities involving asbestos-containing products presents an unreasonable risk, EPA must balance the probability that harm will occur from the activities against the effects of the proposed regulatory action on the availability to society of the benefits of asbestos. EPA has considered these factors in conjunction with the extensive record gathered in the development of this rule. EPA has concluded that the continued manufacture, importation, processing, and distribution in commerce of most asbestos-containing products poses an unreasonable risk to human health. This conclusion is based on information summarized [below].

* * *

Evidence supports the conclusion that substitutes already exist or will soon exist for each of the products that are subject to the rule's bans. In scheduling products for the different stages of the bans, EPA has analyzed the probable availability of non-asbestos substitutes. In the rule, it is likely that suitable non-asbestos substitutes will be available. However, the rule also includes an exemption provision to account for instances in which technology might not have advanced sufficiently by the time of a ban to produce substitutes for certain specialized or limited uses of asbestos.

EPA has calculated that the product bans in this rule will result in the avoidance of 202 quantifiable cancer cases, if benefits are not discounted, and 148 cases, if benefits are discounted at 3 percent. The figures decrease to 164 cases, if benefits are not discounted, and 120 cases, if benefits are discounted at 3 percent, if analogous exposures are not included in the analysis. In all likelihood, the rule will result in the avoidance of a large number of other cancer cases that cannot be quantified, as well as many cases of asbestos-related diseases. Estimates of benefits resulting from the action taken in this rule are limited to mesothelioma and lung and gastrointestinal cancer cases avoided, and do not include cases of asbestosis and other diseases avoided and avoided costs from treating asbestos diseases, lost productivity, or other factors.

EPA has estimated that the cost of this rule, for the 13–year period of the analyses performed, will be approximately $456.89 million, or $806.51 million if a 1 percent annual decline in the price of substitutes is not assumed. This cost will be spread over time and a large population so that the cost to any person is likely to be negligible. In addition, the rule's exemption provision is a qualitative factor that supports the actions taken in this rule. EPA has concluded that the quantifiable and unquantifiable benefits of the rule's staged-ban of the identified asbestos-containing products will outweigh the resultant economic consequences to consumers, producers, and users of the products.

EPA has determined that, within the findings required by Section 6 of TSCA, only the staged-ban approach employed in this final rule will adequately control the asbestos exposure risk posed by the product categories affected by this rule. Other options either fail to address significant portions of the life cycle risk posed by products subject to the rule or are unreasonably burdensome. EPA has, therefore, concluded that the actions taken in this rule represent the least burdensome means of reducing the risks posed by exposure to asbestos during the life cycles of the products that are subject to the bans.

Corrosion Proof Fittings v. EPA
947 F.2d 1201 (5th Cir. 1991)

■ SMITH, CIRCUIT JUDGE.

* * *

Asbestos is a naturally occurring fibrous material that resists fire and most solvents. Its major uses include heat-resistant insulators, cements, building materials, fireproof gloves and clothing, and motor vehicle brake linings. Asbestos is a toxic material, and occupational exposure to asbestos dust can result in mesothelioma, asbestosis, and lung cancer.

* * *

An EPA-appointed panel reviewed over 100 studies of asbestos and conducted several public meetings. Based upon its studies and the public comments, the EPA concluded that asbestos is a potential carcinogen at all levels of exposure, regardless of the type of asbestos or the size of the fiber.
* * *

* * * In 1989, the EPA issued a final rule prohibiting the manufacture, importation, processing, and distribution in commerce of most asbestos-containing products. Finding that asbestos constituted an unreasonable risk to health and the environment, the EPA promulgated a staged ban of most commercial uses of asbestos. The EPA estimates that this rule will save either 202 or 148 lives, depending upon whether the benefits are discounted, at a cost of approximately $450–800 million, depending upon the price of substitutes.

* * *

The EPA's Burden Under TSCA

TSCA provides, in pertinent part, as follows:

> (a) Scope of regulation.—If the Administrator finds that there is a *reasonable basis* to conclude that the manufacture, processing, distribution in commerce, use, or disposal of a chemical substance or mixture, or that any combination of such activities, presents or will present *an unreasonable risk of injury* to health or the environment, the Administrator shall by rule apply one or more of the following requirements to such substance or mixture to the extent necessary to *protect adequately* against such risk using the *least burdensome* requirements. 15 U.S.C. § 2605(c). [Emphasis added.]

As the highlighted language shows, Congress did not enact TSCA as a zero-risk statute. The EPA, rather, was required to consider both alternatives to a ban and the costs of any proposed actions and to "carry out this chapter in a reasonable and prudent manner [after considering] the environmental, economic, and social impact of any action." 15 U.S.C. § 2601(c).

We conclude that the EPA has presented insufficient evidence to justify its asbestos ban. We base this conclusion upon two grounds: the failure of the EPA to consider all necessary evidence and its failure to give adequate weight to statutory language requiring it to promulgate the least burdensome, reasonable regulation required to protect the environment adequately. Because the EPA failed to address these concerns, and because the EPA is required to articulate a "reasoned basis" for its rules, we are compelled to return the regulation to the agency for reconsideration.

1. Least Burdensome and Reasonable

TSCA requires that the EPA use the least burdensome regulation to achieve its goals of minimum reasonable risk. This statutory requirement can create problems in evaluating just what is a "reasonable risk." Congress's rejection of a no-risk policy, however, also means that in certain cases, the least burdensome yet still adequate solution may entail somewhat more risk than other, known regulations that are far more burdensome on the industry and the economy. The very language of TSCA requires that the EPA, once it has determined what an acceptable level of non-zero risk is, choose the least burdensome method of reaching that level.

In this case, the EPA banned, for all practical purposes, all present and future uses of asbestos—a position the petitioners characterize as the "death penalty alternative," as this is the *most* burdensome of all possible alternatives listed as open to the EPA under TSCA. TSCA not only provides the EPA with a list of alternative actions, but also provides those alternatives in order of how burdensome they are. The regulations thus provide for EPA regulation ranging from labeling the least toxic chemicals to limiting the total amount of chemicals an industry may use. Total bans head the list as the most burdensome regulatory option.

By choosing the *harshest remedy* given to it under TSCA, the EPA assigned to itself the toughest burden in satisfying TSCA's requirement that its alternative be the least burdensome of all those offered to it. Since both by definition and by the terms of TSCA the complete ban of manufacturing is the most burdensome alternative—for even stringent regulation at least allows a manufacturer the chance to invest and meet the new, higher standard—the EPA's regulation cannot stand if there is any other regulation that would achieve an acceptable level of risk as mandated by TSCA.

* * *

* * * What concerns us, however, is the manner in which the EPA conducted some of its analysis. TSCA requires the EPA to consider, along with the effects of toxic substances on human health and the environment, "the benefits of such substances or mixtures for various uses and the availability of substitutes for such uses," as well as "the reasonably ascertainable economic consequences of the rule, after consideration for the effect on the national economy, small business, technological innovation, the environment, and public health." § 2605(c)(1)(C–D).

The EPA presented two comparisons in the record: a world with no further regulation under TSCA, and a world in which no manufacture of asbestos takes place. The EPA rejected calculating how many lives a less burdensome regulation would save, and at what cost. Furthermore the EPA, when calculating the benefits of its ban, explicitly refused to compare it to an improved workplace in which currently available control technology is utilized. This decision artificially inflated the purported benefits of the rule by using a baseline comparison substantially lower than what currently available technology could yield.

Under TSCA, the EPA was required to evaluate, rather than ignore, less burdensome regulatory alternatives. TSCA imposes a least-to-most-burdensome hierarchy. In order to impose a regulation at the top of the hierarchy—a total ban of asbestos—the EPA must show not only that its proposed action reduces the risk of the product to an adequate level, but also that the actions Congress identified as less burdensome would not do the job. The failure of the EPA to do this constitutes a failure to meet its burden of showing that it sections not only reduce the risk but do so in the Congressionally-mandated *least burdensome* fashion.

Thus, it was not enough for the EPA to show, as it did in this case, that banning some asbestos products might reduce the harm that could occur from the use of these products. If that were the standard, it would be no standard at all, for few indeed are the products that are so safe that a complete ban of them would not make the world still safer.

This comparison of two static worlds is insufficient to satisfy the dictates of TSCA. While the EPA may have shown that a world with a complete ban of asbestos might be preferable to one in which there is only the current amount of regulation, the EPA has failed to show that there is not some intermediate state of regulation that would be superior to both the currently-regulated and the completely-banned world. Without showing that asbestos regulation would be ineffective, the EPA cannot discharge its TSCA burden of showing that its regulation is the least burdensome available to it.

Upon an initial showing of product danger, the proper course for the EPA to follow is to consider each regulatory option, in the order mandated by Congress, and the costs and benefits of regulation under each option. The EPA cannot simply skip several rungs, as it did in this case, for in doing so, it may skip a less burdensome alternative mandated by TSCA. Here, although the EPA mentions the problems posed by intermediate levels of regulation, it takes no steps to calculate the costs and benefits of these intermediate levels. Without doing this it is impossible, both for the EPA and for this court on review, to know that none of these alternatives was less burdensome than the ban in fact chosen by the agency.

* * *

Furthermore, we are concerned about some of the methodology employed by the EPA in making various of the calculations that it did perform. * * *

* * *

Of * * * concern to us is the failure of the EPA to compute the costs and benefits of its proposed rule past the year 2000, and its double-counting of the costs of asbestos use. In performing its calculus, the EPA only included the number of lives saved over the next 13 years, and counted any additional lives saved as simply "unquantified benefits." The EPA and intervenors now seek to use these unquantified lives saved to justify calculations as to which benefits seem far outweighed by the astronomical costs. For example, the EPA plans to save about three lives with its ban of asbestos pipe, at a cost of $128–227 million (*i.e.,* approximately $43–76 million per life saved).

Although the EPA admits that the price tag is high, it claims that the lives saved past the year 2000 justify the price.

Such calculations not only lessen the value of the EPA's cost analysis, but also make any meaningful judicial review impossible. While TSCA contemplates a useful place for unquantified benefits beyond the EPA's calculation, unquantified benefits never were intended as a trump card allowing the EPA to justify any cost calculus, no matter how high.

The concept of unquantified benefits, rather, is intended to allow the EPA to provide a rightful place for any remaining benefits that are impossible to quantify after the EPA's best attempt, but which still are of some concern. But the allowance for unquantified costs is not intended to allow the EPA to perform its calculations over an arbitrarily short period so as to preserve a large unquantified portion.

Unquantified benefits can, at times, permissibly tip the balance in close cases. They cannot, however, be used to effect a wholesale shift on the balance beam. Such a use makes mockery of the requirements of TSCA that the EPA weigh the costs of its actions before it chooses the least burdensome alternative.

We do not today determine what an appropriate period for the EPA's calculations would be, as this is a matter better left for agency discretion. We do note, however, that the choice of a 13-year period is so short as to make the unquantified period so unreasonably large that any EPA reliance upon it must be displaced.

Under the EPA's calculations, a 20-year-old worker entering employment today still would be at a risk from workplace dangers for more than 30 years after the EPA's analysis period has ended. The true benefits of regulating asbestos under such calculations remain unknown. The EPA cannot choose to leave these benefits high and then use the high unknown benefits as a major factor justifying the EPA action.

We also note that the EPA appears to place too great a reliance upon the concept of population exposure. While a high population exposure certainly is a factor that the EPA must consider in making its calculations, the agency cannot count such problems more than once. For example, in the case of asbestos brake products, the EPA used factors such as risk and exposure to calculate the probable harm of the brakes, and then used, as an *additional* reason to ban the products, the fact that the exposure levels were high. Considering that calculations of the probable harm level, when reduced to basics, simply are a calculation of population risk multiplied by population exposure, the EPA's redundant use of population exposure to justify its actions cannot stand.

Reasonable Basis

In addition to showing that its regulation is the least burdensome one necessary to protect the environment adequately, the EPA also must show that it has a reasonable basis for the regulation. 15 U.S.C. § 2605(a). To some extent, our inquiry in this area mirrors that used above, for many of the methodological problems we have noted also indicate that the EPA did not have a reasonable basis. * * *

Most problematical to us is the EPA's ban of products for which no substitutes presently are available. In these cases, the EPA bears a tough burden indeed to show that under TSCA a ban is the least burdensome alternative, as TSCA explicitly instructs the EPA to consider "the benefits of such substance or mixture for various uses and the availability of substitutes for such uses." § 2605(c)(1)(c). These words are particularly appropriate where the EPA actually has decided to ban a product, rather than simply restrict its use, for it is in these cases that the lack of an adequate substitute is most troubling under TSCA.

As the EPA itself states, "when no information is available for a product indicating that cost-effective substitutes exist, the estimated cost of a product ban is very high." 54 Fed. Reg. at 29,468. Because of this, the EPA did not ban certain uses of asbestos, such as its use in rocket engines and battery separators. The EPA, however, in several other instances, ignores its own arguments and attempts to justify its ban by stating that the ban itself will cause the development of low-cost, adequate substitute products.

As a general matter, we agree with the EPA that a product ban can lead to great innovation, and it is true that an agency under TSCA, as under other regulatory statutes, "is empowered to issue safety standards which require improvements in existing technology or which require the development of new technology." As even the EPA acknowledges, however, when no adequate substitutes currently exist, the EPA cannot fail to consider this lack when formulating its own guidelines. Under TSCA, therefore, the EPA must present a stronger case to justify the ban, as opposed to regulation, of products with no substitutes.

We note that the EPA does provide a waiver provision for industries where the hoped-for substitutes fail to materialize in time. Under this provision, if no adequate substitutes develop, the EPA temporarily may extend the planned phase-out.

The EPA uses this provision to argue that it can ban any product, regardless of whether it has an adequate substitute, because inventive companies soon will develop good substitutes. The EPA contends that if they do not, the waiver provision will allow the continued use of asbestos in these areas, just as if the ban had not occurred at all.

The EPA errs, however, in asserting that the waiver provision will allow a continuation of the status quo in those cases in which no substitutes materialize. By its own terms, the exemption shifts the burden onto the waiver proponent to convince the EPA that the waiver is justified. As even the EPA acknowledges, the waiver only "may be granted by EPA in very limited circumstances."

The EPA thus cannot use the waiver provision to lessen its burden when justifying banning products without existing substitutes. While TSCA gives the EPA the power to ban such products, the EPA must bear its heavier burden of justifying its total ban in the face of inadequate substitutes. Thus, the agency cannot use its waiver provision to argue that the ban of products with no substitutes should be treated the same as the ban of those for which adequate substitutes are available now.

We also are concerned with the EPA's evaluation of substitutes even in those instances in which the record shows that they are available. The EPA explicitly rejects considering the harm that may flow from the increased use of products designed to substitute for asbestos, even where the probable substitutes themselves are known carcinogens. The EPA justifies this by stating that it has "more concern about the continued use and exposure to asbestos than it has for the future replacement of asbestos in the products subject to this rule with other fibrous substitutes." The agency thus concludes that any "regulatory decisions about asbestos which pose well-recognized, serious risks should not be delayed until the risk of all replacement materials are fully quantified."

This presents two problems. First, TSCA instructs the EPA to consider the relative merits of its ban, as compared to the economic effects of its actions. The EPA cannot make this calculation if it fails to consider the effects that alternate substitutes will pose after a ban.

Second, the EPA cannot say with any assurance that its regulation will increase workplace safety when it refuses to evaluate the harm that will result from the increased use of substitute products. While the EPA may be correct in its conclusion that the alternate materials pose less risk than asbestos, we cannot say with any more assurance than that flowing from an educated guess that this conclusion is true.

Considering that many of the substitutes that the EPA itself concedes will be used in the place of asbestos have known carcinogenic effects, the EPA not only cannot assure this court that it has taken the least burdensome alternative, but cannot even prove that its regulations will increase workplace safety. Eager to douse the dangers of asbestos, the agency inadvertently actually may increase the risk of injury Americans face. The EPA's explicit failure to consider the toxicity of likely substitutes thus deprives its order of a reasonable basis.

* * *

UNREASONABLE RISK OF INJURY

The final requirement the EPA must satisfy before engaging in any TSCA rulemaking is that it only take steps designed to prevent "unreasonable" risks. In evaluating what is "unreasonable," the EPA is required to consider the costs of any proposed actions and to "carry out this chapter in a reasonable and prudent manner [after considering] the environmental, economic, and social impact of any action." 15 U.S.C. § 2601(c).

* * *

That the EPA must balance the costs of its regulations against their benefits further is reinforced by the requirement that it seek the least burdensome regulation. While Congress did not dictate that the EPA engage in an exhaustive, full-scale cost-benefit analysis, it did require the EPA to consider both sides of the regulatory equation, and it rejected the notion that the EPA should pursue the reduction of workplace risk at any cost. * * *

Even taking all of the EPA's figures as true, and evaluating them in the light most favorable to the agency's decision (non-discounted benefits, discounted costs, analogous exposure estimated included), the agency's analysis results in figures as high as $74 million per life saved. For example, the EPA states that its ban of asbestos pipe will save three lives over the next 13 years, at a cost of $128–227 million ($43–76 million per life saved), depending upon the price of substitutes; that its ban of asbestos shingles will cost $23–34 million to save 0.32 statistical lives ($72–106 million per life saved); that its ban of asbestos coatings will cost $46–181 million to save 3.33 lives ($14–54 million per life saved); and that its ban of asbestos paper products will save 0.60 lives at a cost of $4–5 million ($7–8 million per life saved). * * *

While we do not sit as a regulatory agency that must make the difficult decision as to what an appropriate expenditure is to prevent someone from incurring the risk of an asbestos-related death, we do note that the EPA, in its zeal to ban any and all asbestos products, basically ignored the cost side of the TSCA equation. The EPA would have this court believe that Congress, when it enacted its requirement that the EPA consider the economic impacts of its regulations, thought that spending $200–300 million to save approximately seven lives (approximately $30–40 million per life) over 13 years is reasonable.

* * *

Conclusion

In summary, of most concern to us is that the EPA has failed to implement the dictates of TSCA and the prior decisions of this and other courts that, before it impose a ban on a product, it first evaluate and then reject the less burdensome alternatives laid out for it by Congress. While the EPA spent much time and care crafting its asbestos regulation, its explicit failure to consider the alternatives required of it by Congress deprived its final rule of the reasonable basis it needed to survive judicial scrutiny.

NOTES AND QUESTIONS

1. *"Least burdensome" regulation.* There is little question that asbestos poses very serious health hazards. Both the EPA and the International Agency for Research on Cancer classify it as a known human carcinogen. Assume TSCA had a different statutory standard for restricting chemicals. How would new production and use of asbestos fare under a health-based standard, such as the Clean Air Act's command to set air quality standards at a level "requisite to protect the public health" with an "adequate margin of safety"? How would new production and use of asbestos fare under the FQPA's standard to regulate down to where there is "reasonable certainty that no harm will result"? Under the "unreasonable risk" standard of TSCA, regulation of this concededly dangerous material came to grief. Why?

The court states that the principal reason was EPA's failure to make a convincing case that the manner of regulation chosen was the "least burdensome." TSCA § 6(a). This standard requires EPA to choose from an array of regulatory alternatives, ranging from a complete ban (most burdensome) to no regulation at all (no burden).[45] Did the Fifth Circuit decide that, to satisfy the "least burdensome" regulation requirement, EPA had to consider the entire range of regulatory options and to calculate the costs and benefits of regulation for each option? Is there a less burdensome way of interpreting "least burdensome"?

2. *Unquantified benefits.* Clearly the main benefit of the asbestos ban is that it will save lives. In a quantitative cost-benefit analysis, this raises three problems. First, the analysis must attempt to place some value, usually economic, on a human life. Assessing the dollar value of a human life is difficult, as we discussed in Chapter 1, though the Fifth Circuit obviously had some views on the subject. Second, even if a value can be assigned to human life, that value will vary over the lifetime of any individual—the remaining life of an infant is presumably worth more than that of a centenarian. A cost-benefit analysis must determine at what age the value of a life is to be calculated. Third, the number of lives saved will increase the longer the regulation is in effect. If one is comparing costs to benefits, during what period of time are the benefits (in lives saved) to be counted? EPA included the number of lives saved over 13 years, and then counted all additional lives saved past that time as "unquantified benefits." The court thought that this was inappropriate, because it permitted the benefits side of the balance to weigh too heavily. In light of the many difficulties accompanying a measurement of benefits counted as human lives saved, was EPA justified in giving great weight to the notion of future unquantified benefits? Or is the court correct in its belief that such benefits should be used only "to tip the balance in close cases"?

3. *Substitutes.* Notice the extensive discussion in *Corrosion Proof Fittings* about substitutes for asbestos. The court explained that EPA "bears a tough burden indeed" when it wants to ban a substance for which no viable substitutes are available. Section 6 of TSCA requires EPA to consider "the benefits of such substance or mixture for various uses and the availability of substitutes for such uses." TSCA § 6(c)(1)(C). According to the Fifth circuit, EPA must not only identify whether a substitute chemical or substitute technology exists, but if it does, EPA must also assess whether new risks may flow from the increased use of substitute products. When substitutes are not readily available, the court explained, EPA must present a stronger case to justify a ban, because the cost of such a ban is high. Is it possible, though, that banning a substance without known substitutes may spur technological progress toward the development of a safer substitute?

Must EPA perform a cost-benefit analysis for a range of potential substitutes that is as extensive as the cost-benefit analysis for the about-to-be-banned substance? What does the Fifth Circuit say about this?

Many environmentalists believe that alternatives analysis (a comparison of one substance with others that might perform the same function)

---

45. A similar requirement is imposed on the Consumer Product Safety Commission, 15 U.S.C. § 2058(f)(3), and CPSC has similarly struggled with judicial review. *See, e.g.,* Gulf S. Insulation v. CPSC, 701 F.2d 1137 (5th Cir. 1983); *see generally* Richard A. Merrill, *CPSC Regulation of Cancer Risks in Consumer Products: 1972–1981,* 67 Va. L. Rev. 1261 (1981).

should be at the heart of the U.S. regulatory process and should be a foundation of precautionary environmental regulation. But who should bear the burden of proof on the availability of substitutes for a product? Should the government prove that safer substitutes exist, or should asbestos manufacturers be required to identify, or possibly develop, safer substitutes? Section 6(c)(1)(C) is the only mention of substitute chemicals in the entire statute. "In this regulatory context, the requirement that the government identify whether safer substitute chemicals exist serves as one more hurdle for regulators considering chemical restrictions. TSCA does not promote a broader, ongoing search for safer alternatives as a routine part of U.S. chemical policy." Sachs, *Jumping the Pond, supra,* at 42.

4. *Saving future lives, at what price?* When the court discusses the meaning of TSCA's "unreasonable risk" requirement, does it use a risk-benefit or cost-benefit analysis? In EPA's justification for the asbestos ban, EPA calculated that the ban would result in the avoidance of 202 quantifiable cancer cases, or 148 cases if benefits are discounted at three percent. We discussed discount rates, which are used so that estimates of future costs and benefits are figured at their present value, at the end of Chapter 1; the higher the discount rate, the smaller the significance of costs and benefits that accrue in the future. Using EPA's numbers, the ban would cost between $2 and $3 million per death avoided. The court, on the other hand, assumes that EPA's figures would result in an expense as high as $74 million per death avoided. Why is there such a large difference in these two numbers?

5. Why did EPA's asbestos rule meet with skeptical disapproval in *Corrosion Proof Fittings*? Perhaps EPA simply failed to follow TSCA's statutory commands and deserved to have its asbestos rule struck down. Another reason might be the court—the Fifth Circuit has a history of rejecting environmental regulations, and it is based in New Orleans, near the heart of the American chemical industry. The date might also matter—all courts have become more exacting in their review of environmental regulations since the mid–1980s, as described in Chapter 3. Which explanation makes the most sense to you?

In any event, *Corrosion Proof Fittings* remains the first—and only—major judicial interpretation of Sections 6(a) and 6(c) of TSCA. EPA never again attempted to restrict any existing chemical under Section 6.[46] What happened after *Corrosion Proof Fittings*? Did EPA give up the fight? Couldn't it have simply redone its analysis of costs and benefits of asbestos to comply with the Fifth Circuit's commands? Almost all observers agree that regulation of toxic chemicals under Section 6 has been crippled since 1991, but is this the fault of EPA, the Fifth Circuit, or Congress (given the complex procedures that Congress inserted in the statute itself)?

Consider some reactions to *Corrosion Proof Fittings*, first from the lawyers who represented industry in the litigation, then from a law professor who is critical of the decision.

46. As we discuss at the end of this chapter, EPA announced in 2010 that it is considering promulgating some Section 6 restrictions for a few chemicals. As this book went to press, no new Section 6 rules had been issued.

While nominally anchored in TSCA's "substantial evidence" test, the Fifth Circuit's approach effectively turned on whether specific choices made by EPA would accomplish more good than harm.

* * *

[The] shortcomings in EPA's decision were compounded by the Agency's failure to weigh the health and safety risks posed by substitute products. While acknowledging that EPA does not have "an affirmative duty to seek out and test every workplace substitute," the court nonetheless held that such a duty does arise "once interested parties introduce credible studies and evidence" of the risks from probable substitute products. The likelihood that EPA's regulation might do more harm than good was an important basis for overturning EPA's friction product and A/C pipe product bans.
* * *

Just as important as what the court did do is what it did not do. The court overturned EPA's ban because many elements of the Agency's action might do more harm than good. In so doing, however, the court expressly eschewed the usual hard look review of the Agency's technical or scientific findings or of the Agency's reasoning process on these issues. For example, the court rejected technical challenges to EPA's cost and benefit calculations and to its decision to treat all types of asbestos the same, stating that "[d]ecisions such as these are better left to the agency's expertise." In declining to scrutinize EPA's reasoning on such technical issues, the court summarized its reviewing role as follows: "On these, and many similar points, the petitioners merely seek to have us reevaluate the EPA's initial evaluation of the evidence. * * * Decisions such as the EPA's decision to treat various types of asbestos as presenting similar health risks properly are better left for agency determination. * * * *" In short, instead of focusing on the agency's decisionmaking process, the Fifth Circuit looked directly at the "Medusa" of EPA's decision, not its reflection, in order to determine whether the Agency had acted reasonably.

* * * The court thus refused to accept lopsided relationships between costs and benefits that a "reasonable mind" would consider unacceptable. It would not sanction product bans when "less burdensome" alternatives appeared more cost-effective. The court also required EPA to target acceptable risk levels above zero and to confront the risk-risk tradeoffs of its actions. Each of these holdings suggests a rule that follows logically from the core principle that agencies act reasonably or rationally only if their actions overall, and at the margin, do more good than harm.

Edward W. Warren & Gary E. Marchant, *"More Good than Harm": A First Principle for Environmental Agencies and Reviewing Courts*, 20 ECOLOGY L.Q. 379, 415–18 (1993).

Professor Tom McGarity, in contrast, has argued that the Fifth Circuit overstepped the proper bounds of the judicial role:

> Just as the courts do not explore in detail the ins and outs of every alternative theory when they resolve a question of law, EPA did not feel that it had to go to such extraordinary analytical lengths to justify banning a substance for which human health risks were extremely well-documented. The court, however, set aside the rule because of the agency's failure to "calculate the costs and benefits" of each of the possible intermediate levels of regulation. Otherwise, the court feared that it could not "know that none of these alternatives was less burdensome than the ban in fact chosen by the agency."

The *Corrosion Proof Fittings* opinion lays out the conclusions of three intelligent lawyers who had been exposed to a complex statute in a complicated rulemaking context for a very limited period of time. The three judges on the panel had no experience with the difficulties encountered in administering a technically complex regulatory program, and they lacked any expertise in the scientific and other analytical methodologies necessary to perform the function that Congress had delegated to EPA. The judges, in short, lacked the breadth and depth of experience and expertise necessary to support such confident assertions about how the agency should go about its assigned business. And they almost certainly got it wrong.

The opinion writer, however, did not stop with his highly questionable analysis of the agency's statute. Noting a dispute over how EPA had compared future costs with future benefits, the court gratuitously offered its wisdom on how the job should be done. Despite very substantial arguments in the relevant economic, legal, and ethical literature that future health benefits should not be discounted to present value, the court made short work of the issue with the extraordinarily simplistic observation that failing to discount benefits would make comparisons difficult. To ease the misguided agency's misgivings, the court offered a single article from *The Economist* "explaining [the] use of discount rates for non-monetary goods." The court followed this arrogant bolt-from-the-blue with an embarrassingly ill-informed critique of EPA's reliance upon the onset of exposure as the time to begin discounting, rather than the time of injury. The court was either unaware of or simply ignored the fact that the time of exposure might be estimated with some degree of accuracy with the aid of employment records and such, whereas the time of injury would have been impossible to predict, given the uncertainties in assessing carcinogenic risks and the long latency period of some carcinogens.

Without any apparent awareness of (or serious interest in) the enormous uncertainties encountered in assessing the risks posed by the agency's adoption of one or more of seven alternative approaches to regulating asbestos, the court sent EPA on a potentially endless analytical crusade in search of the holy grail of the least burdensome alternative that still protected adequately against unreasonable risk. Deferring not one whit to EPA's interpretation of its statute or to its exercise of rulemaking expertise, the court wrote its view of the "proper course for the EPA to follow" into the law governing standard setting under Section 6 of TSCA. The agency could, of course, avoid the analytical nightmare either by adopting options that were sufficiently inoffensive to the regulated industry to avoid legal challenge or by giving up the quest altogether. The agency has apparently adopted the latter option. * * *

In the broader scheme of things, the problem illustrated by the *Corrosion Proof Fittings* opinion is not so much one of judicial incompetence as it is one of judicial overreaching. Many judges would like to see the government play a less intrusive role in private markets, and they have the flexibility under the hard look doctrine to affect regulatory programs radically without being held accountable for the consequences of their actions. Congress can always change the statute to overturn the court, but * * * it is very difficult to get protective legislation enacted. To advocate hard look review in the context of the courts' prescriptive substantive review function is really to advocate greater discretion on the part of judges to substitute their views of appropriate statutory policies and analytical methodologies for those of the agency. In the hands of unsympathetic judges like the author of the *Corrosion Proof Fittings* opinion, this is a license to destroy regulatory programs.

Thomas O. McGarity, *The Courts and the Ossification of Rulemaking: A Response to Professor Seidenfeld*, 75 TEX. L. REV. 525, 547–49 (1997).

Whose characterization of the case do you find most persuasive?

6. *Alternatives to "unreasonable risk."* What alternative statutory standards would you support if you think that "unreasonable risk" is too vague a standard or is too difficult for the agency to prove in practice? Is there a way that TSCA could be revised that would allow EPA to address a chemical's risk without considering countervailing benefits of the chemical? Would this be good policy?

7. *California's Proposition 65 reconsidered.* Now that you've learned about TSCA, take one more look at California's Proposition 65, discussed in the last chapter. Recall that businesses could avoid the warning requirement of Proposition 65 if they showed that the level of actual exposure is below a statutorily based threshold of risk. This shifts the burden of proof to private firms to show *lack* of risk for chemicals known to the state to cause cancer or reproductive toxicity. One of our authors has advocated such a burden shift in TSCA. Shifting the burden of proof, he claims, will mean that chemical manufacturers "will have a keen interest in developing the risk assessment data that will facilitate expeditious approval by government regulators." Noah M. Sachs, *Rescuing the Strong Precautionary Principle*

from its Critics: The Case of Chemical Regulation, 2011 U. of Ill. L. Rev. ____. He also argues that a burden shift would "flip the perverse incentives that occur under a regulatory regime with a governmental burden of proof, in which regulated firms stand to gain by not developing, or by obfuscating, important risk assessment data." *Id.*

Would you support a change to TSCA that shifts the burden of proof on safety to chemical manufacturers, perhaps through a requirement that they show a lack of substantial risk under normal conditions of exposure? If so, how should a burden shift be implemented for chemicals already on the market?

8.   *PCB ban.* Section 6 is also notable for singling out polychlorinated biphenyls (PCBs) for special attention. PCBs had been manufactured and used commercially throughout the 20th century. Because of their stability and their fire and electrical resistance, they were widely used in electrical transformers and capacitors. Epidemiological data and experiments on laboratory animals revealed that exposure to PCBs poses serious carcinogenic risks to humans. PCBs were also found to affect wildlife. Concentrations as low as one part per billion seemed to impair the reproductive capacity of aquatic invertebrates and fish. Since PCBs were often discharged to waterways where they bioaccumulated in fish, animals and humans who eat those fish run a risk of ingesting relatively high concentrations of PCBs. By the time TSCA was enacted in 1976, Congress had been made aware of the dangers associated with PCBs. Section 6(e) therefore specifically addresses the control of PCBs. Although manufacture of PCBs in the United States has ended, they are still a major contaminant in hazardous waste clean-ups and still represent a health risk to humans because of their accumulation in the food chain.

5.   International Developments in Chemical Regulation

The chemical industry is highly globalized. It is dominated by about a dozen multinational firms, and the industry's revenues comprise about 4% of the total economic output of the globe. Chemicals themselves are prone to unintended transport across borders: through rivers, oceans, wildlife, and atmospheric deposition.[47] Given these realities, regulation of chemicals has become an international enterprise.

In 1998, the Rotterdam Convention, discussed *supra* in the section on pesticide regulation, established a prior informed consent regime for imports of many hazardous chemicals and pesticides. In 2001, the international community also adopted the Stockholm Convention on Persistent Organic Pollutants,[48] which bans or heavily restricts 12 chemicals, known as the "Dirty Dozen," including DDT, PCBs, dieldrin, and helptachlor. The

---

47.   The Inuit people of the Canadian arctic and Greenland have some of the highest detected PCB levels in body tissue in the world, despite living thousands of miles from sources of PCBs. PCBs bioaccumulate—concentrate in the foodchain—and the Inuit are exposed through a diet that is heavily reliant on seals and other marine mammals that eat at the top of the ocean food chain. *See* Marla Cone, Silent Snow: The Slow Poisoning of the Arctic 35–52 (2005).

48.   40 I.L.M. 532 (2001).

POPs treaty, as it has come to be known, is the first international effort to ban or restrict toxic chemicals, as opposed to just regulating their trade. The chemicals governed by the treaty "possess toxic properties, resist degradation, bioaccumulate, and are transported, through air, water, and migratory species, across international boundaries and deposited far from their place of release, where they accumulate in terrestrial and aquatic ecosystems."[49] For DDT, the treaty contains provisions allowing countries to opt-out of the global ban in order to use that pesticide for malaria control. The treaty also establishes a scientific review process for adding chemicals to the original list of 12. As of 2010, the Stockholm Convention had 172 parties, and although the United States has signed the treaty, it has not ratified it, in part because of opposition of some Senators to the treaty's process for adding new chemicals. (The original 12 are already banned or highly restricted in the United States, but the process of adding new chemicals raised questions about whether international bodies would limit U.S. sovereignty).

Another important international development in chemical regulation is the Globally Harmonized System (GHS) for Chemical Labeling— nonbinding guidelines developed under the auspices of the UN Environment Program (the third edition GHS guidelines were released in July 2009). The GHS aims to reduce inconsistencies in chemical labeling across national borders, without altering substantive risk management legislation in individual countries. It establishes a unified hazard classification, labeling, and risk communication system. Chemicals will have a uniform Material Safety Data Sheet, with internationally recognized chemical names and hazard data and pictograms representing those hazards. Some products that do not currently carry warnings will require labeling under the GHS, and EPA, which has indicated its intent to implement the GHS, is currently considering how the GHS will affect existing and future pesticide and chemical labels.

Perhaps the most far-reaching international development in chemical regulation is the European Union's enactment in 2006 of a regulation called Registration, Evaluation, and Authorization of Chemicals (REACH).[50] This 800–page statute is probably the most complex law ever enacted in the EU, and it applies in 27 European countries. It replaced over 40 prior directives and regulations that had established a chemical regulatory regime in Europe that was similar to TSCA. For example, under prior law, testing and review requirements were much more stringent for "new" chemicals (those introduced after 1981 in Europe), compared to existing chemicals.

In REACH, the EU eliminated this distinction between new and existing chemicals and made toxicity research and disclosure a precondition for all chemicals to access the European market (the so-called "No Data, No Market" principle). For the most hazardous classes of chemicals, REACH also shifts the burden of proof to industry to demonstrate why the chemicals

---

49. *Id.* (Preamble).

50. The official text of REACH is available in the EU's Official Journal, O.J. L 396/1 (December 30, 2006). A more user-friendly guide to the regulation is available at the European Commission's website: http://ec.europa.eu/environment/chemicals/reach/reach_intro.htm.

should not be banned from the European market. This shift in the burden of proof has been lauded by environmentalists. Industry groups have criticized REACH for imposing extensive research, disclosure, and reporting burdens and for a lack of risk prioritization.

REACH has four major components. In the *registration* stage, producers and importers of chemicals in volumes greater than one ton per year must submit to the European Chemicals Agency a registration dossier listing physical and chemical properties. Additionally, toxicity tests and an exposure assessment must be submitted for chemicals produced or imported in volumes greater than 10 tons per year.[51] In the *evaluation* stage, the European Chemicals Agency assesses dossiers for compliance with REACH and conducts substance evaluations to confirm whether chemicals are substances of "very high concern." Chemicals designated as substances of "very high concern"—due to carcinogenic, mutagenic, or toxic properties, or persistent or bioaccumulative characteristics—are subject to further regulation and public notification.

In the *authorization* process, producers and importers of "very high concern" chemicals must submit additional data on risks, exposures, and potential substitute chemicals. The default presumption in the authorization process is that "very high concern" chemicals must be withdrawn from the market, but authorization for continued use can be granted to applicants who demonstrate either that the chemical's risks can be "adequately controlled," or that no suitable alternative exists and the benefits outweigh the risks. Finally, the *restrictions* process of REACH reconfirms the pre-existing authority of the European Commission to restrict substances posing an unacceptable risk of harm to human health or the environment.

REACH has been called the "anti-TSCA."[52] Can you see why? What are some of the major differences you see between REACH and TSCA? What are the advantages and disadvantages of the European approach to chemical regulation?

REACH is the most extensive effort to date to compile information on chemical risks and overcome what the European Commission calls the "burden of the past" (the lack of data on "existing" chemicals). Most of the toxicity data that will be submitted under REACH will be publicly available on the internet. The actual toxicity testing and the initial risk assessments will be conducted by chemical manufacturers (which many environmentalists have criticized as a flaw in the regulation), and implementing chemical regulation on this scale also requires enormous bureaucratic resources. For example, the European Chemicals Agency is a new entity that had to be staffed with over 200 toxicologists and other scientists to review the data submissions.

What is the impact of REACH on the United States? Consider the following excerpt:

51.   About 146,000 substances were pre-registered by REACH's December 1, 2008, deadline. Preregistration allows substances to continue to be marketed in Europe while the full registration package is prepared.

52.   John S. Applegate, *Synthesizing TSCA and REACH: Practical Principles for Chemical Regulation Reform*, 35 ECOLOGY L.Q. 721, 743 (2008).

Jumping the Pond: Transnational Law and the Future of Chemical Regulation

Noah M. Sachs
62 VAND. L. REV. 1817, 1864–67 (2009)

Under the extraterritorial influence of REACH, the U.S. chemical marketplace may increasingly be governed by European legal norms.

Information disclosure in Europe is the key driver of these effects in the United States. By putting critical toxicity data in the hands of consumers, activists, attorneys, and state regulators in the United States, REACH will likely improve public health and environmental protection and spark substitution of hazardous chemicals, even without legislative changes to TSCA.

REACH will cause regulatory turbulence through four major types of informational spillover effects in the United States. First, U.S. chemical companies may incorporate EU toxicity testing and information disclosure norms into their own internal practices. For example, Dow Chemical announced in early 2008 that it will prepare REACH-qualifying dossiers on all its products, regardless of whether those products are actually being sold in Europe. If other major chemical manufacturers follow, we could see a "regulatory revolution by surprise" in which the EU's own internal legislation quickly becomes the global standard followed by multinational chemical firms.

Second, REACH toxicity data will increasingly shape the chemical purchasing decisions of U.S. manufacturers, retailers, and consumers. * * * REACH may provide a spark for innovations in U.S. product safety that would be impossible to achieve without plentiful background information on chemical risks. U.S. manufacturers that purchase chemicals in bulk will now have the capability to track REACH disclosures in Europe, which may affect the chemical products they buy and the suppliers they choose. U.S. manufacturers may begin to require REACH compliance (or equivalent disclosures of toxicity data) as a condition of their purchases from chemical suppliers in the United States.* * *

The implementation of REACH will also affect U.S. retailers and their customers. Hundreds of chemicals that will likely be subject to authorization under REACH (because of their carcinogenicity, adverse reproductive effects, or potential to bioaccumulate) are widely marketed in the United States. In response to EU decisions naming such substances as "very high concern" chemicals, U.S. retailers may voluntarily withdraw those same substances from the U.S. market, or the chemicals may lose market share—a process that industry insiders call chemical "deselection." * * * As Ernie Rosenberg, President of the U.S. Soap and Detergent Association, has explained, "When you regulate a chemical product, it has a global impact in the global information environment that we live in. An adverse finding about a chemical anywhere creates problems for that chemical everywhere."

A third informational spillover effect from REACH is that U.S. federal regulators can use the toxicity data from Europe in existing regulatory regimes, including TSCA and other environmental laws. There is clearly sufficient overlap between the chemical regulatory regimes in the United States and the EU such that toxicity data disclosed under REACH could, in many cases, have direct legal relevance under TSCA. EPA could rely on data disclosed under REACH, for instance, to support further testing requirements under Section 4 of TSCA. Under Section 11(c) of TSCA, EPA would have the authority to subpoena documents prepared by U.S. firms in the process of complying with REACH. And Section 8(e) of TSCA imposes a mandatory reporting duty when a firm obtains "information which reasonably supports the conclusion" that a chemical "presents a substantial risk of injury to health or the environment." * * *

Finally, information disclosure under REACH is likely to have significant impacts on subnational environmental regulation in the United States. As states consider bans or restrictions on certain classes of chemicals, the toxicity data from Europe—as well as EU decisions on which chemicals are of "very high concern"—is likely to be influential. Additionally, chemical toxicity data disclosed under REACH could be used by plaintiffs' attorneys in the United States as the basis for tort suits over occupational or other chemical exposures. These suits have traditionally been very difficult to bring because of problems in proving causation, long latency periods, and a lack of basic toxicity data on commonly used chemicals. The REACH data that will be generated in Europe over the next decade represents a wealth of information on chemical toxicity that has long been absent from American courtrooms.

---

6. TOWARD TSCA REFORM?

In 2009 and 2010, major changes were taking place in American chemical regulation, both through administrative action at EPA, and, on the horizon, through a possible legislative overhaul of TSCA.

Within the EPA, the largest change has been more aggressive use of the existing statute to respond to chemical risks. The EPA approach involves developing chemical "action plans" targeting chemicals of concern, requiring submission of information needed to understand chemical risks, and increasing public access to chemical information.

The agency has announced action plans to target Bisphenol–A (BPA, used in plastics and food packaging); long-chain perfluorinated chemicals (PFCs, used in non-stick cookware, aerospace applications, and building materials); penta, octa, and decabromodiphenyl ethers (PBDEs, used widely in flame retardants); phthalates (used to soften plastics); and short-chain chlorinated paraffins (used in the metal and plastics industry). The action plans outline risks presented by each chemical and set forth steps EPA plans to take in response to those risks. For example, the action plan for BPA includes potential rulemaking under the little-used TSCA § 5(b)(4) to list BPA as a substance that presents or may present an unreasonable risk to the environment based on its effects on aquatic species. EPA may also issue a test rule for BPA under § 4(a). The PFCs action plan includes assessing the chemicals for a potential rulemaking under TSCA § 6 that could ban or restrict the manufacture, import, processing, and use of PFCs. It remains to be seen whether EPA will follow up on these action plans with actual rulemakings.

EPA is gathering new information on chemical risks by taking a number of additional actions under TSCA Sections 4, 5, and 8, including further reporting and testing of nanoscale substances under TSCA § 8(a) and § 4, as discussed *supra*. In May 2010, EPA Administrator Lisa Jackson also announced that the agency would deny almost all requests to keep the identity of chemicals secret from the public when companies file health and safety studies under TSCA.[53] Moreover, for the first time, the entire TSCA Inventory has been put online.

EPA Administrator Jackson also announced a set of principles that should guide Congress as it considers changes to TSCA.

Remarks to the Commonwealth Club of San Francisco

Lisa P. Jackson, Administrator, U.S. EPA
September 29, 2009

Today, advances in toxicology and analytical chemistry are revealing new pathways of exposure. There are subtle and troubling effects of chemicals on hormone systems, human reproduction, intellectual development and cognition. Every few weeks, we read about new potential threats: Bisphenol A, or BPA—a chemical that can affect brain development and has been linked to obesity and cancer—is in baby bottles; phthalate esters—which have been said to affect reproductive development—are in our medical devices; we see lead in toys; dioxins in fish; and the list goes on. Many states—including California—have stepped in to address these threats because they see inaction at the national level. * * *

Today I'm announcing clear Administration principles to guide Congress in writing a new chemical risk management law that will fix the weaknesses in TSCA. Let me highlight some principles that are of overriding importance:

First, we need to review all chemicals against safety standards that are based solely on considerations of risk—not economics or other factors—and we must set these standards at levels that are protective of human health and the environment.

---

53. Abuse of TSCA's confidentiality provisions has been a recurring problem under the statute. For example, an investigation by the Environmental Working Group found that in the first eight months of 2009, industry kept the identity of chemicals secret from the public in more than half of the health studies submitted to EPA under § 8(e). DAVID ANDREWS, ENVIRONMENTAL WORKING GROUP, OFF THE BOOKS: INDUSTRY'S SECRET CHEMICALS (2009). About 95% of PMNs contain some information that industry claims is confidential, and those claims have rarely been challenged by the agency. *Id.*

Second, safety standards cannot be applied without adequate information, and responsibility for providing that information should rest on industry. Manufacturers must develop and submit the hazard, use, and exposure data demonstrating that new and existing chemicals are safe. If industry doesn't provide the information, EPA should have the tools to quickly and efficiently require testing, without the delays and procedural obstacles currently in place.

Third, both EPA and industry must include special consideration for exposures and effects on groups with higher vulnerabilities—particularly children. Children ingest chemicals at a higher ratio to their body weight than adults, and are more susceptible to long-term damage and developmental problems. Our new principles offer them much stronger protections.

Fourth, when chemicals fall short of the safety standard, EPA must have clear authority to take action. We need flexibility to consider a range of factors—but must also have the ability to move quickly. In all cases, EPA and chemical producers must act on priority chemicals in a timely manner, with firm deadlines to maintain accountability. * * *

Fifth, we must encourage innovation in green chemistry, and support research, education, recognition, and other strategies that will lead us down the road to safer and more sustainable chemicals and processes. All of this must happen with the utmost transparency and concern for the public's right to know.

Finally, we need to make sure that EPA's safety assessments are properly resourced, with industry contributing its fair share of the costs of implementing new requirements.

I take great comfort that the call for change in our chemical management laws is rising from all quarters. A broad coalition of environmental advocates, unions, medical professionals and public health groups—including grass-roots organizations from across the country—has come together to make the case for stronger chemicals regulation.

Industry too, has called for action. Chemical producers are worried not only about facing an inconsistent patchwork of state laws, but believe that their industry can thrive only if the public is confident that their products meet rigorous safety standards. And they want the US to lead the world in chemical risk management, not fall further behind.

Many states—who have been on the leading edge of addressing chemical risks—have also echoed the call for reform. It's not often that the chemical industry, states, and the environmental community agree that the current system is not workable, and have similar visions of how the new system should be shaped. There are certainly differences of opinion and important details to be worked out. But the common ground that exists makes me optimistic that Congress can put a new law in place that has broad support from all the stakeholders.

On April 15, 2010, Senator Frank Lautenberg (D–N.J.) introduced the Safe Chemicals Act of 2010 to overhaul TSCA, largely mirroring the principles outlined above.[54] Companion legislation was introduced in the House of Representatives.[55] The Act would require a minimum toxicity data set for all chemicals and would shift the burden to manufacturers to show, for each chemical, a "reasonable certainty of no harm," defined as a "negligible risk of any adverse effect on the general population or a vulnerable population." The Act borrows this safety standard from the 1996 FQPA. EPA is mandated to compile a "priority list" of at least 300 chemicals for which these safety determinations would be made first, and EPA's ultimate decision about whether the manufacturer has met its burden of proof is not subject to judicial review. EPA's ability to obtain information is broadened considerably. Compare TSCA § 4 to one of the provisions of the Safe Chemicals Act, which states that the EPA Administrator "may, by rule or order, require testing with respect to any chemical substance or mixture … as necessary for making any determination or carrying out any provision of this chapter."[56] While the fate of this legislation remains uncertain, it represents the most advanced effort to date to rethink the basic structure of TSCA.

Consider the Safe Chemicals Act and the principles announced by Administrator Jackson. What changes do you see in the way that officials in the executive and legislative branches are approaching chemical risk assessment and risk management? Are we seeing a shift away from cost-benefit analysis in chemical regulation? Is this wise policy? Are we seeing a shift away from regulation based on a chemical's risks to human health toward regulation based on the intrinsic hazards or properties of chemicals? Note Administrator Jackson's call for "innovation in green chemistry," which involves chemical manufacturers, chemical purchasers, and government scientists searching for safer alternatives to hazardous chemicals. How can law and regulation contribute to that effort?

---

54. Safe Chemicals Act of 2010, S. 3209 (111th Congress).

55. Toxic Chemical Safety Act of 2010, H.R. 5820 (111th Congress).

56. Safe Chemicals Act, § 5.

CHAPTER 5

RESOURCE CONSERVATION AND RECOVERY ACT

A. Introduction

    1. The Background of RCRA

    2. The Structure of RCRA

        a. Subtitle C

        b. Subtitle D

        c. Imminent and Substantial Endangerment Provisions

        d. Recycled Used Oil

        e. Underground Storage Tanks

    3. RCRA and State Hazardous Waste Programs

    4. Researching RCRA

B. Definition of Hazardous Waste

    1. The Dual Definitions: The Relationship Between the Statutory and Regulatory Definitions

        Connecticut Coastal Fishermen's Assn. v. Remington Arms Co., Inc.

    2. The Subtitle C Regulatory Definition of Solid Waste

        a. "Discarded" Materials

            American Mining Congress v. EPA

        b. Recycled Materials

            i. The Matrix

            ii. EPA's Authority to Regulate Recycled Materials Under Subtitle C

                Safe Food and Fertilizer v. EPA

    3. The Subtitle C Regulatory Definition of Hazardous Waste

        a. Listed Wastes

A. INTRODUCTION

We are exposed to hazardous substances in a wide variety of contexts: from food additives, chemical products, pesticides, and even the air we breathe and the water we drink. The Resource Conservation and Recovery Act ("RCRA") was adopted to address the specific threats to public health and the environment from the improper disposal of hazardous by-products of our industrial economy. Unlike other statutes that address problems from hazardous substances and products, RCRA is largely concerned with the management and disposal of "hazardous wastes."

The quantities of hazardous waste generated in the United States are enormous. Estimates of the total amount of hazardous waste vary widely, but, in 2007, EPA reported that over 46.5 million tons of hazardous waste were generated by facilities regulated under RCRA. This does not include hazardous wastes that are not covered by the RCRA hazardous waste program including hazardous waste generated by very small quantity generators and hazardous wastes that do not fall within the RCRA regulatory definition. Almost 60 percent of the total hazardous waste generated in 2007 originated in two states, Louisiana and Texas. *See* 2009 National Biennial RCRA Hazardous Waste Report (based on 2007 Data), Exh. 1–2.

Exhibit 1.2 Rank Ordering of States Based on Quantity of RCRA Hazardous Waste Generated and Number of Hazardous Waste Generators, 2007

State	Hazardous Waste Quantity			Number of Generators			Reported Status	
	Rank	Tons Generated	Percentage	Rank	Number	Percentage	LQG	Non-LQG
LOUISIANA	1	15,892,992	34.0	16	336	2.1	324	12
TEXAS	2	13,272,307	28.4	4	918	5.6	918	0
MICHIGAN	3	2,397,357	5.1	7	682	4.2	536	146
MISSISSIPPI	4	2,239,718	4.8	31	133	0.8	133	0
OHIO	5	1,608,186	3.4	3	942	5.8	784	158
NEW YORK	6	1,267,648	2.7	2	1,181	7.2	896	285
ILLINOIS	7	1,122,937	2.4	6	809	4.9	697	112
TENNESSEE	8	1,079,070	2.3	14	358	2.2	358	0
INDIANA	9	958,019	2.1	9	522	3.2	427	95
NEW MEXICO	10	944,581	2.0	45	43	0.3	37	6
CALIFORNIA	11	809,654	1.3	1	2,312	14.1	2,115	197
NEW JERSEY	12	596,130	1.3	8	573	4.1	644	29
NORTH DAKOTA	13	538,611	1.2	50	13	0.1	13	0
ARKANSAS	14	495,752	1.1	34	117	0.7	106	11
ALABAMA	15	416,916	0.9	24	219	1.3	219	0
PENNSYLVANIA	16	388,782	0.8	5	821	5.0	742	79
WISCONSIN	17	310,293	0.7	10	453	2.8	453	0
KANSAS	18	292,682	0.6	25	203	1.2	162	41
MASSACHUSETTS	19	248,330	0.5	11	449	2.7	425	24
MISSOURI	20	228,109	0.5	18	283	1.7	257	26
FLORIDA	21	152,687	0.3	17	319	2.0	292	27
SOUTH CAROLINA	22	151,431	0.3	19	276	1.7	251	25
WASHINGTON	23	147,246	0.3	13	408	2.5	407	1
KENTUCKY	24	139,878	0.3	21	269	1.6	262	7
OKLAHOMA	25	134,426	0.3	29	164	1.0	0	164
GEORGIA	26	102,636	0.2	16	326	2.0	291	35
MINNESOTA	27	101,690	0.2	23	249	1.5	247	2
NORTH CAROLINA	28	96,009	0.2	12	433	2.6	403	30
VIRGINIA	29	94,833	0.2	19	276	1.7	254	22
UTAH	30	82,829	0.2	37	90	0.6	90	0
WEST VIRGINIA	31	76,577	0.2	32	131	0.8	90	41
OREGON	32	74,965	0.2	26	183	1.1	183	0
PUERTO RICO	33	60,041	0.1	36	104	0.6	95	9
ARIZONA	34	56,708	0.1	27	175	1.1	175	0
COLORADO	35	54,521	0.1	33	120	0.7	104	16
IOWA	36	49,013	0.1	30	159	1.0	134	25
MARYLAND	37	43,506	0.1	34	117	0.7	117	0
NEBRASKA	38	38,720	0.1	39	80	0.5	54	26
CONNECTICUT	39	32,481	0.1	22	268	1.6	259	9
MONTANA	40	29,590	0.1	46	40	0.2	40	0
DELAWARE	41	19,743	0.0	42	55	0.3	45	10
NEVADA	42	10,041	0.0	40	73	0.4	73	0
IDAHO	43	5,638	0.0	44	44	0.3	23	21
NEW HAMPSHIRE	44	5,432	0.0	28	165	1.0	105	60
MAINE	45	5,305	0.0	41	65	0.4	64	1
RHODE ISLAND	46	4,531	0.0	38	88	0.5	70	18
WYOMING	47	4,011	0.0	49	23	0.1	17	6
VIRGIN ISLANDS	48	3,154	0.0	54	1	0.0	1	0
VERMONT	49	2,951	0.0	47	33	0.2	32	1
ALASKA	50	2,532	0.0	43	45	0.3	34	11
HAWAII	51	1,224	0.0	48	29	0.2	27	2
DISTRICT OF COLUMBIA	52	766	0.0	50	22	0.1	19	3
SOUTH DAKOTA	53	750	0.0	52	19	0.1	19	0
GUAM	54	135	0.0	51	21	0.1	14	7
NAVAJO NATION	55	35	0.0	54	1	0.0	1	0
TRUST TERRITORIES	56	1	0.0	54	1	0.0	1	0
Total		46,693,284	100.0		16,349	100.0	14,549	1,800

Note: Columns may not sum due to rounding.

1. THE BACKGROUND OF RCRA

Congress first began to address the problem of disposal of solid waste in 1965. The Solid Waste Disposal Act of 1965 provided limited federal funding to encourage state efforts to manage solid wastes, and a series of other federal statutes that followed provided for additional study, but limited federal regulation, of solid or hazardous waste. In 1976, however, Congress passed the Resource Conservation and Recovery Act (as an amendment to the original Solid Waste Disposal Act) that established a comprehensive "cradle to grave" federal regulatory program targeted at hazardous waste. Congress had a few years before responded to growing environmental concerns by passing The Clean Air Act of 1970 and the Federal Water Pollution Control Act (Clean Water Act) of 1972, and RCRA was seen as closing "the last remaining loophole in environmental law, that of unregulated land disposal of discarded materials and hazardous wastes." H.R.Rep. No. 1491, 94th Cong., 2d Sess. 4, reprinted in 1976 U.S.C.C.A.N. 6238, 6241.

The early years of implementation of RCRA were troubled. Public concern, and therefore the political implications, of the regulation of hazardous waste dramatically increased in the late 1970s as a result of a series of well-publicized incidents. These included the infamous situation at Love Canal. Love Canal was a community in New York that had constructed a school on a former landfill donated to the city by a chemical manufacturing company. Although disposal at the landfill had complied with the then existing laws, problems arose from release of hazardous chemicals at the site. In 1978, President Carter declared Love Canal an emergency area. Additionally, bureaucratic problems within EPA and changes in the administrations from President Carter to President Reagan in 1981 complicated efforts to implement RCRA. *See* James Florio, *Congress as Reluctant Regulator: Hazardous Waste Policy in the 1980's*, 3 Yale J. on Reg. 351 (1986); Marc C. Landy, Marc J. Roberts, and Stephen R. Thomas, *The Environmental Protection Agency: Asking the Wrong Questions: From Nixon to Clinton* (1994). EPA finally promulgated its first major set of RCRA regulations in 1980, but the definition of hazardous waste, the provision that defines the scope of the RCRA program, was not promulgated until 1985.

Concerns about EPA's implementation of RCRA, including a political reaction by a Democratic Congress to President Reagan's revisions to the RCRA program, led to adoption of the Hazardous and Solid Waste Amendments of 1984 ("HSWA"). The HSWA amendments included, among other things, extraordinarily detailed statutory requirements for hazardous waste landfills, the land ban and prohibition on the introduction of liquids in landfills, and stringent requirements on "interim status" hazardous waste disposal facilities.

Implementation difficulties reflect two basic problems inherent in regulating hazardous wastes under RCRA. First, RCRA has a limited jurisdictional scope; for the most part, the statute only regulates hazardous "solid wastes." Consider what this means. A pile of hazardous chemicals stored by a facility for use in its production process is not regulated under RCRA; the same materials if "discarded" may be subject to stringent regulations under RCRA. A hazardous by-product may be sold for "recycling" in ways that produce the same environmental hazards as disposal, but RCRA regulates this by-product only if it is classified as a waste. As we will see, there are no simple or obvious environmental or economic characteristics that distinguish wastes subject to RCRA and products that are not. Yet this distinction, the classification of a material as a hazardous "solid waste," is the key question that defines the scope of the RCRA regulatory program.

Second, there are limited options in dealing with the disposal and management of hazardous waste. The available disposal options all create environmental problems. Placing hazardous waste in landfills creates risks of release to groundwater and effective incineration is technically complex and inevitably involves releases of hazardous constituents into the air.

Recycling and reuse of hazardous wastes has advantages; recycling reduces the quantities of hazardous wastes to may need to be disposed of and can involve recovery of economic value from materials that would otherwise be wastes. But recycling of hazardous wastes can create its own environmental harm and can be used as a "sham" for avoiding the costs associated with proper disposal. Perhaps the best alternative is to avoid the generation of hazardous waste in the first place. This can be accomplished through substitution of less hazardous materials in an industrial process or more efficient use of materials to minimize the wastes that are generated. Lack of information and lack of economic incentives hamper such "pollution prevention" or "waste minimization" efforts. As you review RCRA, consider how the current structure operates to minimize the risks from disposal of hazardous waste and to encourage recycling or pollution prevention as an alternative to disposal.

2. THE STRUCTURE OF RCRA

RCRA contains a number of distinct programs that address the problem of hazardous wastes, non-hazardous wastes and, in some cases, the storage of hazardous products. This chapter largely focuses on the complex set of requirements under Subtitle C, but each of the following programs are relevant to limiting environmental problems from hazardous wastes.

a. SUBTITLE C

The major portion of RCRA (known as the Subtitle C program for its location in the original bill that created RCRA) establishes the primary federal program for the regulation of hazardous wastes. The Subtitle C program is universally referred to as a "cradle to grave" program because it operates to regulate hazardous wastes from their point of generation to their final disposal. As we will see, it establishes separate requirements applicable to generators, transporters and disposers of hazardous waste.

There are several key components of the Subtitle C program. First, Subtitle C addresses only the set of "hazardous wastes" defined by EPA regulation. Other materials may be both hazardous and wastes, but if they do not fall within EPA's regulatory definition of "hazardous wastes" they are not, with one exception discussed below, regulated under the Subtitle C program. Second, Subtitle C establishes a federal permit program for "treatment, storage and disposal facilities" ("TSDFs"). In most cases, hazardous wastes can only be disposed of at a facility that has a federally mandated TSDF permit. Hazardous waste generators and transporters are regulated, but they are not required to have a RCRA permit. Third, the Subtitle C program contains a "manifest" requirement for off-site shipments of hazardous wastes. This "manifest," or tracking document, helps ensure that transported hazardous wastes actually end up at the facility to which they are being sent.

b. SUBTITLE D

RCRA contains a limited federal program that addresses the disposal of non-hazardous solid wastes. Under Subtitle D of RCRA, EPA has established "sanitary landfill" criteria that define standards for a proper solid waste landfill. EPA has promulgated both general "sanitary landfill" criteria and separate and more detailed criteria that apply to construction and operation of "municipal solid waste landfills" ("MSWLFs"). Disposal of non-hazardous wastes at a facility that does not meet federal criteria is classified as "open dumping," and open dumping is prohibited under RCRA.

The quantities of nonhazardous solid wastes generated in the U.S. dwarf the quantities of Subtitle C hazardous wastes, and non-hazardous solid wastes can themselves contain hazardous and toxic constituents. Nonetheless, the Subtitle D program has been of much less significance than the hazardous waste program established under Subtitle C. The most important reason for this is that the RCRA prohibition on "open dumping" is not federally enforceable. Although states and private citizens can bring an open dumping action under RCRA, the federal government cannot. Therefore, the federal government has a limited role in ensuring the proper disposal of non-hazardous solid wastes. This means that EPA has limited options to ensure proper management of a waste if it is excluded from classification as a "hazardous waste" under Subtitle C. It also means that regulation of non-hazardous industrial solid waste is largely a state and local matter.

c. IMMINENT AND SUBSTANTIAL ENDANGERMENT PROVISIONS

In addition to the comprehensive hazardous waste regulatory program established under Subtitle C, RCRA also has separate provisions under which an action can be brought to seek injunctive relief to compel the cleanup of solid or hazard wastes that are creating an "imminent and substantial endangerment." These actions can be brought by the federal government under § 7003(a)(1)(B) or by States and private citizens under § 7002(a)(1)(B). Either of these actions can be brought against a broad class of persons who caused or contributed to the imminent and substantial endangerment.

"Imminent and substantial endangerment" actions are of particular importance since they can be brought to compel the cleanup of materials that do not fall within the class of hazardous wastes regulated under Subtitle C. Additionally, an imminent and substantial endangerment action can be brought to compel the cleanup of wastes, primarily petroleum wastes, that are not covered under the Comprehensive Environmental Response Compensation and Liability Act.

d. RECYCLED USED OIL

Used oil, in most cases, is not defined as a hazardous waste for purposes of regulation under Subtitle C. Given the environmental problems created by the recycling of used oil, Congress gave EPA the authority to regulate the recycling of non-hazardous used oil under Subtitle C. RCRA § 3014. [This is the one exception to the general rule that only EPA defined hazardous wastes are regulated under Subtitle C.] Pursuant to this authority, EPA has established a separate regulatory program that governs the storage, transportation and sale of used oil. *See* 40 C.F.R. Part 279.

e. UNDERGROUND STORAGE TANKS

Leaking underground storage tanks have been a significant source of environmental problems. In 1980, Congress established a separate regulatory program under RCRA that creates a federal program for the construction, monitoring and registration of underground storage tanks. It also establishes separate authority under which the government can require the cleanup of releases from leaking underground storage tanks. 42 U.S.C. §§ 6991 et seq. Unlike the rest of RCRA, the UST program applies to the storage of products, such as petroleum, as well as wastes in underground storage tanks.

3. RCRA AND STATE HAZARDOUS WASTE PROGRAMS

RCRA, like other federal environmental statutes, has a goal of "cooperative federalism," and one of its stated goals is the creation of a "viable federal/state partnership." *See* RCRA § 3001(a)(7). Under RCRA, EPA is responsible for adopting regulations that implement the requirements of Subtitle C, and EPA was initially responsible for issuance of Subtitle C permits. States, however, may receive federal approval of their hazardous waste programs if the programs are "equivalent" to the federal program. *See* 40 C.F.R. §§ 271.9–.16. If approved, the state program operates "in lieu of" the federal program, and the state issues Subtitle C permits to facilities within their borders. RCRA § 3006. EPA does have the authority to withdraw state authorization if the State is no longer "administering or enforcing" a program in accordance with RCRA requirements. *See* RCRA § 3006(e); 40 C.F.R. § 271.22.

All states have been approved to administer the basic RCRA program, but several particular federal/state issues continue to complicate the RCRA Subtitle C scheme. First, RCRA specifically authorizes states to adopt hazardous waste requirements that are "more stringent" than the minimum federal requirements. RCRA § 3009. EPA has taken the position that approved state requirements that are "more stringent" than comparable federal requirements may be federally enforced. In contrast, state requirements that are "broader in scope" than federal requirements are not part of the federally approved program. *See* 40 C.F.R. § 271.1(i)(2). Thus, the federal enforceability of a state hazardous waste restriction may depend on whether the restriction is seen as more stringent or broader in scope than the federal program.

Second, in the Hazardous and Solid Waste Amendments of 1984 ("HSWA"), Congress established many stringent requirements for RCRA that complicate the RCRA picture. EPA regulations issued under the original 1976 provisions of RCRA can in most cases be implemented immediately by states that have approved programs. In contrast, many regulations issued under HSWA authority can be implemented by states only after the state revises its program and the revisions are approved by EPA. *See* 40 C.F.R. § 271.1(f) (list of HSWA issued regulations). This means that even in approved states some portion of the program may still be administered by EPA. A permit applicant may have to deal with both state and federal permit authorities, and state-issued RCRA permits may have a separate section of federally established requirements.

Third, when state programs are approved, RCRA § 3006 states that they operate "in lieu of" the federal program. This has raised issues regarding federal enforcement and the ability to enforce federal requirements in approved states. These issues are also discussed below at section D.5.

4. RESEARCHING RCRA

One of the more frustrating aspects of RCRA is the difficulty in finding answers to basic questions. In most cases, the statute will tell you little about the substantive requirements that apply to hazardous wastes. As with most federal environmental programs, the details are contained in regulations promulgated by the Environmental Protection Agency. EPA's RCRA regulations governing Subtitle C are found generally at 40 C.F.R. Parts 260–273. Part 261 contains provisions that define the scope of solid and hazardous waste for purposes of the Subtitle C program. Part 262 contains requirements applicable to generators. Part 263 applies to transporters and Parts 264–265 contain requirements applicable to permitted TSDFs. The regulations are always an important place to look for answers to RCRA questions, and you *must* review the applicable regulations as you consider the materials in this Chapter. The regulations are available on Westlaw and Lexis and they are also available on the Government Printing Office website, http://www.gpoaccess.gov/cfr/.

The RCRA regulations themselves are, however, frequently confusing and ambiguous. While they may be a place to start, one rarely ends with them. There are a number of other important sources for RCRA answers:

Preambles to EPA regulations. When EPA initially proposes and subsequently promulgates regulations, the regulations are accompanied by a textual discussion of the regulations and, when promulgated, a response to comments. These "preambles" are published in the Federal Register and are essentially the "legislative history" of the regulation. Regulations codified in the Code of Federal Regulations will contain citations to the Federal Registers in which the regulation was promulgated. The preamble will also contain reference to accompanying documents, not published in the Federal Register, that are part of the administrative record prepared by EPA. The preambles particularly can be invaluable sources of EPA's contemporaneous explanation of the scope and operation of regulations.

RCRA guidance documents and interpretative memos. Many of RCRA requirements have been developed, not as promulgated regulations, but through the more informal method of publishing guidance documents and interpretative memos. These documents can be extremely helpful and extremely difficult to find. EPA's "RCRA Online" website is a source for many of these documents. *See http://www.epa.gov/epawaste/ inforesources/online/index.htm*

EPA website. EPA's RCRA website can also sometimes be a useful source of information about RCRA requirements. *See http://www. epa.gov/epawaste/index.htm*

State requirements. Much of RCRA is now administered through State hazardous waste programs. It is always important to review specific State laws and regulations as part of any research into applicable hazardous waste requirements.

B.   DEFINITION OF HAZARDOUS WASTE

Most of the significant provisions of RCRA apply to the class of "hazardous waste." Thus, most RCRA questions begin with a definitional issue—is this material classified as a hazardous waste? As with most questions under RCRA, the answer is rarely simple.

1.   THE DUAL DEFINITIONS: THE RELATIONSHIP BETWEEN THE STATUTORY AND REGULATORY DEFINITIONS

Connecticut Coastal Fishermen's Assn. v. Remington Arms Co., Inc.
989 F.2d 1305 (2d Cir. 1993)

Critical on this appeal is the meaning of the terms "solid waste" and "hazardous waste," as these terms are defined in the Solid Waste Disposal Act, 42 U.S.C. §§ 6901–6992k (1988), as amended by the Resource Conservation and Recovery Act of 1976 (RCRA), and the Hazardous and Solid Waste Amendments of 1984. Defining what Congress intended by these words is not child's play, even though RCRA has an "Alice in Wonderland" air about it. We say that because a careful perusal of RCRA and its regulations reveals that "solid waste" plainly means one thing in one part of RCRA and something entirely different in another part of the same statute.

"When *I* use a word," Humpty Dumpty said in a rather scornful tone, "it means just what I choose it to mean—neither more nor less."

"The question is," said Alice, "whether you *can* make words mean so many different things."

"The question is," said Humpty Dumpty, "which is to be master—that's all."

LEWIS CARROLL, THROUGH THE LOOKING–GLASS ch. 6 at 106–09 (Schocken Books 1987) (1872). Congress, of course, is the master and in the discussion that follows, we undertake to discover what meaning Congress intended in its use of the words solid and hazardous waste.

Remington Arms Co., Inc. (Remington or appellant) has owned and operated a trap and skeet shooting club—originally organized in the 1920s—on Lordship Point in Stratford, Connecticut since 1945. Trap and skeet targets are made of clay, and the shotguns used to knock these targets down are loaded with lead shot. The Lordship Point Gun Club (the Gun Club) was open to the public and it annually served 40,000 patrons. After nearly 70 years of use, close to 2,400 tons of lead shot (5 million pounds) and 11 million pounds of clay target fragments were deposited on land around the club and in the adjacent waters of Long Island Sound. Directly to the north of Lordship Point lies a Connecticut state wildlife refuge at Nells Island Marsh, a critical habitat for one of the state's largest populations of Black Duck. The waters and shore near the Gun Club feed numerous species of waterfowl and shorebirds.

Plaintiff, Connecticut Coastal Fishermen's Association (Coastal Fishermen or plaintiff) brought suit against defendant Remington alleging that the lead shot and clay targets are hazardous wastes under RCRA and pollutants under the Clean Water Act (Act). Remington has never obtained a permit under § 3005 of RCRA for the storage and disposal of hazardous wastes, 42 U.S.C. § 6925, or a National Pollutant Discharge Elimination System (pollution discharge) permit pursuant to § 402 of the Clean Water Act, 33 U.S.C. § 1342. Plaintiff insists that Remington must now clean up the lead shot and clay fragments it permitted to be scattered on the land and in the sea at Lordship Point. Because the debris constitutes an imminent and substantial endangerment to health and the environment under RCRA, we agree.

[Note that the Plaintiffs have brought two distinct RCRA claims. First, Plaintiffs claim that Defendants have a claim under § 7002(a)(1)(A) alleging that Defendants have violated the regulatory requirements of Subtitle C by, among other things, failing to have a TSDF permit. Second, Plaintiffs have claimed a violation of the "imminent and substantial endangerment" provisions of § 7002(a)(1)(B).]

RCRA establishes a "cradle-to-grave" regulatory structure for the treatment, storage and disposal of solid and hazardous wastes. Solid wastes are regulated under Subchapter IV §§ 6941–49a; hazardous wastes are subject to the more stringent standards of Subchapter III §§ 6921–39b. Under RCRA "hazardous wastes" are a subset of "solid wastes." *See* 42 U.S.C. § 6903(5). Accordingly, for a waste to be classified as hazardous, it must first qualify as a solid waste under RCRA. We direct our attention initially therefore to whether the lead shot and clay targets are solid waste.

We consider first the statutory definition of solid waste. RCRA defines solid waste as:

> any garbage, refuse, sludge from a waste treatment plant, water supply treatment plant, or air pollution control facility *and other discarded material* ... resulting from industrial, commercial, mining and agricultural operations, and from community activities ...

42 U.S.C. § 6903(27) [emphasis added]. Remington admits that its Gun Club is a "commercial operation" or a "community activity;" it challenges the district court's finding that the lead shot and clay target debris are "discarded material." The statute itself does not further define "discarded material," and this creates an ambiguity with respect to the specific issue raised by Remington: At what point after a lead shot is fired at a clay target do the materials become discarded? Does the transformation from useful to discarded material take place the instant the shot is fired or at some later time?

The legislative history does not satisfactorily resolve this ambiguity. It tells us that RCRA was designed to "eliminate[ ] the last remaining loophole in environmental law" by regulating the "disposal of discarded materials and hazardous wastes." H.R.Rep. No. 1491, 94th Cong., 2d Sess. 4 (1976), *reprinted in* 1976 U.S.C.C.A.N. 6238, 6241. Further, the reach of RCRA was intended to be broad.

> It is not only the waste by-products of the nation's manufacturing processes with which the committee is concerned: *but also the products themselves once they have served their intended purposes and are no longer wanted by the consumer.* For these reasons the term discarded materials is used to identify collectively those substances often referred to as industrial, municipal or post-consumer waste; refuse, trash, garbage and sludge.

Id. at 2, 1976 U.S.C.C.A.N. at 6240 [emphasis added]. Yet, the legislative history does not tell us at what point products have served their intended purposes. The statutory definition of "disposal" as "the discharge, deposit, injection, dumping, spilling, leaking, or placing of any solid waste or hazardous waste into or on any land or water," 42 U.S.C. § 6903(3), while broad, sheds little light on this question. Remington's focus on RCRA as being intended to address only solid waste "disposal"—in the sense of the affirmative acts of collecting, transporting, and treating manufacturing or industrial by-products—clearly is too narrow because it ignores legislative aim and fails to take into account the often non-voluntary acts of depositing, spilling and leaking. The statute and legislative history do not instruct as to how far the reach of RCRA extends.

The RCRA regulations create a dichotomy in the definition of solid waste. The EPA distinguishes between RCRA's regulatory and remedial purposes and offers a different definition of solid waste depending upon the statutory context in which the term appears. In its *amicus* brief, the EPA tells us that the regulatory definition of solid waste—found at 40 C.F.R. § 261.2(a)—is narrower than its statutory counterpart. The regulations define solid waste as "any discarded material" and further define discarded material as that which is "abandoned." 40 C.F.R. § 261.2(a). Materials that are abandoned have been "disposed of." 40 C.F.R. § 261.2(b). According to RCRA regulations, this definition of solid waste "applies only to wastes that also are hazardous for purposes of the regulations implementing Subtitle C of RCRA." 40 C.F.R. § 261.1(b)(1). As previously noted, Subtitle C [Subchapter III] contains more stringent handling standards for hazardous waste, and hazardous waste is a subset of solid waste.

The regulations further state that the statutory definition of solid waste, found at 42 U.S.C. § 6903(27), applies to "imminent hazard" lawsuits brought by the United States under § 7003. This statement recognizes the special nature of the imminent hazard lawsuit under RCRA.... Consequently, the broader statutory definition of solid waste applies to citizen suits brought to abate imminent hazard to health or the environment.

We recognize the anomaly of using different definitions for the term "solid waste" and that such view further complicates an already complex statute. Yet, we believe on balance that the EPA regulations reasonably interpret the statutory language. Hence, we defer to them. Dual definitions of solid waste are suggested by the structure and language of RCRA. Congress in Subchapter III isolated hazardous wastes for more stringent regulatory treatment. Recognizing the serious responsibility that such regulations impose, Congress required that hazardous waste—a subset of solid waste as defined in the RCRA regulations—be clearly identified. The statute directs the EPA to develop specific "criteria" for the identification of hazardous wastes as well as to publish a list of particular hazardous wastes. By way of contrast, Subchapter IV that empowers the EPA to publish "guidelines" for the identification of problem solid waste pollution areas, does not require explanation beyond RCRA's statutory definition of what constitutes solid waste. Hence, the words of the statute contemplate that the EPA would refine and narrow the definition of solid waste for the sole purpose of Subchapter III regulation and enforcement.

Regulatory Definition of Solid Waste

EPA, as *amicus,* concludes that the lead shot and clay targets discharged by patrons of Remington's Gun Club do not fall within the narrow regulatory definition of solid waste. Again, this issue is one we need not resolve because plaintiff has failed to allege a valid claim, brought under the § 7002(a)(1)(A) citizen suit provision, that Remington violated § 6925 of RCRA. [In other portions of the opinion, the court, among other things, concluded that a citizen suit could not be brought for a "wholly past" violation of RCRA. This and other jurisdictional issues relating to citizen suits brought under § 7002(a)(1)(A) are discussed in the enforcement sections of this chapter.]

Statutory Definition of Solid Waste

As already noted, RCRA regulations apply the broader statutory definition of solid waste to imminent hazard suits. The statutory definition contains the concept of "discarded material," but it does not contain the terms "abandoned" or "disposed of" as required by the regulatory definition. 40 C.F.R. §§ 261.2(a)(2), (b)(1). Amicus interprets the statutory definition of solid waste as encompassing the lead shot and clay targets at Lordship Point because they are "discarded." Specifically, the EPA states that the materials are discarded because they have been "left to accumulate long after they have served their intended purpose." Without deciding how long materials must accumulate before they become discarded—that is, when the shot is fired or at some later time—we agree that the lead shot and clay targets in Long Island Sound have accumulated long enough to be considered solid waste.

NOTES AND QUESTIONS

1.   The court begins its analysis of whether the clay targets and shot were hazardous wastes by looking at the statutory definitions in RCRA itself. Section 1004(5) of RCRA defines a "hazardous waste" as a "solid waste" that has certain hazardous characteristics. As the court notes, hazardous wastes are thus a "subset" of the broader class of solid wastes.

Phrased another way, a material must be a solid waste before it can be a hazardous waste, and the definition of "solid waste" at RCRA § 1004(27) is crucial to establishing the jurisdictional scope of RCRA.

2.   Note that the statutory definition of "solid waste" includes discarded materials that are solid, semi-solid, liquid or a contained gaseous material. We are back to the court's reference to Alice in Wonderland. The phrase "solid waste" means what Congress says it means, and it clearly includes discarded solid materials, wastewaters and other discarded liquids and even, in some cases, gases. *See* 56 Fed. Reg. 5,910, 5,911 (1991) (EPA statement that uncontained gases not associated with solid waste management units are not solid wastes under RCRA); Gallagher v. T.V. Spano Bldg. Corp., 805 F.Supp. 1120 (D. Del. 1992) (methane, formed from the decay of buried materials, was not a "solid waste" under RCRA since it was not a solid, liquid or contained gas). *But see* United States v. Power Eng'g Co., 10 F. Supp. 2d 1145 (D. Colo. 1998) (court held that a chromium liquid mist emitted from air pollution control equipment was a solid waste).

3.   The court also looks to the positions of the Environmental Protection Agency to determine whether the materials constitute solid wastes. As the court notes, EPA has taken the position that solid waste has (at least) two definitions under RCRA. First, EPA has a complex regulatory definition of solid waste at 40 C.F.R. § 261.2, but this definition according to EPA only applies for purposes of determining whether a material is a solid waste regulated under Subtitle C. This regulatory definition would apply to Plaintiff's claim under RCRA § 7002(a)(1)(A) that the Defendant had disposed of hazardous waste in violation of Subtitle C. Second, EPA claims that the broader statutory definition of solid waste applies for purposes of Plaintiff's "imminent and substantial endangerment" claim.

The court in *Connecticut Coastal* accepts the legitimacy of EPA using different definitions of solid waste for purposes of different sections of RCRA. What is the rationale for applying a "broader" statutory definition of solid wastes for imminent and substantial endangerment actions, but a "narrower" regulatory definition for purposes of obligations under Subtitle C?

4.   EPA regulations specify that the regulatory definitions apply solely to define the scope of Subtitle C obligations. 40 C.F.R. § 261.1(a). The broader statutory definition applies to a number of other provisions of RCRA. These include:

"Imminent and substantial endangerment actions." EPA regulations provide that the broader statutory definition applies when the government is bringing an action to abate an "imminent and substantial endangerment" under § 7003. The court in *Connecticut Coastal* held that the statutory definition also applied to citizens bringing an imminent and substantial endangerment action under § 7002(a)(1)(B).

Reporting and record-keeping requirements. Sections 3007 and 3013 of RCRA give EPA authority to engage in inspections and require reporting by persons engaged in management of the statutory class of hazardous wastes, even if those materials are not subject to Subtitle C requirements.

Corrective action. Where there is a release of "hazardous waste" from a facility subject to RCRA Subtitle C permitting requirements, EPA may issue a "corrective action" order to compel cleanup. *See* RCRA §§ 3004(u), 3008(h). EPA has claimed that the statutory definition of hazardous waste applies to determine the scope of these "corrective action" requirements. *See* 55 Fed. Reg. 30789, 30809 (1990).

5.   The statutory definition applies generally to materials that have been "discarded." Although EPA has promulgated a long and complex regulatory definition of solid waste for purposes of Subtitle C, EPA has provided little guidance on the scope of the statutory definition. For purposes of the Subtitle D non-hazardous waste program, EPA has promulgated a definition of solid waste that simply restates the statutory definition. 40 C.F.R. § 257.2. On what sources does the court rely to determine whether the materials are included within the statutory definition of solid waste?

6.   Materials whose intended use involve placement on the ground raise particularly difficult issues under RCRA. In *Connecticut Coastal,* EPA took the position that lead-containing shot and clay targets fell within the *statutory* definition of solid waste since "they had been left to accumulate long after they have served their intended purpose." Courts have held that spent shot is not a solid waste under the statutory definition immediately upon being fired. *See, e.g.,* Water Keeper Alliance v. United States Dep't of Def., 152 F. Supp. 2d 163 (D.P.R. 2001). But how long is too long?

EPA has generally taken the position that materials, like lead shot, do not fall within the "regulatory" definition of solid waste (and are therefore not subject to the complex requirements of Subtitle C) if they are placed on the ground as part of their intended use. *See Cordiano v. Metacon Gun Club,* 575 F.3d 199 (2d Cir. 2009). In *No Spray Coalition v. City of New York,* 252 F.3d 148 (2d Cir. 2001), the court, citing *Connecticut Coastal,* held that pesticides sprayed into the air were not "discarded" since they performed their intended purpose—"reaching and killing mosquitoes." The court in *No Spray Coalition,* however, did not distinguish between claims based on the statutory and regulatory definitions.

2.   The Subtitle C Regulatory Definition of Solid Waste

EPA's regulations, like the statute itself, define hazardous wastes as a "subset" of solid wastes, and a material must first fall within EPA's regulatory definition of "solid waste" before it can be regulated as a hazardous waste under Subtitle C. Thus, EPA's regulatory definition of "solid waste" at 40 C.F.R. § 261.2 is critical for defining the scope of materials that may be subject to stringent regulation under Subtitle C "cradle to grave" regulatory program.

Although RCRA was passed in 1976, EPA's first "interim" regulatory definition of solid waste was not promulgated until 1980. In response to litigation, EPA substantially altered its initial definition in 1985. Although the definition of solid waste has been amended many times since then, the basic structure of EPA's regulatory definition of solid waste has not changed since 1985. *See* Jeffrey M. Gaba, *Separating Chaff from Wheat: Solid Waste and Recycled Materials under RCRA,* 16 Ecology L.Q. 623 (1989).

It is now time to read carefully the regulatory definition of solid waste found at 40 C.F.R. § 261.2. There is no substitute for this careful reading. The regulation is, to be charitable, confusingly written. Many of the difficulties in determining whether a material is classified as a solid waste under Subtitle C can, however, be minimized simply by working through the provisions of the definition.

a. "DISCARDED" MATERIALS

Note the structure of the definition. 40 C.F.R. § 261.2(a)(1) tracks the statutory definition and defines a solid waste as a "discarded" material. 40 C.F.R. § 261.2(a)(2) then defines "discarded" material to include "any material" that is 1) abandoned, 2) recycled, 3) "inherently waste-like," or 4) a "military munition." Each of those terms is further defined, but to be a solid waste that is regulated under Subtitle C a material must fall within one of these four classes.

Abandoned. Under 40 C.F.R. § 261.2(b), a material is "abandoned" if it is "disposed of" or "burned or incinerated" or "accumulated, stored, or treated (but not recycled) before or in lieu of being abandoned by being disposed of, burned, or incinerated." Although determining whether materials have been abandoned can raise difficult issues, this provision probably comports most closely with the common meaning of "discarded." Indeed, the preamble to the 1985 regulation simply states that "[b]y saying 'abandoned,' we do not intend any complicated concept, but simply mean thrown away." 50 Fed. Reg. at 627. If a material is simply thrown away, it is a solid waste under the regulatory definition because it has been abandoned.

Recycled. The regulation defines some, but not all, recycled materials as solid wastes and therefore potentially subject to regulation under Subtitle C as hazardous wastes. The scope of recycled materials covered under by the regulation is defined by application of the "matrix" found at 40 C.F.R. § 261.2(c). Both EPA's legal authority to regulate recycled materials as solid wastes and the application of EPA's regulatory definition to recycled materials will be discussed below.

Inherently waste-like. 40 C.F.R. § 261.2(d) specifies a list of "inherently waste-like" materials that are defined as solid wastes. Do not be confused by the term "inherently waste-like;" this is not a general catch-all that applies to a broad class of waste-like materials. Materials that are solid wastes because they are "inherently waste-like" include only the very small group of materials that EPA has specifically listed in this subsection.

Military munitions. In 1997, EPA addressed the applicability of RCRA to military munitions: unexploded bombs and bomb fragments. Discarded military ordinance is found not only on military installations, but also on privately owned property that was once owned by the military or where military ordinance may have landed during military training exercises. Some types of military munitions are defined as solid waste for purposes of Subtitle C; some types are defined as solid wastes for purposes of the "imminent and substantial endangerment provisions. The regulatory provisions governing military munitions are found at 40 C.F.R. Part 266, Subpart M, §§ 266.270 et seq.

EPA's basic regulatory definition of solid waste was challenged shortly after it was first promulgated.

American Mining Congress v. EPA

824 F.2d 1177 (D.C. Cir. 1987)

These consolidated cases arise out of EPA's regulation of hazardous wastes under the Resource Conservation and Recovery Act of 1976 ("RCRA"), as amended. Petitioners, trade associations representing mining and oil refining interests, challenge regulations promulgated by EPA that amend the definition of "solid waste" to establish and define the agency's authority to regulate secondary materials reused within an industry's ongoing production process. In plain English, petitioners maintain that EPA has exceeded its regulatory authority in seeking to bring materials that are not discarded or otherwise disposed of within the compass of "waste."

I

Congress' "overriding concern" in enacting RCRA was to establish the framework for a national system to insure the safe management of hazardous waste. In passing RCRA, Congress expressed concern over the "rising tide" in scrap, discarded, and waste materials. 42 U.S.C. § 6901 (a)(2). As the statute itself puts it, Congress was concerned with the need "to reduce the amount of waste and unsalvageable materials and to provide for proper and economical solid waste disposal practices." *Id.* § 6901(a)(4). Congress thus crafted RCRA "to promote the protection of health and the environment and to conserve valuable material and energy resources." *Id.* § 6902.

RCRA includes two major parts: one deals with non-hazardous solid waste management and the other with hazardous waste management. Under the latter, EPA is directed to promulgate regulations establishing a comprehensive management system. *Id.* § 6921. EPA's authority, however, extends only to the regulation of "hazardous waste." Because "hazardous waste" is defined as a subset of "solid waste," *id* § 6903(5), the scope of EPA's jurisdiction is limited to those materials that constitute "solid waste." That pivotal term is defined by RCRA as:

> any garbage, refuse, sludge from a waste treatment plant, water supply treatment plant, or air pollution control facility *and other discarded material,* including solid, liquid, semisolid or contained gaseous material, resulting from industrial, commercial, mining, and agricultural operations, and from community activities....

42 U.S.C. § 6903(27) (emphasis added). As will become evident, this case turns on the meaning of the phrase, "and other discarded material," contained in the statute's definitional provisions.

To understand petitioners' claims, a passing familiarity with the nature of their industrial processes is required.

Petroleum. Petroleum refineries vary greatly both in respect of their products and their processes. Most of their products, however, are complex mixtures of hydrocarbons produced through a number of interdependent and sometimes repetitious processing steps. In general, the refining process starts by "distilling" crude oil into various hydrocarbon streams or "fractions." The "fractions" are then subjected to a number of processing steps. Various hydrocarbon materials derived from virtually all stages of processing are combined or blended in order to produce products such as gasoline, fuel oil, and lubricating oils. Any hydrocarbons that are not usable in a particular form or state are returned to an appropriate stage in the refining process so they can eventually be used. Likewise, the hydrocarbons and materials which escape from a refinery's production vessels are gathered and, by a complex retrieval system, returned to appropriate parts of the refining process. Under EPA's final rule, this reuse and recycling of materials is subject to regulation under RCRA.

Mining. In the mining industry, primary metals production involves the extraction of fractions of a percent of a metal from a complex mineralogical matrix (i.e., the natural material in which minerals are embedded). Extractive metallurgy proceeds incrementally. Rome was not built in a day, and all metal cannot be extracted in one fell swoop. In consequence, materials are reprocessed in order to remove as much of the pure metal as possible from the natural ore. Under EPA's final rule, this reprocessed ore and the metal derived from it constitute "solid waste." What is more, valuable metal-bearing and mineral-bearing dusts are often released in processing a particular metal. The mining facility typically recaptures, recycles, and reuses these dusts, frequently in production processes different from the one from which the dusts were originally emitted. The challenged regulations encompass this reprocessing, to the mining industry's dismay.

Against this factual backdrop, we now examine the legal issues presented by petitioners' challenge.

III

We observe at the outset of our inquiry that EPA's interpretation of the scope of its authority under RCRA has been unclear and unsteady.

1

The first step in statutory interpretation is, of course, an analysis of the language itself. As the Supreme Court has often observed, "the starting point in every case involving statutory construction is 'the language employed by Congress.'" In pursuit of Congress' intent, we "start with the assumption that the legislative purpose is expressed by the ordinary meaning of the words used." These sound principles governing the reading of statutes seem especially forceful in the context of the present case. Here, Congress defined "solid waste" as "discarded material." The ordinary, plain-English meaning of the word "discarded" is "disposed of," "thrown away" or "abandoned."[FN7] Encompassing materials retained for immediate reuse within the scope of "discarded material" strains, to say the least, the everyday usage of that term.

FN7. The dictionary definition of "discard" is "to drop, dismiss, let go, or get rid of as no longer useful, valuable, or pleasurable." Webster's Third New International Dictionary, G. & C. Merriam Co. (1981). It bears noting that the term "discarded" is neither inherently difficult to define nor is so intimately tied to knowledge of the industry and the practicalities of regulation that definition requires agency expertise.

Although the "ordinary and obvious meaning of the [statutory] phrase is not to be lightly discounted," we are hesitant to attribute decisive significance to the ordinary meaning of statutory language. To be sure, our inquiry might well and wisely stop with the plain language of the statute, since it is the statute itself that Congress enacts and the President signs into law. But as the Supreme Court recently observed, the "more natural interpretation" (or plain meaning) is not necessarily determinative. And it is not infrequently said, odd as it may seem in a society governed by codified and thus knowable rules, that a matter may be within the letter of a statute but not within its spirit.

The question we face, then, is whether, in light of the National Legislature's expressly stated objectives and the underlying problems that motivated it to enact RCRA in the first instance, Congress was using the term "discarded" in its ordinary sense—"disposed of" or "abandoned"—or whether Congress was using it in a much more open-ended way, so as to encompass materials no longer useful in their original capacity though destined for immediate reuse in another phase of the industry's ongoing production process.

For the following reasons, we believe the former to be the case. RCRA was enacted, as the Congressional objectives and findings make clear, in an effort to help States deal with the ever-increasing problem of solid waste *disposal* by encouraging the search for and use of alternatives to existing methods of disposal (including recycling) and protecting health and the environment by regulating hazardous wastes. To fulfill these purposes, it seems clear that EPA need not regulate "spent" materials that are recycled and reused in an *ongoing* manufacturing or industrial process.[FN11] These materials have not yet become part of the waste disposal problem; rather, *they are destined for beneficial reuse or recycling in a continuous process by the generating industry itself.*

FN11. EPA argues that a narrow reading of "discarded" would "vitiate" RCRA's remedial purpose. EPA Brief at 30–31. We cannot agree. EPA provides no explanation for this remarkable proposition, and we fail to see how not regulating in-process secondary materials in an on-going production process will subvert RCRA's waste disposal management goals.

2

Our task in analyzing the statute also requires us to determine whether other provisions of RCRA shed light on the breadth with which Congress intended to define "discarded." As the Supreme Court reiterated a few years ago, in interpreting a statute, "[w]e do not ... construe statutory phrases in isolation; we read statutes as a whole." The structure of a statute, in short, is important in the sensitive task of divining Congress' meaning.

In its brief, EPA directed us to a number of statutory provisions, arguing that they support its expansive definition of "discarded." This turned out, however, to be a wild goose chase through the labyrinthine maze of 42 U.S.C., for as counsel for EPA commendably recognized at oral argument, those statutory provisions speak in terms of "hazardous" (or "solid") waste." In consequence, EPA's various arguments based on the statute itself are, upon analysis, circular, relying upon the term "solid waste" or "hazardous waste" to extend the reach of those very terms. This, all would surely agree, will not do.

3

After this mind-numbing journey through RCRA, we return to the provision that is, after all, the one before us for examination. And that definitional section, we believe, indicates clear Congressional intent to limit EPA's authority. First, the definition of "solid waste" is situated in a section containing thirty-nine separate, defined terms. This is definitional specificity of the first order. The very care evidenced by Congress in defining RCRA's scope certainly suggests that Congress was concerned about delineating and thus cabining EPA's jurisdictional reach.

Second, the statutory definition of "solid waste" is quite specific. Although Congress well knows how to use broad terms and broad definitions, the definition here is carefully crafted with specificity. It contains three specific terms and then sets forth the broader term, "other discarded material."

In sum, our analysis of the statute reveals clear Congressional intent to extend EPA's authority only to materials that are truly discarded, disposed of, thrown away, or abandoned. EPA nevertheless submits that the legislative history evinces a contrary intent.

Although we find RCRA's statutory language unambiguous, and can discern no exceptional circumstances warranting resort to its legislative history, we will nonetheless in an abundance of caution afford EPA the benefit of consideration of those secondary materials.

4

EPA points first to damage incidents cited by Congress in 1976 as justification for establishing a hazardous waste management system. *See* H.R.Rep. No. 1491, 94th Cong., 2d Sess. at 18, 22 (1976). Neither of the incidents noted by EPA, however, involved commercial, in-process reuse or recycling activities. Instead, both incidents provide clear examples of waste *disposal,* which, of course, indisputably falls within EPA's jurisdiction conferred by RCRA.

EPA next asserts that the "most significant" aspect of the 1976 legislative history is the sense that Congress enacted broad grants of regulatory authority in order to "eliminate[ ] the last remaining loophole in environmental law." To the contrary, a fair reading of the legislative history reveals intimations of an intent to regulate under RCRA only materials that have truly been discarded. Not only is the language of the legislative history fully consistent with the use of "discarded" in the sense of "disposed of," but it strains the language to read it otherwise.

After all is said and done, we are satisfied that the legislative history, rather than evincing Congress' intent to define "discarded" to include in-process secondary materials employed in an ongoing manufacturing process, confirms that the term was employed by the Article I branch in its ordinary, everyday sense.

IV

We are constrained to conclude that, in light of the language and structure of RCRA, the problems animating Congress to enact it, and the relevant portions of the legislative history, Congress clearly and unambiguously expressed its intent that "solid waste" (and therefore EPA's regulatory authority) be limited to materials that are "discarded" by virtue of being disposed of, abandoned, or thrown away. While we do not lightly overturn an agency's reading of its own statute, we are persuaded that by regulating in-process secondary materials, EPA has acted in contravention of Congress' intent.

NOTES AND QUESTIONS

1.   Why were the petroleum refinery and mining materials at issue in *American Mining Congress* "solid wastes" under EPA's regulatory definition? They were certainly not "abandoned." It appears that the petroleum materials were classified as a "solid waste" because they were being "recycled" by being used to produce a fuel. *See* 40 C.F.R. § 261.2(c). The mining materials were classified as solid wastes because they were being recycled by reclamation. *Id.* The application of EPA's regulatory definition to recycled materials is discussed below.

2.   The opinion in *American Mining Congress* is capable of both a broad and narrow reading. In its broadest reading, the court suggested that "discarded material" should be given an ordinary or common sense meaning. This might suggest that RCRA definition of solid waste does not include materials that are being legitimately recycled. The court recognized, however, that some types of recycled material, material that might not in any common sense way be considered discarded, were included within the meaning of solid waste. The court notes that:

> One of RCRA's primary goals is to promote recovery of reusable material that is currently being "needlessly buried." 42 U.S.C. § 6901(c). EPA's argument ignores this objective and, in so doing, overlooks the natural interpretation that those statutory provisions are directed at the recycling of "solid waste" as a way to manage, and indeed benefit from, materials that present a waste management problem by virtue of having been disposed of. 824 F.2d at 1189, n. 17.

Thus, in a narrower reading, the court held only that solid waste could not include recycled materials that were "destined for immediate reuse within the generating industry itself."

EPA read the opinion narrowly and made no significant changes to its regulatory definition. After *AMC*, EPA simply excluded the specific petroleum and refining wastes at issue from classification as a solid waste.

3. A series of case after *AMC* gave a somewhat confused picture of the scope of materials that EPA could define as solid wastes. In *American Petroleum Inst v. EPA,* 906 F.2d 729 (D.C. Cir. 1990), the D.C. circuit held that, consistent with *AMC*, EPA could (and perhaps must) define certain materials as solid wastes if they were being sent for reclamation of their metal content at another industrial facility. In *American Mining Congress v. EPA*, 907 F.2d 1179 (D.C. Cir. 1990) *(AMC II)*, the court held that certain metal bearing sludges that the industrial facility said "might" at some uncertain future time be recycled could be classified as solid wastes. The court indicated that a material was a solid waste if it was 1) not destined for immediate reuse in another part of an industry's ongoing production process and 2) had become part of the waste disposal problem.

In *Association of Battery Recyclers v. EPA,* 208 F.3d 1047 (D.C. Cir. 2000), the D.C. Circuit reaffirmed the basic holding of *American Mining Congress*. *ABR* dealt with an EPA regulation that would have defined certain mining materials as solid wastes if they were stored on the ground before being reintroduced into the mining reclamation process. The court again emphasized the "plain meaning" aspect of *American Mining Congress I* and held that materials that were stored on the ground, even if they created a potential environmental problem, could not be classified as a solid waste if part of a continuous industrial process.

4. Both *AMC I* and *ABR* can be seen as addressing the same basic question: at what point in an industrial process can a material first be classified as a solid waste? EPA has referred to this as the "point of generation" issue. Until a material first exits a "continuous" or "ongoing" production process, *AMC I* and *ABR* suggest that EPA does not have the statutory authority to classify such material as a solid waste. We will more fully consider the scope of EPA's authority to define materials being sent for recycling as solid wastes below.

5. In 2008, EPA added a provision that allows a generator to request that EPA determine that certain reclaimed materials are not solid wastes because they are part of a "continuous industrial process." 40 C.F.R. § 260.30(d). The determination is based on whether the recycling is "legitimate" and a variety of other factors including whether 1) the management of the materials is part of the "continuous primary production process and is not waste treatment," 2) the production process would use the material in a "reasonable time frame," 3) hazardous constituents are reclaimed, rather than released to the environment, in significantly higher levels "than would otherwise be released by the production process," and 4) "other relevant factors." 40 C.F.R. § 260.34(b). This provision is based on the holdings of *AMC I* and *ABR*.

PROBLEMS

Assume that all of the materials below would be classified as hazardous waste if they fell within EPA's regulatory definition of solid waste. Apply EPA's regulatory definition to see how these materials might (or might not) fall within the Subtitle C definition of solid waste.

1. As part of its industrial process, Company X produces a byproduct that it cannot use. It takes the material and throws it in a dumpster to be taken to a municipal landfill. Is the material a solid waste?

2. Company Y uses certain toxic industrial chemicals as part of its industrial process. The chemicals are held in its storage area until they are to be used. Some of the chemicals in the storage area have been held there for years and are no longer suitable for use in the industrial process. Are the old chemicals solid wastes? If so, at what point did they become wastes?

3. Company Z uses a certain toxic chemical that it receives in bulk from a chemical manufacturer. Company Z removes the chemical from the drums in which it is shipped and returns the drums to the manufacturer. There are some residues of the chemical in the drums when they are returned. Are the toxic chemicals in the returned drums a solid waste?

b. RECYCLED MATERIALS

EPA's regulatory definition of solid waste includes materials that are "recycled." The definition, however, is not as broad as it may seem since it has a limited definition of recycling for purposes of coverage under Subtitle C. Nonetheless, it does show that EPA asserts authority to regulate at least some class of materials that are recycled and not abandoned. Let's start by parsing EPA's complex provisions defining the scope of recycled materials that are classified as solid wastes. Then we will address the broader question of EPA's legal authority to regulate recycled materials as solid waste.

i. *The Matrix*

EPA's regulatory definition states that a material is "discarded" if it is recycled, but under this definition a material is considered "recycled" only if it falls within the "matrix" at 40 C.F.R. § 261.2(c). To apply the matrix, you must know two things: the type of material being recycled (the vertical axis) and the type of recycling activity for which it will be used (the horizontal axis). Under the matrix a recycled material is a solid waste if there is an asterisk at the intersection of the type of material and its means of recycling.

The materials covered on the vertical axis (frequently referred to as "secondary materials") are defined in § 261.1(c), and they include the following:

Sludges. "Sludges" are generally defined to include wastes produced by the operation of air or water pollution control equipment.

By-products. A "By-product" is defined as a "material that is not one of the primary products of a production process and is not solely or separately produced by the production process." 40 C.F.R. § 261.1(c)(3). The regulations specifically distinguish "by-products," which may be wastes if recycled, from the category of "co-products" that are not wastes. The definition of by-product states: "The term does not include a co-product that is produced for the general public's use and is ordinarily used in the form it is produced by the process."

Listed commercial chemical products. "Commercial chemical products" as a category of wastes is defined by cross-reference to a group of "off-specification" commercial products that EPA has listed as hazardous waste. Thus, it expressly applies only to a specific list of chemical products that are not suitable for their intended purposes.

Scrap metal. "Scrap metal" is basically defined as "bits and pieces of metal parts." (i.e., big chunks of metal). Thus, scrap metal does not generally include wastes that are simply contaminated with high concentrations of metals.

Under the matrix, these secondary materials can only be solid wastes if they are recycled through the specific means identified by the horizontal list of recycling activities. Each of these types of recycling is separately defined.

Use constituting disposal. "Use constituting disposal" is limited to recycling that involves placement of a product on the land. Spraying waste oil on the ground as a dust suppressant would be recycling through "use constituting disposal." Including materials as ingredients in asphalt that is applied to the ground may also be a type of recycling that would be "use constituting disposal."

Energy recovery/fuel. "Energy Recovery/Fuel" applies to recycling by burning a material for energy recovery or to make a fuel that is burned to produce energy. This category of recycling is different from "incineration" which is a process intended simply to dispose of wastes.

Reclamation. "Reclamation" is defined to include two different types of recycling. First it includes processing to recover valuable materials. An example used by EPA is the recovery of lead from old batteries. The second type of reclamation involves "regeneration" of spent materials. This would include, for example, removing contaminants from a used solvent so that the solvent can be reused. As discussed below, EPA, in 2008, established a series of new exclusions from classification as a solid waste for materials that are reclaimed.

Speculative accumulation. "Speculative Accumulation" essentially involves long-term storage of potentially recyclable materials without actually using them for recycling. Under EPA's definition, speculative accumulation generally occurs if less than seventy-five percent of the accumulated material is recycled in a calendar year.

Although § 261.2(c) and its matrix define materials that are solid wastes if recycled, another section, § 261.2(e), specifies materials that are *not* solid wastes if recycled. This section is quite misleading. It effectively applies only to recycling activities that are not covered under the matrix. In other words, § 261.2(e) "excludes" materials that were never defined as solid wastes in the first place. In fact, EPA initially considered placing this section in a preamble as a description of the application of the matrix. 261.2(e) is, however, useful to understand the type of recycling activities that are not covered under Subtitle C. Secondary materials that are directly used as an ingredient or a product are not classified as solid wastes under the regulatory definition *unless* the recycling is a type covered under the matrix.

EPA has over the years attempted to distinguish legitimate from "sham" recycling. This distinction is somewhat misleading. EPA's regulatory definition of solid waste includes "legitimate" recycling; that is the whole point of the matrix. Thus, under the EPA definition, legitimate recycling may or may not involve a solid waste depending on the application of the matrix. Legitimate recycling covered under the matrix is a solid waste; legitimate recycling not covered under the matrix is not a solid waste.

The purpose of classifying an activity as "sham" recycling is to identify those activities that are, in effect, disposal. If a company "legitimately" recycles materials in ways not covered under the matrix, the materials would not be defined as a solid waste. If, however, the act of recycling is a "sham," the materials involved will be classified as solid wastes because, under EPA's regulatory definition, they are "abandoned."

EPA has issued a series of guidance statements that purport to establish criteria that characterize sham recycling. Through these statements, EPA has identified a number of factors that are relevant to determining whether a transaction involves "sham" recycling. These factors include whether: 1) a secondary material is ineffective or only marginally effective for the claimed use, 2) a secondary material is used in excess of the amount necessary for operating a process, 3) the secondary material is not as effective as that which it is replacing, 4) there is an absence of records concerning the transaction; and 5) the secondary materials are not handled in a manner consistent with their use as raw materials or commercial product substitutes. EPA, in 2008, promulgated a set of "legitimacy criteria" that incorporate elements of this past guidance. 40 C.F.R. § 260.43. *See* Jeffrey M. Gaba, *Rethinking Recycling*, 38 Envt'l L. 1053, 1083 (2008).

PROBLEMS

Assume all of the materials in the following problems would be classified as a hazardous wastes if they are defined as a solid waste.

1. Company A produces a "by-product" as part of its industrial operations. If the by-product is simply discarded it would cost Company A a substantial amount of money to dispose of the by-product as a hazardous waste. This by-product, however, has qualities that make it suitable for use as an "aggregate" in making concrete, and a concrete manufacturer is willing to take the material and use it as an ingredient in making its concrete. Company A would be willing to give the by-product to the concrete manufacturer if legally possible in order to avoid the cost of disposal. If the by-product is "recycled" by being used as an ingredient to make concrete, is it a "solid waste?"

2.   Company B transports natural gas through it pipelines. During the transportation of the natural gas a condensate forms in the pipeline that must be removed. Although it does not contain the same energy content as natural gas, the condensate does have some energy value and can be burned, and Company A is considering selling the natural gas condensate to an industrial facility to burn as a fuel in the facility's boiler. If it were classified as a solid waste the condensate would be considered a hazardous waste because it exhibits the hazard characteristic of "ignitability." Would the natural gas condensate be a "solid waste" if sold for use as a fuel?

3.   Company D operates an air pollution control system that produces a "baghouse" dust. This dust exhibits the toxicity characteristic for lead. If the baghouse dust were simply discarded, it would clearly be hazardous waste since it would be "abandoned." Would baghouse dust be classified as hazardous waste if it was sent to a facility that extracted the lead content for sale? Would it be a hazardous waste if it was sent to be used as an ingredient to make asphalt for use in road construction?

ii.   *EPA's Authority to Regulate Recycled Materials Under Subtitle C*

A fundamental question under RCRA is whether recycled materials can be defined as solid wastes for purposes of regulation under Subtitle C. The issue of the application of Subtitle C to recycled materials raises serious legal and policy concerns. On the one hand, Congress limited the reach of Subtitle C to "discarded" materials, and industrial byproducts that are sold to a third-party for reuse or recycling have some economic value and are not, in an obvious sense, discarded. Further, one of the objectives of RCRA is to encourage recycling, and stringent regulation of recycling activities under RCRA creates economic barriers to recycling. On the other hand, improper recycling activities can create the same environmental problems as disposal and exclusion of regulation of disposal but not recycling creates incentives to engage in "sham" recycling.

EPA has consistently asserted authority to regulate some class of recycled materials as solid wastes. *See, e.g.,* 48 Fed. Reg. 14,472, app. A, at 14,502 (1983). In a 2007 proposal to amend the definition of solid waste, EPA restated its basic justifications for classifying some recyclable materials as solid wastes. *See* 72 Fed. Reg. at 14,176 (2007). First, EPA argues that both the express provisions of RCRA and its legislative history indicate Congress's intent to include recyclable materials under RCRA regulatory authority. Second, EPA claims that hazardous materials stored and transported prior to recycling have the same potential for causing environmental harm as hazardous materials intended for disposal and refers to numerous examples of environmental harms caused by recycling facilities including cases cited by Congress to justify adoption of RCRA. Finally, EPA argues that exempting recycling activities would result in identical materials moving in and out of the RCRA regulatory program depending on their intended use or disposition. This, in EPA's view, is inconsistent with an intention to manage hazardous wastes from "cradle to grave."

Although *American Mining Congress I* held that RCRA did not give EPA the authority to define materials as solid waste if they were part of a "continuous process in the generating industry itself," the majority did not clearly address the broader question of the scope of EPA's authority to define recyclable materials that are no longer part of a continuous industrial process as solid waste. Subsequent cases further addressed the issue of EPA's authority to define recycled materials as solid wastes.

Safe Food and Fertilizer v. EPA
350 F.3d 1263 (D.C. Cir. 2003)

Zinc fertilizers can be produced either from virgin materials or recycled byproducts of certain industrial processes. In the rule under review here, the Environmental Protection Agency resolved that Subtitle C of the Resource Conservation and Recovery Act ("RCRA") would not apply to the recycled materials used to make zinc fertilizers, or to the resulting fertilizers themselves, so long as they met certain handling, storage and reporting conditions and (in the case of the fertilizers themselves) had concentration levels for lead, arsenic, mercury, cadmium, chromium, and dioxins that fall below specified thresholds. Petitioners claim that both the materials and the fertilizer are "hazardous wastes" and that therefore the EPA must regulate them under RCRA's Subtitle C.

A material is a "hazardous waste" under RCRA if it is a "solid waste" as defined in 42 U.S.C. § 6903(27) and is "hazardous" as defined in 42 U.S.C. § 6903(5). Both parties agree that the materials are "hazardous" as that word of art is used under RCRA, although (as we shall see) the EPA does not in fact regard them as posing any material hazard if they comply with the conditions specified by the rule. The issue is whether the materials in question are "solid waste." The EPA has concluded that they are not—that so long as they satisfy the stated conditions, they have not been "discarded" as RCRA's definition of solid waste uses the term.

Merits. RCRA defines "solid waste" to mean:

> any garbage, refuse, sludge from a waste treatment plant, water supply treatment plant, or air pollution control facility and any other *discarded* material.

42 U.S.C. § 6903(27) (emphasis added). Petitioners challenge the EPA's decision that recycled materials complying with the specified conditions are not "discarded" material. We review under the standard principles of *Chevron, U.S.A., Inc. v. Natural Resources Defense Council,* 467 U.S. 837, 104 S.Ct. 2778, 81 L.Ed.2d 694 (1984). Unless the statute resolves the issue, we must uphold the EPA so long as its interpretation is reasonable.

Petitioners assert that, as a matter of plain meaning, the materials in question are "discarded" even though they are recycled in a useful product. They claim that under our cases recycled material destined for immediate reuse within an ongoing industrial process is never considered "discarded," whereas material that is transferred to another firm or industry for subsequent recycling must always be so viewed.

Petitioners misread our cases. We have held that the term "discarded" cannot encompass materials that "are destined for beneficial reuse or recycling in a continuous process by the generating industry itself." *Am. Mining Cong. v. EPA* ("*AMC I*"), 824 F.2d 1177, 1186 (D.C.Cir.1987); see also *Ass'n of Battery Recyclers, Inc. v. EPA*, 208 F.3d 1047, 1056 (D.C.Cir.2000). We have also held that materials destined for future recycling by another industry *may* be considered "discarded"; the statutory definition does not preclude application of RCRA to such materials if they can reasonably be considered part of the waste disposal problem. *Am. Petroleum Inst. v. EPA*, 906 F.2d 729, 740–41 (D.C.Cir.1990); *Am. Mining Cong. v. EPA* ("*AMC II*"), 907 F.2d 1179, 1186–87 (D.C.Cir.1990). But we have never said that RCRA compels the conclusion that material destined for recycling in another industry is necessarily "discarded." Although ordinary language seems inconsistent with treating immediate reuse within an industry's ongoing industrial process as a "discard," see *AMC I,* 824 F.2d at 1185, the converse is not true. As firms have ample reasons to avoid complete vertical integration, see generally Ronald Coase, "The Nature of the Firm," 4 *Economica* 386 (1937), firm-to-firm transfers are hardly good indicia of a "discard" as the term is ordinarily understood.

Thus we turn to the question "whether the agency's interpretation of … 'discarded' [is] permissible, that is, reasonable and consistent with the statutory purpose." The answer depends on the EPA's reasons for finding that the materials involved here should not be regarded as "discarded" so long as they meet its conditions. The EPA's explanation is that market participants treat the exempted materials more like valuable products than like negatively-valued wastes, managing them in ways inconsistent with discard, and that the fertilizers derived from these recycled feedstocks are chemically indistinguishable from analogous commercial products made from virgin materials.

We need not consider whether a material could be classified as a non-discard exclusively on the basis of the market-participation theory. At oral argument EPA counsel rested the agency's case on the combination: market participants' treatment of the materials, together with EPA-required management practices and contaminant limits assuring substantial chemical identity. If this combination is enough to establish that the recycled fertilizers are not "discarded" when used on the land, it follows that feedstocks used to manufacture them are also not "discarded"—and therefore not waste—since the feedstocks are ingredients in a nondiscarded final product.

Petitioners principally attack the legal and factual basis for the EPA's identity principle. As a matter of law, petitioners claim—correctly, as far as we know—that no court has yet endorsed the identity principle that the EPA urges. But this is hardly surprising, as petitioners point to no case where the EPA had both proposed the principle and been challenged. The question, apparently of first impression, is whether the identity principle, when used in conjunction with indicators like market valuation and management practices, is a reasonable tool for distinguishing products from wastes. We find that it is. Nobody questions that virgin fertilizers and feedstocks are products rather than wastes. Once one accepts that premise, it seems eminently reasonable to treat materials that are indistinguishable in the relevant respects as products as well.

But we do not believe that affirmance of the EPA's principle requires literal identity, so long as the differences are so slight as to be substantively meaningless. Here, the apparent differences in the EPA's exclusion ceilings and the contaminant levels in the virgin fertilizer samples lose their significance when put in proper perspective—namely, a perspective based on health and environmental risks.

NOTES AND QUESTIONS

1. In *Safe Food* the court acknowledged EPA's authority to regulate some class of recyclable materials as solid waste if they evidenced an "element of discard." What were the elements of "discard" that justified EPA in classifying both (1) the zinc fertilizer and (2) the zinc containing wastes used to make the fertilizer as solid waste?

2. EPA's authority to regulate some recyclable materials as solid waste has been consistently upheld by the courts. In *United States v. Ilco*, 996 F.2d 1126, 1131–1132 (11th Cir. 1993), for example, the court held that spent batteries subject to recycling by reclaiming their lead components could be considered discarded and therefore classified as solid wastes under RCRA. The court stated that "[p]reviously discarded solid waste, although it may at some point be recycled, nonetheless remains solid waste." Similarly, in *Owen Electric Steel Co. v. Browner*, 37 F.3d 146 (4th Cir. 1994), the court held that metal slag was a "solid waste" even though subsequently recycled.

3. You might think that the issue of determining whether a material is discarded is easy. If someone will pay for them, if they have economic value in the marketplace, how can they be considered to be a discarded waste? The California Supreme Court relied on just such an argument to reject a county's attempt to establish an exclusive franchise to collect recyclable materials under its authority to regulate solid waste management services. The court, in *Waste Management of the Desert v. Palm Springs Recycling Center*, 869 P.2d 440, 443 (Cal. 1994), concluded that a material with "economic value" is not a waste, stating: "If the owner sells his property— that is, receives value for it—the property cannot be said to be worthless or useless in an economic sense and is thus not waste from the owner's perspective." The court further noted: "Property that is sold for value—for example, a recyclable—is not 'discarded' under any traditional understanding of the term. 'Discard' means 'to throw away.' It is not synonymous with the broader term 'dispose,' which means 'To transfer or part with, as by giving or selling.' " *Id.*

EPA, however, has consistently rejected the view that solid wastes can be defined based on a simple criterion of economic value, despite, in EPA's phrase, its "intuitive appeal.". See, e.g., 48 Fed. Reg. 14,472, 14,478–81 (1983). The Agency has rejected this approach because of the obvious possibility of creating sham transactions and the difficulties of enforcement they would entail. There are many ways in which parties can disguise the direction in which money flows in a transaction; a recycler may pay a nominal amount for an item even if the value of the transaction comes from the generator avoiding the cost of disposal. *See, e.g.,* American Petroleum Institute v. EPA, 906 F.2d 729, 741 n.16 (D.C. Cir. 1990) (upholding EPA's authority to regulate metal bearing sludges as solid wastes even if their treatment might produce a valuable product). Thus, the fact that a material has some value does not, at least under RCRA, preclude it from being classified as a solid waste.

4.   EPA has no single theory of "discard." Rather, EPA has at different times and in different regulations advanced a number of criteria that it has used to justify classifying a material as a waste. These include whether (1) a material is similar to a commercial product, (2) the recycling activity is similar to disposal, (3) the amount of toxic materials that will be included in the recycled product is greater than would be present if virgin products were used, (4) the material poses an environmental risk if recycled, (5) the material, prior to recycling, is managed in a manner similar to a virgin product. *See* Jeffrey M. Gaba, *Rethinking Recycling*, 38 ENVT'L L. 1053, 1086 (2008) for a discussion of the ways in which EPA has used these criteria.

3.   The Subtitle C Regulatory Definition of Hazardous Waste

Compared to the problem of defining a material as a solid waste under 40 C.F.R. § 261.2, the classification of a solid waste as a "hazardous" waste is relatively simple. Under § 3001 of RCRA and 40 C.F.R. § 261.3 a solid waste is a hazardous waste if it is either 1) is listed under EPA regulations or 2) exhibits a "hazard characteristic."

a.   LISTED WASTES

A solid waste is considered a hazardous waste under Subtitle C if EPA specifically places it on a hazardous waste "list." EPA regulations contain three different "lists" of hazardous wastes, and each specific listed waste has its own waste code or number. Wastes from "non-specific source" ("F" wastes), 40 C.F.R. § 261.31, generally involve types of wastes, like certain spent solvents, that can originate from a number of different industrial sources. Wastes from "specific sources" ("K" wastes), 40 C.F.R. § 261.32, generally are wastes from specific industrial operations in a particular industry. This includes, for example, certain wastewater sludges generated in the petroleum refining industry). Wastes listed as "commercial chemical products" ("P" and "U" wastes), 40 C.F.R. § 261.33, include listed commercial chemical products that are discarded or are applied to the land or burned as a fuel and that is not their original intended use. This list includes, for example, pesticides that when manufactured are "off-specification" and cannot be used for their original intended purpose.

EPA decides whether to list a waste on one of three bases specified at 40 C.F.R. § 261.11. First, a waste could be listed if it exhibits a "hazard characteristic" discussed below. Second, a waste could be listed if certain types of data show that it is dangerous to humans at low doses. Third, a waste can be listed if it contains a chemical listed in Appendix VIII of the regulation *and* EPA decides to list the waste based on evaluation of a series of factors including its toxicity, potential to bioaccumulate in the environment and the "plausible types of improper management" to which the wastes could be subjected. Each listed waste has a Hazard Code or Codes which indicate the basis on which it is listed. *See* 40 C.F.R. § 161.30(b).

Determining whether a material is regulated under Subtitle C as a "listed" hazardous waste is relatively simple: the generator need only check the lists to see if the material falls within the scope of the listing description. In contrast to the detail of other parts of EPA's hazardous waste regulations, the listing descriptions are relatively terse, and in some cases it can be difficult to determine if EPA intended for a particular waste stream to be included within the scope of listing.

If a waste is covered as a "listed" waste, a generator can have its particular wastes removed from classification as a hazardous waste by filing a "delisting" petition with EPA. To be "delisted" a generator must generally demonstrate that its particular wastes are different from other wastes in this classification and do not meet the criteria for listing.

b. CHARACTERISTIC WASTES

A solid waste can also be classified as a hazardous waste if it exhibits any one of four hazard "characteristics:"

Ignitability. The ignitability characteristic assesses the potential flammability of a waste, and EPA has promulgated test measures applicable to liquids, solids, and compressed gas. Liquids, for example, exhibit the ignitability characteristic if an appropriate sample has a flash point less than 60 degrees Centigrade (140 degrees Fahrenheit).

Corrosivity. The corrosivity characteristic is based on the pH of the material or its ability to corrode steel under specified test conditions. An aqueous waste exhibits the characteristic if a representative sample of the waste has a pH of less than or equal to 2 or greater than or equal to 12.5.

Reactivity. The reactivity characteristic reflects the explosive potential of a waste. EPA has promulgated a number of rather ambiguous criteria for determining whether a waste is reactive. For example, a waste is reactive if it is "readily capable of detonation or explosive decomposition or reaction at standard temperature or pressure."

Toxicity. The Toxicity Characteristic is based on the potential toxicity of the waste. The toxicity characteristic is not, however, as broad as you might think. A waste exhibits the TC only if a sample of the waste contains one of 40 specific constituents at concentrations that are greater than a regulatory threshold. Furthermore, determination of whether a waste exhibits the toxicity characteristic is based on the amount of the specified constituents in an "extract" of the waste. The "Toxicity Characteristic Leachate Procedure" ("TCLP") is EPA's methodology for extracting a liquid sample from a solid waste. The TCLP involves grinding up the solid waste, mixing it with a slightly acidic liquid and then running the mixture through a filter to obtain an extract. The solid waste exhibits the toxicity characteristic if the extract that is produced contains one of the specified constituents at levels above its regulatory threshold.

From 40 C.F.R. § 261.24 Toxicity Characteristic

Table 1—Maximum Concentration of Contaminants for the Toxicity Characteristic

EPA HW No.[1]	Contaminant	CAS No.[2]	Regulatory Level (mg/L)
D004	Arsenic	7440–38–2	5.0
D005	Barium	7440–39–3	100.0
D018	Benzene	71–43–2	0.5
D006	Cadmium	7440–43–9	1.0
D019	Carbon tetrachloride	56–23–5	0.5
D020	Chlordane	57–74–9	0.03
D021	Chlorobenzene	108–90–7	100.0
D022	Chloroform	67–66–3	6.0
D007	Chromium	7440–47–3	5.0
D023	o-Cresol	95–48–7	[4]200.0
D024	m-Cresol	108–39–4	[4]200.0
D025	p-Cresol	106–44–5	[4]200.0
D026	Cresol		[4]200.0
D016	2,4–D	94–75–7	10.0
D027	1,4–Dichlorobenzene	106–46–7	7.5
D028	1,2–Dichloroethane	107–06–2	0.5
D029	1,1–Dichloroethylene	75–35–4	0.7
D030	2,4–Dinitrotoluene	121–14–2	[3]0.13
D012	Endrin	72–20–8	0.02
D031	Heptachlor (and its epoxide)	76–44–8	0.008
D032	Hexachlorobenzene	118–74–1	[3]0.13
D033	Hexachlorobutadiene	87–68–3	0.5
D034	Hexachloroethane	67–72–1	3.0
D008	Lead	7439–92–1	5.0
D013	Lindane	58–89–9	0.4
D009	Mercury	7439–97–6	0.2
D014	Methoxychlor	72–43–5	10.0
D035	Methyl ethyl ketone	78–93–3	200.0
D036	Nitrobenzene	98–95–3	2.0
D037	Pentrachlorophenol	87–86–5	100.0
D038	Pyridine	110–86–1	[3]5.0
D010	Selenium	7782–49–2	1.0
D011	Silver	7440–22–4	5.0
D039	Tetrachloroethylene	127–18–4	0.7
D015	Toxaphene	8001–35–2	0.5
D040	Trichloroethylene	79–01–6	0.5
D041	2,4,5–Trichlorophenol	95–95–4	400.0
D042	2,4,6–Trichlorophenol	88–06–2	2.0
D017	2,4,5–TP (Silvex)	93–72–1	1.0
D043	Vinyl chloride	75–01–4	0.2

NOTES AND QUESTIONS

1.   Under EPA regulations, the generator is responsible for determining whether its wastes are hazardous. 40 C.F.R. § 262.11. Determining whether a waste is listed involves checking the EPA lists; determining whether a waste is a characteristic waste requires a case-by-case assessment of whether the waste exhibits a characteristic. Although a generator may test its wastes to see if they exhibit a hazard characteristic, EPA does not require testing. A generator may rely on its "knowledge of process" to assess whether its wastes exhibit a characteristic. 40 C.F.R. § 262.11(c)(2). If, for example, a generator knows based on its industrial process that its wastes could not exhibit a characteristic (it does not, for example, contain any of the TC constituents), it may simply determine that the waste is not a characteristic waste. If the generator is wrong in its determination, it faces substantial liability for managing a hazardous waste in violation of Subtitle C requirements, but the generator has not violated RCRA simply by failing to test its waste.

2.   When first promulgated, the Toxicity Characteristic only applied to fourteen chemicals, primarily metals and herbicides. Congress responded in 1984 by requiring EPA to study the expansion of the number of constituents covered under the TC. *See* RCRA § 3001(g), (h). EPA subsequently added more than twenty-five additional constituents. Under the current TC, a waste may exhibit the hazard characteristic if an extract of the waste contains one of 40 chemical constituents at levels above their regulatory thresholds.

3.   The Toxicity Characteristic Leachate Procedure ("TCLP") is intended to reflect the effect of disposing of a waste in a municipal landfill—exposure to slightly acid liquids that could cause toxic constituents to leach from the waste. Several cases have challenged the application of the TCLP to wastes that have no history of disposal in municipal landfills. In *Edison Electric Inst. v. EPA*, 2 F.3d 438 (D.C. Cir. 1993), the court held that EPA had not justified application of the TCLP to certain types of mineral processing wastes where there was no evidence that such wastes were likely to be disposed of in a municipal landfill. In *Association of Battery Recyclers v. EPA*, 208 F.3d 1047, 1062 (D.C. Cir. 2000), however, the court upheld EPA's conclusion that the TCLP could reasonably be applied to most of mineral processing wastes based on "an impressive amount of evidence that mineral processing wastes may have been disposed of as hypothesized in the mismanagement scenario modeled in the TCLP."

4.   Determining whether a waste is a "characteristic" hazardous waste involves a case-by-case assessment of whether a sample of the waste exhibits a hazard characteristic. This can involve complex methodological questions. Some of the complexity involves the method for testing whether a sample exhibits a characteristic. EPA has published guidance on appropriate test methods. In addition, there is additional complexity in identifying the sample of the waste that is to be assessed. EPA regulations typically specify a sampling methodology which, if used by the generator, will establish that the generator tested a "representative sample" of its wastes. *See, e.g.* 40 C.F.R. § 261.20(c). A number of courts, however, have upheld

government claims that a generator violated RCRA even if the government data was not gathered in a way that conformed with EPA methodology, if the government could otherwise establish that its sampling methodology produced a representative sample. *See, e.g., United States v. WCI Steel, Inc.,* 72 F.Supp.2d 810(N.D. Ohio 1999).

5. A limited number of listed wastes are designated as "acute hazardous wastes." These listed wastes are designated by Hazard Code (H). 40 C.F.R. § 261.30(b). *See, e.g.,* F020 waste, 40 C.F.R. § 161.31(a). In many cases, "acute hazardous wastes" are subject to more stringent regulatory requirements than other hazardous wastes. *See, e.g,* § 40 C.F.R. § 261.5 (conditionally exempt small quantity generators are largely exempt from regulation if they generate 100 kilogram per month of hazardous waste or one kilogram per month of acute hazardous waste.)

c. MIXTURE AND DERIVED–FROM RULES AND THE CONTAINED–IN INTERPRETATION

EPA's method of defining hazardous waste raises several issues which EPA has had to address.

Mixture rule. What is the status of the mixture of a hazardous waste and a non-hazardous waste? EPA addresses this issue through its "mixture" rule found at 40 C.F.R. § 261.3(a)(2)(iv). Basically, this provision provides that any mixture of a listed waste and a non-hazardous waste is classified as a hazardous waste. This is the case regardless of the quantity of listed waste that is mixed with the non-hazardous waste. In other words, if you mix a teaspoon of a listed hazardous waste with a ton of non-hazardous waste the entire mixture is classified as a hazardous waste under Subtitle C.

In contrast, a characteristic hazardous waste remains hazardous only so long as it exhibits a characteristic, *see* 40 C.F.R. § 261.3(d)(1), and thus a mixture of a characteristic hazardous waste and a non-hazardous waste is hazardous only if the resulting mixture exhibits a hazard characteristic.

Derived-from rule. What is the status of wastes that result from the treatment of hazardous wastes? What is the status, for example, of the sludge produced from the biological treatment of a hazardous waste or the ash produced from the incineration of a hazardous waste? EPA's "derived-from" rule, found at 40 C.F.R. § 261.3(c)(2)(i), operates in a manner similar to the mixture rule: wastes derived-from a listed waste are classified as a hazardous waste, wastes derived from a characteristic waste are hazardous only if the derived-from waste itself exhibits a hazard characteristic. The actual language of the derived-from regulation is confusing since it seems to classify any waste as hazardous if it is derived from either a listed or characteristic hazardous waste. However, the derived-from rule is qualified by 40 C.F.R. § 261.3(d)(1) which provides that a characteristic waste is not classified as hazardous when it no longer exhibits a hazard characteristic.

Contained-in interpretation. A problem not addressed by the mixture and derived-from rules is the status of wastes generated during the remediation of property contaminated with hazardous wastes? What is the status, for example, of contaminated soil that has been excavated as part of the cleanup of property? This issue is not resolved by the mixture rule since the contaminated soil did not arise from the mixture of a hazardous waste and a non-hazardous waste; it resulted from the dumping of a hazardous waste onto the ground, and the ground is not a waste. The contaminated soil became a newly generated waste when it was excavated from the ground. *See Chemical Waste Management v. EPA*, 869 F.2d 1526 (D.C. Cir. 1989). The contaminated soil is not covered by the derived-from rule since it was not generated from the treatment of a hazardous waste.

To deal with this situation, EPA issued a series of guidance documents and statements which announced the "contained-in" interpretation that applies to wastes generated as part of a remediation. Under the contained-in interpretation, a remediation waste is hazardous if it exhibits a characteristic or it "contains" a listed hazardous waste at levels above some undefined "health based" level. *See* Gaba & Stever, Law of Solid Waste, Pollution Prevention and Recycling at 2:67. EPA has never clarified how much "listed wastes" a remediation waste must "contain" to be classified as hazardous.

NOTES AND QUESTIONS

1.   The mixture and derived-from rules were first promulgated in 1980. Eleven years later, the D.C. Circuit, in *Shell Oil v. EPA*, 950 F.2d 741, 752 (D.C. Cir. 1991), held that the rules had never been properly proposed and vacated the rules based on this procedural error. Recognizing the importance of the rules, however, the court stayed its mandate and allowed EPA to reinstate the rules on an "emergency" basis pending their repromulgation. EPA promulgated the rules on an "interim" basis in 1991 and as a final rule in 2001. The mixture and derived-from rules were finally upheld in *American Chemistry Council v. EPA*, 337 F.3d 1060 (D.C. Cir. 2003).

2.   Following *Shell Oil*, a series of cases reversed convictions based on the application of the invalidly promulgated mixture and derived-from rules. *See, e.g., United States v. Goodner Bros.Aircraft, Inc.*, 966 F.2d 380 (8th Cir. 1992); *United States v. Reticel Foam Corp.*, 858 F.Supp. 726 (E.D. Tenn. 1993).

3.   EPA has recognized problems with application of the mixture and derived-from rules: they operate to include materials as hazardous waste that may not, in fact, be hazardous (remember the teaspoon of listed waste in a ton of non-hazardous waste) and exclude materials that are hazardous (characteristic hazardous waste that may be diluted by mixing with non-hazardous waste). Over the years, EPA has undertaken a series of unsuccessful efforts to revise the rules. One proposal, known as the Hazardous Waste Identification Rule, would have adopted a series of "exit" levels that would exclude wastes from being fully regulated as hazardous wastes. Under the HWIR proposal, if a hazardous waste contained hazardous constituents below certain specified levels it would have either been excluded from classification as a hazardous waste or regulated only by a requirement that it be disposed of in a municipal solid waste landfill. 57 Fed. Reg. 21450 (1992). For a variety of reasons, including opposition from

municipalities, EPA abandoned this approach. At the end of over a decade of consideration, the mixture and derived-from rules remain essentially the same as originally promulgated in 1980.

4.   One particular problem arises from the application of the mixture rule. If listed waste is introduced into a wastewater treatment system, the sludge generated during the treatment could be classified as a hazardous waste. EPA has promulgated a series of exclusions from the mixture rule that allow small quantities of listed wastes to be treated in a wastewater treatment system without the resulting sludges being classified as hazardous wastes. *See* 40 C.F.R. § 261.3(a)(2)(iv). To be eligible for the exclusion, however, the wastewater treatment system must be regulated under the Clean Water Act.

5.   A limited number of listed hazardous wastes were listed because they exhibit a hazard characteristic. These listed wastes are designated by the Hazard Codes I (for ignitable), R (for reactive), C (for corrosive), or E (for toxicity characteristic). Do not confuse the Hazard Code T (for toxicity) with the Hazard Code E (for the Toxicity Characteristic). Listed wastes designated by the Hazard Code T were listed based on a general assessment of their toxicity and not a specific numerical threshold like the toxicity characteristic. The few listed hazardous wastes designated because they exhibit a hazard characteristic of ignitability, reactivity or corrosivity (sometimes referred to as ICR wastes) are treated like characteristic wastes for purposes of the mixture and derived-from rules. *See* 40 C.F.R. § 261.3(g). *See* Jeffrey Gaba, *The Mixture and Derived–From Rules under RCRA: Once a Hazardous Waste, Always a Hazardous Waste?*, 21 Envt. L. Rep. 10033 (1991) (in amendments to the regulations, EPA extended this position to the derived-from as well as the mixture rule).

6.   Although the "contained-in" interpretation is largely found in guidance documents and other EPA statements, EPA has promulgated a regulation incorporating a form of the contained-in rule for one particular application: there is a "contained-in" rule that governs the classification of a limited group of "hazardous debris." *See* 40 C.F.R. § 261.3(f)(2). Hazardous debris generally includes natural or manufactured material that is over 2.5 inches in diameter. *See* 40 C.F.R. § 268.2(g),(h). This specific rule would not, therefore, generally apply to remediation wastes consisting of soil or groundwater.

PROBLEMS

1.   Company A generates a solid waste that contains high concentrations of lead. The plant manager, through her knowledge of the industrial process, knows that the total concentration of lead in the waste must exceed the 5.0 milligrams per liter threshold that applies to the "toxicity" characteristic. Is the waste a RCRA hazardous waste?

2.   Company B generates a waste "halogenated spent solvent." The plant manager, through her knowledge of the industrial process, knows that this spent solvent falls within the listing description of listed waste F–001. Is this waste a RCRA hazardous waste?

3. Company C generates a "byproduct" of its industrial operations. The plant manager does not know the types or concentrations of contaminants in the sludge. Is the byproduct a hazardous waste and what actions would be necessary to make this determination?

4. A facility, as part of its industrial process, generates a wastewater that exhibits the TC characteristic. This wastewater is sent to a wastewater treatment system that is regulated under the Clean Water Act. The sludge produced by the wastewater treatment system is periodically removed for disposal. This sludge itself does not exhibit the characteristic. Is the sludge a hazardous waste?

4. EXCLUSIONS FROM CLASSIFICATION AS A SOLID AND HAZARDOUS WASTE

Although a material may be classified as a hazardous waste under EPA regulations, EPA has also promulgated a series of exclusions from coverage under Subtitle C. The most significant of these are found at 40 C.F.R. § 261.4 which contains exclusions both from classification as a solid waste, § 261.4(a), and exclusions from classification as a hazardous waste, § 261.-4(b). The effect of either class of exclusions is to exempt the material from regulation as a hazardous waste under Subtitle C. Some of the more significant exclusions include the following.

a. HOUSEHOLD HAZARDOUS WASTE

The definition of hazardous waste includes abandoned materials that exhibit a hazard characteristic, and many discarded household materials may technically fall within the class of hazardous waste. EPA had no interest in applying the Subtitle C regulatory scheme to the vast number of individual households, and in its earliest RCRA regulations EPA excluded "household waste" from classification as a hazardous waste under Subtitle C. The statutory basis for this exclusion is not clear. There was no explicit exclusion of household wastes in RCRA when it was adopted in 1976. In 1984, Congress adopted a cryptic "clarification of household waste exclusion" which, under some circumstances, exempts municipal waste incinerators burning municipal solid waste from regulation under Subtitle C. 42 U.S.C. § 6921(i). Whatever its legal justification, the household waste exclusion is an important element of RCRA.

"Household waste" is excluded from classification as a hazardous waste under 40 C.F.R. § 261.4(b)(1). This provision excludes:

> Household waste, including household waste that has been collected, transported, stored, treated, disposed, recovered (e.g., refuse-derived fuel) or reused. "Household waste" means any material (including garbage, trash and sanitary wastes in septic tanks) derived from households (including single and multiple residences, hotels and motels, bunkhouses, ranger stations, crew quarters, campgrounds, picnic grounds and day-use recreation areas).

Note that the exclusion is not limited to wastes generated by "households." It also applies to waste from various sources, such as hotels and motels, that generate wastes similar to households. EPA has, however, specifically stated that wastes from retail stores, office buildings, restaurants and shopping centers do not fall within the scope of the household waste exclusion. *See* 49 Fed. Reg. 44,978 (1984).

As noted, Congress, in 1984, "clarified" the scope of the household waste exclusion by specifically exempting "resource recovery facilities" that generate energy by burning municipal solid waste from regulation under Subtitle C. In other words, municipal solid waste incinerators that burn hazardous household and other municipal wastes are not subject to regulation as hazardous waste incinerators under Subtitle C. This provision, however, does not directly address the issue of the status of ash "derived-from" the treatment of hazardous municipal solid waste. In *City of Chicago v. Environmental Defense Fund*, 511 U.S. 328 (1994), the Supreme Court resolved a dispute among the circuits when it concluded that ash generated at municipal incinerators is not exempt from classification as a hazardous waste. As a result, municipal incinerator ash that exhibits a hazard characteristic will be classified as a hazardous waste.

b. DOMESTIC SEWAGE EXCLUSION

Both the statutory definition of "solid waste" and EPA regulations exclude materials that are introduced into a municipal sewer system from classification as a solid waste. *See* RCRA § 1003(24), 40 C.F.R. § 261.-4(a)(1). This "domestic sewage exclusion" means that hazardous materials dumped into the sewer system are not regulated under Subtitle C of RCRA. These materials are not necessarily unregulated, but they are regulated, if at all, through the "pretreatment" requirements of the Clean Water. The domestic sewage exclusion acts to allocate control between two different federal environmental statutes. Hazardous wastes shipped off site for treatment or disposal are regulated under RCRA; the same material if introduced into a municipal sewer system is excluded from regulation under RCRA and is regulated under the Clean Water Act.

The domestic sewage exclusion is not limited to domestic wastes. 40 C.F.R. § 261.4(a)(1) excludes not only domestic sewage but also "[a]ny mixture of domestic sewage and other wastes that passes through a sewer system to a publicly-owned treatment works for treatment." This means that a hazardous industrial material introduced into a municipal sewer system (known as a "publicly-owned treatment works" or "POTW") is not subject to regulation under RCRA.

At what point does an industrial waste "mix" with domestic sewage for purposes of the domestic sewage exclusion? EPA has generally taken the position that the exclusion applies at the point which the materials enter the sewer system, regardless of where the later mixing takes place. Recognizing the difficulties in identifying the point of mixing, the Agency has stated:

> EPA has, therefore, decided that a waste falls within the domestic sewage exemption when it first enters a sewer system that will mix it with sanitary wastes prior to storage or treatment by a POTW. EPA recognizes that this interpretation brings various wastes within the

exemption before they are actually mixed with sanitary wastes. In light of the fact that the wastes will be mixed prior to treatment and that the mixture will be properly treated by the POTW, EPA believes that the need for administrative clarity in this otherwise complicated regulatory program warrants such an approach.

45 Fed. Reg. 33,097 (1980).

c.   NPDES POINT SOURCE

In addition to regulating materials introduced into municipal sewers, the federal Clean Water Act also regulates the "direct discharge" of pollutants into waters of the United States. Dischargers are required to obtain a federally mandated National Pollutant Discharge Elimination System ("NPDES") permit that limits the quantity or concentration of pollutants that may be discharged. Under both the statutory definition of solid waste and EPA regulations, a discharge that is subject to regulation under n NPDES permit is excluded from classification as a solid waste. *See* § 1003(24), 40 C.F.R. § 261.4(a)(2). This avoids double regulation; if a discharge is regulated under an NPDES permit, it is not subject to regulation under RCRA.

This exclusion, however, applies only to the discharge itself. A "comment" to 40 C.F.R. § 261.4(a)(2) states:

> This exclusion applies only to the actual point source discharge. It does not exclude industrial wastewaters while they are being collected, stored or treated before discharge, nor does it exclude sludges that are generated by industrial wastewater treatment.

Therefore, wastes in an industrial wastewater treatment system are not excluded from classification as a solid waste. Since sludges in a wastewater treatment system may be hazardous wastes, they may be subject to regulation under Subtitle C. *See, e.g., United States v. Dean,* 969 F.2d 187 (6th Cir. 1992) (discharges into a lagoon prior to subsequent discharge into waters of the U.S. were not point source discharges and were not excluded from classification as a hazardous wastes.)

EPA has, however, adopted a regulation that excludes an "active" wastewater treatment unit from the need to obtain a Subtitle C hazardous waste permit. 40 C.F.R. § 270.1(c)(2)(v). EPA regulations define "wastewater treatment unit" to include only certain types of confined, tank systems. 40 C.F.R. § 270.2. Once the wastewater treatment unit is shut down or if the sludges are removed from the system, any hazardous wastes are subject to Subtitle C requirements.

d.   "SPECIAL WASTES"

In the earliest days of RCRA, EPA proposed to suspend the regulation of certain high volume/low toxicity wastes, which it called "special wastes." These included wastes from the oil and gas exploration and production wastes, mining wastes, wastes from burning fossil fuels and cement kiln dust. EPA later withdrew this proposal, but Congress intervened. In 1980, RCRA was amended to require EPA to suspend regulation of these wastes while it studied whether to classify the wastes as hazardous waste. RCRA §§ 3001(b)(2)–(3).

EPA has excluded oil and gas exploration and production wastes from classification as a hazardous waste, but note that this exclusion applies only to wastes produced by drilling for oil and gas, such as drilling muds and cuttings and produced water; it is not an exclusion of petroleum or used oil. 40 C.F.R. § 261.4(b)(5). EPA has also excluded certain mining wastes produced from the "extraction, beneficiation and storage of ores and minerals," 40 C.F.R. § 261.4(b)(7), and, in some cases, cement kiln dust, 40 C.F.R. § 261.4(b)(8).

The Comprehensive Environmental Response Compensation and Liability Act ("CERCLA") generally provides for the cleanup of "hazardous substances," and CERCLA defines hazardous substances by cross-reference to other environmental statutes. CERCLA § 101(14). One basis on which a material might be a hazardous substance is if it is classified as a hazardous waste under RCRA, "but not including any waste the regulation of which [under RCRA] has been suspended by an Act of Congress." CERCLA § 101(14)(C). This refers to the "special wastes." Industry undoubtedly thought that this provision would also exclude the RCRA special wastes from being CERCLA hazardous substances, but courts have uniformly held that RCRA special wastes can be CERCLA hazardous substances if they fall under some other basis for classification as a hazardous substance. Thus, mining wastes, excluded from classification as a hazardous waste under RCRA, can be addressed as hazardous substances under CERCLA if they contain lead or asbestos, both toxic pollutants under the Clean Water Act. *See, e.g., Eagle–Picher Indus. v. EPA*, 759 F.2d 922 (D.C. Cir. 1985). CERCLA also generally excludes petroleum and crude oil from classification as a hazardous substance. CERCLA § 101(14). Note, that this CERCLA "petroleum exclusion" is totally different from the exclusion of oil and gas exploration and production wastes from classification as a hazardous waste under RCRA. There is no "petroleum exclusion" from RCRA.

5. CONTINGENT MANAGEMENT

Many of the exclusions from classification as a hazardous waste are "conditional:" a material is excluded from regulation as a hazardous waste only if certain conditions are met. This allows regulation, but avoids the "stigma" that comes with designating a material as a hazardous waste. This technique of "contingent management" is being increasingly used by EPA to regulate hazardous materials without classifying them as "hazardous wastes." You can see that many of the later exclusions in 40 C.F.R. § 261.4(b) are subject to long and complex conditions. Other conditional exclusions are found at 40 C.F.R. 261.38–.40.

"Contingent management" raises troubling issues. Through this process, EPA establishes regulations on "non-hazardous" wastes that it could not otherwise impose under Subtitle D of RCRA. Further, through "contingent management" EPA may impose conditions that may not be as stringent as those that would be required if the material were classified as a hazardous waste. The use of the technique also raises the possibility that the breach of a single condition of the exclusion will subject the generator to the full set of penalties for mismanagement of what is now, as a result of violation of the condition, a hazardous waste.

Gaba, Regulation by Bootstrap: Contingent Management of Hazardous Wastes under the Resource Conservation and Recovery Act

18 Yale J. of Regulation 85 (2001)

The concept of contingent management is deviously simple, or in EPA's terms a "creative, affordable and common sense approach." EPA excludes a waste from classification as hazardous on the condition that it is managed in compliance with specific regulatory requirements. In other words, EPA establishes a set of requirements that apply to a waste that, by virtue of the exclusion, is classified as a non-hazardous solid waste. Non-compliance with the requirements converts the waste into a hazardous waste, and the party who violated the conditional requirements becomes subject to the full Subtitle C requirements. Thus, EPA achieves regulation and enforcement without the stigmatizing effects of classification as hazardous waste. EPA has used or proposed the use of contingent management in a number of instances.

EPA has articulated its legal rationale for the contingent management approach in a number of recent rule-makings. The basic premise of conditional regulation is that EPA need not list a waste as hazardous, even if it is inherently toxic, if there is no "need" for regulation. Relying on the statutory language of §§ 1004(5) and 3001 and the listing criteria in 40 C.F.R. § 261.11, EPA has concluded that it may determine not to list a waste if mismanagement is implausible or if the waste is otherwise adequately regulated. This statement itself is an unremarkable restatement of the statutory and regulatory listing criteria.

The remarkable extension of this rationale is EPA's claim that it may therefore adopt a set of regulations under RCRA that themselves remove the risk of plausible mismanagement. It is one thing to say that a waste will not be listed as a hazardous waste because existing data do not show a threat of mismanagement or that regulations legally adopted under other regulatory schemes minimize the threat of mismanagement. It is quite another to claim legal authority, not otherwise available to regulate a non-hazardous waste, to create the very conditions that justify a decision not to regulate a waste as hazardous in the first place. It is even more remarkable to claim authority to avoid legal requirements, such as "land disposal restrictions," which would otherwise apply if the waste were classified as hazardous.

Indeed, there is a quality of optical illusion about EPA's approach; it is both appealing and disturbing. Viewed from one perspective, it is simply an attempt to define those conditions under which wastes will satisfy the criteria for classification as a hazardous waste. Viewed from another perspective, it is EPA's imposition of an entire regulatory program on materials without either invoking the statutory requirement for classification as a hazardous waste or complying with mandatory statutory consequences that flow from that classification.

The legality of "contingent management" has not been fully resolved. In *Military Toxics Project v. EPA*, 146 F.3d 948 (D.C. Cir. 1998), the court upheld EPA's authority to "conditionally" exempt certain military munitions from classification as a hazardous waste. The conditional exclusions in that case, however, involved compliance with existing regulations imposed by the Department of Defense and Department of Transportation. No court has yet addressed the issue of whether EPA can exclude a waste from classification as a hazardous waste based on conditions that EPA itself has established under RCRA.

PROBLEM

Company A generates a liquid waste containing levels of benzene that would meet the Toxicity Characteristic for classification as a hazardous waste. The Company has three alternatives for dealing with the waste. First, it can send the waste off-site for disposal. Second, it can treat the waste in an on-site wastewater treatment system that is regulated under a National Pollutant Discharge Elimination System ("NPDES") permit. Third, it can put the dump the waste into its industrial sewer that connects to the municipal sewage treatment works. Is the waste regulated as a RCRA hazardous waste under any of these options?

C. REGULATION OF HAZARDOUS WASTES UNDER SUBTITLE C

Subtitle C is said to regulate hazardous waste from "cradle to grave," and it contains regulatory requirements applicable to each step in the hazardous waste management process from generation, to transportation, to disposal.

1. GENERATORS

Generators are those entities whose actions result in a material initially being regulated as a hazardous waste. *See* 40 C.F.R. § 260.10 (Definition of "Generator"). Although not subject to a federal permit requirement, generators are subject to significant regulatory requirements. EPA regulations focus on regulating generators who produce a significant amount of hazardous waste. Large quantity generators ("LQG"), generally those producing 1000 kilograms per month or more of hazardous waste, and small quantity generators ("SQG"), those producing between 100 and 1000 kg/month of hazardous waste, are subject to similar set of requirements. Small quantity generators are subject to slightly less stringent requirements relating to reporting, training and on-site accumulation. In contrast, "conditionally exempt small quantity generators" ("CESQG"), generators who produce 100 kg/month of hazardous waste or less, are largely exempt from regulation under Subtitle C. Do not confuse small quantity generators, largely subject to full regulation under Subtitle C, with conditionally exempt small quantity generators.

Classification of generator status is made on a month-by-month basis. In other words, if, in any one month, a generator produces more than 100 kg/month of hazardous waste it will be subject to full RCRA regulation for that month.

EPA Summary of Generator Requirements

http://www.epa.gov/epawaste/hazard/generation/summary.htm

	CESQGs	SQGs	LQGs
Quantity Limits	≤100 kg/month ≤1 kg/month of acute hazardous waste ≤100 kg/month of acute spill residue or soil §§ 261.5(a) and (e)	Between 100–1,000 kg/month § 262.34(d)	≥1,000 kg/month 1 kg/month of acute hazardous waste 100 kg/month of acute spill residue or soil Part 262 and § 261.5(e)
EPA ID Number	Not required § 261.5	Required § 261.12	Required § 262.12
On–Site Accumulation Quantity	≤1,000 kg ≤1 kg acute ≤100 kg of acute spill residue or soil §§ 261.5(f)(2) and (g)(2)	≤6,000 kg § 262.34(d)(1)	No limit
Accumulation Time Limits	None § 261.5	≤180 days or ≤270 days (if greater than 200 miles) §§ 262.34(d)(2) and (3)	≤90 days § 262.34(a)
Storage Requirements	None § 261.5	Basic requirements with technical standards for tanks or containers §§ 262.34(d)(2) and (3)	Full compliance for management of tanks, containers, drip pads, or containment buildings § 262.34(a)
Sent To:	State approved or RCRA permitted/interim status facility §§ 261.5(f)(3) and (g)(3)	RCRA permitted/interim status facility § 262.20(b)	RCRA permitted/interim status facility § 262.20(b)
Manifest	Not required § 261.5	Required § 261.20	Required § 261.20
Biennial Report	Not required § 261.5	Not required § 262.44	Required § 262.41
Personnel Training	Not required § 261.5	Basic training required § 262.34(d)(5)(iii)	Required § 262.34(a)(4)
Contingency Plan	Not required § 261.5	Basic plan § 262.34(d)(5)(i)	Full plan required § 262.34(a)(4)

	CESQGs	**SQGs**	**LQGs**
Emergency Procedures	Not required § 261.5	Basic plan § 262.34(d)(5)(iv)	Full plan required § 262.34(a)(4)
DOT Transport Requirements	Yes (if required by DOT)	Yes §§ 262.30–262.33	Yes §§ 262.30–262.33

a.   LARGE AND SMALL QUANTITY GENERATORS

i.   *Identification*

Perhaps the single most important obligation on a generator is to identify whether it produces a hazardous waste. As discussed above, the question of whether a material is classified as a RCRA Subtitle C hazardous waste can be difficult to answer, but the responsibility is placed on the generator to make that determination. Generators are also required to determine each waste code classification that applies to its wastes. If a waste is listed and exhibits several hazard characteristics, the generator is required to identify each of the applicable waste codes. This is important in order to satisfy "land disposal restrictions" discussed below. Generators are not required to test their wastes to see if they exhibit a hazard characteristic, they may rely on their "knowledge of process" to make the determination, but the generator is responsible for correctly classifying its wastes.

ii.   *Reporting and Recordkeeping*

Each large and small quantity generator is required to notify the government and receive a hazardous waste generator "identification number." Obtaining a RCRA ID number is not like obtaining a permit; the ID number is simply issued by the government upon notification that the facility is a RCRA generator. The ID number is used to identify the generator in its reports and manifests.

In addition to the one-time notification of its status as a generator, large quantity generators are required to submit biennial reports to the government regulatory authority that contain information about the amount and types of wastes the large quantity generator produces.

iii.   *On-site Accumulation and Treatment*

Although "treatment, storage or disposal" of a hazardous waste can generally only be done at a federally permitted RCRA facility, generators are allowed to accumulate wastes on-site for a limited period of time without a permit. For a large quantity generator, wastes may be accumulated for up to ninety days; for a small quantity generator, on-site accumulation may occur for up to 180 days. Wastes accumulated on-site are subject to management requirements and each accumulation site must identify the date at which accumulation commenced. Generators accumulating wastes on-site are also subject to certain personnel training and emergency response planning requirements.

EPA regulations allow on-site accumulation, but they are silent as to whether a facility may, without obtaining a TSDF permit, treat its wastes on-site during that period to avoid the need for off-site disposal. In a series of preamble statements and policy guidance documents, EPA has taken the position that hazardous wastes may be treated during the accumulation period without triggering permit requirements. See, e.g., 57 Fed Reg. 37194 (August 18, 1992); RCRA Training Manual, Introduction to Generators, EPA530–K–05–011 (May 2007) at 8. EPA's regulations defining solid waste also exclude, in certain circumstances, materials that are reclaimed on-site. *See* 40 C.F.R. §§ 261.2(a)(ii), 261.4(a)(23).

iv.   *Off–Site Shipment*

Hazardous wastes may not be stored, treated or disposed on-site beyond the accumulation period without triggering the need to obtain a RCRA TSDF permit. Generators who do not have a TSDF permit must ship wastes off-site for disposal or treatment. Off-site shipments are subject to a variety of requirements: generators may in most cases only send the wastes to a facility that has a TSDF permit; the wastes must be packaged and labeled in compliance with EPA requirements; generators may only send wastes using transporters that have an EPA ID number.

Additionally, the wastes must be accompanied by a signed EPA "manifest." This manifest is a key component of the system. In addition to specifying the TSDFs to which the waste may be shipped and information about the waste, the manifest is the tracking document that ensures that the waste actually ends up at the specified facility. The generator, along with each transporter, must sign the manifest. When received by the final TSDF, a signed copy of the completed manifest must be returned to the original generator. If the generator has not received the signed copy of the manifest within a certain number of days (35 days for a large quantity generator, 90 days for a small quantity generator) of initial shipment of the waste, the generator must file an "exception report" to the government.

EPA Form 8700-22 (Rev. 3-05) — Uniform Hazardous Waste Manifest (VOID)

v. Waste Minimization and Pollution Prevention

RCRA, the federal Pollution Prevention Act and EPA policy statements all indicate that "waste minimization," also referred to as "pollution prevention," is preferred to disposal or recycling of waste. Perhaps the most significant "waste minimization" element of RCRA is the high cost of disposal of hazardous waste at a permitted TSDF; these costs create economic incentives to minimize the amount of hazardous wastes generated.

EPA regulations require generators to certify that they have taken steps to minimize their wastes. A large quantity generator must certify that: "I have a program in place to reduce the volume and toxicity of waste generated to the degree I have determined to be economically practicable and I have selected the practicable method of treatment, storage, or disposal currently available to me which minimizes the present and future threat to human health and the environment." 40 C.F.R. § 262.27(a). A small quantity generator, in contrast, need only certify that it has made a "good faith" effort "to minimize my waste generation and select the best waste management method that is available to me and that I can afford." 40 C.F.R. § 262.27(b). Note that the RCRA manifest requires that generators to certify that they have complied with these requirements. This certification is contained in manifests used by generators, and large quantity generators are also required to certify in their biennial reports that they have complied with their waste minimization requirements.

Despite the requirement for formal certification, the waste minimization requirements are largely contentless. The legislative history of the waste minimization provision indicates that criteria for satisfying the certification are to be established by generators and are not subject to review by EPA. S. Rep. No. 284, 98th Cong., 1st Sess. 66 (1983). In draft guidance, EPA has declined to give any interpretation of the key term "economically practicable." 54 Fed. Reg. 25,056 (1989). In other words, generators may be required to document some efforts at waste minimization, but there may be no federal requirements under RCRA on the content of such efforts.

b. CONDITIONALLY EXEMPT SMALL QUANTITY GENERATORS

EPA regulations largely exempt from regulation those generators that produce 100 kilograms per month or less of hazardous waste (approximately one 55 gallon drum of waste). *See* 40 C.F.R. § 261.5. These generators are known as "conditionally exempt small quantity generators" ("CESQGs"). CESQGs are not required to obtain ID numbers; they are not required to dispose of their hazardous waste in a permitted TSDF; they are not subject to manifest requirements, and they may accumulate up to a total of 1000 kilograms of hazardous waste on-site without a RCRA storage permit.

CESQGs are, however, required to properly dispose or recycle its wastes. This can be done by disposal of the hazardous waste at a municipal solid waste landfill. This CESQG requirement is one reason, together with the household hazardous waste exclusion, that municipal solid waste landfills may receive substantial quantities of hazardous waste.

Classification as a CESQG is made on a month-by-month basis. If a facility generates more than 100 kilograms of hazardous waste in one month, that waste is subject to the full requirements of Subtitle C. EPA does not, however, apply the mixture rule to CESQG wastes. *See* 40 C.F.R. § 261.5(h). Thus a conditionally exempt small quantity generator can mix small amounts of listed wastes with other non-hazardous wastes without the entire mixture counting towards the quantity of wastes generated.

NOTES AND QUESTIONS

1. *On-site Management of Wastes.* As a general matter, generators cannot treat, store or dispose of hazardous wastes on-site without obtaining

a Subtitle C permit. As noted, however, EPA policy statements indicate that a generator may engage in treatment of wastes during the "accumulation" period without triggering the need for a permit. Additionally, as discussed below, EPA regulations provide a "conditional exemption" that allows generators to reclaim "hazardous secondary materials" on-site." 40 C.F.R. § 261.2(a)(ii); § 261.4(a)(23). The exclusion exempts the materials from being classified as a solid waste, and therefore any permit requirement for treatment of hazardous wastes is avoided.

2. *Universal wastes.* The regulatory requirements that apply to generators and transporters of hazardous waste can act as an impediment to recycling. To minimize these disincentives, EPA has established special rules for a limited class of "universal wastes." *See* 40 C.F.R. Part 273. The universal wastes rules establish minimal requirements for persons who generate, store, and transport certain batteries, pesticides, and mercury-containing equipment. Although a main objective of the rules is to encourage increased recycling of these wastes, the rules apply regardless of whether the wastes are being managed for recycling or disposal.

3. *Generator pollution prevention requirements.* Although RCRA imposes only limited "pollution prevention" obligations on generators, pollution prevention and waste minimization are explicit goals of RCRA. *See* RCRA § 1003(b). Congress also adopted the Pollution Prevention Act of 1990 that explicitly adopts a national policy to encourage pollution prevention:

> The Congress hereby declares it to be the national policy of the United States that pollution should be prevented or reduced at the source whenever feasible; pollution that cannot be prevented should be recycled in an environmentally safe manner, whenever feasible; pollution that cannot be prevented or recycled should be treated in an environmentally safe manner whenever feasible; and disposal or other release into the environment should be employed only as a last resort and should be conducted in an environmentally safe manner.

42 U.S.C. § 13101(b). Despite its goals, the Pollution Prevention Act contains almost no substantive pollution prevention requirements. Its only mandatory provision that affects industry is a requirement that facilities filing toxic chemical release forms under Title III of the Emergency Planning Community Right-to-Know Act ("EPCRA") information on source reduction and recycling activities. 42 U.S.C. § 13106(a). *See* Jeffrey M. Gaba and Donald Stever, The Law of Solid Waste, Pollution Prevention and Recycling § 9:6.

In 1989, EPA issued a Pollution Prevention Policy Statement that states EPA's intention to encourage source reduction and, secondarily, recycling, to reduce pollution 54 Fed. Reg. 3,845 (1989). EPA has established an Office of Pollution Prevention that provides pollution prevention grants and provides information "clearinghouse" and technical assistance to persons seeking to recycle materials. *See* www.epa.gov/oppt/p2home/.

Another way in which RCRA promotes recycling is through its Federal procurement requirements. Under the provisions of § 6002 of RCRA and

Executive Order 12873, EPA issues Comprehensive Procurement Guidelines and Recovered Materials Advisory Notices that specify purchasing requirements for federal agencies that require the purchase of specified item manufactured with recycled materials. *See* 40 C.F.R. Part 247.

2. TRANSPORTERS

EPA establishes a limited set of requirements on the off-site transportation of hazardous waste. 40 C.F.R. Part 263. Hazardous waste transporters are not required under RCRA to obtain a permit, but they must obtain an EPA Identification number, transport wastes only if it the wastes are accompanied by a manifest, and deliver the wastes only to another transporter or permitted TSDF facility. The regulations authorize transporters to store hazardous waste without a permit for up to ten days during transit. Each transporter must sign the manifest when it is passed to the next transporter or permitted TSDF. EPA and the Department of Transportation have established consistent requirements for packaging and labeling of hazardous wastes in transit. EPA regulations impose requirements on the transporter to provide notification and take immediate response if there is a release of hazardous wastes in transit.

3. TSDFs

Most facilities that "treat, store or dispose" of hazardous wastes are required to obtain a RCRA TSDF permit. This permit requirement applies, for example, to facilities at which hazardous waste is permanently disposed of, such as hazardous waste landfills or incinerators. The permit requirement also applies to facilities that "treat" hazardous waste to reduce its toxicity or that "store" hazardous waste prior to disposal or treatment.

Obtaining a RCRA TSDF permit can be costly and time-consuming. The permit itself can contain a range of requirements designed to minimize the environmental threats from the waste, and the permit process itself is complex and time-consuming.

a. PERMIT REQUIREMENTS

Facilities that are required to obtain a RCRA permit are subject to a range of permit obligations. In addition to a variety of general requirements involving personnel training, recordkeeping and reporting, RCRA TSDFs are required to comply with requirements addressing the following issues:

i. *Technology Standards*

EPA regulations establish a variety of technology requirements that vary depending on the type of TSDF. Hazardous waste "landfills" are subject to very detailed requirements that specify the number and composition of "liners" that must be placed in the landfill prior to receiving hazardous waste. These liners are designed to limit the capacity of hazardous wastes to leach from the landfill and enter groundwater. In most cases, hazardous waste landfills are required to have two or "double" liners. Between the two liners, facilities are required to have a "leak detection" system to indicate if there has been a breach in the first liner. Hazardous waste incinerators are subject to complex technical requirements on the operation of the incinerator and limitations on the emissions of hazardous constituents from incomplete incinerations. Tank systems used to store hazardous wastes are also subject to specific requirements on construction and containment in the event of releases.

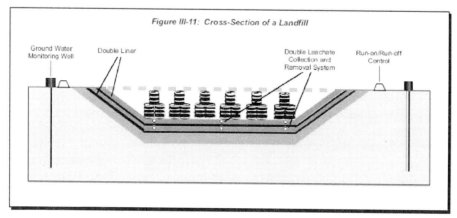

From RCRA Orientation Manual at III–67.

ii.   Closure and Post–Closure Requirements

One of the major concerns associated with operation of a hazardous waste disposal facility is that the operator will abandon the facility once it can no longer obtain a profit by receiving new wastes. As part of the process of initially obtaining a TSDF permit, facilities are generally required to prepare plans for closure of the facility and post-closure management of the facility.

iii.   Financial Assurance

To assure that there is adequate money to undertake closure and post-closure care, facilities obtaining a RCRA permit are generally required to satisfy "financial assurance" requirements. These provisions are complex, but they allow the permittee to document the future availability of adequate money through a variety of techniques such as bonds or financial commitments of parent companies.

Facilities obtaining a TSDF permit are also required to provide financial assurance that they can, within specified limits, provide compensation for personal injury or property damage resulting from an accidental release from the facility.

iv.   Groundwater Monitoring and Corrective Action for Releases

RCRA permits will contain a variety of requirements that ensure that a facility will identify any releases of hazardous wastes and take steps to correct the release. In the case of landfills, these requirements involve placement and sampling of groundwater monitoring wells to detect increases of hazardous constituents resulting from releases from the facility.

v.   Corrective Action for SWMUs.

Facilities seeking RCRA permits are required identify and clean past releases of "hazardous waste or constituents." from "solid waste management units" (SWMUs) located at the facility. *See generally* Joseph F. Guida, "Corrective Action under the Resource Conservation and Recovery Act," 44 Sw. L.J. 1331 (1991) for an excellent discussion of the corrective action program. This "corrective action" requirement not only applies to past releases at SWMUs regardless of when the material was placed in the unit, but the cleanup requirement extends to areas of the facility that are not used as a TSDF. EPA has interpreted these sections to allow corrective action even when the release does not involve materials defined as hazardous wastes under its regulatory definition. The "corrective action" program in fact expands Subtitle C to allow regulation of materials containing "hazardous constituents" and materials that are hazardous wastes under the statutory definition in 1003(5). *See* 55 Fed. Reg. 30798, 30809 (1990). The RCRA permit will typically will contain enforceable requirements relating to cleanup of the SWMUs identified during the permit process.

b.   PERMIT PROCESS

All RCRA permits were initially issued by EPA, but RCRA allows States to seek delegation of permit issuing authority to facilities within their jurisdiction. EPA approves a State request for permit issuance authority if the State demonstrates that it has authority to issue RCRA permits that is substantially equivalent to the federal requirements. Today, all 50 states have authority to issue RCRA permits, and facilities seeking a RCRA permit apply to the applicable State permitting authority.

Under EPA regulations, a facility seeking a TSDF permit must submit a two part permit application. Part A contains general information about the facility, such as the facility name and location and the type of hazardous waste it will handle. Part A of the application is submitted on a standard form. In contrast, Part B of the application can be extremely long and complex, and contains detailed information including geologic, hydrologic and other technical information about the facility and proposed waste management practices. Part B of the permit application can consist of many volumes of information.

The EPA permit issuance process involves a number of steps including:

- Informal meeting prior to application
- Permit submission
- Permit review
- Preparation of the draft permit
- Taking public comment
- Finalizing the permit.

See RCRA Orientation Manual: Chapter III Managing Hazardous Waste—RCRA Subtitle C, Permitting of Treatment, Storage and Disposal Facilities, III–111–117, http://www.epa.gov/waste/inforesources/pubs/orientat/rom3.-pdf

A "final" RCRA permit is generally subject to an administrative appeal process which may include some form of adjudicatory hearing. These hearings can resemble mini-trials and are subject to their own rules of procedure. If appealed, a RCRA permit is only "final" after it has completed the agency review process, and, at that point, the permit may be subject to judicial review.

NOTES AND QUESTIONS

1. *Exceptions to the permit requirement.* Although the RCRA TSDF permit requirement is one of the most important components of the Subtitle C cradle-to-grave program, there are significant exceptions. The following are some, but not all, of the situations in which hazardous waste can be treated, stored or disposed of without a RCRA permit:

- On-site treatment or storage during the generator accumulation period;
- Management of materials that are excluded from classification as a hazardous waste;
- Disposal of hazardous wastes generated by a Conditionally Exempt Small Quantity Generator;
- Storage during transportation of the waste;
- Activities that are specifically authorized under a "permit-by-rule." Certain activities, including operation of an active wastewater treatment facility or an "elementary neutralization" unit, can be conducted without a RCRA permit;
- Operation under permits issued under certain other statutes. Disposal of hazardous waste through underground injection into a well is governed by permits issued under the Safe Drinking Water Act and ocean disposal of wastes, if authorized, would be governed by the Ocean Dumping provisions of the Marine Protection Research and Sanctuaries Act;
- Recycling processes governed by 40 CFR Part 268, including, for example, the burning of hazardous wastes in "boilers and industrial furnaces," are subject to special regulations that may not require a RCRA permit;
- EPA has established a special regulatory program applicable to a designated group of "universal wastes" to facilitate the collection and recycling of certain specified hazardous wastes. These designated "universal wastes," include, for example, mercury containing switches. Universal waste storage and recycling facilities are exempt from RCRA permit requirements.
- On-site management of hazardous waste as part of an emergency response to a release or as part of remediation conducted under the Comprehensive Environmental Response Compensation and Liability Act.

2. *Interim status.* When RCRA was first adopted in 1976, Congress recognized that there would be a transition period during which EPA would be issuing regulations and facilities would be preparing to meet requirements to obtain a TSDF permit. RCRA therefore contained provisions for facilities to obtain "interim status" to receive hazardous wastes without fully satisfying the requirements to obtain final TSDF permit. Facilities initially seeking interim status essentially had only to notify EPA of their existence and submit a permit application. Interim status was available to facilities in existence as of November, 1980. *See* RCRA § 3005(e)(1). Congress modified RCRA to require land disposal facilities that had obtained interim status facilities before November 1984 to meet minimum requirements for groundwater protection and financial assurance within a year of the November 1984 cutoff or close. *See* RCRA § 3005(e)(2).

Although most interim status facilities have now either closed or received a final permit, there is at least one situation in which "interim status" may still be available. Facilities that are in existence when EPA first promulgates regulations making them subject to Subtitle C may obtain interim status. *See* RCRA § 3005(e)(1)(A)(ii); 40 C.F.R. § 270.10(e). Thus, if EPA adds a new listed hazardous waste, facilities that "treat, store or dispose" of this newly listed waste may obtain interim status for a period until they receive a final RCRA permit. Facilities that obtained interim status (or should have obtained interim status) were subject to requirement to undertake "corrective action" to clean up their facility under § 3008(v) of RCRA.

3. *Duration / Transfer / Modification of permits.* RCRA permits can be issued for a maximum of 10 years. 40 C.F.R. § 270.5(a). Permittees that, for example, sell a permitted facility must separately apply for a transfer of the permit to the new owner or operator of the facility. 40 C.F. R. § 270.40.

RCRA permits can be modified for cause by the permit authority or on the request of the permittee. RCRA regulations provide varying procedures for "Class 1, Class 2, and Class 3" modifications of permits. *See* 40 C.F.R. § 270.42. Class 1 permit modifications, such as permit transfers, have limited procedural obligations. Class 2 and Class 3 have increasingly stringent procedural requirements including expanded requirements for public notice and opportunity for a public hearing. The regulations contain an Appendix which lists the classification of various types of permit modifications.

4. RCRA *Preemption and More Stringent State Requirements.* RCRA does not preempt the field of hazardous waste regulation, and it has an express "savings clause" authorizes States to adopt requirements that are more stringent than those established by RCRA. RCRA § 3009. One court has stated that "RCRA sets a floor, not a ceiling for State regulation of hazardous waste." *Old Bridge Chemicals, Inc. v. New Jersey Dept. of Environmental Protection* 965 F.2d 1287, 1296 (3d Cir. 1992) (upholding more stringent state regulation of recycled hazardous waste). Federal requirements, however, apply in case of conflict with a State. *See, e.g., Boyes v. Shell Oil Products, Co.,* 199 F.3d 1260 (11th Cir. 2000) (State provisions regarding remediation of underground storage tanks are preempted to the

extent they directly conflict with federal requirements). Additionally, there are complex enforcement issues relating to the effect of state enforcement on federal authority. These issues are discussed below in the section D.4.

5. *EPA/State Joint Permitting.* Although all States have RCRA permitting authority, in some cases EPA must also be involved in permit issuance. Certain RCRA regulations issued under the requirements of the 1984 Hazardous and Solid Waste Amendments ("HSWA") cannot be implemented by a State until the State revise its hazardous waste programs to reflect the changes and obtains EPA approval of the revised regulations. *See* 40 C.F.R. § 271.1(f) (list of HSWA issued regulations). Until the State has received approval of these revisions, EPA remains responsible for inclusion of those provisions in the state-issued RCRA permit. This means that in many cases, a RCRA permit will contain one set of state issued requirements and a separate section for federally imposed requirements, and a permit applicant may be required to deal both with the State and EPA. When EPA issues a revised RCRA regulation, the preamble will typically include a description of which changes can be immediately implemented by States and which are implemented by EPA until the State revises its regulations and receives EPA approval.

4.   Land Disposal Restrictions

"Land disposal" of hazardous waste is generally considered the most environmentally threatening form of disposal. It is difficult to permanently contain hazardous wastes in a landfill and hazardous constituents may leach into the groundwater. Although hazardous waste landfills can be granted a TSDF permit, EPA has established stringent requirements for liners to prevent leaking and for monitoring to detect releases.

In the 1984 Hazard and Solid Waste Amendments, Congress amended RCRA to limit the use of land disposal. Under the "land disposal restriction" ("LDR") provisions of § 3004(d)–(k) and (m), (also known as the "land ban" provisions) land disposal of hazardous waste is generally prohibited except in two cases. First, land disposal is allowed at a facility that has petitioned for and received a no migration variance. These "no migration" variances can be granted to facilities that satisfy detailed requirements to demonstrate that hazardous wastes cannot migrate from the facility. *See* 40 C.F.R. § 268.6. Most of the approved "no migration" variances have been granted for underground injection of hazardous waste into formations located deep underground. *See Introduction to Land Disposal Restrictions,* EPA503–K–05–013 (Sept. 2005), http://www.epa.gov/osw/inforesources/pubs/hotline/training/ldr05.pdf.

The second basis on which hazardous wastes may be land disposed is far more common. Land disposal is authorized if the hazardous waste has been treated to the level or by the method of treatment that EPA has determined will "substantially diminish the toxicity or substantially reduce the likelihood of migration of hazardous constituents from the waste," RCRA § 3004(m); 40 C.F.R. § 268.40. EPA has implemented the "substantially diminish" standard by authorizing the land disposal of wastes that have been "pretreated" to meet standards based on "best demonstrated available technology" ("BDAT") prior to land disposal. These pretreatment requirements in some cases require a generator to treat wastes so that they contain no greater than specified concentrations of hazardous constituents. EPA has promulgated a long list of "universal treatment standards" ("UTS") that set maximum concentrations for hazardous constituents. *See* 40 C.F.R. § 268.40. In other cases, the LDR specifies a specific type of treatment, such as metals reclamation, that must be used. *See* 40 C.F.R. §§ 268.40, 268.42. EPA has also established a general "dilution prohibition" that prohibits attainment of pretreatment requirements through dilution of the wastes. *See* 40 C.F.R. § 268.3.

To comply with the land disposal restrictions, a generator is now required, among other things, to:

- determine all of the various bases on which the waste might be considered hazardous,

- identify each "underlying hazardous constituent" which is defined to include specific constituents listed in the Universal Treatment Standard table that are "reasonably expected to be present" at a level above the UTS standard,

- check the regulations to determine the necessary pretreatment requirements and apply the most stringent of the applicable standards,

- satisfy certain notice requirements relating to compliance with the land ban requirements.

One of the most confusing parts of the LDR requirements is their application to characteristic wastes. Under EPA regulations, a characteristic waste is no longer hazardous waste once it ceases to exhibit a hazard characteristic. *See* 40 C.F.R. § 261.3(c),(d)(1). Nonetheless, LDRs can continue to apply to a waste that is no longer hazardous if it was originally classified as a characteristic waste. Therefore, to apply LDR's the generator must determine the initial "point of generation" of the hazardous waste. If a waste exhibited a hazard characteristic at the point it first became a waste it is subject to LDR requirements even if it subsequently no longer exhibits a characteristic.

For most Toxicity Characteristic wastes there are specific required forms of treatment or UTS treatment levels for the "underlying chemical constituents." For most ICR [ignitable, corrosive, reactive] wastes, the treatment standards include "deactivation" (or removal of the hazard characteristic) and treatment of the "underlying chemical constituents" to UTS levels. For some limited number of ICR wastes specific treatment methods are required. Dilution is not allowed as a means of meeting standards unless the dilution occurs as part of treatment in a Clean Water Act treatment system.

The application of LDR's to characteristic wastes was addressed in *Chemical Waste Management v. EPA.*

Chemical Waste Management v. EPA

976 F.2d 2 (D.C. Cir. 1992)

The Hazardous and Solid Waste Amendments of 1984 instituted a ban on the land disposal of classes of hazardous wastes unless certain conditions are met. Those amendments require the Environmental Protection Agency to follow a phased schedule for implementing the ban. In this case we consider various challenges to regulations implementing the final portion of this program, the so-called "third-third" rule, which largely covers the land disposal of wastes deemed hazardous because they possess certain defined characteristics.

I. STATUTORY AND REGULATORY BACKGROUND

Subtitle C of the Resource Conservation and Recovery Act sets out a comprehensive regulatory system governing the treatment, storage, and disposal of hazardous wastes. Wastes are deemed hazardous in one of two ways: they possess one of the four hazardous characteristics identified by the EPA in 40 C.F.R. Part 261, Subpart C ("characteristic wastes"), *see id.* § 261.3(a)(2)(i) (1991), or they have been found to be hazardous as a result of an EPA rulemaking. *See id.* Part 261, Subpart D ("listed wastes").

The four characteristics identified as hazardous are ignitability, corrosivity, reactivity, and extraction procedure ("EP") toxicity. The hazards presented by ignitable, corrosive, and reactive ("ICR") wastes are primarily, though not exclusively, the results of their physical properties. *See* 45 Fed.Reg. 33,066, 33,107–10 (1980). EP characteristic wastes contain toxic constituents. *Id.* at 33,107–12. These wastes remain hazardous until they cease to exhibit any of the characteristics identified in Subpart C. Characteristic wastes comprise over fifty percent of all the hazardous wastes generated in the United States each year.

Although the EPA may list a waste if it possesses one of the four characteristics described above, in practice it will only list specific wastes that are either acutely hazardous or possess high levels of toxic constituents. A listed waste loses its hazardous status only after a petition for its "delisting" is approved by the EPA in a notice-and-comment rulemaking.

"Once a waste is listed or identified as hazardous, its subsequent management is regulated" under subtitle C of RCRA. *American Petroleum Inst. v. EPA,* 906 F.2d 729, 733 (D.C.Cir.1990) ("*API*"). The waste enters RCRA's "cradle-to-grave" regulatory system; and "the waste's treatment, storage, and disposal is usually regulated by permit." *American Mining Congress v. EPA,* 907 F.2d 1179, 1182 (D.C.Cir.1990) ("*AMC II*"); *see also* RCRA §§ 3001–3004, 42 U.S.C. §§ 6921–6924. The management of a hazardous waste continues "until such time as it ceases to pose a hazard to the public." *Shell Oil,* 950 F.2d at 754.

Because "certain classes of land disposal facilities are not capable of assuring long-term containment of certain hazardous wastes," RCRA § 1002(b)(7), Congress amended subtitle C in 1984 to prohibit land disposal of many hazardous wastes. The Hazardous and Solid Waste Amendments of 1984, ("1984 Amendments"), gave the EPA significant authority to regulate land disposal. The statute expressed a general policy preference that "reliance on land disposal should be minimized or eliminated." RCRA § 1002(b)(7). A prohibition on disposal would apply unless the waste is treated so as to minimize the short-term and long-term threats to human health and the environment posed by toxic and hazardous constituents, RCRA § 3004(m), or unless the EPA finds that no migration of hazardous constituents from the facility will occur after disposal. *Id.* § 3004(g)(5).

The 1984 Amendments specifically required the EPA to follow a phased schedule to implement the land disposal ban. They forbade the land disposal of hazardous wastes containing solvents and dioxins after November 8, 1986. RCRA § 3004(e). A select list of other wastes were barred from land disposal after July 8, 1987 ("California list" wastes). *Id.* § 3004(d). Finally, the amendments ordered the Agency to rank all remaining hazardous wastes on the basis of their intrinsic hazard and the volume generated annually and to divide the list into three parts. *Id.* § 3004(g)(4). The Administrator was then charged with the task of promulgating final regulations for each third of the list. *See id.* § 3004(g)(5). Unless the Administrator promulgated regulations for wastes in the last third of the list by May 8, 1990, they could not be land disposed. *Id.* § 3004(g)(6)(C).

Under the 1984 Amendments, the final regulations must:

> prohibit[ ] one or more methods of land disposal of the hazardous wastes listed on such schedule except for methods of land disposal which the Administrator determines will be protective of human health and the environment for as long as the waste remains hazardous.... For the purposes of this paragraph, a method of land disposal may not be determined to be protective of human health and the environment (except with respect to a hazardous waste which has complied with the pretreatment regulations promulgated under subsection (m) of this section) unless, upon application by an interested person, it has been demonstrated to the Administrator, to a reasonable degree of certainty, that there will be no migration of hazardous constituents from the disposal unit or injection zone for as long as the wastes remain hazardous.

RCRA § 3004(g)(5). The Administrator must also promulgate treatment standards, compliance with which will authorize land disposal, at the same time he publishes the land ban. The treatment regulations shall:

> specify[ ] those levels or methods of treatment, if any, which substantially diminish the toxicity of the waste or substantially reduce the likelihood of migration of hazardous constituents from the waste so that short-term and long-term threats to human health and the environment are minimized.

Id. § 3004(m)(1).

The regulations under review implement the land-ban program for the last third of the ranked list of wastes, the "third-third." They largely consist of treatment standards for characteristic wastes. The final rule also modifies regulations governing characteristic wastes that are managed in treatment systems regulated through National Pollutant Discharge Elimination System permits issued under the Clean Water Act as well as regulations affecting those disposed of in underground injection wells regulated under the Safe Drinking Water Act. The rule establishes a variety of compliance requirements as well.

II. TREATMENT STANDARDS FOR CHARACTERISTIC WASTES

Industry petitioners contend that RCRA does not provide authority for the EPA to mandate treatment of characteristic wastes after their ignitability, corrosiveness, reactivity, or EP toxicity has been addressed. They make a straightforward argument: Subtitle C regulations attach to a waste only when it is hazardous. The moment a waste ceases to meet the regulatory definition of a hazardous waste, the EPA loses its authority to regulate further. Thus, in industry petitioners' view, RCRA's cradle-to-grave system covers waste only if it remains hazardous throughout its life and at the moment of its burial.

Industry petitioners point to a welter of provisions in RCRA where the words "hazardous waste" are used as proof that the statute applies only to waste defined as hazardous. Subtitle C, they explain, is entitled "Hazardous Waste Management," and the entire subtitle addresses that problem—the management of *hazardous* waste. They add that some statements by the EPA have suggested the same reading of the statute.

In their view, the 1984 Amendments did not change this boundary. They point out that land disposal is defined in part as "any placement of such hazardous waste in a landfill, [or] surface impoundment," RCRA § 3004(k), that section 3004(g) similarly "prohibit[s] one or more methods of land disposal of [ ] hazardous wastes," and, finally, that section 3004(m) authorizes land disposal of hazardous waste that has been treated, suggesting to industry petitioners that the provision specifically authorizes only the disposal of wastes that remain hazardous after treatment. Thus, they conclude, the disposal restrictions can apply only to wastes that are hazardous at the moment of disposal.

In its brief, the EPA reiterates the rationales stated in its final rule: The key provisions of the land-ban program, sections 3004(g)(5) and (m), can be read as allowing the Agency to apply land disposal restrictions at any time it wishes; those provisions at a minimum contemplate activity that occurs before land disposal; section 3004(m)(1) requires treatment to avoid the prohibition on land disposal; and treatment must take place, by definition, before disposal occurs. This reading, the EPA adds, dovetails with the concern expressed in the report accompanying the Senate version of the 1984 Amendments, that hazardous waste not be diluted and then disposed of in landfills. The Agency reasons that the subtitle C program can attach at the point of generation, and the broad language of section 3004(m)(1) allows additional treatment to remove risks posed by wastes beyond those inherent in the characteristic.

To succeed in their *Chevron* step one argument, industry petitioners must show that Congress "has directly spoken to the precise question at issue" and has "unambiguously expressed [its] intent." We find little support in the statute or our prior decisions for the notion that Congress mandated the line industry petitioners draw. These petitioners believe that the definition of a hazardous waste acts as a revolving regulatory door, allowing continual entrance and egress from RCRA's requirements. The key provisions of the statute support a contrary view—that hazardous waste becomes subject to the land disposal program as soon as it is generated.

In *HWTC III,* the Chemical Manufacturer's Association ("CMA") attacked treatment standards for solvents under the land disposal program because the EPA required treatment of all solvents, not simply those deemed unsafe. The CMA argued that this regime could result in treatment "below established levels of hazard," and therefore was an unreasonable interpretation of the Act. We disagreed, noting that section 3004(m) demands that treatment minimize risks to health and the environment. Treatment might be unreasonable, we added, if the EPA required treatment of wastes that "posed no threat to human health or the environment." That was not the case in *HWTC III,* nor is it true here.

We conclude that, in combination, sections 3004(g)(5) and (m) provide the EPA with authority to bar land disposal of certain wastes unless they have been treated to reduce risks beyond those presented by the characteristics themselves. We also find the Agency's assertion of regulatory authority over the wastes from the moment they are generated to be "based on a permissible construction of the statute."

NOTES AND QUESTIONS

1. *Technology-based LDRs.* Most LDR standards are set at levels that can be achieved by use of "best demonstrated available technology" ("BDAT"). This is a form of technology-based standard, and the LDR standard is based on what technology can achieve, not the environmental or human health need for the standard. In *Hazardous Waste Treatment Council v. EPA*, 886 F.2d 355 (D.C. Cir. 1989) (referred to as *HWTC III* by the court in *Chemical Waste Management* above), the court addressed industry claims that EPA could not set LDRs based on BDAT technology standards. Industry argued that LDR standards could not require treatment beyond some health "screening level." The court upheld EPA's authority to implement the provisions of RCRA § 3004(m) through use of technology-based standards stating:

> The statute directs EPA to set treatment standards based upon either "levels or methods" of treatment. Such a mandate makes clear that the choice whether to use "levels" (screening levels) or "methods" (BDAT) lies within the informed discretion of the agency, as long as the result is "that short-term and long-term threats to human health and the environment are minimized." To "minimize" something is, to quote the Oxford English Dictionary, to "reduce [it] to the smallest possible amount, extent, or degree." But Congress recognized, in the very

amendments here at issue, that there are "long-term uncertainties associated with land disposal," 42 U.S.C. § 6924(d)(1)(A). In the face of such uncertainties, it cannot be said that a statute that requires that threats be minimized unambiguously requires EPA to set levels at which it is conclusively presumed that no threat to health or the environment exists.

886 F.2d at 361.

2. *LDRs and characteristic waste.* As the court noted in *Chemical Manufacturers Assn,* the same logic applies to the application of LDRs to characteristic wastes. After a waste is once designated as hazardous waste, EPA has the authority to impose LDRs that "minimize" the threat to human health and the environment. EPA has since generally set LDRs for ignitable, reactive and corrosive characteristic wastes as "deactivation"—removal of the characteristic. But EPA treats Toxicity Characteristic wastes differently. Since the levels that define the Toxicity Characteristic are not set at a point where there is no risk to human health and the environment, EPA has set LDRs that require treatment of "underlying hazardous constituents" below levels that define the Toxicity Characteristic and for toxic constituents not included in the list of TC pollutants.

EPA has given the following "case study" on the application of LDRs to Toxicity Characteristic wastes:

CASE STUDY: DECHARACTERIZED WASTES AND THE REQUIREMENT TO TREAT FOR UNDERLYING HAZARDOUS CONSTITUENTS

A facility generates an industrial nonwastewater that contains benzene, acetone, and methanol. The generator determines that their waste is not listed on its origin, but upon testing the waste, determines that it fails the TCLP for benzene. As a result, the waste is identified as D018. According to the LDR treatment standard for D018, the benzene in the waste must be treated to a standard of 10 mg/kg, and the waste must also be treated for acetone and methanol underlying hazardous constituents. The generator decides to treat the waste in containers at the facility. After treatment, the benzene meets the 10 mg/kg standard and no longer exhibits a characteristic. Although the waste is technically no longer a hazardous waste, it must be treated for the acetone and methanol underlying hazardous constituents before it can be land disposed.

RCRA Orientation Manual, III–96.

3. *LDR Variances.* Wastes may also be land disposed if EPA has issued a variance or based on a finding by EPA of inadequate disposal capacity. RCRA § 3004(h)(3). Under EPA regulations, a case-by-case variance from otherwise applicable LDRs may be granted if the LDRs are "not achievable" or "inappropriate." 40 C.F.R. § 268.44. EPA has stated that an LDR variances might be appropriate for wastes generated during the remedia-

tion of existing contaminated sites since application of LDRs to remediation wastes might discourage remediation of existing sites. In *Louisiana Action Network v. EPA*, 172 F.3d 65 (D.C. Cir. 1999), the court upheld EPA's authority to base a variance on such considerations.

4. *LDRs and Clean Water Act wastewater treatment systems.* The court in *Chemical Waste Management* also invalidated elements of EPA's LDR regulations that exempted characteristic wastes treated in wastewater treatment systems from LDR requirements. This holding produced considerable controversy, and in March 1996, Congress amended RCRA by the adoption of the Land Disposal Program Flexibility Act (LDPFA). RCRA § 3004(g)(7)–(11). The LDPFA essentially overruled this portion of the *Chemical Waste Management* decision by allowing the disposal of characteristic wastes in Clean Water Act equivalent wastewater treatment systems or underground disposal wells. It provides, among other things, that land disposal restrictions do not apply to decharacterized wastes which are managed under the CWA required treatment (NPDES permit or pretreatment) As a result, if the waste is treated in such a system, it is not regulated subject to LDRs unless it exhibits a characteristic at the point of its disposal.

5. REGULATORY REQUIREMENTS FOR RECYCLED HAZARDOUS MATERIALS

As we have noted, RCRA has competing objectives: to ensure proper management of hazardous wastes and to encourage recycling as an alternative to disposal. This creates a conflict since classifying hazardous recyclable material as a solid waste under the regulatory definition potentially subjects recycling to the complex Subtitle C regulatory scheme, but excluding hazardous recyclable materials from regulation creates a potentially large loophole for environmentally harmful recycling processes. EPA regulatory scheme addresses this conflict by asserting RCRA jurisdiction over recycled hazardous waste through its regulatory definition but by adopting, in many cases, reduced requirements for recycled hazardous wastes.

EPA establishes these special requirements on recycled hazardous wastes in a number of different ways. First, EPA has established "contingent" exemptions from classification as a hazardous waste for materials that are recycled. Through these exemptions, EPA establishes specific requirements that must be met for the materials to be excluded from regulation under Subtitle C. This process of "contingent management" is discussed above. Second, under 40 C.F.R. § 261.6 EPA has established reduced regulatory requirements on recycling activities applicable to recycled hazardous wastes unless regulated under other provisions. Third, EPA has established tailored regulatory requirements in 40 C.F.R. Part 266 that apply to specific types of recycling.

a. GENERAL PROVISIONS REGULATING RECYCLING ACTIVITY

In 40 C.F.R. § 261.6, EPA has established the general regulatory requirements that generally apply to the recycling of hazardous wastes unless EPA has established specific requirements in Part 266. There are a number of important elements of this reduced set of regulatory requirements.

- EPA does not generally regulate the recycling process itself. 40 C.F.R. § 261.6(c)(1) (2008) states: "(The recycling process itself is exempt from regulation except as provided in § 261.6(d))." Therefore, once a recyclable material enters the recycling process, application of the Subtitle C requirements in most case ends. Unless the recycling facility stores hazardous waste prior to insertion in the recycling process, the facility will not need a TSDF permit.

- EPA does not generally assert RCRA jurisdiction over products produced from regulated recyclable solid wastes. 40 C.F.R. § 261.3(c)(2)(i) includes the statement: "(However, materials that are reclaimed from solid wastes and that are used beneficially are not solid wastes and hence are not hazardous wastes under this provision unless the reclaimed material is burned for energy recovery or used in a manner constituting disposal.)" With the significant exceptions of hazardous waste derived fuels and products derived from hazardous waste that are applied to the land, products produced from the recycling of hazardous wastes are not themselves regulated as hazardous wastes.

- EPA exempts certain types of recycled hazardous waste from any regulation at all. Recycled scrap metal, for example, is totally exempt from the regulatory requirements that would otherwise apply to hazardous waste. See 40 C.F.R. § 261.-6(a)(3).

Determining the applicability of the reduced requirements specified in § 261.6 can be complex.

United States v. Rineco Chemical Industries
Not Reported in F.Supp., 2009 WL 801608

The United States of America brings this civil action against Rineco Chemical Industries, Inc. ("Rineco") under the Resource Conservation and Recovery Act ("RCRA"). The United States seeks injunctive relief and civil penalties against Rineco for violations of RCRA Sections 3005(a) and 3010, and Arkansas Pollution Control and Ecology Commission ("APCEC") Regulation No. 23, which incorporates federal regulations approved by the Environmental Protection Agency ("EPA") pursuant to RCRA that are part of the federally-enforceable State hazardous waste program relating to the generation, transportation, treatment, storage, handling, and disposal of hazardous waste.

I

Rineco owns and operates a facility in Benton, Arkansas that is engaged in the generation, treatment, and storage of hazardous waste. Rineco is the largest single-site hazardous waste fuel blending facility in the United States and receives more than 400 different types of listed and characteristic solid phase and liquid phase hazardous wastes at its facility from a large number of generators of hazardous waste.

Rineco applied for and obtained a permit to operate a hazardous waste management facility at its Benton facility, RCRA Permit No. 28H–M001. Located at this facility is a Thermal Metal Wash Recycling Unit ("TMW"). The TMW is protected by Rineco Patent No. 7,341,155 B2 ("Patent"), which "relates generally to waste processing, and more particularly to systems and methods for processing heterogeneous waste materials."

The operation of the TMW, which does not have a RCRA permit, is at the center of the United States' claims in this action. The United States claims the primary purpose of the TMW is to convert a chemical soup of hazardous waste streams into hazardous waste derived fuel ("HWDF") for sale to boiler and industrial furnaces ("BIFs"), an activity it claims requires a RCRA permit. Rineco, however, claims the TMW is designed to recycle metal from hazardous and non-hazardous materials, an activity it claims is exempt from regulation and does not require a RCRA permit.

II

The United States asserts five claims for relief in its original complaint concerning operation of the TMW: (1) unauthorized operation of RCRA treatment unit; (2) unauthorized operation of RCRA storage unit; (3) unauthorized operation of RCRA disposal unit; (4) failure to notify of hazardous waste activity; and (5) failure to provide financial assurances. Rineco moves for summary judgment on each of those claims, its central argument being that the TMW does not require a RCRA permit as the TMW is engaged in the recycling process and, thus exempt from regulation under APCEC Regulation No. 23 § 261.6(c)(1).

a

The Court has carefully considered the matter and agrees with the United States that Rineco's hazardous waste activities are not eligible for the recycling process exemption as a matter of law because, under APCEC Regulation No. 23 § 261.6(a),[FN10] as an intermediary to a BIF, Rineco is not eligible for the recycling exemption set forth in APCEC Regulation No. 23 § 261.6(c)(1).[FN11] Under § 261.6(a)(2)(ii), recyclable materials, *i.e.* hazardous wastes burned for energy recovery in BIFs, are not subject to the requirements for generators, transporters, and storage facilities listed in §§ 261.6(b) and 261.6(c), but instead are regulated under Subparts C through H of Part 266. Under Subpart H of Part 266, "[o]wners and operators of facilities that store or treat hazardous waste that is burned in a boiler or industrial furnace are subject to the applicable provisions of Sections 264, 265, and 270 of this regulation."APCEC Regulation No. 23 § 266.101(c)(1). The Subpart H regulations provide that "[t]hese standards apply to storage and treatment by the burner as well as to storage and treatment facilities operated by intermediaries (processors, blenders, distributors, etc.) between the generator and the burner."*Id.* Rineco is an intermediary fuel blender that treats hazardous wastes in the TMW that are sold to and burned for energy recovery in BIFs, including cement kilns, which are regulated under Part 266, Subpart H. Thus, the exemption set forth in § 261.6(c)(1) is inapplicable to Rineco.

FN10. APCEC Regulation No. 23 § 261.6(a) provides in part:

> (a)(1) Hazardous wastes that are recycled are subject to the requirements for generators, transporters, and storage facilities of paragraphs (b) and (c) of this section, except for the materials listed in paragraphs (a)(2) and (a)(3) of this section. Hazardous wastes that are recycled will be known as "recyclable materials."

> (2) The following recyclable materials are not subject to the requirements of this section but are regulated under subsections C through H of section 266 of this regulation and all applicable provisions in section 270 of this regulation and 40 CFR Part 124:

> (i) Recyclable materials used in a manner constituting disposal (subsection C);

> (ii) Hazardous wastes burned for energy recovery in boilers and industrial furnaces that are not regulated under subsection O of section 264 or 265 of this regulation (subsection H).

FN11. APCEC Regulation No. 23 § 261.6(c)(1) provides:

> (c)(1) Owners or operators of facilities that store recyclable materials before they are recycled are regulated under all applicable provisions of subsections A through L, AA, BB, and CC of sections 264 and 265, and under sections 266, 268, and 270 of this regulation and 40 CFR Part 124, and the notification requirements under section 3010 of RCRA, except as provided in paragraph (a) of this section. (The recycling process itself is exempt from regulation except as provided in § 261.6(d).)

Rineco concedes that recyclable materials subject to APCEC Regulation No. 23 § 261.6(a) do not qualify for the recycling exemption but argues that § 261.6(a) does not apply in the instant case because Rineco only recycles metal in the TMW. While Rineco admits that a substantial percentage of oil and char resulting from the treatment process in the TMW is blended into HWDF and sent to BIFs where it is burned for energy recovery, Rineco contends that only the percentage of metal resulting from the treatment process should be counted as recyclable materials in assessing whether § 261.6(a) applies and that focusing on the other materials exiting the TMW that are sent for use as fuel is a "red herring." In support of this argument, Rineco relies on a passage in EPA's Office of Solid Waste and Emergency Response Memorandum 9521.1994(01), entitled "Regulation of Fuel Blending and Related Treatment and Storage Activities" (the "Guidance"), which provides as follows:

> There may be some recycling operations at a fuel blending facility that

are exempt from permitting, even though the fuel blending process itself is not exempt. The exemption is only available to units that are solely engaged in permit-exempt recycling; if the reclaimed materials are sometimes sent for use as a fuel, then the recycling unit would be subject to the permitting standards.

Rineco, states that "[a]s the [G]uidance explains, if the reclaimed materials are themselves sometimes sent for use as a fuel, then the recycling unit would be subject to permitting standards (*i.e.* the unit would not "solely" be engaged in recycling activities)." In contrast, states Rineco, "if the reclaimed materials are *never* sent for use as a fuel, like the reclaimed metal in this case, the recycling unit exemption would apply."Rineco states that because the material recycled in the TMW is metal, and metal recycled in the TMW is never burned for energy recovery, § 261.6(a)(2)(ii) does not apply to metal recycling in the TMW. Consequently, states Rineco, the materials placed into the TMW are subject to the general requirements of APCEC Regulation No. 23 § 261.6, including the recycling unit exemption in § 261.6(c)(1), and the TMW would be exempt from regulation under RCRA.

The Court rejects Rineco's assertion that the word "solely" in the Guidance exclusively refers to the ultimate use of the recycled material and that the focus should be exclusively on the percentage of metal generated from the TMW while ignoring all other outputs from the treatment process. Clearly, metal is not the only material recycled in the TMW, and APCEC Regulation No. 23 § 261.6(a)(2) specifically provides that recyclable materials, *i.e.* hazardous wastes burned for energy recovery in BIFs, are not subject to this section. Rineco points to the word "reclaimed" in the Guidance, but in the preamble to the hazardous waste regulations EPA explained that although "commercial products reclaimed from hazardous wastes are products, not wastes, and so are not subject to the RCRA Subtitle C regulations," waste-derived fuel resulting from the reclamation process continues to be governed by RCRA:

> We caution, though, as we did in the proposal, that this principle does not apply to reclaimed materials that are not ordinarily considered to be commercial products, such as waste-waters or stabilized wastes. The provision also does not apply when the output of the reclamation process is burned for energy recovery or placed on the land. These activities are controlled by the provisions of the definition dealing with using hazardous wastes as ingredients in fuel or land-applied products. For instance, if a spent solvent is treated and blended with oil to sell as a fuel, that waste-derived fuel is still subject to RCRA jurisdiction.

50 Fed.Reg. 614, 634 n. 20, Final Rule–Hazardous Waste Management System: Definition of Solid Waste, January 4, 1985. Thus, if reclaimed materials from the TMW are sometimes sent for use as a fuel, as indisputably occurs with oil and char, then the TMW cannot be exempt from the RCRA permitting requirements of Part 266, Subpart H.

There is certainly evidence in the record showing that a substantial percentage of the output from the TMW is not metal, even though the recovery of metal clearly takes place and is one of the purposes of the TMW. While the metal recycled in the TMW is not burned for energy recovery, the deposition testimony of three former Rineco employees (whom Rineco describes as "disgruntled") and certain Rineco documents support the United States' contention that a substantial percentage of oil and char resulting from the treatment process in the TMW is blended into HWDF and sent to BIFs where it is burned for energy recovery. Certain Rineco documents concerning operation of the TMW corroborate the testimony of Rineco's former Production Chemist and Directors of Operations. Between 2003 and 2008, the annual TMW Mass Balance Reports show that the TMW treatment process produced more than twice as much oil and char as metal.

In sum, the Court determines that Rineco's TMW unit does not qualify for the recycling process exemption set forth in APCEC Regulation No. 23 § 261.6(c)(1) because, under APCEC Regulation No. 23 § 261.6(a)(2)(ii), hazardous wastes that are burned for energy recovery in a BIF (as are the wastes managed in Rineco's TMW unit), are subject to APCEC Regulation No. 23 Part 266, Subpart H. Were the Court to uphold Rineco's interpretation, any hazardous waste treatment unit that processed an incidental amount of recovered material that is not burned for energy recovery would qualify for the recycling exemption. Such an interpretation is contrary to the regulations and RCRA's purpose to ensure the proper treatment, storage and disposal of hazardous waste so as to minimize the present and future threat to human health and the environment.

b

The Court additionally agrees with the United States that the TMW is not eligible for the recycling exemption for a second reason because substantial hazardous wastes that are treated in the TMW are destroyed by thermal treatment and not recycled in the TMW. With respect to such activity, EPA has stated:

> [W]e wish to clarify that materials being burned in incinerators or other thermal treatment devices, other than boilers and industrial furnaces, are considered to be "abandoned by being burned or incinerated" under § 261.2(a)(1)(ii), whether or not energy or material recovery also occurs.... In our view, any such burning (other than in boilers and industrial furnaces) is waste destruction subject to regulation either under Subpart O of Part 264 or Subpart O and P of Part 265. If energy or material recovery occurs, it is ancillary to the purpose of the unit-to destroy wastes by means of thermal treatment-and so does not alter the regulatory status of the device or the activity.

48 Fed.Reg. 14472, 14484, Proposed Rules, April 4, 1983.

Rineco claims that burning cannot occur in the TMW because the "materials are indirectly heated in an oxygen-depleted chamber."Rineco's use of the phrase "oxygen-depleted" is ambiguous, however, and Rineco has provided no actual evidence that oxygen is absent from the TMW. Rineco's own documentation evidences destruction or burning of materials in the TMW. In any case, it is undisputed that vapor from the TMW is vented to the TOU where it is destroyed through burning and incineration. Thus, a portion of inputs to the TMW are volatilized by the high temperature, vented to the TOU, and destroyed through burning and incineration. In addition, the presence of substantial char shows that the destruction of organic materials takes place in the TMW. Accordingly, the exemption for the recycling process found at APCEC Regulation No. 23 § 261.6(c)(1) does not apply because certain of the organic hazardous wastes processed in the TMW are not recycled but instead are destroyed by thermal treatment.

NOTES AND QUESTIONS

1.   The Arkansas regulations discussed in the case are identical to the EPA regulations found at 40 C.F.R. § 261.6(a) and 261.6(c). Note that this case involved federal prosecution for violation of State regulations. The enforcement issues associated with prosecution of RCRA violations in States with "approved" hazardous waste programs are discussed below.

2.   *Rineco* in part deals with the question of the applicability of the "recycling process" exemption (found as a parenthetical in § 261.6(c)(1)) to recycling processes that produce both exempt materials (reclaimed metals) and regulated materials (hazardous waste fuels). Note the reliance both by Rineco and the court on EPA guidance documents and decades old preambles to resolve this basic question.

3.   Would Rineco have escaped regulation of its recycling process if it had simply disposed of the oil and char as a hazardous waste rather than recycling the material by using it as a fuel?

4.   The court notes that Rineco's argument would result in exempting a recycling process from regulation if an "incidental amount" of the output were metal and the rest a hazardous waste derived fuel. Is the opposite also true? Does the court's interpretation subject an otherwise exempt recycling process to regulation if only an "incidental amount" of the output were used as a hazardous waste derived fuel?

b.   CONDITIONAL EXEMPTION OF RECLAMATION

Reclamation is the form of recycling that either 1) allows a material, such as a spent solvent, to be "regenerated" and reused or 2) removes a valuable product from an otherwise discarded material, such as removing valuable lead from old batteries. In regulations issued in late 2008, EPA substantially changed the regulation of the reclamation of hazardous wastes. As discussed above, EPA excludes what it calls "hazardous secondary materials" from classification as a solid waste (and therefore excluded from classification as a hazardous waste) if the material is reclaimed on-site or at a facility that is "under the control" of the generator. There are certain limited conditions that must be satisfied to obtain this exclusion. *See* 40 C.F.R. § 161.2(a)(2)(ii); § 261.4(a)(24).

EPA also established a complex "conditional exemption" for hazardous secondary materials that are reclaimed off-site by "third-party" reclaimers. 40 C.F.R. § 261.4(25). In EPA's view, third-party reclaimers do not have the same financial incentives to properly manage hazardous materials, 73 Fed.

Reg. 64,677–79 (2008), and to be excluded from classification as a solid waste, hazardous secondary materials sent for reclamation by third parties must satisfy a number of conditions including, among others, 1) an obligation for the generator to use "reasonable efforts" to assess compliance by the third-party reclaimer, 2) a requirement that the third-party reclaimer manage the hazardous secondary material in a manner "at least as protective" as analogous raw materials, and 3) the third-party reclaimer must document "financial assurance" to address releases of the hazardous materials, closure of the facility and compensation to persons injured by a release. *See* Jeffrey M. Gaba, *Rethinking Recycling,* 38 Envt'l L. 1053, 1080–1083 (2008).

c. TAILORED REGULATION OF RECYCLING ACTIVITIES: PART 266

40 C.F.R. Part 266 contains a set of detailed regulatory requirements that apply to a number of recycled hazardous wastes. Part 266 has separate regulatory requirements for hazardous wastes that are recycled by "use constituting disposal," precious metal recovery, reclamation of spent lead-acid batteries, and hazardous waste burned for energy recovery in boilers and industrial furnaces.

i. BIF Rules

EPA's regulation of the "recycling" of hazardous wastes by burning as a fuel in "boilers and industrial furnaces" ("BIFs") is among the most controversial of the tailored regulatory requirements. Hazardous waste if burned in an incinerator for destruction would be subject to the full set of Subtitle C requirements and the incinerator would be subject to stringent RCRA permit requirements. Burning hazardous waste as a "fuel," however, is not disposal, but a form of recycling.

Although EPA's definition of solid waste established that hazardous materials recycled by burning for energy recovery could be hazardous wastes, EPA was reluctant to prohibit the burning of hazardous waste as fuel. EPA initially prohibited the burning of hazardous wastes in nonindustrial boilers, such as boilers located in apartment and office buildings, schools, hospitals, but it exempted the burning of hazardous wastes in industrial boilers and industrial furnaces from substantive regulation when the purpose of that burning was for energy recovery. *See* 50 Fed. Reg. 631, 647–48 (1985). In 1984, Congress amended RCRA to require EPA to establish standards for facilities burning hazardous waste as fuel "as may be necessary to protect human health and the environment." RCRA § 3004(q).

In 1991 EPA promulgated comprehensive regulations in Part 266, Subpart H that regulate the burning of wastes in boilers and industrial furnaces. The BIF regulations establish requirements that are substantially similar to those imposed on incinerators.

Regulated BIFs, for example, must obtain operating permits and hazardous waste burned in the BIF are subject to the RCRA manifest requirement. The regulations impose air emission requirements that are identical to that required of incinerators burning hazardous waste for destruction and EPA has also promulgated emission limits for BIFS under its authorities in the Clean Air Act. BIFs are also subject to financial responsibility and closure requirements identical to incinerators.

ii. Use Constituting Disposal

40 C.F.R. Part 266 Subpart C contains specific requirements applicable to hazardous wastes that are recycled by being applied to or placed on the land. EPA calls this activity "Use Constituting Disposal." EPA's special restrictions on recycling by land application are hardly surprising. Perhaps the paradigm example of the environmental problems raised by recycling is Times Beach, Missouri, where dioxin-contaminated oil was "recycled" as a dust suppressant by being sprayed on the ground.

The Part 266 "use constituting disposal" regulations apply to hazardous wastes that are themselves directly placed on the land or to simple mixtures that include hazardous wastes which are directly applied to the land. Thus, use of a hazardous sludge as a road base material, for example, is regulated under this Subpart. The rules, however, not only apply to the direct land application of the hazardous wastes themselves but also, in some cases, to the land application of products made from recyclable materials. EPA has drawn a rather difficult line between hazardous waste derived products that are regulated and those that are not. In general, the regulations provide that a product is regulated under Part 266 if the product, with the exception of commercial fertilizer, is the result of the simple mixing of hazardous wastes with other substances.A hazardous waste derived product is not subject to regulation if the hazardous waste contained in the product has undergone some chemical reaction that binds the hazardous waste and if the product is sold for the general public's use.

United States v. Marine Shale Processors

81 F.3d 1361 (5th Cir. 1996)

From 1923 to 1985, Southern Wood Piedmont Company operated several wood treatment facilities designed primarily to manufacture railroad ties and telephone poles. These facilities treated wood with preservatives such as creosote and pentachlorophenol, leaving behind acres of soil contaminated with toxic wastes. Facing slackening demand, SWP in 1985 decided to close its facilities and clean up its waste sites. It sought to avoid regulation under the Resource Conservation and Recovery Act, 42 U.S.C. §§ 6901–92k, and liability under The Comprehensive Environmental Response, Compensation & Liability Act, 42 U.S.C. §§ 9601–75, by recycling its contaminated soil into a product covered by an EPA regulation known as the Product Rule. See 40 C.F.R. § 266.20(b). If SWP were successful in recycling its hazardous waste into a product covered by the Product Rule, the resulting material could be placed on the ground without violating RCRA. Relying in part on its own investigation and in part on letters from the Louisiana Department of Environmental Quality stating that Marine Shale Processors, Inc. was a legitimate recycler of hazardous waste, SWP contracted with MSP to dispose of SWP's contaminated soil.

II

According to the United States, the federal Product Rule exempts a product produced for the general public's use only if the product emerges from a process of legitimate, as opposed to sham, recycling. 40 C.F.R. § 261.6(a)(2) declares that "recyclable materials used in a manner constituting disposal" are "not subject to [regulation as listed or characteristic wastes] but are regulated under subpart[ ] C … of part 266." The Product Rule appears in Subpart C of part 266; this regulation provides,

> Products produced for the general public's use that are used in a manner that constitutes disposal and that contain recyclable materials are not presently subject to regulation if the recyclable materials have undergone a chemical reaction in the course of producing the products so as to become inseparable by physical means and if such products meet the [treatment standards for land disposal] for each recyclable material (i.e. hazardous waste) that they contain.

40 C.F.R. § 266.20(b) [alterations added]. Accordingly, in order to be exempt from regulation under the Product Rule, a substance must (1) be produced for the general public's use, (2) used in a manner that constitutes disposal, (3) contain recyclable materials, (4) have undergone a chemical reaction during the production process so as to be inseparable by physical means, and (5) meet land ban standards for each hazardous waste it contains. The United States focuses on the third element.

The third element of the Product Rule requires that the substance at issue contain recyclable materials. "Hazardous wastes that are recycled will be known as 'recyclable materials.'" 40 C.F.R. § 261.6(a)(1). "A material is "recycled" if it is used, reused, or reclaimed." 40 C.F.R. § 261.1(c)(7). "A material is 'used or reused' if it is … [e]mployed as an ingredient (including use as an intermediate) in an industrial process to make a product." 40 C.F.R. § 261.1(c)(5)(I). Accordingly, in order for its substance to meet the third element of the product rule, a facility must have employed the hazardous waste as an ingredient in an industrial process to make a product. Mercifully, the regulatory definitions end here; the regulations do not define the terms "ingredient" or "industrial process."

The United States points out that EPA has consistently interpreted the Product Rule to include a requirement that the substance at issue be produced from a process of legitimate, as opposed to sham, recycling. According to these documents, sham recycling, as opposed to legitimate recycling, occurs when the hazardous waste purportedly recycled contributes in no significant way to the production of the product allegedly resulting from the recycling. One EPA publication, in the midst of discussing an example involving the recycling of hazardous waste to produce aggregate in an aggregate kiln, states that legitimate recycling is occurring if "the prohibited hazardous wastes and their hazardous constituents do contribute legitimately to producing aggregate." In other words, the sham versus legitimate recycling inquiry focuses on the purpose or function the hazardous waste allegedly serves in the production process. If the waste does not in fact serve its alleged function in the process, then sham recycling is occurring.

Although the text of 40 C.F.R. § 266.20(b) itself does not mention sham or legitimate recycling, the distinction is inherent in the language "[e]mployed as an ingredient ... in an industrial process to make a product" in 40 C.F.R. § 261.1(c)(5)(I). A hazardous waste is not "employed as an ingredient" if it contributes in no legitimate way to the product's production. EPA's interpretation of its own regulation as including a distinction between sham and legitimate recycling is entitled to deference. *Ford Motor Credit Co. v. Milhollin,* 444 U.S. 555, 566, 100 S.Ct. 790, 797, 63 L.Ed.2d 22 (1980). In this case, the interpretative exercise is fairly straightforward. A substance cannot be an ingredient in making something if it is merely along for the ride.

We agree with the United States that the district court should not have entered a Rule 54(b) partial judgment without deciding whether MSP was engaging in sham versus legitimate recycling. To illustrate our reasoning, we provide the following examples. Hypothetical Facility A generates a large amount of liquid organic waste. In order to rid itself of the waste, Facility A heats the liquid to very high temperatures in the presence of oxygen, causing the carbon and hydrogen in the organic waste to burn away. The temperatures in the heating device are so high as to make irrelevant any heat contribution from the burning of the organic waste. Facility A has incinerated, not recycled, its organic waste. To the extent that Facility A has made a product, it has done so without using its hazardous waste.

Hypothetical Facility B also generates a large amount of liquid organic waste. In order to rid itself of the waste, the facility dumps the substance into soil. Facility B then digs up the soil containing the waste and heats it to very high temperatures in the presence of oxygen, causing the carbon and hydrogen in the organic waste to burn. The temperatures in the heating device are so high as to make irrelevant any heat contribution from the burning of the organic waste. The soil, however, conglomerates together and forms something that Facility B calls "aggregate." Under such circumstances, Facility B has not recycled its hazardous waste. The only difference between Facilities A and B is that Facility B dumped its waste in soil first. If the organic waste provides neither energy nor materials, then the organic material contributes nothing to the production of the "aggregate." Facility B could have manufactured the exact same "aggregate" by dumping virgin soil into its heating device.

SWP argues that producing a product is recycling. This contention ignores the fact that the hazardous waste in MSP's "feedstocks" may simply be along for the ride. At bottom, SWP's argument depends on the idea that soil contaminated with organic waste is a fundamentally distinct substance from the organic waste itself. We do not agree. *See Chemical Waste*

Management, Inc. v. Environmental Protection Agency, 869 F.2d 1526, 1539 (D.C.Cir.1989) (holding that EPA could reasonably reject the argument that "an agglomeration of soil and hazardous waste is to be regarded as a new and distinct substance"). Incineration does not cease to be incineration when one dumps the waste to be incinerated into a temporary medium like soil.

In *Marine Shale Processors, Inc. v. United States Environmental Protection Agency,* 81 F.3d 1371, 1382–83, we held that EPA could conclude that MSP is burning its organic wastes for destruction, and thus that the waste is not recycled or reclaimed or reused. This holding supports our conclusion that, at minimum, an issue of fact exists as to whether SWP's organic waste is a legitimate ingredient in the production of any Marine Shale product. Accordingly, we vacate the district court's Rule 54(b) judgment and remand for further proceedings.

NOTES AND QUESTIONS

1. An issue in *Marine Shale* was whether the materials were being legitimately recycled to make a product applied to the land. As discussed above in section B.2.b.ii, EPA has adopted a series of policies on the distinction between "sham" and "legitimate" recycling.

2. The court notes, but does not discuss, an additional requirement. A product applied to the land that is made from a hazardous waste is exempt from regulation only if the hazardous waste has undergone a "chemical reaction" and become "inseparable" by physical means. EPA has provided little guidance on what constitutes a sufficient "chemical reaction," but in a preamble discussing the exemption, EPA stated:

> Examples of hazardous waste-derived products in which contained wastes have undergone chemical bonding, and so are deferred from regulation, are waste-derived cement and asphalt. In these processes, the constituents polymerize and so are essentially inseparable by physical means.

50 Fed. Reg. 646 (1985).

3. *Pesticides.* The regulations do *not* apply to pesticides or pesticide applications. EPA has stated that pesticides, when applied to the land in accord with label instructions, are not wastes but products and thus outside the jurisdiction of RCRA. 50 Fed. Reg. 628 n. 15 (1985).

4. *Waste-derived fertilizers.* EPA has established specific conditional exemptions both for zinc-containing hazardous wastes that are used as an ingredient to make fertilizers and for the fertilizers themselves, and these materials are not subject to the requirements applicable to other hazardous wastes that are recycled by "use constituting disposal." 40 C.F.R. § 266.-20(d)(1). As discussed above, the court in *Safe Food and Fertilizer v. EPA,* 350 F.3d 1263 (D.C. Cir. 2003), the court upheld EPA's decision to conditionally exclude these materials from classification as a solid waste.

D. GOVERNMENT ENFORCEMENT

The effectiveness of any regulatory program for control of hazardous wastes ultimately depends on the threat of sanctions for non-compliance.

RCRA provides the federal government with an array of enforcement tools. Section 3008 of RCRA provides for three means of enforcement. Under § 3008(a), the Administrator of EPA may issue an "administrative order" requiring payment of a civil penalty and compliance with the requirements of RCRA. Section 3008(a) also authorizes the federal government to file a "civil action" in federal district court for imposition of civil penalties and injunctive relief. Section 3008(d) and (e) provide criminal sanctions for violation of RCRA requirements or for "knowing endangerment." As discussed above, however, every State has been delegated RCRA authority and every State is required, as a condition of delegation, to have its own authority to prosecute for violation of State adopted hazardous waste requirements. *See* 40 C.F.R. § 271.16. As important as federal enforcement may be, States have the primary role in the enforcement of RCRA related requirements.

EPA also has other enforcement related authorities. Under § 3007 and 3013, the Administrator has authority to issue enforceable requests for information and gives authority to obtain entry into facilities for investigation. Under § 7003, the Administrator can issue an order to respond to an "imminent and substantial endangerment" from the release of a solid or hazardous waste. This authority does not, however, require a finding of a violation of RCRA requirements.

1.   ADMINISTRATIVE ORDERS

Under Section 3008(a)(1), the Administrator of EPA is authorized to issue an "order assessing a civil penalty for any past or current violation, requiring compliance immediately or within a specified time period, or both." RCRA provides for civil penalties for up to $25,000 per day per violation, but, in fact, potential penalties are higher. Under the Federal Civil Penalties Adjustment Act, 28 U.S.C. § 2461, EPA adjusts available civil penalties to account for inflation. As of January 2009, the maximum civil penalty for violation of RCRA had been adjusted to $37,500. *See* 40 C.F.R. § 19.4. This adjusted amount applies to both administrative penalties and civil penalties available in a civil action brought in federal district court.

Far more enforcement proceedings are initiated through administrative orders than through civil or criminal judicial proceedings. Among other reasons, EPA prefers administrative orders since it controls their issuance and management of the proceeding. Judicial actions brought by the United States under RCRA must be handled by the Department of Justice, and EPA must refer RCRA civil actions to DOJ lawyers for filing and prosecution.

The process of issuance an administrative order is typically commenced by EPA through serving an administrative complaint. EPA procedures call for "informal negotiations" to resolve the dispute, and most RCRA administrative orders are resolved through a negotiated agreement that contains agreed penalties and corrective action requirements. These negotiated orders are issued by EPA as "administrative orders on consent." Recipients of an administrative complaint can, however, request an adjudicatory hearing before an Administrative Law Judge, and parties can appeal the decision of the ALJ to the EPA Environmental Appeals Board. Only after the completion of this review process is there a "final" administrative order. EPA has its own set of "civil procedures" governing the conduct of this administrative process. *See* 40 C.F.R. Part 40.

In assessing administrative penalties, the § 3008(a)(3) provides that EPA should take into account "the seriousness of the violation and any good faith efforts to comply with applicable requirements," but EPA has developed a formal "RCRA Civil Penalty Policy" which guides its lawyers in determining the initial proposed penalty and negotiation of a final agreed penalty. http://www.epa.gov/compliance/resources/policies/civil/rcra/rcpp2003–fnl.pdf. In order to effectively negotiate with EPA, lawyers need to be familiar with the details of the Penalty Policy. Briefly, under the Penalty Policy, EPA determines the number of violations and calculates a proposed penalty by assigning a "gravity" component based on the seriousness of the violation. In addition, the proposed penalty also includes an "economic benefit" component that seeks to recapture any economic benefit received from non-compliance, and adjustment based on equitable factors. There are limited downward adjustments of the "gravity" component of the penalty under the Penalty Policy. The policy authorizes limited reduction of the proposed penalty based on the "litigation risk" avoided by settlement. Additionally, the Policy allows a downward adjustment based on the alleged violator's "ability to pay;" EPA essentially states that it does not want a penalty to force a violator into bankruptcy.

EPA also allows a downward adjustment of a proposed penalty based on an approved "Supplemental Environmental Project" ("SEP") undertaken by the alleged violator. The SEP policy allows the gravity component of the penalty to be reduced by a portion of the cost of approved environmental projects. *See* 63 Fed. Reg. 24796 (1998). *See generally* Gaba & Stever, The Law of Solid Waste, Pollution Prevention and Recycling §§ 9.17–9.21. The credit for the SEP does not result in a dollar for dollar reduction of the penalty; typically a dollar spent on a SEP will result in an $0.80 reduction in penalty. The penalty reduction only applies to the gravity component of a proposed penalty, and EPA will always seek penalties that recover, at a minimum, the economic benefit received from non-compliance. To be approved, the supplemental project must, among other things, be voluntary and in addition to any legal requirements, and there must be a "nexus" between the project and the alleged violation. EPA's Penalty Policy identifies specific categories of projects that might qualify as SEPs. One category is "pollution prevention." EPA states that "[t]hese SEPs involve changes so that the company no longer generates some form of pollution. For example, a company may make its operation more efficient so that it avoids making a hazardous waste along with its product." *See* http://www.epa.gov/compliance/civil/seps/. This is another one of the limited mechanisms by which EPA promotes waste minimization and pollution prevention.

2. CIVIL ACTIONS

Section 3008(a)(1) gives EPA the alternative of instituting a "civil action" in federal district court against "any person who violates any requirement" of Subtitle C of RCRA. As noted, a civil action is filed and handled by the Department of Justice and not EPA. Courts are authorized to impose civil penalties and to issue injunctive relief. Civil penalties can be up to the inflation adjusted maximum of $37,500 per day per violation. RCRA § 3008(g). The statute does not specify factors to be considered in assessing penalties, and determination of penalties is committed to the discretion of the court. Some courts have indicated that they will be guided by the statutory factors specified in § 3008(a)(3) ("seriousness" and "good faith") that apply to EPA's imposition of administrative penalties. *See,e.g., United States v. Environmental Waste Control,* 710 F.Supp. 1172 (N.D. Ind. 1989).

3. Criminal Enforcement

RCRA also provides for criminal sanctions for certain violations. Under § 3008(d), persons are criminally liable for "knowing" violations of certain RCRA requirements.

United States v. Dean

969 F.2d 187 (6th Cir. 1992)

Defendant Gale E. Dean appeals his convictions on one count of conspiracy to violate the Resource Conservation and Recovery Act (RCRA), 42 U.S.C. §§ 6901 *et seq.,* in violation of 18 U.S.C. § 371; one count of failure to file documentation of hazardous waste generation, storage, and disposal as required by 42 U.S.C. § 6928(d)(4); and one count of storage of spent chromic acid without a permit, one count of storage and disposal of chromic acid rinse water and wastewater sludges in a lagoon without a permit, and one count of disposal of paint sludge and solvent wastes in a pit without a permit, all in violation of 42 U.S.C. § 6928(d)(2)(A).

I

Defendant's convictions arose out of the operation of the General Metal Fabricators, Inc. (GMF) facility in Erwin, Tennessee, which engaged in metal stamping, plating, and painting. The facility utilized hazardous chemicals and generated hazardous waste. The owners of GMF, Joseph and Jean Sanchez; as well as Dean, the production manager; and Clyde Griffith, the plant manager; were indicted for conspiracy to violate RCRA, and, individually, for violations of various sections of the statute. The district court granted defendant's motion to sever his trial from that of the other defendants.

RCRA provides a comprehensive system of oversight of hazardous materials, a system centered upon requirements that facilities utilizing such materials obtain permits, and maintain proper records of the treatment, storage, and disposal of hazardous substances. No permit was sought for the GMF facility. The hazardous waste disposal practices at GMF were discovered by chance by state waste-management authorities whose attention was caught, while driving to an appointment at another facility, by two 55–gallon drums abandoned among weeds on GMF's property.

As production manager, Dean had day-to-day supervision of GMF's production process and employees. Among his duties was the instruction of employees on hazardous waste handling and disposal. Numerous practices at GMF violated RCRA. GMF's plating operations utilized rinse baths, contaminated with hazardous chemicals, which were drained through a pipe into an earthen lagoon outside the facility. In addition, Dean instructed employees to shovel various kinds of solid wastes from the tanks into 55–gallon drums. Dean ordered the construction of a pit, concealed behind the facility, into which 38 drums of such hazardous waste were tossed. The contents spilled onto the soil from open or corroded drums. Chemical analyses of soil and solid wastes, entered by stipulation at trial, revealed that the lagoon and the pit were contaminated with chromium. In addition, the pit was contaminated with toluene and xylene solvents. All of these substances are hazardous. Drums of spent chromic acid solution were also illegally stored on the premises.

Defendant was familiar with the chemicals used in each of the tanks on the production lines, and described to authorities the manner in which the contents of the rinse tanks were deposited in the lagoon. Material Safety Data Sheets (MSDS) provided to GMF by the chemical manufacturer clearly stated that various chemicals in use at GMF were hazardous and were subject to state and federal pollution control laws. The MSDS were given to investigators by Dean, who demonstrated his knowledge of their contents. The MSDS delivered with the chromic acid made specific reference to RCRA and to related EPA regulations. Dean informed investigators that he "had read this RCRA waste code but thought it was a bunch of bullshit."

II

A

Dean assigns as error numerous aspects of the proceedings in the trial court. We shall address first a number of contentions going to the scope and elements of RCRA's criminal provisions, which we think of primary importance among the issues raised by defendant. The first of these issues arises in connection with defendant's contention that the trial court erred in denying his motion for an acquittal on Count 4, because there was no evidence that defendant knew of RCRA's permit requirement. Defendant's characterization of the evidence is inaccurate; but moreover, we see no basis on the face of the statute for concluding that knowledge of the permit requirement is an element of the crime. The statute penalizes:

Any person who:

    ....

(2) knowingly treats, stores, or disposes of any hazardous waste identified or listed under this subchapter—

(A) without a permit under this subchapter or pursuant to title I of the Marine Protection, Research, and Sanctuaries Act (86 Stat. 1052); or

(B)   in knowing violation of any material condition or requirement of such permit; or

(C)   in knowing violation of any material condition or requirement of any applicable interim status regulations or standards

42 U.S.C. § 6928(d)(2). Defendant was convicted of violating subsection 6928(d)(2)(A).

The question of interpretation presented by this provision is the familiar one of how far the initial "knowingly" travels. Other courts of appeals have divided on this question. In *United States v. Johnson & Towers, Inc.*, 741 F.2d 662 (3d Cir.1984), the Court of Appeals for the Third Circuit concluded that knowledge of the permit requirement was an element of the crime, observing:

> Treatment, storage or disposal of hazardous waste in violation of any material condition or requirement of a permit must be "knowing," since the statute explicitly so states in subsection (B). It is unlikely that Congress could have intended to subject to criminal prosecution those persons who acted when no permit had been obtained irrespective of their knowledge (under subsection (A)), but not those persons who acted in violation of the terms of a permit unless that action was knowing (subsection (B)). Thus we are led to conclude either that the omission of the word "knowing" in (A) was inadvertent or that "knowingly" which introduces subsection (2) applies to subsection (A).

Id. at 668 (footnote omitted).

The Court of Appeals for the Ninth Circuit disagreed with the Third Circuit in *United States v. Hoflin*, 880 F.2d 1033 (9th Cir.1989). The Ninth Circuit noted first the well-established principle of statutory construction that courts will "give effect, if possible, to every clause and word of a statute," pointing out that the Third Circuit's reading of subsection 6928(d)(2)(A) would render mere surplusage the word "knowing" in subsections 6928(d)(2)(B) and (C). The Ninth Circuit also disagreed with the Third Circuit that there was anything illogical about reading subsections 6928(d)(2)(B) and (C) to have a knowledge requirement but subsection 6928(d)(2)(A) to have none. The Ninth Circuit observed that the permit requirement is intended to give the EPA notice that oversight of a facility is necessary (and, by implication, the force of the statutory scheme would be greatly diminished by exempting all who claimed ignorance of the statute's requirements). The difference in *mens rea* between the subsections signifies the relative importance, in the estimation of Congress, of the twin requirements of obtaining a permit and complying with the permit. This ranking is consistent with the greater likelihood that compliance *with* the permit will be monitored. The Court of Appeals for the Fourth Circuit agreed with the Ninth Circuit in *United States v. Dee*, 912 F.2d 741 (4th Cir.1990).

All of the courts to address this question have reasoned by analogy from the holding of the Supreme Court in *United States v. International Minerals*

& Chemical Corp., 402 U.S. 558, 91 S.Ct. 1697, 29 L.Ed.2d 178 (1971). In that case, the indictment was brought under 18 U.S.C. § 834(f), which penalizes knowing violation of any regulation. The regulation at issue, enacted by the Interstate Commerce Commission, required shipping papers to reflect certain information concerning corrosive liquids being shipped. The question before the Supreme Court was whether knowledge of existence of the regulation was an element of the crime. The Court held that it was not, turning its decision upon the maxim that ignorance of the law is no excuse. The Court concluded its opinion by stating, with equal force here, that when "dangerous or deleterious devices or products or obnoxious waste materials are involved, the probability of regulation is so great that anyone who is aware that he is in possession of them or dealing with them must be presumed to be aware of the regulation." The Court of Appeals for the Third Circuit mitigated its holding in *Johnson & Towers* somewhat in light of *International Minerals,* holding that knowledge of RCRA would be imputed to employees above a certain level of responsibility (no guidance was given concerning the level of responsibility required, on grounds that there was insufficient evidence in the record on the responsibilities of the employees at issue).

We agree with the reasoning of the Court of Appeals for the Ninth Circuit in *Hoflin.* The "knowingly" which begins § 6928(d)(2) cannot be read as extending to the subsections without rendering nugatory the word "knowing" contained in subsections 6928(d)(2)(B) and (C). Subsection 6928(d)(2)(A) requires knowing treatment (or knowing storage, or knowing disposal) of hazardous waste. It also requires proof that the treatment, or storage, or disposal, was done without a permit. It does not require that the person charged have known that a permit was required, and that knowledge is not relevant.

As to subsections 6928(d)(2)(B) and (C), the requirements are different. Here, the statute clearly requires in addition that if one is to be charged under 6928(d)(2)(B) with violating the terms of a permit or under 6928(d)(2)(C) with violating regulations then one must be aware of the additional requirements of the permit or regulation. To us the statute is clear, makes sense and does not contain the ambiguities or inconsistencies found by others.

The Court of Appeals for the Third Circuit hypothesized in the alternative that Congress inadvertently omitted the word "knowing" from subsection 6928(d)(2)(A), because, the court opined, the plain language reading of section 6928(d)(2) to which we adhere resulted in an "unlikely" statutory scheme. A general review of the reasonableness of legislative choices, however, is not among our statutory construction tools. The inquiry ends with a cogent means of reading the plain language of the statute. The *Hoflin* court, moreover, adequately addressed the reasons Congress might have had for crafting the statute in this manner. Finally, we note that statutes which are designed to protect the public health and safety (as is RCRA, *Johnson & Towers,* 741 F.2d at 668) have consistently been distinguished in Supreme Court precedent as more likely candidates for diminished *mens rea* requirements.

We do not agree with the suggestion in *Johnson & Towers* that section 6928(d)(2)(A) is in fact a strict liability crime if knowledge of the permit requirement need not be shown. The provision applies by its terms to any person who "*knowingly* treats, stores or disposes of hazardous waste." 42 U.S.C. § 6928(d)(2) (emphasis ours). The Supreme Court's pronouncement in *International Minerals,* quoted above, stands for the proposition that persons involved in hazardous waste handling have every reason to be aware that their activities are regulated by law, aside from the rule that ignorance of the law is no excuse. In this case, the documentation provided by the chemical manufacturer abundantly illustrates one means by which knowledge of hazardous waste laws is communicated. Accordingly, even absent the requirement of proof that the defendant knew of RCRA's permit provisions, the statute does not impose strict liability. The district court did not err in declining to grant defendant's motion for acquittal based on his alleged ignorance of RCRA's permit requirement.

B

Defendant also contends that the district court should have granted his motion for acquittal because subsection 6928(d)(2)(A) was not intended to reach employees who are not "owners" or "operators" of facilities. By its terms, the provision applies to "any person." "Person" is a defined term meaning "an individual, trust, firm, joint stock company, corporation (including a government corporation), partnership, association, State, municipality, commission, political subdivision of a State, or any interstate body." 42 U.S.C. § 6903(15).

Defendant would be hard pressed to convince the court that he is not an "individual." He argues, however, that because only owners and operators of facilities are required to obtain permits, the penalty imposed for hazardous waste handling without a permit by subsection 6928(d)(2)(A) must apply only to owners and operators.

This contention is unpersuasive for numerous reasons. Of primary importance is the fact that it is contrary to the unambiguous language of the statute. We agree with the Third Circuit that "[h]ad Congress meant in § 6928(d)(2)(A) to take aim more narrowly, it could have used more narrow language." *United States v. Johnson & Towers, Inc.,* 741 F.2d 662 (3d Cir.1984). Second, while defendant's argument at first glance has logical appeal in relation to subsection 6928(d)(2)(A), the relevant language "any person" prefaces § 6928(d) generally. A number of separate crimes are set out in § 6928(d), several of them having nothing to do with the permit requirement (*e.g.,* failure to maintain requisite documentation or to comply with regulations). Defendant's argument would accordingly impose a limitation on all of the crimes set out in § 6928(d) on a ground relevant to few of them. Third, even the logical appeal of the assertion does not withstand scrutiny. The fact that Congress chose to impose the permit requirement upon owners and operators does not undercut the value of further assuring permit compliance by enacting criminal penalties which would lead others to make inquiry into the permit status of facilities. Given that "[s]uch wastes typically have no value, yet can only be safely disposed of at considerable cost," *United States v. Hoflin*, 880 F.2d 1033, 1038 (9th Cir.1989), facilities generating hazardous waste have a strong incentive to evade the law. Moreover, clean-up of the resulting environmental damage almost always involves far greater cost than proper disposal would have, and may be limited to containing the spread of the harm. Defendant argues that employees are the least likely persons to know facilities' permit status. However, employees of a facility are more able to ascertain the relevant facts than the general public, which the statute is intended to protect. In light of these factors, it was entirely reasonable for Congress to have created broad criminal liability. Fourth, it is far from clear that defendant is in fact not an "operator" of GMF, a term defined in the regulations to mean "the person responsible for the overall operation of a facility." 40 C.F.R. § 260.10 (1991). Finally, we agree with the Court of Appeals for the Third Circuit that this result is also supported by the decision of the Supreme Court in *United States v. Dotterweich*, 320 U.S. 277, 64 S.Ct. 134, 88 L.Ed. 48 (1943), and by the legislative history. We conclude that employees may be criminally liable under § 6928(d).

C

[4] Defendant contends that he should have been acquitted on Count 3 because the chromic acid at issue was not "hazardous waste" as required by 42 U.S.C. § 6928(d)(2)(A), set out above. The term "hazardous waste" is defined as:

> [A] solid waste, or combination of solid wastes, which because of its quantity, concentration, or physical, chemical, or infectious character-istics may—
>
> (A)   cause, or significantly contribute to an increase in mortality or an increase in serious irreversible, or incapacitating irreversible, illness; or
>
> (B)   pose a substantial present or potential hazard to human health or the environment when improperly treated, stored, transported, or disposed of, or otherwise managed.

42 U.S.C. § 6903(5). Count 3 involved spent chromic acid solution which was being stored in drums at the facility. Dean contends that the chromic acid was not "hazardous" within the meaning of § 6903(5), apparently on the ground that the chromic acid did not pose a danger to human health in the conditions under which it was being stored at GMF. *American Mining Congress v. EPA*, 907 F.2d 1179, 1191 (D.C.Cir.1990), upon which defendant relies, contains nothing supporting this proposition, and is directed at an inapposite question of law.

Defendant does not deny that the "chemical ... characteristics" of chromic acid involve a threat to human health, as was prominently stated in the MSDS provided by its vendor. It is not apparent from the plain language of the statute that it requires, as defendant would read it, that a hazardous waste present a threat to human health as a result of the manner in which it is being stored. We note that the definitions of "disposal" and "storage" under the statute are distinguished by the fact that the former is defined to mean placing the waste in a location where environmental contamination may result, while the latter is defined as "containment" of waste in a manner not constituting disposal, *i.e.,* such that environmental contamination will not result. *See,* 42 U.S.C. §§ 6903(3), 6903(33). A substance contained in a manner which does not threaten environmental contamination presumably would not present a threat to human health. Substances being "stored" would accordingly not be "hazardous," therefore storage could never be a predicate for a RCRA violation. This result is clearly contrary to the terms of the statute, and highlights the fallacy in defendant's argument.

Moreover, construing the statute to penalize storage of hazardous substances without a permit, without regard to whether the means of storage is itself unsafe, is in keeping with the statute's purposes. The requirement of a permit is intended to remedy the danger to the public health (underscored by the events in this case) presented by facilities whose generation of hazardous waste is unknown to authorities charged with monitoring the handling of wastes, for the protection of the environment.

NOTES AND QUESTIONS

1. *Scienter.* As *Dean* suggests, there has been some confusion over the element of scienter in RCRA criminal prosecutions. The court states that its holding does not make RCRA a "strict liability" statute and some knowledge is necessary for liability under § 3008(d)(2). Given the holding in *Dean,* what must a defendant "know" in order to be criminally liable under § 3008(d)(2)(A) for disposal of hazardous waste without a permit? Consider the following:

- What if a defendant does not "know" that a hazardous material it disposes of is defined as a hazardous waste under 40 C.F.R. § 261.3;
- What if a defendant believes that the liquid it is disposing of is distilled water, but the material is, in fact, a hazardous waste under § 261.3;
- What if a defendant knows that a material is a hazardous waste but does not know that federal law prohibits disposal except in a permitted facility?

2. *Persons liable.* Both civil and criminal liability under § 3008 can be imposed on "persons." Who is included among the class of "persons" who can be held liable? The word "person" is defined broadly in RCRA to include, among others, individuals, corporations, and state governments, RCRA § 1003(15), and, as noted in *Dean,* individuals can be held liable for disposal without a permit even if they are not the "owner/operator" responsible for obtaining the permit.

One issue that has arisen is the extent to which an officer of a corporation can be held personally liable for criminal acts committed on behalf of the corporation when that officer did not have personal knowledge of the individual act, but had the authority to control the activity. In other words, can "responsible corporate officers" be held personally liable under RCRA by virtue of their position within a corporation? The Supreme Court has recognized that a standard of "strict liability" can be applied to statutes which promote public health or safety, and that in such strict liability statutes, a corporate officer can be held liable for the conduct of the corporation even without personal knowledge of the conduct. *See United States v. Dotterweich,* 320 U.S. 277 (1942) (President of corporation held criminally liable under the Food Drug and Cosmetic Act for sale of adulterated and misbranded drugs by corporation without proof the president had knowledge of the sale).

RCRA is not, however, a strict liability statute, and some form of "knowledge" is necessary for criminal liability. In *United States v. Mac-Donald & Watson Waste Oil Co.,* 933 F.2d 35 (1st Cir. 1991), for example, the court rejected imposing criminal liability on a corporate officer simply because of his authority to manage environmental activities within the corporation. Courts, however, have recognized that corporate officers can be held criminally liable based on evidence from which it could be inferred that they had actual knowledge of and authority to control the illegal conduct or if knowledge could be inferred through "willful blindness," deliberate efforts by corporate officers to shield themselves from knowledge of criminal activities.

The court in *MacDonald & Watson,* for example, stated:

> We agree with the decisions ... that knowledge may be inferred from circumstantial evidence, including position and responsibility of defendants such as corporate officers, as well as information provided to those defendants on prior occasions. Further, willful blindness to the facts constituting the offense may be sufficient to establish knowledge. However, the district court erred by instructing the jury that proof that a defendant was a responsible corporate officer, as described, would suffice to conclusively establish the element of knowledge expressly required under [RCRA].

933 F.2d at 55.

In *Dean,* the court upheld the conviction of the defendant Dean for "knowingly" disposing of hazardous wastes. Dean, the plant Production Manager, had day-to-day responsibility for production and employees, ordered acts of disposal of hazardous wastes and had knowledge of the hazardous nature of the chemicals.

What arguments would you make (and what additional facts would you want to obtain) as prosecutor or defense lawyer in prosecution under § 3008(d)(1)(A) of:

- a plant employee who was ordered to dig the pit and bury the drums,

- the President of the company.

3. *Knowing endangerment.* § 3008(e) also imposes criminal liability on a person who treats, stores or disposes of a RCRA hazardous waste or of used oil and who "knows at that time that he thereby places another person in imminent danger of death or serious bodily injury." *See United States v. Hansen,* 262 F.3d 1217 (11th Cir. 2001) (discussing elements of proof

necessary to show that defendants knew that conduct created an imminent danger of death or serious bodily injury). The financial penalties and maximum jail sentence for "knowing endangerment" are far higher than those imposed by the criminal liability provisions of § 3008(d).

4. Given the complexity of EPA's regulatory definition of solid and hazardous waste, it should come as no surprise that defendants have in criminal cases asserted as a that the regulatory requirements are so vague and unclear that prosecution would violate constitutional requirements of due process. In one case, the defendant quoted a statement of the former head of the RCRA program that "RCRA is a regulatory cuckoo land of regulation.... I believe we have five people in the agency who understand what 'hazardous waste' is." United States v. White, 766 F.Supp. 873, 882 (E.D. Wash. 1991). The court rejected the due process defense. *See also United States v. Elias,* 269 F.3d 1003 (9th Cir. 2001) (definition of "reactivity" characteristic not unconstitutionally vague); *United States v. Hajduk,* not reported in F.Supp., 2005 WL 3237308 (D. Colo. 2005) (same).

5. *Enforcement requires information.* Generators and transporters have regulatory requirements that involve submission of information, and TSDFs have substantial reporting requirements. Additionally, RCRA provides additional sources of authority for EPA and its authorized representatives to gather information. John A. Hamill, Sr., *EPA's Investigative Tools: An Insider's Perspective,* 4 J. Envtl. L. & Litig. 85 (1989). Under § 3007, EPA has the authority both to require submission of requested information and to gain access to a facility to allow review and copying of records and for inspection and sampling at the facility.); *National–Standard Co. v. Adamkus,* 881 F.2d 352 (7th Cir. 1989) (upholding inspection authority under § 3007 to investigate the presence of hazardous waste at a site). Fourth Amendment protections apply to government "search and seizures," but the Supreme Court has authorized a process of issuance of administrative warrants in situations where traditional probable cause might not apply. *See Marshall v. Barlow's, Inc.,* 436 U.S. 307 (1978).

Additionally, RCRA § 3013 authorizes EPA to require the "owner or operator" of a facility where there may be "hazardous wastes" that may present an imminent and substantial endangerment "to conduct such monitoring, testing, analysis, and reporting with respect to such facility or site as the Administrator deems reasonable to ascertain the nature and extent of such hazard."

Violations of orders issued pursuant to § 3007 are enforceable through the administrative, civil or criminal remedies available under § 3008. *See United States v. JG–24, Inc.,* 478 F.3d 28 (1st Cir. 2007) (entity could be found liable for civil penalties for failure to provide a written response to EPA's information request under § 3007(a), notwithstanding the fact that EPA gained access to and conducted an inspection of the facility after information request was made). Violation of an order issued under § 3013 can be enforced through the civil enforcement available under § 3013(e).

Both RCRA §§ 3007 and 3013 apply to management or releases of "hazardous waste." EPA has stated that for purposes of its authority under

§§ 3007 and 3013, "hazardous waste" includes materials that fall within the broad statutory definition. Thus persons may be subject to information requests and facility inspections even if they manage materials that do not fall within the regulatory definitions of solid and hazardous waste.

6. *Environmental audits and self-reporting.* Compliance with RCRA requirements is facilitated by some process of internal compliance review by industrial facilities. A decision to engage in an internal evaluation of environmental compliance, an "environmental audit," raises several concerns. First, if a violation is discovered, is there any advantage to voluntarily reporting the violation to the government? Second, If a facility generates documents containing information about its compliance with environmental laws, will those documents by discoverable by the government through its information gathering authority and by the government or private parties in civil litigation. Neighbors suing in tort for injuries allegedly resulting from groundwater contamination, for example, would obviously like to obtain discovery of any internal documents about compliance held by a defendant. It can be very difficult to structure environmental audits so that they are protected by attorney-client or work-product privileges.

To minimize the potential risks of performing internal environmental audits, EPA in 2000 issued a revised policy titled "Incentives for Self-Policing: Discovery, Disclosure, Correction and Prevention of Violations," 65 Fed. Reg. 19618 (2000). The policy contains a number of elements. First, it states that EPA will not "routinely" request copies of environmental audit reports prepared by a facility. This is obviously not complete protection from a government request for the information; it is simply a policy against routinely including a request for any existing audits as part of government investigations of a facility. It is certainly no protection from a request for discovery by the government or private parties during civil litigation. Second, the policy provides that EPA will not refer violations for criminal prosecution if the entity discloses the violation in compliance with the policy.

Third, the policy provides incentives for reporting by providing for some penalty mitigation for self-reported violations. The policy states that EPA will eliminate the "gravity" component of any proposed penalty if the entity has "self-reported" pursuant to the terms of the policy. To obtain a penalty reduction, the policy requires, among other things, that (1) the violation was identified as part of a "systematic" policy of environmental compliance review either through an environmental audit program or a policy of due diligence review, (2) the violation is promptly disclosed, typically within 21 days of discovery, (3) the disclosure was voluntary, and (4) the violation is corrected within 60 days of discovery. Additionally, the policy provides that it does not apply to any violations that produce serious actual harm or may present an imminent and substantial endangerment to human health or the environment. If the violation was not discovered as part of a "systematic" review, but the entity otherwise complies with the policy, the gravity component will be reduced by 75%.

The EPA policy provides less than complete incentives to identify and voluntary disclose violations. To further encourage discovery and self-reporting of violations, a large number of states have adopted provisions that provide a statutory "privilege" that protects environmental audits from disclosure in many situations. A few states have also adopted "immunity" statutes that actually provide immunity from civil penalties for self-reported violations. There is a wide variation in State environmental audit privilege and immunity statutes regarding the scope of the privilege and the prerequisites for asserting a privilege or immunity. *See* Kenneth A. Manaster and Daniel P. Selmi, State Environmental Law § 16:30, Self–Auditing and Self–Reporting.

EPA has consistently opposed such formal privilege and immunity statutes. The preamble to the EPA policy states that:

> The Agency remains firmly opposed to statutory and regulatory audit privileges and immunity. Privilege laws shield evidence of wrongdoing and prevent States from investigating even the most serious environmental violations. Immunity laws prevent States from obtaining penalties that are appropriate to the seriousness of the violation, as they are required to do under Federal law. Audit privilege and immunity laws are unnecessary, undermine law enforcement, impair protection of human health and the environment, and interfere with the public's right to know of potential and existing environmental hazards.

65 Fed. Reg. 19618, 19623 (2000).

Consider the problems faced by a lawyer in advising a client whether to undertake an investigation of potential environmental problems and, if violations are discovered, on whether the client should voluntarily disclose the violations to EPA. What advise might you give prior to undertaking an internal examination of environmental compliance?

4.   Federal/State Enforcement Issues

RCRA § 3006(b) provides that States with approved RCRA programs are authorized "to carry outs such program in lieu of the Federal program under Subtitle C in such State." This language has raised questions about EPA's ability to enforce RCRA in States with approved programs. Section 3008(a)(2) suggest that EPA has a continuing enforcement role in States with approved program; that section requires that EPA give notice to an approved State prior to seeking enforcement of a violation of Subtitle C through administrative or civil action. EPA has consistently taken the position that the federal government may enforce RCRA requirements where a State has failed to undertake enforcement. EPA's authority to bring enforcement actions for violation of RCRA requirements in such circumstances has generally been recognized. *See United States v. Elias*, 269 F.3d 1003 (9th Cir. 2001); *United States v. Conservation Chem. Co.*, 660 F.Supp. 1236 (N.D. Ind. 1987).

Far more controversial has been EPA's authority to "overfile"—to undertake federal enforcement against an alleged violator where a State has previously undertaken prosecution for the same violation. EPA regulations specifically "note" that EPA may undertake enforcement action in approved States if a state enforcement action imposes penalties that are "substantially inadequate" in comparison to the amounts that EPA may impose. 40 C.F.R. § 271.16(c).

United States v. Power Engineering Co.
303 F.3d 1232 (10th Cir. 2002)

The State of Colorado brought an enforcement action against defendants Power Engineering Company, Redoubt Limited, and Richard Lilienthal (collectively referred to as "PEC") for violations of the Colorado Hazardous Waste Management Act. Plaintiff United States, acting on behalf of the Environmental Protection Agency ("EPA"), filed its own lawsuit against PEC for the same violations, seeking financial assurances. The district court denied PEC's motion for summary judgment, finding that the EPA's lawsuit was not barred by statute or by res judicata. We exercise jurisdiction pursuant to 28 U.S.C. § 1292(a)(1) and AFFIRM.

I. Background

Power Engineering Company has operated a metal refinishing and chrome electroplating business in Denver, Colorado since 1968. Redoubt Limited owns land and buildings leased and used by Power Engineering. Richard Lilienthal is an officer of both Power Engineering and Redoubt, as well as the sole shareholder of both companies. Each month Power Engineering produces over 1000 kilograms of waste, including arsenic, lead, mercury, and chromium. This waste is covered by the Resource Conservation and Recovery Act ("RCRA"), and is defined as "hazardous." After the Colorado Department of Public Health and Environment ("CDPHE") learned of a discharge of hexavalent chromium into the Platte River, it conducted inspections of PEC and discovered that chromium emanating from PEC was contaminating the groundwater. It also found that PEC treated, stored, and disposed of hazardous wastes without a permit. CDPHE issued a notice of violation on June 11, 1993, and an Initial Compliance Order in July 1994. CDPHE issued a Final Administrative Compliance Order on June 13, 1996, requiring PEC to comply with hazardous waste laws, implement a cleanup plan for chrome-contaminated soil, conduct frequent inspections, and submit periodic reports.

PEC failed to comply with this order, and CDPHE issued an Administrative Penalty Order on December 23, 1996, assessing civil penalties of $1.13 million. When PEC refused to pay the penalties, CDPHE brought suit in state court to force compliance with both orders. The Colorado state court found on March 23, 1999 that the Final Administrative Compliance Order and the Administrative Penalty Order were enforceable as a matter of law.

Before CDPHE issued its Final Administrative Compliance Order, the EPA had requested that CDPHE enforce RCRA's financial assurance requirements against PEC. The EPA notified CDPHE that it would bring its own enforcement action if CDPHE failed to do so. When CDPHE did not demand financial assurances, the EPA filed its own suit against PEC.

The EPA and PEC filed cross-motions for summary judgment. PEC argued that the RCRA statute and res judicata barred the EPA from "overfiling"—which has been defined in this context as "[t]he EPA's process of duplicating enforcement actions." *Harmon Indus. v. Browner,* 191 F.3d 894, 898 (8th Cir.1999). The district court granted summary judgment for the EPA and held that PEC must provide $2,119,044 in financial assurances and obtain liability coverage for accidental occurrences. PEC appeals the district court's grant of summary judgment.

II. *Discussion*

A. *Permissibility of Overfiling*

PEC contends that the district court erred in not following the Eighth Circuit's interpretation of RCRA in *Harmon.* Under RCRA, a state may apply to the EPA for authorization to administer and enforce its own hazardous waste program if its program is equivalent to the federal program and provides adequate enforcement. 42 U.S.C. § 6926(b), (c). The *Harmon* court held that RCRA allows the EPA to overfile after providing notice to the authorized state only if the EPA withdraws authorization or if the state fails to initiate an enforcement action.

A state program authorized pursuant to RCRA operates "in lieu of" the federal program. 42 U.S.C. § 6926(b). PEC contends that the "in lieu of" language renders the EPA powerless to file a separate lawsuit when a state has been authorized to run its own program and initiates its own enforcement action. The EPA disagrees and interprets RCRA in its regulations to allow such overfiling. 40 C.F.R. §§ 271.16(c) note, 271.19; *see also United States v. Power Eng'g Co.,* 125 F.Supp.2d 1050, 1061 (D.Colo.2000) (discussing the history and context of these regulations).

The EPA argues that Congressional intent to allow overfiling is demonstrated by 42 U.S.C. § 6928(a), which conditions EPA enforcement only on providing notice to an authorized state: "[T]he [EPA] Administrator may issue an order assessing a civil penalty for any past or current violation.... [T]he Administrator shall give notice to the State in which such violation has occurred prior to issuing an order or commencing a civil action under this section." As another circuit court held, "Read in context, section [6928(a)] ... simply conditions the exercise of [federal] authority on the provision of prior notice." *Wyckoff Co. v. EPA,* 796 F.2d 1197, 1201 (9th Cir.1986).

The EPA finds support for this interpretation in RCRA's citizen suit provision, which explicitly limits authority for citizen suits. This provision states, "No [citizen suit] may be commenced ... if the [EPA] or State has commenced and is diligently prosecuting a civil or criminal action...." 42 U.S.C. § 6972(b)(1). No similar language is included in section 6928, which only requires notice. "[W]here Congress includes particular language in one section of a statute but omits it in another section of the same Act, it is generally presumed that Congress acts intentionally and purposely in the disparate inclusion or exclusion." *Brown v. Gardner,* 513 U.S. 115, 120, 115 S.Ct. 552, 130 L.Ed.2d 462 (1994). Because Congress explicitly prohibits citizens from duplicating a federal or state RCRA action in section 6972(b)(1), but omits such language from section 6928, the statute suggests that Congress intended to prohibit duplicative citizen suits but not duplicative federal suits.

PEC argues, however, that several provisions of RCRA support its interpretation that RCRA unambiguously prohibits overfiling. PEC relies largely on section 6926(b), which provides that, once a state's hazardous waste program has been approved under RCRA, "[s]uch State is authorized to carry out such program in lieu of the Federal program under this subchapter in such State and to issue and enforce permits...." 42 U.S.C. § 6926(b). PEC argues that, because an authorized state program operates "in lieu of" the federal program, the EPA may not file an enforcement action after a state has done so. The linchpin of PEC's argument "is that the term 'program' in § 6926 incorporates the exclusive responsibility to enforce criminal provisions penalizing the disposal of hazardous wastes." *United States v. Elias,* 269 F.3d 1003, 1009 (9th Cir.2001) (quoting *United States v. MacDonald & Watson Waste Oil Co.,* 933 F.2d 35, 44 (1st Cir.1991)). The statute, however, does not define the term "program," and the meaning of the term is ambiguous. *Wyckoff Co. v. EPA,* 796 F.2d 1197, 1200 (9th Cir.1986). The EPA argues that "program" refers only to the administration of the regulatory program, and not to enforcement. It argues that section 6926(b) simply provides that once authorization has taken place, state requirements replace federal requirements, because the state requirements may be more stringent. *Cf.* 40 C.F.R. § 271.1(i) (allowing states to adopt more stringent and extensive requirements than the federal requirements).

The wording of section 6926(b) lends support to the EPA's interpretation. The administration of authorized state programs and the enforcement of state regulations are addressed in separate clauses of the relevant sentence: "[An authorized] State is authorized to carry out [its] program in lieu of the Federal program under this subchapter in such State *and* to issue and enforce permits for the storage, treatment, or disposal of hazardous waste...." 42 U.S.C. § 6926(b) (emphasis added). Because "in lieu of" appears in the first clause rather than the second, the language can reasonably be interpreted as saying that the state is authorized to carry out its program in lieu of the federal program, and that the state is authorized to issue and enforce permits. If enforcement were considered part of carrying out a program, the second clause would be superfluous, and we cannot "construe a statute in a way that renders 'words or phrases meaningless, redundant, or superfluous.' "

The only other circuit court of which we are aware that has directly addressed the question acknowledged that "the EPA is correct that the 'in lieu of' language refers to the program itself." *Harmon,* 191 F.3d at 899. The *Harmon* court nonetheless found that "the administration and enforcement of the program are inexorably intertwined." *Id.* at 899. This interpretation fails to account for the placement of "enforcement" and "in lieu of" in separate clauses of section 6926(b), and it does not adequately consider the structure of the statute. Section 6926 addresses the administration and enforcement of state regulations by authorized states, while the federal enforcement of such regulations is addressed in a different part of the statute-section 6928. Given this statutory structure, the EPA's conclusion that administration and enforcement of RCRA are not inexorably intertwined—and that authorization of a state program therefore does not deprive the EPA of its enforcement powers—is not unreasonable.

Even if we were to find that administration and enforcement were inexorably intertwined, we could only reach the *Harmon* court's ultimate holding by "harmonizing" different sections of the statute:

> Harmonizing the section 6928(a)(1) and (2) language that allows the EPA to bring an enforcement action in certain circumstances with section 6926(b)'s provision that the EPA has the right to withdraw state authorization if the state's enforcement is inadequate manifests a congressional intent to give the EPA a secondary enforcement right in those cases where a state has been authorized to act that is triggered only after state authorization is rescinded or if the state fails to initiate an enforcement action.

191 F.3d at 899. This interpretation goes well beyond the plain language of the statute. While *Harmon* correctly states that section 6928(a) limits the EPA's right to bring an enforcement action to "certain circumstances," the only explicit limitation is that the EPA must provide prior notice to authorized states. 42 U.S.C. § 6928(a)(2). Withdrawal of authorization for a state program is an "extreme" and "drastic" step that requires the EPA to establish a federal program to replace the cancelled state program. Nothing in the text of the statute suggests that such a step is a prerequisite to EPA enforcement or that it is the only remedy for inadequate enforcement.

PEC also relies upon section 6926(d) in support of its position that the statute does not allow overfiling. That section provides:

(d) Effect of a State permit

> Any action taken by a State under a hazardous waste program authorized under this section shall have the same force and effect as action taken by the [EPA] under this subchapter.

42 U.S.C. § 6926(d). The *Harmon* court, construing "the Act as a whole," found that this section applies broadly to any action authorized under this subchapter, including enforcement:

> The state authorization provision substitutes state action (not excluding enforcement action) for federal action. It would be incongruous to conclude that the RCRA authorizes states to implement and administer a hazardous waste program "in lieu of" the federal program where only the issuance of permits is accorded the same force and effect as an action taken by the federal government.... Nothing in the statute suggests that the "same force and effect" language is limited to the issuance of permits but not their enforcement.

191 F.3d at 900. According to this interpretation, the statute substitutes state enforcement action for EPA enforcement action and therefore does not

permit an EPA lawsuit when a state has initiated an enforcement suit. This interpretation reads too much into the provision. The provision must be read in the context of the language and design of the statute as a whole. Section 6926 addresses the authorization of state programs, not federal enforcement. The heading of subsection 6926(d) also suggests that the provision is more limited. While the title of a statutory subsection "is not part of the law itself, ... it can be used to interpret an ambiguous statute." Again, it is ambiguous whether "program" includes enforcement. *Wyckoff,* 796 F.2d at 1200. The statutory heading, "Effect of a State permit," suggests that this subsection only intends for state permits to have the "same force and effect" as federal permits.

In our judgment, limiting the "same force and effect" language to the issuance of permits is not "incongruous" with RCRA as a whole. *Harmon,* 191 F.3d at 900. It would be reasonable to conclude that Congress simply intended for section 6926(d) to clarify that recipients of state-issued permits need not obtain a permit from the EPA. Thus, it is reasonable to conclude that while subsection 6926(d) prevents the EPA from denying the effect of a state permit, it does not prevent the EPA from taking action when a violation occurs.

PEC also argues that the language of the citizen suit provision supports its interpretation. That provision states that no citizen suit may be brought if "the [EPA] Administrator *or* State" is diligently pursuing a lawsuit. 42 U.S.C. § 6972(b)(1) (emphasis added). PEC contends that the choice of the word "or" instead of "and/or" indicates that Congress did not contemplate competing actions between the EPA and an authorized state. *Harmon,* 191 F.3d at 901. This distinction is ambiguous at most. The word "and" is unnecessary in this context, because the statute clearly states that a lawsuit by either entity is sufficient to bar a citizen suit. Even without the word "and," the statute clearly prohibits citizen suits when both the EPA and a state are diligently pursuing an action.

In sum, PEC's position is arguably supported by the "in lieu of" and "same force and effect" language of section 6926, as well as the "or" instead of "and/or" language of section 6972(b)(1). On the other hand, PEC's interpretation contradicts the plain language of section 6928, the wording of section 6926(b), and the structure of the statute. Moreover, PEC's result is only reached by "harmonizing" sections 6928 and 6926 in a rather strained manner. Given these ambiguities and contradictions, we find that Congress has not "directly spoken to the precise question at issue." *Chevron,* 467 U.S. at 842, 104 S.Ct. 2778. Because RCRA is ambiguous regarding whether EPA overfiling is permissible, we must defer to the EPA's reasonable interpretation "even if we would have reached a different result had we construed the statute initially." We find that the EPA's interpretation of RCRA has substantial support in the text of the statute and is therefore a reasonable interpretation of the statute.

NOTES AND QUESTIONS

1. Under § 3006(a), an approved State hazardous waste "program" operates in lieu of the federal program. In *Power Engineering,* the court

stated that the scope of the approved state "program" was the "linchpin" of the defendant's argument that federal overfilling was not authorized in an approved State. How did the court describe the scope of an approved State "program" under RCRA? Under the logic in *Power Engineering,* if EPA gives notice to an approved State and the State does not initiate an enforcement action, can EPA issue an administrative order against a permittee that was violating the terms of its State-issued permit? Is there additional information you would need to know about the terms of the permit that were being violated?

2.   If EPA is authorized to issue an administrative order or the Justice Department files a civil action, what are the statutory or regulatory violations that would be alleged in the federal order or complaint—the State or federal requirements?

3.   The court in *Power Engineering* in part relied on RCRA § 3008(a)(2) to conclude that EPA could bring a civil enforcement action in an approved State. Section 3008(a)(2) requires EPA to give notice to an approved State prior to issuing an "administrative order or seeking a civil penalty," but the section is silent about criminal enforcement. Nonetheless, courts have held that the government's criminal enforcement authority under § 3008(d) is still available for violations occurring in approved States. *See United States v. Elias,* 269 F.3d 1003 (9th Cir. 2001); *United States v. MacDonald & Watson,* 933 F.2d 35 (1st Cir. 1991).

4.   As indicated in *Power Engineering*, there is a split among the courts over the legitimacy of EPA overfiling. Federal overfiling was upheld in *Power Engineering* but rejected in *Harmon Indus. v. Browner,* 191 F.3d 894 (8th Cir. 1999). The Supreme Court has not resolved this split, and thus, the potential for federal overfilling following a State prosecution for a hazardous waste violation will vary depending on the federal circuit in which the violation occurs. *See* Joel A. Mintz, *Enforcement "Overfiling" in the Federal Courts: Some Thoughts on the Post–Harmon Cases,* 21 Va. Envtl. L.J. 425 (2003).

5.   In addition to the statutory argument that federal overfilling is not authorized because the state program operates "in lieu of" the federal program, the courts have also split on whether principles of "res judicata" prohibit federal prosecution for the same acts that formed the basis of the State prosecution. In general, the enforcement actions of a State will not bar a subsequent federal enforcement under principles of res judicata, unless the federal government has sufficient control over the state litigation. *See United States v. Montana,* 440 U.S. 147 (1979). The courts in *Harmon* and *Power Engineering* also split on the question of whether EPA's delegation of authority under RCRA constituted sufficient control over State enforcement to justify application of res judicata to subsequent federal enforcement.

E.   CITIZEN SUITS

One of the more extraordinary aspects of U.S. environmental policy is the substantial authority conferred on private citizens to prompt compliance. Perhaps reflecting concerns both with the resources available and the political limitations on government enforcement, RCRA § 7002 contains several different causes of action under which private citizens can sue for non-compliance with RCRA requirements or for creating environmental risk.

1. § 7002(A)(1)(A): VIOLATION OF RCRA REQUIREMENTS

a. VIOLATION OF SUBTITLE C OF RCRA

RCRA § 7002(a)(1)(A) authorizes any citizen to sue in federal district court where any "person" is alleged to be in violation of any "any permit, standard, regulation, condition, requirement, prohibition, or order" of RCRA. Thus, § 7002(a)(1)(A) would authorize a private enforcement action against someone who was alleged to be violating Subtitle C by disposing of hazardous waste without a permit.

Section 7002(a)(1)(A) authorizes the classic citizen suit—a citizen acting as a "private attorney general" to enforce the requirements of RCRA. Remedies available under § 7002(a)(1)(A) include injunctive relief to compel compliance with RCRA requirements and civil penalties payable to the federal treasury. § 7002(e) does, however, authorize the award of costs and attorneys' fees to the prevailing or substantially prevailing party.

There are significant statutory prerequisites to a § 7002(a)(1)(A) citizen suit:

Notice and delay. § 7002(b)(a)(1) requires that a prospective plaintiff provide written notice of the proposed citizen suit to the EPA, the State in which the alleged violation occurs and to the alleged violator. For alleged violations of Subtitle C requirements, the complaint may be filed immediately after notice. For alleged violations of non-Subtitle C violations (such as "open dumping" violations of Subtitle D non-hazardous waste requirements, discussed below), the plaintiff must wait ninety days before filing the complaint. The Supreme Court has held that this delay requirement is jurisdictional. *See Hallstrom v. Tillamook,* 493 U.S. 20 (1989). EPA has promulgated regulations that specify the content of notices for citizen suits brought under § 7002(a)(1)(A). *See* 40 C.F.R. Part 254.

The different delay requirements applicable to § 7002(a)(1)(A) actions for alleged Subtitle C and non-Subtitle C violations create a problem when a complaint alleges both types of violations. Many courts have allowed these "hybrid" complaints to proceed without delay. *See, e.g., Dague v. City of Burlington,* 935 F.2d 1343, 1351 (2d Cir. 1991); *Building and Constr. Trades Council of Buffalo, N.Y. and Vicinity v. Downtown Dev., Inc.,* 448 F.3d 138 (2d Cir. 2006) (to avoid the delay requirement, complaint must allege a violation of Subtitle C rather than a generalized allegation of disposal of hazardous waste.)

Current violation. A citizen suit under § 7002(a)(1)(A) may be brought where the defendant is alleged to be "in violation" at the time the complaint is filed. The Supreme Court, in a citizen suit under similar provisions of the Clean Water Act, held that a citizen suit can therefore not be brought where the violations are "wholly past" at the time of filing the complaint. Courts have extended this requirement to RCRA § 7002(a)(1)(A) actions. For example, in *Connecticut Coastal Fishermen's Assn.*, discussed above, the Plaintiffs' had asserted that the Defendant was violating RCRA by disposing of the regulatory class of hazardous waste without a permit. The court, citing *Gwaltney*, dismissed this § 7002(a)(1)(A) count since it concluded that allegations of prior acts of disposal of lead shot or clay targets did not constitute a continuing violation of Subtitle C. *See also Chemical Weapons Group v. U.S. Dept. of Defense*, 61 Fed. Appx. 556 (10th Cir. 2003) (*Gwaltney* prohibition on citizen suits for "wholly past" violations applies to citizen suits under § 7002(a)(1)(A) of RCRA). Although a § 7002(a)(1)(A) action may only be available if there is a continuing violation, several courts have held that the current presence of previously disposed of hazardous waste constitute a continuing violation of RCRA. *See, e.g., California v. M & P Investments*, 308 F.Supp.2d 1137 (E.D. Cal. 2003); *City of Toledo v. Beazar Materials and Services, Inc.*, 833 F.Supp. 646 (N.D. Ohio 1993).

Diligent government prosecution. A citizen suit under § 7002(a)(1)(A) is precluded if the federal or state government has commenced and is "diligently prosecuting" a civil or criminal action in federal or state court regarding the alleged violation. RCRA § 7002(b)(1)(B). Although § 7002(b)(1)(B) does not expressly bar citizen suits where States have taken administrative enforcement actions, some courts have held that federal courts should "abstain" from preceding where a State action is pending. *See, e.g, Coalition for Health Concern v. LWD, Inc.*, 60 F.3d 1188 (6th Cir. 1995) (applying "Burford abstention" doctrine).

Standing. In addition to the statutory prerequisites under § 7002(a)(1)(A) and § 7002(b)(1), plaintiffs in a citizen suit must also satisfy federal constitutional requirements for standing.

NOTES AND QUESTIONS

1. There has been controversy over whether a citizen suit for violation of Subtitle C requirements can be brought in a state that has an approved RCRA program. Courts have split on this issue. In *Sierra Club v. Chemical Handling Corp.*, 824 F.Supp. 195 (D. Colo. 1993), for example, the court held that a § 7002(a)(1)(A) actions could be brought for violation of Colorado hazardous waste requirements RCRA requirements since they had become "effective" under RCRA upon the program's approval by EPA. *See also Glazer v. American Ecology Environmental Services*, 894 F.Supp. 1029 (E.D. Tex. 1995). In contrast, other courts have held that Subtitle C requirements are not enforceable by citizen suit in approved States. *See, e.g., Dague v. City of Burlington*, 935 F.2d 1343 (2d Cir. 1991), rev'd in part on other grounds, 505 U.S. 557 (1992); In *Heath v. Ashland Oil Inc.*, 834 F.Supp. 971 (S.D. Ohio 1993), the court held that citizens could not bring a citizen suit for violation of federal requirements in an approved State, but the court did not reach the issue of whether a citizen suit could be brought for violation of the approved State requirements.

2. RCRA contains several other significant causes of action for violation of the requirements of RCRA. RCRA § 7006(a) provides for "judicial review" of regulations issued by EPA under RCRA. Review of EPA regula-

tions is in the D.C. Circuit, and a petition for review must generally be filed within 90 days of promulgation of the regulation. Additionally, RCRA § 7006(b) provides for "judicial review" of any action by EPA in issuing, denying or modifying a permit under Subtitle C or in authorizing or revoking a State permit program. Judicial review of these actions is in the appropriate Circuit Court of Appeals and a petition for review must generally be filed within 90 days of the action. State-issued RCRA permits are reviewable only in State court.

The citizen suit provision of § 7002(a) also has another important cause of action to note. RCRA § 7002(a)(2) provides for a citizen suit against the Administrator when he is alleged to have failed to perform a "non-discretionary" duty required under RCRA. An action under § 7002(a)(2) would not be brought to review an action taken by the Administrator, but rather to compel the Administrator to take an action that he or she is required, but has failed to take. Many of EPA's initial RCRA regulations were issued under a court ordered deadline established when EPA was sued under § 7002(a)(2) for failure to promulgate regulations as required by RCRA. *See State of Illinois v. Gorsuch,* 530 F.Supp. 340 (D.D.C. 1981) (denying EPA an extension of court-ordered deadline for promulgation of RCRA hazardous waste regulations); 47 Fed. Reg. 32274, 32278 (1981) (promulgation of RCRA TSDF permit regulations and discussing requirement to issue under court order).

b.   OPEN DUMPING

RCRA § 7002(a)(1)(A) authorizes a citizen suit for violations of the requirements of RCRA including the prohibition on the "open dumping" of non-hazardous solid wastes found in RCRA § 4005(a). Thus, § 7002(a)(1)(A) provides a basis for citizen suits involving the disposal of solid wastes that do not meet the regulatory definition of "hazardous waste" under Subtitle C. In 1984, Congress amended § 4005(a) specifically to provide that the open dumping prohibition "shall be enforceable" under the citizen suit provisions of § 7002(a). *See generally* Jeffrey M. Gaba and Donald E. Stever, The Law of Solid Waste, Pollution Prevention and Recycling § 3:26.

"Open dumping" is generally defined as the disposal of wastes at a facility that does not meet "sanitary landfill" criteria promulgated by EPA pursuant to its authority in RCRA § 4004. See RCRA § 1003(14); 40 C.F.R. § 257.2. 40 CFR Part 257 contain general criteria applicable to most sanitary landfills. Disposal of wastes on property that does not meet the applicable Part 257 sanitary landfill criteria promulgated pursuant to RCRA § 4004 would constitute prohibited "open dumping."

South Road Assoc. v. IBM Corp.

216 F.3d 251 (2d Cir. 2000)

South Road Associates ("SRA") as landlord has sued International Business Machines Corporation ("IBM"), the former long-term lessee of its property, under the citizen-suit provisions of the Resource Conservation and Restoration Act ("RCRA") alleging that IBM's storage of chemical wastes on the site resulted in contamination of the surrounding soil, bedrock and groundwater, and amounted to a violation of RCRA's open-dumping provisions.

A. Facts

From the mid–1950s until spring 1994, IBM leased and occupied a parcel of real property in Poughkeepsie, New York. South Road Associates acquired the property around 1979. In 1981, SRA and IBM entered into a five-year lease, which was renewed for additional periods until it was allowed to expire on February 28, 1994.

IBM used the property for manufacturing, parts-cleaning, storage, shipping and other commercial operations. RCRA classifies certain substances as "solid wastes" in 42 U.S.C. § 6903(27), and classifies a subset of solid wastes as "hazardous wastes" in 42 U.S.C. § 6903(5). At the Poughkeepsie site, IBM used some chemicals classified as solid wastes and some that were also classified as hazardous wastes. IBM stored these solid and hazardous wastes on the property, some of them in underground storage tanks that are alleged to be leaking the wastes into the surrounding soil, bedrock and groundwater.

IBM first discovered the leakage in or about 1981. An internal investigation from 1982 to 1984 showed contamination of soil, bedrock and groundwater. In 1987, the New York State Department of Environmental Conservation ("NYSDEC") declared the site to be a Class 2 environmental hazard, *i.e.,* a "significant threat to the public health and environment," pursuant to N.Y. Envtl. Conserv. Law § 27–1301*et seq.*

During the 1980s, beginning before the intervention of the NYSDEC, IBM conducted a remediation program to reduce contamination on the property. SRA alleges that this remediation program:

(1) failed to discover (or remedy) all of the contamination, so that contamination levels continued at the time of the suit to exceed the maximum contaminant levels ("MCLs") allowable under 40 C.F.R. § 257.3–4(a), (c)(2)(i)–(ii); and

(2) used contaminated soil as fill in a soil excavation project that was part of the remediation program, thereby worsening rather than fixing the contamination.

In March 1993, however, IBM successfully petitioned the NYSDEC to modify the status of the site from Class 2 to Class 4, which relieved IBM of any state-imposed environmental obligation at the site except for continued monitoring. At the time of the filing of this suit, IBM continued to monitor the site under the New York State Inactive Hazardous Waste Disposal Site Program. SRA retook possession of the property on March 1, 1994.

RCRA Citizen Suits

SRA brought its federal claims in the form of a citizen suit under RCRA, pursuant to 42 U.S.C. § 6972(a)(1)(A), which provides that "any person may commence a civil action on his own behalf""against any person … who is alleged to be *in violation of* any permit, standard, regulation, condition, requirement, prohibition, or order" under the solid waste disposal provisions. *Id.* (emphasis added).

SRA alleges that IBM is in violation of 42 U.S.C. § 6945(a) and 40 C.F.R. § 257.3–4(a), each of which constitutes a part of RCRA's prohibition on open dumps and open dumping. The open issue is whether IBM's actions constitute present violations of those regulations or prohibitions, within the meaning of § 6972(a)(1)(A) (and as construed by *Remington Arms*). That is because 40 C.F.R. § 257.3–4(a) is a "regulation" under RCRA, and 42 U.S.C. § 6945(a) (set forth in part below) is a "prohibition" under RCRA:

> *Upon promulgation of criteria under section 6907(a)(3)* of this title, any solid waste management practice or disposal of solid waste or hazardous waste which constitutes the open dumping of solid waste or hazardous waste is prohibited, except in the case of any practice or disposal of solid waste under a timetable or schedule for compliance established under this section. The prohibition contained in the preceding sentence shall be enforceable under section 6972 of this title against persons *engaged in the act of open dumping.*

42 U.S.C. § 6945(a) [emphasis added]. Thus SRA can maintain this action only if IBM was at the time of filing "engaged in the act of open dumping."

"Open dumping" is defined in two places. First, it is among RCRA's statutory definitions in 42 U.S.C. § 6903. Second, by virtue of the "promulgation of criteria under section 6907(a)(3),"42 U.S.C. § 6945(a), we consider the definition in RCRA regulations.

The statute defines an "open dump" by elimination as "any facility … where solid waste is disposed of *which is not* a sanitary landfill which meets the criteria promulgated under section 6944 of this title *and which is not* a facility for disposal of hazardous waste." 42 U.S.C. § 6903(14)(emphases added). The chemicals alleged to be on the property are "solid waste" within the definition of 42 U.S.C. § 6903(27), and the process by which those chemicals contaminated the local environment falls within the statutory definition of "disposal," The question becomes whether SRA's property falls within one of the two statutory exceptions emphasized above in the quoted text of § 6903(14). We put aside for now (and ultimately decide that we need not reach) the question of whether SRA's Poughkeepsie site is a "facility for the disposal of hazardous waste," and instead examine the other exception in the definition of open dumping, for facilities that meet the criteria promulgated on the authority of § 6944.

Subsection 6944(a) mandates the promulgation of "regulations containing criteria for determining which facilities shall be classified as sanitary landfills and which shall be classified as open dumps." 42 U.S.C. § 6944(a).

Thus both the statutory prohibition on open dumps and dumping (§ 6945(a)) and the statutory definition (§ 6903(14)) define "open dump" by reference to regulatory criteria promulgated by the Environmental Protection Agency ("EPA"). Though SRA alleges a violation of § 6945, the wording of that section (and the statutory provisions implicated thereby) does not say whether an ongoing violation of the open-dumping provisions requires ongoing conduct. We therefore look to the regulatory criteria for classifying solid waste disposal facilities and practices.

2. Regulatory criteria

Promulgated on the authority of 42 U.S.C. §§ 6907(a)(3) and 6944(a), 40 C.F.R. pt. 257 lists criteria for determining what is, and what is not, an open dump. Facilities and practices that fail to fulfill the criteria delineated in §§ 257.1 through 257.4 are considered (respectively) open dumps and open dumping. *See* 40 C.F.R. § 257.1(a)(1)–(2). Facilities that satisfy those criteria are considered sanitary landfills. *See* 42 U.S.C. § 6944(a).

Because open dumps are prohibited by § 6945(a), and because failing any criterion listed in §§ 257.1 through 257.4 automatically renders a facility an open dump, *failure to satisfy any one criterion itself violates RCRA.* And because non-compliance with any one of the "Criteria for Classification of Solid Waste Disposal Facilities and Practices," 40 C.F.R. pt. 257, will cause one to be "in violation of ... [a] regulation, condition, requirement, [or] prohibition" of RCRA and therefore subject to suit under § 6972(a)(1)(A), these criteria operate as independent prohibitions under RCRA.

The complaint alleges that at the time of suit, IBM was in violation of 40 C.F.R. § 257.3–4, which provides (in relevant part) that "[a] facility or practice shall not contaminate an underground drinking water source beyond the solid waste boundary." 40 C.F.R. § 257.3–4(a). We assume that SRA's complaint adequately pleads the existence of an "underground drinking water source" and chemical expansion beyond the "solid waste boundary," as respectively defined in 40 C.F.R. § 257.3–4(c)(4)(i)–(ii) and 40 C.F.R. § 257.3–4(c)(5).

According to SRA, it is the fact of M.C.L. exceedances—caused by IBM's past acts, but still present at the site and causing groundwater contamination—that constitutes a violation of the provision requiring that a facility or practice "not contaminate" the groundwater. We conclude that that is not enough. The term "contaminate" is defined: " '[c]ontaminate' means *introduce* a substance that would cause" M.C.L. exceedances. 40 C.F.R. § 257.3–4(c)(2) (emphasis added). What is prohibited by the statute and the regulation (read together) is the act of introducing a substance that causes M.C.L. exceedances, not the action of the M.C.L. exceedances on the environment.

Accordingly, the complaint does not plead that IBM is engaged in the forbidden act of open dumping *unless* the complaint alleges that IBM is introducing substances that would cause exceedances.

D. *The alleged violation*

The final question is whether the facts alleged by SRA, if true, would state a judicially cognizable claim for a violation of 40 C.F.R. § 257.3–4(a)-that is, whether SRA, notwithstanding its defective theory of the case, nevertheless alleges that IBM at the time of filing continued to introduce substances that made the M.C.L. exceedances worse. After careful examination of the complaint and SRA's brief, we believe SRA has failed to do so.

At oral argument, counsel for SRA appeared to claim that SRA's complaint *does* allege continuing introduction of solid wastes onto the property, possibly in connection with IBM's remediation of the site. We can find no such allegation. SRA failed to present such a theory at oral argument before the district court, and nowhere in its complaint or its brief does SRA allege that introduction of waste onto the property was ongoing at the time of filing:

> The complaint alleges that introduction of contaminating wastes took place during IBM's lease, not afterward. This historical act cannot support a claim for violation of 42 U.S.C. § 6945(a) and 40 C.F.R. § 257.3–4(a).

NOTES AND QUESTIONS

1. To establish that "open dumping" occurred a plaintiff must demonstrate that a facility does not satisfy the Part 257 criteria. *South Road Assoc.* involved a claim that the facility violated 40 C.F.R. § 257.3–4(c)(2)—a discharge that contaminated an underground drinking water source beyond the facility boundary. This criterion has a specific numerical component. According to the court in *South Road Assoc.*, an entity violates this criterion if it introduces a substance to an "underground drinking water source" that exceeds "Maximum Contaminant Levels" ("MCLs") promulgated under the federal Safe Drinking Water Act at the solid waste boundary.

Other criteria are more general. 40 C.F.R. § 257.3–8(d) requires that the landfill not allow "uncontrolled access." How does one establish that access is "controlled" or "uncontrolled?" *See Covington v. Jefferson Cty.*, 358 F.3d 626 (9th Cir. 2004) (assessing alleged violations of Sanitary Landfill criteria involving contamination of groundwater, open burning, application of periodic cover, buildup of explosive gases, and uncontrolled access).

2. Not all of the Part 257 criteria are applicable to establishing "open dumping." As noted by the court, the term "open dump" is defined to include a facility that does not meet sanitary landfill criteria promulgated under § 4004. Two of the Part 257 sanitary landfill criteria, discharges in violation of the Clean Water Act (§ 257.3–3(a),(b)) and violations of State Implementation Plans under the Clean Air Act (§ 257.3–7(b)), were promulgated under the authority of a different section, § 1008(a)(3), and EPA has taken the position that violation of these two criteria are not enforceable requirements for purposes of establishing open dumping. *See Long Island Soundkeeper Fund v. New York Athletic Club*, 1996 WL 131863 (S.D.N.Y. 1996); Jeffrey M. Gaba and Donald E. Stever, The Law of Solid Waste, Pollution Prevention and Recycling, § 3:17.

3. Although the prohibition on "open dumping" of non-hazardous waste is enforceable by States and by citizens, it is not enforceable by the federal government. The federal enforcement provisions of § 3008 are generally limited to violation of Subtitle C requirements. *See* RCRA

§ 3008(a) and (g) (authorizing federal enforcement of the requirements of "this subchapter" [i.e. Subtitle C]); § 3008(d) and (e) (generally imposing criminal liability relating to treatment, storage or disposal of Subtitle C hazardous wastes.) The enforcement provisions of § 3008 do not, however, give the federal government authority to enforce the Subtitle D requirements applicable to disposal of non-hazardous solid waste, including the prohibition on "open dumping." *See, e.g.,* 46 Fed. Reg. 29,064 (1981); Gaba & Stever, The Law of Solid Waste, Pollution Prevention and Recycling, § 3:25. Thus, EPA has a limited enforcement role regarding implementation of state controls over non-hazardous industrial solid waste.

4. EPA has also promulgated detailed sanitary landfill criteria specifically applicable to Municipal Solid Waste Landfills (MSWLFs). 40 C.F.R. Part 258. Additionally, EPA has promulgated sanitary landfill criteria that apply to "non-municipal, non-hazardous waste" facilities that may receive wastes from Conditionally Exempt Small Quantity Generators. These criteria, found at 40 C.F.R. Part 257, Subpart B, generally apply to facilities receiving construction and demolition wastes. *See* 61 Fed. Reg. 34,252 (1996).

2. Imminent and Substantial Endangerment

In 1984, Congress amended RCRA to provide a powerful additional basis for a citizen suit. Under § 7002(a)(1)(B), a citizen or a State may also bring an action for injunctive relief where certain persons have caused or contributed to "the past or present handling, storage, treatment, transportation, or disposal of any solid or hazardous waste which may present an imminent and substantial endangerment to health or the environment." A § 7002(a)(1)(B) "imminent and substantial endangerment" action is fundamentally different from a citizen suit under § 7002(a)(1)(A) that is based on a violation of requirements of RCRA. A § 7002(a)(1)(B) action does not depend on a violation of a RCRA requirement; it depends on showing a current "imminent and substantial endangerment" from the presence of solid or hazardous waste. RCRA § 7002(a)(1)(B) thus gives private parties a basis to go to federal court to compel others to cleanup releases of waste.

In order to establish a prima facie case under § 7002(a)(1)(B) for an "imminent and substantial endangerment," it has generally been held that a plaintiff must demonstrate three elements.

- The alleged endangerment stems from a solid or hazardous waste as defined by the statutory, not regulatory, definitions in RCRA;
- Conditions that may present an imminent and substantial endangerment; and
- Defendant has contributed to or is contributing to such handling, storage, treatment, transportation, or disposal.

Citizen suits under § 7002(a)(1)(B) are also subject to statutory prerequisites. § 7002(b)(2). These prerequisites differ in significant ways from those that apply to § 7002(a)(1)(A) actions.

Notice and delay. § 7002(a)(1)(B) actions require prior notice, but they are subject to a 90 day delay requirement unless they are an action "respecting" a violation of Subtitle C. Since a § 7002(a)(1)(B) action does not require an allegation of a Subtitle C requirement, the 90 day delay requirement is a significant, and jurisdictional, requirement in most cases.

Current violation. Although a § 7002(a)(1)(B) action must be based on a current condition creating an "imminent and substantial endangerment," courts have not required demonstration of a current violation of RCRA requirements.

Government remediation actions. § 7002(b)(2)(B) and (C) bar a citizen "imminent and substantial endangerment" action if the federal or state governments have commenced a specific list of actions to remedy the conditions creating the imminent and substantial endangerment. These actions include actions taken under the Comprehensive Response Compensation and Liability Act ("CERCLA") or, in the case of States, their own prior "imminent and substantial endangerment action" under § 7002(a)(1)(B).

Standing. Plaintiffs bringing a § 7002(a)(1)(B) action must satisfy constitutional standing requirements. *See, e.g., Maine People's Alliance and Natural Resources Defense Council v. Mallinckrodt, Inc.,* 471 F.3d 277 (1st Cir. 2006).

Interfaith Community Organization v. Honeywell International, Inc.
399 F.3d 248 (3d Cir. 2005)

I. BACKGROUND FACTS

Starting in 1895, Mutual Chemical Company of America ("Mutual"), later the largest chrome manufacturer in the world, operated a chromate chemical plant in Jersey City, New Jersey. Its process resulted in a waste residue that had a high pH and high concentrations of hexavalent chromium. Mutual piled this waste at a tidal wetlands site along the Hackensack River. The piling of the waste created a land-mass (the "Site") which is the subject of this appeal. The Site consists of some 1,500,000 tons of the waste, 15 to 20 feet deep, on some 34 acres. The Site's high pH prevents the hexavalent chromium from reducing naturally to its less-toxic trivalent form, and enhances its ability to leach freely into surface water and groundwater. The hexavalent chromium is highly soluble, a known carcinogen to humans, and toxic to the environment.[FN1]

> FN1. As the District Court found, the United States Environmental Protection Agency ("EPA") classifies hexavalent chromium in the first quartile of known human carcinogens, more potent than arsenic, benzene, and PCBs. It is toxic not only to humans, but also animals and lower life forms, including benthic organisms. The New Jersey Department of Environmental Protection ("NJDEP") has made similar determinations.

Mutual continued dumping until 1954, when it was succeeded by the Allied Corporation, in turn succeeded by AlliedSignal, Inc., and then Honeywell. The site was never cleaned up.

The State of New Jersey first sought a permanent remedy for the Site in 1982, about the time a "green stream" and "yellowish-green plumes" were observed in surface water on the Site. In 1983, a Honeywell official described it as an "extremely contaminated site, visible to the naked eye" with "yellow water ... draining into the Hackensack River," and concluded "there's something terribly not right with the site." Honeywell did not act, however, until seven years later, about two years after NJDEP had ordered it to do so. The result was not a permanent remedy but rather an "interim" measure consisting of poured concrete and asphalt over 17 acres of the Site and a plastic liner "cap" over the remaining 17 acres. This was intended to last only five years while a permanent remedy was to be studied and implemented. Honeywell had told NJDEP that the interim measure would not prevent all discharges, even assuming proper maintenance; in any event, as the District Court found, and as we discuss *infra,* the interim measure was constantly in need of repair, having succumbed to, among other things, a phenomenon called "heaving" caused by the waste.

In a 1993 consent order arising from litigation over the Site, AlliedSignal promised $60 million towards a permanent containment solution and NJDEP reserved the right to compel a full cleanup at higher cost. The order also stated that the permanent remedy would be put in place through the NJDEP's usual process, which was to: (I) delineate, or identify, all of the conditions needing remedy; (ii) analyze remedial alternatives and select a remedy; and (iii) take "remedial action." The District Court found, and the record shows, that these steps were not taken or completed.

In 1995, a local community organization, Interfaith Community Organization ("ICO"), and five individual plaintiffs sued Honeywell's predecessor AlliedSignal and the then-owners of the Site under the citizen suit provision of RCRA, § 6972(a)(1)(B), alleging the Site "may present an imminent and substantial endangerment to health or the environment." At the conclusion of a two-week bench trial, the District Court found for plaintiffs and enjoined Honeywell to clean up the Site through excavation of the contamination.

B. *Imminent and Substantial Endangerment*

1. *Legal Standard*

Honeywell contends it did not violate § 6972(a)(1)(B). As we have already noted, a person may bring suit under this provision

> against any person ... who has contributed or who is contributing to the past or present handling, storage, treatment, transportation, or disposal of any solid or hazardous waste which may present an imminent and substantial endangerment to health or the environment.

42 U.S.C. § 6972(a)(1)(B). This provision explicitly allows the consideration of environmental or health effects arising from waste and authorizes suit any time there may be a present threat—an imminent and substantial endangerment—to health or the environment. To prevail under § 6972(a)(1)(B), a plaintiff must prove:

> (1) that the defendant is a person, including, but not limited to, one

who was or is a generator or transporter of solid or hazardous waste or one who was or is an owner or operator of a solid or hazardous waste treatment, storage, or disposal facility; (2) that the defendant has contributed to or is contributing to the handling, storage, treatment, transportation, or disposal of solid or hazardous waste; and (3) that the solid or hazardous waste may present an imminent and substantial endangerment to health or the environment.

Because Honeywell concedes that it is legally responsible for the Site and that chromium is both a solid and a hazardous waste under RCRA, the only remaining issue is whether it "may present an imminent and substantial endangerment to health or the environment." The meaning of this statutory language has been summarized as follows:

The operative word ... [is] "may"....

[P]laintiffs need only demonstrate that the waste ... "may present" an imminent and substantial threat.... Similarly, the term "endangerment" means a threatened or potential harm, and does not require proof of actual harm.... The endangerment must also be "imminent" [meaning] threatens to occur immediately.... Because the operative word is "may," however, the plaintiffs must [only] show that there is a potential for an imminent threat of serious harm ... [as] an endangerment is substantial if it is "serious" ... to the environment or health.

United States v. Price, 688 F.2d 204, 213–14 (3d Cir.1982) (concluding § 6972(a)(1)(B) contains "expansive language" conferring upon the courts the authority to grant affirmative equitable relief to the extent necessary to eliminate any risk posed by toxic wastes").

This approach, we believe, is most faithful to the statutory language, especially as to the word "substantial." *See, e.g., United States v. Union Corp.,* 259 F.Supp.2d 356, 399–400 (E.D.Pa.2003) (observing that RCRA's "substantial" requirement " 'does not require quantification of the endangerment (*e.g.,* proof that a certain number of persons will be exposed ... or that a water supply will be contaminated to a specific degree)' ") (quoting *United States v. Conservation Chemical Co.,* 619 F.Supp. 162, 194 (W.D.Mo.-1985)). For the reasons we discuss *infra,* we believe that decisions such as *Parker, Cox, Union Corp.,* and *Conservation Chemical* define "substantial" in a manner consistent with the statutory language, the legislative history, and the plain meaning of that word. *See, e.g., Cox,* 256 F.3d at 300 (stating that "an endangerment is 'substantial' if it is 'serious' "); *Union Corp.,* 259 F.Supp.2d at 400 (stating that a RCRA "endangerment is substantial if there is some reasonable cause for concern that someone or something may be exposed to a risk of harm ... if remedial action is not taken."). We do not disagree that, given RCRA's language and purpose, Congress must have intended that "if an error is to be made in applying the endangerment standard, the error must be made in favor of protecting public health, welfare and the environment." *Conservation Chemical,* 619 F.Supp. at 194.

Here, the District Court added four additional requirements to the endangerment showing. These held plaintiffs to a higher than needed showing for success on the merits under § 6972(a)(1)(B). The additional requirements were as follows:

> [A] site "may present an imminent and substantial endangerment" within the meaning of RCRA where: (1) there is a potential population at risk; (2) the contaminant at issue is a RCRA "solid" or "hazardous waste"; (3) the contaminant is present at levels above that considered acceptable by the state; and (4) there is a pathway for current and/or future exposure.

263 F.Supp.2d at 838.

At least two of these requirements are irreconcilable with § 6972(a)(1)(B). The first requirement requires a "population," but § 6972(a)(1)(B)'s disjunctive phrasing, "*or* environment," means a living population is not required for success on the merits, as we discuss *infra*. The third requirement, apparently intended by the District Court to give quantitative meaning to the word "substantial" in § 6972(a)(1)(B), is similarly without support. The word "substantial" is not defined by the statute or its legislative history. Turning to a dictionary, we find that "substantial" means "having substance" and "not imaginary"; only as the last of several definitions does the dictionary offer "of considerable size or amount." *Webster's New Universal Unabridged Dictionary* 1817 (2d ed.-1983). These definitions do not support one particular type of quantification measurement, such as the District Court's requirement that there be an exceedance of state standards. Honeywell, tacitly following *Cox,* 256 F.3d at 300, equates "substantial" with "serious," which also does not support one particular type of quantification measurement. As noted, the word "substantial" is not defined by the statute or its legislative history, and we have not found any binding authority which stands contrary to this analysis. It is thus difficult to see how § 6972(a)(1)(B) justifies the kind of hurdle created by the District Court's third quantitative requirement—let alone the even *higher* requirements for "substantial" that Honeywell argues for, without citation.

Honeywell's arguments actually provide an additional reason why we will not read state standards into the language of this federal law. Honeywell contends that its conceded discharges into the Hackensack River could not possibly be "substantial" because New Jersey has not yet established a remedial standard for river sediment chromium. We do not believe that Congress intended § 6972(a)(1)(B) to be dependent upon the states in such a manner, and the statutory language provides no support for such dependency.

When Congress enacted RCRA in 1976, it sought to close "the last remaining loophole in environmental law, that of unregulated land disposal of discarded materials and hazardous wastes." H.R.Rep. No. 1491, 94th Cong., 2d Sess. 4, *reprinted in* 1976 U.S.C.C.A.N. 6238, 6241. As we have noted, there is no definition or explanation of the meaning of "substantial," but a discussion of RCRA's amendments observes that § 6972(a)(1)(B) is " 'intended to confer upon the courts the authority to eliminate any risks posed by toxic wastes,' " S.Rep. No. 98–284, 98th Cong., 1st Sess. at 59

(1983) (quoting *Price,* 688 F.2d at 213–14), and further that courts should "recogniz[e] that risk may be assessed from suspected, but not completely substantiated, relationships between imperfect data, or from probative preliminary data not yet certifiable as fact." *Id.* (internal quotations and citations omitted). This supports neither the District Court's particular quantitative requirement nor the even higher and more narrow quantitative standards that Honeywell would have us impose.

Decisions of the other courts of appeals are not to the contrary. None require a particular quantitative showing as a *sine qua non* for liability. *See Parker,* 386 F.3d at 1015 (considering evidence of contamination at levels requiring landfill operator to notify state agency but determining substantiality on totality of the evidence); *Cox,* 256 F.3d at 299–301 (finding endangerments at two dumps on totality of the evidence; considering evidence of exceedences as to only one dump); *Dague,* 935 F.2d at 1356 (affirming endangerment finding without considering any quantitative evidence).

2. *Evidence of Endangerment*

Having analyzed the meaning of the statute, we turn now to the straightforward clear error analysis before us. The District Court first found that the amounts of hexavalent chromium for which Honeywell was responsible far exceeded all applicable NJDEP contamination standards for soil, groundwater, surface water, and river sediments adjacent to the Site. The evidence shows this finding was not clearly erroneous.

There was also evidence, relevant to several of the District Court's findings, that Honeywell had expressly informed NJDEP at the time of Honeywell's installation of its "interim" measures that they could not prevent all discharges of chromium contamination from the Site, but would rather only "substantially reduce" discharges through their "various routes." The evidence showed that these measures, as built and maintained, were now severely compromised because the 17–acre plastic liner, or "cap," had been used years beyond its intended useful life and was ripped and leaking due to, among other things, wind damage. Similarly, the asphalt portion of the cap used to cover the remaining 17 acres of the site was buckled and cracked in numerous places due to "heaving" caused by the chromium at the Site.

Even assuming *arguendo* the District Court clearly erred with respect to its findings relating to human endangerment, the findings with respect to environmental endangerment are manifestly correct on this record. That is all that is required under § 6972(a)(1)(B), which imposes liability for endangerments to the environment, including water in and of itself. *See, e.g.,* 42 U.S.C. § 6903(3) (defining "disposal" to include waste discharges "into or on any land or water" where waste is "emitted into the air or discharged into any waters, including groundwaters"). Honeywell does not argue otherwise, concedes direct exposure pathways, and faces evidence of, *inter alia,* concentrations of contamination in groundwater to be on the order of hundreds if not thousands of times greater than the relevant state standard would allow. Indeed, Honeywell concedes the groundwater at the

Site is in "danger" because it is so highly contaminated by hexavalent chromium. Chromium from its Site is also discharging into the Hackensack River, which, like groundwater, is part of the environment in and of itself.

IV.   PROPRIETY OF THE INJUNCTION

Honeywell argues the District Court erred in enjoining Honeywell to clean up its Site through excavation and removal of the contaminated waste. In addition to the findings of fact we have already discussed, the District Court also found, specific to remedy, that a permanent solution (as opposed to an interim solution) was necessary within the meaning of the statute to eliminate the established endangerments; that NJDEP had already independently come to the same conclusion; that injunctive relief, as opposed to some other form of relief, was necessary to obtain a remedy that was permanent; that Honeywell presented no credible evidence at trial that either a containment "cap" or shallow groundwater treatment, or both, would be an effective permanent remedy; and that excavation and removal of the contamination from the Site was necessary within the meaning of the statute to ensure a permanent remedy. The evidence shows that experts presented all other conceivable remedial options known to be potentially available, and, on the basis of computer modeling and other factual and scientific grounds, they demonstrated why none were appropriate for the site except excavation. These included capping, encapsulation, reactive barriers, vitrification, solidification and stabilization, bioremediation, chemical reduction, chemical stabilization, chemical extraction, electrokinetics, soil washing, and, finally, "pump and treat" remedies.

The injunction's language, read in conjunction with the District Court's findings, confirms the necessity for the injunction within the meaning of RCRA. The injunction only orders Honeywell to excavate and remove contaminated soil and then "remedy" those river sediments that have been contaminated with chromium residue from the Site. As to deep groundwater, the injunction only requires Honeywell to study the contamination, and provides that, once that study is complete, the District Court will order additional remedial actions only if "necessary." Given the record in this case, the injunction is reasonable and narrow, as it requires only what is necessary now to abate the established endangerments.

Honeywell next argues that the injunction does not serve a public interest. In its brief, Honeywell poses the question as follows: even if cleaning up hexavalent chromium would be "better" for humans living near the site "and for some barnacles and clams in the Hackensack River ... is it worthwhile to move over 1,500,000 tons of fill" and replace it with "over 1,500,000 tons of clean fill?" Honeywell asserts that environmental agencies would answer this question in the negative, and that therefore the District Court erred in reaching a different conclusion.

Without a doubt, the injunction will require the movement of a substantial amount of fill. Nevertheless, Honeywell's framing of the issue misses the point in several respects: the 1,500,000 tons of fill are all contaminated with a hazardous waste; plaintiffs have satisfied the standard for liability; and the evidence they adduced persuaded the District Court that a cleaning up through excavation was necessary, even in light of the monetary and other costs associated with that remedy, including the use of hazardous waste landfill capacities. The record shows the District Court considered the cost-benefit analysis evidence appropriately and made findings consistent with the public interest as reflected in the applicable statutory scheme.

In passing RCRA, Congress established a national policy to "minimize the present and future threat to human health and the environment" from wastes of the type found at Honeywell's Site, 42 U.S.C. § 6902, and Congress has instructed that § 6972 "is intended to allow citizens exactly the same broad substantive and procedural claim for relief which is already available to the United States under section 7003." S.Rep. No. 98–284, 98th Cong., 1st Sess., at 59 (1983). We have previously determined that "due to the nature of the hazards presented by disposal sites, section 7003 is intended to confer upon the courts the authority to grant affirmative equitable relief to eliminate any risks posed by toxic wastes." *Price,* 688 F.2d at 213–14. As such, Honeywell's claim that the District Court "ignore[d] the judgment of Congress, deliberately expressed in legislation" is without merit.

Honeywell's final argument is that the District Court improperly overrode an ongoing administrative process. As discussed *supra,* the District Court's findings as to Honeywell's dilatory tactics and NJDEP's inability to deal effectively with those tactics are not clear error. Indeed, a fair reading of the record casts strong doubt as to whether there *is* a process to override in this case. Honeywell next suggests that NJDEP's presence alone precludes a judicial remedy, given Congress' preference for agency-directed cleanups. Not only does the statute not bar the remedy here, but Congress has rejected Honeywell's argument outright. *See* S.Rep. No. 98–284, 98th Cong., 1st Sess. at 57 (1983) "[C]itizens need not exhaust or rely upon other resources or remedies before seeking relief under these amendments. As with Section 7003, these amendments are to be an alternative and supplement to other remedies." Courts should consider the availability of other alternatives, as the District Court did here, but there is no requirement to defer to them, notwithstanding Honeywell's protestations otherwise. *Id.*

More fundamentally, Honeywell argues the remedial injunction usurps agency power. The reconciliation of such power in the injunctive context, however, is not difficult. Honeywell has violated the statute; and, despite Honeywell's argument to the contrary, nothing in the statute precludes the nature of the injunctive relief ordered here. Depending on the particular characteristics of a given RCRA site, as found by a district court on a case-by-case basis, particular types of injunctive relief may not be circumscribed by arguments as to what an agency might have done. "The comprehensiveness of [a court's] equitable jurisdiction is not to be denied or limited in the absence of a clear and valid legislative command." Here, the enforcement language of § 6972(a)(1)(B) is generous: it says that a district court may, *inter alia,* "order ... such other action as may be necessary" to remedy a violation of the statute. Nothing in this language precludes, as part of this enforcement authority, measures such as those required by the District Court here. Certainly we have not been cited to authority requiring otherwise.

VI. CONCLUSION

We have considered all of the other arguments advanced by the parties and conclude that no further discussion is necessary. Enough time has already been spent in the history of this matter and the time for a clean-up has come. Accordingly, the judgment of the District Court will be affirmed.

NOTES AND QUESTIONS

1. The remedy approved in *Interfaith Community Org.* involved injunctive relief—actual remediation and additional study. The Supreme Court has held that § 7002(a)(1)(B) does not authorize recovery of response costs incurred by the plaintiff in remediating the endangerment prior to bringing the action. *See Meghrig v. KFC Western, Inc,* 516 U.S. 479 (1996). Courts later held that response costs cannot be recovered under § 7002(a)(1)(B) even if they were incurred after the complaint was filed. *See, e.g., Avondale Federal Savings Bank v. Amoco Oil Co.,* 170 F.3d 692 (7th Cir. 1999). CERCLA, discussed in Chapter 6, provides several causes of action for recovery of response costs.

2. An action under § 7002(a)(1)(B) can be brought if there is an "imminent and substantial endangerment" from any "solid or hazardous waste." Thus, a § 7002(a)(1)(B) action is not limited to Subtitle C hazardous wastes. Nor does it require that the waste be a hazardous waste; a plaintiff may show that an "imminent and substantial endangerment" result from a "solid waste." As discussed above in section B.1, it is the statutory and not regulatory definition of solid waste that applies, and thus a § 7002(a)(1)(B) action may, but need not, involve parsing the regulatory definition of solid waste at 40 C.F.R. § 261.2. *See Comite Pro Rescate de la Salud v. Puerto Rico Aqueduct & Sewer Auth.,* 888 F.2d 180 (1st Cir. 1989) (discussing rationale for use of the broader statutory definition in a § 7002(a)(1)(B) action).

The material must, however, still be a solid waste. Is a hazardous product or a hazardous material that is intentionally applied to the land a "solid waste" for purposes of § 7002(a)(1)(B)? As we have seen, in *Connecticut Coastal* above, the court concluded that at some point lead shot and clay targets could be a solid waste if left long enough in the environment. In *No Spray Coalition v. City of New York,* 252 F.3d 148 (2d Cir. 2001), the court held that a § 7002(a)(1)(B) action could not be brought with respect to pesticide sprayed into the air since the pesticide was not "discarded" it performed its intended purpose—"reaching and killing mosquitoes."

In *Safe Air for Everyone v. Meyer,* 373 F.3d 1035 (9th Cir. 2004), the court held that grass residue left after harvesting was not a solid waste for purposes of § 7002(a)(1)(B). Largely relying on the logic of D.C. Circuit cases addressing the regulatory definition of hazardous wastes, the court applied a test for waste that included an assessment of (1) whether the material is "destined for beneficial reuse or recycling in a continuous process by the generating industry itself, (2) whether the materials are being actively reused, or whether they merely have the potential of being reused, and (3) whether the materials are being reused by their original owner, as opposed to being used by a salvager or reclaimer.

3. Are products that have unintentionally leaked into the environment a "solid waste" under § 7002(a)(1)(B)? Most courts have held that products that have leaked from underground storage tanks are "solid wastes" under § 7002(a)(1)(B). *See, e.g, Zands v. Nelson*, 779 F.Supp. 1254 (S.D. Cal. 1991)(the release of petroleum into the soil constituted disposal of a solid waste and therefore could properly be the subject of an action under § 7002(a)(1)(B)). The applicability of § 7002(a)(1)(B) to releases of petroleum is particularly significant since the "petroleum exclusion" limits the applicability of CERCLA in those situations.

4. Plaintiffs in a § 7002(a)(1)(B) action must show that the solid waste "may present an imminent and substantial endangerment," and as indicated in *Interfaith Community Org.* most courts have adopted an expansive interpretation of the phrase. It would presumably be satisfied by demonstrating a current risk of serious future harm. As the court noted, a § 7002(a)(B) action is not limited to threats to human health; it may also involve endangerment of the "environment." In *Aiello v. Town of Brookhaven*, 136 F. Supp. 2d 81 (E.D.N.Y. 2001). the court, quoting Henry David Thoreau, found that aesthetic injuries resulting from the visual blight of polluted water at a landfill were relevant in establishing an imminent and substantial endangerment.

Although a § 7002(a)(1)(B) action may require only a risk of harm, what conditions create that risk? The court in *Interfaith Community Org.* rejected a need to demonstrate that a population was actually exposed, but then relied on evidence that there was a "pathway" by which humans could be exposed to the contamination to uphold a finding of an "imminent and substantial endangerment."

What if there is no threat of exposure to humans? Is there an "imminent and substantial endangerment" when the contamination is contained and there is not likelihood of human exposure? In *Price v. United States Navy*, 39 F.3d 1011 (9th Cir. 1994), the court held that there was no imminent and substantial endangerment from contaminated material possibly located under the sealed foundation of a house.

Is there an "imminent and substantial endangerment" from contaminated groundwater, if everyone in the area gets there water from a public water supply? In *Leister v. Black & Decker (U.S.), Inc.*, 117 F.3d 1414 (4th Cir. 1997), the court held that there was no imminent and substantial endangerment from trichloroethylene (TCE) and tetrachloroethylene (PCE) that were present on the property and in groundwater. The court wrote:

> Although the Leisters direct our attention to evidence that TCE and PCE are still present on the Property and on their dairy farm, there is simply no evidence in the record—expert or otherwise—to suggest that the presence of these substances poses a current serious threat of harm. Indeed, the Leisters' own evidence suggests that drinking water from the Leisters' wells—the most direct pathway of exposure—presents no

threat to health because of filtration systems. In the absence of affirmative proof of an immediate serious threat of harm, the Leisters' RCRA claim under § 6972(a)(1)(B) must fail.

See also Two Rivers Terminal, L.P. v. Chevron USA, 96 F. Supp. 2d 432, 446 (M.D. Pa. 2000).

In *Scotchtown Holdings LLP v. Town of Goshen*, 2009 WL 27445 (S.D.N.Y. 2009), the court rejected an "imminent and substantial endangerment" action brought by a developer. The groundwater on the developer's property was contaminated with road salt at levels that would mean it could not be approved for human consumption. The court held that since the water could not be used for human consumption it could not create an imminent and substantial endangerment. The noted that this creates a "catch–22;" the water cannot be approved for use because it is contaminated, and it is not an "imminent and substantial endangerment" because it cannot be used.

5. The "imminent and substantial endangerment" must exist at the time the action is brought, and therefore a § 7002(a)(1)(B) action may not be brought for conditions that have already been remediated. *See Meghrig v. KFC Western, Inc.*, 516 U.S. 479 (1996). This creates a nice dilemma. Clean up a condition that creates an imminent and substantial endangerment and you have lost your cause of action under § 7002(a)(1)(B); wait and the imminent and substantial endangerment continues.

6. RCRA § 7002(b)(2)(B) specifies the situations in which a State action will bar an action under § 7002(a)(1)(B); these include situations in which the State has commenced its own action under § 7002(a)(1)(B) or is taking certain actions under CERCLA. The section does not prohibit a citizen suit simply because the State is addressing the situation under other authority. In *Interfaith Community Org.*, the court concluded that it was appropriate to allow a § 7002(a)(1)(B) to proceed although the State was addressing the same conditions in an administrative action. The defendants had argued that if court issued relief under § 7002(a)(1)(B) it would "usurp" State authority, and relying on the doctrine of "Burford Abstention," at least one court has declined to exercise federal jurisdiction where there was an on-going State proceeding addressing the conditions. *See Space Age Fuels v. Standard Oil Co. of Ca.*, 1996 WL 160741 (D. Ore. 1996). *But see PMC v. Sherwin–Williams Co.*, 151 F.3d 610, 618 (7th Cir. 1998) (declining to apply Burford Abstention in 7002(a)(1)(B) action).

7. Although EPA has promulgated regulations governing the content of a notice letter for purposes of a § 7002(a)(1)(A), these regulations do not apply to a § 7002(a)(1)(B) action. In *Board of Cty Comm. Of Cty of La Plata v. Brown Group Retail, Inc.*, 598 F.Supp.2d 1185 (D.Colo. 2009), the court noted the absence of an EPA regulation governing the requirement of a notice letter under § 7002(a)(1)(B) and held that notice was adequate if it was sufficient, among other things, to inform the defendant of "the nature of the ongoing problems on the facility site and of its potential responsibility for those problems."

8. Section 7002(a)(1)(B) provides a cause of action against a person who "has contributed or is contributing" to an imminent and substantial

endangerment. The section provides that person includes any "past or present generator, past or present transporter and past or present owner or operator of a treatment, storage or disposal facility.

Courts have broadly interpreted to scope of parties who may be liable for contributing to an imminent and substantial endangerment. *See generally Cox v. City of Dallas, Tex.*, 256 F.3d 281 (5th Cir. 2001), (an extensive discussion of the meaning of "contributed" in its discussion of the municipal liability under § 7002(a)(1)(B) for releases from dumps used by the city). In *Zands v. Nelson*, 779 F.Supp. 1254 (S.D. Cal. 1991), the court held that liability for releases from underground storage tanks (USTs) extended to 1) persons who owned land during the time that USTs leaked, 2) the operators of the pumps that leaked, and 3) the installers of the leaking tanks. But liability has limits. At least one court has held that a person who bought land after a release from an UST without knowledge of the release and who did not add contaminants would not be liable as a "contributor." *See First San Diego Properties v. Exxon Co.*, 859 F.Supp. 1313 (S.D. Cal. 1994). In *Sycamore Indus. Park Assoc. v. Ericsson, Inc.*, 546 F.3d 847 (7th Cir. 2008). the court held that a seller of a building containing a heating system with asbestos insulation did not "contribute" to any handling or storage of a waste. In the court's view, "RCRA requires active involvement in handling or storing of materials to be liable."

9. Section 7002(a)(1)(B) specifically provides that "persons," includes "past or present" generators, transporters and TSDFs, and courts have held that § 7002(a)(1)(B) applies to acts committed prior to adoption of RCRA. *See Tanglewood East Homeowners v. Charles–Thomas, Inc.*, 849 F.2d 1568 (5th Cir. 1988) (language of § 7002(a)(1)(B) allows injunctive relief based on "past or present conduct.")

PROBLEM

Your client, PropCo, purchased Blackacre about three years ago. PropCo planned to subdivide the Blackacre and construct and sell homes. During the process of developing the property, PropCo learned that the former owner disposed of chrome and zinc containing wastes that have leached into groundwater beneath the property. Focusing exclusively on § 7002 of RCRA, what possible cause of actions are available to the landowner to either compel the former owner to clean up the existing contamination, to compensate the landowner if it undertakes a cleanup itself, or to recover damages for loss of property value from the presence of the wastes? What information might you need to know in evaluating the availability of these causes of action?

F. INTERNATIONAL TRADE IN HAZARDOUS WASTE

The issue of hazardous waste is not purely a domestic one. As domestic costs for disposal of hazardous waste rise, there are economic incentives to find places where the cost of disposal are lower, and increasing quantities of hazardous wastes and recyclables are subject to international trade. There are many notorious examples of problems arising from this trade. In 2006 at least 10 people died when hazardous waste was disposed of in Abidjan, the capital of the Ivory Coast. The waste was reported as a

> mix of petrochemical waste transported by a Panamanian-registered tanker chartered by the Dutch firm Trafigura. The pitch-black sludge found its way from Amsterdam—via Estonia and Nigeria—to Ivory Coast aboard the Korean-built and Greek-managed Probo Koala.

Ivory Coast Tragedy Exposes Toxic Flow to Poor, NPR website (Oct. 4, 2006), http://www.npr.org/templates/story/story.php?storyId=6354149. In 1987, 8,000 barrels of hazardous waste from Italian companies were imported into Nigeria. The barrels, found in storage in the port of Lagos, contained toxic waste including polychlorinated biphenyls, and they were ultimately returned to Europe. Widespread protests accompanied the return of the wastes, and the incident helped prompt adoption of the Basel Convention on the international trade in hazardous waste, discussed below. http://www.ban.org/about_ basel_ ban/chronology.html.

The issue of international trade in recyclable materials also raises particular problems. A report of the General Accountability Office has described issues relating to the recycling electronic waste. The report noted:

> A growing concern is the international trade in hazardous recyclables, including electronic wastes. Recent surveys conducted on behalf of the United Nations Environment Programme found that used electronics imported from the United States are dismantled in many developing countries under unsafe health conditions. Other investigations have corroborated disassembly practice in some Asian countries involving the open-air burning of wire to recover copper and open acid baths for separating metals. These practices expose people to lead and other hazardous materials. China, in particular, has been at the center of much of the world's attention regarding electronic waste export issues since 2002, when environmental groups first exposed egregious electronics-recycling and disposal practices in Guiyu and other areas in southeastern China.

GAO, Electronic Waste: EPA Needs to Better Control Harmful U.S. Exports Through Stronger Enforcement and More Effective Regulation 6 GAO–08–1044 (August 2008).

Although international trade in hazardous waste and recyclables raises particular concerns when it involves transfers of waste from developed countries to less developed countries, much of the trade involves transfers among the developed countries of the Organization for Economic Cooperation and Development ("OECD") that include, among others, most European countries and the United States. As of 1990, over 90% of wastes exported from the United States went to either Canada or Mexico. *See* Grant L. Kratz, *Implementing the Basel Convention into U.S Law: Will It Help or Hinder Recycling Efforts?"* 6 B.Y.U. J. Pub. L. 323 (1992).

Charts prepared for the United Nations Environment Programme ("UNEP") shows the growth of the international trade in hazardous wastes and recyclables.

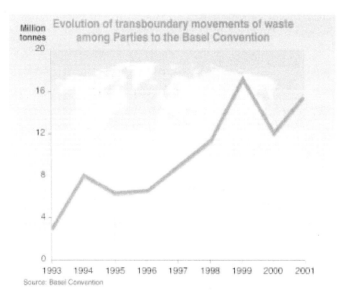

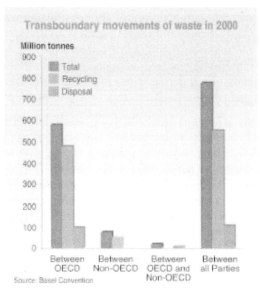

http://www.grida.no/publications/vg/waste/page/2865.aspx

The international trade in hazardous wastes and recyclables raises difficult questions of international law and environmental protection. Proper regulation of hazardous wastes and recyclables involve complex technical and policy questions and can involve trade-offs of environmental risk for economic development. International principles of "state sovereignty" suggest that the decision to accept hazardous waste should be made by the government involved. In fact, most of the legal instruments discussed below involve some form of "notice and consent" regime in which notice must be given to a receiving country prior to the export of covered hazardous materials, but export is allowed if there is formal "consent" by the government of the receiving country. Thus, regulation of the trade in hazardous waste and recyclables largely rests on the political decisions of the country receiving the waste.

1.   REGULATION OF THE EXPORT AND IMPORT OF HAZARDOUS WASTES UNDER RCRA

Section 3017 of RCRA establishes basic requirements for the import and export of hazardous waste. The statute prohibits the export of hazardous waste unless 1) the exporter satisfies certain "notice and consent" requirements or 2) U.S. and importing country have established a treaty authorizing the export. RCRA § 3017(a). "Notice and consent" systems, common among the multi-lateral and bi-lateral treaties discussed below, basically require notification of intent to export wastes and a requirement that officials of the receiving country provide consent to the shipment.

a.   REGULATION OF EXPORTS UNDER RCRA

There are two main components of EPA regulations dealing with the export of wastes. First, 40 C.F.R. Part 262 contain specific regulatory requirements dealing with the export of "hazardous wastes." 40 C.F.R. Part 262, Subpart E contains generally applicable requirements for the export of hazardous wastes for disposal or recycling. 40 C.F.R. Part 262, Subpart H contains specific requirements applicable to the export of hazardous wastes for recycling to countries in the Organization for Economic Cooperation and Development (except Mexico and Canada). The regulations establish the following basic requirements:

- The "primary" exporter of a Subtitle C hazardous waste must provide notification of its intent to export at least sixty days prior to export. 40 C.F.R. § 262.53. The primary exporter is the person who is required to originate the manifest under RCRA or comparable state regulations. 40 C.F.R. § 262.51. The notification must be sent to EPA and it must contain certain general information about the waste and the countries through which the waste will transit and the country that will finally receive the waste.

- EPA, in conjunction with the State Department, is responsible for providing notification to the receiving country and any countries though which the waste will transit.

- The waste may be exported if the receiving country consents to the shipment. Upon receipt of the consent EPA will issue an "Acknowledgment of Consent," and this document must accompany the shipment. If the receiving country objects to the shipment, EPA must notify the primary exporter.

- A primary exporter must file an "exception report" with EPA if the exporter has not received (1) a signed copy of the manifest from the transporter within forty-five days of the date the wastes were accepted for transport by the initial transporter, or (2) a written confirmation from the consignee that the wastes have been received within ninety days of the date the wastes were accepted for transport by the initial transporter, or (3) the waste is returned to the United States.

Second, EPA in 2008 promulgated a regulation that conditionally excludes exported "hazardous secondary materials" from classification as a solid waste. 40 C.F.R. § 261.4(a)(25). This exclusion imposes similar "notice and consent" requirements that apply to the export of non-excluded wastes. Since these materials are excluded from classification as a solid waste, they may now avoid coverage under other laws or treaties, such as the OECD requirements discussed below, that are triggered by a domestic classification of a material as a solid or hazardous waste.

In addition to the general RCRA regulations governing exports of hazardous waste, EPA has also established specific requirements on the export of certain wastes. EPA has, for example, established specific "notification and consent" requirements applicable to the export of cathode ray tubes (CRTs) for recycling. 40 C.F.R. §§ 261.39(a)(5), 261.40, 261.41. EPA has also established specific export requirements for small quantity handlers of universal wastes. 40 C.F.R. § 273.20(a).

b. REGULATION OF THE IMPORTS UNDER RCRA

The regulations governing the import of hazardous waste into the United States impose essentially the same requirements on imported hazardous waste that are applicable to wastes generated in the U.S. 40 C.F.R. Part 262, Subpart F. Thus, imported hazardous wastes are subject to similar manifest, transport and disposal requirements as domestically generated hazardous waste. There are, however, some special requirements applicable to the completion of the manifest accompanying these wastes. 40 C.F.R. § 262.60(b)

2. REGULATION OF THE IMPORT AND EXPORT OF HAZARDOUS WASTE UNDER INTERNATIONAL TREATIES

a. BILATERAL TREATIES WITH CANADA AND MEXICO

The U.S. has entered into a number of bilateral treaties that authorize the import and export of wastes and recyclable materials. By far the most significant of these are U.S. treaties with Canada and Mexico since, as of 1990, over 90 percent of U.S. international trade in hazardous wastes involves these two countries. *See* Grant L. Kratz, "Implementing the Basel Convention into U.S Law: Will It Help or Hinder Recycling Efforts?," 6 B.Y.U. J. Pub. L. 323 (1992). The Canada/U.S. Agreement, originally entered in 1986, establishes a "notice and consent" system for transboundary shipments of "hazardous waste" for "treatment, storage or disposal." Notification requires submission of limited information, and if no objection or conditions are imposed within 30 days of receipt of notice, consent is presumed. Agreement Between the Government of Canada and the Government of the United States of America Concerning the Transboundary Movement of Hazardous Waste, Oct. 28, 1986, U.S.-Can., T.I.A.S. No. 11,099, http://www.epa.gov/epaoswer/osw/internat/agree.htm. The Mexico/U.S. Agreement, like the Canada/U.S. Agreement, is based on notice and consent requirements. Notification must be provided to the designated government authorities, but notice must be provided 45 days prior to shipment and consent is not presumed. Annex III to the Agreement on Cooperation for the Protection and Improvement of the Environment in the Border Area, Agreement of Cooperation Between the United States of America and the United Mexican States Regarding the Transboundary Shipments of Hazardous Wastes and Hazard Substances, http://www.epa.-gov/epaoswer/osw/internat/agree.htm. *See generally* Jeffrey M. Gaba and Donald E. Stever, The Law of Solid Waste, Pollution Prevention and Recycling, § 9:66.1.

b. ORGANIZATION FOR ECONOMIC COOPERATION AND
    DEVELOPMENT

EPA has also adopted Subpart H to 40 C.F.R. Part 262 that governs the import and export of recyclable wastes to countries in the Organization for Economic Cooperation and Development (OECD). The regulations implement various OECD Decisions regarding the movement of recyclable materials within the OECD. *See* Council Decision C(2001)107/FINAL Concerning the Control of Transfrontier Movements of Wastes Destined for Recovery Operations. The Subpart H regulations apply to recyclable wastes that are transferred between countries in the OECD. For purposes of this requirement, those countries include: Australia, Austria, Belgium, Denmark, Finland, France, Germany, Greece, Iceland, Ireland, Italy, Japan, Luxembourg, the Netherlands, New Zealand, Norway, Portugal, Spain, Sweden, Switzerland, Turkey, the United Kingdom, and the United States. The regulations also address the transit of recyclable wastes across the OECD countries.

These regulations are based on "notice and consent," but they establish different requirements based on classification of the regulated materials as either "green" or "amber" wastes. Under these regulations covered materials include "wastes" that are defined as hazardous wastes under RCRA and are either subject to the RCRA manifest requirement or to the universal waste management standards. 40 C.F.R. § 262.80(a). Thus, exported hazardous secondary materials that are "conditionally excluded" from classification as solid wastes and hazardous wastes generated by "conditionally exempt small quantity generators" are not subject to these requirements.

c. BASEL CONVENTION ON THE TRANSBOUNDARY MOVEMENTS
    OF HAZARDOUS WASTE AND THEIR DISPOSAL

The Basel Convention on the Control of Transboundary Movements of Hazardous Wastes and their Disposal was adopted in 1989 and went into force in 1992. Basel Convention on the Control of Transboundary Movements of Hazardous Wastes and Their Disposal, U.N.E.P. Doc. I.G.80/3 (March 22, 1989), reprinted in 28 I.L.M. 657 (1989). The Basel Convention, the primary multilateral instrument dealing with international shipments of wastes, itself establishes a "notice and consent" regime with some additional teeth. It purports to prohibit the export of wastes to countries that do not ensure "environmentally sound management" of the wastes.

Basel Convention, Arts. 4.2(e), 4.8. As of April 2005, 167 countries were parties to the Convention.

The U.S. signed, but has not yet ratified, the Basel Convention and is therefore not directly bound by its provisions. Ratification of the Convention is seen as requiring some revisions to U.S. domestic law, and since the administration of the first President Bush, legislation has been introduced to amend RCRA to conform to the Convention. None have been adopted.

Although the U.S. has not ratified the Convention, it still has significant implications for the import and export of wastes from the U.S. First, under the terms of the Convention, parties who have ratified the Convention may not trade in wastes with a non-party unless the two countries have a suitable bi-lateral agreement. Basel Convention Arts. 4.5, 11. In other words, the Basel Convention on its face prevents ratifying parties, other than perhaps Mexico, Canada, and the OECD countries, from exporting waste to or importing wastes from the United States

NOTES AND QUESTIONS

1.   The reliance on "notice and consent" rather than a requirement that importing countries meet some minimum level of environmental regulation of suggests that the international community accepts the proposition that individual countries may rationally make different decisions regarding both the acceptability and level of regulation for management of hazardous wastes. The principle in international law of "state sovereignty" suggests that individual countries be allowed to exercise their own judgment about environmental policies at least with respect to environmental effects that occur within their borders.

Why might one country choose to accept hazardous wastes for disposal or recycling which another country might reject?

2.   The export of hazardous wastes for disposal or recycling to less developed countries raises a number of particularly troubling issues. Less developed countries, it has been argued, have less technical capacity to manage or supervise disposal or recycling operations or the expertise to make informed decisions. The poverty of many LDCs and the costs of disposal in more tightly regulated countries, however, make the economic incentives to export the wastes substantial. In 1988, Guinea–Bissau was offered $600 million dollars to accept shipments of hazardous waste. This amount was four times greater than Guinea–Bissau' s then gross national product. Zada Lipman, Trade in Hazardous Waste: Environmental Justice Versus Economic Growth, http://www.ban.org/Library/lipman.html#fn14

Concerns about transfer of developed countries wastes for disposal in less developed countries have produced calls for total bans on the practice. The "Basel Ban" is an amendment to the Basel Convention that would prohibit the export of hazardous wastes from developed countries (including OECD countries) to other less developed countries. The Basel Ban has not yet been ratified by a sufficient number of parties to go into effect. The Bamako Convention represents another mechanism to restrict the trade in hazardous wastes with less development countries. The Bamako Convention ratified by over a dozen members of the African Union prohibits the import of hazardous wastes from non-signatories into Africa.

Are there reasons to treat trade in hazardous wastes any differently that we treat trade in more conventional products?

3. We live in a world where the dominant economic theory supports unrestricted trade among countries. Stemming in part from the analysis of the economist David Ricardo in the 18th century, conventional economic theory has supported the idea that the free movement of goods among nations will produce greater wealth for all trading countries. This is the foundation for the World Trade Organization and General Agreement on Tariffs and Trade ("WTO/GATT") regime that has acted to reduce tariffs and trade barriers among international trading partners. Under WTO/GATT, virtually all countries have voluntarily surrendered a measure of control over domestic policy to obtain the presumed wealth generating advantages of a system of international free trade. These limitations on state sovereignty are embodied in the "trade disciplines" contained in WTO/GATT that restrict governments from imposing certain types of domestic regulations or charges affecting international trade. Thus, the "most favored nation" provisions of Art. I of GATT prohibit a WTO member from establishing trade barriers that favor one WTO member over another. The "national treatment" provisions of Art. III prohibit GATT members from adopting regulations or fees that favor its domestic products over imports from other GATT members. Environmental exceptions in Art. XX(b) and (g) provide uncertain authority for countries to allow their environmental policies to override the trade disciplines.

In a wide variety of contexts, the WTO/GATT has acted to limit a nation's ability to impose environmentally based restrictions on imports, and WTO/GATT has implications for the control on the international trade in hazardous wastes and recyclables. In 2008, for example, a panel of the WTO invalidated Brazil's prohibition on the import of waste tires. *See* Brazil—Measures Affecting Imports of Retreaded Tyres, WT/DS332/R (12 June 2007); Colm Patrick McInerney, *From Shrimps and Dolphins to Retreaded Tyres: An Overview of the World Trade Organization Disputes, Discussing Exceptions to the Trading Rules*, 22 N.Y. Int'l L.Rev. 153 (Winter 2009).

The relationship between "multinational environmental agreements" ("MEAs"), such as the Basel Convention, and WTO/GATT raises issues that are currently unresolved. *See* Tanya Katrina A. Lat, *Testing the Limits of GATT Art. XX(B): Toxic Waste Trade, Japan's Economic Partnership Agreements, and the WTO*, 21 Geo. Int'l Envtl. L.Rev. 367 (Winter 2009). The WTO is specifically attempting to address this relationship. *See http://www.wto. org/english/tratop_e/envir_e/envir_neg_mea_e.htm#relationship.*

G.   ENVIRONMENTAL JUSTICE

Environmental Justice is the fair treatment and meaningful involvement of all people regardless of race, color, national origin, or income with respect to the development, implementation, and enforcement of environmental laws, regulations, and policies. EPA has this goal for all communities and persons across this Nation. It will be achieved when everyone enjoys the same degree of protection from environmental and health hazards and equal access to the decision-making process to have a healthy environment in which to live, learn, and work.

Environmental Protection Agency, Environmental Justice Home, http://www.epa.gov/oecaerth/environmentaljustice/

1.   The Issue of Environmental Justice

The issue of Environmental justice involves an assessment of the distribution of benefits and burdens in society. Our industrial society produces tremendous benefits in terms of creation of wealth; it also creates burdens in the form of industrial pollution. Environmental justice involves identifying who is subject to harm, if that harm is in some sense "disproportionate" or otherwise unfair, and a proper legal response to any problems that are identified.

Environmental justice is also about wealth, power and discrimination. It would not be surprising if the poorest and least powerful in society bore a disproportionate share of the burden. It would also not be surprising if groups who have historically been subject to discrimination and racism might also be subject to a disproportionate share of environmental harms. As discussed below, the Environmental Justice movement grew out of the Civil Rights movement, and it has a both an equitable and legal focus on racial and ethnic discrimination.

Carlton Waterhouse, Abandon All Hope Ye that Enter? Equal Protection, Title VI, and the Divine Comedy of Environmental Justice
20 Fordham Envtl. L.Rev. 51 (2009)

Environmental Justice Background

The Environmental Justice movement began as a continuation of the civil rights movement, and focused on the prevalence of racism in the environmental arena. Its national prominence can be traced to Warren County, North Carolina, which under the leadership of Congressman Walter Fauntleroy mirrored the "campaigns" of the civil rights movement. Organizers fighting against the placement of a hazardous waste landfill in the area protested and used civil disobedience to challenge what they understood was "environmental racism." After a truck driver traversed the state from the northern to the southern border and back again discharging waste oils along the shoulders of Interstate Highway 85, state officials decided to place a toxic waste landfill in Warren County to hold the contaminated soils gathered from across the state. Protestors challenged the action as racism because the site selected was in the county with the largest black population of the state near a black residential area. Congressman Fauntleroy was arrested along with 500 others during the protest. Upon his return to Washington he requested a General Accounting Office (GAO) study examining the demographics of communities with hazardous waste sites in the southeast.

The 1985 GAO study found that three out of five hazardous waste landfills in the southeast region were located in predominantly black or Latino areas. It was soon followed by a 1987 report, entitled "Toxic Waste and Race" by the Commission for Racial Justice of the United Church of Christ. That report was more extensive than the GAO study. It looked at the list of uncontrolled toxic waste sites contained in the Environmental Protection Agency Comprehensive Environmental Response, Compensation and Liability Information System (CERCLIS) database and mapped them unto zip codes across the country. Using census data, the study then correlated the zip codes with waste sites and the demographic data for nearby residents. Beyond analyzing the racial makeup of residents, the study also examined residential income to assess its relative significance in the location of waste sites. Report author, Charles Lee, and others, reported in the study that regardless of their income African–Americans disproportionately lived in zip codes with uncontrolled toxic waste sites. Within a year, a book by sociologist Robert Bullard of the Clark Atlanta University in Atlanta, Georgia, entitled "Dumping in Dixie" provided an academic examination of a historic and continuing phenomenon that relegated many undesirable waste disposal and polluting facilities to predominantly black areas. With the GAO study, Commission for Racial Justice report, and Professor Bullard's book bolstering their claims, local activists and more prominent civil rights leaders began to draw attention to racial disparities in the siting of pollution related facilities. In response to growing awareness and pressure, in 1990, Environmental Protection Agency (hereinafter "EPA") Administrator William Reilly, commissioned an agency task force to determine what relationship existed between race and pollution. Rejecting the activists' claims that EPA and others participated in environmental racism; the Administrator adopted the name "Environmental Equity" to describe the concerns raised by activists.

Because the southeast region represented a focal point of environmental racism claims, the EPA's Region Four office in Atlanta became a major battlefield in the controversy. When the EPA's Draft Environmental Equity report was issued in 1992, the author had been an attorney in the EPA Region Four Office of Regional Counsel for less than one year. Coinciding with the issuance of the report, regional personnel and local organizers convened a meeting of activists from across the region to come and discuss their concerns with EPA personnel. At the well-attended meeting, one of the concerns raised was the EPA's decision to study "environmental equity" instead of "environmental racism."

Though couched in semantic terms, this disagreement reflected a fundamental difference in the understanding that they and the EPA had over the issue. Activists felt that race affected the decisions of corporations and state officials in choosing sites for unwanted pollution. Though activists lacked direct evidence of racial animus, they believed that the disparity in siting shown by the preceding studies and their own experience confirmed the phenomenon. On the other hand, the EPA's position reflected the view that racism was a charged word and that the behavior of their grant recipients, personnel, and others should not be so described absent clear evidence to that effect. The disagreement escalated when the director of the Commission for Racial Justice, Benjamin Chavis Jr., popularized the phrase "environmental racism." The issue continued to play out in the following three new contexts: studies contesting racial disparity in siting, federal court cases brought under the Equal Protection Clause of the Fourteenth Amendment and Title VI of the Civil Rights Act, and administrative complaints filed with the EPA alleging Title VI violations by EPA grant recipients. Nonetheless, both the EPA and activists accepted "Environmental Justice" to describe their concern and the apparent disagreement faded.

The EPA created an Office of Environmental Justice in the agency Administrator's Office. It was tasked with investigating the issue and educating agency personnel on how to approach citizens' concerns. The first director, Clarice Gaylord, had a Ph.D. in atmospheric science and brought a scientific perspective and background to the issue. She was assisted in the task with corresponding regional directors. In Region Four, where a substantial number of "Environmental Justice" hot spots existed, Vivian Malone Jones was hired to direct the office. A love-hate relationship soon developed as William Clinton was elected President of the United States, and the EPA announced that "Environmental Justice" was one of its top five priorities. The EPA soon became the agency that Environmental Justice activists loved to hate. Serving as a clearinghouse for activists to voice their concerns, the EPA modified many of its policies and practices of community relations and took substantial strides to give voice to the concerns raised by "EJ communities." The agency provided numerous grants, sponsored several conferences and created a National Environmental Justice Advisory Council (NEJAC) to inform the agency on ways to achieve its Environmental Justice goals.

One of the greatest benefits of these developments was the raised awareness gained by Native American, African–American, Latino, and other community members near Superfund sites and other pollution related facilities. During this time period, communities began to share stories, ideas, and knowledge to assist each other in learning about the risks they faced and the tools to decrease or eliminate them. In 1994, President William Clinton supported these developments across the federal government by issuing Executive Order 12898, directing federal agencies to identify and address disproportionately high and adverse human health effects affecting minority and low income populations.

Under this regime, Environmental Justice became an exercise in community relations for the EPA, state agencies, and corporations. Rather than the development of an environmental policy that attended to the alleged disparity in pollution exposure, the Environmental Justice movement raised the awareness of community members concerning their role in environmental decision-making and forced agency officials to develop a more effective means of dealing with the concerns of "minority" and "low income" populations. This represented a genuine improvement over the status quo. In fact, at the local level the Environmental Justice movement has provided well organized communities with access to funds, education, resources and great deal more respect and consideration from public officials and corporations. Unfortunately, the fundamental discord remained and today represents the primary basis of federal courts' all but unanimous rejection of Environmental Justice claims under both the Fourteenth Amendment and Title VI. Moreover, the EPA's failure to find a single Title VI violation by any of its grant recipients since its 1997 decision to dedicate staff and resources to investigating Title VI complaints flows from the same discord.

NOTES AND QUESTIONS

1. *Environmental racism or Environmental Justice?* As discussed by Professor Waterhouse, the history of this movement involves a dispute over characterization of the problem and thus a dispute over legal theory and remedy. The term "environmental racism" suggests the link to the civil rights movement and the conscious or unconscious racial and ethnic discrimination that might lie at the heart of disparities in hazardous waste siting decisions.

It is improper to discriminate based on race—both law and justice agree. But is it "unjust" to site facilities in areas with cheaper land if the consequence will be a "disproportionate" impact on the poor? Certainly it is fair to assume that the poor are less able to obtain the technical and legal support necessary to contest siting decisions. It also is a fair concern that the poor have less clout in the political and administrative process of siting. Issues of discrimination against the poor have been an aspect of Environmental Justice concerns. In 1994, President Clinton issued Executive Order 12898 that addresses Environmental Justice concerns arising from disproportionate impacts on "minority populations and low income populations." Sec. 1–1. As discussed below, few legal remedies, however, exist for claims of discrimination based on wealth.

Environmental Justice suggests a link to the philosophical concern with "distributive justice." The concept of distributive justice, with roots going back to Aristotle, focuses on treating "like things in a like manner" or treating "equals, equally." Thus, Environmental Justice involves consideration of the principles that determine whether a distribution of benefits and burdens is fair or just? A focus on distributive justice raises complex questions with few clear answers. *See* Jeffrey M. Gaba, *Taking "Justice and Fairness" Seriously: Distributive Justice and the Takings Clause*, 40 Creighton L. Rev. 569, 576–583 (2007).

2. *The issue of proof.* The Environmental Justice movement starts from the proposition that racial or ethnic minorities or the poor are "disproportionately" affected by adverse industrial activities such as the siting of facilities that generate hazardous waste. As discussed in the excerpt above, the Environmental Justice movement gained impetus as a result of a series of studies that purported to establish that adverse

industrial activities were located in poor or minority communities in numbers higher than their proportion overall.

But "disproportion" requires a calculation of a proportion—the percentage of racial or ethnic minorities in the affected area in relation to the percentage of the racial or ethnic minority in some larger population. If, hypothetically, the percentage of African–Americans in an area adjacent to hazardous waste generators was 40% and the percentage of African–Americans in the population as a whole was 13%, one might conclude that African–Americans were disproportionately affected.

The problem of demonstrating disproportion comes, in part, from the difficulty in identifying both the proper numerator and denominator of the equation. What is the appropriate area to define as the affected area? What is the appropriate comparison population? In identifying the composition of the population affected by a hazardous waste landfill should we be using zip code, census tract or some other set of boundaries? The choice can affect the percentages of racial or ethnic minorities who are seen to be affected by the siting decision. *See* Paul Mohai, *The Demographics of Dumping Revisited: Examining the Impact of Alternate Methodologies in Environmental Justice Research,* 14 Va. J. Envtl.L. 615 (1995). In its Guidance on Investigating Title VI Complaints, discussed below, EPA suggests that the "affected population may be categorized, for example, by likely risk or measure of impact above a threshold of adversity, or by the sources or pathways of the adverse impacts." 65 Fed. Reg. 39650, 39681(2000) (EPA Draft Revised Guidance for Investigating Title VI Administrative Complaints Challenging Permits). Thus, identification of the affected population may require information about the actual environmental effects of the activity. Other data would be needed to identify the "race, color or national origin" of the affected population.

The EPA Guidance suggests that the comparison population, the denominator, might in some cases be the local community and in others the nation as a whole.

3. *The issue of causation.* Assuming that adverse industrial activities are disproportionately located in minority or poor neighborhoods, why might that be the case? The legal response might depend on the cause. An obvious explanation is that siting decisions, like other decisions in society, might be infected by racism—the entities initially selecting the proposed location of their activity and the government officials involved in permitting and enforcement might consciously or unconsciously be influenced by racism and stereotypes.

Alternatively, it is possible that land use decisions, especially the siting of adverse industrial activities, follow the market. The cost of land might correlate with decisions to locate adverse activities, and the location of the adverse activity further depresses prices leading to increased likelihood that additional adverse activities will follow. If the poor and minorities also tend to disproportionately be located in areas of lower land prices, then it is the price of land that is the "confounder"—the variable that independently correlates with the proportion of poor and minorities and the location of adverse industries. The 1987 Church of Christ study mentioned above, however, found that race, rather than income, was more closely associated with the composition of communities near adverse industries.

Professor Vicki Breen has identified another concern with relying on studies that demonstrate a current disproportionate impact. It is possible, she has noted, that the disproportion arose after the initial siting. If the initial siting of adverse industries affects land values, it is possible that the area would subsequently have a greater percentage of the poor or minorities if they moved in the area after the initial siting of the facility reduced land values. Professor Breen and colleagues subsequently conducted "longitudinal" studies that attempted to identify the change in composition of communities over time. She characterized her results as follows:

> As detailed below, we found no substantial evidence that the facilities that began operating between 1970 and 1990 were sited in areas that were disproportionately African American. Nor did we find any evidence that these facilities were sited in areas with high concentrations of the poor; indeed, the evidence indicates that poverty is negatively correlated with sitings. We did find evidence that the facilities were sited in areas that were disproportionately Hispanic at the time of the siting. The analysis produced little evidence that the siting of a facility was followed by substantial changes in a neighborhood's socioeconomic status or racial or ethnic composition.

Vicki Been and Francis Gupta, *Coming to the Nuisance or Going to the Barrios? A Longitudinal Analysis of Environmental Justice Claims*, 24 ECOLOGY L.Q. 1, 9 (1997). *But see* Robert D. Ballard, et al., *Toxic Wastes and Race at Twenty: Why Race Still Matters After All of these Years*, 38 ENVTL. L. 371, 373 (2008) (claiming that subsequent studies "nearly put to rest" the chicken/egg problem of which came first and that "disproportionately high percentages of minorities and low-income populations were present at the time the commercial hazardous waste facilities were sited.")

4. *The issue of remedy.* If adverse environmental consequences flow from the siting of adverse industrial activities, why should it matter if those areas are disproportionately composed of racial or ethnic minorities? Should the issue be phrased as proper protection from environmental harms regardless of the racial or ethnic composition of the community? This would focus legal challenges on the adequacy of the environmental protection afforded, rather than the potential discriminatory motives that might have motivated the disproportion.

If the problem arises from the fact of disproportion, what is the appropriate remedy? In the context of disproportionate provision of resources, such as adequate roads or adequate housing, to racial or ethnic minorities or the poor, the solution has been to require the government to more fairly distribute these resources. *See, e.g., Southern Burlington Cty NAACP v. Township of Mt. Laurel*, 67 N.J. 151, 336 A.2d 713 (1975) (requiring communities to provide "fair share" of low and moderate income housing). In the context of disproportionate allocation of adverse industries, is the remedy to require some form of fairer distribution—requiring or preferring location of adverse uses in richer or more majority communities?

If the problem of disproportion arises from the lack of political power or economic resources to challenge the siting of adverse uses, the remedy might be provision of compensating resources, such as grants to hire experts to contest siting decisions. EPA has, for example, provided "technical assistance grants" to provide resources to help community groups participate in Superfund site decisions. *See* CERCLA § 117(e), 40 C.F.R. Part 35. EPA has consistently identified increased public participation opportunities as a response to Environmental Justice concerns.

2.   JUDICIAL RESPONSE

A challenge for the Environmental Justice movement is finding a basis in law to contest siting decisions that might disproportionately affect racial or ethnic minorities or the poor. Finding an effective legal basis for an Environmental Justice claim has proved difficult.

Consider the legal analysis (and procedural history) of the following Environmental Justice case. The case involves a challenge to the decision of the New Jersey Department of Environmental Protection to issue air quality permits to the St. Louis Cement Co. ("SLC"). SLC proposed to operate a cement grinding facility in the Waterfront South area of Camden, New Jersey. In a prior opinion, the court described the situation as follows:

> SLC's proposed facility will emit certain pollutants into the air. These pollutants will include particulate matter (dust), mercury, lead, manganese, nitrogen oxides, carbon monoxide, sulphur oxides and volatile organic compounds. The GBFS [granulated blast furnace slag] will arrive by barge at a Camden port facility. Trucks will then deliver the GBFS to SLC's proposed facility in Waterfront South, a distance of approximately three miles. The GBFS will then be processed and transported back to the port by truck. Annually, there will be approximately 35,000 inbound delivery trucks arriving at SLC's proposed facility and approximately 42,000 outbound truck deliveries departing from the facility. Inbound truck deliveries will occur on about eighty days per year with approximately 500 truck deliveries per day. Outbound truck departures from the SLC facility will occur on approximately 225 days per year, with about 200 trucks departing per day. The contemplated truck routes pass through the Waterfront South Community.

> The population of Waterfront South is 2,132, forty-one percent of whom are children. Ninety-one percent of the residents of Waterfront South are persons of color. Specifically, sixty-three percent are African–American, 28 percent are Hispanic, and nine percent are non-Hispanic white. The residents of Waterfront South suffer from a disproportionately high rate of asthma and other respiratory ailments.

> The Waterfront South neighborhood is already a popular location for the siting of industrial facilities. It contains the Camden County Municipal Utilities Authority, a sewage treatment plant, the Camden

County Resource Recovery facility, a trash-to-steam plant, the Camden Cogen Power Plant, a co-generation plant, and two United States Environmental Protection Agency ("EPA") designated Superfund sites. Four sites within one-half mile of SLC's proposal facility are currently being investigated by the EPA for the possible release of hazardous substances. The NJDEP has also identified fifteen known contaminated sites in the Waterfront South neighborhood.

...[T]he NJDEP granted the necessary air permits to SLC to allow its proposed facility to begin operations. In doing so, the NJDEP considered only whether the facility's emissions would exceed technical emissions standards [National Ambient Air Quality Standards or NAAQS] for specific pollutants, especially dust.

South Camden Citizens in Action v. New Jersey Dept. of Environmental Protection, 145 F.Supp.2dd 446, 450–451 (D.N.J. 2001)

The challenge to the permitting of the facility continued in a series of subsequent decisions.

South Camden Citizens in Action v. New Jersey Dept. of Environmental Protection
254 F.Supp.2d 486 (D.N.J. 2003)

I.   INTRODUCTION

Approximately two years ago, South Camden Citizens in Action, and the individual Plaintiffs who reside in a South Camden, New Jersey neighborhood, known as "Waterfront South," asked this Court to issue a preliminary injunction enjoining the construction and operation of a proposed cement grinding facility, which they claimed would have a disparate impact on the residents of their community in violation of Title VI of the Civil Rights Act of 1964, 42 U.S.C. § 2000d–1. Since then, the boundaries of Title VI jurisprudence have been narrowed well beyond what was initially thought to be appropriate by this Court. With this lawsuit now before this Court for the second time, I must consider the Defendants' motions to dismiss Plaintiffs' remaining claims pursuant to Fed.R.Civ.P. 12(b)(6). Plaintiffs' remaining claims are: (1) intentional discrimination in violation of both § 601 of Title VI of the Civil Rights Act of 1964, 42 U.S.C. § 2000d, and 42 U.S.C. § 1983 and the Fourteenth Amendment (First and Third Counts, Second Amended Complaint); (2) discriminatory impact on the basis of race, color, and national origin in violation of the Fair Housing Act, Title VIII of the Civil Rights Act of 1968, 42 U.S.C. §§ 3601 *et seq.* (Fourth Count, Second Amended Complaint); (3) Private Nuisance and Public Nuisance against the Defendant–Intervenor, St. Lawrence Cement Co., LLC only (Fifth and Sixth Counts, respectively, Second Amended Complaint).

II.   PROCEDURAL HISTORY

This is the third published opinion I have filed in the course of adjudicating the claims asserted by Plaintiffs, South Camden Citizens in

Action and the individual residents of a community located in South Camden, New Jersey, known as "Waterfront South" (collectively, "the SCCIA Plaintiffs"), that Defendants, New Jersey Department of Environmental Protection ("NJDEP") and NJDEP Commissioner Robert Shinn ("Shinn"), now Bradley M. Campbell ("Campbell") (collectively, "the NJDEP Defendants"), *inter alia,* violated Title VI of the Civil Rights Act of 1964, 42 U.S.C. § 2000d ("Title VI"), by granting Defendant–Intervenor, St. Lawrence Cement Co.'s ("SLC"), application for air permits to operate a proposed cement grinding facility without considering the potential adverse, disparate impact of their permitting decision on the residents of "Waterfront South," an impoverished and largely minority neighborhood in Camden, New Jersey. *See South Camden Citizens in Action v. New Jersey Dep't of Envtl. Prot.,* 145 F.Supp.2d 446 (D.N.J.2001) (Orlofsky, J.) ("*SCCIA I*"); *South Camden Citizens in Action v. New Jersey Dep't of Envtl. Prot.,* 145 F.Supp.2d 505 (D.N.J.) (Orlofsky, J.) ("*SCCIA II*"), *rev'd, South Camden Citizens in Action v. New Jersey Dep't of Envtl. Prot.,* 274 F.3d 771 (3d Cir.2001), *cert. denied,* 536 U.S. 939, 122 S.Ct. 2621, 153 L.Ed.2d 804 (2002). The basic facts underlying the SCCIA Plaintiffs' claims are set forth in great detail in this Court's earlier Opinions, and will only be repeated here when necessary to provide context. A brief recitation of the procedural history, however, is warranted to explain the current procedural posture of this case.

On February 13, 2001, the SCCIA Plaintiffs moved for a preliminary injunction and declaratory relief against the NJDEP Defendants. In their original verified Complaint, the SCCIA Plaintiffs alleged that the NJDEP Defendants violated Title VI and the regulations promulgated by the United States Environmental Protection Agency ("EPA") to implement Title VI when the NJDEP issued air pollution control permits to SLC to operate a cement grinding facility without regard to the discriminatory effect it would have on their neighborhood, Waterfront South, an impoverished, minority community located in South Camden, which was already suffering from the cumulative environmental effects of the numerous industrial facilities situated in and around it.

Subsequently, on April 19, 2001, I granted the SCCIA Plaintiffs' motion for a preliminary injunction and declaratory relief. In doing so, I relied on controlling case law in this Circuit which held that a private right of action existed under § 602 of Title VI,. I determined that, *inter alia,* SCCIA had established a reasonable likelihood that the operation of the proposed cement grinding facility which would emit various pollutants and require the annual ingress and egress of nearly 80,000 delivery trucks would have an adverse, disparate impact on the residents of the Waterfront South neighborhood based on their race, color, or national origin.

Five days later, on April 24, 2001, however, the United States Supreme Court decided the case of *Alexander v. Sandoval,* 532 U.S. 275, 121 S.Ct. 1511, 149 L.Ed.2d 517 (2001), in which a five justice majority held that: "Neither as originally enacted nor as later amended does Title VI display an intent to create a freestanding private right of action to enforce regulations promulgated under § 602." *Id.* at 293, 121 S.Ct. 1511. In response to the Supreme Court's decision in *Sandoval,* which effectively overruled this

Court's decision rendered five days earlier, the SCCIA Plaintiffs argued that my decision of April 19, 2001, which granted preliminary injunctive relief, could stand on alternative legal grounds. In particular, the SCCIA Plaintiffs maintained that their claim of disparate impact, originally brought under § 602 of Title VI, could be properly brought under 42 U.S.C. § 1983 ("§ 1983"). On April 26, 2001, I granted the SCCIA Plaintiffs' motion for leave to amend the complaint to seek to enforce Title VI's disparate impact regulations pursuant to § 1983.

Thereafter, after considering the supplemental briefs filed by the parties, on May 10, 2001, in a Supplemental Opinion and Order granting the SCCIA Plaintiffs preliminary injunctive and declaratory relief, I held that the EPA's Title VI implementing regulations, codified at 40 C.F.R. §§ 7.1 *et seq.*, created rights which are enforceable under § 1983.

In a divided two to one decision, the United States Court of Appeals for the Third Circuit disagreed, and on December 17, 2001, reversed this Court's Opinion and Order of May 10, 2001, granting preliminary injunctive relief, and remanded the case for further proceedings. *See South Camden Citizens in Action v. New Jersey Dep't of Envtl. Prot.,* 274 F.3d 771 (3d Cir.2001), *cert. denied,* 536 U.S. 939, 122 S.Ct. 2621, 153 L.Ed.2d 804 (2002). Judge Greenberg, writing for a two judge majority, held that the EPA's Title VI implementing regulations, by themselves, did not create rights which are enforceable under § 1983. *Id.* at 790–91. Rather, Judge Greenberg held that the alleged right of which a plaintiff claims to have been deprived must be found in the statute itself. Judge Greenberg observed: "It was of paramount importance that Congress intended to create such a right in the statute, with the regulation then defining the right that Congress already conferred through the statute." *Id.* at 788.

Following the remand to this Court, the SCCIA Plaintiffs filed a motion for leave to file a Second Amended Complaint.

IV. DISCUSSION

A. INTENTIONAL DISCRIMINATION UNDER § 601 OF TITLE VI AND THE EQUAL PROTECTION CLAUSE

The SCCIA Plaintiffs first allege that the NJDEP Defendants, "who are the recipients of federal financial assistance and subject to the requirements of Title VI, intentionally discriminated against the plaintiffs and other African–American and Hispanic residents of Waterfront [South] and the adjoining communities on the basis of race, color, and national origin" in violation of § 601 of Title VI. Second Amended Compl. ¶ 101.[FN4]

FN4. Specifically, the SCCIA Plaintiffs contend that the evidence of intentional discrimination can be found in the following thirteen allegations set forth in the Second Amended Complaint:

a. The DEP and Commissioner Shinn [now Campbell] knew that the residents of Waterfront South and the surrounding neighborhoods were predominately African–American and Hispanic.

b. The DEP and Commissioner Shinn [now Campbell] knew that

the siting of the SLC facility in Waterfront South would have an adverse impact upon these African–American and Hispanic residents.

c. The DEP and Commissioner Shinn [now Campbell] choose to use the NAAQS and related environmental standards as the criteria for determining whether a permit should be issued, knowing that such a limited analysis could not reveal that the permitting of the SLC facility would create a discriminatory impact on plaintiffs.

d. The DEP and Commissioner Shinn [now Campbell] refused to conduct a disparate impact analysis because they contended that the operation of this facility would not have any negative impact upon the Waterfront South community.

e. The DEP and Commissioner Shinn [now Campbell] were fully aware of the requirements of Title VI and of their obligations, as recipients of federal assistance, to comply with their assurances to the EPA that they will meet such requirements. They knew that their use of the NAAQS and related environmental standards as the sole criteria was not consistent with the EPA's Guidances for recipients of financial assistance and was in violation of Title VI.

f. The DEP and Commissioner Shinn [now Campbell] knew of the region's non-compliance with the EPA's proposed standard for PM–2.5 and that the scientific evidence on which the EPA proposed standard was based. The DEP and Commissioner Shinn [now Campbell] also knew that SLC would emit significant levels of PM–2.5.

g. The DEP and Commissioner Shinn [now Campbell] failed to consider the health effects of SLC's PM–2.5 emissions in making its [sic] determination that there would be no adverse effects from SLC operations, and to inform the public about such health effects.

h. The DEP and Commissioner Shinn [now Campbell] knew of the region's non-compliance with the NAAQS for ozone and that the emissions from diesel trucks and SLC's other emissions would tend to increase the level of non-compliance and cause adverse health effects on the residents.

i. The DEP and Commissioner Shinn [now Campbell] issued the permits to SLC even though they knew of the illegal discriminatory impact it would have upon plaintiffs and other African–American and Hispanic residents.

j. The DEP and Commissioner Shinn [now Campbell] have engaged in a statewide pattern and practice of granting permits to polluting facilities to operate in communities where most of the residents are African–American and/or Hispanic to a greater extent than in predominately white communities, resulting in discriminatory impact on the grounds of race, color, and national origin.

k. The DEP and Commissioner Shinn [now Campbell] have failed to develop or implement a procedure that ensures there will be no discrimination in their permitting decisions or to provide for meaningful public participation for residents of communities affected by the permitting decisions.

l. The DEP and Commissioner Shinn [now Campbell] failed to translate documents which were made available in English into Spanish, even though they knew or should have known that a significant number of the affected people are Hispanic and have limited English proficiency, so that they require Spanish language materials to be available for meaningful participation in the permit process.

m. The DEP and Commissioner Shinn's [now Campbell] prior history of permitting decisions and their issuance of the permit to SLC despite knowledge of its discriminatory effects demonstrate that defendants intended to and did discriminate against plaintiffs on the basis of race, color, and national origin.

Section 601 of Title VI provides:

No person in the United States shall, on the ground of race, color, or national origin, be excluded from participation in, be denied the benefits of, or be subjected to discrimination under any program or activity receiving Federal financial assistance.

42 U.S.C. § 2000d.

In addition, the SCCIA Plaintiffs allege that by intentionally discriminating against them on the basis of race, color, and national origin, the NJDEP Defendants violated the Equal Protection Clause of the Fourteenth Amendment and § 1983. Section 1983 provides, in relevant part:

Every person who, under color of any statute, ordinance, regulation, custom, or usage, of any State ... subjects, or causes to be subjected, any citizen of the United States or other person within the jurisdiction thereof to the deprivation of any rights, privileges, or immunities secured by the Constitution and laws, shall be liable to the party injured in an action at law, suit in equity, or other proper proceeding for redress....

42 U.S.C. § 1983.

The Supreme Court has made it clear that "the reach of Title VI's protection extends no further than the Fourteenth Amendment." In order to state a claim upon which relief can be granted under either § 601 of Title VI or the Equal Protection Clause of the Fourteenth Amendment and § 1983, a party must allege that he or she was the target of purposeful, invidious discrimination. *See Alexander v. Sandoval,* 532 U.S. 275, 285, 121 S.Ct. 1511, 149 L.Ed.2d 517 (2001) (rejecting any application of § 601 of Title VI that extends beyond intentional discrimination) even if a neutral law has a disproportionately adverse effect upon a racial minority, it is unconstitutional under the Equal Protection Clause only if that impact can be traced to a discriminatory purpose."). In order to conclude that the SCCIA Plaintiffs have failed to state a claim of intentional discrimination, I must find "beyond a doubt" that no set of facts alleged in the Second Amended Complaint would entitle them to relief.

A plaintiff who seeks recovery under a theory of purposeful discrimination must demonstrate that governmental authority implemented the facially neutral policy at issue " 'because of,' not merely 'in spite of,' its adverse effects upon an identifiable group."

> Determining whether invidious discrimination was a motivating factor demands a sensitive inquiry into such circumstantial and direct evidence of intent as may be available. The impact of the official action whether "it bears more heavily on one race than another," *Washington v. Davis, supra,* 426 U.S. at 242, 96 S.Ct. at 2049 may provide an important starting point. Sometimes a clear pattern, unexplainable on other grounds than race, emerges from the effect of the state action even when the governing legislation appears neutral on its face.

Arlington Heights, 429 U.S. at 266, 97 S.Ct. 555. The Supreme Court, however, has recognized that "disproportionate impact is not the sole touchstone of invidious racial discrimination," *id.* at 265, 97 S.Ct. 555, but rather, "is often probative of why the action was taken in the first place since people usually intend the natural consequences of their actions."

In addition to disproportionate impact, the other factors indicative of a discriminatory animus include: (1) the "historical background of the decision," *Arlington Heights,* 429 U.S. at 267, 97 S.Ct. 555 (observing that the historical background of a state action is an "evidentiary source, particularly if it reveals a series of official action taken for invidious purposes"); (2) any "departures from the normal procedural sequence also might afford evidence that improper purposes are playing a role," *id.*; (3) any "[s]ubstantive departures ... particularly if the factors usually considered important by the decisionmaker strongly favor a decision contrary to the one reached," *id.*; and (4) the foreseeability of the consequences of the state action, *see Columbus Bd. of Educ. v. Penick,* 443 U.S. 449, 465, 99 S.Ct. 2941, 61 L.Ed.2d 666 (1979) ("[A]ctions having foreseeable and anticipated disparate impact are relevant evidence to prove the ultimate fact, forbidden purpose."). *See also Baker v. City of Kissimmee,* 645 F.Supp. 571, 585 (M.D.Fl.1986) ("These factors, probative of discriminatory intent include: (1) the nature and magnitude of the disparity itself ...; (2) foreseeability of the consequences of the [state] actions; (3) legislative and administrative history of the decision-making process; and (4) knowledge, in that a defendant's actions would be known to have caused [a] discriminatory impact....").

Once a plaintiff has established that the state actor harbored a discriminatory intent, the burden shifts to the state actor to show that the same decision would have resulted in the absence of a discriminatory animus.

In their motion to dismiss, the NJDEP Defendants contend that the SCCIA Plaintiffs have failed to state a claim of intentional discrimination upon which relief can be granted under the applicable statutory and constitutional provisions. Specifically, the NJDEP Defendants argue that the SCCIA Plaintiffs' allegations are legally deficient because they have merely alleged that Defendants knew or were deliberately indifferent to the disparate impact the siting of the cement grinding facility would have on the residents of Waterfront South. *See* Defs. NJDEP and Bradley M. Campbell's Br. in Support of Motion to Dismiss under Fed.R.Civ.P. 12(b)(6) at 11 ("NJDEP Br."). According to the NJDEP Defendants, "these allegations [do not] meet the legal test for a private cause of action under Title VI because they do not contend that the New Jersey Defendants issued the permits for St. Lawrence *because* the area's residents are Black or Hispanic." *Id.* at 12 (emphasis in original). The NJDEP Defendants further argue that "an intentionally discriminatory motive [cannot] be reasonably inferred from the complaint because it is incontrovertible that the air pollution criteria that were applied in South Camden to St. Lawrence are uniformly applicable throughout New Jersey and even nationally." *Id.* at 12–13.

In response, the SCCIA Plaintiffs contend that not only are allegations of disparate impact "highly relevant and probative of discriminatory motive," but also that they have alleged "numerous other circumstances which support a finding of intent, including DEP's historical practices and the specific sequence of events leading to the issuance of the permit," as well as NJDEP's "knowledge of the discriminatory impact of its actions...." Moreover, the SCCIA Plaintiffs contend that the NJDEP's justification for issuing the permits, namely that it acted within the parameters of federal environmental laws and did not violate the National Ambient Air Quality Standards ("NAAQS"), goes to the merits of the case, and has no bearing upon whether the SCCIA Plaintiffs have stated a claim upon which relief can be granted pursuant to Fed.R.Civ.P. 12(b)(6).

I agree with the SCCIA Plaintiffs that the Second Amended Complaint contains allegations sufficient to state a cause of action of intentional discrimination under both § 601 of Title VI and the Fourteenth Amendment. In support of their claim that the NJDEP Defendants purposefully and invidiously discriminated against them on the basis of their race, color, and national origin, the SCCIA Plaintiffs allege facts which, if proven true, would show not only that the operation of the cement grinding facility would have a disparate impact upon the predominantly minority community of Waterfront South, but also that the NJDEP was well-aware of the potential disproportionate and discriminatory burden placed upon that community and failed to take measures to assuage that burden. *See supra* Note 2 of this Opinion. As I have already noted, the controlling decisions of the Supreme Court and the Third Circuit make it clear that a case of intentional discrimination is often based upon the type of circumstantial evidence which the SCCIA Plaintiffs allege in the Second Amended Complaint, namely, disparate impact, history of the state action, and foreseeability and knowledge of the discriminatory onus placed upon the complainants. The NJDEP Defendants disregard the fact that, in addition to alleging disparate impact and knowledge, the SCCIA Plaintiffs also maintain that the NJDEP has historically "engaged in a statewide pattern and practice of granting permits to polluting facilities to operate in communities where most of the residents are African–American and/or Hispanic to a greater extent than in predominately white communities."

Furthermore, it is inappropriate at this stage of these proceedings to argue the merits of the case, as the NJDEP Defendants have done in their moving papers. Indeed, "a complaint requires only a 'short and plain statement' to show a right to relief, not a detailed recitation of the proof that will in the end establish such a right." If the NJDEP Defendants acted within the parameters of the law in issuing air permits to SLC, they will have the opportunity to present supporting evidence to this Court in a motion for summary judgment, or ultimately at trial.

In sum, I conclude that the SCCIA Plaintiffs have stated a claim of intentional discrimination upon which relief can be granted under either § 601 of Title VI or the Equal Protection Clause of the Fourteenth Amendment and § 1983 because I cannot say "beyond doubt" that there is no set of facts alleged in the Second Amended Complaint, which if proven, would entitle them to relief. Accordingly, I shall deny the NJDEP Defendants' motion to dismiss the First and Third Counts of the Second Amended Complaint, to the extent that they allege that the NJDEP Defendants intentionally discriminated against the SCCIA Plaintiffs in violation of both § 601 of Title VI and the Equal Protection Clause of the Fourteenth Amendment and § 1983.

B. UNLAWFUL DISCRIMINATION UNDER THE FAIR HOUSING ACT

The SCCIA Plaintiffs' allegation that the NJDEP Defendants violated the Fair Housing Act presents a more difficult issue. Specifically, the SCCIA Plaintiffs contend that: "By granting the permits to SLC, DEP has caused a diminution in both the quantity and quality of the available housing stock in the Waterfront South neighborhood, which has a discriminatory impact on the Waterfront South residents on the basis of race, color, and national origin in violation of Title VIII [of the Civil Rights Act of 1968, 42 U.S.C. § 3604(a)]." Second Amended Compl. ¶ 117. Whether the SCCIA Plaintiffs have stated a claim upon which relief can be granted under the Fair Housing Act is contingent upon one issue: Does the NJDEP provide a service to the residents of Waterfront South in a manner contemplated by the Fair Housing Act? While the question is not free from doubt, I ultimately conclude that the NJDEP does not provide such a service.

The Fair Housing Act, Title VIII of the Civil Rights Act of 1968, 42 U.S.C. §§ 3601 et seq., prohibits "both direct discrimination and practices with significant discriminatory effects" on the availability of housing. The relevant provisions of Title VIII make it unlawful:

(a) To refuse to sell or rent after the making of a bona fide offer, or to refuse to negotiate for the sale or rental of, or otherwise make unavailable or deny, a dwelling to any person because of race, color, religion, sex, familial status, or national origin.

(b) To discriminate against any person in the terms, conditions, or privileges of sale or rental of a dwelling, or in the provision of services or facilities in connection therewith, because of race, color, religion, sex, familial status, or national origin.

42 U.S.C. § 3604(a)–(b). According to floor debates in the Senate, which ultimately enacted the legislation that became the Fair Housing Act, the underlying policy behind Title VIII is to encourage the dispersion of urban ghettos and to create more integrated neighborhoods.

1. Have the SCCIA Plaintiffs Stated a Claim under § 3604(a) of the Fair Housing Act?

That being said, however, it is not true that the tentacles of Title VIII extend beyond the availability of housing or related services. The NJDEP Defendants contend that they have taken no action to deny the residents of Waterfront South the sale or rental of residential property or to evict them from their homes. In response, the SCCIA Plaintiffs maintain in their moving papers that their situation is analogous to a "constructive eviction." SCCIA Br. at 22. According to the SCCIA Plaintiffs, the permitting of the cement grinding facility by the NJDEP is an act which rendered the Waterfront South neighborhood uninhabitable.

I conclude that in granting SLC permits to operate a cement grinding facility, the NJDEP's actions at most had an indirect effect on the availability of housing in the Waterfront South community. A survey of the case law in this area reveals that, in order to have a cognizable claim under § 3604(a), plaintiffs must establish a far closer nexus between housing availability and the challenged action.

Similarly, in this case, assuming the truth of the allegations the SCCIA Plaintiffs assert in the Second Amended Complaint for the purposes of this motion only, the NJDEP's decision to grant air pollution permits to SLC which authorized the construction of the cement grinding facility had, at most, a remote impact on the availability of housing in the Waterfront South community. The NJDEP has not evicted citizens of that community from their residences or denied them the right to rent or purchase housing. If I were to extend the scope of § 3604(a) beyond its plain language—to reach any official decision which has an indirect effect on the availability of housing—the effect would be, as the Fourth Circuit observed in *Jersey Heights,* to "warp the statute into a charter of plenary review." 174 F.3d at 192. Even a broad reading of § 3604(a) does not support such a result. I conclude, therefore, that the SCCIA Plaintiffs have failed to state a claim which relief can be granted under § 3604(a) of Title VIII.

2. Have the SCCIA Plaintiffs Stated a Claim under § 3604(b) of the Fair Housing Act?

More interestingly, the SCCIA Plaintiffs claim that the NJDEP was providing a service to the residents of Waterfront South, which in turn would bring the NJDEP under the umbrella of § 3604(b) of Title VIII. Specifically, they maintain that because the NJDEP "is responsible for the promotion of environmental protection and the prevention of pollution of the environment of the State … [and] oversees sanitary engineering and sewerage systems in New Jersey," it "qualifies as a 'governmental unit' which provides services [directly related to housing] much like garbage collection." SCCIA Br. at 19–20. The SCCIA Plaintiffs analogize the circumstances in this case to those presented in *Campbell v. City of Berwyn,* 815 F.Supp. 1138, 1144 (N.D.Ill.1993), where the district court held that citizens who alleged that the city's termination of police protection interfered with their right to fair housing sufficiently stated a claim under § 3604(b). The *Campbell* court further observed that § 3604(b) "applies to services generally provided by governmental units such as police and fire protection or garbage collection." *Id.* at 1143–44 (quoting *Southend Neighborhood Improvement Ass'n,* 743 F.2d at 1210).

The NJDEP Defendants contend, on the other hand, that the NJDEP does not provide the type of services contemplated by § 3604(b), and, therefore, the SCCIA Plaintiffs have failed to state a cognizable claim under that provision of Title VIII. Similar to their argument that the SCCIA Plaintiffs failed to state a claim under § 3604(a), the NJDEP Defendants contend that the granting of industrial air pollution permits is simply too far removed to fall within the scope of the remedial objectives of § 3604(b).

I conclude that the NJDEP Defendants have the better argument. If I were to accept the SCCIA Plaintiffs' argument that § 3604(b) extends to the decision of every governmental agency that may have an indirect impact on housing, Title VIII would be "a civil rights statute of general applicability rather than one dealing with the specific problems of fair housing." Although the NJDEP clearly provides a number of valuable services to the citizens of the State of New Jersey by enacting regulations and overseeing their implementation, it does not follow that it provides specific residential services. The NJDEP is not responsible for door-to-door ministrations such as those provided by police departments, fire departments, or other municipal units. The SCCIA Plaintiffs, therefore, have failed to state a cognizable claim under § 3604(b).

NOTES AND QUESTIONS

1. The plaintiffs at various stages of the *South Camden* litigation raised claims of violation of 1) the Equal Protection Clause of the U.S. Constitution, 2) § 601 of the Civil Rights Act of 1964, 3) § 602 of the Civil Rights Act of 1964, 4) 42 U.S.C. § 1983, 5) § 3604(a) of the Fair Housing Act, and 6) § 3604(b) of the Fair Housing Act. Based on the procedural history and the courts disposition of claims in this case, which of these claims are available to a plaintiff challenging the siting of a hazardous waste facility and, if available, what type of information would be necessary to support the claim?

2. Plaintiffs claimed that New Jersey officials had intentionally discriminated on the basis of race when granting an air permit to the cement facility. If proved, intentional discrimination on the basis of race or national origin would constitute a violation of the Equal Protection clause of the Federal constitution and a violation of § 601 of the Civil Rights Act. Many of the Plaintiffs' allegations of discriminatory intent were premised on the fact that the State knew both the environmental harms from permitting the

plant and the racial composition of the community. Is knowledge of discriminatory impact sufficient to prove discriminatory intent? What other factors were relevant in the court's decision not to dismiss the claim at this stage in the proceedings?

3.   The alleged adverse impacts from permitting the cement plant arose, in part, from the fact that there were many other industrial facilities operating in the area. Plaintiffs, among other things, were alleging that it was the cumulative impact of the cement plant and operation of the other facilities that resulted in discriminatory impact on residents of the area. If the operations of the permittee alone would not produce a discriminatory impact, how should issuance of its permit be affected by pre-existing activities?

4.   Plaintiffs also alleged that operation of the cement plant would create a public and private nuisance. Nuisance, both public and private, is a tort that can be invoked to seek compensation or injunction from damages caused by environmental harm. Nuisance, however, is not per se an Environmental Justice claim; the elements of proof of a nuisance do not necessarily involve claims of discriminatory impact or intent.

3.   ADMINISTRATIVE RESPONSE

If there are limited causes of action to challenge in court actions that create environment justice concerns, what options are available for administrative agencies, such as EPA, to address Environmental Justice issues? In 1994, President Clinton issued Executive Order 12898 that, among other things, directed executive agencies to include Environmental Justice concerns in their decision making and to implement the requirements of the Executive Order "to the greatest extent practicable and permitted by law." The Executive Order expressly states that it does not, itself, create any private rights. EPA's response to Environmental justice claims, particularly in the context of federal and state RCRA permitting, involves a search for existing statutory authority available to EPA.

a.   ENVIRONMENTAL JUSTICE THROUGH RCRA

EPA has concluded that it has no independent authority to address Environmental justice in its permitting decisions. Any authority it may have must be found in the provisions of the statutes themselves. The following is a portion of an EPA memorandum addressing the scope of its authority under RCRA to address Environmental Justice concerns in permitting.

December 1, 2000

MEMORANDUM

SUBJECT: EPA Statutory and Regulatory Authorities Under Which Environmental Justice Issues May Be Addressed in Permitting

This memorandum analyzes a significant number of statutory and regulatory authorities under the Resource Conservation and Recovery Act, the Clean Water Act, the Safe Drinking Water Act, the Marine Protection, Research, and Sanctuaries Act, and the Clean Air Act that the Office of

General Counsel believes are available to address Environmental Justice issues during permitting. The use of EPA's statutory authorities, as discussed herein, may in some cases involve new legal and policy interpretations that could require further Agency regulatory or interpretive action. Although the memorandum presents interpretations of EPA's statutory authority and regulations that we believe are legally permissible, it does not suggest that such actions would be uniformly practical or feasible given policy or resource considerations or that there are not important considerations of legal risk that would need to be evaluated. Nor do we assess the relative priority among these various avenues for addressing Environmental Justice concerns. We look forward to working with all your offices to explore these matters in greater detail.

I.   Resource Conservation and Recovery Act (RCRA)

RCRA authorizes EPA to regulate the generation, transportation, treatment, storage, and disposal of hazardous wastes and the management and disposal of solid waste. EPA issues guidelines and recommendations to State solid waste permitting programs under RCRA sections 1008(a), 4002, or 4004 and may employ this vehicle to address Environmental Justice concerns. The primary area where Environmental Justice issues have surfaced, however, is in the permitting of hazardous waste treatment, storage, and disposal facilities (e.g., incinerators, fuel blenders, landfills). Pursuant to RCRA section 3005, EPA is authorized to grant permits to such facilities if they demonstrate compliance with EPA regulations.

Upon application by a State, EPA may authorize a State's hazardous waste program to operate in lieu of the Federal program, and to issue and enforce permits. The State's program must be equivalent to the Federal program to obtain and retain authorization. When EPA adopts more stringent RCRA regulations (including permit requirements), authorized States are required to revise their programs within one year after the change in the Federal program or within two years if the change will necessitate a State statutory amendment. 40 CFR § 271.21(e). EPA and most authorized States have so-called "permit shield" regulations, providing that, once a facility obtains a hazardous waste permit, it generally cannot be compelled to comply with additional requirements during the permit's term.

The scope of EPA's authority to address Environmental Justice issues in RCRA hazardous waste permits was directly addressed by the Environmental Appeals Board (EAB) in Chemical Waste Management, Inc., 6 E.A.D. 66, 1995 WL 395962 (1995) (http://www.epa.gov/eab/disk11/cwmii.pdf). The Board found "that when the Region has a basis to believe that operation of the facility may have a disproportionate impact on a minority or low-income segment of the affected community, the Region should, as a matter of policy, exercise its discretion to assure early and ongoing opportunities for public involvement in the permitting process." Id. at 73. It also found that RCRA allows the Agency to "tak[e] a more refined look at its health and environmental impacts assessment in light of allegations that operation of the facility would have a disproportionately adverse effect on the health or environment of low-income or minority populations." Id. at 74. Such a close evaluation could, in turn, justify permit conditions or denials based on disproportionately high and adverse human health or environmental effects, while "a broad analysis might mask the effects of the facility on a disparately affected minority or low-income segment of the community." Id. However, while acknowledging the relevance of disparities in health and environmental impacts, the Board also cautioned that "there is no legal basis for rejecting a RCRA permit application based solely upon alleged social or economic impacts upon the community." Id. at 73.

Consistent with this interpretation, there are several RCRA authorities under which EPA could address Environmental Justice issues in permitting:

A. Hazardous Waste Treatment, Storage, and Disposal

1.   RCRA section 3005(c)(3) provides that "[e]ach permit issued under this section shall contain such terms and conditions as the Administrator (or the State) determines necessary to protect human health and the environment." EPA has interpreted this provision to authorize denial of a permit to a facility if EPA determines that operation of the facility would pose an unacceptable risk to human health and the environment and that there are no additional permit terms or conditions that would address such risk. This "omnibus" authority may be applicable on a permit-by-permit basis where appropriate to address the following health concerns in connection with hazardous waste management facilities that may affect low-income communities or minority communities:

a.   Cumulative risks due to exposure from pollution sources in addition to the applicant facility;

b.   Unique exposure pathways and scenarios (e.g., subsistence fishers, farming communities); or

c.   Sensitive populations (e.g., children with levels of lead in their blood, individuals with poor diets).

2.   RCRA section 3013 provides that if the Administrator determines that "the presence of any hazardous waste at a facility or site at which hazardous waste is, or has been, stored, treated, or disposed of, or the release of any such waste from such facility or site may present a substantial hazard to human health or the environment," she may order a facility owner or operator to conduct reasonable monitoring, testing, analysis, and reporting to ascertain the nature and extent of such hazard. EPA may require a permittee or an applicant to submit information to establish permit conditions necessary to protect human health and the environment. 40 CFR § 270.10(k). In appropriate circumstances, EPA could use the authority under section 3013 or 40 CFR § 270.10(k) to compel a facility owner or operator to carry out necessary studies, so that, pursuant to the "omnibus" authority, EPA can establish permit terms or conditions necessary to protect human health and the environment.

3.   RCRA provides EPA with authority to consider Environmental Justice issues in establishing priorities for facilities under RCRA section 3005(e), and for facilities engaged in cleaning up contaminated areas under the RCRA corrective action program, RCRA sections 3004(u), 3004(v), and

3008(h). For example, EPA could consider factors such as cumulative risk, unique exposure pathways, or sensitive populations in establishing permitting or clean-up priorities.

4.   EPA adopted the "RCRA Expanded Public Participation" rule on December 11, 1995. See 60 Fed. Reg. 63417. RCRA authorizes EPA to explore further whether the RCRA permit public participation process could better address Environmental Justice concerns by expanding public participation in the permitting process (including at hazardous waste management facilities to be located in or near low-income communities or minority communities).

5.   In expanding the public participation procedures applicable to RCRA facilities, EPA also would have authority to expand the application of those procedures to the permitting of:

(a) publicly owned treatment works, which are regulated under the Clean Water Act; (b) underground injection wells, which are regulated under the Safe Drinking Water Act; and (c) ocean disposal barges or vessels, which are regulated under the Marine Protection Research and Sanctuaries Act. These facilities are subject to RCRA's permit by rule regulations, 40 CFR § 270.60, and are deemed to have a RCRA permit if they meet certain conditions set out in the regulations. 40 CFR § 270.60.

6.   EPA's review of State-issued permits provides additional opportunities for consideration of Environmental Justice concerns. Where the process for a State-issued permit does not adequately address sensitive population risks or other factors in violation of the authorized State program, under the regulations EPA could provide comments on these factors (in appropriate cases) during the comment period on the State's proposed permit on a facility-by-facility basis. 40 CFR § 271.19(a). Where the State itself is authorized for RCRA "omnibus" authority and does not address factors identified in EPA comments as necessary to protect human health and the environment, EPA may seek to enforce the authorized State program requirement. 40 CFR § 271.19(e) Alternatively, if the State is not authorized for "omnibus" authority, EPA may superimpose any necessary additional conditions under the "omnibus" authority in the federal portion of the permit. These conditions become part of the facility's RCRA permit and are enforceable by the United States under RCRA section 3008 and citizens through RCRA section 7002.

7.   RCRA section 3019 provides EPA with authority to increase requirements for applicants for land disposal permits to provide exposure information and to request that the Agency for Toxic Substances and Disease Registry conduct health assessments at such land disposal facilities.

8.   RCRA section 3004(o)(7) provides EPA with authority to issue location standards as necessary to protect human health and the environment. Using this authority, EPA could, for example, establish minimum buffer zones between hazardous waste management facilities and sensitive areas (e.g., schools, areas already with several hazardous waste

management facilities, residential areas). Facilities seeking permits would need to comply with these requirements to receive a permit.

9. RCRA-permitted facilities are required under RCRA section 3004(a) to maintain "contingency plans for effective action to minimize unanticipated damage from any treatment, storage, or disposal of ... hazardous waste." Under this authority, EPA could require facilities to prepare and/or modify their contingency plans to reflect the needs of Environmental Justice communities that have limited resources to prepare and/or respond to emergency situations.

10. RCRA additionally provides EPA with authority to amend its regulations to incorporate some of the options described in 1 through 6 above so they become part of the more stringent federal program that authorized States must adopt.

b. EPA TITLE VI REGULATIONS

EPA, like other federal agencies, has promulgated regulations that define the obligations of recipients of EPA "assistance" under Title VI of the Civil Rights Act of 1964. 40 C.F.R. Part 7. These regulations prohibit State agencies that receive funding from EPA from discriminating "on the basis of race, color, national origin, or sex" 40 C.F.R. § 7.30. This prohibition would apply, for example, to all States that have been delegated RCRA permitting authority. The consequence for violation of this prohibition by a State would include potential loss of permitting authority. In 2006, EPA issued final guidance to recipients of EPA funds on steps they can take to ensure compliance with the EPA Title VI regulations. See Title VI Public Involvement Guidance for EPA Assistance Recipients Administering Environmental Permitting Programs ("Recipient Guidance"), 71 Fed. Reg. 14207 (2006). The guidance focuses on recipient efforts to ensure public participation, voluntary resolution of Environmental Justice disputes and use of existing authorities to address Environmental Justice concerns.

EPA provides a mechanism for persons complaining of Title VI violations by State agencies to petition EPA for review of their complaints, and an administrative petition to EPA alleging Title VI violations exists as a mechanism for asserting Environmental Justice complaints. *See* Luke W. Cole, *Civil Rights, Environmental Justice and the EPA: The Brief History of Administrative Complaints under Title VI of the Civil Rights Act of 1964*, 9 J. of Envtl.L. & Litig. 309 (1994). In 2000, EPA also issued "revised draft guidance" on its handling of Title VI complaints. *See* Draft Revised Guidance on Investigating Title VI Administrative Complaints Challenging Permits, 65 Fed. Reg. 39650 (2000) ("Draft Investigative Guidance"). The Draft Investigative Guidance provides a framework for submission of Title VI complaints and their review by EPA's Office of Civil Rights.

The reaction by both the Environmental Justice community and industry to EPA's Draft Investigative Guidance was almost uniformly negative. Robert Bullard, who performed one of the earliest studies on Environmental Justice, described the described the draft guidance as a "total disaster." Robert D. Bullard, Guidance in Two Words: Total Disaster, ENVTL. F.,

Sept./Oct. 2000, at 49. Criticisms focused on the level and burden of proof necessary to support a Title VI claim and the burdens that the methodology for establishing disproportionate impact imposed on claimants. Industry complained about the vagueness of the guidelines. See Bradford C. Mank, The Draft EPA Recipient and Revised Investigative Guidances: Too Much EPA Discretion and a More Difficult Standard for Complaintants?, 30 ENVT. L. REPTR. 11144 (Dec. 2000).

One commentator has described the effect of EPA's Title VI petition process:

> In light of the numerous criticisms of the guidance by industry representatives, one might expect that complainants would have a reasonable chance of success through administrative channels. However, that has not been the case. As of February 7, 2002, there were forty-four administrative complaints pending with the EPA, of which thirty-six had been accepted for investigation. Of the eighty closed cases, nine were dismissed after acceptance and sixty-eight (85%) were rejected for investigation for failure to meet the regulatory requirements. Since the program's inception, no investigation has resulted in a victory for the complainant. Further frustrating Environmental Justice complainants, Congress has prohibited the EPA from investigating several Title VI complaints until the final guidance is issued. Even if a complaint is accepted for investigation, winning is no easy task in light of the many shortcomings of the EPA guidance documents, such as the unclear definition of "disparate impact" and the vague explanation of what constitutes an "equally effective" less discriminatory alternative or acceptable mitigation to justify an otherwise unacceptable project. Furthermore, a victory for a complainant may not be meaningful if the only relief is revocation of EPA funding with no guarantee that such a penalty will ensure pollution reduction or elimination of the disparate effects of the polluting activity. Essentially, the administrative complaint process has not yet advanced effective limits for discriminatory effects nor has it created any meaningful causes of action for aggrieved parties.

Janet V. Siegel, *Negotiating for Environmental Justice: Turning Polluters Into "Good Neighbors" through Collaborative Bargaining,* 10 N.Y.U. ENVTL. L.J. 147, 164 (2002).

Another commentator has suggested some more positive consequences from the actions spurred by State agency attempts to comply with EPA's Title VI requirements:

> To the extent that it forces permitting authorities to assess and document disparate adverse impacts, EPA's Title VI regulations will likely have three significant effects. First, if an assessment indicates disparate impacts, states may be in violation if they have not taken all available means to minimize this impact. This will, however, focus on the state's legal authorities under other statutes.

> Second, identification of potential environmental concerns is likely to result in increased opportunities for public participation in the

permit process. Whatever limits there are regarding the states' ability to impose substantive permit limitations, there should be little issue that states can provide broader opportunities for public participation in appropriate cases. EPA's Draft Recipient Guidance encourages "meaningful public participation and outreach."

Third, and perhaps more importantly, Title VI may force the public airing and recognition of disparate impacts and environmental injustice. The remedy following such a showing is likely to be more political than legal. Information has its own power, and political pressure will almost certainly follow from state documentation of impacts. Voluntary acceptance by the permittee of restrictions to minimize impacts is likely. Additionally, "voluntary" abandonment of proposed facilities by the applicant in the face of local opposition is also possible. Information produced by Title VI analysis may also form the impetus for subsequent changes to law to allow greater restrictions on facilities producing disparate impact. All in the environmental community are aware of the power of public information. Thus, the ultimate effect of the application of EPA's Title VI regulations (either through a private cause of action or through EPA decisions) may be more political than legal.

Jeffrey M. Gaba, *South Camden and Environmental Justice: Substance, Procedure and Politics*, 32 ENVT. L.REPTR. 11073, 11077–11078 (Sept. 2001).

NOTES AND QUESTIONS

1.   Other environmental statutes may also provide an opportunity to raise Environmental Justice concerns. The National Environmental Policy Act ("NEPA"), 42 U.S.C. §§ 4321 et seq., requires preparation of an "Environmental Impact Statement" ("EIS") for federal actions that significantly affect the quality of the human environment. Guidance issued by the President's Council on Environmental Quality requires consideration of Environmental Justice issues in an EIS. See Environmental Justice: Guidance under the National Environmental Policy Act, Council on Environmental Quality, Dec. 1997, /www.epa.gov/compliance/resources/policies/ej/ej _ guidance_ nepa_ ceq1297.pdfev. When agencies include an Environmental Justice analysis in an EIS, courts have been willing to consider the adequacy of the analysis. *See, e.g., See, e.g., Coliseum Square Ass'n, Inc. v. Jackson*, 465 F.3d 215 (5th Cir.2006); Communities Against Runway Expansion v. Federal Aviation Agency, 355 F.3d 678 (D.C. Cir. 2004).

2.   The EPA memorandum addresses authorities available under RCRA to address Environmental Justice concerns. How many of those authorities address the issue of "disproportion" or discrimination? Most of the cited RCRA provisions authorize consideration of environmental impacts, including impacts on sensitive populations. How does information about the racial or ethnic identity of exposed populations affect implementation of this authority? If adverse impacts on human health or the environment are documented should the response be different if they occur among minority or low income communities?

Income or ethnicity may affect calculation of risk. Part of risk assessment involves an "exposure assessment" or a determination of the pathways by which individuals may be exposed to pollutants. Environmental Justice claims have involved challenges to assumptions about exposure. *See* Catherine A. O'Neill, *Variable Justice: Environmental Standards, Contaminated Fish, and "Acceptable" Risk to Native Peoples,* 19 Stan. Envtl.L.J. 3 (2000).

3.   Who can be victims of environmental injustice under EPA's regulations? Executive Order 12898 addresses environmental justice concerns arising from disproportionate impacts on "minority populations and low income populations." Sec. 1–1. EPA's Title VI regulations, however, address discrimination based on "race, color, national origin, or sex." The prohibition on discrimination on the basis of "race, color or national origin" implements the requirements of Title VI of the Civil Rights Act. The prohibition on discrimination based on sex is based on § 13 of the Federal Water Pollution Control Act. *See* 49 Fed. Reg. 1656 (1984). There may be distinct sources for claims of discrimination against Native Americans. *See* Catherine A. O'Neill, *Protecting the Tribal Harvest: The Right to Catch and Consume Fish,* 22 J. Envtl. L. & Litig. 131 (2007). Although disproportionate siting of adverse industries in low-income communities raises environmental justice concerns, there are limited legal bases for challenging discrimination against the poor.

4.   EPA's Guidance on Investigation of Title VI complaints identifies "informal" methods of resolving allegations of discrimination. The formal remedies for an alleged violation are limited. EPA may withdraw funding received by the State, but consider EPA's statement regarding the proper action where environmental justice concerns are raised by issuance of a permit:

> EPA believes it will be a rare situation where the permit that triggered the complaint is the sole reason a discriminatory effect exists; therefore, denial of the permit at issue will not necessarily be an appropriate solution. Efforts that focus on all contributions to the adverse disparate impact, not just the permit at issue, will likely yield the most effective long-term solutions.

65 Fed. Reg. 39650, 39700 (2000).

CHAPTER 6

CLEAN–UP: THE COMPREHENSIVE ENVIRONMENTAL RESPONSE, COMPENSATION, AND LIABILITY ACT

Of all the statutes that have been passed to address the problem of toxic substances and hazardous wastes, the Comprehensive Environmental Response, Compensation, and Liability Act (CERCLA) has had perhaps the most profound effect on the environmental law landscape. It authorizes and funds the remediation of inactive, leaking hazardous waste sites, and it defines the nature and scope of liability for past environmental harms. Since potential CERCLA liability is huge and the statute itself is no model of legislative draftsmanship, it has spawned thousands of lawsuits, and hundreds of judicial decisions attempting to interpret its terms. From this body of case law one can derive the "law of CERCLA," which is the topic of this chapter.

The chapter begins with a summary of CERCLA, so that we can have a broad conception of what CERCLA and the Superfund are, before delving into details. Then the chapter addresses all the key component parts of CERCLA. We start with the CERCLA cornerstones—its blueprint for action (the National Contingency Plan and National Priorities List), actions that may be taken to clean up contaminated sites (removal and remedial actions), and the availability *vel non* of judicial review of these actions. Next, the chapter explains CERCLA's unique liability scheme, which ensures that when private parties linked to the site can be identified, the costs of clean-up are borne by those parties responsible for the contaminated waste site, and its imminent or potential harm to the environment. If such parties cannot be found, the Superfund is used, and that is the focus of the next section of the chapter. Finally, we review the various kinds of costs for which parties may find themselves liable, and the procedures for assigning and allocating liability.

A. OVERVIEW

Before one embarks on an analysis of the many provisions that constitute CERCLA, it might be helpful to begin with a brief overview of the statute. The next section provides a brief discussion of what CERCLA does, how it does it, and why it was passed. This overview also explains what the Superfund is, what a Superfund site is, and how such sites are cleaned up. Additionally, the structure and organization of CERCLA's interlocking parts will be discussed.

1. What Is CERCLA?

CERCLA's current regulatory scheme is the result of three major enactments. The original Comprehensive Environmental Response, Compensation and Liability Act, Pub. L. No. 96–510, 94 Stat. 2767, was enacted in 1980. In 1986, Congress reauthorized and revised CERCLA in the Superfund Amendments and Reauthorization Act (SARA), Pub. L. 99–499, 160 Stat. 1615. In 2002, CERCLA was amended again with the Small Business Liability Relief and Brownfields Revitalization Act (Brownfields Act), Pub. L. No. 107–118, 115 Stat. 2356. Known collectively as CERCLA, 42 U.S.C. §§ 9601–9675, the statutes address three main issues: the identification, investigation, and remediation of contaminated sites; and the allocation of financial responsibility for clean-up activities; and the support of voluntary cleanup and redevelopment of contaminated sites.

The passage of CERCLA represents the final piece of Congress's mosaic of environmental legislation. The National Environmental Policy Act of 1969 (NEPA) required federal agencies to consider, in advance of making decisions, the environmental impacts of these decisions. The 1970 Clean Air Act (CAA) regulated air pollution. The 1972 Clean Water Act (CWA) sought to control polluted discharges in rivers and lakes. The Resource Conservation and Recovery Act of 1976 (RCRA) regulated toxic and hazardous discharges to land and groundwater. But no statute addressed pre-existing environmental harms, especially those caused by the threat from hazardous waste disposal sites. The purpose of CERCLA was to address acts occurring in the past, in order to prevent environmental disasters in the future. It is not a traditional regulatory statute, like the CAA, CWA, or RCRA. It is a remediation statute that imposes liability for past conduct with present effects.

There are numerous interactions between the remediation and liability aspects of CERCLA, but they are conceptually and statutorily quite separate. The remediation aspect of CERCLA identifies the kinds of sites ("facilities") that require attention, sets priorities among them, provides for their analysis, and finally specifies in some detail the nature and degree of clean-up activities. These parts of CERCLA look very much like the regulatory regimes we have already examined, and you will find many familiar issues.

The liability aspect of CERCLA is new and unique in toxics regulation. In essence, CERCLA is a retrospective statute that uses tort-like liability to reach a range of private parties to pay the costs of cleaning up hazardous waste sites. CERCLA is not primarily regulatory or preventive, like RCRA which provides for cradle-to-grave control of current activities regarding hazardous waste. Instead, CERCLA is *remedial*. It is designed to repair past waste disposal practices. If parties responsible for hazardous waste sites can be identified and located, they will be liable for both past and future clean-up costs of these sites, as well as the cost of preventing spills and releases of toxic and hazardous waste into the environment. *O'Neil v. Picillo*, 883 F.2d 176 (1st Cir. 1989). If such parties cannot be found (*e.g.*, when hazardous waste sites have been abandoned by their original owners), or if the owners of the site have become bankrupt, the Superfund created by CERCLA serves as a monetary source from which the government may finance clean-up of these "orphan" sites.

Although the text of CERCLA is ambiguous about the liability it imposes, subsequent court interpretations have established that the nature of the liability is *strict*; the scope of the liability is *joint and several*; and the effect of the liability is *retroactive*. Consequently, fault and causation are largely irrelevant; a person responsible for a small percentage of the site's waste could be liable for 100% of the clean-up costs; and a party may be liable for extensive clean-up costs for disposal practices occurring pre-CERCLA that were legal at the time the disposal took place.[1] Not only is the liability scheme in CERCLA strict, broad, and backwards looking, it is also subject to only a few statutory defenses: acts of God; acts of war; acts or omissions of a third party not in contractual privity with the person asserting the defense; innocent landowners (or innocent purchasers) who can demonstrate causation by a third party and adequate precautions by the buyer; and lenders who did not participate in the management of the waste site.

If a party's actions with respect to a waste site satisfy CERCLA's liability triggers (*i.e.*, there is a threatened release of a hazardous substance from a "facility"—a site or area where a hazardous substance

> **CERCLA LIABILITY**
> Nature ⇒ STRICT
> Scope ⇒ JOINT & SEVERAL
> Effect ⇒ RETROACTIVE

has been deposited), and if the party becomes—a Potentially Responsible Party "PRP" (*i.e.*, an owner, operator, etc.), then CERCLA provides that this unfortunate soul is liable for "all costs of removal or remedial action incurred by the United States Government or a State or an Indian tribe not inconsistent with the [NCP]." § 107(a)(4)(A).[2] Courts have interpreted the "all costs" phrase quite literally, so that where the government takes action to investigate or monitor a release, or pays a contractor to perform work under agency direction, all these costs can be reimbursed. Most courts also allow the government to recover enforcement-related costs, indirect costs, such as rent and clerical supplies, and overhead, such as travel and legal expenses. Attorneys' fees are expressly authorized for government response actions, but are not in private cost recovery actions. In *Key Tronic Corp. v.*

---

1. United States v. Northeastern Pharmaceutical Chem. Corp., 810 F.2d 726, 734 (8th Cir. 1986) (Congress intended for CERCLA to apply to pre-CERCLA acts, and such retroactivity does not violate due process).

2. CERCLA § 107(a)(4)(B) creates a similar right in any private party, with the additional requirement that private parties bear the responsibility of demonstrating that costs incurred were consistent with the NCP. The government's costs are presumably recoverable unless a private defendant proves inconsistency with the NCP.

United States, 511 U.S. 809 (1994), the Supreme Court ruled that attorney's fees incurred in prosecuting a CERCLA liability action are not a "necessary cost of response," but did allow recovery of fees incurred by an attorney in tracking down other PRPs.

Another provision of CERCLA, § 107(a)(4)(c), "imposes on PRPs the duty to pay for injury to, destruction of, or loss of natural resources. * * * " The federal government, the states and local governments, and Indian tribal governments are designated as trustees empowered to sue for natural resource damages. Although cost recovery claims have dominated actions involving CERCLA, liabilities associated with natural resource damage claims may eventually exceed the billions of dollars spent on cleaning up waste sites. This is because (1) the term "natural resources" is given an extremely broad definition in the statute's definition section; (2) unlike recovery of response costs, the government need not expend money to recover natural resource damages; and (3) the appropriate measure of damages is not just the diminution of use values, but rather the cost of restoration and replacement of the damaged land and ecosystem. The potential cost to private parties found liable for this kind of clean-up and restoration action could be crippling. *See, e.g., Kennecott Utah Copper Corp. v. U.S. Dept. of Interior*, 88 F.3d 1191, 1217 (D.C. Cir. 1996).

CERCLA pursues three objectives: (1) it prevents further contamination and release of toxic substances by requiring prompt clean-up of existing hazardous waste sites; (2) it ensures that the costs of cleaning up these sites are borne by "responsible" parties; and (3) its sweeping liability provisions help to deter future environmental releases by imposing high costs on careless waste management and disposal practices. *B.F. Goodrich Co. v. Murtha*, 958 F.2d 1192 (2d Cir. 1992). On the other hand, CERCLA does *not* provide a cause of action, like a new toxic tort, to compensate for personal or economic injuries resulting from hazardous waste contamination. *Exxon Corp. v. Hunt*, 475 U.S. 355, 375 (1986). Nor does it provide clear and explicit guidance about how its provisions should be interpreted. Congress left much of CERCLA ambiguous, so the judiciary has created a kind of federal common law of CERCLA.

> **THREE OBJECTIVES OF CERCLA**
>
> 1) prevents contamination and releases of toxic substances
>
> 2) ensures costs for cleanup are borne by responsible parties
>
> 3) deters future environmental releases

Within CERCLA's vague and ambiguously drafted framework, the U.S. Congress created a two-pronged approach to meeting its twin objectives— cleaning up hazardous waste sites and recovering costs. On the one hand, the *federal government* (through the EPA) was given authority to respond to hazardous releases at abandoned and inactive waste disposal sites. The federal government may rely on the Superfund to clean up a site and then seek reimbursement from any responsible parties, or it may proceed directly against responsible parties, or it may encourage "voluntary" clean-up by threatening responsible parties with court action and sanctions if they do

> **STEPS THAT CAN BE TAKEN BY THE FEDERAL GOVERNMENT**
>
> 1) initiate clean up itself
>
> 2) require that responsible parties take the appropriate action
>
> 3) encourage responsible parties to engage in the appropriate clean up

not agree to the EPA's chosen action. On the other hand, *private parties* may spend their own money to clean-up, then sue those responsible to recover those clean-up costs. Even if private parties are partially responsible themselves, they may sue other responsible parties for their share of clean-up costs. *See* Susan R. Poulter, *Clean-up and Restoration: Who Should Pay?*, 18 J. LAND RESOURCES & ENVTL. L. 77 (1998).

If either the government or a private party can identify and locate a party responsible for the hazardous waste site, that responsible party is subject to a particularly stringent form of liability. Under CERCLA, liability is *not* determined by traditional tort principles, which require some degree of causative link between the defendant's conduct and the actual harm to another person. It was thought that this principle would obstruct clean-up of sites where multiple parties disposed of toxic substances years or decades before anyone became aware of the hazardous nature of the site. By the time the site's threat to the public and the environment becomes known, it may be impossible to identify the persons who actually contaminated it (or their relative share of the contamination). Even when parties who were responsible for the contamination are located, they may be incapable of shouldering the costs due to bankruptcy or insolvency.

As a result, CERCLA imposes liability when there is a causal link between certain classes of defendants—generally site owners and waste generators—the release of a hazardous substance, and the incurrence of clean-up costs. Neither harm (other than incurring clean-up costs) nor carelessness or illegality of the defendant's conduct need be proven. Defendants are also jointly and severally liable, so that, in theory at least, a person responsible for only a tiny percentage of the waste at a site can be liable for the total cost of cleaning it up if no other PRPs can be located.[3] Moreover, the courts have interpreted CERCLA as imposing retroactive liability, which means that potentially responsible parties (PRPs) are liable for conduct occurring before CERCLA's 1980 enactment. *United States v. Olin Corp.*, 107 F.3d 1506 (11th Cir. 1997). This result is consistent with CERCLA's purpose of cleaning up all hazardous sites, regardless of when they were created.

2.   WHAT IS THE SUPERFUND?

The other distinguishing feature of CERCLA, besides its unique liability scheme, is its revolving trust fund, the "Superfund." As originally

---

3.   Some courts have decided that clean-up costs may be apportioned among PRPs if (1) the defendant satisfies the burden of proving that responsibility and/or harm is divisible, (2) responsibility for the contamination and/or harm from the site is in fact divisible, and (3) the other PRPs contributing to the site may be found. *United States v. Alcan Aluminum Corp.*, 964 F.2d 252 (3d Cir. 1992). Other courts have suggested that if a current site owner were able to prove that none of the hazardous substances found at the site were fairly attributable to it, such an owner's apportioned share of the clean-up costs could be zero. *United States v. Rohm & Haas Co.*, 2 F.3d 1265 (3d Cir. 1993).

envisioned, the Superfund exists to finance government-directed clean-up efforts, to pay claims arising from clean-up activities of private parties who are not liable as PRPs under CERCLA, and to compensate federal and state governments for damages to natural resources caused by a hazardous waste site. The Superfund receives its money from excise taxes on companies such as the petroleum and chemical industries.

To determine which sites are worthy of Superfund dollars, CERCLA authorizes the EPA to create a list of the worst hazardous waste sites in the country, the National Priorities List (NPL). To determine which sites should be placed on the NPL, EPA employs a Hazard Ranking System (HRS) which assigns a score to each site, based on a few salient risk assessment criteria (*e.g.*, potential for contaminating drinking water, for producing public health hazard, or for destroying sensitive ecosystems). Once a site is placed on the NPL, the National Contingency Plan (NCP) establishes the procedures and standards for responding to releases of hazardous substances from the site. CERCLA authorizes two kinds of responses: (1) short-term "removal" actions designed to alleviate immediate dangers, and (2) long-term "remedial" actions meant to provide a more permanent remedy.

Together, the NPL and NCP determine the *kinds of actions* that may be taken at hazardous waste sites and the ability of government and private parties to *recover costs* for cleaning up such sites. Placement of a site on the NPL is a prerequisite only to use of Superfund monies for clean-up; a non-federal party can always use its own money to clean up a facility and then, if possible, recover from responsible parties. However, a federal, state, or tribal government's costs of cleaning up a waste site are recoverable from other responsible parties *unless* the defendant in a cost-recovery action shows an inconsistency with the NCP, *United States v. Northeastern Pharmaceutical & Chemical Co., Inc.*, 810 F.2d 726, 747 (8th Cir. 1986), while a private party can only recover costs for their clean-up actions if such actions are demonstrated to be in substantial compliance with the NCP.

The following recounts how the failed Summitville mine in Colorado came to be listed on the NPL.

THE SUMMITVILLE STORY: A SUPERFUND SITE IS BORN

Luke J. Danielson, Laura Alms, and Alix McNamara
24 ENVTL. L. REP. 10388 (1994)

From the top of the Summitville mine's defunct heap leach, a mass of leached-out gold ore hundreds of feet high, the signs of environmental disaster are visible everywhere. The leach pad, a pond-like structure covering 46 acres, contains over nine million tons of ore. Murky green water collects in pools along the heap's border, and milky water drains from old tunnels. Long coils of black pipe, once used to pump cyanide solution onto the heap, are now used to percolate water through the cyanide- and metal-laden ore as part of a detoxification process that will take years and millions of tax dollars to complete. Trailers filled with portable water treatment systems dot the site, and the scar of the open pit is visible for miles. The contrast with the surrounding landscape, where the austere, rugged peaks of Colorado's San Juan Mountains slope into miles of pristine wilderness, is dramatic.

In just eight years, the Summitville mine has progressed from initial permitting [as an ongoing mining operation] to an U.S. Environmental Protection Agency (EPA) emergency response site. Soon, it will land on the Comprehensive Environmental Response, Compensation, and Liability Act (CERCLA) national priorities list.

* * *

Summitville began construction of the heap leach pad and liner in the fall of 1985 and continued construction throughout the winter of 1985–86. Many of the problems that would later plague the mine during its operating life resulted directly from the company's decision to complete construction of the liner during the winter. Critical to the success of a heap leaching operation is an impermeable liner under the crushed ore material. This liner has two functions. First, it collects the "pregnant" cyanide solution that has percolated through the heap in order to convey it to the processing plant where the gold is ultimately removed from the solution. Second, it prevents the solution from entering the environment.

Despite the importance of the liner for environmental control, the permit did not restrict winter installation. Liner construction occurred through the depth of the 1985 winter. This ill-advised winter construction, compounded by frequent snow slides, led to liner rips and tears and inadequately sealed seams that culminated in cyanide leaks soon after the company began initial operations in June 1986. A recent Canadian Broadcasting Corporation report describes the severe problems experienced during winter construction:

The pad was built under nightmarish conditions—sub-zero temperatures, 35 feet of snow, and avalanches that crashed into the construction site. In the words of one report, the pad liner froze, buckled, cracked, and eventually leaked.

* * *

The regulators' optimism that the company had committed itself to a program that would remedy some of the site's worst problems was dashed in December 1992, when the company declared bankruptcy without warning, terminating its commitment to pay for continuing operation of the water treatment plant and the complex system of pumps and pipes that was keeping massive active discharges of contaminants from overflowing the heap. The company's withdrawal from its agreements with 11 days' notice was a supreme act of corporate irresponsibility. The bankrupt mining operation left both state and federal regulators, without any advance warning, heirs to an abandoned mine at the beginning of one of the most severe winters in recent history. The timing of the bankruptcy was extremely unfortunate and has been the subject of much deserved criticism.

* * *

Since assuming control of the site, EPA has spent over $10.8 million on monitoring. During the winter, EPA was spending an average of $30,000 a day to prevent heap overflow. Overall costs during the winter totaled $3.5 million dollars. It is estimated that clean-up could cost up to $120 million. The immediate project of moving the six million-ton waste pile to an acceptable location is in itself an enormous engineering task.

The expected Superfund listing of Summitville is triggering a rash of litigation. Galactic [the parent of the mining company], its officers, other mining companies whose only involvement in Summitville may have been a little core drilling or sampling, landowners, engineering consultants, and others are girding for battle over their relative responsibilities for on-site conditions. For EPA, state regulators, lawyers, potential criminal defendants, and the various mining companies who will be PRPs at this site, Summitville will go on for a long time.

Without a Superfund, the Summitville mine site could never have been cleaned up. The State of Colorado did not have the necessary funds to pay the costs of preventing the cyanide from killing everything downstream; state regulators had failed to secure an adequate performance bond; the principal PRP itself, the Summitville Mining Company, was bankrupt. The Superfund is therefore essential to the eventual success of CERCLA. Although more solvent mining companies, such as Galactic, may also become PRPs at the Summitville site, protracted litigation among these companies with respect to their relative "contribution" shares will delay the United States recovering its costs paid out of the Superfund.

But has Superfund been a success? When Congress succeeded in passing the major amendments to CERCLA in 1986, the Superfund Amendments and Reauthorization Act (SARA), the size of the Superfund was expanded to $8.5 billion. Most of this was to be raised by a so-called "Superfund tax" on certain industries (*e.g.*, petroleum and chemical) whose products were judged to create most of the clean-up problem. At the end of 1995, Congress failed to reach agreement on CERCLA reauthorization, and the Superfund tax expired. Between 1996 and 2000, Congress continued to consider CERCLA reauthorization bills, but was unable to achieve consensus. CERCLA remains a statute in need of reauthorization. The EPA's efforts under CERCLA, as well as the Superfund, have been able to continue only because of a continuing resolution originally enacted in 1996. Technically, the Superfund has always been something of an accounting charade; however, since the Superfund tax expired, the EPA's CERCLA operations have been funded at only 75 percent of prior levels, curtailing clean-up activities at hundreds of NPL sites and forcing a dramatic reduction in remediation activities. *See* Kathleen Chandler Schmid, *The Depletion of the Superfund and Natural Resource Damages,* 16 N.Y.U. Envtl. L.J. 483 (2008).

At its peak in 1993, Superfund reached $3.6 billion, but because of Congress' refusal to reauthorize the tax, the fund ran dry in 2003. After 2003, funding to pay for orphaned sites, which account for 606 of the 1279 sites across the nation, came directly from public money. Logically, the dwindling of the fund bears correlation to the rate of contaminated site clean up, which was 89 in 1999, but only 19 in 2009. In June of 2010, a bill was introduced in Congress aimed rejuvenating the Superfund. The bill would impose a 9.7 cent a barrel tax on crude oil and refined oil products, excise taxes of 22 cents to $4.87 a ton on certain chemicals, and an income tax of .12 percent on certain corporations' modified alternative minimum taxable income above $2 million. In all, the Bill is aimed at raising an estimated $18.0 billion over 10 years.

In addition to suffering from inadequate funding and a failure by Congress to reauthorize CERCLA, the Superfund clean-up process can be criticized because of the long period of time that can elapse between the time a site comes to the EPA's attention, and the time when remedial work is completed. Nearly four years can pass from the time a citizen or a state notifies the EPA of a possible CERCLA site, before that site is assessed and then receives a sufficiently high score on the HRS to be placed on the NPL for Superfund clean-up. After listing, there must be a remedial investigation and feasibility study completed before the EPA issues a Record of Decision (ROD) detailing the clean-up action that will be taken. This can take five years or more. The clean-up of the site can then begin, but it is not complete until a remedial "design" is finished and subsequent remedial "action" has physically removed (or halted) the contamination from the site. This clean-up work can last four or more years. What is the total elapsed time between discovery of site and its clean-up? On average, that elapsed time is between 13 to 15 years.[4] The major steps in the Superfund process are illustrated below.

AVERAGE TIME TO COMPLETE STEPS

IN SUPERFUND CLEANUP PROCESS

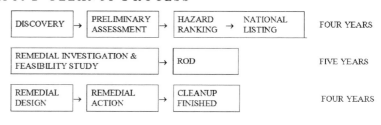

Figure 6.1

CERCLA has also been criticized because of its high administrative costs. The Rand Corporation concluded that of $2.6 billion paid out of the Superfund by the EPA through 1988, only $1.6 billion were devoted to remedial investigations and response actions at waste sites. J. Acton, Understanding Superfund: A Progress Report (1989). The remainder ($1 billion) had been spent on transaction costs—administration, management, laboratory, and litigation expenses. Of this $2.6 billion paid out of Super-fund, EPA had recovered $230 million of its costs through settlements at 328 sites.

Both the Congress and EPA have tried to accelerate the clean-up process and reduce transaction costs. To speed up clean-ups, SARA imposed timetables and statutory deadlines for EPA to complete preliminary assessments and site inspections; it also directed EPA to begin 275 remedial investigation and feasibility studies, 175 remedial clean-up actions within three years of enactment, and an additional 200 in the next two years. To lower administrative costs, EPA has established presumptive remedies and other administrative improvements, encouraged settlements among private parties, and ratified allocations of costs initiated by PRPs. EPA has also been experimenting with non-judicial solutions in which neutral mediators negotiate allocations of responsibility.

---

4. Further delays can occur if administrative and judicial challenges are brought by PRPs while the EPA is engaged in the clean-up process.

3. HOW TO CLEAN UP A CONTAMINATED SITE

CERCLA and the Superfund are meant to accomplish one central goal, which is the prevention of "releases" of hazardous substances from specific sites where soil or groundwater is, or may be, contaminated. A PRP or the EPA has several options available to it when contemplating how to remove the threat posed by a contaminated waste site. Each carries with it certain dangers that must be factored into the eventual clean-up decision. The most logical option is to remove the source of the threat, treat it, and then dispose of it, either on-site or at an off-site commercial facility. The removal option has the advantage of controlling the source of the environmental threat, but it also has disadvantages. Sometimes the site is so large, and the contamination so pervasive, that removal of all contamination is virtually impossible; removal is usually extremely expensive; and the mere act of removing and/or transporting large amounts of hazardous substances can itself harm the environment or the public.

The standard techniques for managing the hazards of Superfund sites are described in the following excerpt, which also emphasizes the hazards inherent in clean-up activities:

> * * * the clearest way to understand the sources of the physical effects of remediation is to see a clean-up project for what it is—a construction site and industrial operation. Construction and transportation risks account for the great majority of the fatalities suffered by remediation workers. Cleaning up Superfund sites also requires some or all of the following kinds of operations:
>
> 1) restricting site access and imposing institutional controls to limit post-remediation land use;
>
> 2) decontaminating, decommissioning (shutting down), and demolishing buildings and other structures;
>
> 3) handling hazardous materials in tanks, ponds, pits, drums, and other containers;
>
> 4) managing contaminated media such as soil, sediment, surface water, and groundwater;
>
> 5) treating wastes or contaminated media to stabilize, compact, or neutralize it; and
>
> 6) transporting hazardous materials away from a site and transporting construction and treatment equipment and materials to it.
>
> * * *
>
> [R]emediation risks consist of both (i) the toxic and unfamiliar risks associated with the hazard that triggered the clean-up in the first place, and (ii) the mechanical or accident-related risks associated with the physical demands of construction and transportation work. * * *
>
> [Finally, there are several] different receptors of risks. * * *

The primary receptors of remedial risks are (i) project workers, including both those regularly employed at the site and transportation workers; (ii) the general public, including immediate neighbors, affected area population, and residents of transportation corridors; and (iii) the natural world, especially sensitive ecosystems like wetlands in and around the site. * * *

John S. Applegate & Steven M. Wesloh, *Short Changing Short–Term Risk: A Study of Superfund Remedy Selection*, 15 YALE J. ON REG. 269, 277–79 (1998).

To avoid some of the problems inherent in clean up activities, *in situ* treatment methods are now being tried. If the site is capable of being enclosed and surrounded, it may be "impounded," often by wrapping it with several impermeable layers of some plastic product. Impoundments work only if the site can in fact be encased, and if the encasement is truly impermeable and capable of resisting the most toxic of volatile substances. Impoundments are usually surrounded by monitoring wells, so that any leakage into groundwater can be detected.

A more sophisticated and experimental clean-up option entails the on-site treatment of hazardous wastes to alter their chemical and toxic nature. This can occur in a number of ways, ranging from adding chemicals or bacteria to alter the molecular structure of the wastes, to circulating gas through soil in order to remove harmful chemicals when they react with the gas, to sending electrical charges into contaminated soil. When a Superfund site is an enormous mile-deep pit filled with lethal water, some of these *in situ* options seem very appropriate.

Figure 6.2–Berkeley Pit, Butte, Montana

Butte Breaks New Ground to Mop Up a World–Class Mess
JIM ROBBINS
New York Times, *July 21, 1998.*

So much copper was dug from the mountain this city in the Rockies was built on, it was dubbed the Richest Hill on Earth.

Now the copper is largely gone, and the bill for a century's worth of mining has come due. The mountains and waterways around Butte are so contaminated they make up the largest Superfund complex in the country. The contamination is so widespread and difficult to deal with that company scientists have been forced to look for new solutions. Butte has, in essence, become a giant test laboratory for clean-up technologies.

The heart of the problem is in the city of Butte itself, which is next to one of the largest open-pit mines in the world. The mine was abandoned in 1979 and the Atlantic Richfield Co. stopped pumping water out of the pit in 1981. As maroon-colored water pours into the pit through mining tunnels that honeycomb the remains of the mountain, and more washes in from the surface, the water carries large amounts of sulfuric acid and a variety of heavy metals, including zinc, nickel, cadmium and arsenic, and especially high levels of copper.

In 1995, 342 snow geese landed on the water and never took off again. Burns in the esophagus indicated they died from drinking the water. "It's basically acid," said Michael Tuck, president of MSE Technology Applications, a company owned by the Montana university system and funded by grants from the Department of Energy, the National Aeronautics and Space Administration and other Federal agencies. "And it has the potential to contaminate wells and creeks."

* * *

Any solution will be less than perfect. Berkeley Pit's poisonous brew is expected to pollute the surrounding aquifer by 2022 if nothing is done.

Atlantic Richfield plans to spend $48 million to build two plants to treat the water indefinitely at a cost of $14 million a year. The plan is to add lime to the water and neutralize the sulfuric acid, allowing the metal to precipitate out. But the process creates 1,000 tons of lime sludge each day, which would be dumped backed into the pit or stored in a lagoon.

MSE Technology Applications is studying other ways to treat the water, and to remove copper and other metals in order to help offset treatment costs. MSE looked at some 150 proposals and was evaluating 15 that seemed most promising.

One idea that works, at least chemically, is another precipitation scheme, in which sulfides are added to the brew. This makes the metal ions heavier, which means the most valuable metals, copper and zinc, precipitate out and could be sold. It would reduce the sludge to 300 tons a day, from 1,000. "Chemistry is straightforward, but the economics of building a treatment plant are another matter," said Mary Ann Harrington–Baker, manager of MSE's Heavy Metals Program.

* * *

Down the valley from the pit, is Silver Bow Creek, the small meandering stream where gold was originally found. Seven smelters lined the creek at one time. Thousands of tons of tailing laden with heavy metals were dumped along its banks. This stream was so polluted that 26 of its 30 miles had no fish.

Atlantic Richfield moved and buried the tailings, and planned to build a plant to treat the water with lime. Instead, engineers designed and built a two to three-acre artificial wetland, complete with cattails. Contaminated water from the creek is pumped into a reservoir behind the wetland and seeps through the mud at the rate of three to five feet per day.

Bacteria in the mud consume carbon and oxygen from decaying plants. Once they deplete the oxygen, the bacteria begin to eat the sulfur from the acid mine drainage and make it more alkaline. As the water becomes more alkaline, the zinc and copper precipitate out. The water flows through another artificial swamp, where it is re-oxygenated, forcing out the methane and hydrogen sulfide gases.

"Contrasted with a system with a lot of lime, it's cost effective," said Sandy Stash, who directs the clean-up operation for Atlantic Richfield in Montana, "but it's not cheap."

After a Superfund site is cleaned up, and the levels of contamination are brought down so that neither human health nor the environment is threatened, the next question is what to do with the site in its post-Superfund state. If humans are to live on the site, then additional remediation work might be necessary. If the site is to return to a natural condition, human intervention may be needed to jump start nature. For example, at the former Bunker Hill smelter site in Idaho, logging and sulphur dioxide emissions had denuded the nearby hillsides. To minimize erosion of lead-contaminated soil and to restore the forest, EPA has ordered a massive revegetation program that will take three years and cost about $8 million.

As you study the law of CERCLA, it is important to remember that it all comes down to moving, incinerating, treating, or encapsulating chemicals, soil, and water. The physical demands of these activities drive the risks and costs which in turn drive the regulatory system.

B.   CERCLA IN CONTEXT

CERCLA was the last of the major environmental statutes enacted during the "Environmental Decade," 1969–1980. At the beginning of that period, between 1969 and 1972, Congress required that certain procedures be followed to assess the environmental impacts of major governmental actions. It also established programs for regulating air and water pollution, and for protecting drinking water. By the mid–1970s, scientific and medical knowledge had grown considerably. It was now possible to detect chemicals in the environment at levels one part per billion and lower. This was unheard of 20 years before. The medical community was beginning to establish links between numerous chemical substances and negative health effects, especially cancer. Soon policymakers began to suspect that very low levels of many toxic chemicals in the environment could pose a threat to public health. As we have seen, one statutory response to that discovery was the enactment of federal laws to regulate the sale and production of toxic substances, in order to control market access to products that might contain chemicals harmful to humans. Among the prime examples of this kind of statute are the Federal Insecticide, Fungicide, and Rodenticide Act of 1947 (FIFRA), and the Toxic Substances Control Act of 1976 (TSCA), discussed above in Chapters 7 and 8, respectively. The Resource Conservation and Recovery Act of 1976 (RCRA), covered in Chapter 9, was designed to prevent the active disposal of toxic wastes onto the soil and into groundwater. However, RCRA, like FIFRA and TSCA, did not address the threat posed to humans and the environment from *past* waste disposal practices.

1.   Love Canal and the Statute's History

The problem of inadequate hazardous waste disposal was dramatically brought home to America by the Love Canal disaster. As the case study in Chapter 9 explains, the Love Canal site was a classic abandoned waste dump. Standard disposal practice for factories, refineries, and mines was simply to place hazardous wastes in barrels, drums, or open pits and then to bury and abandon them. Consistent with this tradition, for ten years the Hooker Chemical Company had dumped tens of thousands of tons of chemical waste into an old canal, covered it, and had given the site to the local board of education. The new owners built a school on the land and sold the remainder to homebuilders. After a series of illnesses began to plague the area, investigators discovered that toxic chemicals migrating from the canal had contaminated the subsoil and groundwater, and had even seeped into residential basements. Panic set in, the Love Canal story made national headlines, the area's residents were hastily evacuated, and the problem of non-active waste sites was placed at the doorstep of Congress.

Three questions had to be addressed. First, how grave was the problem of hazardous waste dumps? Before CERCLA was enacted, both the EPA and congressional subcommittees estimated (based on surveys of the largest chemical manufacturers) that there could be between 1,500 and 2,000 dump sites across the United States that contained wastes so hazardous that they threatened human health.[5] The EPA concluded that virtually all of the hazardous wastes generated in this country were being disposed of improperly, and that there were over 3,000 new spills of toxic chemicals each year. Second, who should pay for the clean-up of hazardous waste sites? There were two choices: (1) the federal government could bear the cost, perhaps by creating a clean-up fund through the imposition of a tax on classes of industries that tended to dispose of hazardous waste, or (2) the private parties responsible for the waste dumps could be liable for clean-up costs, if a formula could be devised for determining who exactly was responsible.[6] Third, if a waste site was not an "orphan site" (one whose owners had disappeared), what mechanism should be established for reaching a range of liable private parties to pay clean-up costs that often run into the tens of millions of dollars per site?

With respect to the first question, the fact that CERCLA was passed at all reflected congressional concern that the problem of environmental contamination from hazardous waste sites was indeed national in scope, and was both grave and threatening. As we saw at the beginning of this

---

5.   After CERCLA's enactment, EPA compiled an inventory of over 35,000 sites contaminated by past dumping of hazardous wastes. Of these, over 10,000 sites still require further federal investigation to determine if they should be placed on the National Priority List. By 1999, there were nearly 1400 on the NPL. The remainder of the sites are subject to clean-up by private parties or clean-up under state law.

6.   In the case of the Love Canal, the federal government paid for relocating its residents, while the Occidental Petroleum Company, owner of the Hooker Chemical Company, paid for the remediation work.

chapter, the second question was answered by establishing a program that combined the ideas of federal responses to locations containing hazardous substances, as well as private party liability for past and ongoing releases of such substances. We also saw that the third question was answered by imposing strict, joint and several, and retroactive liability on parties deemed "responsible" for the contaminated sites.

CERCLA's structure was modeled on section 311 of the Clean Water Act, which establishes a revolving fund for use by the Coast Guard and EPA to respond to oil spills (and, after 1978, hazardous substance spills) into navigable waters. It applies the principle of strict liability to persons responsible for releases of "harmful quantities" of oil.[7] Within § 311 are the seeds of CERCLA. Section 311(b)(5) requires any person "in charge" of a vessel or facility discharging harmful quantities of oil to report the discharge to the EPA or Coast Guard.[8] Section 103 of CERCLA requires reporting of releases of hazardous substances to the National Response Center. Under § 311(c), the federal government may respond to the discharge or threatened discharge of oil or other hazardous substances into navigable waters, so long as the action is consistent with the National Contingency Plan (NCP). The initial costs of clean-up may be paid out of the Oil Spill Liability Trust Fund. In a similar fashion, section 104 of CERCLA authorizes response action consistent with the NCP. Section 111 of CERCLA creates a Superfund which can be used to finance governmental response actions, and to reimburse private parties for costs incurred in carrying out the NCP. Section 311(f) imposes liability for clean-up costs and natural resources damages on owners or operators of vessels or facilities from which spills have occurred or are threatened. Section 107 of CERCLA imposes liability on current and past owners and operators of facilities where hazardous substances are released, or threatened to be released.[9]

KEY PROVISIONS OF CERCLA

§ 101   *Definitions*–"facility"; "release"; "disposal"; "hazardous substance."

§ 104   *Removals* and *remedial action* authorized if consistent with the National Contingency Plan (NCP).

§ 105   National Contingency Plan requires establishment of hazard *ranking system* and a National Priorities List (NPL).

---

7.   The term National *Contingency* Plan, is a vestige of CERCLA's origins. The original NCP dealt exclusively with oil spills; oil and hazardous substance spills on water are now a small part of the NCP. *See* 40 C.F.R. §§ 300, 300–335.

8.   What is a harmful quantity of oil? *See United States v. Chotin Transp., Inc.*, 649 F.Supp. 356 (S.D. Ohio 1986) (20 gallons spilled into the Ohio River may be harmful).

9.   Like CERCLA's liability scheme, § 311(f) of the CWA incorporates principles of strict liability, *Steuart Transp. Co. v. Allied Towing Corp.*, 596 F.2d 609, 613 (4th Cir. 1979), as well as joint and several liability where the harm is indivisible. United States v. M/V Big Sam, 681 F.2d 432, 439 (5th Cir. 1982).

§ 106 *Abatement* orders may be issued if actual or potential releases create imminent and substantial endangerment.

§ 107 *Liability* is imposed on potentially responsible parties (PRPs), defined as owners, operators, arrangers, and transporters of hazardous waste, for all costs of removal or remedial action incurred by the federal government not inconsistent with the NCP, for other response costs incurred by any person consistent with the NCP, or for damages to natural resources.

§ 111 Creates a *Superfund* to finance governmental response actions, and to reimburse private parties for costs incurred in carrying out the NCP.

§ 113 Prevents pre-enforcement *judicial review* of response actions; permits private *contribution* actions against PRPs.

§ 116 Sets out *schedules* for listing sites on the NPL, for undertaking remedial investigation and feasibility studies, and for taking remedial clean-up action at sites.

§ 121 Fixes *standards for CERCLA clean-ups*. There is a preference for permanent solutions where the site must be cleaned up to a level meeting a "legally applicable or relevant and appropriate standard, requirement, criteria or limitation" (*ARARs*) found in federal environmental law, or state law if it is more restrictive than federal law.

§ 122 Articulates standards for government-initiated *settlements* with PRPs.

The Clean Water Act also contains an "imminent hazard" provision authorizing EPA to seek administrative and judicial action against those causing these hazards. 33 U.S.C. § 1364 (a). However, The CWA's provisions regarding spills do not extend to spills or discharges of contaminated materials onto land,[10] Therefore, CERCLA was a huge expansion of the oil spill provisions, but its passage in 1980 was nevertheless extremely hurried. The actual language was the product of a last-minute compromise by a small bipartisan group of influential senators. With virtually no debate, the statute passed in a lame-duck session by the Senate, and the House then agreed to accept the Senate version without even holding a conference committee. The result was unclear draftsmanship and very little legislative history. Many judges have in fact assumed that Congress left much of CERCLA vague so that the courts would, by their decisions construing its language, develop a federal common law to supplement the statute. Whether intended or not, this is in fact what happened on the liability side

---

10. The Oil Pollution Act of 1990, Pub. L. 101–380, parallels § 311 of the CWA. Both assume that the party responsible for the oil spill should be the one who should pay for the costs of cleaning it up, and that the government should be able to recover any public monies that had to be spent.

of CERCLA, which is managed by the courts through litigation. The preclusion of most judicial review of remedy selection has, by contrast, resulted in very little judicial guidance on the regulatory side, which is managed administratively.

The two amendments to CERCLA since 1980 have not significantly altered its original structure though they have clarified (often by ratifying judicial or administrative practice) some major provisions. The Superfund Amendments and Reauthorization Act of 1986 (SARA) sorted out several liability issues, established a methodology for deciding the nature and degree of clean-up, and increased the Superfund amount to $8.5 billion. It also made a number of procedural changes designed to accelerate the clean-up process. Chief among these were provisions facilitating contribution among responsible parties and encouraging settlements. An obscure amendment enacted in 1996 (as part of the Asset Conservation, Lender Liability, and Deposit Insurance Protection Act, Pub. L. No. 104–208) clarified the scope of lender liability and provided additional protections for fiduciaries.

2.   CERCLA AND RCRA

As noted above, RCRA was passed to provide a comprehensive structure for managing hazardous and non-hazardous solid wastes, primarily at active waste disposal sites. CERCLA, on the other hand, was intended to address ongoing problems associated with past improper waste disposal activities.

> Unlike [CERCLA], RCRA is not principally designed to effectuate the clean-up of toxic waste sites or to compensate those who have attended to the remediation of environmental hazards. *Cf. General Electric Co. v. Litton Industrial Automation Systems, Inc.,* 920 F.2d 1415, 1422 (C.A.8 1990) (the "two * * * main purposes of CERCLA" are "prompt clean-up of hazardous waste sites and imposition of all clean-up costs on the responsible party"). RCRA's primary purpose, rather, is to reduce the generation of hazardous waste and to ensure the proper treatment, storage, and disposal of that waste which is nonetheless generated, "so as to minimize the present and future threat to human health and the environment." 42 U.S.C. § 6902(b).

Meghrig v. KFC Western, Inc., 516 U.S. 479, 483 (1996). Despite this difference in focus, there are still similarities and overlap between CERCLA and RCRA. Jurisdictionally, there is a great deal of potential overlap, since CERCLA incorporates RCRA's list of hazardous wastes, and RCRA includes corrective action provisions for cleaning up RCRA-permitted facilities. This provides EPA with remedial choices when the contaminated site is also a "treatment, storage, and disposal facility" (TSDF) regulated under RCRA. TSDFs are subject to strict RCRA requirements, including the need to obtain a permit before wastes can be received, and the need to take corrective actions to clean up uncontrolled wastes that may be hazardous. EPA may choose to rely on either CERCLA or RCRA to bring about a clean-up at a TSDF.[11] If EPA proceeds under CERCLA, the owner/operator may object, because CERCLA actions are often more public and less flexible, and because the owner/operator then becomes a PRP from whom response costs may be recovered. Despite these concerns, the rule is that RCRA does not limit CERCLA, and CERCLA may have applicability to a RCRA TSDF. *Apache Powder Co. v. United States*, 968 F.2d 66 (D.C. Cir. 1992) (EPA may include a TSDF subject to RCRA on the CERCLA National Priorities List). *See also Chemical Waste Management, Inc. v. Armstrong World Industries, Inc.*, 669 F.Supp. 1285 (E.D. Pa. 1987) (a TSDF allegedly in violation of RCRA may nonetheless seek cost recovery under CERCLA).

There is also a striking similarity between RCRA § 7003, which empowers EPA to clean up hazardous waste sites that pose an "imminent and substantial endangerment to health or the environment," and CERCLA § 106(a), which empowers EPA to issue a responsible party an abatement order when an actual or threatened release of hazardous substances presents an "imminent and substantial endangerment" to health or the environment. Initially, RCRA § 7003 was understood to apply only to active hazardous waste sites. In 1984, Congress amended RCRA so that § 7003 was applicable to both "past and present handling, storage, treatment, or disposal" of hazardous wastes.[12] As a result, EPA sometimes uses RCRA § 7003 and CERCLA § 106(a) in tandem when it confronts a particularly dangerous waste disposal site.[13] If EPA can identify a PRP at such a site, it might also proceed under the cost-recovery provisions of CERCLA § 107 (setting out liability standards when cost recovery actions are initiated for clean-up expenses).

CERCLA § 106 is available only to the federal government; states and private parties seeking abatement must use RCRA's citizen suit provision, § 7002(a)(1)(B) in conjunction with § 7003. *See Sealy Connecticut, Inc. v. Litton Industries*, 989 F.Supp. 120, 123 (D. Conn. 1997) (present owner could bring RCRA § 7002 action against prior owner, even though present owner was a CERCLA PRP). Private parties may not obtain compensatory relief for personal injury or property under § 7003 or § 7002, since these RCRA provisions are equitable. CERCLA § 107 is the preferred statutory provision for recovery of clean-up costs. RCRA § 7003 may also be broader than CERCLA, since it includes within its reach those who "contribute" to the practices that create the endangerment; RCRA's provisions also extend to non-hazardous "solid waste"; and RCRA is not subject to CERCLA's petro-

---

11.   EPA usually declines to address waste problems at RCRA TSDFs under CERCLA, in large part because a non-CERCLA response conserves the Superfund. *See, e.g.,* 54 Fed. Reg. 41,004 (1989).

12.   Some earlier RCRA cases assumed that § 7003 applied just to inactive sites, because a contrary interpretation would have limited the government's ability to respond to "disasters precipitated by earlier poor planning." *United States v. Waste Industries, Inc.*, 734 F.2d 159 (4th Cir. 1984).

13.   That RCRA is primarily intended to correct present hazardous waste practices, while CERCLA is more focused on past disposal actions, still has relevance in two contexts: (1) when parties bring an action under both RCRA and a *state* waste management statute, where the state statute is a prospective regulatory regime, Acme Printing Ink Co. v. Menard, Inc., 870 F.Supp. 1465 (E.D. Wis. 1994); and (2) when an RCRA remedy might interfere with a CERCLA clean-up. McClellan Ecological Seepage Situation v. Perry, 47 F.3d 325 (9th Cir. 1995).

leum exclusion (CERCLA §§ 101(14) and 101(33)). Moreover, CERCLA has been interpreted to require that the "hazardous substances" exist in sufficient concentrations to subject a party to response costs. *Amoco Oil Co. v. Borden, Inc.*, 889 F.2d 664 (5th Cir. 1989). On the other hand, the "hazardous substances" subject to CERCLA cover a broader range of materials than RCRA's "hazardous wastes." The CERCLA term includes RCRA hazardous wastes as well as substances regulated under the Clean Air Act (CAA), the Clean Water Act (CWA), and the Toxic Substances Control Act. § 101(14); *State of California v. Summer Del Caribe, Inc.*, 821 F.Supp. 574 (N.D. Cal. 1993).

3.   CERCLA AND STATE LAW

CERCLA has something of a love-hate relationship with state law. On the one hand, CERCLA liability is a logical statutory extension of state common law tort doctrine. Moreover, it contains a broad savings clause, which provides that nothing in the statute "shall affect * * * the obligations or liabilities of any person under * * * State law, including common law, with respect to releases of hazardous substances or other pollutants or contaminants." § 302(d). This savings clause is to prevent the creation of an inference that CERCLA is intended to be the exclusive remedy for harms that also violate the statute. CERCLA was not intended to wipe out the common law of toxic torts. *See PMC, Inc. v. Sherwin–Williams Co.*, 151 F.3d 610, 618 (7th Cir. 1998); *Gordon v. United Van Lines, Inc.*, 130 F.3d 282, 288–89 (7th Cir. 1997). Nor does CERCLA preempt state statutes that do not conflict with federal cleanup objectives. *Marsh v. Rosenbloom*, 499 F.3d 165 (2d Cir. 2007) (finding CERCLA's six year statute of limitations did not preempt Delaware statute imposing three year wind-up period following dissolution of corporation, because Delaware's limitation on a corporation's capacity to be sued did not significantly interfere with the goals of CERCLA). It is therefore common for actions against parties responsible for contaminating a waste site to be grounded both in CERCLA and state statutory and common law.

On the other hand, CERCLA does preempt state laws and actions arising under state common law that would have the effect of preventing the accomplishment of federal statutory clean-up goals. *See, e.g.,* Gregory Romano, *"Shovel First and Lawyers Later": A Collision Course for CERCLA Clean-ups and Environmental Tort Claims*, 21 WM & MARY ENVTL. L. & POLICY REV. 421 (1997); *Arrest the Incinerator Remediation, Inc. v. Ohm Remediation Services, Corp.*, 5 F. Supp.2d 291 (M.D. Pa. 1998) (CERCLA preempts private state law nuisance action seeking to block ongoing clean-up of Superfund site); *In re Pfohl Bros. Landfill Litigation*, 68 F. Supp. 2d 236, 249 (W.D.N.Y. 1999) (CERCLA preempts state statute of limitations that would otherwise have removed liability from those who Congress intended to be responsible for clean-up costs); *BASF Corp. v. Central Transport, Inc.*, 830 F.Supp. 1011 (E.D. Mich. 1993) (CERCLA preempts state law which otherwise would have limited the liability of a dissolved corporation under § 107).

Even though CERCLA builds upon, and is a direct extension of, common law principles of strict liability for abnormally dangerous activities, it alters traditional common law tort doctrine in several ways. It often goes farther than traditional tort law, allowing the government and private plaintiffs to do things that would be quite difficult for the common law to do.

4.   CERCLA's EXTRATERRITORIALITY APPLICATION

Although Congress has the authority to enact legislation governing entities and locations outside of the United States, there is a general presumption that unless a federal statute explicitly states that it applies outside the boundaries of the United States, it will not be read to apply to other nations or territories. CERCLA does not explicitly state that it can be applied beyond the United States' domestic borders. In *Pakootas v. Teck Cominco Metals, Ltd.*, 452 F.3d 1066 (9th Cir. 2006), the Ninth Circuit addressed whether a Canadian mining company could be required to clean up the Columbia River after it discharged hazardous substances that migrated downstream into the state of Washington. *See also* Jordan Diamond, *How CERCLA's Ambiguities Muddled the Question of Extraterritoriality in Pakootas v. Teck Cominco Metals, Ltd.*, 34 ECOLOGY L.Q. 1013 (2007).

Pakootas v. Teck Cominco Metals, Ltd.

452 F.3d 1066 (9th Cir. 2006)

■ GOULD, CIRCUIT JUDGE:

Joseph A. Pakootas and Donald R. Michel (collectively "Pakootas") filed suit to enforce a Unilateral Administrative Order (Order) issued by the United States Environmental Protection Agency (EPA) against Teck Cominco Metals, Ltd. (Teck), a Canadian corporation. The Order requires Teck to conduct a remedial investigation/feasibility study (RI/FS) in a portion of the Columbia River entirely within the United States, where hazardous substances disposed of by Teck have come to be located. We decide today whether a citizen suit based on Teck's alleged non-compliance with the Order is a domestic or an extraterritorial application of the Comprehensive Environmental Response, Compensation, and Liability Act (CERCLA), 42 U.S.C. §§ 9601–9675. We hold that because CERCLA liability is triggered by an actual or threatened release of hazardous substances, and because a release of hazardous substances took place within the United States, this suit involves a domestic application of CERCLA.

In August of 1999, the Colville Tribes petitioned the EPA under § 9605 to conduct an assessment of hazardous substance contamination in and along the Columbia River in northeastern Washington state. The EPA began the site assessment in October 1999, and found contamination that included "heavy metals such as arsenic, cadmium, copper, lead, mercury and zinc." The EPA... concluded that the Upper Columbia River Site (the Site) was eligible for listing on the National Priorities List (NPL).

Teck owns and operates a lead-zinc smelter ("Trail Smelter") in Trail, British Columbia. Between 1906 and 1995, Teck generated and disposed of hazardous materials, in both liquid and solid form, into the Columbia River. These wastes, known as "slag," include the heavy metals arsenic, cadmium, copper, mercury, lead, and zinc, as well as other unspecified hazardous materials. Before mid–1995, the Trail Smelter discharged up to 145,000 tons of slag annually into the Columbia River. Although the discharge took place within Canada, the EPA concluded that Teck has arranged for the disposal of its hazardous substances from the Trail Smelter into the Upper Columbia River by directly discharging up to 145,000 tonnes of slag annually prior to mid–1995. Effluent, such as slag, was discharged into the Columbia River through several outfalls at the Trail Smelter.... The slag was carried downstream in the passing river current and settled in slower flowing quiescent areas. A significant amount of slag has accumulated and adversely affects the surface water, ground water, sediments, and biological resources of the Upper Columbia River and Lake Roosevelt. Technical evidence shows that the Trail Smelter is the predominant source of contamination at the Site. The physical and chemical decay of slag is an ongoing process that releases arsenic, cadmium, copper, zinc, and lead into the environment, causing harm to human health and the environment.

We begin by considering how this litigation fits within the CERCLA statutory framework. CERCLA sets forth a comprehensive scheme for the cleanup of hazardous waste sites, and imposes liability for cleanup costs on the parties responsible for the release or potential release of hazardous substances into the environment.

To ensure the prompt cleanup of hazardous waste sites, CERCLA gives four options to the EPA: (1) the EPA can investigate and remediate hazardous waste sites itself under § 9604, and later seek to recover response costs from the potentially responsible parties (PRPs) under § 9607; (2) the EPA can initiate settlement negotiations with PRPs under § 9622; (3) the EPA can file suit in federal district court to compel the PRPs to abate the threat if there is an "imminent and substantial" threat to public health or welfare under § 9606(a); or (4) the EPA can issue orders directing the PRPs to clean up the site under § 9606(a). In this case, the EPA chose the fourth approach, and issued the Order to Teck under § 9606(a).

If a party receives an order and refuses to comply, enforcement options are available. First, the EPA may bring an action in federal district court to compel compliance, using the contempt powers of the district court as a potential sanction for non-compliance. § 9606(a). Second, the EPA may bring an action in federal district court seeking to impose fines of up to $25,000 for each day that the party fails to comply with the order. § 9606(b)(1). Third, the EPA may initiate cleanup of the facility itself under § 9604, and the party responsible for the pollution is potentially liable for the response and cleanup costs, plus treble damages. § 9607(c)(3).

Here, the EPA has not sought to enforce the Order through any of the mechanisms described above. Rather, Pakootas initiated this suit in federal district court under § 9659, the citizen suit provision of CERCLA. Section 9659(a)(1) provides a cause of action for any person to commence a civil action "against any person ... who is alleged to be in violation of any standard, regulation, condition, requirement, or order which has become effective pursuant to this chapter." Section 9659(c) gives the district court the power "to order such action as may be necessary to correct the violation, and to impose any civil penalty provided for the violation." Further, § 9613(h)(2), the "timing of review" provision of CERCLA, grants federal courts jurisdiction to review an order issued under § 9606(a) when a party seeks to enforce the order.

Teck's primary argument is that, in absence of a clear statement by Congress that it intended CERCLA to apply extraterritorially, the presumption against extraterritorial application of United States law precludes CERCLA from applying to Teck in Canada. We need to address whether the presumption against extraterritoriality applies only if this case involves an extraterritorial application of CERCLA. So a threshold question is whether this case involves a domestic or extraterritorial application of CERCLA.

Unlike other environmental laws such as the Clean Air Act, and the Resource Conservation and Recovery Act (RCRA), CERCLA is not a regulatory statute. Rather, CERCLA imposes liability for the cleanup of sites where there is a release or threatened release of hazardous substances into the environment. CERCLA liability attaches when three conditions are satisfied: (1) the site at which there is an actual or threatened release of hazardous substances is a "facility" under § 9601(9); (2) a "release" or "threatened release" of a hazardous substance from the facility has occurred, § 9607(a)(4); and (3) the party is within one of the four classes of persons subject to liability under § 9607(a).

* * *

Assuming that Teck is an arranger under § 9607(a)(3), we consider whether the fact that the act of arranging in Canada for disposal of the slag makes this an extraterritorial application of CERCLA. Teck argues that because it arranged in Canada for disposal, that is, the act of arranging took place in Canada even though the hazardous substances came to be located in the United States, it cannot be held liable under CERCLA without applying CERCLA extraterritorially.

* * *

Here, the operative event creating a liability under CERCLA is the release or threatened release of a hazardous substance. See § 9607(a)(4). Arranging for disposal of such substances, in and of itself, does not trigger CERCLA liability, nor does actual disposal of hazardous substances. A release must occur or be threatened before CERCLA is triggered. A party that "arranged for disposal" of a hazardous substance under § 9607(a)(3) does not become liable under CERCLA until there is an actual or threatened release of that substance into the environment. Arranging for disposal of hazardous substances, in itself, is neither regulated under nor prohibited by CERCLA. Further, disposal activities that were legal when conducted can nevertheless give rise to liability under § 9607(a)(3) if there is an actual or threatened release of such hazardous substances into the environment. See *Cadillac   Fairview/California,   Inc.   v.   United   States*   (Cadillac

Fairview/California I), 41 F.3d 562, 565–66 (9th Cir.1994) (holding that a party that sold a product to another party "arranged for disposal" of a hazardous substance); Cadillac Fairview/California, Inc. v. Dow Chem. Co. (Cadillac Fairview/California II), *299 F.3d 1019, 1029 (9th Cir.2002)* (characterizing the conduct at issue in Cadillac Fairview/California I as "legal at the time").

The location where a party arranged for disposal or disposed of hazardous substances is not controlling for purposes of assessing whether CERCLA is being applied extraterritorially, because CERCLA imposes liability for releases or threatened releases of hazardous substances, and not merely for disposal or arranging for disposal of such substances. Because the actual or threatened release of hazardous substances triggers CERCLA liability, and because the actual or threatened release here, the leaching of hazardous substances from slag that settled at the Site, took place in the United States, this case involves a domestic application of CERCLA.

Our conclusion is reinforced by considering CERCLA's place within the constellation of our country's environmental laws, and contrasting it with RCRA. Unlike [CERCLA], RCRA is not principally designed to effectuate the cleanup of toxic waste sites or to compensate those who have attended to the remediation of environmental hazards. RCRA's primary purpose, rather, is to reduce the generation of hazardous waste and to ensure the proper treatment, storage, and disposal of that waste which is nonetheless generated, "so as to minimize the present and future threat to human health and the environment." *Meghrig*, 516 U.S. at 483, 116 S.Ct. 1251 (quoting § 9602(b)) (internal citation omitted). RCRA regulates the generation and disposal of hazardous waste, whereas CERCLA imposes liability to clean up a site when there are actual or threatened releases of hazardous substances into the environment. It is RCRA, not CERCLA, that governs prospectively how generators of hazardous substances should dispose of those substances, and it is the Canadian equivalent of RCRA, not CERCLA, that regulates how Teck disposes of its waste within Canada.

Here, the district court assumed, but did not decide, that this suit involved extraterritorial application of CERCLA because "[t]o find there is not an extraterritorial application of CERCLA in this case would require reliance on a legal fiction that the 'releases' of hazardous substances into the Upper Columbia River Site and Lake Roosevelt are wholly separable from the discharge of those substances into the Columbia River at the Trail Smelter." However, what the district court dismissed as a "legal fiction" is the foundation of the distinction between RCRA and CERCLA. If the Trail Smelter were in the United States, the discharge of slag from the smelter into the Columbia River would potentially be regulated by RCRA and the Clean Water Act. And that prospective regulation, if any, would be legally distinct from a finding of CERCLA liability for cleanup of actual or threatened releases of the hazardous substances into the environment from the disposal site, here the Upper Columbia River Site. That the Trail Smelter is located in Canada does not change this analysis, as the district court recognized.

CERCLA is only concerned with imposing liability for cleanup of hazardous waste disposal sites where there has been an actual or threatened release of hazardous substances into the environment. CERCLA does not obligate parties (either foreign or domestic) liable for cleanup costs to cease the disposal activities such as those that made them liable for cleanup costs; regulating disposal activities is in the domain of RCRA or other regulatory statutes.

We hold that applying CERCLA here to the release of hazardous substances at the Site is a domestic, rather than an extraterritorial application of CERCLA, even though the original source of the hazardous substances is located in a foreign country.

Similarities to the Common Law

1. Under CERCLA, an "owner" PRP is liable for clean-up costs irrespective of negligence or fault. Liability may also be imposed on an owner PRP regardless of whether the government has been able to prove actual harm (as opposed to threatened harm or risk) stemming from the site. Some jurisdictions have likewise deemed property owners subject to strict liability notwithstanding that they had not disposed of any waste during their tenure on the now contaminated property. *See, e.g., State of New York v. Shore Realty Corp.*, 759 F.2d 1032, 1051 (2d Cir. 1985); RESTATEMENT (SECOND) OF TORTS § 839.

2. CERCLA provides that companies that arrange for the disposal of hazardous waste may be PRPs and be liable for clean-up costs. Similarly, some courts have decided that a company's decision to generate wastes, and to dispose of these wastes, either by itself or through an independent contractor, may be an "abnormally dangerous activity" giving rise to common law strict liability. *See, e.g., United States v. Hooker Chemicals and Plastics Corp.*, 722 F. Supp. 960 (N.D. N.Y. 1989) (generate and dispose of wastes on company's own property); *Sterling v. Velsicol Chemical Corp.*, 647 F. Supp. 303 (N.D. Tenn. 1986) (same); *Kenney v. Scientific, Inc.*, 497 A.2d 1310 (N.J.Super.,1985) (through independent contractor).

3. CERCLA provides for recovery, by the government, for natural resource damages, which encompass environmental harms to "public" natural resources not owned by private parties. The common law also recognizes that a nuisance can be "public," when there is an "unreasonable interference with a right common to the general public." RESTATEMENT (SECOND) OF TORTS § 821B. As with CERCLA natural resources damages claims, such public rights are usually protected by a public body. *State of New York v. Schenectady Chemicals, Inc.*, 479 N.Y.S.2d 1010 (N.Y.A.D. 3 Dept. 1984).

Extensions of the Common Law

1. As any first-year law student knows, the common law of torts usually requires a proximate causal linkage between the plaintiff's injury and the defendant. It was noted in Chapter 5 (Toxic Torts), that one of the chief difficulties in bringing a tort action against an entity that has discharged some hazardous substance into the environment is demonstrat-

ing that: (1) the substance under control of the defendant eventually wound up inside, or somehow made contact with, the plaintiff, and (2) once there, it caused some harm, such as cancer. The drafters of CERCLA rightly saw that individuals injured by the release of hazardous wastes faced substantial barriers to recovery under the common law, since proving the above two causation elements would be an especially high barrier to overcome. In response, CERCLA establishes a dramatically relaxed standard of proof of causation.

To establish CERCLA § 107 liability, only two conditions must be met: (1) a release of a hazardous substance must cause the incurrence of response costs, and (2) the defendant must fall within one of four categories of responsible parties based on relationship to the waste or to the site, rather than on the quality of the defendant's conduct. The first condition does not require proof that the defendant's hazardous waste actually migrated to the plaintiff's property; it is sufficient that legitimate response costs were incurred by the defendant. *Dedham Water Co., Inc. v. Cumberland Farms Dairy, Inc.*, 972 F.2d 453 (1st Cir. 1992). The second condition assumes that CERCLA's strict liability standard is satisfied regardless of the ignorance, action, or inaction of the defendant; all that is relevant is the defendant's status with respect to the waste.

2.   Another problem facing plaintiffs who wish to bring a common law toxic tort action is that there is usually a long latency period between the time of initial exposure to the harmful substance and the manifestation of the physical harm or illness. This is especially true of cancer. Since many cancers can occur years or decades after the plaintiff's contact with the cancer-causing substances, the relevant statute of limitations may have run before the plaintiff is aware of any injury. To address this long-latency issue, CERCLA § 309 provides that for injuries caused by exposure to hazardous substances, state statutes of limitations for *state law* causes of action do not begin to run until the plaintiff has reason to know that the injury was caused by exposure to a hazardous substance.[14] *Freier v. Westinghouse Electric Corp.*, 303 F.3d 176 (2d Cir. 2002) (holding CERCLA § 9658 provides that discovery of the cause of injury becomes the uniform accrual date for state law claims based on exposure to hazardous substances, including state survival claims and wrongful death claims).

3.   Under the common law, it is quite difficult for a property owner to pursue a strict liability claim against a former owner who has contaminated the property with hazardous waste. This is because of the *caveat emptor*

14.   Section 113 (g) sets out the period of time in which various CERCLA actions must be brought: (1) natural resources damages (within 3 years from the date of the discovery of the loss); (2)(A) cost recovery for removal action (within 3 years after completion of the action); (2)(B) cost recovery for remedial action (within 6 years after initiation of physical on-site construction); (3) contribution (within 3 years of date of judgment for a cost recovery action).

While § 113(g)(2)(B) provides that "initial action" to recover costs must be commenced within 6 years for remedial action, any "subsequent action ... for further response costs may be maintained at any time during the response action...." "Sometimes it is difficult to determine whether an action is 'initial' or 'subsequent' to an initial action". *See United States v. Navistar Intern. Transp. Corp.*, 152 F.3d 702 (7th Cir. 1998) (government action to recover oversight costs was "initial action," notwithstanding the government's earlier action to establish liability of third party, because government never previously asserted any claim against a PRP).

doctrine, which holds that a vendee is required to make inspection of the property prior to purchase, so that the vendor is not responsible to the vendee for the property's "defective" condition existing at the time of transfer. *See, e.g., Philadelphia Electric Co. v. Hercules, Inc.*, 762 F.2d 303 (3d Cir. 1985); RESTATEMENT (SECOND) OF TORTS § 352. CERCLA deals with the *caveat emptor* problem in two ways. First, contracting parties may allocate environmental risks between themselves by contract. § 107(e)(1); *Olin Corp. v. Yeargin, Inc.*, 146 F.3d 398, 407–08 (6th Cir. 1998). Second, CERCLA permits one of the "responsible parties" (*i.e.*, the current owner) to sue other responsible parties (*e.g.*, the prior owner) for reimbursement of costs of clean-up in a contribution action. § 113(f)(1).

4. In a common law tort action, the winning plaintiff's damages are typically determined by calculating the plaintiff's loss. The damage assessment under CERCLA § 107(a)(4)(A) is not this traditional measure of damages; instead, it is based on the actual total costs of environmental remediation. Moreover, damage awards under the common law rarely include corrective action that will ultimately benefit society, or nature (not parties to the typical lawsuit). CERCLA § 107(c) permits damages for injury to natural resources, while § 107(d) includes as damages the total costs of health assessments to members of the public who may have been adversely affected by the waste site.

C. THE CLEAN–UP CORNERSTONES

CERCLA is built on four cornerstones of remedial action. On one side of the CERCLA structure are the two basic components of the statute's blueprint for action—the *National Contingency Plan* (NCP) and the *National Priorities List* (NPL). These establish the procedures and standards for responding to releases of hazardous substances (the NCP) and for determining priorities among releases and threatened releases (the NPL). On the other side of the foundation are the two kinds of clean-up or response actions that may be taken once a release or threatened release has been confirmed. These are "removal" and "remedial" actions. "Removal" and "remedial" actions are defined in sections 101(23) and (24) of CERCLA. Removal actions prevent or minimize immediate threats posed by a release; remedial actions concern the final, long-term management of the site.

1. THE NATIONAL CONTINGENCY PLAN (NCP)

CERCLA § 105 states that clean-ups of hazardous waste sites are to be governed by a master plan, called the National Contingency Plan (NCP). *Redwing Carriers, Inc. v. Saraland Apartments*, 94 F.3d 1489 (11th Cir. 1996). The purpose of the NCP is to "establish procedures and standards for responding to releases of hazardous substances, pollutants, and contaminants," § 105(a), including methodologies for identifying sites most in need of remediation, analyses for determining the risks to human health and the environment posed by waste sites, requirements for state and community involvement in decision-making, systems for selecting cost-effective remedies, guidance for remedial actions that use Superfund money, and standards for judging the extent and scope of a clean-up. The NCP also allocates authority among federal, state, and local governments for implementing the plan's clean-up provisions.

To ensure that the NCP has teeth, CERCLA provides that response costs cannot be recovered if the response actions violate the NCP. Governmental parties (the EPA, states, or Indian tribes) can only recover "costs of removal or remedial action" which are "not inconsistent with the [NCP]." § 107(a)(4)(A). Private plaintiffs can recover only response costs which are "consistent with the [NCP]." § 107(a)(4)(B); *ABB Indus. Systems, Inc. v. Prime Technology, Inc.*, 32 F. Supp. 2d 38 (D.Conn. 1998). What might this distinction in language mean? For present purposes, it means that the NCP is to be followed in any clean-up action. Later, when we consider liability and cost recovery, we will explore the distinction in more detail.

a. EVOLUTION OF THE NCP

The original 1980 version of CERCLA called for revision of the existing NCP for oil spills to create a "national hazardous substance response plan." This plan was to detail a step-by-step process for dealing with a contaminated waste site, and to establish standards for determining the remediation measures to be deployed. The 1986 SARA amendments called for additional revision of the NCP, particularly in the area of remedy selection. The post–1986 NCP was also to give preference to remedial actions that "permanently and significantly" reduced the volume, mobility, and toxicity of the contaminants from a site. SARA also ordered the development of a Hazard Ranking System to be used to determine which sites may be added to the NPL. The new ranking system incorporates a risk assessment methodology that requires the EPA to accurately assess the relative "degree of risk to human health and the environment posed by sites and facilities subject to review." § 105(c)(1).

The current product of these statutory commands is the 1990 National Contingency Plan.[15] *See* 40 C.F.R. part 300. The 1990 NCP has several important components:

National Response System—The discharge of oil, or the release of hazardous substances in reportable quantities, triggers a regulatory and statutory duty to notify the National Response Center. The reporting requirements, set forth in CERCLA § 103(a), require that any person who knows of a release of a "reportable quantity" of a hazardous substance must notify the National Response Center. The reportable quantity varies, depending on the nature of the contaminant involved.[16] A lead agency is

---

15. Numerous challenges to the 1990 NCP were rejected in *State of Ohio v. U.S. EPA*, 997 F.2d 1520 (D.C. Cir. 1993).

16. Only an actual release of a hazardous substance into the environment triggers the reporting requirement; § 103 does not apply to threats of a release. *See* The *Fertilizer Institute v. EPA*, 935 F.2d 1303 (D.C. Cir. 1991). The release reporting requirement ensures "that the government, once timely informed, will be able to move quickly to check the spread of a hazardous release." *United States v. Carr*, 880 F.2d 1550 (2d Cir. 1989). There are penalties for failing to report. § 109; *United States v. Freter*, 31 F.3d 783 (9th Cir. 1994). CERCLA reporting requirements have nothing to do with whether a polluter is liable for clean-up costs. *United States v. Alcan Aluminum Corp.*, 990 F.2d 711 (2d Cir. 1993).

assigned, which then designates an On–Scene Coordinator (OSC) and Regional Project Manager (RPM) to direct response efforts. Together the OSC and RPM coordinate clean-up activities at the site, manage costs paid out of the Superfund, and ensure compliance with the NCP. State and local participation in response planning is provided by commissions and committees created under the Emergency Planning and Community Right-to-Know Act of 1986, 42 U.S.C.§ 11001 *et seq.*

Removals and remedial actions—The NCP articulates three steps that must be taken in order to clean up a hazardous waste site. First, those sites deemed worthy of some kind of clean-up job must be identified. This step is accomplished through the site identification and preliminary inspection assessment process (which entails listing on the Comprehensive Environmental Response Compensation and Liability Information System—the CERCLIS list of over 30,000 sites), and then listing on the NPL (over 1400 sites). Second, a decision must be made as to whether the CERCLA "response" should be an emergency "removal" or long-term "remedial" action. If the latter, a "remedial investigation/feasibility study" must be conducted to determine how best to clean up the site. Third, for remedial actions, the NCP requires that the remedy eventually chosen be cost-effective, a permanent solution, protective of human health and environment, and compatible with "applicable or relevant and appropriate" legal standards. *See* § 121.

Enforcement—The NCP provides guidance to the parties who may enforce various CERCLA provisions. If the EPA wishes to proceed under § 106 administrative abatement authority when there is a threat that a release presents an "imminent and substantial endangerment," the NCP lays out what must appear in the administrative record. When private parties undertake response costs, the NCP spells out when such private actions are "consistent with the NCP" for purposes of cost recovery lawsuits under § 107. When natural resources damages are claimed, CERCLA authorizes that officials may "act on behalf of the public as trustees for natural resources." § 107(f)(2). The NCP identifies who these trustees are and sets out their responsibilities.

Even though the NCP seems quite detailed–and it is far more detailed than the statute–the myriad subissues that arise in individual clean-up actions are resolved by reference to hundreds of CERCLA "guidance documents." Guidance, which need not be subjected to the rulemaking requirements of the Administrative Procedure Act, is issued at both the national and regional levels, and the result is an enormous body of "law" and practice that must be consulted in choosing response actions.

b. NCP PROCEDURES

The NCP establishes procedures which the EPA and other government agencies must follow when responding to a contaminated waste site through either a removal or remedial action. This lengthy step-by-step process lays out what must be done, and who should do it, from the time a site is initially discovered to when the clean-up commences. The key stages in the process are as follows:

Preliminary assessment and site investigation—The first step leading to implementation of NCP procedures is, of course, the initial identification of a site that possibly contains hazardous waste. A site can be identified by neighbors, employees, site owners, interested passers by, environmental organizations, local, state, or federal officials. After identification of the suspect site, the OSC and lead agency (often EPA, but sometimes a state agency) then go through a series of steps to determine if the site poses an immediate threat to the public health, or if instead it warrants a long-term federal response, or if no action is needed. More specifically, these steps are:

- *Removal site evaluation*—a quick assessment to see if the problem at the site requires an immediate clean-up, that is, a "removal" action;

- *Preliminary assessment*—an assessment that either eliminates the site from further investigation if it poses no threat, or if there is a threat, a determination whether permanent remedial action is needed;

- *Site investigation*—a more thorough on-site and off-site field investigation of the release or threatened release to decide whether the site should be placed on the NPL for remedial action.[17] If EPA determines that no further response action is needed no additional federal action will be taken absent new developments or the discovery of new information.

Removal actions—Where a rapid response is necessary, the NCP imposes few procedural barriers. Removal actions are addressed more fully below.

Remedial investigation and feasibility study—If remedial action appears to be required at a site (regardless of whether removal action is taken), a remedy must be selected. The remedial investigation and feasibility study (RI/FS) is the pre-decision assessment that permits selection of an appropriate remedy. The remedial investigation and feasibility study take place concurrently, although they deal with separate evaluations. The remedial investigation is, in essence, a data acquisition exercise about the conditions at the site. In EPA jargon, the RI is used to "characterize" the site. It considers the nature of the hazardous substances there, and their threat to "human and environmental receptors," based on estimates of actual or potential exposure.[18]

The feasibility study analyzes remedial alternatives for a response that will satisfy CERCLA's clean-up criteria. Like an environmental impact statement, it typically proposes a few alternative remedies (including no

---

17. CERCLA allows the EPA to order any person to furnish information relating to the hazardous substances at the site (§ 104(e)). EPA personnel may also enter such sites and collect soil and groundwater samples. § 104(e)(5)(B); *United States v. Long*, 687 F.Supp. 343 (S.D. Ohio 1987). Is it a "taking" if EPA has access to private property to monitor contaminated groundwater by wells drilled on private land? *Hendler v. United States*, 38 Fed. Cl. 611 (1997) (no); *Juliano v. MOSSWMA*, 983 F.Supp. 319 (N.D. N.Y. 1997) (yes).

18. The remedial investigation is intended to be a risk assessment, which considers "potential threats to human health and the environment" and establishes "acceptable exposure levels for use in developing remedial alternatives." 40 C.F.R. § 300.430(d)(4).

action) and evaluates them according to the substantive requirements of the NCP. The RI/FS does not choose the remedy, but it does permit a remedy to be selected that will be protective of human health and the environment, and conform to applicable federal and environmental standards.[19]

Proposed plan—SARA added a final pre-decision step to enhance public participation in the remedy selection process. The proposed plan (PP) announces EPA's initial conclusions from the RI/FS process, that is, it announces EPA's preferred remedy. This is then made available for public commentary before a final decision is made[20] and state concurrence.[21]

Record of decision—The record of decision (ROD) memorializes EPA's final remedy selection. It is, in fact, the PP as modified in response to public comments, and it *includes* a response to all significant comments. The ROD describes the site and its risks; alternative remedial actions available; why the final remedy was chosen; how the action complies with the NCP; the remediation goals for the site; the extent to which hazardous substances will remain after the clean-up is done; and how community involvement affected the final plan.[22]

Remedial design and remedial action—The final stage prior to a construction and clean-up contract being awarded to a private contractor to implement the remedy is the "remedial design/remedial action" (RD/RA) step. This sets out the actual design of the remedy, and the construction that will take place to achieve the remedy's clean-up goal. After the RD/RA step, construction begins and eventually is completed. Compare EPA's progress between 1993 and 1997.

c. NCP SUBSTANTIVE STANDARDS

There are two substantive aspects of determining the appropriate remedial action at a Superfund site–the method of clean-up (the actual remedy, so to speak–excavation, incineration, capping, liners, etc.), and the degree of clean-up (sometimes called the "how clean is clean" question). These two standards must comply with the mandate set out in § 121. The two are interlinked, as the remedy is selected in large part on the basis that it will satisfy applicable clean-up goals, and clean-up goals are often chosen on the basis of available remedies. In drafting the NCP, the EPA combined

---

19. While the risk assessment portion of the RI/FS is done by the EPA, much of investigation and site assessment is done by the PRPs (when they can be found) and their contractors. The public also plays a role in the RI/FS process. The NCP requires the lead agency conduct interviews in the community, and prepare a community relations plan which ensures opportunities for public involvement in site-related decisions.

20. *See* § 117(a); *VME Americas, Inc. v. Hein–Werner Corp.*, 946 F.Supp. 683 (E.D. Wis. 1996) (property owners allege that state agency did not comply with NCP requirement for public notice, and that therefore recovery of response costs was precluded).

21. Section 104(c)(3) prevents EPA from taking remedial action if the relevant state has not agreed that it will play a role with respect to future maintenance of the remedial action; § 121(f) requires that states have "meaningful" involvement in the selection of remedies.

22. RODs are not planning documents; they provide an after-the-fact rationale for the remedy selected. As we will soon see, CERCLA prevents judicial challenges to remedy selection before implementation. § 113(h). As a result, courts rarely decide cases where the plaintiffs argue that the remedy goes too far (when the plaintiff is a PRP) or not far enough (when the plaintiff is a citizen group), despite the centrality of these issues to CERCLA.

the two sets of statutory factors into nine criteria, each of which was assigned a particular weight in remedy selection. Interestingly, detailed remedy selection criteria are relative newcomers to the statute. The 1980 CERCLA offered little guidance on remedy selection, so the 1986 SARA added section 121 to clarify the standards that EPA is to apply. The criteria themselves are discussed below when we address the cleanup, which is called a "response." There are two kinds of response actions contemplated by the NCP: "removal" actions and "remedial" measures. § 104(a).

2.   THE NATIONAL PRIORITIES LIST

CERCLA may be used to clean-up any contaminated site, but Congress also wanted to identify and clean up the most dangerous sites in the United States. This goal is accomplished by § 105(a)(8)(B), which requires that a National Priorities List (NPL) be established. By the close of the 20th century, there were over 1,400 sites on the NPL, including those on private and public (usually federal) property. Both the United States Congressional Budget Office and the General Accounting Office estimate that there could be as many as 3,000 new non-federal sites eventually added to the NPL from the large inventory of sites listed in the CERCLA Information System (CERCLIS).

The road to the NPL generally begins with the Preliminary Assessment and Site Identification (PA/SI) phase of the NCP. One of the purposes of the PA/SI is to determine if a site is such a potential hazard that it warrants an NPL listing. The most commonly used mechanism for placing a site on the NPL is through a modeling system known as the Hazard Ranking System (HRS). The HRS assigns a numerical "score" to each site based on (1) various risk assessment criteria (*e.g.*, the likelihood of release, the nature of the hazardous substance, the probability of dilution, the distance from the site to the threatened target, and the nature of the endangerment to human population or environment); and (2) the potential exposure "pathways" to threatened humans and the environment (*e.g.*, soil, surface water, ground-water, and air). The resulting HRS score represents an estimate of "the probability and magnitude of harm * * * from exposure to hazardous substances as a result of contamination of groundwater, surface water, [soil], or air." *Eagle–Picher Industries v. U.S. EPA*, 759 F.2d 905 (D.C. Cir. 1985). Sites compiling a score of 28.50 or greater are eligible for the NPL list.[23]

a.   CONSEQUENCES OF AN NPL LISTING

In theory, inclusion of a site or facility on the NPL list entails no liability, no fault, and no necessary legal consequences. The EPA could therefore assume a rather casual attitude about NPL listing, since it is only the first step in a process that requires further studies, investigation, public comment, and remedial evaluation under the NCP. *Honeywell Int'l., Inc. v.*

---

23.   Under § 105(a)(8)(B), states may designate sites or facilities that pose the greatest danger to "public health or welfare or the environment," regardless of their HRS score. If the Agency for Toxic Substances and Disease Registry issues a health advisory recommending "disassociation" of individuals from the site, that site may be listed on the NPL even if its HRS score is below 28.50. 40 C.F.R. § 300.425(c)(3).

E.P.A., 372 F.3d 441 (D.C. Cir. 2004) (finding that EPA's listing of a site on the NPL did not obligate the agency to discuss, or give notice, of potential remedial actions to be taken at the site). The listing itself does not even definitively set the borders of the site, since the full extent of the contamination will usually be revealed only after more rigorous assessment of the pollution problem. Indeed, it is not uncommon for the EPA to enlarge the area of the site if, after exploration, the area of contamination is more widespread than originally assumed. *Washington State Dept. of Transp. v. EPA*, 917 F.2d 1309 (D.C. Cir. 1990).

While an NPL listing is necessary for the EPA to use Superfund money for remedial action, the NPL is not a pre-condition to a number of other clean-up options available under CERCLA. Among the more important non-NPL actions are:

- EPA may perform short term *removal* actions with Superfund money. *State of New York v. Shore Realty Corp.*, 759 F.2d 1032, 1045–47 (2nd Cir. 1985).

- EPA may order parties to undertake short and long-term clean-up measures pursuant to its abatement authority under § 106. See 40 C.F.R. § 300.425(b)(4).

- State governments, local governments, or private parties may clean up a site and then bring a § 107 action to recover their response costs. *New York v. General Elec. Co.*, 592 F.Supp. 291 (N.D.N.Y. 1984);

- Settlement through consent decrees can take place under § 122.

In other words, the NPL is an important element of CERCLA, but it is by no means a prerequisite or threshold for CERCLA-based action.

To the site owner, however, listing on the NPL is *very* significant.[24] To be on the NPL means that the EPA has determined that from nearly 40,000 sites on the CERCLA Information System list, this site poses a sufficient degree of concern about threats to health or the environment to warrant a full federal investigation and possible response. The NPL-listing is a prerequisite to EPA's use of Superfund money to pay for the cost of long-term, permanent remedial actions. 40 C.F.R. § 300.425(b). Since these Superfund-subsidized remedial actions are reserved for only the gravest and most dangerous sites, an owner finding the site on the NPL is left with the sinking feeling that it will almost certainly be the focus of a major EPA CERCLA clean-up action. Whether or not that actually comes to pass, it is usually very different to sell or borrow against NPL-listed property, for obvious reasons.

b. POST–DESIGNATION CONCERNS

A site's designation on the NPL does not necessarily mean that the hazardous substance is cleaned up immediately and that the PRPs problems

---

24. The consequences of NPL listing and the resulting incentive to litigate the listing decision are discussed in John S. Applegate, *How to Save the National Priorities List from the D.C. Circuit—and Itself*, 9 J. of Natural Res. & Envtl. Law 211 (1994).

are over. What happens when the clean-up process is slow? What about newly discovered waste? A PRP might find itself fighting on two fronts after designation on the NPL. On one side, it will be dealing with its cleanup duties under CERCLA, and on the other it might be fighting non-CERCLA common law litigation, brought by plaintiffs such as residents of contaminated communities. The following case study describes the ongoing problems of a PRP, Cotter Corporation, after it was listed as a Superfund site in 1983.

Toxic Plume of Uranium Heading Towards Arkansas River

In 2005, Cañon City residents took a survey of 239 residents who live near Cotter Corporation's uranium mill and found 150 reported cases of cancer, 26 miscarriages, 28 neurological problems, 19 kidney problems, and 42 lung problems. Three years later, in May 2008, the Havens Family Clinic alerted Colorado Department of Public Health and Environmental officials to the possible connection between the ailments and pollution from the mill. Since then, the U.S. Department of Health and Human Services has begun a comprehensive review of public health in Cañon City and the EPA is taking another look the residents' use of groundwater for drinking and cooking uses.

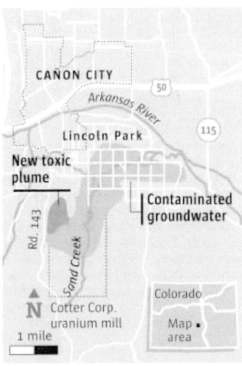

Two months after the state of Colorado was alerted to the possible connection between the illnesses and pollution from the mill, state regulators and Cotter mill operators confirmed a new plume of uranium-contaminated groundwater had spread from the mill, under a golf course, and towards Cañon City and the Arkansas River. In July 2008, state officials issued a "notice of violation" which gave Cotter 60 days to develop a remedy. Currently, no remedy is in place because mill operators are still searching for the source of the pollution.

So far, no contaminants have reached the Arkansas River or homes, and mill operators have attempted to cut off the contaminated plume. Although state regulators and health officials are confident that people are safe, residents cannot help but suspect contaminated groundwater is the source of the large number of unexplained illnesses that have afflicted their community. Bruce Finley, "Toxic Plume Spurs Study of Public Health," *The Denver Post*, October 19, 2008.

Residents and Employees Fear Increased Cancer Risk

The health problems caused by hazardous substances can range from aches and pains in some to fatal cancer in others. The two most common hazardous substances found at the mill site and in the groundwater of Lincoln Park are uranium and molybdenum, but as many as 19 hazardous substances have been detected in the area. When uranium is ingested or breathed in, microscopic particles deposit themselves in the lungs, kidneys, bones and soft tissues, causing cancers and other diseases in those organs. Molybdenum increases uric acid and causes gout-like symptoms when ingested. Two decay products of uranium, radon and radium, can also cause serious health problems such as bone and lung cancer.

Statistics compiled from Lincoln Park residents do not show significantly higher cancer rates in the area, but they do point to a higher than expected level of lung cancer cases. 74 lung cancer cases existed in the 17-year period of the study in Lincoln Park—normal incidence of the disease would have caused 66 cases. The study also documented nine cases of brain cancer, five thyroid cancer cases and 24 lymphomas—all of which are higher rates than expected for the diseases, but not statistically significant. Jackie Hutchins, *"Questions and Cancers,"* CAÑON CITY DAILY RECORD, Oct. 18, 2002, at 4.

Employees of the mill also developed health problems, including long-time chemist, Lynn Boughton, who died from lymphoma in 2001. Boughton worked at the mill for 21 years and during that time became increasingly sicker and sicker. After leaving Cotter in 1979, Boughton learned that 100,000 tons of waste generated from the nuclear bombs that destroyed Hiroshima and Nagasaki in 1945 had been transferred to Cotter in open railroad cars in the late 1960s. Boughton claimed "that Cotter officials never told him—or anyone else at the mill—that the material was actually the Manhattan Project residue and a product of the most radioactive ore on earth ... and that the mill's process was not equipped to detect or remove those materials." B.J. Plasket, *"Family Dream Went Bad Fast,"* CAÑON CITY DAILY RECORD, Oct. 18, 2002, at 10. Cotter officials have since acknowledged that the waste generated from the Manhattan Project were brought to Cotter and some still remains in the detention ponds at the site.

In September of 1989, Lynn Boughton and 550 other Lincoln Park residents filed a $500 million federal suit against Cotter. See *Boughton v. Cotter Corp.*, 65 F.3d 823 (10th Cir. 1995). The plaintiffs eventually agreed to an undisclosed settlement which Boughton accepted, but was not thrilled about. In 1996, Boughton filed a workers compensation claim against Cotter, claiming that his health problems were caused by exposure to radiation at the mill. As part of the process, samples of tissue were removed from Boughton and were found to have 700 times normal radiation levels found in the human body. As a result, a judge ordered Cotter to pay Boughton $500,000—but by the time Boughton received the check from Cotter he had only one year to live. Plasket at 11.

History of the Mill and Cleanup

Cotter Corporation began extracting uranium from ore through an alkaline leach process in when it built its mill in Cañon City, Colorado in

1958. Once uranium yellowcake was stripped from the ore, the ore was discarded—leaving toxic and radioactive tailings. The tailings would then be dumped into an impoundment pond, which, prior to 1982, was unlined. The lack of a "lining," consisting of an earth and clay barrier with a plastic overlay, allowed uranium and molybdenum contamination to bleed into the groundwater and surface soils of the neighboring Lincoln Park community. This practice occurred for more than two decades.

Groundwater beneath the mill and Lincoln Park was shown to contain uranium and molybdenum in excess of permissible quantities. Cotter's monitoring data indicate that a plume of contaminants are extending from the mill, along Sand Creek, and into private wells of about 200 residents in Lincoln Park. As a result, residents were exposed to the contaminants either through ingestion of dust or ingestion of the groundwater. Ultimately, the waters of Sand Creek flow into the Arkansas River.

Due to the contamination, the EPA announced that it was placing the mill and Lincoln Park to its National Priority List (NPL) in May of 1983. Prior to its listing, Cotter Corporation took several actions challenging the proposed listing on the NPL. In August 1983, Cotter filed suit in U.S. District Court seeking injunctive and declaratory relief aimed at preventing listing. The Court denied the preliminary injunction request, and Cotter appealed unsuccessfully to the Tenth Circuit Court of Appeals. The EPA filed a motion to dismiss Cotter's request for permanent injunction and declaratory relief from the U.S. District Court in March 1984, and Cotter found itself permanently listed on the NPL in September of 1984.

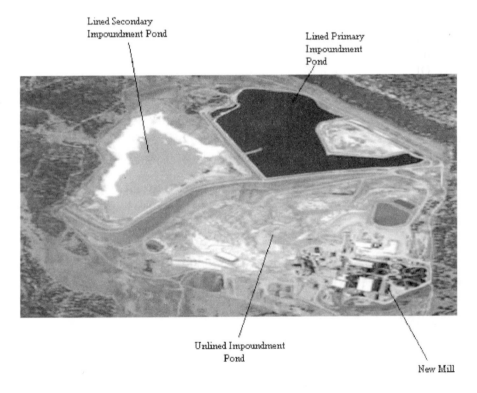

Lined Secondary Impoundment Pond

Lined Primary Impoundment Pond

Unlined Impoundment Pond

New Mill

At the same time Cotter was fighting its sites' listing on the NPL, it was also being sued by the state of Colorado for $50 million. The state claimed that the mill had polluted the land, air and water surrounding the mill site. As part of its suit against Cotter, the state performed a study of the area and found a contaminant plume in the groundwater contained levels of uranium and molybdenum up to 2,000 times above natural levels. Additionally, the study found that new "lined" tailings impoundments were leaking pollutants into the ground. Colorado and Cotter arrived at a settlement in 1988; Cotter would pay $11 million for future monitoring and cleanup of the site and surrounding area, and the state of Colorado would oversee the cleanup process. This settlement received much criticism—including that from the EPA, who called the cleanup " 'seriously deficient' and openly questioned the credibility of the proposed cleanup ... [It] called the plan 'loosely defined and open-ended' ... and it claimed the settlement plan ... left out many pollutants, saying 'the only constituents for which standards have been set are uranium and molybdenum." B.J. Plasket, *"Did the State Share Blame?"* CAÑON CITY DAILY RECORD, Oct. 18, 2002, at 38. In addition, Lincoln Park residents criticized the settlement, wondering how the cleanup cost estimated at $50 million could be reduced to $11 million. On this basis, hundreds of Lincoln Park residents brought suit against Cotter over the next few years, although they were largely unsuccessful. See *Dodge v. Cotter Corp.*, 328 F.3d 1212 (10th Cir. 2003).

Cotter's Cleanup Progress

Two areas were specified for cleanup under the Remedial Action Plan: the onsite area around the mill (OU1) and the offsite Lincoln Park community (OU2). The Remedial Action Plan requires Cotter to 1) cleanup both OU1, and OU2 and 2) monitor groundwater and air. Cleanup on the mill included source control measures as well as measures to prevent contaminated ground water from migrating from the mill to Lincoln Park. The Plan also required regular monitoring of uranium and molybdenum in Lincoln Park groundwater through monitoring wells. Additionally, Cotter took measures to minimize the likelihood of human exposure to groundwater in the Lincoln Park community. These measures included conducting a water use survey in the late 1980s, provision of municipal water to residents using groundwater, and semi-annual reviews of residents' applications for new water wells.

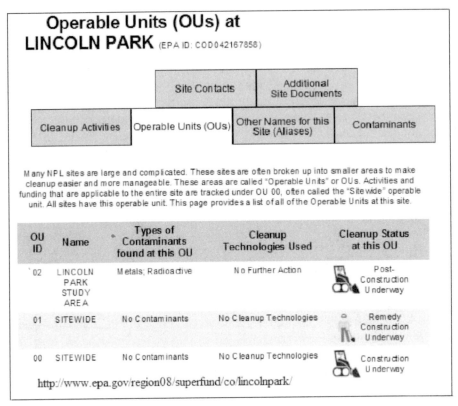

Progress of a sites' cleanup can be monitored on the EPA's Superfund website, where each site has a detailed profile of the contaminants, the methods used for cleanup, and the current cleanup status of the site. In September of 2007, the EPA prepared a five-year review pursuant to CERCLA § 121 and the National Contingency Plan. The purpose of the review was to ensure that human health and the environment are being protected by the remedial actions being implemented. The review found that many of the Remedial Action Plan's proposed cleanup activities had been completed, including: giving eligible residents of Lincoln Park the option of connecting to city water, moving contaminated soils to lined impoundment ponds, and creating a barrier to minimize migration of contaminated groundwater. However, the review also found that cleanup is not complete— there is still the issue of the plume of uranium-contaminated groundwater heading towards the Arkansas River.

c. DELISTINGS AND DELETIONS

For site owners and for PRPs, NPL listing is extremely bad news. Moreover, there is no administrative procedure in place for bringing about a "delisting" of an area that is not in fact contaminated and therefore improperly listed *ab initio*. The only way to delist a site that has been added to the NPL is to overturn EPA's listing decision in court.[25] Since NPL-listing

---

25. Specifically, in the D.C. Circuit Court of Appeals—*see* § 113(a); *United States v. M. Genzale Plating, Inc.*, 723 F.Supp. 877, 884 (E.D.N.Y. 1989).

is done by rulemaking, affected parties can obtain pre-enforcement judicial review. Hence, NPL listing decisions have engendered a surprisingly large amount of litigation.[26] While challengers have enjoyed some success in this litigation, EPA's decision to put a site on the list may be judicially changed only if proven to be arbitrary and capricious. Under this standard, most courts defer to the EPA.[27] An EPA decision to list a site on the NPL will usually only be reversed if the agency makes a listing call based either on (1) criteria other than those specified by statute,[28] or (2) assumptions about the nature and extent of contamination that are not supported by the record.[29]

Sites can be deleted from the NPL for a number of reasons, such as completion of all necessary response actions. But even when a site has been deleted, EPA can restore the NPL listing if it is discovered that the threat of dangerous releases remains due to a flawed clean-up. The EPA's goal for the year 2000 is the deletion of 650 sites from the NPL.

3. REMOVAL ACTIONS

Relatively simple, short-term clean-ups at sites posing an immediate "threat to the public health or welfare" (40 C.F.R. § 300.415(b)) are called removal actions. *ABB Indus. Systems, Inc. v. Prime Technology*, 32 F. Supp. 2d 38, 42 (D. Conn. 1998). *Village of Milford v. K–H Holding Corp.*, 390 F.3d 926, 934 (6th Cir. 2004) (determining removal actions include "such actions as may be necessary to monitor, assess, and evaluate the release or threat of release of hazardous waste" and the characterization of hazardous waste as posing an "immediate threat" is not required for finding the costs of an action recoverable as removal costs). In theory, none of these responses are intended to be effective in the long term; rather, they are expected to be superseded by a permanent remedy. They include actions like installation of fences and warning signs; removal of drums, barrels, or tanks that may leak or spill; excavation or removal of highly contaminated soils that could migrate; stabilizing dikes or impoundments; and evacuating individuals threatened by a release.

ANTHRAX TRIGGER'S CERCLA'S EMERGENCY RESPONSE?

CERCLA's emergency removal actions are defined in *APWU v. Potter*, 343 F.3d 619 (2d Cir. 2003). The New York Metro Area Postal Union filed a complaint after learning that letters containing anthrax were processed at the Morgan Processing and Distribution Center before ultimately being delivered to the NBC Studios and the New York Post in New York City. The appellate court agreed with the district court's finding that the anthrax contamination did not fall within CERCLA's definition of emergency removal actions. The court held that emergency removal actions under CERCLA are those where:

---

26. *See* Applegate, *National Priorities List, supra* note 24.

27. *See, e.g., Board of Regents of Univ. of Washington v. EPA*, 86 F.3d 1214 (D.C. Cir. 1996); 957 F.2d 882 (D.C. Cir. 1992).

28. *Mead Corp. v. Browner*, 100 F.3d 152, 153–55 (D.C. Cir. 1996).

29. *National Gypsum v. EPA*, 968 F.2d 40 (D.C. Cir. 1992)

(i) action must be taken within hours of the discovery of the possible release of a pollutant, contaminant, or hazardous substance, and

(ii) the lead federal agency is unable to perform the removal action itself in a timely matter.

Here, the situation did not call for action within hours, and the USPS was able to perform the removal action itself. By the time the anthrax release was discovered, and the USPS became aware that removal action might be necessary, more than a month had already elapsed. Because there was no true emergency, the anthrax contamination did not fall within CERCLA's definition, the appellate court held that the USPS's removal action was sufficient.

If you were a postal worker, would you be satisfied with the Second Circuit's finding that anthrax contamination did not warrant emergency removal actions, based on USPS's reaction to the discovery?

An important part of EPA's initial investigation of a site is to ascertain whether the immediacy of the threat requires removal action, or whether there is a long-term risk sufficient for an NPL-listing and remedial action.[30] As noted above, this threshold determination is important since the NCP prevents the EPA from undertaking remedial actions unless the site qualifies for an NPL-listing. The EPA may spend Superfund dollars on removal actions for sites that are not on the NPL. So a site must be labeled as worthy of either removal or remedial action as an initial step. But how does EPA make that call?

The language of CERCLA provides some guidance. CERCLA § 101(23) defines "removal" to include clean-up actions necessary to deal with a threatened release. These essential measures designed to "dispose of removal material" and "prevent or mitigate damage to the public health or welfare or to the environment." This statutory definition blurs the line between temporary fixes (removals) and permanent ones (remedial action). Case law is equally unhelpful in separating the two response actions. *Compare General Electric Co. v. Litton Industrial Automation Services, Inc.*, 920 F.2d 1415, 1418–19 (8th Cir. 1990) (excavation work was removal action), *with Channel Master Satellite Systems, Inc. v. JFD Electronics Corp.*, 748 F.Supp. 373, 384–86 (E.D.N.C. 1990) (excavation was remedial action). *State of Colorado v. Sunoco, Inc.*, (337 F.3d 1233 (10th Cir. 2003) (installing monitoring wells constituted removal, rather than remedial action).

The NCP compounds the definitional confusion between the two concepts. Removal action may be undertaken whenever there is a "threat," based on potential exposure to hazardous substances, contamination of

---

30. In 1993, EPA adopted the Superfund Accelerated Clean-up Model which places sites into three categories—(1) non-NPL-sites which need time-critical action; (2) NPL-caliber sites deserving of non-emergency early action; and (3) NPL sites where remedial responses are justified.

drinking water supplies or ecosystems, or high levels of hazardous substances in soils that may migrate. 40 C.F.R. § 300.415(b)(2). The same conditions trigger the need for more permanent remedial measures. The NCP defines the term "removal" extremely broadly as well, encompassing any response actions that might be taken when there is a release or a threatened release from a contaminated site. 40 C.F.R. § 300.5. Neither the NCP definition nor the implementing regulations require that removals be limited to short-term, emergency threats. Indeed, pursuant to § 104(a)(2), the EPA must undertake removal actions that are also consistent with "the efficient performance of long-term remedial action."

Because there is so much overlap between removal and remedial action, EPA may be tempted to perform full and permanent "remedial" clean-ups at a non-NPL site under its removal authority. There are two incentives for this approach: (1) the Superfund may be used to finance removal actions at sites not listed on the NPL, and (2) the procedures for removal actions allow the EPA to act more quickly than it may under its remedial action authority. However, courts have tried to keep the types of actions separate and have discouraged remedial clean-ups labeled as removals. Several cases seem to establish that early sampling, surveillance, and assessment studies are removal actions, especially when they are interim actions undertaken in emergency settings to address an immediate threat. *Hanford Downwinders Coalition, Inc. v. Dowdle*, 71 F.3d 1469 (9th Cir. 1995); *State of California v. Celtor Chemical Corp.*, 901 F.Supp. 1481 (N.D. Cal. 1995). Responses to non-urgent situations are considered remedial actions. *Yellow Freight System, Inc. v. ACF Industries, Inc.*, 909 F. Supp. 1290 (E.D. Mo. 1995). One non-judicial limit on EPA's removal authority is found in § 104(c)(1). This section provides that removal action at a site cannot continue after $2 million has been spent for response work, or one year has elapsed from the date of the initial agency response.[31]

If it is determined that removal action is needed, activity proceeds as follows. First, the action must "begin as soon as possible to * * * prevent * * * mitigate, or eliminate the threat. * * *" 40 C.F.R. § 300.415(b)(3). Second, the public should be informed of the action, and be allowed to provide a certain amount of input to the decision makers. 40 C.F.R. § 300.415(m). Third, when the removal action is being planned, the NCP provides that all Superfund-financed removal actions are, to the extent practicable, to meet the "applicable or relevant and appropriate requirements" (ARAR's) that determine the clean-up standard. ARAR compliance is only necessary for those actions that are directly part of the removal action, but not for other clean-up steps that are not encompassed by the removal plan. Fourth, when the response action is removal in nature, the party seeking cost recovery must prove that its actions were in "substantial compliance" with those portions of the NCP pertaining to removal actions. *Morrison Enterp. v. McShares*, Inc., 13 F. Supp. 2d 1095, 1115 (D. Kan. 1998). Fifth, the owner, operator, or PRP must provide EPA with relevant

31. However, two statutory exceptions swallow the limitation. The § 104(c)(1) limits are not applicable if EPA finds that additional response action is required, or that continuation of the removal action is consistent with the subsequent remedial action.

information about the site and the nature of the hazardous substances there and with physical access to the site. § 104(e); *United States v. Omega Chemical Corp.*, 156 F.3d 994, 999–1000 (9th Cir. 1998).

If the removal action is completed by EPA, it will file suit to recover its costs if a PRP is available. Section 107 provides that a PRP "shall be liable for all costs of removal * * * incurred by the United States Government. * * *" A frequently litigated question, which will be taken up again later in this chapter, is whether a PRP should be required to repay the EPA for costs that are not directly connected to the actual clean-up. For example, should a PRP be liable for the government's "oversight costs"—the costs incurred by the EPA in monitoring private parties' compliance with their legal obligations during a removal action?

RECOVERABLE COSTS

The question of whether oversight costs are recoverable is a subset of the larger problem of whether indirect and administrative costs should be recoverable for either removal or remedial actions. For example, should the government's indirect overhead costs for a removal action be recoverable? The language of CERCLA is completely silent on this issue. *See National Cable Television Ass'n, Inc. v. United States*, 415 U.S. 336, 342 (1974), interpreted by *Skinner v. Mid–America Pipeline Co.*, 490 U.S. 212, 224 (1989) (before the federal government may impose financial burdens on private parties, "Congress must indicate clearly its intention to delegate to the Executive the discretionary authority to recover administrative costs not inuring directly to the benefit of regulated parties").

---

4.   REMEDIAL ACTIONS

The other response action contemplated by CERCLA is remedial action, generally encompassing more extensive, long-term, permanent clean-ups of contaminated sites. *See Public Service Co. of Colorado v. Gates Rubber Co.*, 175 F.3d 1177 (10th Cir. 1999) (cleanup was remedial where landowner engaged in lengthy study of the site, expended $9 million, took four years to complete cleanup, and intended a permanent remedy); *State of Minnesota v. Kalman W. Abrams Metals, Inc.*, 155 F.3d 1019, 1025 (8th Cir. 1998) (permanent nature of remedy and the "leisurely manner" in which the clean-up problem was addressed made it a remedial action). CERCLA § 101(24) defines "remedial action" as actions that are "consistent with permanent remedy," taken "instead of or in addition to removal actions" so as to "prevent or minimize the release of hazardous substances. * * *" Remedial actions may include removing contaminated groundwater, excavating contaminated soil, disposing of hazardous materials offsite, constructing barriers above, below, or around sites to prevent migration, and relocating residents. The NCP forbids the EPA from undertaking such clean-up measures unless the site subject to remediation is listed on the NPL. Remediation is therefore the mandated response action at the approximately 1,400 NPL sites. For these sites, deemed the most dangerous in the

United States, clean-up will be slow (10–20 years from discovery to completion) and costly ($25–$30 million per site on average).

For remedial actions, the EPA must take care to comply with all the procedural and substantive requirements of the NCP.[32] As is the case with removal actions, EPA is authorized under § 107 to sue any of the parties responsible for the contamination to recover EPA's costs of performing remediation activities.

PROBLEM

Read sections 121(a), (b) and (d) of CERCLA that call for the promulgation of cleanup criteria. Now take a look at how EPA implemented the criteria in the NCP:

Nine criteria for evaluation. The analysis of alternatives under review shall reflect the scope and complexity of site problems and alternatives being evaluated and consider the relative significance of the factors within each criteria. The nine evaluation criteria are as follows:

(A) *Overall protection of human health and the environment.* Alternatives shall be assessed to determine whether they can adequately protect human health and the environment, in both the short- and long-term, from unacceptable risks posed by hazardous substances, pollutants, or contaminants present at the site by eliminating, reducing, or controlling exposures to levels established during development of remediation goals * * *. * * *

(B) *Compliance with ARARs.* The alternatives shall be assessed to determine whether they attain applicable or relevant and appropriate requirements under federal environmental laws and state environmental or facility siting laws or provide grounds for invoking one of the waivers * * *.

(C) *Long-term effectiveness and permanence.* Alternatives shall be assessed for the long-term effectiveness and permanence they afford, along with the degree of certainty that the alternative will prove successful. * * *

(D) *Reduction of toxicity, mobility, or volume through treatment.* The degree to which alternatives employ recycling or treatment that reduces toxicity, mobility, or volume shall be assessed, including how treatment is used to address the principal threats posed by the site. * * *

---

32. Section 104(c) provides that EPA may not implement remedial action unless the state in which the site is located—

- agrees to pay 10 percent of clean-up costs;

- assures maintenance of the site upon completion of remedial action;

- demonstrates a 20–year capacity for the treatment and destruction of all resulting wastes.

(E) *Short-term effectiveness.* The short-term impacts of alternatives shall be assessed considering the following:

(1) Short-term risks that might be posed to the community during implementation of an alternative;

(2) Potential impacts on workers during remedial action and the effectiveness and reliability of protective measures;

(3) Potential environmental impacts of the remedial action and the effectiveness and reliability of mitigative measures during implementation; and

(4) Time until protection is achieved.

(F) *Implementability.* The ease or difficulty of implementing the alternatives shall be assessed by considering the [(1) technical feasibility, (2) administrative feasibility, and (3) availability of services and materials, including adequate off-site treatment].

(G) *Cost.* The types of costs that shall be assessed include [(1) capital costs, (2) annual operation and maintenance costs, and (3) present value of future costs].

(H) State [government] acceptance. * * *

(I) *Community acceptance.* This assessment includes determining which components of the alternatives interested persons in the community support, have reservations about, or oppose. * * *

40 C.F.R. § 300.430(e)(9)(iii), (f)(1)(i). These are the nine criteria used to select a remedy. How does the EPA's statement of NCP criteria differ from § 121 in form? In substance? Is it an improvement over the statute? Does it emphasize the same policies as the statute? The NCP has been held to be consistent with the statute. *Ohio v. EPA*, 997 F.2d 1520 (D.C. Cir. 1993).

Under the NCP, the most important considerations in selecting a remedy are the "protection of human health and the environment," the "applicable or relevant and appropriate" federal and state standards, permanence of remedies (including the preference for treatment), and cost effectiveness. Others have a lesser role—"state and community acceptance" because it is regarded as a modifying factor that only comes into play when a remedy has been tentatively selected, and "short-term effectiveness" because, as two commentators have suggested, the criterion is poorly understood and significantly complicates the analysis.[33] "Implementability" is in effect a catch-all for various practical, common sense considerations in selecting a remedy. Only the four most important remedy-selection considerations warrant extended discussion.

---

33.   John S. Applegate & Steven M. Wesloh, *Short Changing Short–Term Risk: A Study of Superfund Remedy Selection*, 15 YALE J. OF REG. 269 (1998).

a. PROTECTIVENESS

The protection of human health and the environment, the first of the NCP threshold criteria, must be met before a remedial alternative is acceptable. § 121(b)(1); 40 C.F.R. § 300.430(f)(1)(i)(A). Protectiveness means the acceptable exposure level representing concentrations to which humans (including sensitive ones) may be exposed without adverse effect. 40 C.F.R. § 300.430(e)(2)(i)(A)(1).

To make this determination, EPA performs a two-part risk assessment analysis. For known or suspected carcinogens, the appropriate level for CERCLA sites is defined in the NCP as a range between 10^{-4} to 10^{-6} individual lifetime excess cancer risk. *See United States v. Burlington Northern Railroad Co.* 200 F.3d 679 (10th Cir. 1999) (a risk level of 1 in 100,000 does not mean that 100,00 people need to be exposed for one person to contract cancer; it means that for every person exposed there is a .00001% chance the person will get cancer). The toxicity portion of the equation is based, of course, on the contaminants of concern. The exposure portion is based on a "reasonable maximum exposure" (RME) scenario which calculates the amount of exposure to the harm-producing substances that may still remain after remediation is completed, and the likelihood that it still poses a risk to human health. This calculation of exposure is based on the cumulative effect of multiple contaminants, the potential for human exposure to toxic pathways from the site in light of exposure frequency and duration, the sensitivities of the population that may be in contact with the site, as well as some uncertainty factors.[34] The"protectiveness" goal is met when there would be a less than 1 in 500 chance that an individual exposed to a cleaned up Superfund site would receive exposure greater than the RME.[35]

b. ARARS

One of the most difficult questions under CERCLA is how clean the waste site should be once the remedial action is finished. The most specific guidance in section 121(d)(2) is that any "legally applicable" or "relevant and appropriate" rule under federal or state law (ARAR) must be achieved for on-site clean-ups or explicitly waived for specific reasons. The ARAR concept is an extremely important element of CERCLA because it does not judge the suitability of a clean-up according to some ad hoc, case-by-case measure, but according to either existing federal standards, such as those arising under RCRA, the Safe Drinking Water Act (SDWA), the Clean Water Act, and the Toxic Substance Control Act, or their state counterparts (if more stringent than federal standards).[36] The ARAR requirement is also an extremely

---

34. One of the most important current issues in remedy selection is the choice of scenarios based on the anticipated future use of a site.

35. Although § 121(b)(1) requires protection of both human health and the environment, EPA's risk assessment analysis has largely ignored the risks to the environment. The rationale here is probably that humans are either more sensitive than ecosystems, or more important.

36. *See, e.g., State of Missouri v. Independent Petrochemical Corp.*, 104 F.3d 159 (8th Cir.

complex element of CERCLA, because it often involves adapting standards that were not originally developed for clean-up purposes, an exercise akin to fitting a square peg in a round hole.

The NCP makes a distinction between "applicable" and "relevant and appropriate" requirements. An "applicable" requirement includes "those clean-up standards, standards of control, and other substantive requirements * * *under federal environmental or state * * *laws that specifically address a hazardous substance. * * * " This language means that if a law would be legally enforceable at the site, regardless of CERCLA remediation, it must be attained unless grounds for a waiver exist.[37] "Relevant and appropriate" requirements are "clean-up standards * * * that, while not 'applicable,' * * * address problems sufficiently similar to those encountered at the CERCLA site that they use is well suited to the particular site." 400 C.F.R. § 300.5. Unlike "applicable" requirements, which are largely objective, "relevant and appropriate" requirements are discretionary, and assume that "best professional judgment" will be used to decide if a given clean-up requirement addresses problems at the site (*i.e.*, is relevant), and is suited to the particular characteristics of the site (*i.e.*, is appropriate). EPA also uses a third category, "to be considered," for standards that are neither applicable nor suitable for direct adoption, but which may provide useful guidance.

An ARAR, particularly one based on an "applicable" requirement, can come from any number of federal or state laws. Most commonly, an ARAR is pegged to a health or risk-based numerical value, such as the maximum contaminant levels set under the SDWA that establish limits on contaminants in the water of a public water system. 42 U.S.C. § 300(f) et seq. An ARAR can be a technology or activity-based requirement, such as RCRA's land disposal restrictions for RCRA "hazardous wastes" (which may have been disposed of at a CERCLA site). If a RCRA waste has been dumped at a CERCLA site, the RCRA requirement is the applicable requirement even if the wastes were disposed of at the site prior to the statutory date that they were deemed hazardous. *Chemical Waste Management, Inc. v. United States EPA*, 869 F.2d 1526, 1535–7 (D.C. Cir. 1989). Location-specific ARARs are also possible, if a legal restriction is triggered solely because the hazardous substance is in a specified location, such as a wetland, a protected wildlife habitat, or a water body subject to an anti-degradation law under state law. *United States v. Akzo Coatings of America, Inc.*, 949 F.2d 1409, 1439–50 (6th Cir. 1991).

1997) (a post-ROD county ordinance imposing stricter standards than federal law could not be an ARAR, since ARARs are frozen on the date of the ROD); *United States v. City and County of Denver*, 100 F.3d 1509, 1513 (10th Cir. 1996) (local zoning law in conflict with a CERCLA remedial order cannot be an ARAR).

37. Section 121(d)(4) permits waiver of an ARAR if one of a number of conditions are present, such as—compliance with the ARAR will result in greater risk than alternative options; compliance with an ARAR is technically impractical; the ARAR derives from state law, but the state has not consistently applied it.

PROBLEM
THE SAFE DRINKING WATER ACT

CERCLA § 121(d)(2)(a)(I) designates as an ARAR "any standard, requirement, criteria, or limitation" under the SDWA. The SDWA establishes two potential ARAR standards: maximum contaminant levels (MCLs), which represent the maximum permissible levels of contaminants that can be in the public water system; and maximum contaminant level goals (MCLGs), which are health-based goals, set without regard to their achievability or cost. EPA has determined that MCLGs of zero are not "appropriate" and therefore may not be ARARs. Instead, MCLs will become the applicable ARARs, even though the MCL ARAR would permit a site with contaminated groundwater to be declared clean when its groundwater still contained some detectable levels of the contaminant. In *State of Ohio v. EPA*, 997 F.2d 1520 (D.C.Cir. 1993), the court upheld EPA's decision to exclude zero-based MCLGs as ARARs. In light of this decision, consider the following questions:

- If an MCL is the ARAR, and not a MCLG of zero, some risk remains because MCLs may tolerate pollutants in groundwater at very low levels. Is this result consistent with CERCLA's goals?

- If MCLs are ARARs for groundwater, should the standard be met anywhere in the groundwater, or just at the drinking water tap?

- Should MCLs be an ARAR when the contaminated groundwater is otherwise unsuitable as drinking water (*e.g.*, if it is naturally saline)?

c.   CASE STUDY: ARARS AND PCBS

EPA is often called upon to remediate hazardous substances found at abandoned, or sometimes operational, municipal dumps. These dumpsites are characterized by large volumes of extremely heterogeneous, mostly non-hazardous waste material. However, some hazardous wastes are frequently present, sometimes in high concentrations. For example, if electrical equipment manufacturer had disposed of PCB-containing articles and waste materials at the dump, there are typically some areas of the landfill with very high levels of PCB contamination and many areas with some contamination.

PCB-contaminated landfills present difficult practical and legal clean-up problems. The practical problem begins with characterization: the large volume of waste means that sampling the entire site is extremely expensive and may well be impractical. Moreover, the excavation and treatment of such volumes of waste is even more expensive. Alternatively, transportation to a licensed hazardous waste facility is not only expensive, but it involves transportation risks associated with moving thousands of truckloads of waste over highways—and there is a great deal of resistance to the idea that moving landfill risk from one neighborhood to another. Consequently, EPA's policy is to attempt to locate the worst of the contamination ("hot spots," in EPA jargon), treat and/or transport it elsewhere, and to place a weatherproof cap on the remainder of the landfill to limit further migration of water though the landfill.

The principal legal difficulty lies in determining the appropriate ARARs. The NCP requires ARARs to be identified, as follows:

(1) The lead and support agencies shall identify requirements applicable to the release or remedial action contemplated based upon an objective determination of whether the requirement specifically addresses a hazardous substance, pollutant, contaminant, remedial action, location, or other circumstance found at a CERCLA site.

(2) If, based upon paragraph (g)(1) of this section, it is determined that a requirement is not applicable to a specific release, the requirement may still be relevant and appropriate to the circumstances of the release. In evaluating relevance and appropriateness, the factors in paragraphs (g)(2)(i) through (viii) of this section shall be examined, where pertinent, to determine whether a requirement addresses problems or situations sufficiently similar to the circumstances of the release or remedial action contemplated, and whether the requirement is well-suited to the site, and therefore is both relevant and appropriate. The pertinence of each of the following factors will depend, in part, on whether a requirement addresses a chemical, location, or action [*i.e.*, the three types of ARARs]. The following comparisons shall be made, where pertinent, to determine relevance and appropriateness:

(i) The purpose of the requirement and the purpose of the CERCLA action;

(ii) The medium regulated or affected by the requirement and the medium contaminated or affected at the CERCLA site;

(iii) The substances regulated by the requirement and the substances found at the CERCLA site;

(iv) The actions or activities regulated by the requirement and the remedial action contemplated at the CERCLA site;

(v) Any variances, waivers, or exemptions of the requirement and their availability for the circumstances at the CERCLA site;

(vi) The type of place regulated and the type of place affected by the release or CERCLA action;

(vii) The type and size of structure or facility regulated and the type and size of structure or facility affected by the release or contemplated by the CERCLA action;

(viii) Any consideration of use or potential use of affected resources in the requirement and the use or potential use of the affected resource at the CERCLA site.

(3) In addition to applicable or relevant and appropriate requirements, the lead and support agencies may, as appropriate, identify other advisories, criteria, or guidance to be considered for a particular release. The "to be considered" (TBC) category consists of advisories, criteria, or guidance that were developed by EPA, other federal agencies, or states that may be useful in developing CERCLA remedies. * * *

40 C.F.R. § 300.400(g)(2); *see also* 40 C.F.R. § 300.5 (defining "relevant and appropriate requirements"). One of the very few judicial decisions on the meaning of "relevant and appropriate" construed it broadly:

> Even if Michigan's anti-degradation law were not applicable to this site, its consideration would certainly be "relevant and appropriate." Among possible factors to be considered, the environmental media ("groundwater"), the type of substance ("injurious") and the objective of the potential ARAR ("protecting aquifers from actual or potential degradation)," are all "relevant" in this case because they pertain to the conditions of the Rose Site. Moreover, considering the aforementioned factors, the use of Michigan's anti-degradation law is well-suited to the site at issue and therefore "appropriate" in this case.

United States v. Akzo Coatings of America, 949 F.2d 1409, 1445 (6th Cir. 1991).

At first blush, one would think that the appropriate analogy is other hazardous waste landfills. The relevant TSCA (why TSCA?) and RCRA regulations require that PCB landfills have not just a cap, but also a bottom liner, leachate collection system, relatively impermeable bedrock. They also limit the concentrations of PCBs in the landfill; concentrations higher than 100 ppm must be incinerated. 40 C.F.R. part 761. The cap-in-place remedy obviously does not meet these standards.

Consider the following arguments that may be used by EPA to justify not following the PCB regulations:

(a) The regulations in question were designed for new, as opposed to existing, landfills. Therefore, by their own terms, they are not "applicable" and need not be followed.

(b) New and existing landfills are fundamentally different; therefore, regulations the apply to new landfills are not even "relevant and appropriate" to existing ones? (In considering this argument, you will need to think about *why* new and existing landfills are different, and whether those distinctions should or should not make a *legal* difference.)

(c) PCB disposal regulations need not be literally followed because they are only "relevant and appropriate," not "applicable." EPA treats potentially relevant requirements on a sliding scale from "applicable," which must be followed absolutely; to "relevant and appropriate, which EPA tries to follow; to "to be considered," which EPA can freely choose to follow or not.

(d) Capping in place is the equivalent of on-site disposal of remediation waste; therefore, EPA need not meet the requirements of other hazardous waste disposal laws. (Hint: *see* 42 U.S.C. § 9621(e).)

(e) Even if the PCB disposal regulations are an ARAR, EPA can waive them. (The NCP's waiver requirements can be found at 40 C.F.R. § 300.-430(f)(1)(ii)(c).)

d. PERMANENCE

While protectiveness and compliance with ARARs clean-up goal are "threshold" criteria, long-term effectiveness and "permanence" constitute one of the "primary balancing criteria" which may be used to decide among different clean-up strategies. A closely related balancing criteria is "reduction of toxicity, mobility, or volume through treatment." Both are designed to assure that remedial action will in fact be final, that the problem will not reappear several years in the future. Thus, the statute states a distinct preference that "treatment" or other "permanent" solutions are a "principal part" of any remedy.

EPA endorses a guideline that achieves between 90 to 99 percent reductions in toxicity or mobility. Such a strict standard is driven by the realization that over 26% of the NPL are expected to become residential, while 80% will likely have residents surrounding the site. 60 Fed. Reg. 29595, 29596 (June 5, 1995). On the other hand, the NCP assumes that some residual hazardous waste will still exist after clean-up is completed. It presumes the permanence standard is satisfied if the "threat posed by the hazardous substances remaining can be adequately managed by "engineering or institutional controls." These are seemingly contradictory impulses: treatment because people are likely to come into contact with the contamination in the future, and yet acceptance of significant amounts of residual contamination. Reliance on the exposure scenarios of a limited future use adds to the conundrum—how can the preference for treatment and permanence be reconciled with remedies that deliberately leave waste in place?

e. COST

CERCLA § 121(a), (b)(1) requires that a remedy be "cost effective." This is an especially slippery term that can have multiple meanings. The NCP and EPA have seized upon two alternative interpretations that are mirror images of each other. On the one hand, a cost-effective remedy is simply a means of achieving a predetermined clean-up goal. EPA decides what level of environmental and health protection is appropriate (*i.e.*, a level that is protective and permanent), and then it may select the remedy that is the cheapest effective way of obtaining that level. Alternative comparable technologies that are more costly than others will be rejected.[38] On the other hand, cost can help decide the appropriate level of environmental clean-up (the goal) by being weighed against the benefits conferred by that level. If the costs are disproportionate to the benefits, the clean-up standard itself can be ratcheted down. In this way, "cost-effectiveness" becomes a surrogate for a cost-benefit analysis.

---

38. "[T]he decisionmaker should both compare the cost and effectiveness of each alternative individually and compare the cost and effectiveness of alternatives in relation to one another." 55 Fed. Reg. 8728 (Mar. 8, 1990).

NOTES AND QUESTIONS

1.   Are health and environmental returns justified in terms of their expense?[39] You will recall the different cost-benefit standards discussed in Chapter 3. Which is the better interpretation of the statute?

2.   How are permanence and cost to be reconciled? In fact, cost, not permanence, is the most important factor for three critical parties: PRPs, who must pay for the clean-up; states, which must provide 10 percent of the cost that PRPs do not pay; and EPA, which has limited available funding and wishes to conserve the Superfund. J.H. HIRD, SUPERFUND: THE POLITICAL ECONOMY OF ENVIRONMENTAL RISK 144 (1994). This covers just about all of the interested parties (who is excepted?), so although permanence is a variable that is equally weighed along with cost, cost-effectiveness has come to dominate the legal preferences for treatment of CERCLA sites. Is this a betrayal of the goals of CERCLA—or does it simply bring CERCLA into line with the other statutes we have studied?

> *Come run the hidden pine trails of the forest*
>
> *Come taste the sunsweet berries of the earth*
>
> *Come revel in all the riches all around you*
>
> *And for once never wonder what they're worth.*
>
> STEPHEN SCHWARTZ, *Color of the Wind,* on WALT DISNEY PICTURES' POCAHONTAS (Wonderland Music Co., 1995).

3.   When the EPA is determining costs and cost-effectiveness of a proposed remedy, should any of the following be considered?

- The cost of no clean-up at all (the contaminated sited becomes a "scorched earth" no-use zone, isolated from all human contact and most pathways to the natural environment).

- The opportunity cost of an expenditure on the site (the environmental clean-up opportunities foregone by spending money on one waste site and not on other sites).

- The cost of alternative remedies that do not require site clean-up (the cost of providing bottled water to a community whose well water supplies have been contaminated).

- The cost of the remedy compared to the value of the cleaned up property (should a site be cleaned up if the remedial costs will be hundreds of times the ultimate economic worth of the remediated site?).

- Long-term of costs of operating water treatment or waste disposal facilities, or of restricting access to sites at which contamination remains.

---

39.   "A remedy shall be cost-effective if its costs are proportional to its overall effectiveness." 40 C.F.R. § 300.430(f)(1)(ii)(1). *But see Northwest Resource Information Center, Inc. v. Northwest Power Planning Council,* 35 F.3d 1371, 1394 (9th Cir. 1994) (achievement of biological objectives in a least-cost manner does not require a cost-benefit analysis).

5. Judicial Review

There are several reasons why a private party might wish to bring a lawsuit challenging a decision under CERCLA. The general public, including environmental organizations, may believe that an EPA regulation is too lax or may be concerned that a specific clean-up operation will be inadequate. By contrast, a PRP may wish to attack a rule or a particular clean-up decision for being too harsh. In such cases, two CERCLA provisions are key. Section 310(a) "giveth"—it permits suits against (1) any person alleged to be in violation of any CERCLA rule, or (2) any federal official who has failed to perform a non-discretionary act under CERCLA. Section 113(h) "taketh away"—it restricts federal court jurisdiction to entertain challenges to EPA decisions with respect to the clean-ups of a hazardous waste site. It bars most pre-implementation review, and possibly even pre-enforcement review.

In addition to the critical restrictions found in section 113(h), if a citizen suit alleges a violation of CERCLA, notice of the alleged violation must be given to the EPA, to the relevant state, and the perpetrator of the violation. Section 310(d)(1). Moreover, the cause of action may not be based upon past violations; the defendant must be in violation at the time of the litigation, or the violation must be likely to recur. *Lutz v. Chromatex, Inc.*, 718 F.Supp. 413 (M.D. Pa. 1989). The notice provision, therefore, gives governmental defendants an opportunity to take the demanded action, and private defendants the opportunity to sin no more without facing litigation.

CERCLA section 113(h) provides that "[n]o Federal court shall have jurisdiction under Federal law * * * to review any challenges to removal or remedial action selected" by the EPA under sections 104 or 106(a) except in cost-recovery or enforcement lawsuits in which money or response actions are actually demanded. *Gopher Oil Co. v. Bunker*, 84 F.3d 1047, 1051 (8th Cir. 1996); *Arkansas Peace Ctr. v. Arkansas Department of Pollution Control & Ecology*, 999 F.2d 1212, 1216 (8th Cir. 1993). Federal courts have interpreted section 113(h) to mean that they have no jurisdiction to review challenges to removal or remedial actions *until those actions have been completed. Clinton County Comm'rs v. EPA*, 116 F.3d 1018 (3d Cir. 1997) (en banc) (overruling a prior case permitting preemptive challenges in special circumstances), *cert. denied sub nom. Arrest the Incinerator Remediation Inc. v. EPA*, 522 U.S. 1045 (1998); *Schalk v. Reilly*, 900 F.2d 1091, 1095 (7th Cir. 1990) ("The obvious meaning of this statute is that when a remedy has been selected, no challenge to the clean-up may occur prior to the completion of the remedy."). In other words, pre-implementation review is forbidden. *Alabama v. EPA*, 871 F.2d 1548 (11th Cir. 1989); *Oil, Chemical & Atomic Workers Int'l Union v. Peña*, 18 F.Supp.2d 6, 21 (D.D.C. 1998). *See generally* Michael P. Healy, *The Effectiveness and Fairness of Superfund's Judicial Review Preclusion Provision*, 15 Va. Envtl. L. J. 271 (1995–1996); Michael P. Healy, *Judicial Review and CERCLA Response Actions: Interpretive Strategies in the Face of Plain Meaning*, 17 Harv. Envtl. L. Rev. 1 (1993).

Why would Congress have imposed such a barrier to lawsuits that wish to limit EPA's clean-up expenditures in advance? After all, pre-implementation review might prevent excessive, and possibly *ultra vires*, expenditures. It also might prevent the implementation of remedies which themselves posed serious dangers to the community.[40] The answer is that, in enacting section 113(h), "Congress intended to prevent time-consuming litigation which might interfere with CERCLA's overall goal of effecting the prompt clean-up of hazardous waste sites." *United States v. City and County of Denver*, 100 F.3d 1509, 1514 (10th Cir. 1996); *Clinton County Comm'rs v. U.S. EPA*, 116 F.3d 1018, 1022–25 (3d Cir. 1997). Therefore, once an activity has been classified as a section 104 removal or remedial action, section 113(h) "amounts to a blunt withdrawal of federal jurisdiction." *Hanford Downwinders Coalition, Inc. v. Dowdle*, 71 F.3d 1469, 1474 (9th Cir. 1995). *But see Frey v. EPA*, 403 F.3d 828, 834 (7th Cir. 2005) (concluding that § 113(h) is not an open ended prohibition to citizen's suits; and therefore, following initial clean-up, in order to halt a lawsuit under § 113(h), the EPA "must point to some objective referent that commits it and other responsible parties to an action or plan."). The rule apparently is to clean up first and ask questions later.

Some courts have taken this philosophy to its logical extreme. In *Voluntary Purchasing Groups, Inc. v. Reilly*, 889 F.2d 1380 (5th Cir. 1989), the court barred pre-enforcement review. According to the court, the PRPs at the site could not challenge a fully implemented clean-up decision until EPA had filed a cost recovery action against them. Despite the fact that a post-implementation, pre-enforcement lawsuit could not halt the already completed remedy, the court concluded there was "no indication [that section 113(h)] only applies when a delay in clean-up would ensue." 889 F.2d at 1388–89.

Section 113(h) also precludes "any challenges" to CERCLA removal and remedial actions, not simply those brought under the provisions of CERCLA itself. *Frey v. EPA,* 270 F.3d 1129 (7th Cir. 2001) (precluding citizens from bringing air pollution enforcement action where citizens failed to exhaust their administrative remedies and the state diligently pursued cleanup of the sites). *McClellan Ecological Seepage Situation v. Perry*, 47 F.3d 325, 329 (9th Cir. 1995) ("Section 113 withholds federal jurisdiction to review any of [plaintiff's] claims, including those made in citizen suits under non-CERCLA statutes, that are found to constitute 'challenges' to ongoing CERCLA clean-up actions."); *United States v. State of Colorado*, 990 F.2d 1565, 1577 (10th Cir. 1993).

While the courts have been under considerable pressure to find (or permit) exceptions to section 113(h), they have by and large held the line on broad preclusion. In *United States ex. rel. Costner v. URS Consultants, Inc.*, 153 F.3d 667 (8th Cir. 1998), the court permitted a False Claims Act suit alleging that EPA's clean-up contractors had submitted fraudulent bills for services to the government. However, it made the limitations of its ruling clear:

---

40. A panel of the Third Circuit permitted pre-implementation review for this reason, *United States v. Princeton Gamma–Tech, Inc.*, 31 F.3d 138 (3d Cir. 1994), but it was overruled by *Clinton County,* 116 F.3d 1018 (3d Cir. 1997), infra.

In *Arkansas Peace* [999 F.2d 1212 (8th Cir. 1993)], we determined that plaintiffs' claims, "although couched in terms of a RCRA violation," constituted a challenge to the EPA removal action so as to invoke the section 113(h) bar. In that case, however, plaintiffs sought and had been granted a preliminary injunction against incineration activity at the Vertac site. *Here, relators seek neither review of nor injunction against any remedial activity on the site.* Instead, they allege fraud and seek civil penalties on behalf of the United States. Resolution of this suit in relators' favor "would not involve altering the terms of the clean-up order," but would result only in financial penalties for alleged fraud regarding payments sought and received for past completed work. Thus, the complaint does not seek to interfere with the remediation process ongoing at the site, nor is the suit "directly related to the goals of the clean-up itself." *McClellan*, [47 F.3d 325 (9th Cir. 1995)]. Accordingly, we hold that relators' FCA suit does not constitute a section 113(h)-barred challenge to remedial action at the Vertac site. 153 F.3d at 675 (emphasis added).

NOTES AND QUESTIONS

1.   Several other circuits have addressed the issue of what constitutes a challenge under section 113(h). None have identified a particular test to be used in making this determination. *Compare United States v. Colorado*, 990 F.2d 1565, 1575 (10th Cir. 1993) (action by the state to enforce a compliance order under its state waste management act, issued pursuant to its EPA-delegated authority to enforce state hazardous waste laws under RCRA was not a challenge to a CERCLA response action under section 113(h)), *with McClellan Ecological Seepage Situation v. Perry*, 47 F.3d 325 (9th Cir. 1995) (section 113(h) barred an environmental group's challenges based on both RCRA and the Clean Water Act); *Boarhead Corp. v. Erickson*, 923 F.2d 1011, 1021–22 (3d Cir. 1991) (section 113(h) barred an action under the National Historic Preservation Act seeking to stay a CERCLA response action pending determination of whether the property at issue qualified for historic site status); *Schalk v. Reilly*, 900 F.2d 1091, 1095 (7th Cir. 1990) (section 113(h) barred private citizens from bringing a CERCLA citizens suit challenging a consent decree between the EPA and the PRP alleging violation of the National Environmental Policy Act for failure to prepare an environmental impact statement).[41]

2.   In one other situations courts have been willing to carve out exceptions to the ban on pre-implementation review. In *United States v. Akzo Coatings of America*, 949 F.2d 1409, 1424 (6th Cir. 1991), the court allowed non-settling PRPs to attack remedies incorporated into negotiated consent decrees under section 106. This holding is based upon one of the exceptions to section 113(h), which permits judicial review where EPA

---

41.   Does the § 113(h) ban extend to constitutional challenges to remedial action taken under CERCLA? *Compare Reardon v. EPA*, 947 F.2d 1509, 1514–17 (1st Cir. 1991) (facial challenges allowed), *with Barmet v. Aluminum Corp. v. Reilly*, 927 F.2d 289, 293 (6th Cir. 1991) (§ 113(h) precludes even constitutional challenges).

moves to compel remedial action under section 106. The *Akzo* court reasoned that in light of this exception, courts should be able to inquire into the acceptability of remedies in the consent decree that is about to be entered in court under section 106. *See,* 949 F.2d at 1424 n.11.

3. Does section 113(h) also preclude state court challenges to CERCLA cleanup? *See Fort Ord Toxics Project, Inc. v. California EPA*, 189 F.3d 828 (9th Cir. 1999) (no state court determination allowed as only federal courts have jurisdiction to adjudicate challenges to CERCLA clean-up).

D. Liability

The first purpose of CERCLA is to protect the public and the environment by responding to hazardous spills and releases of contaminated waste and by bringing about a prompt clean-up of hazardous waste sites. The foregoing section discussed how the four clean-up cornerstones of CERCLA (the NCP, NPL, and remedial and removal actions) accomplish this task. But Congress was not content with simply decontaminating waste sites, especially when the costs of the clean-up would be borne by EPA (*i.e.,* the American taxpayer) and the Superfund (*i.e.,* companies taxed to finance the Fund). Accordingly, CERCLA's second purpose is to ensure that the costs of clean-up efforts are borne by responsible parties. The Act accomplishes this goal by providing mechanisms for reaching a range of liable parties. CERCLA, in short, creates a new cause of action, so it must set out (or at least imply) the nature of the liability, the identity of who may be liable, the triggers for liability, remedy, and the defenses to liability. If the conditions to liability are met, and the defenses are unavailable, the consequence, according to section 107(a)(4), is that the responsible party is liable for three types of costs incurred as a result of a release or threatened release of hazardous waste: (1) governmental response costs (incurred by the federal government, Indian tribes, or states); private party response costs (incurred by private parties if consistent with the NCP); and damages to natural resources. We now discuss how persons may find themselves liable under CERCLA, as well as the elements of damages for which PRPs may be liable.

PROBLEM
INTERPRETING SECTION 107

1. Read section 107(a) and (b) to identify the sources of the elements of a CERCLA cause of action (nature of liability, persons liable, triggers, remedy, and defenses). Were you able to find them all?

2. Does the organization of section 107 confuse matters?

3. Now, relying on the statutory language, see if you can state succinctly the elements of a CERCLA cause of action.

4. Finally, identify the key terms in section 107(a) and (b) and refer to section 101, the definitions. Which terms are statutorily defined? What are the effects of the definitions? Do they expand or restrict liability? Both?

1. THE STANDARD OF LIABILITY

Although section 107(a) merely states that certain "person[s]" meeting CERCLA's test for responsible parties "shall be liable," this phrase has been interpreted by the courts to impose (1) strict, (2) joint and several, and (3) retroactive liability. All of these elements were established in judicial decisions shortly after CERCLA was enacted. *See, e.g., United States v. Chem–Dyne Corp.*, 572 F.Supp. 802 (S.D. Ohio 1983). Since Congress had the opportunity to modify these results in the 1986 SARA, its failure to do so must be considered an affirmance of these interpretations.

a. STRICT LIABILITY

The standard of liability under section 107(a) is strict liability, even though the statute nowhere expressly demands this result. Section 101(32) merely states that the term "liability" is to be the same as "the standard of liability which obtains under [§ 311 of the Clean Water Act]." Since most pre-CERCLA courts had interpreted § 311 as imposing strict liability, the same was imposed under CERCLA. This means that a plaintiff, governmental or private, need not prove that the release of hazardous substances was due to the defendant's negligent conduct, nor that the defendant's conduct was intentional or unreasonable. Under a CERCLA strict liability theory, proof of only four central elements is needed to establish the defendant's responsibility for response costs: the site is a "facility"; the defendant is a responsible "person"; release or threatened release of a "hazardous substance" has occurred; and the release has caused the plaintiff to "incur response costs." *Westfarm Assoc. v. Washington Suburban Sanitation Com'n*, 66 F.3d 669 (4th Cir. 1995); *Akzo Coatings, Inc. v. Ainger Corp.*, 909 F.Supp. 1154 (N.D. Ind. 1995).

Another important consequence of strict liability is that causation, normally a central component to a common law toxic tort action, is relevant in a completely new way. Current and prior owners and operators of hazardous waste sites, as well as generators of hazardous wastes, may be liable irrespective of whether they in fact caused the presence or release of hazardous waste. *United States v. Hercules, Inc.*, 247 F.3d 706 (8th Cir. 2001), *cert. denied sub nom.* (finding chemical manufacturer to be a generator who arranged for disposal—an "arranger" under CERCLA § 9607(a)(3)—and was therefore correctly held jointly and severally liable). Instead, the required linkage is whether the *release* (or threat of release) caused response costs to be incurred. *New York v. Shore Realty Corp.*, 759 F.2d 1032 (2d Cir. 1985); *United States v. Monsanto*, 858 F.2d 160, 167–69 (4th Cir. 1988); *United States v. Alcan Aluminum Corp.*, 964 F.2d 252, 264–66 (3d Cir. 1992); *Textron, Inc. by and through Homelite v. Barber*, 903 F. Supp. 1558 (W.D. N.C. 1995). This very weak causation requirement has several benefits: (1) companies are given a powerful incentive to internalize their waste clean-up costs; (2) clean-up costs will usually be borne by the businesses that generate and dispose of the wastes, not by affected neighbors or taxpayers; and (3) the Superfund (*i.e.,* taxpayer money) is conserved. The cost is that a generator of wastes or owner of a facility can be liable even if it was not at fault or if it took "every precaution in the disposal of its wastes," *O'Neil v. Picillo*, 682 F.Supp. 706, 720–21 (D.R.I. 1988), *aff'd*, 883 F.2d 176 (1st Cir. 1989), since due care is not a defense to strict liability. This has struck some observers—notably PRPs—as unfair. Moreover, the strict liability standard stands in the way of some good faith cleanup efforts.

b. JOINT AND SEVERAL LIABILITY

Apart from imposing strict liability, CERCLA § 107(a) has been universally interpreted as allowing joint and several liability among potentially responsible parties. *United States v. Chem–Dyne Corp.*, 572 F.Supp. 802 (S.D. Ohio 1983). As every first year torts student knows, liability that is joint and several means that the entire burden can be shifted to any contributor to the harm, even one that has only a tiny role, leaving to that party the task of seeking contribution from other defendants, if possible. Because CERCLA is silent on the issue, early CERCLA cases assumed that Congress intended the courts to exercise their discretion in deciding whether to impose joint and several liability. The central question became whether, in light of general tort principles apportioning liability among multiple defendants,[42] the harm can be said to be sufficiently divisible or severable. Early cases like *Chem–Dyne*, with leaking landfills in mind, expected that divisibility could be shown only in rare cases.

United States v. Monsanto
858 F.2d 160 (4th Cir. 1988)

"Under common law rules, when two or more persons act independently to cause a single harm for which there is a reasonable basis of apportionment according to the contribution of each, each is held liable only for the portion of harm that he causes. When such persons cause a single and indivisible harm, however, they are held liable jointly and severally for the entire harm. We think these principles * * * represent the correct and uniform federal rule applicable to CERCLA cases." *Id.* at 171–72.

Nevertheless, the potentially high cost of remediation gave defendants in a § 107(a) CERCLA liability suit a continuing incentive to try to show that the harm is divisible, and conversely, rebut the plaintiff's argument that it is indivisible. *See In re Bell Petroleum Services, Inc.*, 3 F.3d 889, 902–03 (5th Cir. 1993) (it is the defendant's burden to establish a reasonable basis by which to apportion liability, or to establish that distinct harms exist). This considerable burden can be met only at the atypical hazardous waste site, where the defendant's waste has produced a separate, identifiable harm which is distinct from all other harms, or where it is possible to determine the defendant's separate contribution to the single harm, for example, where many generators of the same kind of toxic waste in a non-leaking site can calculate the exact percentage of the total quantity of waste for which they were responsible.[43]

---

42. RESTATEMENT (SECOND) OF TORTS § 433A is the most influential tort principle.

43. If there are many migration paths from the waste site, it is not possible to know what

CERCLA defendants have discovered that it is quite difficult to meet the burden of proving divisibility. *O'Neil v. Picillo,* 883 F.2d 176 (1st Cir. 1989); *United States v. Dico,* 979 F. Supp. 1255, 1259–61 (S.D. Iowa 1997); *Cooper Industries, Inc. v. Agway, Inc.*, 956 F. Supp. 240 (N.D. N.Y. 1997). *But see Dent v. Beazer Materials & Services, Inc.*, 993 F. Supp. 923, 946 (D.S.C. 1995) (burden met for showing reasonable basis for division of liability when one party was "the only cause of the harm inflicted on the environment") *aff'd* 156 F.3d. *United States v. Alcan Aluminum Corp.,* 315 F. 3d 179 (2d Cir. 2003) (determining defendant failed to prove that harm was divisible where defendant merely argued that the waste it created was minimal and "benign"). Divisibility is almost impossible to show in the usual abandoned waste site, which has been contaminated by numerous, commingled hazardous substances, often by multiple parties. *United States v. Vertac Chemical Corp.*, 966 F. Supp. 1491 (E.D. Ark. 1997); *United States v. Wallace,* 961 F. Supp. 969 (N.D. Tex. 1996). When a defendant fails to establish a reasonable basis as a matter of fact for apportioning liability among potentially responsible parties, a court may find any given defendant jointly and severally liable for *any* hazardous substance that is found at the site, whatever its source, and regardless of that defendant's percentage contribution to the overall waste problem at the site. *United States v. Township of Brighton*, 153 F.3d 307, 317 (6th Cir. 1998); *Town of Windsor v. Tesa Tuck, Inc.*, 919 F. Supp. 662 (S.D. N.Y. 1996). *Chem–Nuclear Systems v. Bush,* 292 F.3d 254 (D.C. Cir. 2002) (finding that party responsible for 80 drums of hazardous waste was not entitled to reimbursement absent proof beyond a preponderance of the evidence that additional waste at the site was not also attributable to the same source). And when § 107(a) liability is joint and several, no equitable defenses apply. *Aluminum Co. of America v. Beazer East, Inc.,* 124 F. 3d 551, 562–3 (3d Cir. 1997).

THE HARSH REALITY OF STRICT, JOINT AND SEVERAL LIABILITY

In *PMC, Inc. v. Sherwin–Williams Co.*, 151 F.3d 610 (7th Cir. 1998), the court decided that, as between a purchaser and seller who both concededly dumped toxic wastes at a site, the seller was liable for 100 percent of the total clean-up cost. Although the seller argued that this result was unfair (after all, the purchaser had admitted dumping wastes at the site on a number of occasions after the sale), the appeals court was unimpressed:

> [The purchaser's] spills may have been too inconsequential to affect the cost of cleaning up significantly, and in that event a zero allocation to [the purchaser] would be appropriate. * * * Granted, it might seem an invitation to purchasers of polluted sites to do a little polluting deliberately, in the hope of not having to pay anything to clean it up; but in the first place, this is a risky strategy, since it might induce the judge to exercise his equitable

---

generator is responsible for the waste leaking into one or more of these pathways.

> discretion against the wise guy; and in the second place, the
> deliberate disposal of wastes without a permit is forbidden by
> RCRA. 42 U.S.C. § 6928(d)(2).
>
> 151 F.3d at 616.

While *strict liability* has the advantage of transferring the costs of environmental damage to those in the best position to reduce risks (by higher insurance premiums or safer disposal practices), *joint and several* liability may have several disadvantages. Karl Tilleman & Shane Swindle, *Closing the Book on CERCLA Section 107 "Joint and Several" Claims by Liable Private Parties*, 18 VA. ENVT'L L. REV. 159 (1999). It may be very unfair to make one party responsible for the cost of an entire clean-up when it can be demonstrated that there are several parties who caused the problem. *See* J. Hyson, *"Fairness" and Joint and Several Liability in Government Cost Recovery Actions Under CERCLA*, 21 HARV. ENVTL. L. REV. 137 (1997). A party liable for the lion's share of the clean-up cost may be, at one end of the spectrum, a deep pocket responsible party who contributed a tiny fraction of the hazardous waste. Or, at the other end of the spectrum, 100 percent liability can fall on a small-fry generator of wastes, a naïve purchaser of the contaminated property, or a former lessee with only fleeting contact with the waste site, each of whom had little to do with dumping significant waste quantities there. Moreover, joint and several liability may actually act as a disincentive for those involved with hazardous waste to take precautions. If one dumping wastes can escape liability altogether if a co-dumper is saddled with 100 percent responsibility for the ultimate clean-up, then there is little reason to prevent releases, and even less reason to settle with other responsible parties. *See* Richard Epstein, *Two Fallacies in the Law of Joint Torts*, 73 GEO. L. J. 1377 (1985).

The potential harshness of joint and several liability did not escape the attention of Congress. In SARA in 1986, Congress chose to leave the case law alone, thereby permitting courts to resolve the liability issue on the basis of the predominant "divisibility" rule discussed above; however, it added two important provisions designed to mitigate the sometimes unfair consequences of joint and several liability. First, EPA is directed to offer early settlements to defendants who are responsible for only a small portion of the harm, so-called *de minimis* settlements. § 122(g). Second, there is now a statutory cause of action in *contribution*, which permits courts to "allocate response costs among liable parties using such equitable factors as the court determines are appropriate." § 113(f)(1). The latter provision, which will be discussed more fully later in this chapter, has become the main tool for softening the blow for defendants who fail to satisfy the divisibility test.

In addition some courts have tried to moderate the impact of joint and several liability in appropriate cases. Both the Second and Third Circuits inject causation into the liability question (although the burden of proof remains on the defendant) by permitting an otherwise responsible party to avoid § 107(a) liability if it can prove that its wastes, when mixed with other hazardous wastes, "did not [or could not] contribute to the release and the resultant response costs [or contributed at most to only a divisible portion of the harm]." *United States v. Alcan Aluminum Corp.*, 990 F.2d 711, 722 (2d Cir. 1993); *United States v. Alcan Aluminum Corp.*, 964 F.2d 252, 270–1 (3d Cir. 1992).[44] Other cases have attempted to shield certain parties from joint and several liability by suggesting that "passive owners" (*e.g.*, ones who purchased a site without adequate pre-purchase investigation, but who did not contribute any wastes to it) may escape liability if they "were able to prove that none of the hazardous substances found at the site were fairly attributable to it. * * * [If this were shown] we might well conclude that apportionment was appropriate and [the passive owners'] apportioned share would be zero." *United States v. Rohm & Haas Co.*, 2 F.3d 1265, 1280 (3d Cir. 1993).[45] Still others have stretched joint and several liability doctrine to find the harm to be divisible and the resulting liability capable of apportionment. The leading case is *In the Matter of Bell Petroleum Services, Inc.*, 3 F.3d 889 (5th Cir. 1993). In *Bell Petroleum*, three parties had successively operated a business that discharged one contaminant (chromium) into groundwater. The Fifth Circuit decided it could apportion damages based on circumstantial evidence of the volumes of chromium-contaminated water discharged by each party. Other lower courts, more cautiously, have found that harms were divisible for purposes of a § 107(a) action where in no chemicals similar to those found at the site were released during the party's prior ownership of the site, *Dent v. Beazer Materials and Services, Inc.*, 156 F.3d 523, 530–1 (4th Cir. 1998), and where the facility involved "distinct pollutants" that were "geographically separated." *Memphis Zane May Assocs. v. IBC Mfg. Co.*, 952 F. Supp. 541 (W.D. Tenn. 1996); *United States v. Broderick Investment Co.*, 862 F. Supp. 272 (D. Colo. 1994) (harm divisible based on geographic considerations).

In *Burlington Northern and Santa Fe Ry. Co v. United States,* 129 S. Ct. 1870 (2009), the Court recognized that CERCLA does not mandate joint and several liability in every case, and that apportionment is proper when there is a "reasonable basis" for determining the contribution of each cause to a single harm.

---

44. Unfortunately, this so-called *Alcan* defense will likely only benefit financially well-off, technically sophisticated defendants. *See* Harris and Milan, *Avoiding Joint and Several Liability Under CERCLA*, 23 ENV. REP. 1726, 1728 (1992):

"If *Alcan's* holding becomes widely followed, EPA response actions will become more like private contribution actions. Potentially responsible parties will need to retain toxicologists, environmental chemists, and clean-up cost specialists to aid in proving the harm caused by a particular waste."

45. In part because this *dicta* flies in the face of CERCLA's strict liability premise, it has not been followed elsewhere—and did not even permit the defendant in the *Rohm & Haas* case to avoid liability, since it failed to meet its burden of providing a reasonable basis for determining its relative contribution to the harm. In fact, the third circuit explicitly overruled *Rohm and Haas* in 2005. *U.S. v. E.I. Dupont De Nemours and Co. Inc.*, 432 F.3d 161 (3d Cir. 2005), which held that CERCLA authorizes United States to recover costs incurred in overseeing private party removal and remedial actions, to extent such costs are consistent with National Contingency Plan. *Id. at* 162–63.

Burlington Northern and Santa Fe Railway Co. v. United States

129 S.Ct. 1870 (2009)

■ STEVENS, JUSTICE.

In 1960, Brown & Bryant, Inc. (B & B) began operating an agricultural chemical distribution business, purchasing pesticides and other chemical products from suppliers such as Shell Oil Company (Shell). Using its own equipment, B & B applied its products to customers' farms. B & B opened its business on a 3.8 acre parcel of former farmland in Arvin, California, and in 1975, expanded operations onto an adjacent .9 acre parcel of land owned jointly by the Atchison, Topeka & Santa Fe Railway Company, and the Southern Pacific Transportation Company (now known respectively as the Burlington Northern and Santa Fe Railway Company and Union Pacific Railroad Company (Railroads). Both parcels of the Arvin facility were graded toward a sump and drainage pond located on the southeast corner of the primary parcel. Neither the sump nor the drainage pond was lined until 1979, allowing waste water and chemical runoff from the facility to seep into the ground water below.

During its years of operation, B & B stored and distributed various hazardous chemicals on its property. Among these were the herbicide dinoseb, sold by Dow Chemicals, and the pesticides D–D and Nemagon, both sold by Shell. Dinoseb was stored in 55-gallon drums and 5-gallon containers on a concrete slab outside B & B's warehouse. Nemagon was stored in 30-gallon drums and 5-gallon containers inside the warehouse.

When B & B purchased D–D, Shell would arrange for delivery by common carrier, f.o.b. destination. When the product arrived, it was transferred from tanker trucks to a bulk storage tank located on B & B's primary parcel. From there, the chemical was transferred to bobtail trucks, nurse tanks, and pull rigs. During each of these transfers leaks and spills could—and often did—occur. Although the common carrier and B & B used buckets to catch spills from hoses and gaskets connecting the tanker trucks to its bulk storage tank, the buckets sometimes overflowed or were knocked over, causing D–D to spill onto the ground during the transfer process. Aware that spills of D–D were commonplace among its distributors, in the late 1970's Shell took several steps to encourage the safe handling of its products. Shell provided distributors with detailed safety manuals and instituted a voluntary discount program for distributors that made improvements in their bulk handling and safety facilities. Later, Shell revised its program to require distributors to obtain an inspection by a qualified engineer and provide self-certification of compliance with applicable laws and regulations. B & B's Arvin facility was inspected twice, and in 1981, B & B certified to Shell that it had made a number of recommended improvements to its facilities.

Despite these improvements, B & B remained a "sloppy operator." Over the course of B & B's 28 years of operation, delivery spills, equipment failures, and the rinsing of tanks and trucks allowed Nemagon, D–D and dinoseb to seep into the soil and upper levels of ground water of the Arvin facility. In 1983, the California Department of Toxic Substances Control (DTSC) began investigating B & B's violation of hazardous waste laws, and the United States Environmental Protection Agency (EPA) soon followed suit, discovering significant contamination of soil and ground water. Of particular concern was a plume of contaminated ground water located under the facility that threatened to leach into an adjacent supply of potential drinking water.

Although B & B undertook some efforts at remediation, by 1989 it had become insolvent and ceased all operations. That same year, the Arvin facility was added to the National Priority List, and subsequently, DTSC and EPA (Governments) exercised their authority under 42 U.S.C. § 9604 to undertake cleanup efforts at the site. By 1998, the Governments had spent more than $8 million responding to the site contamination; their costs have continued to accrue. In 1991, EPA issued an administrative order to the Railroads directing them, as owners of a portion of the property on which the Arvin facility was located, to perform certain remedial tasks in connection with the site. The Railroads did so, incurring expenses of more than $3 million in the process. Seeking to recover at least a portion of their response costs, in 1992 the Railroads brought suit against B & B in the United States District Court for the Eastern District of California. In 1996, that lawsuit was consolidated with two recovery actions brought by DTSC and EPA against Shell and the Railroads. The District Court entered a judgment in favor of the Governments, holding that both the Railroads and Shell were potentially responsible parties (PRPs) under CERCLA—the Railroads because they were owners of a portion of the facility, and Shell because it had "arranged for" the disposal of hazardous substances through its sale and delivery of D–D.

Although the court found the parties liable, it did not impose joint and several liability on Shell and the Railroads for the entire response cost incurred by the Governments. The court found that the site contamination created a single harm but concluded that the harm was divisible and therefore capable of apportionment. Based on three figures—the percentage of the total area of the facility that was owned by the Railroads, the duration of B & B's business divided by the term of the Railroads' lease, and the Court's determination that only two of three polluting chemicals spilled on the leased parcel required remediation and that those two chemicals were responsible for roughly two-thirds of the overall site contamination requiring remediation—the court apportioned the Railroads' liability as 9% of the Governments' total response cost. Based on estimations of chemicals spills of Shell products, the court held Shell liable for 6% of the total site response cost.

The Governments appealed the District Court's apportionment, and Shell cross-appealed the court's finding of liability.

* * *

On the subject of apportionment, the Court of Appeals found "no dispute" on the question whether the harm caused by Shell and the

Railroads was capable of apportionment. The court observed that a portion of the site contamination occurred before the Railroad parcel became part of the facility, only some of the hazardous substances were stored on the Railroad parcel, and "only some of the water on the facility washed over the Railroads' site." With respect to Shell, the court noted that not all of the hazardous substances spilled on the facility had been sold by Shell. Given those facts, the court readily concluded that "the contamination traceable to the Railroads and Shell, with adequate information, would be allocable, as would be the cost of cleaning up that contamination." Nevertheless, the Court of Appeals held that the District Court erred in finding that the record established a reasonable basis for apportionment. Because the burden of proof on the question of apportionment rested with Shell and the Railroads, the Court of Appeals reversed the District Court's apportionment of liability and held Shell and the Railroads jointly and severally liable for the Governments' cost of responding to the contamination of the Arvin facility.

We granted certiorari to determine whether Shell and the Railroads were properly held liable for all response costs incurred by EPA and the State of California. We must determine whether the Railroads were properly held jointly and severally liable for the full cost of the Governments' response efforts.

The seminal opinion on the subject of apportionment in CERCLA actions was written in 1983 by Chief Judge Carl Rubin of the United States District Court for the Southern District of Ohio. *United States* v. *Chem–Dyne Corp.,* 572 F. Supp. 802. After reviewing CERCLA's history, Chief Judge Rubin concluded that although the Act imposed a "strict liability standard," *id.,* at 805, it did not mandate "joint and several" liability in every case. See *id.,* at 807. Rather, Congress intended the scope of liability to "be determined from traditional and evolving principles of common law." *Id.,* at 808. The *Chem–Dyne* approach has been fully embraced by the Courts of Appeals, and following *Chem–Dyne,* the Courts of Appeals have acknowledged that "[t]he universal starting point for divisibility of harm analyses in CERCLA cases" is § 433A of the Restatement (Second) of Torts. Under the Restatement, "when two or more persons acting independently cause a distinct or single harm for which there is a reasonable basis for division according to the contribution of each, each is subject to liability only for the portion of the total harm that he has himself caused. But where two or more persons cause a single and indivisible harm, each is subject to liability for the entire harm." RESTATEMENT (SECOND) OF TORTS, § 875; Prosser, at 315–316." *Chem–Dyne Corp.,* 572 F. Supp., at 810. In other words, apportionment is proper when "there is a reasonable basis for determining the contribution of each cause to a single harm." Restatement (Second) of Torts § 433A(1)(b), p. 434 (1963–1964).

Not all harms are capable of apportionment, however, and CERCLA defendants seeking to avoid joint and several liability bear the burden of proving that a reasonable basis for apportionment exists. See *Chem–Dyne Corp.,* 572 F. Supp., at 810. When two or more causes produce a single, indivisible harm, "courts have refused to make an arbitrary apportionment for its own sake, and each of the causes is charged with responsibility for the entire harm." RESTATEMENT (SECOND) OF TORTS § 433A, Comment *i*, p. 440 (1963–1964).

Neither the parties nor the lower courts dispute the principles that govern apportionment in CERCLA cases, and both the District Court and Court of Appeals agreed that the harm created by the contamination of the Arvin site, although singular, was theoretically capable of apportionment. The question then is whether the record provided a reasonable basis for the District Court's conclusion that the Railroads were liable for only 9% of the harm caused by contamination at the Arvin facility.

The District Court criticized the Railroads for taking a " 'scorched earth,' all-or-nothing approach to liability," failing to acknowledge any responsibility for the release of hazardous substances that occurred on their parcel throughout the 13–year period of B & B's lease. According to the District Court, the Railroads' position on liability, combined with the Governments' refusal to acknowledge the potential divisibility of the harm, complicated the apportioning of liability. Yet despite the parties' failure to assist the court in linking the evidence supporting apportionment to the proper allocation of liability, the District Court ultimately concluded that this was "a classic 'divisible in terms of degree' case, both as to the time period in which defendants' conduct occurred, and ownership existed, and as to the estimated maximum contribution of each party's activities that released hazardous substances that caused Site contamination." Consequently, the District Court apportioned liability, assigning the Railroads 9% of the total remediation costs.

The District Court calculated the Railroads' liability based on three figures. First, the court noted that the Railroad parcel constituted only 19% of the surface area of the Arvin site. Second, the court observed that the Railroads had leased their parcel to B & B for 13 years, which was only 45% of the time B & B operated the Arvin facility. Finally, the court found that the volume of hazardous-substance-releasing activities on the B & B property was at least 10 times greater than the releases that occurred on the Railroad parcel, and it concluded that only spills of two chemicals, Nemagon and dinoseb (not D–D), substantially contributed to the contamination that had originated on the Railroad parcel and that those two chemicals had contributed to two-thirds of the overall site contamination requiring remediation. The court then multiplied .19 by .45 by .66 (two-thirds) and rounded up to determine that the Railroads were responsible for approximately 6% of the remediation costs. "Allowing for calculation errors up to 50%," the court concluded that the Railroads could be held responsible for 9% of the total CERCLA response cost for the Arvin site.

The Court of Appeals criticized the evidence on which the District Court's conclusions rested, finding a lack of sufficient data to establish the precise proportion of contamination that occurred on the relative portions of the Arvin facility and the rate of contamination in the years prior to B & B's addition of the Railroad parcel. The court noted that neither the duration of the lease nor the size of the leased area alone was a reliable measure of the harm caused by activities on the property owned by the Railroads, and—as the court's upward adjustment confirmed—the court had relied on estimates rather than specific and detailed records as a basis for its conclusions.

Despite these criticisms, we conclude that the facts contained in the record reasonably supported the apportionment of. The District Court's detailed findings make it abundantly clear that the primary pollution at the Arvin facility was contained in an unlined sump and an unlined pond in the southeastern portion of the facility most distant from the Railroads' parcel and that the spills of hazardous chemicals that occurred on the Railroad parcel contributed to no more than 10% of the total site contamination, some of which did not require remediation. With those background facts in mind, we are persuaded that it was reasonable for the court to use the size of the leased parcel and the duration of the lease as the starting point for its analysis. Although the Court of Appeals faulted the District Court for relying on the "simplest of considerations: percentages of land area, time of ownership, and types of hazardous products," these were the same factors the court had earlier acknowledged were *relevant* to the apportionment analysis.

The Court of Appeals also criticized the District Court's assumption that spills of Nemagon and dinoseb were responsible for only two-thirds of the chemical spills requiring remediation, observing that each PRP's share of the total harm was not necessarily equal to the quantity of pollutants that were deposited on its portion of the total facility. Although the evidence adduced by the parties did not allow the court to calculate precisely the amount of hazardous chemicals contributed by the Railroad parcel to the total site contamination or the exact percentage of harm caused by each chemical, the evidence did show that fewer spills occurred on the Railroad parcel and that of those spills that occurred, not all were carried across the Railroad parcel to the B & B sump and pond from which most of the contamination originated. The fact that no D–D spills on the Railroad parcel required remediation lends strength to the District Court's conclusion that the Railroad parcel contributed only Nemagon and dinoseb in quantities requiring remediation.

The District Court's conclusion that those two chemicals accounted for only two-thirds of the contamination requiring remediation finds less support in the record; however, any miscalculation on that point is harmless in light of the District Court's ultimate allocation of liability, which included a 50% margin of error equal to the 3% reduction in liability the District Court provided based on its assessment of the effect of the Nemagon and dinoseb spills. Had the District Court limited its apportionment calculations to the amount of time the Railroad parcel was in use and the percentage of the facility located on that parcel, it would have assigned the Railroads 9% of the response cost. By including a two-thirds reduction in liability for the Nemagon and dinoseb with a 50% "margin of error," the District Court reached the same result. Because the District Court's ultimate allocation of liability is supported by the evidence and comports with the apportionment principles outlined above, we reverse the Court of Appeals' conclusion that the Railroads are subject to joint and several liability for all response costs arising out of the contamination of the Arvin facility.

For the foregoing reasons . . . we conclude that the District Court reasonably apportioned the Railroads' share of the site remediation costs at 9%. The judgment is reversed, and the cases are remanded for further proceedings consistent with this opinion.

NOTES AND QUESTIONS

1.   Several courts have already applied the apportionment holding of *Burlington Northern*. For example, in *Evansville Greenway and Remediation Trust v. Southern IN Gas and Elec. Co., Inc.*, 661 F.Supp.2d 989 (S.D. Ind. 2009), on summary judgment, the court reserved the question of apportionment for trial, thereby allowing "each side to present evidence relevant to its own and its opponents' different interpretations of *Burlington Northern*." *Id.* at 1012; *see also Appleton Papers Inc. v. George A. Whiting Paper Co.*, No. 08–C–16, 2009 WL 3931036 (E.D. Wis. Nov. 18, 2009).

2.   What implications does the apportionment holding of *Burlington Northern* have for the theory of joint and several liability under CERCLA? Could an argument be made that the Federal government must bear the burden of the orphaned shares of insolvent companies if apportionment can be proven? Does this defeat the purpose of imposing joint and several liability?

c.   RETROACTIVE LIABILITY

As if strict and joint and several liability were not enough, CERCLA has also been consistently interpreted to impose retroactive liability, that is, the statute's liability standards apply to hazardous wastes deposited years (or decades) before its enactment. Private parties responsible for dumping such wastes prior to 1980 have found themselves subject to CERCLA's tough clean-up rules and cost recovery actions even though at the time of the dumping activity it may have been perfectly legal to discard wastes at a site now listed on the NPL.[46] Not surprisingly, defendants fighting CERCLA's liability provisions have frequently attacked the Act's sweeping retroactive effect on constitutional grounds. To date, all these constitutional challenges have been unsuccessful. *See, e.g., United States v. Monsanto*, 858 F.2d 160, 173–74 (4th Cir. 1988); *United States v. Northeastern Pharmaceutical & Chemical Co.*, 810 F.2d 726, 732–34 (8th Cir. 1986); *United States v. Shell Oil Co.*, 605 F.Supp. 1064, 1069 (D. Colo. 1985).

These cases conclude that CERCLA did not create retroactive liability at all, because it simply imposed post-enactment prospective obligations for past, pre-enactment private actions. Alternatively, since one of the triggers of CERCLA liability is a present or threatened *release*, CERCLA can be understood to apply prospectively to remedy current problems, not punish past conduct. *See, e.g., Usery v. Turner Elkhorn Mining Co.*, 428 U.S. 1 (1976); *Concrete Pipe & Products of California, Inc. v. Construction Laborers Pension Trust for Southern California*, 508 U.S. 602 (1993). Following two other Supreme Court cases on retroactivity in other settings, *Landgraf v.*

---

46.   In fact, however, most major Superfund sites involve disposal practices that were irresponsible by any standard.

USI Film Products, 511 U.S. 244 (1994) and *Eastern Enterprises v. Apfel*, 524 U.S. 498 (1998) (plurality), some have seen an opening for a renewed attack on CERCLA. Bruce Howard, *Environmental Law: CERCLA Retroactivity*, The National Law Journal, (Jan. 4, 1999); T. Waugh, *CERCLA's Retroactivity: Has the Door Been Opened for a Reevaluation of Whether CERCLA Applies to Preenactment Activities?*, 14 J. of Natural Resources and Envt'l Law 31 (1999). So far, however, the lower courts have continued to uphold CERCLA's constitutionality. *Combined Properties / Greenbriar Ltd. Partnership v. Morrow*, 58 F. Supp. 2d 675 (E.D. Va. 1999); *United States v. Alcan Aluminum Corp.*, 49 F. Supp. 2d 96 (N.D.N.Y. 1999).

2. Potentially Responsible Parties

We now consider the potential defendants in CERCLA actions. CERCLA liability applies to four classes of parties:

(1) the "owner and operator" of a hazardous waste site or "facility";

(2) "any person who at the time of disposal of any hazardous substance owned or operated" a site or facility where "hazardous substances were disposed of";

(3) "any person who by contract, agreement, or otherwise arranged for disposal or treatment, or who arranged with a transporter for transport for disposal or treatment" of hazardous substances; or

(4) "any person who accepts or accepted any hazardous substances for transport" to "facilities * * * or sites" for disposal or treatment.

§ 107(a). These "potentially responsible parties," or PRPs, may be liable for all of the costs specified by the statute, under the standards of liability just described. Note especially that these categories are not exclusive. There is no reason that a PRP cannot be liable cumulatively or alternatively under any category that fits.

The actual task of determining who fits into these categories has been arduous, spawning hundreds of lawsuits. Some of the questions have arisen from the vague contours of the four statutory categories of PRPs, and we will address them first. We then address other questions that have arisen in the context of particular *types* of defendants—corporations, secured lenders, and others—whose characteristics fit awkwardly with the statutory categories. For example,

- should a truly innocent purchaser of a contaminated site become an "owner" and thereby a liable PRP?

- May a purchaser of such a site avoid liability by selling it to some unsuspecting buyer?

- Is the parent corporation of a subsidiary that owns a hazardous waste site also an "owner"?

- Is a successor corporation responsible for the liabilities that took it over?

- May a company be an "operator" if it does not actively manage the day-to-day activities of the waste disposal site?

- Is a lender who makes loans to a waste-disposal business an "operator"?

- Is the sale of a not-yet contaminated product an act that constitutes "arrang[ing] for disposal"?

Like the standards of liability, early PRP decisions tended to read the PRP provisions quite expansively in order to accomplish the statute's broad remedial design, but later decisions have retreated somewhat. Unlike the standards of liability, in regard to PRP provisions, Congress has decisively stepped in to resolve some of the more glaring problems with the original statute.

a.   CURRENT OWNER/OPERATOR

Section 107(a)(1) imposes liability on the "owner and operator" of a facility. Although the presence of the word "and" indicates that this is a conjunctive test (the owner must also operate the facility or site), the courts have read it to be disjunctive in context, that is, *either* present owners *or* operators may be liable. *Redwing Carriers, Inc. v. Saraland Apartments*, 94 F.3d 1489, 1498 (11th Cir. 1996). If one wishes to receive guidance on the question of who is an "owner," and who is an "operator," the statute's basic definition is spectacularly unhelpful in its circularity. Section 101(20)(A) defines "owner or operator" as "any person owning or operating." One is left with the commonsense notion that Congress must have intended to hold strictly liable those parties whose status put them in a position to do something about the waste at the site—the present owner has most immediate control over how the land is used, and the operator in some way manages the activity that resulted in the release of hazardous substances. For these two parties, it should be immaterial that they might not have caused the problem, or that they could have been ignorant of it. The more troubling issue is, of course, that a present owner/operator may still be liable even though that party neither owned nor operated the site or facility at the time of the disposal or release of the hazardous substance there. *State of New York v. Shore Realty Corp.*, 759 F.2d 1032, 1043–44 (2d Cir. 1985); *City of Phoenix v. Garbage Services Co.*, 816 F.Supp. 564 (D. Ariz. 1993).

i.   Owners

A current owner is liable under § 107(a)(1) so long as that owner holds title in fee simple. In that case, it is irrelevant that the waste disposal was done by someone other than the owner, such as a lessee. *United States v. Monsanto Co.*, 858 F.2d 160, 168 (4th Cir. 1988); Anthony Fejfar, *Landowner–Lessor Liability Under CERCLA*, 53 Md. L. Rev. 157 (1994). The hard cases with respect to ownership involve lesser property interests. Easement holders are usually not owners if they exercise little control over the waste site. *Long Beach Unified School Dist. v. Dorothy B. Godwin California Living Trust*, 32 F.3d 1364 (9th Cir. 1994); *Comment, Extending Liability Under CERCLA: Easement Holders and the Scope of Controls*, 87 Nw. U. L. Rev. 992 (1993). Lessees may be liable as an owner if they maintain substantial "site control." *United States v. A & N Cleaners & Launderers, Inc.*, 788 F.Supp. 1317, 1330–34 (S.D. N.Y. 1992). Corporate owners and shareholders may likewise find themselves liable as § 107(a) "owners" if they influence or control waste disposal decisions. *Lansford–Coaldale Joint Water Auth. v. Tonolli Corp.*, 4 F.3d 1209, 1225 (3d Cir. 1993) (partial owner of a corporation may be liable under CERCLA); *State of Idaho v. Bunker Hill Co.*, 635 F.Supp. 665, 670–72 (D. Idaho 1986) (parent corporation liable for actions of subsidiary); *Donahey v. Bogle*, 987 F.2d 1250 (6th Cir. 1993) (sole shareholder with sufficient authority to prevent contamination may be an "owner"), *vacated sub nom. Livingstone v. Donahey*, 512 U.S. 1201 (1994) (case remanded to Sixth Circuit, in light of *Key Tronic Corp. v. United States*, 510 U.S. 1031 (1993)). *See generally* E.C. Birg, *Redefining "Owner or Operator" Under CERCLA to Preserve Traditional Notions of Corporate Law*, 43 EMORY L.J. 771 (1994).[47]

WHEN DOES A PERSON BECOME AN "OWNER?"

A contaminated site might be bought and sold multiple times after it poses a threat due to the hazardous substances that have been dumped there. Sometimes ownership is fleeting—a party could own the site only for a few months before it is sold. When the waste site is subject to many changes of ownership in a short period of time, the question arises as to when an owner becomes a current owner for purposes of § 107(a)(1). Current ownership could be based on who the owner was at the time the site first became contaminated, the time the site was identified as a threat, the time the site was NPL-listed, or the time a CERCLA liability lawsuit was filed. *United States v. Fleet Factors Corp.*, 901 F.2d 1550, 1554 (11th Cir. 1990) (time complaint is filed).

Three common relationships to property have given rise to much CERCLA litigation:

Secured creditors—One class of passive owners who have tried to resist CERCLA liability are lenders and secured creditors. There is an explicit statutory exclusion from the "owner or operator" category of a person "who, without participating in * * * management * * * holds indicia of ownership primarily to protect his security interest in the * * * facility."[48]

---

47. *See also* Fishbein Family Partnership v. PPG Indus., Inc., 871 F.Supp. 764 (D.N.J. 1994) (stock ownership alone does not establish "owner" status).

Similarly, limited partners have been found not to be "owners" under applicable state law, and therefore not "owners" under § 107(e). Redwing Carriers, Inc. v. Saraland Apartments, 94 F.3d 1489 (11th Cir. 1996). Some fiduciaries holding title for another may be an "owner," such as a trustee of a testamentary trust. Briggs & Stratton Corp. v. Concrete Sales & Services, 20 F. Supp. 2d 1356, 1367 (M.D. Ga. 1998); City of Phoenix v. Garbage Services Co., 816 F.Supp. 564 (D. Ariz. 1993); W.C. Santos, *Trustee Liability in CERCLA: Confronting the Problems and Proposing Solutions,* 19 WM. & MARY ENVTL. LAW AND POLICY REV. 69 (1994). Other fiduciaries, such as executors or conservators, have far less power and control than trustees, and they are not "owners." Castlerock Estates, Inc. v. Estate of Walter S. Markham, 871 F.Supp. 360, 366 (N.D. Cal. 1994).

48. CERCLA § 101(20)(A)(iii). This section has been subject to a 1992 EPA interpretative

Nonetheless, one important case found liable a secured creditor whose "involvement with the management of the facility is sufficiently broad to support the inference that it could affect hazardous waste disposal decisions if it so chose." *United States v. Fleet Factors Corp.*, 901 F.2d 1550, 1558 (11th Cir. 1990). Subsequent cases, as well as the EPA, have backed off the *Fleet Factors* result by immunizing secured creditors who do not actually participate in the management of the contaminated site. *United States v. McLamb*, 5 F.3d 69 (4th Cir. 1993); *Lansford–Coaldale Water Auth. v. Tonolli Corp.*, 4 F.3d 1209; (3d Cir. 1993); *Organic Chemical Site PRP Group v. Total Petroleum*, 58 F. Supp. 2d 755 (W.D. Mich. 1999); J.S. Flood, *The EPA's Interpretative Rule on CERCLA § 101(20)(A): Does it Create a Safe Harbor for Secured Lenders?*, 24 Rutgers L.J. 511 (1993).

Lessor / Lessee Liability—As an owner of the site, a lessor may be liable for contamination caused by the lessee. *United States v. Monsanto*, 858 F.2d 160, 168–69 (4th Cir. 1988). A lessee may also qualify as an "owner" for purposes of § 107(a). *United States v. A & N Cleaners and Launderers, Inc.*, 788 F.Supp. 1317 (S.D. N.Y. 1992). Lessees may therefore be liable under CERCLA, particularly if they could control decisions regarding disposal of waste at the site. *Nurad, Inc. v. Hooper & Sons Co.*, 966 F.2d 837, 842 (4th Cir. 1992) (lessee was an "operator"); *see also United States v. Saporito*, 684 F.Supp.2d 1043 (N.D. Ill. 2010) (finding equipment lessor to be an "owner" under CERCLA, and therefore liable for remediation costs). *But see Commander Oil Corp. v. Barlo Equipment Corp.*, 215 F.3d 321, 332 (2d Cir. 2000) (denying liability of sublessor for contamination of property because "he had not managed, directed, or conducted operations specifically related to pollution"). A lessee might be able to escape liability if the contamination was entirely caused by the lessor, and preceded the lessee's tenancy. *Cf. Westwood Pharmaceuticals, Inc. v. National Fuel Gas Dist. Corp.*, 964 F.2d 85, 89 (2d Cir. 1992).

Innocent Purchaser Liability—If a buyer of contaminated land becomes the "owner" of the waste site, that purchaser may become liable under § 107(a). To prevent this result in the case of truly innocent purchasers, the SARA amendments clarified that such buyers can be relieved of liability if they did not have knowledge of the hazardous substances when the land was acquired, and if at acquisition the buyer conducted "all appropriate inquiry into the previous ownership and uses of the property." § 101(35)(B). This provision requires environmental assessments prior to purchase. Inadequate preacquisition inquiry voids the innocent purchaser defense. *See, e.g., In re Hemingway Transport, Inc.*, 993 F.2d 915, 933 (1st Cir. 1993). Purchasers should also be advised to consult relevant insurance policies prior to acquisition. *See* David M. Smith, *Sudden Exposure: Accessing Historic Insurance Policies for the Environmental Liabilities Associated With Newly Acquired Properties or Acquisitions*, 25 Ecology L. Q. 439 (1998).

Is there a common element in the resolution of these questions about who is an "owner?" What is the "touchstone" for determining whether someone is an owner? Does the touchstone make sense?

---

rule, and a clarifying CERCLA amendment, both of which will be addressed later in the chapter under "lender liability."

ii. Operators

Non-owners can be liable if they are termed "operators." An operator is one who has the legal authority to control the activities at the site, and who actually exercises that control. Most cases do not find individuals or entities liable under § 107(a)(1) unless they had "substantial control" or "authority" over the activities of another party who produced the pollution, and in fact exercised that authority, either by personally performing the tasks necessary to dispose of the hazardous wastes, or by directing others to perform those tasks. *American Cyanamid Co. v. Capuano*, 381 F.3d 6, 23 (1st Cir. 2004) (finding operator liability where operator developed the idea for using the site, prepared the site for dumping, arranged for waste to be dumped at the site, showed transporters where to dump on the site, and collected payment for allowing dumping). *United States v. Gurley*, 43 F.3d 1188, 1193 (8th Cir. 1994); *FMC Corp. v. United States Dept. of Commerce*, 29 F.3d 833 (3d Cir. 1994); *Lansford–Coaldale Joint Water Authority v. Tonolli Corp.*, 4 F.3d 1209, 1221 (3d Cir. 1993). If there is not "active involvement" in the activity that produces the contamination, "operator" liability will not attach. *Geraghty and Miller, Inc. v. Conoco, Inc.*, 27 F. Supp. 2d 918, 924–925 (S.D. Tex. 1998) (environmental contractor not an operator who was employed merely to investigate and assist in construction of a facility for remedying contamination in the soils), *aff'd in part, rev'd in part*, 234 F.3d 917 (5th Cir. 2000) (reversed on portion of decision barring counterclaim due to statute of limitations); *Washington v. United States*, 930 F.Supp. 474, 483 (W.D. Wash. 1996) (no liability if party had only contractual relationship to entity engaged in waste disposal, where the contractual relationship was limited to managing costs, not instructing the polluting entity whether, or how, to dispose of its wastes).

If the necessary control is present, then a wide range of parties can be held liable as a § 107(a)(1) operator:

- *Tenants–Clear Lake Properties v. Rockwell Intern. Corp.*, 959 F.Supp. 763 (S.D. Tex. 1997) (as current operator, tenant was liable under CERCLA even absent showing that tenant had ability to control facility at time of release of hazardous substance); *Pierson Sand & Gravel, Inc. v. Pierson Township*, 851 F.Supp. 850, 854 (W.D. Mich. 1994) (lessee's control over the operation makes it liable).

- *Contractors–Ganton Technologies, Inc. v. Quadion Corp.*, 834 F.Supp. 1018, 1021–22 (N.D. Ill. 1993) (contractors hired to clean up hazardous wastes can be operators if they make the contamination worse).

- *Trust Fund Beneficiaries–State of North Carolina ex rel. Howes v. W.R. Peele, Sr. Trust*, 876 F.Supp. 733 (E.D. N.C. 1995) (if an individual is an "operator" PRP, the trust fund beneficiary of that PRP can be liable as well).

- *Estates–United States v. Martell*, 887 F. Supp. 1183, 1188 (N.D. Ind. 1995) (estate of deceased operator may be liable).

- *Agents–Redwing Carriers, Inc. v. Saraland Apartments*, 94 F.3d 1489 (11th Cir. 1996) (property management agent that prepares budgets, inspects, and performs repair work is an operator).

- *Transporters–Browning–Ferris Ind. of Ill. v. Ter Maat*, 13 F. Supp. 2d 756, 765 (N.D. Ill. 1998), *aff'd in part, rev'd in part*, 195 F.3d 953, 955 (7th Cir. 1999) (upholding district court's allocation of responsibility to transporter) (transporter may also be liable as operator where transporter was joint-operator of the contaminated waste site).

- *Corporate Officers and Directors–United States v. Lowe*, 29 F.3d 1005 (5th Cir. 1994) (a corporate official is liable as an operator, because the official created the harmful condition, and might receive indemnification under corporate bylaws).

- *Corporations–Sidney S. Arst. Co. v. Pipefitters Welfare Educ. Fund*, 25 F.3d 417, 421–22 (7th Cir. 1994) (corporation "operates" hazardous waste site, not an individual within the corporation, when the individual did not directly and personally engage in the conduct that led to the environmental damage).[49]

Governmental entities can also be liable as operators. One leading case, *FMC Corp. v. U.S. Department of Commerce*, 29 F.3d 833 (3d Cir. 1994) (*en banc*) found that the United States qualified as an operator of the plaintiff's facility where it required a company to manufacture a product that yielded a hazardous waste product and maintained a significant degree of control over the production process through regulations and on-site inspectors. The court also concluded that the federal government could be liable when it "engaged in regulatory activities extensive enough to make it an operator * * * even though no private party could engage in the regulatory activities at issue." *Id.* at 840. Although the *FMC Corp.* case hinted that the government could be liable under CERCLA merely for its regulatory activities, subsequent cases have tended to reject such arguments. *See United States v. Town of Brighton*, 153 F.3d 307, 315–16 (6th Cir. 1998) (mere regulation does not suffice to make a government entity liable, but actual operation and "macromanagement" does); *Washington v. United States*, 930 F. Supp. 474, 483 (W.D. Wash. 1996) (government's contractual relationship with company that caused hazardous waste problem insufficient for operator liability where there was no "[a]ctive involvement in the activity that produce[d] the contamination"); *Delaney v. Town of Carmel*, 55 F. Supp. 2d 237 (S.D.N.Y. 1999) (government entities liable as operators only upon a showing of actual and substantial control); *United States v. American Color & Chemical Corp.*, 858 F.Supp. 445 (M.D. Pa. 1994) (United States not an "operator" when it is acting in a regulatory capacity to bring about a clean-up).

---

49. The direct liability provided by CERCLA for corporations is distinct from the *derivative liability* that results from piercing the corporate veil. The United States Supreme Court has concluded that if a subsidiary that operates, but does not own, a waste site is so pervasively controlled by its parent for a sufficiently improper purpose to warrant veil piercing, the parent may be held derivatively liable for the subsidiary's acts as an operator. *United States v. Bestfoods*, 524 U.S. 51, 118 S.Ct. 1876, 1886 n.10 (1998).

Courts that have differed in finding operator liability have often differed on the test of control. Some courts hold that a party may be an operator simply because that party had the legal authority to control and make decisions about the site in which case it is irrelevant that control may not have been exercised. They have "decline[d] to absolve from CERCLA liability a hypothetical party who possessed the authority to abate the damage * * * but who declined to actually exercise that authority by undertaking efforts at a clean-up." *Nurad Inc. v. William E. Hooper & Sons Co.*, 966 F.2d 837, 842 (4th Cir. 1992). *See also Pierson Sand & Gravel, Inc. v. Pierson Township*, 851 F.Supp. 850, 855 (W.D. Mich. 1994), *aff'd* 89 F.3d 835 (6th Cir. 1996) (applying "authority" test in concluding that township was operator in leasing property and contracting with the owner to operate a landfill); *Nutrasweet Co. v. X–L Engineering Corp.*, 933 F.Supp. 1409 (N.D. Ill. 1996) (corporate official is operator who has knowledge of the waste disposal activity, and authority to prevent it, but acquiesces); *State of California v. Celtor Chemical Corp.*, 901 F.Supp. 1481 (N.D. Cal. 1995) (same). This line of authority stands in contrast to courts that have adopted an "actual control" test. Under this test, two conditions must be met before operator liability attaches: (1) the defendant had the authority to determine whether and how there would be a disposal of hazardous wastes, and (2) that defendant actually exercised the authority, either by personally performing the tasks necessary to dispose of the wastes, or by directing others to perform the tasks. *United States v. Gurley*, 43 F.3d 1188, 1193 (8th Cir. 1994); *Lansford–Coaldale Joint Water Auth. v. Tonolli Corp.*, 4 F.3d 1209, 1220–24 (3d Cir. 1993); K.C. 1986 *Ltd. Partnership v. Reade Manufacturing*, 33 F. Supp. 2d 1143 (W.D. Mo. 1998); *Maxus Energy Corp. v. United States*, 898 F.Supp. 399 (N.D. Tex. 1995).

Without some level of involvement in day-to-day operations, entities are not operators even though they may have had the power to control the waste disposal practices of another party. *United States v. Consolidated Rail Corp.*, 729 F.Supp. 1461 (D. Del. 1990) (no operator liability even though defendant initially set up the operations at the waste site and pre-approved shipments of hazardous wastes there). Conversely, one who is "in charge" or who supervises the operations at a site is an "operator." *United States v. Northeastern Pharmaceutical & Chemical Co.*, 810 F.2d 726, 743–44 (8th Cir. 1986). One of the central components of the "actual control" test is that CERCLA "operator" liability cannot be triggered simply by being in a position to prevent contamination. *Long Beach Unified School Dist. v. Godwin California Living Trust*, 32 F.3d 1364 (9th Cir. 1994). *See also Z & Z Leasing, Inc. v. Graying Reel, Inc.*, 873 F.Supp. 51, 54–55 (E.D. Mich. 1995) (mere capacity to influence hazardous waste decisions does not suffice to establish operator status). An important corollary of the actual control test is that the rationale affirmative acts are a prerequisite to liability; omissions will not suffice. *United States v. Township of Brighton*, 153 F.3d 307, 315 (6th Cir. 1998).[50]

---

50. The actual control test also means that those who supply materials to a hazardous waste facility, or design and build such a facility, are likely not "operators." *See Edward Hines Lumber Co. v. Vulcan Materials Co.*, 861 F.2d 155 (7th Cir. 1988):

In 1998, the United States Supreme Court had occasion to take up the meaning of "operator" under CERCLA in *United States v. Bestfoods*, 524 U.S. 51 (1998).

> [W]e * * * again rue the uselessness of CERCLA's definition of a facility's "operator" as "any person * * * operating" the facility, 42 U.S.C. § 9601(20)(A)(ii), which leaves us to do the best we can to give the term its "ordinary or natural meaning." In a mechanical sense, to "operate" ordinarily means "[t]o control the functioning of; run: *operate a sewing machine*." AMERICAN HERITAGE DICTIONARY 1268 (3d ed. 1992); *see also* WEBSTER'S NEW INTERNATIONAL DICTIONARY 1707 (2d ed. 1958) ("to work; as, to *operate* a machine"). And in the organizational sense more obviously intended by CERCLA, the word ordinarily means "[t]o conduct the affairs of; manage: *operate a business*." AMERICAN HERITAGE DICTIONARY, *supra*, at 1268; *see also* WEBSTER'S NEW INTERNATIONAL DICTIONARY, *supra*, at 1707 ("to manage"). So, under CERCLA, an operator is simply someone who directs the workings of, manages, or conducts the affairs of a facility. To sharpen the definition for purposes of CERCLA's concern with environmental contamination, an operator must manage, direct, or conduct operations specifically related to pollution, that is, operations having to do with the leakage or disposal of hazardous waste, or decisions about compliance with environmental regulations.
>
> * * *
>
> In our enquiry into the meaning Congress presumably had in mind when it used the verb "to operate," we recognized that the statute obviously meant something more than mere mechanical activation of pumps and valves, and must be read to contemplate "operation" as including the exercise of direction over the facility's activities.

524 U.S. at 66–71.

NOTES AND QUESTIONS

1.   Why *not* hold the government liable as an operator for regulating a facility? Even if such a rule were considered too broad, could certain *types* of regulation give rise to liability? What about failure to regulate?[51]

2.   What test does the *Bestfoods* case seem to adopt: "authority to control" or "actual control"? Which test is the better one? It depends, presumably on the purposes of CERCLA—what are the relevant purposes of

---

"The statute does not fix liability on slipshod architects, clumsy engineers, poor construction contractors, or negligent suppliers of on-the-job training.... The liability falls on owners and operators; architects, engineers, construction contractors, and instructors must chip in only to the extent they have agreed to do so by contract." *Id* at 157.

51.   *Compare United States v. Dart Indus.*, 847 F.2d 144, 146 (4th Cir. 1988) (declining to classify local government as operator merely for failing to regulate adequately), with *CPC International, Inc. v. Aerojet–General Corp.*, 731 F.Supp. 783, 788–89 (W.D. Mich. 1989) (government may be an operator if it assumes clean-up responsibilities, but fails to finish the job, thereby increasing remediation costs).

CERCLA, and which test best serves them? Which test is best coordinated with the meaning of "owner"—should the tests for the two terms be parallel or complimentary?

3. Suppose that your client has her eye on a piece of property, which she strongly suspects is contaminated, which she would like to use for future expansion of her chain of sports equipment stores. The client would ordinarily purchase the property now, but she does not want to incur the risks of CERCLA liability until she knows that her business is expanding. Can you think of ways that she might prevent the sale of the property to another business, without becoming an owner or operator? Would an option contract work?

b. PAST OWNERS/OPERATORS "AT THE TIME OF DISPOSAL"

Section 107(a)(2) states that a PRP may be "any person who at the time of disposal of any hazardous substance owned or operated any facility at which such hazardous substances were disposed of." Under this provision, *past* owners and operators may be liable. CERCLA therefore creates two categories of PRPs—those that currently own or operate the waste site/facility, and those that did so in the past. This latter, "past owner/operator" category, in turn can be divided into two further classes. In the first class, the easy case, a person owned the land at the time a "disposal of any hazardous substance" took place. Section 101(29) of CERCLA defines "disposal" by borrowing RCRA's broad definition, which includes "the discharge, deposit, injection, dumping, spilling, leaking, or placing of * * * hazardous waste into or on any land or water. * * * " RCRA § 1004(3). So, if a party owned land on which wastes were "deposited" or "dumped" or "discharged" that party would be a past owner PRP under § 107(a)(2). *See National Acceptance Co. v. Regal Products, Inc.*, 838 F.Supp. 1315, 1319–20 (E.D. Wis. 1993).

Note that the RCRA definition includes both active (dumping, placing) and passive (leaking, spilling) means of entry into the environment. Thus, the second class of past owner/operator, the more difficult case, involves persons who owned or operated the waste site *after* the time the initial disposal took place but *before* the time the CERCLA liability lawsuit is filed. The question facing courts considering this second class is whether such past owners/operators may also be liable under § 107(a)(2) if the wastes may have, without human intervention, migrated further into the soil or groundwater during the alleged PRP's ownership or operation of the site. Courts have split on this issue. If CERCLA intended that term to apply only during a one-time occurrence deposit of hazardous wastes, then passive past owners are immunized from liability. If "disposal" includes any migration or movement of the wastes after they have been dumped at the site, then passive owners/operators may be liable. The RCRA definition (§ 1004(3)) uses words like "deposit" and "injection" and "dumping," which suggest a single occurrence. However, the definition also uses the word "leaking," and assumes that there may be disposal when the hazardous waste "enter[s] the environment." These phrases presume that a "disposal" is present as a result of a process that may occur over a lengthy period of time.

The leading case opting for an interpretation of "disposal" sufficiently broad to include passive owners is *Nurad, Inc. v. William E. Hooper & Sons Co.*, 966 F.2d 837 (4th Cir. 1992). The court believed that the "disposal" definition contemplates action that has a passive component, encompassing the leakage or spillage of hazardous waste without any active human participation. *See also Redwing Carriers, Inc. v. Saraland Apartments*, 94 F.3d 1489, 1508 (11th Cir. 1996); *State ex rel. Howes v. W.R. Peele, Sr. Trust*, 876 F.Supp. 733, 747 (E.D. N.C. 1995). One rationale for these decisions is that absent liability for passive disposal, there would be no disincentive for past owners who did nothing while hazardous wastes slowly contaminated the surrounding environment.

Other courts refuse to follow the *Nurad* rationale. These define "disposal" more narrowly to require that a person introduce ("place") formerly controlled or contained hazardous substances into the environment. Under this interpretation, only prior owners or operators who had a relationship with the site at the time the hazardous substances were actively added may be liable. *Bob's Beverage, Inc. v. Acme Inc.*, 264 F.3d 692 (6th Cir. 2001) (finding predecessor warehouse owner not liable for response costs, and its action of replacing the septic system did not cause a "disposal" of hazardous waste). *ABB Industrial Systems, Inc. v. Prime Technology, Inc.* 120 F.3d 351 (2d Cir. 1997) (CERCLA definition of "disposal" does not mention leaching); *United States v. CDMG Realty Co.*, 96 F.3d 706 (3d Cir. 1996) (since definitional terms "discharge" and "deposit" and "dumping" require some human action, courts should similarly construe terms "spilling" and "leaking," which then negates a definition of "disposal" encompassing gradual passive migration of contaminants); *Joslyn Manufacturing Co. v. Koppers Co., Inc.*, 40 F.3d 750 (5th Cir. 1994) (no active disposal occurred during defendant's ownership of the site).

Several rationales support the "active disposal" cases. Since CERCLA's primary policy is to enforce a "polluter pays" principle, prior owners and operators should not be liable for mere passive migration since these parties are not true polluters. *Carson Harbor Village, Ltd. v. Unocal Corp.*, 270 F.3d 863 (9th Cir. 2001) (en banc) (determining gradual passive migration of contamination through the soil not to be "disposal"). Also, the two terms that arguably justify liability for passive owners/operators—"leak" and "spill"—both seem to assume something other than slow passive migration of wastes. *See Idylwoods Assocs. v. Mader Capital, Inc.*, 915 F.Supp. 1290 (W.D. N.Y. 1996). A "leak" usually requires a discharge from some measurable opening, not a diffuse movement of a substance. A "spill" also suggests a rapid torrent, not a passive migration over the course of several years. *In re Tutu Wells Contamination Litigation*, 994 F.Supp. 638, 668 (D. Virgin Islands 1998). Moreover, an interpretation of "disposal" that includes passive disposal might gut the so-called "innocent landowner" defense found in § 101(35)(A). This defense protects purchasers who acquire land "after disposal" of a hazardous substance and who have no knowledge of the contamination. If otherwise innocent buyers could not assert the § 101(35)(A) because they are liable as passive owners, then the innocent purchaser defense would largely become a nullity. *United States v. CDMG*

Realty Co., 96 F.3d 706, 716 (3d Cir. 1996); *United States v. Petersen Sand & Gravel, Inc.*, 806 F.Supp. 1346 (N.D. Ill. 1992). *See generally* Craig May, Note, *Taking Action—Rejecting the Passive Disposal Theory of Prior Owner Liability Under CERCLA*, 17 VA. ENVTL. L. J. 385 (1998); Andrew R. Klein, *Hazardous Waste Clean-up and Intermediate Landowners: Reexamining the Liability–Based Approach*, 21 HARV. ENVTL. L. REV. 337 (1997).

Figure 6.3–Is this a "spill?"[52]

NOTES AND QUESTIONS

1.   Can you think of other reasons for adopting the active or passive disposal theory? Can you make anything of the difference between "disposal" and "release," another term in the statute? (You will first need to figure out what "release" means and how it is used.)

2.   Can you develop an argument based on the language of section 107(a)(2)? Why is past ownership qualified by "at the time of disposal," while present ownership is not? Who was Congress trying to protect? Does that suggest an answer to the passive-active question?

52.   Photo by Greg Lief (photos@gregleif.com, http://www.greglief.com).

c. GENERATORS OF WASTE–PERSONS WHO "ARRANGED FOR DISPOSAL OR TREATMENT"

A third PRP category is set out in § 107(a)(3): persons who "by contract, agreement, or otherwise arranged for disposal or treatment, or arranged with a transporter for disposal or treatment, of hazardous substances" which they "owned or possessed." Arrangers—typically, the generators of the waste—are the first cause of the contaminated site that will be subject to a CERCLA clean-up. Prior to CERCLA, generators could rid themselves of hazardous waste simply by hiring a waste hauler who would take care of it: out of sight, out of mind. With the advent of arranger liability, a generator of wastes cannot ignore how the wastes will eventually be treated or discarded; if a hazardous substance generated by a private party is sent to a site where a release occurs (or threatens), that party is subject to CERCLA liability.

The language of § 107(a)(3) has become one of the most frequently litigated provisions of CERCLA, in part because it is unclear in several important respects (a trait is shares with other parts of CERCLA), and in part because it is the provision that creates by far the largest universe of PRPs.[53]

The language of § 107(a)(3) makes a person liable where there has been an arrangement for "disposal" of hazardous substances "at any [site] * * * containing such hazardous substances." The word "such," in referring to the "hazardous substances" contained at the dump site, could be read to require either that the site contain the waste generated by the defendant, or that hazardous substances like those found in the defendant's waste must be found there. Most courts have rejected the "proof of ownership" requirement, and have adopted instead a four-element test for generator liability:

>   (1) the generator in some fashion disposed of its hazardous substances at the site in question;

>   (2) the site now contains hazardous substances *like* those disposed by the generator

>   (3) there has been a release (or threat of release) of some hazardous substance (not necessarily the generator's or wastes like the generator's);

>   (4) which has caused the incurrence of response costs.

United States v. Monsanto Co., 858 F.2d 160, 169 (4th Cir. 1988); *United States v. Mottolo*, 695 F.Supp. 615, 625 (D.N.H. 1988); *United States v. Wade*, 577 F.Supp. 1326 (E.D. Pa. 1983).

A few core issues predominate the analysis of generator liability:

Is it relevant that the generator was not at fault and acted with due care?—The general rule of strict liability applies with respect to generators

---

53.   There are about 1400 NPL sites, so the number of present and even past owners is relatively circumscribed. But many of those sites had dozens or even hundreds of waste contributors.

who took every precaution in the disposal of their wastes. They are liable if the transporter of the wastes, or some subsequent entity who disposed of the wastes, left behind a contaminated waste site. *See Pierson Sand & Gravel, Inc. v. Pierson Township*, 851 F.Supp. 850, 855 (W.D. Mich. 1994), *aff'd* 89 F.3d 835 (6th Cir. 1996) (arranger liability may attach even though defendant did not know the substances would be deposited at a particular site); *Acme Printing Ink Co. v. Menard, Inc.*, 881 F.Supp. 1237, 1249 (E.D. Wis. 1995) (defendant subject to generator liability even though it did not choose the destination of the waste); *United States v. Parsons*, 723 F.Supp. 757, 761–62 (N.D. Ga. 1989) (generator liable although it had insisted that proper disposal practices be followed).

What does it mean to require that the hazardous substances be "owned or possessed" by the arranger?—To be found liable as an arranger-generator, the party must have had actual or constructive "ownership" or "possession" of the hazardous wastes. While the ownership prong is satisfied if the generator retains formal title to the product throughout its journey to the site, *United States v. Aceto Agr. Chemicals Corp.*, 872 F.2d 1373, 1375 (8th Cir. 1989); *United States v. Vertac Chemical Corp.*, 966 F.Supp. 1491, 1501 (E.D. Ark. 1997), proof of continuing ownership is not a prerequisite to liability. *Cadillac Fairview/California, Inc. v. United States*, 41 F.3d 562, 565 (9th Cir. 1994). Since the "owned or possessed" requirement is written in the disjunctive, possession alone can satisfy § 107(a)(3), where constructive possession suffices. *United States v. Northeastern Pharmaceutical & Chemical Co., Inc.*, 810 F.2d 726, 743 (8th Cir. 1986). Constructive possession is present if the generator had the authority or duty to exercise control of the hazardous substance, *Briggs & Stratton Corp. v. Concrete Sales & Services, Inc.*, 990 F.Supp. 1473, 1479 (M.D. Ga. 1998), or was actively involved in the decision to dispose of waste. *General Electric Co. v. AAMCO Transmissions, Inc.*, 962 F.2d 281, 286 (2d Cir. 1992); *Berg v. Popham*, 412 F.3d 1122 (9th Cir. 2005) ("[A]ctual involvement in the decision to dispose of waste" encompasses actions such as (1) recommending the use of hazardous chemical, and (2) designing and installing the system that disposes of the waste). While the "authority to control" test usually demands that the authority be exercised by affirmative act, in some cases it may be satisfied by authority and failure to act. *Redwing Carriers, Inc. v. Saraland Apartments*, 94 F.3d 1489, 1506 (11th Cir. 1996).

Are some parties excused from arranger liability?—Most courts agree that it is consistent with CERCLA's remedial purpose to interpret the loose language of § 107(a)(3) broadly and to extend liability beyond the typical manufacturer who hired a contractor or arranged with a transporter to dispose of its wastes at a dump site. Thus, while generators are the principal target of section 107(a)(3), a party need not have generated the waste to be found liable. *See, e.g., GenCorp, Inc. v. Olin Corp.,* 390 F.3d 433 (6th Cir. 2004) (finding arranger liability even when company did not realize it would create hazardous waste at the time it entered into its business agreement to build and operate a manufacturing plant, because company "necessarily approached this reality" when it approved the plant's construction plans which provided that the waste would be placed in drums and buried at an offsite location); *United States v. Mottolo*, 629 F.Supp. 56, 60 (D.N.H. 1984); *United States v. Parsons*, 723 F.Supp. 757, 762 (N.D. Ga. 1989) (liability attaches to one who simply possessed drums of waste and arranged with another company to transport them elsewhere); *United States v. Bliss*, 667 F.Supp. 1298, 1303 (E.D. Mo. 1987) (party who actively participated as a broker in the disposal of its customer's waste is liable). The question arises whether the large number of persons or entities who may have some control or relationship with the waste between its generation and ultimate disposal are also be liable. The cases tend to require some decisional nexus with the disposal of the hazardous materials, or some affirmative action influencing or profiting from the transactions leading to the disposal. *See, e.g., Morton Int'l, Inc. v. A.E. Staley Mfg. Co.*, 343 F.3d 669 (3d Cir. 2003) (explaining that the most important factors in determining arranger liability are *ownership* or *possession* of waste, *knowledge* that processing will release a hazardous substance, or *control* over the production process); *South Florida Water Management Dist. v. Montalvo*, 84 F.3d 402, 406–09 (11th Cir. 1996) (factors such as intent, ownership, and actual knowledge are relevant in deciding "arranger" liability); *United States v. Vertac Chemical Corp.*, 46 F.3d 803, 810–812 (8th Cir. 1995) (United States was not an arranger when it did not control the production of a hazardous substance, but merely contracted for its production); *Chatham Steel Corp. v. Brown*, 858 F.Supp. 1130, 1144 (N.D. Fla. 1994) (if a party does not have some control over the location and method of disposal, it should not be liable). Other courts have ruled that the mere ability or opportunity to control the disposal of hazardous substances does not make an entity an arranger; it is the *obligation* to exercise such control that is critical. *General Electric Co. v. AAMCO Transmissions, Inc.*, 962 F.2d 281, 286 (2d Cir. 1992); *United States v. Davis*, 1 F. Supp. 2d 125, 130–1 (D.R.I. 1998). The rationale behind these decisions has permitted courts to reject arranger liability for a number of parties who have been only indirectly connected with the disposal decision. *See, e.g., Concrete Sales & Services, Inc. v. Blue Bird Body Co.*, 211 F.3d 1333 (11th Cir. 2000) (determining that absent evidence that manufacturer took action or had any intent to dispose of hazardous substances, manufacturer was not an arranger when it loaned money to a facility it knew generated hazardous waste); *Redwing Carriers, Inc. v. Saraland Apartments*, 94 F.3d 1489 (11th Cir. 1996) (limited partners who promised to clean up); *United States v. TIC Investment Corp.*, 68 F.3d 1082, 1091 (8th Cir. 1995) (parent corporation did not incur arranger liability for a subsidiary's off-site disposal practices); *City of North Miami v. Berger*, 828 F.Supp. 401, 414 (E.D. Va. 1993) (attorneys who provided advice to owner of contaminated site not arrangers). Nor are parties liable as arrangers when unanticipated events produce contamination. *Amcart Indust. Corp. v. Detrex Corp.*, 2 F.3d 746, 751 (7th Cir. 1993) ("No one arranges for an accident."); *RSR Corp. v. Avanti Development, Inc.*, 68 68 F. Supp. 2d 1037 (S.D. Ind. 1999) (no arranger liability where event causing the release was an unanticipated fire).

In 2009, the Supreme Court discussed the meaning of § 9607(a)(3) when it determined whether Shell Oil Company was properly held liable as an entity that had "arranged for disposal" of hazardous substances within the meaning of § 9607(a)(3).

Burlington Northern and Santa Fe Railway Co. v. United States
129 S.Ct. 1870 (2009)

* * *

[See discussion of facts and procedure on page 517]

* * *

The Court of Appeals acknowledged that Shell did not qualify as a "traditional" arranger under § 9607(a)(3), insofar as it had not contracted with B & B to directly dispose of a hazardous waste product. Nevertheless, the court stated that Shell could still be held liable under a " 'broader' category of arranger liability' if the "disposal of hazardous wastes [wa]s a foreseeable byproduct of, but not the purpose of, the transaction giving rise to" arranger liability. Relying on CERCLA's definition of "disposal," which covers acts such as "leaking" and "spilling," 42 U.S.C. § 6903(3), the Ninth Circuit concluded that an entity could arrange for "disposal" "even if it did not intend to dispose" of a hazardous substance. Applying this theory of arranger liability to the District Court's findings of fact, the Ninth Circuit held that Shell arranged for the disposal of a hazardous substance through its sale and delivery of D-D. Under such circumstances, the court concluded, arranger liability was not precluded by the fact that the purpose of Shell's action had been to transport a useful and previously unused product to B & B for sale. We granted certiorari to determine whether Shell was properly held liable as an entity that had "arranged for disposal" of hazardous substances within the meaning of § 9607(a)(3).

CERCLA imposes strict liability for environmental contamination upon four broad classes of PRPs: (1) the owner and operator of a vessel or a facility, (2) any person who at the time of disposal of any hazardous substance owned or operated any facility at which such hazardous substances were disposed of, (3) any person who by contract, agreement, or otherwise arranged for disposal or treatment, or arranged with a transporter for transport for disposal or treatment, of hazardous substances owned or possessed by such person, by any other party or entity, at any facility or incineration vessel owned or operated by another party or entity and containing such hazardous substances, and (4) any person who accepts or accepted any hazardous substances for transport to disposal or treatment facilities, incineration vessels or sites selected by such person, from which there is a release, or a threatened release which causes the incurrence of response costs, of a hazardous substance.... 42 U.S.C. § 9607(a). Once an entity is identified as a PRP, it may be compelled to clean up a contaminated area or reimburse the Government for its past and future response costs.

In these cases, it is undisputed that the Railroads qualify as PRPs under both §§ 9607(a)(1) and 9607(a)(2) because they owned the land leased by B & B at the time of the contamination and continue to own it now. The more difficult question is whether Shell also qualifies as a PRP under § 9607(a)(3) by virtue of the circumstances surrounding its sales to B & B. To determine whether Shell may be held liable as an arranger, we begin with the language of the statute. As relevant here, § 9607(a)(3) applies to an entity that "arrange[s] for disposal … of hazardous substances." It is plain from the language of the statute that CERCLA liability would attach under § 9607(a)(3) if an entity were to enter into a transaction for the sole purpose of discarding a used and no longer useful hazardous substance. It is similarly clear that an entity could not be held liable as an arranger merely for selling a new and useful product if the purchaser of that product later, and unbeknownst to the seller, disposed of the product in a way that led to contamination. See *Freeman* v. *Glaxo Wellcome, Inc.*, 189 F.3d 160, 164; *Florida Power & Light Co.* v. *Allis Chalmers Corp.*, 893 F.2d 1313, 1318. Less clear is the liability attaching to the many permutations of "arrangements" that fall between these two extremes—cases in which the seller has some knowledge of the buyers' planned disposal or whose motives for the "sale" of a hazardous substance are less than clear. In such cases, courts have concluded that the determination whether an entity is an arranger requires a fact-intensive inquiry that looks beyond the parties' characterization of the transaction as a "disposal" or a "sale" and seeks to discern whether the arrangement was one Congress intended to fall within the scope of CERCLA's strict-liability provisions.

Although we agree that the question whether § 9607(a)(3) liability attaches is fact intensive and case specific, such liability may not extend beyond the limits of the statute itself. Because CERCLA does not specifically define what it means to "arrang[e] for" disposal of a hazardous substance, under the plain language of the statute, an entity may qualify as an arranger under § 9607(a)(3) when it takes intentional steps to dispose of a hazardous substance. See *Cello–Foil Prods., Inc.*, 100 F.3d at 1231 ("[I]t would be error for us not to recognize the indispensable role that state of mind must play in determining whether a party has 'otherwise arranged for disposal … of hazardous substances.' ").

The Governments do not deny that the statute requires an entity to "arrang[e] for" disposal; however, they interpret that phrase by reference to the statutory term "disposal," the Act broadly defines as "the discharge, deposit, injection, dumping, spilling, leaking, or placing of any solid waste or hazardous waste into or on any land or water." 42 U.S.C. § 6903(3). The Governments assert that by including unintentional acts such as "spilling" and "leaking" in the definition of disposal, Congress intended to impose liability on entities not only when they directly dispose of waste products but also when they engage in legitimate sales of hazardous substances knowing that some disposal may occur as a collateral consequence of the sale itself. Applying that reading of the statute, the Governments contend that Shell arranged for the disposal of D-D within the meaning of § 9607(a)(3) by shipping D-D to B & B under conditions it knew would result in the spilling of a portion of the hazardous substance by the purchaser or common carrier. Because these spills resulted in wasted D-D, a result Shell anticipated, the Governments insist that Shell was properly found to have arranged for the disposal of D-D.

While it is true that in some instances an entity's knowledge that its product will be leaked, spilled, dumped, or otherwise discarded may provide evidence of the entity's intent to dispose of its hazardous wastes, knowledge alone is insufficient to prove that an entity "planned for" the disposal, particularly when the disposal occurs as a peripheral result of the legitimate sale of an unused, useful product. In order to qualify as an arranger, Shell must have entered into the sale of D-D with the intention that at least a portion of the product be disposed of during the transfer process by one or more of the methods described in § 6903(3). Here, the facts found by the District Court do not support such a conclusion.

Although the evidence adduced at trial showed that Shell was aware that minor, accidental spills occurred during the transfer of D-D from the common carrier to B & B's bulk storage tanks after the product had arrived at the Arvin facility and had come under B & B's stewardship, the evidence does not support an inference that Shell intended such spills to occur. To the contrary, the evidence revealed that Shell took numerous steps to encourage its distributors to *reduce* the likelihood of such spills, providing them with detailed safety manuals, requiring them to maintain adequate storage facilities, and providing discounts for those that took safety precautions. Although Shell's efforts were less than wholly successful, given these facts, Shell's mere knowledge that spills and leaks continued to occur is insufficient grounds for concluding that Shell "arranged for" the disposal of D-D within the meaning of § 9607(a)(3). Accordingly, we conclude that Shell was not liable as an arranger for the contamination that occurred at B & B's Arvin facility.

* * *

NOTES AND QUESTIONS

1. In *Burlington Northern*, the Supreme Court suggested that courts conduct a fact-intensive review of the parties' intent when determining "arranger" liability. Several lower courts have translated this suggestion into practice. *Appleton Papers Inc. v. George A. Whiting Paper Co.,* No. 08–C–16, 2009 WL 5064049 (E.D. Wis., December 16, 2009) (finding that the defendants lacked the requisite intent to impose arranger liability); *United States v. Washington State Dep't of Transp.,* 665 F.Supp.2d 1233 (W.D. Wash. 2009) (holding that the defendant's liability turned on a fact-intensive inquiry that the parties had yet to conduct).

2. Applying prior case law and the holding of *Burlington Northern*, one scholar created several illustrations of situations that may or may not create arranger liability:

- A enters "into a transaction for the sole purpose of discarding a used and no longer useful hazardous substance." A is liable as an arranger.

- *A*, the original owner of Facility 1 and the generator of contaminated mud there, sold the property to B. B subsequently arranged for disposal of the waste mud at Facility 2, owned and operated by C. C sued A, alleging that by selling Facility 1, A had "arranged for" disposing of the site's leftover contaminated waste mud. Even though in selling the entire property to B, A also sold whatever waste existed on Facility 1, A did not arrange for the disposal of the waste mud from Facility 1 to Facility 2. A is not liable as an arranger.

- *A* sells used transformers containing the hazardous substance PCB to B. B subsequently, unbeknownst to A, disposes of the transformers in a way that leads to contamination. A is not liable as an arranger.

- *A* is aware that minor, accidental spills occurred during the transfer of a product containing a hazardous substance from a common carrier to B's bulk storage tanks after the product had arrived at the facility and had come under B's stewardship. This knowledge does not support an inference that A intended such spills to occur. A is not liable as an arranger for the contamination that occurred at B's facility.

Alfred R. Light, *Restatement for Arranger Liability Under CERCLA: Implications of Burlington Northern for Superfund Jurisprudence*, 11 VT. J. ENVTL. L. 371, 376 (2009).

Do sales of a product give rise to liability?—One recurring question is whether the sale of a product that might later be dumped or discarded is tantamount to arranging the disposal of a hazardous substance. Courts have wrestled with articulating a test for determining when a party is engaged in the sale of a product (that has some use to the buyer) and the disposal of waste. Some jurisdictions simply ask whether the ultimate disposal of the product was intended or caused by its sale, or whether its disposal was a transaction, or event, that was independent of the sale. This "intent-causation" test seems most appropriate with respect to products, such as asbestos materials or PCB-contaminated transformers, that were sold not because the seller wanted or intended to rid itself of a hazardous substance, but because the seller intended for the product to satisfy some market demand. *Prudential Ins. Co. v. United States Gypsum Co.*, 711 F.Supp. 1244, 1254 (D.N. J. 1989) (asbestos); *Florida Power & Light Co. v. Allis Chalmers Corp.*, 893 F.2d 1313 (11th Cir. 1990) (PCBs).

Most courts have adopted the "useful product" test. The purpose of the test is to protect potentially responsible parties who were engaged in the sale of a useful product, as opposed to parties who were merely trying to get rid of something because it had, in effect, become waste. *See Carter–Jones Lumber Co. v. Dixie Distributing Co.*, 166 F.3d 840 (6th Cir. 1999) (buyer of transformers was "arranger" when evidence showed transformers were being scrapped rather than reused); *AM Int'l, Inc. v. International Forging Equip. Corp.*, 982 F.2d 989, 998–99 (6th Cir. 1993). The idea behind the test is to sort out a legitimate sales transaction from a disguised arrangement for disposal. *Compare Freeman v. Glaxo Wellcome, Inc.,* 189 F.3d 160 (2d Cir. 1999) (if a party merely sells a "virgin" product, without additional evidence that the transaction includes an arrangement for the ultimate disposal of a hazardous substance, CERCLA liability will not be imposed); *RSR Corp. v. Avanti Development, Inc.,* 68 F. Supp. 2d 1037 (S.D. Ind. 1999) (selling a useful marketable product that will not necessarily enter the environment as waste is not a disposal by an arranger), *with* EPA by and through *U.S. v. TMG Enterprises,* 979 F.Supp. 1110, 1123–4 (W.D. Ky. 1997) (arranger liability attaches when company no longer had any use for its product, and then sold it to another party, thereby creating a threat that hazardous substances contained in the product would be released during disposal); *Pneumo Abex Corp. v. Bessemer and Lake Erie Railroad Co.,* 921 F.Supp. 336 (E.D. Va. 1996) (sale of worn bearings was disposal when seller made decision to send bearings to facility that processed hazardous wastes); *New York v. General Electric Co.,* 592 F.Supp. 291, 297 (N.D. N.Y. 1984) (sale of contaminated waste oil to a drag strip for use as a dust control agent was simply an arrangement to relieve the buyer of the waste).

"USEFUL PRODUCT" TEST

In *California Dept. of Toxic Substances v. Alco Pacific, Inc.,* 508 F.3d 930 (9th Cir. 2007), the court looked at three factors to determine whether slag from a lead processing facility was a useful product:

(1) "the commercial reality and value of the product in question;

(2) a factual inquiry into the actions of the seller in order to determine the intent underlying the transaction; and

(3) whether the material in question was a principal product or by-product of the seller."

After considering these variables, the court decided that a reasonable fact finder could infer that slag was waste, rather than a useful product.

The Ninth Circuit has employed a third test, which asks whether the material being arranged for disposal would qualify as a "solid waste" under RCRA. In *Catellus Development Corp. v. United States,* 34 F.3d 748 (9th Cir. 1994), it was found that the seller of spent automotive batteries to a lead reclamation plant could be liable for arranging for a disposal, primarily because spent batteries would be considered solid waste under RCRA. *See also Cadillac Fairview/California, Inc. v. United States,* 41 F.3d 562 (9th Cir. 1994) (rubber companies who sold contaminated styrene back to chemical company for reprocessing were "arrangers" because reprocessing called for removal/release of hazardous substances).

Who are arrangers by "contract, agreement, or otherwise"?—In what has to be one of the most sweeping interpretations of arranger liability, the court in *United States v. Aceto Agricultural Chemicals Corp.,* 872 F.2d 1373, 1379 (8th Cir. 1989), found that producers who contracted with another company to formulate commercial grade pesticides had "arranged for" the releases that occurred at the formulator's factory site. This conclusion was based on the assumption that the escape of contaminated waste products was "inherent" in what the formulator did. (The mixing of pesticides for commercial use is not necessarily a precision activity.) The formulators had caused the wastes to be released as a result of the contract with the producers, while the producers had retained title to the pesticide at all times. Moreover, the final product had been shipped back to the producer or to the producer's customers. *In accord Jones–Hamilton Co. v. Beazer Materials & Services*, 973 F.2d 688 (9th Cir. 1992); *United States v. Vertac Chemical Corp.*, 966 F.Supp. 1491, 1501 (E.D. Ark. 1997). The prevailing view, however, is that the *Aceto* rule is too extreme. *See South Florida Water Management Dist. v. Montalvo*, 84 F.3d 402, 406–09 (11th Cir. 1996) (landowners who contracted with crop dusting company to have their fields sprayed with pesticides had not arranged for the company to spill pesticide wastes). Most courts demand that the alleged arranger have some direct participation in the waste disposal action. The nature of the connection between the alleged arranger and the disposal varies by jurisdiction:

- Exercised direct control over disposal–*United States v. Vertac Chemical Corp.*, 46 F.3d 803, 811 (8th Cir. 1995); *General Electric Co. v. AAMCO Transmissions, Inc.*, 962 F.2d 281 (2d Cir. 1992).
- Made decision to dispose of the hazardous substance–*Edward Hines Lumber Co. v. Vulcan Materials Co.*, 685 F.Supp. 651, 654–6 (N.D. Ill. 1988).
- Had knowledge that disposal would occur–*United States v. North Landing Line Construction Co.*, 3 F. Supp. 2d 694, 701 (E.D. Va. 1998).
- Evidence of actual intent to dispose of the wastes–*United States v. Cello–Foil Prods., Inc.*, 100 F.3d 1227 (6th Cir. 1996); *Struhan v. City of Cleveland*, 7 F. Supp. 2d 948, 952 (N.D. Ohio 1998). *But see Mathews v. Dow Chemical Co.*, 947 F.Supp. 1517, 1524 (D. Colo. 1996) (rejecting test that focuses exclusively on the intent of the arranger).

NOTES AND QUESTIONS

1.   What strikes you as unusual about the four elements of generator liability? What elements make it so broad?

Why such a broad test for liability? Wouldn't a more narrowly tailored provision meet the needs of a polluter pays statute? What would a more narrowly tailored provision look like?

Is there any way for generators to avoid liability if plaintiffs need not trace the contaminants in the site to the generator? Consider four arguments:

(i) The generator can try to prove that its wastes are not at all similar to the wastes released at the site.

(ii) The generator can try to prove that there was at the site no release of hazardous substances that are similar to its hazardous substances.

(iii) The generator can demonstrate that its wastes do not contain hazardous substances. *B.F. Goodrich Co. v. Murtha*, 840 F.Supp. 180 (D. Conn. 1993).

(iv) The generator can try to prove that its particular wastes never in fact arrived at the contaminated site. *But see United States v. Bliss*, 667 F.Supp. 1298 (E.D. Mo. 1987) (generators liable if "trace" amounts of their waste were in mixtures that were deposited at a site).

2. You have by now seen several instances in which the test for liability turns on the ability or obligation to control or make decisions regarding the hazardous waste in question. Why is control or decisionmaking authority so important? If CERCLA's purpose is simply to find a deep pocket for clean-up, why complicate matters with questions of control and authority?

3 Which test would you adopt for distinguishing between wastes and products? Wouldn't it make most sense to adopt the RCRA test as a way of reconciling the two statutes and simplifying administration?

With RCRA still in mind, how should CERCLA handle the problem— central to RCRA's definitional provisions—of sham recycling? Should intent govern, or should it be irrelevant?

4. Section 107(a)(3) makes liable as a PRP a person who "arranged for * * * treatment" of hazardous substances. Does this language make liable parties who arrange for the treatment of hazardous substances, whether or not such substances are waste? Or does it encompass only those parties who arrange for the treatment of hazardous substances which are also waste? Section 101(29) of CERCLA incorporates by reference RCRA's definition of "treatment": "The term 'treatment,' when used in connection with hazardous waste, means any method, technique or process * * * designed to change the * * * character or composition of any hazardous waste so as to neutralize such waste or so as to render such waste nonhazardous. * * *" RCRA § 1004. Does this definition refer to a party arranging for the processing of *discarded* hazardous substances, or processing resulting in the discard of hazardous substances? *See Pneumo Abex v. High Point Thomasville & Denton*, 142 F.3d 769, 774 (4th Cir. 1998).[54]

d. TRANSPORTERS INVOLVED IN SITE SELECTION

The fourth PRP category imposes liability on those who accept hazardous substances for transport "to disposal * * * sites selected by such person."§ 107(a)(4). Like past owners, the category is qualified. The "selected by" language excuses transporters or shippers for releases during transportation resulting from circumstances beyond their control. *United States v. M/V Santa Clara I*, 887 F.Supp. 825 (D.S. C. 1995). Here, Congress wanted to include as PRP only transporters who helped cause the pollution problem by picking up the hazardous substance and then dumping it at

---

54. In *Shell Oil Co. v. Environmental Protection Agency*, 950 F.2d 741 (D.C. Cir. 1991), the court found that a resource recovery process was not a "treatment" as that term is defined in RCRA.

locations of their choice. *See, e.g., United States v. Bliss*, 667 F.Supp. 1298, 1303 (E.D. Mo. 1987). This category includes both legitimate "full service" waste disposal companies who transport and dispose of their customers' hazardous waste, and so-called midnight dumpers who dispose of wastes illegally. However, transporter liability is not so far-reaching that anyone who has ever transported waste material to a site becomes a PRP, even if the material was wholly innocuous. To impose liability, a CERCLA plaintiff must prove that a defendant transported material containing a hazardous substance to the site. *Prisco v. A & D Carting Corp.*, 168 F.3d 593, 605 (2d Cir. 1999).

Although CERCLA § 107(a) specifies four distinct classes of PRPs, the lines blur with respect to the "owner" and "transporter" categories. *See, e.g., Atlantic Richfield Co. v. Blosenski*, 847 F.Supp. 1261 (E.D. Pa. 1994) (owner of site may be liable as transporter). On the other hand, there are distinctions between arrangers and transporters. An arranger-generator may be several transactions away from a decision to dump wastes, particularly in a sales context, but the transporter usually has direct control with, and influence over, the decision to dump at a waste site. Nonetheless, despite the transporter's closer ties to the dump site, the liability of transporters is not as extensive as that of arrangers. *United States v. Hardage*, 750 F.Supp. 1444, 1458 (W.D. Okl. 1990). Indeed, some courts have suggested that transporters may not be liable as arrangers under § 107(a)(3). *United States v. Western Processing Co.*, 756 F.Supp. 1416 (W.D. Wash. 1991). Of course, one key difference between arranger and transporter liability is that CERCLA limits PRP status to those who transport to "[disposal] sites selected by such person." The "selected by" language excuses transporters or shippers for releases during transportation resulting from circumstances beyond their control. *United States v. M/V Santa Clara I*, 887 F.Supp. 825 (D.S. C. 1995).

Two interpretative issues have arisen regarding transporter liability. First, because CERCLA § 101(26) defines "transport" to include "the movement of a hazardous substance by any mode," does CERCLA liability attach to a person who does not move the hazardous substances over some distance, but who merely spreads it further after it has already been dumped? *See Kaiser Aluminum & Chemical Corp. v. Catellus Development Corp.*, 976 F.2d 1338 (9th Cir. 1992) (building contractor who excavated a development site and spread contaminated soil was engaged in the transportation of hazardous materials). Second, how much role must a transporter play in the actual "selection" of the dump site? *See B.F. Goodrich v. Betkoski*, 99 F.3d 505, 520 (2d Cir. 1996) (a transporter is only liable if it has substantial input into the choice of the site), *modified by* 112 F.3d 88 (2d Cir. 1996) (clarifying decision on rehearing); *United States v. USX Corp.*, 68 F.3d 811, 825 (3d Cir. 1995) (transporter liability may not be imposed "solely on the basis of an officer's or shareholder's active involvement in the corporation's day to day affairs [but instead this corporate personnel must] actually participate in the liability-creating conduct"); *Tippins, Inc. v. USX Corp.*, 37 F.3d 87, 94 (3d Cir.1994) (transporter liable who has substantial input into which site is ultimately chosen).

e. CORPORATIONS

i. Officers, Directors, and Employees

In some cases it appears that CERCLA's remedial purposes would be better served if liability were imposed not only on the company that was an owner, operator, arranger, or transporter, but also on personnel within that company (officers, directors, and employees), or on corporate entities that have some relationship to that company, such as parent corporations (for subsidiaries), successor corporations (for businesses subsequently acquired), and dissolved corporations (dissolved prior to the filing of the CERCLA claim). Under traditional corporate law, owners of a corporation may be held personally liable only if a court believes it proper to "pierce the corporate veil" because the corporation is something less than a bona fide independent entity.

Rather than resort to "veil piercing" theories in CERCLA cases, courts have ruled that individuals owning or working for a corporation may be personally liable as "operators" or "arrang[ers] for disposal" under § 107(a), if certain conditions are met. *See Sidney S. Arst Co. v. Pipefitters Welfare Educ. Fund*, 25 F.3d 417, 420 (7th Cir. 1994) ("the direct, personal liability provided by CERCLA is distinct from the derivative liability that results from piercing the corporate veil"). The theory is that the term "person" in CERCLA includes both corporations and individuals, and does not exclude corporate officers or employees. Since individuals within a corporation may be liable for torts they personally commit, individuals may likewise be liable under § 107 if they personally participated in the conduct that violated CERCLA. *See, e.g., Riverside Market Dev. Corp. v. International Bldg. Prods., Inc.*, 931 F.2d 327, 330 (5th Cir. 1991) ("CERCLA prevents individuals from hiding behind the corporate shield when, as 'operators,' they themselves actually participate in the wrongful conduct prohibited by the Act"); *United States v. Kayser–Roth Corp.*, 910 F.2d 24, 26 (1st Cir. 1990); *United States v. Northeastern Pharmaceutical & Chemical Co., Inc.*, 810 F.2d 726, 743–4 (8th Cir. 1986).

When operator liability is alleged, courts have had some difficulty with the correct standard to apply to corporate officers or employees. At the one extreme is the view that the only issue is whether the individual had the authority to control the hazardous substances that were ultimately released into the environment. If such capacity existed, then the individual within the corporation is liable, regardless of whether control was in fact never exercised. *See, e.g., United States v. Carolina Transformer Co.*, 978 F.2d 832 (4th Cir. 1992) (if president was in charge of company and responsible for its operations, he was an "operator" under CERCLA because he had the power to prevent the release of hazardous waste); *Nurad, Inc. v. Hooper & Sons Co.*, 966 F.2d 837, 844 (4th Cir. 1992). At the other extreme are cases concluding that an individual qualifies as an operator only if she had *both* the authority to control the activity that resulted in the release and exercised that authority. *See, e.g., Riverside Market Development Corp. v. International Building Products, Inc.*, 931 F.2d 327 (5th Cir. 1991) (majority shareholder not an "operator" if not actually involved with the handling of hazardous substances); *Raytheon Constructors, Inc. v. Asarco Inc.*, 368 F.3d 1214 (10th Cir. 2003) (determining individual's involvement in purchase of successor mining company did not serve as basis for operator liability with respect to predecessor mining company). A middle ground approach considers several criteria:

    (1) the individual's degree of authority with respect to hazardous waste disposal;

    (2) the individual's position in the corporate hierarchy;

    (3) actual responsibility undertaken for waste disposal practices; and

    (4) evidence of responsibility undertaken and neglected, as well as affirmative attempts to prevent hazardous waste disposal.

See Kelley v. Thomas Solvent Co., 727 F.Supp. 1532 (W. D. Mich. 1989).

Corporate officers, directors, or employees may also become PRPs if they are deemed to be "arrangers." Courts may impose arranger liability if the individual either "owned or possessed" the wastes at issue. Ownership may stem from that party's ownership rights to the corporation that conducted the disposal operation. Possession follows if the individual alleged to be an arranger had actual control over the wastes, approved an arrangement for their transportation, and was directly responsible for deciding how and where they would be discarded. *United States v. Northeastern Pharmaceutical & Chemical Co.*, 810 F.2d 726 (8th Cir. 1986).

ii. Parent–Subsidiary

For many years, the courts split on the circumstances under which a parent corporation could be held responsible for its subsidiary's CERCLA liability without piercing the corporate veil. Finally, in 1998 the United States Supreme Court stepped in and resolved the conflict in the circuits among three competing theories of liability.

United States v. Bestfoods
524 U.S. 51 (1998)

■ JUSTICE SOUTER delivered the Opinion of the Court.

In 1957, Ott Chemical Co. (Ott I) began manufacturing chemicals at a plant near Muskegon, Michigan, and its intentional and unintentional dumping of hazardous substances significantly polluted the soil and ground water at the site. In 1965, respondent CPC International Inc. incorporated a wholly owned subsidiary to buy Ott I's assets in exchange for CPC stock. The new company, also dubbed Ott Chemical Co. (Ott II), continued chemical manufacturing at the site, and continued to pollute its surroundings. CPC kept the managers of Ott I, including its founder, president, and principal shareholder, Arnold Ott, on board as officers of Ott II. Arnold Ott and several other Ott II officers and directors were also given positions at CPC, and they performed duties for both corporations.

* * *

It is a general principle of corporate law deeply "ingrained in our economic and legal systems" that a parent corporation (so-called because of control through ownership of another corporation's stock) is not liable for the acts of its subsidiaries. * * * Thus it is hornbook law that the exercise of the "control" which stock ownership gives to the stockholders * * * will not create liability beyond the assets of the subsidiary. That "control" includes the election of directors, the making of by-laws * * * and the doing of all other acts incident to the legal status of stockholders. Nor will a duplication of some or all of the directors or executive officers be fatal. * * * Although this respect for corporate distinctions when the subsidiary is a polluter has been severely criticized in the literature, * * * nothing in CERCLA purports to reject this bedrock principle, and against this venerable common-law backdrop, the congressional silence is audible * * * The Government has indeed made no claim that a corporate parent is liable as an owner or an operator under § 107 simply because its subsidiary is subject to liability for owning or operating a polluting facility.

But there is an equally fundamental principle of corporate law, applicable to the parent-subsidiary relationship as well as generally, that the corporate veil may be pierced and the shareholder held liable for the corporation's conduct when, *inter alia*, the corporate form would otherwise be misused to accomplish certain wrongful purposes, most notably fraud, on the shareholder's behalf. * * * Nothing in CERCLA purports to rewrite this well-settled rule, either. CERCLA is thus like many another congressional enactment in giving no indication "that the entire corpus of state corporation law is to be replaced simply because a plaintiff's cause of action is based upon a federal statute," *Burks v. Lasker*, 441 U.S. 471, 478 (1979), and the failure of the statute to speak to a matter as fundamental as the liability implications of corporate ownership demands application of the rule that "[i]n order to abrogate a common-law principle, the statute must speak directly to the question addressed by the common law," *United States v. Texas*, 507 U.S. 529, 534 (1993) (internal quotation marks omitted). The Court of Appeals was accordingly correct in holding that when (but only when) the corporate veil may be pierced, may a parent corporation be charged with derivative CERCLA liability for its subsidiary's actions.

If the act rested liability entirely on ownership of a polluting facility, this opinion might end here; but CERCLA liability may turn on operation as well as ownership, and nothing in the statute's terms bars a parent corporation from direct liability for its own actions in operating a facility owned by its subsidiary. As Justice (then-Professor) Douglas noted almost 70 years ago, derivative liability cases are to be distinguished from those in which "the alleged wrong can seemingly be traced to the parent through the conduit of its own personnel and management" and "the parent is directly a participant in the wrong complained of." Douglas & Shanks, *Insulation from Liability Through Subsidiary Corporations*, 39 Yale L.J. 193, 207, 208 (1929). In such instances, the parent is directly liable for its own actions. * * * The fact that a corporate subsidiary happens to own a polluting facility operated by its parent does nothing, then, to displace the rule that the parent "corporation is [itself] responsible for the wrongs committed by its agents in the course of its business," *Mine Workers v. Coronado Coal Co.*, 259 U.S. 344, 395, 42 S.Ct. 570, 577, 66 L.Ed. 975 (1922), and whereas the rules of veil-piercing limit derivative liability for the actions of another corporation, CERCLA's "operator" provision is concerned primarily with direct liability for one's own actions. *See, e.g., Sidney S. Arst Co. v. Pipefitters Welfare Ed. Fund*, 25 F.3d 417, 420 (C.A.7 1994) ("the direct, personal liability provided by CERCLA is distinct from the derivative liability that results from piercing the corporate veil") (internal quotation marks omitted). It is this direct liability that is properly seen as being at issue here.

Under the plain language of the statute, any person who operates a polluting facility is directly liable for the costs of cleaning up the pollution. *See* 42 U.S.C. § 9607(a)(2). This is so regardless of whether that person is the facility's owner, the owner's parent corporation or business partner, or even a saboteur who sneaks into the facility at night to discharge its poisons out of malice. If any such act of operating a corporate subsidiary's facility is done on behalf of a parent corporation, the existence of the parent-subsidiary relationship under state corporate law is simply irrelevant to the issue of direct liability.

* * *

[We] * * * think that the appeals court erred in limiting direct liability under the statute to a parent's sole or joint venture operation, so as to eliminate any possible finding that CPC is liable as an operator on the facts of this case.

By emphasizing that "CPC is directly liable under section 107(a)(2) as an operator because CPC actively participated in and exerted significant control over Ott II's business and decision-making," 777 F. Supp., at 574, the District Court applied the "actual control" test of whether the parent "actually operated the business of its subsidiary," *id.*, at 573, as several Circuits have employed it.

* * *

The well-taken objection to the actual control test, however, is its fusion of direct and indirect liability; the test is administered by asking a question about the relationship between the two corporations (an issue going to indirect liability) instead of a question about the parent's interaction with the subsidiary's facility (the source of any direct liability). If, however, direct liability for the parent's operation of the facility is to be kept distinct from derivative liability for the subsidiary's own operation, the focus of the enquiry must necessarily be different under the two tests. "The question is not whether the parent operates the subsidiary, but rather whether it operates the facility, and that operation is evidenced by participation in the activities of the facility, not the subsidiary. Control of the subsidiary, if extensive enough, gives rise to indirect liability under piercing doctrine, not direct liability under the statutory language." Oswald, Bifurcation of the Owner and Operator Analysis under CERCLA, 72 Wash. U.L.Q. 223, 269 (1994). The District Court was therefore mistaken to rest its analysis on

CPC's relationship with Ott II, premising liability on little more than "CPC's 100–percent ownership of Ott II" and "CPC's active participation in, and at times majority control over, Ott II's board of directors." 777 F. Supp., at 575. The analysis should instead have rested on the relationship between CPC and the Muskegon facility itself.

In addition to (and perhaps as a reflection of) the erroneous focus on the relationship between CPC and Ott II, even those findings of the District Court that might be taken to speak to the extent of CPC's activity at the facility itself are flawed, for the District Court wrongly assumed that the actions of the joint officers and directors are necessarily attributable to CPC. The District Court emphasized the facts that CPC placed its own high-level officials on Ott II's board of directors and in key management positions at Ott II, and that those individuals made major policy decisions and conducted day-to-day operations at the facility: "Although Ott II corporate officers set the day-to day operating policies for the company without any need to obtain formal approval from CPC, CPC actively participated in this decision-making because high-ranking CPC officers served in Ott II management positions." *Id.*, at 559.)

* * *

In imposing direct liability on these grounds, the District Court failed to recognize that it is entirely appropriate for directors of a parent corporation to serve as directors of its subsidiary, and that fact alone may not serve to expose the parent corporation to liability for its subsidiary's acts.

* * *

This recognition that the corporate personalities remain distinct has its corollary in the well established principle [of corporate law] that directors and officers holding positions with a parent and its subsidiary can and do "change hats' to represent the two corporations separately, despite their common ownership. * * * Since courts generally presume that the directors are wearing their "subsidiary hats' and not their "parent hats' when acting for the subsidiary, it cannot be enough to establish liability here that dual officers and directors made policy decisions and supervised activities at the facility. The Government would have to show that, despite the general presumption to the contrary, the officers and directors were acting in their capacities as CPC officers and directors, and not as Ott II officers and directors, when they committed those acts. The District Court made no such enquiry here, however, disregarding entirely this time-honored common law rule.

In sum, the District Court's focus on the relationship between parent and subsidiary (rather than parent and facility), combined with its automatic attribution of the actions of dual officers and directors to the corporate parent, erroneously even if unintentionally, treated CERCLA as though it displaced or fundamentally altered common law standards of limited liability. Indeed, if the evidence of common corporate personnel acting at management and directorial levels were enough to support a finding of a parent corporation's direct operator liability under CERCLA, then the possibility of resort to veil piercing to establish indirect, derivative liability for the subsidiary's violations would be academic. There would in essence be a relaxed CERCLA-specific rule of derivative liability that would banish traditional standards and expectations from the law of CERCLA liability. But, as we have said, such a rule does not arise from congressional silence, and CERCLA's silence is dispositive.

[The Court then remanded the case to the trial court to make further factual findings about the CPC agent's role in Ott II's environmental affairs. The critical fact that needed to be resolved on remand is whether the CPC agent made CPC liable as a parent corporation, since the agent's actions show that CPC managed, directed, and conducted Ott II's operations that are specifically related to waste disposal.]

NOTES AND QUESTIONS

1. Does federal common law or state law govern parent or subsidiary liability, according to the Court? *Carter–Jones Lumber Co. v. LTV Steel Co.,* 237 F.3d 745, 747 (6th Cir. 2001) (citing *Bestfoods* for the proposition that state law should be used to determine whether to pierce a corporate veil in the context of a CERCLA case). *But see Board of Trustees, Sheet Metal Workers' Nat'l Pension Fund v. Elite Erectors, Inc.,* 212 F.3d 1031, 1038 (7th Cir. 2000) (holding federal common law should apply when determining whether to pierce a corporate veil in CERCLA cases), and *United States v. Davis,* 261 F.3d 1, 53–54 (1st Cir. 2001) (adopting Connecticut successor liability law when determining liabilities under CERCLA, "so long as it is not hostile to the federal interests animating CERCLA."). Which, in your view, is the better rule? Why?

2. The *Bestfood's* decision turned on whether a parent could be liable as an "operator" for the acts of its subsidiary. *See also United States v. Kayser–Roth Corp.* 272 F.3d 89 (1st Cir. 2001) (finding parent corporation liable under CERCLA as operator of subsidiary's textile manufacturing facility because it controlled subsidiary's environmental affairs). CERCLA imposes a different liability test regarding parent corporations in the context of being an "arranger for disposal." Consider the following explanation set forth in *United States v. TIC Investment Co.,* 68 F.3d 1082, 1091–92 (8th Cir.1995):

> "[S]ubsection (a)(2) requires only that the person operate the facility where disposal occurs * * *; by contrast, subsection (a)(3) requires that the person arrange for the disposal.
>
> Therefore while a parent corporation need only have the authority to control, and exercise actual or substantial control, over the operations of its subsidiary in order to incur direct [operator] liability, we believe that, in order for a parent corporation to incur direct arranger liability for a subsidiary's off-site disposal practices, there must be some causal connection or nexus between the parent corporation's conduct and the subsidiary's arrangement for disposal, or the off-site disposal itself."

The *United States v. TIC Investment Co.* case deals with direct liability, not derivative liability. Direct, personal liability provided by CERCLA is distinct from the derivative liability that results from piercing the corporate veil. *Sidney S. Arst Co. v. Pipefitters Welfare Educ. Fund*, 25 F.3d 417 (7th Cir. 1994). Some courts have concluded that it is within the intent of CERCLA, and consistent with *Bestfoods*, to impute derivative arranger liability upon a parent corporation if their corporate veil can be pierced, and if their subsidiary can be adjudged an arranger. *AT & T Global Information v. Union Tank Car Co.*, 29 F. Supp. 2d 857, 863 (S.D. Ohio 1998). *See also United States v. Wallace*, 961 F.Supp. 969 (N.D. Tex. 1996) (derivative liability does not require actual participation in wrongful conduct).

3. Does *Bestfoods* cast doubt on the current understanding that corporate officers may be reached as "operators," considered above in section (i)? In other words, must CERCLA plaintiffs use state veil-piercing law instead of the federal definition of "operator"? What difference would it make? *See Donahey v. Bogle*, 129 F.3d 838 (6th Cir. 1997) (holding that when a single individual owns 100 percent of a corporation's stock, that person could not be liable under CERCLA unless the elements necessary to pierce the corporate veil were present).

iii. Successor Corporations

If one corporate entity purchases or "takes over" another corporate entity, two CERCLA liability questions arise. First, can the corporation that has been acquired by another avoid liability as a result of the transaction? The answer is a clear *no*. CERCLA has a prohibition on transferring liability (in the absence of an indemnification agreement) in order to prevent companies from divesting themselves of direct liability by shifting responsibility for their waste problem to another corporation. § 107(e); *Harley-Davidson, Inc. v. Minstar, Inc.*, 41 F.3d 341, 342–44 (7th Cir.1994).

Second, is a successor corporation responsible for the waste disposal practices of the corporate entity it has acquired? While the issue is not resolved by the plain language of CERCLA, *Smith Land and Improvement Corp. v. Celotex Corp.*, 851 F.2d 86, 91 (3d Cir.1988), courts agree that Congress intended successor liability to apply. *B.F. Goodrich v. Betkoski*, 99 F.3d 505 (2d Cir. 1996); *United States v. Carolina Transformer Co.*, 978 F.2d 832 (4th Cir. 1992). CERCLA's definition of "person" is broadly written to include a "firm, corporation, association * * * [or] commercial entity." § 101(21). Congress itself has directed the judiciary to apply a rule of construction to the United States Code that requires, when the word "association" is used "in reference to a corporation, [it] shall be deemed to embrace the words 'successors and assigns.'" 1 U.S.C.A. § 5. Moreover, they have ample opportunity to examine the potential liabilities of the target corporation.

Where the successor only buys the assets of its predecessor, the question is more complicated. The general common law rule is that an asset purchaser does not acquire the liabilities (*e.g.*, PRP liabilities under CERCLA) of the seller. *See, e.g., City Management Corp. v. U.S. Chemical Co.*, 43 F.3d 244, 256 (6th Cir. 1994). In the CERCLA context, however, there are four exceptions to this general rule. Each of the exceptions is detailed below.

1. *The purchaser expressly or impliedly agrees to assume liabilities.*—To fall within this exception, courts are interested in whether the purchase agreement contains language transferring "all liabilities." This phrase is usually construed to include environmental liability under CERCLA. *Philadelphia Electric Co. v. Hercules, Inc.*, 762 F.2d 303, 309–10 (3d Cir. 1985). Another factor indicating that a successor intends to assume the predecessor's environmental liability is the successor's knowledge of the pollution problems at the site it has acquired. *United States v. Iron Mountain Mines, Inc.*, 987 F.Supp. 1233, 1243 (E.D. Cal. 1997).

2. *The transaction is a "de facto" merger or consolidation.*—Courts consider several factors in deciding whether to characterize a purported sale of assets as a *de facto* merger.

- Is there continuity of management, personnel, physical location, assets, and general business operations?

- Is there a continuity of shareholders resulting from the successor corporation paying for the acquired assets with shares of its own stock?

- Has the purchasing corporation assumed the obligations of the seller necessary for uninterrupted continuation of business operations?

See North Shore Gas Co. v. Salomon Inc., 152 F.3d 642 (7th Cir. 1998), *overruled by Envision Healthcare, Inc. v. PreferredOne Ins. Co.*, 604 F.3d 983 (7th Cir. 2010) (overruling on basis that district court did not abuse its discretion in abstaining from reaching the merits of insurance broker's suit). *Louisiana–Pacific Corp v. Asarco, Inc.*, 909 F.2d 1260, 1264 (9th Cir.1990).

3. *The purchaser is a mere "continuation of the seller.*—The mere continuation exception to successor non-liability applies when a corporation otherwise liable under a law like CERCLA transfers its assets to another corporation, so that post-transfer there is only one corporation with stock, stockholders, and directors identical to the acquired corporation. Since this exception is easily avoided by either continuing the predecessor corporation in some form, or altering the stock, shareholders, or directors between the two entities, successors can often escape CERCLA liability by invoking the normal rule that purchasers are not responsible for the liabilities of acquired corporations. *See, e.g., United States v. Vermont American Corp.*, 871 F.Supp. 318 (W.D. Mich. 1994); *Blackstone Valley Elec. Co. v. Stone & Webster, Inc.*, 867 F.Supp. 73 (D. Mass.1994).

In order to make more flexible and fact-specific the scope of successor liability, some courts have broadened the "mere continuation" exception with a "substantial continuation" (or "continuity of enterprise") standard. This exception requires the plaintiff to establish that the predecessor and successor share continuity of employees, supervisory personnel, location, product, company name, and assets, as well as holding itself out as a continuation of the seller.

THE SUBSTANTIAL CONTINUITY TEST

What do courts consider when applying this test? One federal circuit court of appeals has articulated a check-list of relevant factors.

"Proper application of the substantial continuity test to protect the policy concerns of CERCLA first requires a consideration of whether the successor corporation retains the same employees, the same supervisory personnel, the same production facilities in the same location, the same product, the same name, a continuity of assets and general business operations, and holds itself out as a continuation of the previous enterprise." *See K.C. 1986 Ltd. Partnership v. Reade Mfg.*, 472 F.3d 1009, 1022 (8th Cir. 2007).

In the absence of such a continuity of the seller's enterprise, successor liability does not attach. *See Oner II, Inc. v. United States EPA*, 597 F.2d 184 (9th Cir. 1979); *United States v. Carolina Transformer Co.*, 978 F.2d 832 (4th Cir. 1992); *Andritz Sprout–Bauer, Inc. v. Beazer East. Inc.*, 12 F Supp. 2d 391, 405–406 (M.D. Pa.1998). Some courts adopting the "substantial continuation" exception also require the acquiring company to have actual notice of its potential liabilities. *Louisiana–Pacific Corp. v. Asarco, Inc.*, 909 F.2d 1260 (9th Cir. 1990); *Hunt's Generator Committee v. Babcock & Wilcox Co.*, 863 F.Supp. 879, 883 (E.D.Wis. 1994).

    4. *The transaction is an effort to fraudulently escape liability.*—Many jurisdictions reject the broader "substantial continuation" exception on the basis that when it has been applied to hold an asset purchaser liable, there has almost always been some fraudulent intent or collusion, in which case the purchaser would have been liable under the fraudulently-entered transaction exception. *Atchison, Topeka & Santa Fe Ry. v. Brown & Bryant, Inc.*, 159 F.3d 358 (9th Cir. 1997). For example, in the leading "substantial continuation" case, *United States v. Carolina Transformer Co.*, 978 F.2d 832 (4th Cir. 1992), the children of the seller's owner were the sole shareholders of the successor, giving the "unmistakable impression that the transfer * * * was part of an effort to continue the business in all material respects yet avoid the environmental liability." 978 F.2d at 339–41.

    Consider why establishing successor liability is important to the effectiveness of CERCLA. Is it fair to hold the successor liable? *See* Fox, *Corporate Successors Under Strict Liability: A General Economic Theory and the Case of CERCLA*, 26 WAKE FOREST L. REV. 183 (1991).

iv. Dissolved Corporations

    CERCLA makes "persons" liable as PRPs, but does not explicitly include dissolved corporations within the statute's definition of "persons." The question that emerges is whether dissolution under state law, coupled with the typical state law prohibition against corporations being sued within two years of their dissolution, defeats a CERCLA § 107(a) claim against a former owner.

Does CERCLA preempt state laws that prevent dissolved corporations from being sued? On the one hand, Federal Rule of Civil Procedure 17(b) states that a corporation's capacity to be sued must be determined by the state law where it was organized. If a dissolved corporation is no longer a legal entity pursuant to state law and Rule 17 (b), then it follows that a § 107(a) lawsuit must fail. On the other hand, if such state law stands as an obstacle to the accomplishment of CERCLA, then the state rule is preempted. The courts are divided on the preemption issue. Some say that since Rule 17(b) is a "procedural" rule, it is not superseded by CERCLA's substantive imposition of liability. *See, e.g., U.S. Bank Nat. Ass'n v. U.S. E.P.A.,* 563 F.3d 199 (6th Cir. 2009); *Levin Metals corp. v. Parr–Richmond Terminal Co.,* 817 F.2d 1448, 1451 (9th Cir. 1987); *Citizens Elec. Corp. v. Bituminous Fire & Marine Ins. Co.,* 68 F.3d 1016 (7th Cir. 1995). Other courts hold that CERCLA preempts state laws, which could limit liability under CERCLA. They argue that the difference between statutes defining substantive liability (CERCLA) and those defining capacity to be sued (Rule 17(b) and state law) is a distinction without a difference. Why? *See United States v. Sharon Steel Corp.,* 681 F.Supp. 1492, 1497 (D. Utah 1987); *Town of Oyster Bay v. Occidental Chem. Corp.,* 987 F.Supp. 182 (E.D. N.Y 1997). Is it relevant that although Congress did not include dissolved corporations within its statutory scheme of liability, it did provide that PRPs should be held liable for clean-up costs "[n]otwithstanding any other provision or rule of law" (§ 107(a))?

If CERCLA does preempt state law, then to what extent may dissolved corporations be subject to § 107(a) liability? In addressing this issue, the courts have differentiated between "dead" corporations (dissolved entities) and those that are "dead and buried" (dissolved and all assets distributed). Most courts have held that only dead corporations can be amenable to suit. *Idylwoods Assocs. v. Mader Capital, Inc.,* 915 F.Supp. 1290, 1304 (W.D. N.Y. 1996). The rationale here is that dead and buried corporations are no longer entities that can be sued or defend themselves against suit, and therefore should be excused from CERCLA liability. *Burlington Northern and Santa Fe Ry Co. v. Consolidated Fibers, Inc.* 7 F. Supp. 2d 822, 828 (N.D. Tex. 1998). Other courts have refused to recognize any distinction between the CER-CLA liability of dead, and dead and buried, corporations. These courts emphasize that the language of CERCLA places no limitation on the term "corporation" as used in the statute. *United States v. SCA Services of Indiana, Inc.,* 837 F.Supp. 946, 953 (N.D. Ind. 1993). Which approach is more persuasive? How do you think the problem of dissolved corporations should be handled?

f. LENDERS

Lender liability under CERCLA has had a convoluted history. Lenders initially escaped liability due to an exclusion in the definition of "owner or operator." *See* § 101(20) (excluding as "owners" or "operator" a person who held "indicia of ownership" in a facility in order to protect a "security interest," without "participating in the management" of the facility). However, the case law of the early 1990s expansively held the lender's "capacity to influence" the borrower's operational decisions could create liability. *See e.g. United States v. Fleet Factors Corp.*, 901 F.2d 1550, 1557 (11th Cir. 1990) (a secured creditor could be liable if its involvement with the waste site leads to the inference that it could affect hazardous waste disposal decisions if it so chose). Some cases even suggested that liability could attach if the lender acquired the property through foreclosure. *See e.g., Guidice v. BFG Electroplating and Manufacturing Co.*, 732 F.Supp. 556 (W.D. Pa. 1989).

The pendulum swung the other way when in 1992 the EPA issued an interpretative rule rejecting the test that the lender's *capacity* to influence waste disposal decisions was sufficient, without the lender's active participation, to hold a lender liable under CERCLA. 40 C.F.R. § 300.1100(c), (d). This rule also allowed lenders to escape liability for both foreclosure and repurchase at a foreclosure sale, so long as (1) these were simply mechanisms for protecting security interests, and (2) the foreclosing lender acted quickly to divest itself of the property. In 1994, lenders again faced CERCLA liability when a D.C. Circuit panel struck down the EPA interpretative rule because CERCLA did not delegate to EPA authority to define through regulation the scope of § 107 liability. *Kelley v. EPA*, 15 F.3d 1100 (D.C. Cir. 1994). Once again, lenders' rights to control borrowers' waste sites could, in some jurisdictions, create owner/operator liability under CERCLA.

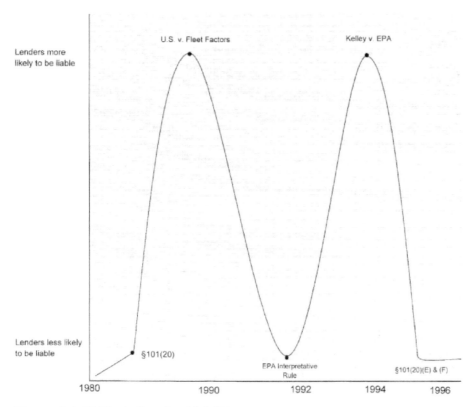

Figure 6.4–Shifts in Lender Liability

Finally, in 1996 Congress altered the extent of lender exposure to liability when it statutorily amended CERCLA. The Asset Conservation,

Lender Liability, and Deposit Insurance Protection Act of 1996 rejects the capacity-to-influence test. Now, the lender must be "actually participating in the management or operational affairs" of the borrower. § 101(20)(F)(i)(I–II). Moreover, a lender will not become an owner/operator simply by acquiring contaminated property by foreclosure, or by undertaking related post-foreclosure activities. Similar to the EPA interpretative rule, the lender must try to resell or transfer the contaminated facility or waste site "at the earliest practicable, commercially reasonable time. * * * " § 101(20)(E)(ii). For now, the ups and downs of lender liability appear to have stabilized, though the application of this rule in particular cases continues to be litigated. More important, lenders continue to insist on inquiry into the environmental condition of mortgaged property or property pledged as collateral, not so much to protect themselves from liability, but mainly to assure that their security does not become worthless because contamination is found.[55]

g.   FIDUCIARIES, ESTATES, AND BENEFICIARIES

A "fiduciary" is defined by CERCLA to include trustees, executors, administrators, custodians, guardians, conservators, or personal representatives. § 107(n)(5)(A). A fiduciary may be liable as a PRP. *Canadyne–Georgia Corp. v. Nationsbank, N.A.*, 183 F.3d 1269 (11th Cir. 1999) (trustee who held legal title to pesticide manufacturing business is an owner of plant site for CERCLA purposes). CERCLA does provide some protection since the liability cannot exceed the sum of the assets held in a fiduciary capacity. *Briggs & Stratton Corp. v. Concrete Sales & Services*, 20 F. Supp. 2d 1356, 1368 (M.D. Ga. 1998). Moreover, a fiduciary may conduct response actions at the contaminated site, and administer an already-contaminated facility, without incurring personal liability under CERCLA.[56] There is no private right of action against a fiduciary. § 107(n)(5)(A)(i), (n)(5)(B).

CERCLA does not expressly impose liability on the estates of those found to be PRPs. The definitions section fails to include as a "person" a beneficiary of an inheritance. § 101(21). Instead, Congress endorsed traditional rules of property descent by creating an exception to § 107 liability within the "innocent landowner defense." § 107(b)(3). Under this defense, which is discussed in detail below, a person who inherits contaminated property, thereby becoming an "owner" and a PRP, is entitled to assert the innocent landowner defense and escape liability. *Witco Corp. v. Beekhuis*, 38 F.3d 682, 689 (3d Cir. 1994). Thus, beneficiaries do not become PRPs under CERCLA simply because they inherited a hazardous waste site from someone who was a PRP. *Norfolk Southern Ry. Co. v. Shulimson Bros. Co.*, 1 F. Supp. 2d 553, 557–58 (W.D. N.C. 1998).

h.   FEDERAL, STATE, AND LOCAL GOVERNMENTS

In addition to individuals and businesses, a "person" under section 107(a) may also be the "United States Government, [a] State, municipality,

55.   *See* William Buzbee, *CERCLA's New Safe Harbors for Banks, Lenders, and Fiduciaries*, 26 Envtl. L. Rptr. 10656 (1996).

56.   These protections are not applicable if the fiduciary's negligence contributes to the release of a hazardous substance. § 107(n)(1)–(4).

commission, political subdivision of a state, or any interstate body."
§ 101(21). In the case of the federal government, CERCLA waives sovereign
immunity for facilities owned and operated by the federal government, such
as military facilities, which are considered in Chapter 12, *infra*. Section
120(a)(1) also provides that the United States is subject to CERCLA to the
same extent as any private, nongovernmental entity. Should the federal
government be able to impose joint and several liability on private PRPs,
even when federal agencies are themselves PRPs? *See United States v.
Hunter,* 70 F. Supp. 2d 1100 (C.D. Cal. 1999) (yes); *United States v. Newmont
USA Ltd.,* 504 F. Supp. 2d 1050 (E.D. Wash. 2007). The waiver of sovereign
immunity is, however, inapplicable when the United States acts in a
regulatory capacity (*e.g.,* when EPA performs § 104 remedial work). *See In
re Paoli Railroad Yard PCB Litigation*, 790 F.Supp. 94 (E.D. Pa. 1992), *aff'd*
980 F.2d 724 (3d Cir. 1992).

Although states are expressly included within the definition of "person"
subject to CERCLA liability, several doctrines reduce their risk. When a
private PRP sues a state for "contribution" under § 113(f), such a suit runs
up against the case of *Seminole Tribe of Florida v. Florida*, 517 U.S. 44
(1996). *Seminole Tribe* holds that Congress cannot abrogate, by statutes
passed under the commerce power, the states' Eleventh Amendment immunity from private suits. This case seems to prevent private parties from
suing states for contribution under § 113(f).[57] Apart from constitutional
limitations on certain private litigation, states may avoid CERCLA liability
by demonstrating that the waste site was only regulated, but not owned, by
the state. *United States v. Dart Industries*, 847 F.2d 144 (4th Cir. 1988). On
the other hand, a state may be liable if it selected a site for hazardous waste
disposal and controlled operations at the site. *United States v. Stringfellow*,
31 E.R.C. 1315 (C.D. Cal. 1990). Municipalities can be liable under
§ 107(a)(3) for having arranged to dispose of municipal solid waste at sites
where CERCLA response actions take place. *B.F. Goodrich v. Murtha*, 958
F.2d 1192, 1205–06 (2d Cir. 1992) (industrial PRPs can bring a contribution
action against towns that sent municipal waste to a landfill subject to a
CERCLA response action); *New Jersey v. Gloucester Env. Mgt. Serv.*, 821
F.Supp. 999 (D. N.J. 1993) (PRPs can bring contribution claim against
municipalities that arranged for dumping of municipal and household waste
at landfills); *Goodrich Corp. v. Town of Middlebury,* 311 F.3d 154 (2d Cir.
2002) (finding municipalities that contributed to waste mixture at landfill
sites were "liable parties," and therefore subject to contribution claims from
non-municipal parties). However, in an emergency, a municipal government
may be immune from liability arising as a result of action taken in response
to that emergency. *AMW Materials Testing, Inc. v. Town of Babylon*, 584 F.3d
436 (2d Cir. 2009) (finding city immune from damages claimed when city fire
department responded to fire that released hazardous substances).

---

57. The Supreme Court's decision in *Florida Prepaid Postsecondary Education Expense
Board v. College Savings Bank* [Florida Prepaid I], 527 U.S. 666 (1999), would seem to confirm
this interpretation. *See also Burnette v. Carothers*, 192 F.3d 52 (2d Cir. 1999) (state's Eleventh
Amendment immunity barred homeowners' CERCLA claim against state officers for response
costs).

3. TRIGGERS FOR LIABILITY

As we have seen, to make a prima facie case of liability under § 107, the plaintiff must prove that (1) a "hazardous substance," (2) has been "release[d]" or there is a "threat" that it may be released, (3) from a "facility", and that the release (4) causes the plaintiff (the government or some "other person") to incur "response costs" which are "not inconsistent with" (or "consistent with") the NCP. These four conditions are sometimes considered jurisdictional in nature, and they have been the topic of numerous interpretative battles in court. Each of the four liability triggers is now considered.

a. HAZARDOUS SUBSTANCES

A CERCLA "hazardous substance" includes a broad range of pollutants, contaminants, and wastes. Since the statute uses the term "substance," CERCLA liability can even be triggered when there is no "waste." *Uniroyal Chemical Co., Inc. v. Deltech Corp.*, 160 F.3d 238, 245 (5th Cir. 1998). But since hazardous substances are commonly found in hazardous wastes, and since hazardous wastes are so ubiquitous, as a practical matter CERCLA has primary applicability to wastes. *See, e.g., Transportation Leasing Co. v. State of California*, 861 F.Supp. 931 (C.D. Cal. 1993) (wastes from governmental, commercial, and residential activities can be hazardous substances). To the extent municipal wastes contain a hazardous substance, and there is a release or threatened release, such wastes fall within the CERCLA liability framework. To the consternation of local governments, CERCLA may even impose liability on municipalities disposing of household waste that contains hazardous substances. *B.F. Goodrich v. Murtha*, 958 F.2d 1192 (2d Cir. 1992).

Chemicals are designated as "hazardous substances" in three ways. First, § 101(14) incorporates lists of substances regulated under other federal environmental statutes, such as RCRA, the Clean Water Act, the Clean Air Act, and TSCA. Second, § 102(a) permits EPA to designate any substance that "may present substantial danger" as hazardous.[58] Mixtures of hazardous and non-hazardous substances qualify as "hazardous" under CERCLA if somewhere within it there is a CERCLA hazardous substance. *B.F. Goodrich v. Betkoski*, 99 F.3d 505, 515 (2d Cir. 1996) ("It is enough that a mixture of waste solution contains a hazardous substance for that mixture to be deemed hazardous under CERCLA.") *modified* by 112 F.3d 88 (2d Cir. 1996) (clarifying decision on rehearing).

Does it follow from this "mixture" rule that if copper is a listed hazardous substance, a person who drops a copper penny at a waste site can therefore be responsible for cleaning up the site? *See United States v. Wade*, 577 F.Supp. 1326, 1339–41 (E.D. Pa. 1983) (yes, but not for much of it.) In other words, is there is some minimum level of concentration or quantity which must exist before CERCLA liability can be triggered? This question becomes important when PRPs face staggering clean-up costs for wastes that contain hazardous substances in such minute amounts that they

---

58. The resulting EPA list contains close to 2,000 hazardous substances. 40 C.F.R. § 302.4, Table 302.4.

cannot be considered dangerous. Courts that have addressed this question universally agree that CERCLA's definition of hazardous substance has no minimum level requirement. *See United States v. Alcan Aluminum Corp.*, 990 F. 2d 711, 720 (2d Cir.1993); *United States v. Alcan Aluminum Corp.*, 964 F.2d 252, 260–63 (3d Cir. 1992); *B.F. Goodrich Co. v. Murtha*, 958 F.2d 1192, 1199–1201 (2d Cir. 1992). The primary rationale for this conclusion is that the CERCLA definition refers simply to "any substance," § 101(14), and the accompanying EPA regulations give no minimum levels.

PROBLEM

1. Is there any argument available to a PRP that finds itself liable for clean-up costs when the actual quantity of hazardous substance in a waste mixture is so small that there could be no risk to human health and the environment? Consider § 107(a)(4), discussed later in this chapter, which defines a liable person as one responsible for a release "which causes the incurrence of response costs." When there is very little hazardous substance in a waste deposit, but EPA orders a clean-up anyway, what is the "cause" of the incurrence of the response costs? Does the release of the wastes pose a serious enough threat to justify the response, in which case the PRP's wastes have caused the need to incur response costs? Or is the response caused by the agency's overzealousness? If the latter is true, can the PRP then argue that the "release" has not caused the incurrence of response costs? *Compare Amoco Oil Co. v. Borden, Inc.*, 889 F.2d 664, 669 (5th Cir. 1989) (possibly a good argument), *with A & W Smelter and Refiners, Inc. v. Clinton*, 146 F.3d 1107, 1110–11 (9th Cir. 1998) (the argument reads too much into the word "causes" in § 107(a)(4)).

2. Should courts be more receptive to this argument, or would it unduly undermine CERCLA's liability scheme?

The petroleum exclusion. Petroleum products are expressly exempted from the definition of "hazardous substance" in § 101(14). Although petroleum-based wastes may contain other toxic constituents, they were exempted because petroleum product spills into navigable waters were already covered by § 311 of the Clean Water Act and because at the time Congress was considering CERCLA, it was also debating a parallel land-based oil-spill bill (which never passed). As a result, much petroleum contamination on land would be outside the scope of CERCLA liability, except that courts have tended to interpret the petroleum exclusion quite narrowly.

A defendant bears the burden of proving that it is not liable based on the petroleum exclusion. *Organic Chemicals Site PRP Group v. Total Petroleum, Inc.*, 6 F. Supp. 2d 660, 663 (W.D. Mich. 1998). The easiest way to meet this burden is to show that an otherwise hazardous substance is inherent (that is, occurs naturally) in petroleum. *Wilshire Westwood Assoc. v. Atlantic Richfield Corp.*, 881 F.2d 801 (9th Cir. 1989); *United States v. Poly–Carb, Inc.*, 951 F.Supp. 1518, 1526 (D. Nev. 1996); *Niecko v. Emro Mktg. Co.*, 769

F.Supp. 973, 981–82 (E.D. Mich. 1991). The petroleum exclusion also applies if the hazardous substance is added during the refining or production process, *United States v. Gurley*, 43 F.3d 1188, 1199 (8th Cir. 1994), if there is no indication that the petroleum products were used waste oil or that they were contaminated with hazardous substances, *Foster v. United States*, 926 F.Supp. 199, 205–06 (D. D.C.), or if petroleum products are mixed with soil that itself is nonhazardous. *Southern Pacific Trans. Co. v. Caltrans.*, 790 F.Supp. 983, 985–86 (C.D. Cal. 1991).

Because the judiciary has sought to limit the scope of the petroleum exclusion (in order to extend CERCLA's reach to some petroleum-based wastes), several theories may now be employed if one wishes to affix liability despite the presence of petroleum at the waste site or facility.[59] Among these are:

- No petroleum exclusion for waste oil contaminated with hazardous substances other than those which are constituents of petroleum in greater than normal concentrations—*ACME Printing Ink Co. v. Menard*, 881 F.Supp. 1237, 1251 (E.D. Wis. 1995).

- While useful petroleum products fall within the exclusion, petroleum that has been contaminated by a waste product, or that has been commingled with other hazardous substances, is not within the exclusion—*Cose v. Getty Oil Co.*, 4 F.3d 700 (9th Cir. 1993) (subsurface crude oil tank bottom waste not covered by the exclusion); *Diversified Services, Inc. v. Simkins Inds.*, 974 F.Supp. 1448, 1454 (S.D. Fla. 1997) (petroleum commingled with other sources of contamination not within the exclusion); *Mid Valley Bank v. North Valley Bank*, 764 F.Supp. 1377, 1382–84 (E.D. Cal. 1991) (non-useful waste oil combined with hazardous substances is adulterated waste oil not protected by the exclusion).

- The exclusion does not apply to petroleum products that have been contaminated by hazardous substances after refining, during the manufacturing process—*City of New York v. Exxon Corp.*, 766 F.Supp. 177 (S.D. N.Y. 1991).

- While the exclusion applies to petroleum containing indigenous hazardous substances in its natural or refined state, it does not apply to petroleum to which hazardous substances have been added through use—*United States v. Alcan Aluminum Corp.* 964 F.2d 252 (3d Cir.1992); *Ekotek Site PRP Cmte. v. Self*, 932 F.Supp. 1319 (D. Utah 1996); *United States v. Amtreco, Inc.*, 846 F.Supp. 1578, 1584 (M.D. Ga. 1994).

- The exclusion does not apply to waste oil sludges that have become contaminated with hazardous substances generated through chemical reactions between the waste oil and the tanks in which they were stored—United States v. Western Processing Co., Inc., 761 F.Supp. 713 (W.D. Wash. 1991).

---

59. Petroleum is not excluded from RCRA, however. Therefore, if one of the foregoing rationales does not apply, EPA can often use RCRA's corrective action authority (*see* Chapter 9, *supra*) for the petroleum component of a waste site.

b. RELEASE OR THREATENED RELEASE

The term "release" is broadly defined to include "any spilling, leaking, * * *emitting, * * * discharging, * * * escaping, leaching, dumping, or disposing into the environment. * * * " § 101(22). Courts have interpreted this language to cover virtually all avenues by which pollutants can escape and do damage to human health or the environment. All that seems needed is some kind of *movement* of hazardous substances into the general environment. *See, e.g., Westfarm Assocs. Ltd. Partnership v. Washington Suburban Sanitary Comm.*, 66 F.3d 669, 680–81 (4th Cir. 1995) (PCE leaking from sewers is a release); *United States v. M/V Santa Clara I*, 887 F.Supp. 825 (D. S. Ct. 1995) (the loss overboard a ship of arsenic trioxide is a release); *Elf Atochem North America, Inc. v. United States*, 868 F.Supp. 707, 711–13 (E.D. Pa 1994) (waste entering pipes that lead to outdoor waste pit has been released); *HRW Systems, Inc. v. Washington Gas Light Co.*, 823 F.Supp. 318 (D. Md. 1993) (hazardous substances found in soil have *ipso facto* been released); *State of Vermont v. Staco, Inc.*, 684 F.Supp. 822, 832–33 (D. Vt. 1988) (the escape of mercury from a plant used to make thermometers in the clothing of workers is a release). Despite the breadth of the term, however, there are some exceptions in CERCLA and in the case law:

- The statutory definition in § 101(22) excludes releases in the workplace, emissions from motor vehicles, nuclear material from a processing site, and "the normal application of a fertilizer."

- CERCLA § 104(a)(3) instructs federal authorities not to initiate removal or remedial actions in response to a release of a "naturally occurring substance in its unaltered form," from "products which are part of the structure of, and result in exposure within, residential * * * business or community structures," or into "public or private drinking water supplies due to deterioration of the system through ordinary use."

- Parties who previously controlled property are not liable for a release if there has been passive migration of hazardous chemicals spilled by their predecessor. *ABB Ind. Systems, Inc. v. Prime Technology*, 120 F.3d 351 (2d Cir. 1997); *Foster v. United States*, 922 F.Supp. 642 (D. D.C. 1996) (defendant must have some control over the disposal to be liable).

- Although "abandonment" is a form of release (*e.g.,* discarding barrels or closed receptacles), it is not a release if the defendant merely transfers possession of the closed receptacle to some other entity. *A & W Smelter and Refiners, Inc. v. Clinton*, 146 F.3d 1107, 1111–1112 (9th Cir. 1998).

- Hazardous substances that merely flow through adjacent property are not considered a "release" or "disposal" because they are not "set in motion by human agency." *Niagara Mohawk Power Corp. v. Jones Chem., Inc.*, 315 F.3d 171, 178 (2d Cir. 2003).

Can you see any common themes, or is it just a collection of special cases?

Section 107 also reaches parties whose action creates a "threatened release." *See also* §§ 104(a)(1), 106(a). Most courts require that two conditions be met before such potential future releases trigger liability: (1) there must be evidence of the *presence* of a hazardous substance at a facility, and (2) there should be evidence of unwillingness of a party to assert control over the substances. *G.J. Leasing Co. v. Union Elec. Co.*, 854 F.Supp. 539, 561 (S.D. Ill. 1994), *aff'd* 54 F.3d 379 (7th Cir. 1995); *Amland Properties Corp. v. ALCOA*, 711 F.Supp. 784, 793 (D. N.J.1989). Why the second requirement?

Should there be some quantitative level that must be reached before a release of a hazardous substance triggers CERCLA liability? After all, some hazardous substances, like radionuclides, are used and produced in thousands of locations throughout the United States. The courts are split on this issue. *Compare Nutrasweet Co. v. X–L Engineering Corp.*, 933 F.Supp. 1409 (N.D. Ill. 1996) (there is no minimum quantitative requirement for a release); *Prisco v. State of New York*, 902 F.Supp. 374 (S.D. N.Y 1995) (very low levels of concentration of hazardous waste can be a release), *with United States v. Ottati & Goss, Inc.*, 900 F.2d 429, 438 (1st Cir. 1990) (release must exceed naturally occurring levels); *Amoco Oil Co. v. Borden, Inc.*, 889 F.2d 664, 670 (5th Cir. 1989) (only quantitative levels in a release that correspond to CERCLA "ARAR" clean-up standards may give rise to § 107 liability). Recall that the courts have uniformly found that there is no quantitative limit on "hazardous substance"—why not adopt the same policy here?

THE PROBLEM OF ASBESTOS I

Although asbestos has been EPA-listed as a hazardous substance under CERCLA (40 C.F.R. table 302.4), should a past construction project using asbestos subject the builder to § 107(a) liability for including within the structure a "hazardous substance"? Some courts have concluded that a release of a hazardous substance within a building is not a release "into the environment" under § 107(a)(4) (holding liable parties who cause a release) and § 101(22) (defining "release"). *See Covalt v. Carey Canada, Inc.*, 860 F.2d 1434, 1436–37 (7th Cir. 1988). Other courts hold that one who constructs a building with asbestos does not "dispose of" asbestos under § 107(a)(2). *See 3550 Stevens Creek Assoc. v. Barclays Bank*, 915 F.2d 1355, 1361 (9th Cir. 1990). Also, § 104(a)(3)(B) withholds Superfund expenditures when there is a "release" of asbestos from residential, business or community buildings. If someone undertakes asbestos removal from a structure, does CERCLA apply?

---

c.   FACILITY

Section 101(9) defines "facility" to include "any site or area where a hazardous substance has been deposited, stored, disposed of, or placed, or otherwise come to be located." Thanks to the catch-all language "come to be located," rather than serve as any kind of substantive limitation, the term "facility" includes "every conceivable area where hazardous substances may be found." *State of New York v. General Elec. Co.*, 592 F.Supp. 291, 296 (N.D.

N.Y. 1984). Thus, it has been interpreted to cover sewer pipes, manufacturing equipment, 220 miles of highway, a dragstrip, mine tailings at the base of a dam, and mines. Most attempts to limit the term "facility" have failed. Moreover, it is irrelevant that the facility is an ongoing disposal site and so could be regulated under RCRA. *See, e.g., Mardan Corp. v. C.G.C. Music, Ltd.*, 600 F.Supp. 1049, 1053–54 (D. Ariz. 1984), *aff'd* 804 F.2d 1454 (9th Cir. 1986).

The real issue in defining "facility," therefore, is the *scope* of the site to be cleaned up. At one extreme, a large geographic area (*e.g.,* all property under the control of a PRP) could be defined as a facility based on the presence of a hazardous substance in one portion of it. At the other extreme, the facility could be defined with such precision to include only those specific cubic meters of a PRP's property where hazardous substances were deposited or eventually found. The words of the statute suggest that the bounds of a facility should be defined at least in part by the bounds of the contamination. *See* § 101(9) (defining a facility where the hazardous substances were "deposited, stored, disposed of. * * * "). *See also e.g., Northwestern Mut. Life Ins. Co. v. Atlantic Research Corp.*, 847 F.Supp. 389, 395–96 (E.D. Va. 1994) ("What matters for purposes of defining the scope of the facility is where hazardous substances * * * [have] otherwise come to be located."); *ACC Chemical Co. v. Halliburton Co.*, 932 F.Supp. 233 (Iowa 1995) (where PCE had been pumped from a truck into a landfill at a manufacturing site, the relevant facility was the manufacturing site, not the truck); *Nurad, Inc. v. Hooper & Sons Co.*, 966 F.2d 837, 842–43 (4th Cir. 1992) (facility limited to portion of property that had been contaminated). However, an area that cannot reasonably or naturally be divided into multiple parts or functional units should be defined as a single "facility," even if it contains parts that are non-contaminated. *United States v. 150 Acres of Land,* 204 F.3d 698 (6th Cir. 2000) (parcels not separate when they were transferred on the same deed, and all were in the same undeveloped state; irrelevant that parcels were separate on land records); *United States v. Township of Brighton*, 153 F.3d 307, 313 (6th Cir. 1998) (even though most dumping was in southwest corner of property, entire property is a facility where some hazardous material was moved throughout the property); *Clear Lake Props. v. Rockwell Int'l Corp.*, 959 F.Supp. 763, 767–68 (S.D. Tex. 1997) (rejecting argument that surface structures constitute separate facility from subsurface soil and groundwater); *Sierra Club v. Seaboard Farms Inc.,* 387 F.3d 1167 (10th Cir. 2004) (holding that a farm complex as a whole, as opposed to every barn, waste lagoon, and land application area within the complex, constituted a single "facility").

THE PROBLEM OF ASBESTOS II

One important limitation on the reach of "facility" is the CERCLA definitional exclusion for a "consumer product in consumer use." This

> language has been consistently interpreted as excluding from CER-
> CLA liability the costs of removal of asbestos-containing materials
> from the structure of buildings. *Kane v. United States*, 15 F.3d 87 (8th
> Cir. 1994); *Dayton Independent School Dist. v. United States Mineral
> Products*, 906 F.2d 1059, 1065–66 (5th Cir. 1990). The exclusion does
> not, however, apply to a housing subdivision where asbestos was found
> in the soil and air, *United States v. Metate Asbestos Corp.*, 584 F.Supp.
> 1143, 1148 (D. Ariz. 1984), or to a site contaminated with asbestos. *CP
> Holdings, Inc. v. Goldberg–Zoino & Assoc., Inc.*, 769 F.Supp. 432 (D.
> N.H. 1991).

Courts have relied upon several commonsense principles to declare a
large area to be a single facility:

- The entire parcel is a facility if contamination extended throughout
  property, and property was never subdivided or leased to different
  tenants.—*Axel Johnson, Inc. v. Carroll Carolina Oil Co.*, 191 F.3d
  409 (4th Cir. 1999).

- The entire parcel is facility when there is no way of telling exactly
  where on the parcel the hazardous substances are located.—*In re
  Approximately Forty Acres in Tallmadge Township*, 566 N.W.2d 652,
  656 (Mich.Ct.App.1997).

- The entire area is facility where each of its quadrants are
  contaminated.—*Northwestern Mut. Life Ins. Co. v. Atlantic Research Corp.*, 847 F.Supp. 389, 399 (E.D. Va. 1994).

- If hazardous substances came to be located in several locations at a
  site, divided into five distinct geographical areas, the relevant
  facility was entire site and therefore defendants who asserted
  contribution claim were not required to establish liability for contribution with respect to each area within the site.—*Akzo Coatings,
  Inc. v. Aigner Corp.*, 960 F.Supp. 1354 (N.D. Ind. 1996).

- If the federal government incurs response costs in cleaning up
  certain parcels on a site that housed hazardous materials, and
  wishes to place a lien upon all of the site under § 107(1) of CERCLA,
  the defendant's property should be treated as a single unit, in order
  not to limit the strength of the lien provision as a CERCLA cost
  recovery tool.—*United States v. Glidden Co.*, 3 F. Supp. 2d 823, 831
  (N.D. Ohio 1997), *aff'd sub nom. United States v. 150 Acres of Land*,
  204 F.3d 698, 711 (6th Cir. 2000).[60]

The definition of the site has regulatory as well as financial
consequences. The most important is that on-site disposal of remediation

---

60. *But see Union Carbide Corp. v. Thiokol Corp.*, 890 F.Supp. 1035, 1042–43 (S.D. Ga.
1994) (where solid waste management units are geographically distinct from the landfill,
contain a variety of wastes not present in the landfill, and may require different clean-up
actions than the landfill, then they should be considered separate facilities from the landfill).

waste (*e.g.*, contaminated soils) need not go through state or federal licensing processes (*e.g.*, under RCRA) for waste disposal. § 121(e).

THE PROBLEM OF ASBESTOS III

Although asbestos has been EPA-listed as a hazardous substance under CERCLA (40 C.F.R. table 302.4), should a past construction project using asbestos subject the builder to § 107(a) liability for including within the structure a "hazardous substance"? Some courts have concluded that a release of a hazardous substance within a building is not a release "into the environment" under § 107(a)(4) (holding liable parties who cause a release) and § 101(22) (defining "release"). *See Covalt v. Carey Canada, Inc.*, 860 F.2d 1434, 1436–37 (7th Cir. 1988). Other courts hold that one who constructs a building with asbestos does not "dispose of" asbestos under § 107(a)(2). *See 3550 Stevens Creek Assoc. v. Barclays Bank*, 915 F.2d 1355, 1361 (9th Cir. 1990). *Also*, § 104(a)(3)(B) withholds Superfund expenditures when there is a "release" of asbestos from residential, business or community buildings.

Another problem regarding asbestos the term "facility." One important limitation on the reach of "facility" is the definitional exclusion for a "consumer product in consumer use." This language has been consistently interpreted as excluding from CERCLA liability the costs of removal of asbestos-containing materials from the structure of buildings. *Kane v. United States*, 15 F.3d 87 (8th Cir. 1994); *Dayton Independent School Dist. v. United States Mineral Products*, 906 F.2d 1059, 1065–66 (5th Cir. 1990). The exclusion does not, however, apply to a housing subdivision where asbestos was found in the soil and air, *United States v. Metate Asbestos Corp.*, 584 F.Supp. 1143, 1148 (D. Ariz. 1984), or to a site contaminated with asbestos. *CP Holdings, Inc. v. Goldberg–Zoino & Assoc., Inc.*, 769 F.Supp. 432 (D. N.H. 1991).

---

d. CAUSES THE INCURRENCE OF RESPONSE COSTS

If there is a "release or threatened release" of a "hazardous substance" at a "facility," liability cannot attach unless the above conditions "cause" the "incurrence of response costs." This final liability trigger is comprised of three elements: (1) the actions of the PRP must have brought about (however indirectly) the release or threatened release; (2) the release or threatened release must have caused response costs to be incurred; and (3) the costs incurred must be within the scope of recoverable response costs. Element (3) is discussed in the section that follows. Elements (1) and (2), however, warrant closer examination, because their idea of causation seems to require linkages between the PRP and the release or threatened release, and between the release or threatened release and incurred response costs.[61]

---

61. *See generally* John Nagle, *CERCLA, Causation, and Responsibility*, 78 MINN. L. REV. 1493 (1994).

Connection between a PRP and a release—As noted above in the discussion of CERCLA's strict liability scheme (particularly with respect to arranger-generator liability), courts typically need only one connection between the PRP and the release or threatened release: the PRP delivered hazardous substances to the site where there is

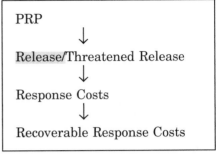

now, or may be, a release. There need be no specific linkage established between the delivery and the threat of release, or between the release and environmental damage. *See, e.g., United States v. Wade*, 577 F.Supp. 1326, 1333 (E.D. Pa. 1983). Plaintiffs do not need to "trace ownership of" or "fingerprint" the wastes, or prove conclusively that the hazardous substances at the site originated with the PRP-defendant. Courts are justifiably concerned about the difficulties in requiring such connections at sites where there are multiple contributors of waste. *See, e.g., United States v. Alcan Aluminum Corp.*, 990 F.2d 711, 720 (2d Cir. 1993); *State of New York v. Shore Realty Corp.*, 759 F.2d 1032, 1044 (2d Cir. 1985); *Town of Oyster Bay v. Occidental Chemical Corp.*, 987 F.Supp. 182, 195 (E.D. N.Y. 1997) ("Causation is not required to establish liability under CERCLA.").

Since a defendant normally cannot disprove the presumed causal link between the defendant's conduct and the release or threat of release, the next best defense is to argue, in the case of more than one defendant, that the harm is divisible, and that each defendant should be liable just for the harm attributable to that defendant's wastes. As noted above in the discussion of joint and several liability, most courts have interpreted CERCLA to impose such liability when the environmental harm is indivisible, but to allow for apportionment when two or more persons independently are responsible for a single harm that is divisible. *In re Bell Petroleum Servs., Inc.*, 3 F.3d 889, 895 (5th Cir. 1993); *United States v. R.W. Meyers, Inc.*, 889 F.2d 1497, 1507 (6th Cir. 1989). Such divisibility analysis, however, is different from the fairness- or equity-based analysis used for contribution and apportionment of liability. The court bases its decision on fact-based considerations, such as the ability to divide clean-up responsibilities geographically, *United States v. Broderick Investment Co.*, 862 F.Supp. 272, 275–77 (D. Colo. 1994), or on a volumetric basis, *In the Matter of Bell Petroleum Services, Inc. v. Sequa Corp.*, 3 F.3d 889 (5th Cir. 1993), *appeal after remand*, 64 F.3d 202 (5th Cir. 1995), rather than on equitable allocation principles. *United States v. Township of Brighton*, 153 F.3d 307, 318–19 (6th Cir. 1998).

Connection between a release and incurred response costs—In order to establish CERCLA liability, a plaintiff must show that the defendant falls within one of the four categories of PRPs, that the site is a "facility," and that there is a "release or a threatened release of hazardous substances at the facility." The final element that must be proven is that the plaintiff must have incurred costs in responding to the release or threatened release. *B.F.*

Goodrich v. Betkoski, 99 F.3d 505, 514 (2d Cir. 1996), *modified* by 112 F.3d 88 (2d Cir. 1996) (clarifying decision on rehearing). It is not a defense that the particular hazardous substance attributable to a *specific defendant* is not linked to the plaintiff's response costs. *Prisco v. A & D Carting Corp.*, 168 F.3d 593, 603 (2d Cir. 1999). But the plaintiff must establish that the release/threatened release caused *the plaintiff* to incur response costs. *Kalamazoo River Study Group v. Rockwell Intern.*, 171 F.3d 1065 (6th Cir. 1999). The plaintiff is not required to show that operators actually dumped waste, or had knowledge of dumping or leaking, in order to recover for response costs. *Crofton Ventures Ltd. Partnership v. G & H Partnership & Cyphers*, 258 F.3d 292 (4th Cir. 2001).

Especially when the release is merely threatened, the question arises whether there is a sufficient causal link between the defendant's conduct that gives rise to the threat and the incurrence of response costs. Since most courts do not require the plaintiff to show that the defendant's wastes caused the threat, the plaintiff instead must demonstrate that response costs were incurred *because of* the threat of release. This causation standard is met if the plaintiff can show a good faith belief that clean-up actions were necessary in light of the threat, and a clean-up response that is objectively reasonable. *Lansford–Coaldale Joint Water Auth. v. Tonolli Corp.*, 4 F.3d 1209, 1216–20 (3d Cir. 1993); *Dedham Water Co., Inc. v. Cumberland Farms Dairy, Inc.*, 972 F.2d 453 (1st Cir. 1992). As one leading decision states: "[w]e believe that the question of whether a release has caused incurrence of response costs should rest on a factual inquiry into the circumstances of the case [where the relevant inquiry is] whether the particular hazard justified any response action." *Amoco Oil Co. v. Borden, Inc.*, 889 F.2d 664, 670 (5th Cir. 1989).

The difficult next question, of course, is determining whether response costs incurred are "justified." The *Amoco* case states that the liability requirement is met if it is shown that "any release violates * * * any applicable [ARAR], including the most stringent." *But see United States v. Western Processing Co.*, 734 F. Supp. 930, 942 (W.D. Wash. 1990) (government need not show particular defendant's waste caused ARAR to be violated).

The courts are somewhat split on the issue of which party has the burden of proving or disproving the causal nexus between the release and the incurrence of response costs. On the one hand, some jurisdictions assume that after the plaintiff makes a prima facie case of defendant's-conduct-causing-a-release (typically met by showing that defendant dumped waste at the site and hazardous substances in that waste are also at the site), then "the burden of proof falls on the defendant to disprove causation." *Westfarm Assocs. Ltd. Partnership v. Washington Suburban Sanitary Com'n*, 66 F.3d 669, 681 (4th Cir. 1995); *Town of New Windsor v. Tesa Tuck, Inc.*, 919 F.Supp. 662, 669 (S.D. N.Y. 1996). On the other hand, several jurisdictions not only hold that the plaintiff must establish causation between a release and incurrence of response costs; these cases have also concluded that such causation is *not* shown if response costs are incurred merely because of a finding of hazardous substances above background levels. *United States v. DICO, Inc.*, 136 F.3d 572, 577–79 (8th Cir. 1998), vacated, 136 F.3d 572 (8th Cir. 1998), *vacated*, 136 F.3d 572 (8th Cir. 1998) (vacated because owner failed to exhaust administrative remedies as to counterclaim); *Licciardi v. Murphy Oil U.S.A. Inc.*, 111 F.3d 396, 398 (5th Cir. 1997).

Some observers are concerned that the causal link between release and costs will become a back-door way of introducing a threshold test based on the quantity, concentration, or risk of release of hazardous substances. The *Licciardi* case, in particular, may be headed in that direction. Would such a threshold test be a bad thing? If one is introduced, should it be based on quantity, concentration, or risk—or all of them, or something else? And, where should the threshold test be located in the statutory structure—here, or elsewhere?

4. RECOVERABLE COSTS

Section 107 provides that once a PRP has been found liable, it is responsible for "all costs of removal or remediation action," by the government. § 107(a)(4)(A).[62] These costs can be in the tens of millions of dollars. Moreover, where applicable, a PRP may also be liable for "damages * * * to * * * natural resources." § 107(a)(4)(C),[63] which may total hundreds of millions of dollars. The two questions we now address are: (1) What does "all costs" mean? (2) What are, and how does one measure, "damages to natural resources"?

a. "ALL COSTS"

The operative words in § 107(a)(4)(A) and (B) are "all," and "any." Read literally, the government is authorized to recover for all and any expenditures incurred as part of a clean-up operation. These costs include expenses for investigating, monitoring, and assessing a release, as well as the government's payments reimbursing contractors who actually do the § 104 remediation work. *Johnson County Airport Com'n v. Parsonitt Co., Inc.*, 916 F.Supp. 1090 (D. Kan. 1996). Recoverable costs may entail "indirect" costs, such as planning, overhead, and oversight costs. *See, e.g., United States v. Chromalloy American Corp.*, 158 F.3d 345, 351–52 (5th Cir. 1998); *United States v. Lowe*, 118 F.3d 399 (5th Cir. 1997); *United States v. R.W. Meyer, Inc.*, 889 F.2d 1497, 1503 (6th Cir. 1989); *Browning–Ferris Ind., Inc. v. Ter Maat*, 13 F. Supp. 2d 756, 769 (N.D. Ill. 1998); *Goodrich Corp. v. Town of Middlebury*, 311 F.3d 154 (2d Cir. 2002) (allowing the government to obtain pre-judgment interest under § 107(a)(4)); *Franklin County Convention Facilities Auth. v. Am. Premier Underwriters, Inc.*, 240 F.3d 534, 549 (6th

---

62. Section 107(a)(4)(A) also provides that such costs shall be "not inconsistent" with the NCP.

The costs recoverable for response actions by private parties are governed by § 107(a)(4)(B) and they are slightly more restricted in two ways: First, only "necessary costs" may be recovered; second, the costs must be "consistent with" the NCP (as opposed to "not inconsistent" in paragraph (A)). These differences are examined in detail in connection with private party cost-recovery actions in section E(3).

63. Section 107(a)(4)(D) also makes PRPs liable for health effects studies carried out by the Agency for Toxic Substances and Disease Registry, part of the Centers for Disease Control, pursuant to § 107(i).

Cir. 2001) (finding costs incurred in identifying potentially responsible parties are recoverable).

Some courts have rejected medical monitoring and evacuation costs as outside the scope of CERCLA, on the theory that recoverable costs should be limited to remediation efforts, not victims' relief. *In re Burbank Envir. Litigation*, 42 F. Supp. 2d 976 (C.D. Cal. 1998) (private medical monitoring costs not recoverable); *Price v. United States Navy*, 39 F.3d 1011 (9th Cir. 1994); *Daigle v. Shell Oil Co.*, 972 F.2d 1527 (10th Cir. 1992); *Romeo v. General Chemical Corp.*, 922 F.Supp. 287 (N.D. Cal. 1994). *But see Pneumo Abex Corp. v. Bessemer and Lake Erie R.R. Co.*, 936 F.Supp. 1250 (E.D. Va. 1996) (medical monitoring costs recoverable). Other courts have permitted recovery for monitoring of a release, but not the oversight of the monitoring of others. *United States v. Rohm & Haas Co.*, 2 F.3d 1265 (3d Cir. 1993), *overruled sub nom. U.S. v. E.I. Dupont De Nemours and Co. Inc.*, 432 F.3d 161 (3d Cir. 2005) (overruled on the grounds that that CERCLA authorizes United States to recover costs incurred in overseeing private party removal and remedial actions, to extent such costs are consistent with National Contingency Plan). While some courts have left open the question of whether unreasonable, unnecessary, or excessive costs can be recovered, *Matter of Bell Petroleum*, 3 F.3d 889, 907 n.26 (5th Cir. 1993), others have simply assumed that the modifier "all" permits recovery of even apparently unreasonable costs. *United States v. Hardage*, 982 F.2d 1436 (10th Cir. 1992).[64]

Future costs are another important issue. While CERCLA does not contemplate awards of future monetary damages, § 113(g)(2) permits courts to enter a declaratory judgment on liability for "further response costs or damages." *United States v. Hughes, Hubbard & Reed*, 68 F.3d 811 (3d Cir. 1995); *Kelley v. E.I. DuPont de Nemours & Co.*, 17 F.3d 836 (6th Cir. 1994); *United States v. Davis*, 20 F. Supp. 2d 326, 332 (D.R.I. 1998). When there is such a judgment, PRPs may be liable to CERCLA plaintiffs for future costs not inconsistent with the NCP. *Laidlaw Waste System, Inc. v. Mallinckrodt, Inc.*, 925 F.Supp. 624 (E.D. Mo. 1996).

CERCLA LIENS

Section 107(l)(1) provides that "[a]ll costs and damages for which a person is liable to the United States * * * shall constitute a lien in favor of the United States" upon all real property owned by the PRP which is subject to a removal or remedial action. Since the lien is imposed without normal procedural safeguards (prior notice or pre-deprivation hearing), one leading case has found that the section violates procedural due process. *Reardon v. United States*, 947 F.2d 1509 (1st Cir. 1991).

---

64. The government is entitled to recover its attorneys' fees and other costs of litigation. *United States v. Bell Petroleum Services, Inc.*, 734 F.Supp. 771 (W.D. Tex. 1990), *rev'd on* other grounds, 3 F.3d 889 (5th Cir. 1993).

b. "NOT INCONSISTENT WITH THE NATIONAL CONTINGENCY PLAN"

CERCLA also requires that the governmental party's[65] actions giving rise to the costs to be recovered be "not inconsistent with" the NCP. § 107(a)(4)(A). This double-negative construction has been read to mean that the *challenger* of the costs of a removal or remedial action has the burden of proving that costs incurred were inconsistent with the NCP. This is generally a difficult task. PRPs may succeed only if they can show that the NCP's substantive or procedural requirements were not followed, making the government's clean-up orders arbitrary and capricious. Moreover, pre-enforcement suits are generally forbidden by CERCLA § 113(h), *Lone Pine Steering Committee v. United States EPA*, 600 F.Supp. 1487, 1493 (D.N.J. 1985), so a challenger is in the position of asking EPA to redo the remedy and asking taxpayers to foot more of the bill. Most courts are extremely reluctant to second guess the EPA's choice of remedy. *United States v. Northeastern Pharmaceutical & Chemical Co., Inc.*, 810 F.2d 726 (8th Cir. 1986) (choice of a particular clean-up method is within discretion of government). For PRPs, this presumption means that so long as response costs are in accord with the NCP, (1) there is no obligation on the United States to minimize its response costs to benefit PRPs liable for the costs, *United States v. Akzo Nobel Coatings, Inc.*, 990 F.Supp. 892 (E.D. Mich. 1998), and (2) all costs expended on these NCP-consistent remedies are recoverable. *United States v. Hardage*, 982 F.2d 1436, 1443 (10th Cir. 1992).

Although the deck is certainly stacked against PRPs wishing to assert that certain costs are inconsistent with NCP, it is still possible for PRPs to avoid paying unreasonable costs. *See, e.g., State of Minnesota v. Kalman W. Abrams Metals, Inc.*, 155 F.3d 1019, 1024–25 (8th Cir. 1998) (state clean-up was arbitrary and capricious and inconsistent with NCP for failure to do feasibility study before selecting remedy). The leading case is *In re Bell Petroleum Services, Inc.*, 3 F.3d 889 (5th Cir. 1993). The NCP provides for an alternate water supply when there was a "substantial danger to public health or the environment," but the otherwise liable PRP successfully argued that the administrative record failed to demonstrate any "substantial danger." The court was unpersuaded by EPA's position that costs incurred during remediation should be accepted by courts, since EPA had in place internal agency audits and other self-regulating systems:

Acceptance of the EPA's position would effectively prohibit judicial review of the EPA's expenditures. In short, we would give the EPA a blank check in conducting response actions. We seriously doubt that Congress intended to give the EPA such unrestrained spending discretion. Moreover, such unbridled discretion removes any restraint upon the conduct of the EPA in exercising its awesome powers; if the EPA knows there are no economic consequences to it, its decisions and conduct are likely to be less responsible. 3 F.3d at 906–07.

---

65. Private parties' costs must be "consistent with" the NCP. § 107(a)(4)(B). The meaning of this difference in language is addressed below in connection with private cost recovery actions.

Inconsistency may also be present if there is a government violation of the NCP's procedural standards. Failure to comply with the NCP requirement for public notice and comment can be grounds for precluding recovery of response costs. *VME Americas, Inc. v. Hein–Werner Corp.*, 946 F.Supp. 683 (E.D. Wis. 1996). If the government incurs response costs for remedial work without conducting an adequate remedial investigation (the RI/FS) or evaluating alternative remedies, there is inconsistency with the NCP. Such costs are non-recoverable for being arbitrary and capricious. *Washington State Dept. of Transp. v. Washington Natural Gas Co.*, Pacificorp., 59 F.3d 793 (9th Cir. 1995).

c.   NATURAL RESOURCE DAMAGES

Apart from "all costs of removal and remedial action," a PRP may also discover that it is liable for "damages for injury to, destruction of, or loss of natural resources." § 107(a)(4)(C). Such natural resource damage (NRD) claims can be staggering—sometimes twice to three times the amounts involved in a cost-recovery claim. There are four immediate differences between cost-recovery and natural resource damage actions. First, the government need not spend any money first in order to seek natural resource damages. Second, any monetary recovery received for such damages may only be used to "restore, replace, or acquire the equivalent of such natural resources." § 107(f)(1). Third, there is an exception to the normal rule of unlimited retroactive CERCLA liability, in that § 107(f)(1) precludes recovery where the release, and damages from the release, occurred prior to CERCLA's enactment. Fourth, § 113(g) sets out special statutes of limitations for natural resource damage claims.[66]

What does the statutory terminology mean? The following sections explore each of § 107(a)(4)(C)'s terms in detail.

i.   *"Natural Resources"*

The words "natural resources" are broadly defined in § 101(16) to include "land, fish, wildlife, biota, air, water, ground water, drinking water supplies, and other such resources" that "belong * * * to, [are] managed by, held in trust by, * * * or otherwise controlled by the United States [,] * * * any State or local government, any foreign government, [or] Indian tribe. * * *" This language encompasses virtually all effects a hazardous substance can have on nature, so long as that which is affected is somehow owned or controlled or held in trust by a government entity.

ii.   *Injuries Caused by a Release*

Section 107(a)(C) of CERCLA requires that natural resources damages "result[] from [a] release." In order to satisfy this statutory standard of causation, the Department of Interior—which was given authority to issue

---

66.   For federal facilities, facilities on the NPL, and those subject to remedial action, the statute of limitations does not begin to run until three years after completion of remedial work. For all other sites, the statute runs three years after the discovery of the loss, or the date on which regulations are promulgated for assessing natural resource damages, whichever is later. *See* 43 C.F.R. § 11.91(e).

NRD regulations—has established criteria that must be proven by the party bringing the natural resource damage claim. The party must show that the injury alleged to have occurred is a "commonly documented" response to releases of such hazardous substances; that the hazardous substances are known to cause such injury in field studies or controlled experiments; and that the injury can be measured by practical techniques and has been "adequately documented in scientific literature." 43 C.F.R. § 11.62(f)(2). Other limitations on natural resource damages include: (1) damages must be based on an actual injury to the state's legal interest, and (2) all damages recovered by the state must be used solely to restore, replace, or acquire resources and could not be used for other purposes. CERCLA preempts state law claims that would permit use of such recoveries for other purposes. *State of New Mexico et al v. General Elec. Co.*, 467 F.3d 1223 (10th Cir. 2006).

Although these criteria have been sustained, *State of Ohio v. U.S. Dept. of Interior*, 880 F.2d 432 472 (D.C. Cir. 1989) (*Ohio II*), questions persist about the standard of proof required to demonstrate that natural resources injuries "result[] from" a particular release. Specifically, should the causation-of-injury standard be less demanding than that of the common law? And should CERCLA § 301(c)(2)'s requirement that "best available procedures" be used to determine natural resources damages permit speculative assessments of causation? In 1998, the United States Court of Appeals for the District of Columbia considered both questions.

> * * * Regarding causation, this court has repeatedly held that CERCLA is ambiguous on the precise question of what standard of proof is required to demonstrate that natural resource injuries were caused by, or "result[] from," a particular release. *See Ohio II*, 880 F.2d at 472 ("[W]hile we agree with petitioners that Congress expressed dissatisfaction with the common law as a norm in several areas of damage assessment, we conclude that CERCLA is at best ambiguous on the question of whether the causation-of-injury standard under § 107(a)(4)(C) must be less demanding than that of the common law."); *Kennecott*, 88 F.3d at 1224 ("CERCLA left it to Interior to define the measure of damages in natural resources damage assessment cases. * * * While the statutory language requires some causal connection between the element of damages and the injury—the damages must be 'for' an injury 'resulting from a release of oil or a hazardous substance'—Congress has not specified precisely what that causal relationship should be.") (citation omitted).
>
> Similarly, we find nothing in the "resulting from" language of subsections 107(a)(4)(C) and 301(c)(1), or other provisions of CER-CLA, to indicate that the Congress unambiguously intended a particular kind or quantity of causation and injury proof as a prerequisite to recovery of natural resources damages. While we have noted that the "best available procedures" language of subsection 301(c)(2) indicates that it would be inconsistent with CERCLA to permit "unduly speculative assessments," *Ohio II*, 880 F.2d at 462, we have never held that simply because assessments

procedures are in some measure "speculative" or "predictive" they are contrary to CERCLA's "best available procedures" admonition. Rather, predictive submodels that represent rational scientific judgments about the probability that a particular release will cause a specific type and amount of injury are consistent with the Congress's intent to develop a "standardized system for assessing such damage which is efficient as to both time and cost." S.REP. No. 96–848, at 85 (1980); cf. Ohio II, 880 F.2d at 455 ("[S]upport for the proposition that Congress adopted common-law damage standards wholesale into CERCLA is slim to nonexistent.").

National Ass'n of Manufacturers v. Department of the Interior, 134 F.3d 1095, 1105 (D.C. Cir. 1998).

PROBLEM

1. What is the law of National Resources Damage causation after the *National Association of Manufacturers* case?

2. Can you apply the *National Association of Manufacturers* test to the following facts, where the question is whether a party's "release" has caused a "specific type * * * of injury"?

Outside of Denver is a 40 square mile area once called the most polluted spot in the world. This is the Rocky Mountain Arsenal, where for several decades both the Shell Oil Company (which was making pesticides) and the United States Army (which was making nerve gas) discharged toxic and dangerous wastes into unlined lagoons. When birds or mammals (*e.g.,* chipmunks and prairie dogs) drank from the lagoons, they became sick, and usually died. When the Army and Shell stopped their operations, the poisoned waters in the lagoons eventually seeped into the ground water, where they remain to this day. The surface waters in the lagoons on the site have been replaced by water from rain and snowfall. A thriving animal population has emerged on the now abandoned Arsenal grounds. Bald eagles find this 40 square miles is perfect habitat to nest and raise their young. Mule deer have invaded the site. The Arsenal grounds have become a part of the National Wildlife Refuge System.

3. What are the "natural resources damages" at the Arsenal, and who, or what, is the cause?

---

iii. Who May Bring Suit

Unlike the rest of section 107, which permits any responder to sue, only certain public "trustees" may sue for natural resources damages—the United States, the states, and Indian tribes (and local governments if specifically authorized by state law). § 107(F)(1); *Artesian Water Co. v. Government of New Castle County*, 851 F.2d 643, 649 (3d Cir. 1988). Conversely, public trustees recover for damages to private property or other "purely private" interests. *Ohio II*, 880 F.2d at 460; *Exxon Corp. v. Hunt*, 475 U.S. 355, 375 (1986) (compensation to "third parties for damage resulting from hazardous substance discharges * * * [is] clearly beyond the scope of CERCLA").

It is not always easy to determine whether a particular loss of natural resources is "private" or "public." Consider the case of a release of hazardous substances in the Great Lakes, or marine environments within the jurisdiction of a coastal state, that kill game or fish. CERCLA defines "natural resources" to encompass "fish" and "wildlife." § 101(16). Case law assumes that a state has a sovereign interest in natural resources within its boundaries. *Alaska Sport Fishing Assoc. v. Exxon Corp.*, 34 F.3d 769, 773 (9th Cir. 1994). If the release kills so much fish or game in the Great Lakes or coastal marine environments that they are no longer usable for commercial purposes, is the adverse effect of the release on harvesting activities a "purely private" loss for which the public trustee may not recover? Does it make any difference that commercial hunting and fishing operations there may not pay anything to the state for the privilege of exploiting public fish and game stocks? *See National Assoc. of Manufacturers v. U.S. Dept. of Interior*, 134 F.3d 1095, 1114 (D.C. Cir. 1998).

iv.   "Damages"

Section 107(a)(4)(C) provides that public trustees may recover "damages for injury to, destruction of, or loss of natural resources. * * *," while § 107(f)(1) cautions that these damages "shall not be limited by the sums which can be used to restore or replace such resources."

CERCLA DAMAGES AND STATE LAW

Does § 107(a)(4)(C) preempt states from bringing actions for money damages against PRPs under state law?

In *New Mexico v. General Elec. Co.,* 467 F.3d 1223 (10th Cir. 2006), the court denied the state from seeking unrestricted money damages for contamination to groundwater, because such a reward would conflict with CERCLA's comprehensive natural resources damages scheme:

"An unrestricted award of money damages does not restore or replace contaminated natural resources. ... We hold CERCLA's comprehensive NRD scheme preempts any state remedy designed to achieve something other than the restoration, replacement, or acquisition of the equivalent of a contaminated natural resource. ... Under the logic of the State's approach, hazardous waste sites need never be cleaned up as long as PRPs are willing or required to tender money damages to a state as trustee." *Id.* at 1247–48.

Furthermore, CERCLA § 301(c) directs the Department of Interior to promulgate two kinds of assessment methodologies for measuring natural resources damages: Type A rules "for simplified assessments requiring minimal field observation;" and Type B rules "for conducting [more complex] assessments in individual cases to determine the type and extent of short- and long-term injury, destruction or loss."[67]

When the Interior Department was prescribing methods for estimating the amount of money to be sought for natural resources damages that would comply with §§ 301(c) and 107(f)(1), several questions arose.

- Should natural resources damages be based on restoration/replacement costs, or the diminution-of-use value?

- If use values are relevant, as of when should these be calculated?

- Should use values be limited to market prices, or may measurement techniques be employed, such as "contingent valuation," which sets up hypothetical markets to elicit an individual's economic valuation of a natural resource?[68]

- May "non-use" values be used to calculate natural resource damages, for example, "option" and "existence" value, which measure an individual's willingness to pay to avoid an injury to a natural resources site, even if the individual will never visit (use) the site?[69]

The Interior Department's initial "Type B" regulations for assessing natural resources damages provided that the dollar amounts recoverable would be either restoration/replacement costs, or diminution of use values, whichever was less. These regulations chose to measure "use" values in large part according to market values. Only when it or a similar resource is not traded in a market would contingent valuation be acceptable. The regulations also largely excluded non-use values in the damages calculation. The case that follows, *Ohio II*, analyzes whether these regulations comport with CERCLA and with sound economic methodology.[70]

Ohio v. Department of the Interior [Ohio II]
880 F.2d 432 (D.C. Cir. 1989)

■ WALD, CHIEF JUDGE, and SPOTTSWOOD W. ROBINSON III and MIKVA, CIRCUIT JUDGES.

* * *

III. The "Lesser–Of" Rule

The most significant issue in this case concerns the validity of the regulation providing that damages for despoilment of natural resources

67. Damage assessments made pursuant to these regulations enjoy a rebuttable presumption of validity. § 107(F)(2)(c).

68. *See* B. Binger, R. Coppole, & Elizabeth Hoffman, *The Use of Contingent Valuation Methodology in Natural Resource Damage Assessments: Legal Fact and Economic Fiction,* 89 NORTHWESTERN U.L. REV. 1029 (1995).

69. Option value is the dollar amount an individual is willing to pay, although the individual is not using a resource, but wishes to reserve the option to use that resource in the future. Existence value is the dollar amount an individual is willing to pay although that individual does not ever plan to use the resource.

70. *See generally* Douglas Williams, *Valuing Natural Environments: Compensation, Market Norms, and the Idea of Public Goods,* 27 CONN. L. REV. 365 (1995).

shall be "the *lesser of*: restoration or replacement costs; or diminution of use values." 43 C.F.R. § 11.35(b)(2) (1987) (emphasis added).

State and Environmental Petitioners challenge Interior's "lesser of" rule, insisting that CERCLA requires damages to be at least sufficient to pay the cost in every case of restoring, replacing or acquiring the equivalent of the damaged resource (hereinafter referred to shorthandedly as "restoration"). Because in some—probably a majority of—cases lost-use-value will be lower than the cost of restoration, Interior's rule will result in damages award too small to pay for the costs or restoration.

* * *

Although our resolution of the dispute submerges us in the minutiae of CERCLA text and legislative materials, we initially stress the enormous practical significance of the "lesser of" rule. A hypothetical example will illustrate the point: imagine a hazardous substance spill that kills a rookery of fur seals and destroys a habitat for seabirds at a sealife reserve. The lost use value of the seals and seabird habitat would be measured by the market value of the fur seals' pelts (which would be approximately $15 each) plus the selling price per acre of land comparable in value to that on which the spoiled bird habitat was located. Even if, as likely, that use value turns out to be far less than the cost of restoring the rookery and seabird habitat, it would nonetheless be the only measure of damages eligible for the presumption of recoverability under the Interior rule.

* * *

Interior's "lesser of" rule operates on the premise that, as the cost of a restoration project goes up relative to the value of the injured resource, at some point it becomes wasteful to require responsible parties to pay the full cost of restoration. The logic behind the rule is the same logic that prevents an individual from paying $8,000 to repair a collision-damaged car that was worth only $5,000 before the collision. Just as a prudent individual would sell the damaged car for scrap and then spend $5,000 on a used car in similar condition, DOI's rule requires a polluter to pay a sum equal to the diminution in the use value of a resource whenever that sum is less than restoration cost. What is significant about Interior's rule is the point at which it deems restoration "inefficient." Interior chose to draw the line not at the point where restoration becomes practically impossible, nor at the point where the cost of restoration becomes grossly disproportionate to the use value of the resource, but rather at the point where restoration cost exceeds—by any amount, however small—the use value of the resource. Thus, while we agree with DOI that CERCLA permits it to establish a rule exempting responsible parties *in some cases* from having to pay the full cost of restoration of natural resources, we also agree with Petitioners that it does not permit Interior to draw the line on an automatic "which costs less" basis.

Interior's "lesser of" rule squarely rejects the concept of any clearly expressed congressional preference for recovering the full cost of restoration from responsible parties. The challenged regulation treats the two alternative measures of damages, restoration cost and use value, as though the choice between them were a matter of complete indifference from the statutory point of view: thus, in any given case, the rule makes damages turn solely on whichever standard is less expensive. * * *

Based on the discussion that follows, we conclude that CERCLA unambiguously mandates a distinct preference for using restoration cost as the measure of damages, and so precludes a "lesser of" rule which totally ignores that preference.

The strongest linguistic evidence of Congress' intent to establish a distinct preference for restoration costs as the measure of damages is contained in § 107(f)(1) of CERCLA. That section states that natural resource damages recovered by a government trustee are "for use only to restore, replace, or acquire the equivalent of such natural resources." It goes on to state: "The measure of damages in any action under [§ 107(a)(C)] shall not be limited by the sums which can be used to restore or replace such resources."

By mandating the use of all damages to restore the injured resources, Congress underscored in § 107(f)(1) its paramount restorative purpose for imposing damages at all. It would be odd indeed for a Congress so insistent that all damages be spent on restoration to allow a "lesser" measure of damages than the cost of restoration in the majority of cases. * * *

In this connection, it should be noted that Interior makes no claim that a "use value" measure will provide enough money to pay for *any* of the three uses to which all damages must be assigned: restoration, replacement, *or acquisition of an equivalent resource.* Nor could Interior make such a claim, because its "lesser of" rule not only calculates use value quite differently from restoration or replacement cost but it also fails to link measurement of use value in any way to the cost of acquiring an equivalent resource. For example, Interior could not possibly maintain that recovering $15 per pelt for the fur seals killed by a * * * release would enable the purchase of an "equivalent" number of fur seals.

The same section of CERCLA that mandates the expenditures of all damages on restoration * * * provides that the measure of damages "shall not be limited by" restoration costs. § 107(f)(1). This provision obviously reflects Congress' apparent concern that its restorative purpose for imposing damages not be construed as making restoration cost a damages ceiling. But the explicit command that damages "shall not be limited by" restoration costs also carries in it an implicit assumption that restoration cost will serve as the basic measure of damages in many if not most CERCLA cases. It would be markedly inconsistent with the restorative thrust of the whole section to limit restoration-based damages, as Interior's rule does, to a minuscule number of cases where restoration is cheaper than paying for lost use.

* * *

The legislative history of CERCLA confirms that restoration costs were intended to be the presumptive measure of recovery. Senate proponents of the legislation, in the committee report and on the Senate floor, repeatedly emphasized that their primary objective in assessing damages for public resources was to achieve restoration.

Interior justifies the "lesser of" rule as being economically efficient. Under DOI's economic efficiency view, making restoration cost the measure of damages would be a waste of money whenever restoration would cost more than the use value of the resource. Its explanation of the proposed rules included the following statement:

> [I]f use value is higher than the cost of restoration or replacement, then it would be more rational for society to be compensated for the cost to restore or replace the lost resource than to be compensated for the lost use. Conversely, if restoration or replacement costs are higher than the value of uses foregone, it is rational for society to compensate individuals for their lost uses rather than the cost to restore or replace the injured natural resource.

50 Fed. Reg. at 52,141. *See also* 51 Fed. Reg. at 27,704 ("lesser of" rule "promotes a rational allocation of society's assets").

This is nothing more or less than cost-benefit analysis: Interior's rule attempts to optimize social welfare by restoring an injured resource only when the diminution in the resource's value to society is greater in magnitude than the cost of restoring it. * * *

The fatal flaw of Interior's approach, however, is that it assumes that natural resources are fungible goods, just like any other, and that the value to society generated by a particular resource can be accurately measured in every case—assumptions that Congress apparently rejected. As the foregoing examination of CERCLA's text, structure and legislative history illustrates, Congress saw restoration as the presumptively correct remedy for injury to natural resources. To say that Congress placed a thumb on the scales in favor of restoration is not to say that it forswore the goal of efficiency. "Efficiency," standing alone, simply means that the chosen policy will dictate the result that achieves the greatest value to society. Whether a particular choice is efficient depends on *how the various alternatives are valued.* Our reading of CERCLA does not attribute to Congress an irrational dislike of "efficiency"; rather, it suggests that Congress was skeptical of the ability of human beings to measure the true "value" of a natural resource. Indeed, even the common law recognizes that restoration is the proper remedy for injury to property where measurement of damages by some other method will fail to compensate fully for the injury. Congress' refusal to view use value and restoration cost as having equal presumptive legitimacy merely recognizes that natural resources have value that is not readily measured by traditional means. Congress delegated to Interior the job of deciding at what point the presumption of restoration falls away, but its repeated emphasis on the primacy of restoration rejected the underlying premise of Interior's rule, which is that restoration is wasteful if its cost exceeds—by even the slightest amount—the diminution in use value of the injured resource.

* * *

vi. The Hierarchy of Assessment Methods

The regulations establish a rigid hierarchy of permissible methods for determining "use values," limiting recovery to the price commanded by the resource on the open market, unless the trustee finds that "the market for the resource is not reasonably competitive." 43 C.F.R. § 11.83(c)(1). If the trustee makes such a finding, it may "appraise" the market value in accordance with the relevant sections of the "Uniform Appraisal Standards for Federal Land Acquisition," *see* 43 C.F.R. § 11.83(c)(2). Only when neither the market value nor the appraisal method is "appropriate" can other methods of determining use value be employed, *see* 43 C.F.R. § 11.83(d).

* * * While it is not irrational to look to market price as one factor in determining the use value of a resource, it is unreasonable to view market price as the exclusive factor, or even the predominant one. From the bald eagle to the blue whale and snail darter, natural resources have values that are not fully captured by the market system. DOI's own CERCLA 301 Project Team recognized that "most government resources, particularly resources for which natural resource damages would be sought[,] may often have no market." DOI has failed to explain its departure from this view. Indeed, many of the materials in the record on which DOI relied in developing its rules regarding contingent valuation expressed the same idea; it is the incompleteness of market processes that gives rise to the need for contingent valuation [CV] techniques. * * *

* * *

Neither the statute nor its legislative history evinces any congressional intent to limit use values to market prices. On the contrary, Congress intended the damage assessment regulations to capture fully all aspects of loss. CERCLA section 301(c)(2) commands Interior to "identify the best available procedures to determine [natural resource] damages, including both direct and indirect injury, destruction or loss." 42 U.S.C. § 9651(c)(2). The Senate CERCLA report stated that assessment procedures should provide trustees "a choice of acceptable damage assessment methodologies to be employed [and should] select the most accurate and credible damage assessment methodologies available." S.Rep. No. 848, 96th Cong., 2d Sess. 85–86 (1980). The current rules defeat this intent by arbitrarily limiting use values to market prices.

On remand, DOI should consider a rule that would permit trustees to derive use values for natural resources by summing up all reliably calculated use values, however measured, so long as the trustee does not double count. Market valuation can of course serve as one factor to be considered, but by itself it will necessarily be incomplete. In this vein, we instruct DOI that its decision to limit the role of non-consumptive values, such as option and existence values, in the calculation of use values rests on an erroneous construction of the statute.

* * * First, section 301(c)(2) requires Interior to "take into consideration factors including, *but not limited to* * * * use value." 42 U.S.C. § 9651(c)(2) (emphasis added). The statute's command is expressly not

limited to use value; if anything, the language implies that DOI is to include in its regulations other factors in addition to use value. Second, even under its reading of section 301(c), DOI has failed to explain why option and existence values should be excluded from the category of recognized use values. Indeed, the CERCLA 301 Project Team draft referred to option and existence values as "non-consumptive use values" (emphasis added). Option and existence values may represent "passive" use, but they nonetheless reflect utility derived by humans from a resource, and thus, prima facie, ought to be included in a damage assessment. DOI is entitled to rank methodologies according to its view of their reliability, but it cannot base its complete exclusion of option and existence values on an incorrect reading of the statute.

* * *

XIII. Contingent Valuation

* * *

The CV process "includes all techniques that set up hypothetical markets to elicit an individual's economic valuation of a natural resource." CV involves a series of interviews with individuals for the purpose of ascertaining the values they respectively attach to particular changes in particular resources. Among the several formats available to an interviewer in developing the hypothetical scenario embodied in a CV survey are direct questioning, by which the interviewer learns how much the interviewee is willing to pay for the resource; bidding formats, for example, the interviewee is asked whether he or she would pay a given amount for a resource and, depending upon the response, the bid is set higher or lower until a final price is derived; and a "take or leave it" format, in which the interviewee decides whether or not he or she is willing to pay a designated amount of money for the resource. CV methodology thus enables ascertainment of individually-expressed values for different levels of quality of resources, and dollar values of individuals' changes in well-being. The regulations also sanction resort to CV methodology in determining "option" and "existence" values.

Industry Petitioners' complaint is limited to DOI's inclusion of CV in its assessment methodology. They claim fatal departures from CERCLA on grounds that CV methodology is inharmonious with common law damage assessment principles, and is considerably less than a "best available procedure." * * *

* * *

The primary argument of Industry Petitioners is that the possibility of bias is inherent in CV methodology, and disqualifies it as a "best available procedure." In evaluating the utility of CV methodology in assessing damages for impairment of natural resources, DOI surveyed a number of studies which analyzed the methodology, addressed the shortcomings of various questionnaires, and recommended steps needed to fashion reliable CV assessments. For example, an early study by the Water Resources Council advised that questions in CV surveys be "carefully designed and pretested," a warning DOI was quick to heed.

Industry Petitioners urge, however, that even assuming that questions are artfully drafted and carefully circumscribed, there is such a high degree of variation in size of the groups surveyed, and such a concomitant fluctuation in aggregations of damages, that CV methodology cannot be considered a "best available procedure." We think this attack on CV methodology is insufficient in a facial challenge to invalidate CV as an available assessment technique. The extent of damage to natural resources from releases of oil and hazardous substances varies greatly, and though the impact may be widespread and severe, it is in the mission of CERCLA to assess the public loss. Certainly nothing in CV methodology itself shapes the injury inflicted by an environmental disaster, or influences identification of the population affected thereby. The argument of Industry Petitioners strikes at CERCLA, not CV's implementation, and can appropriately be considered only by Congress.

Similarly, we find wanting Industry Petitioners' protest that CV does not rise to the status of a "best available procedure" because willingness-to-pay—a factor prominent in CV methodology—can lead to overestimates by survey respondents. The premise of this argument is that respondents do not actually pay money, and likely will overstate their willingness-to-pay. One study relied upon by Industry Petitioners hypothesizes that respondents may "respond in ways that are more indicative of what they would like to see done than how they would behave in an actual market," and also observes that the converse is possible. The simple and obvious safeguard against overstatement, however, is more sophisticated questioning. Even as matters now stand, the risk of overestimation has not been shown to produce such egregious results as to justify judicial overruling of DOI's careful estimate of the caliber and worth of CV methodology.

NOTES AND QUESTIONS

1. *Ohio II* made short work of Interior's regulations—which was not too surprising because they were promulgated by the Reagan Administration which was extremely hostile to natural resource damages at all. In *Colorado v. U.S. Dept. of Interior*, 880 F.2d 481 (D.C. Cir. 1989), the Interior Department's Type A regulations were invalidated in part for the same reasons that the *Ohio II* case invalidated much of the Type B regulations. The revised Type A regulations were later upheld in *National Assoc. of Manufacturers v. U.S. Dept. of Interior*, 134 F.3d 1095 (D.C. Cir. 1998).

2. Do you agree with the court's resolution of these issues? Was there merit to the effort to introduce efficiency and market valuation into the assessment of damages? Was Congress acting wisely in its emphasis on restoration?

3. Assume that a release of a hazardous substance in Year 0 will require a restoration project costing $10 million in Year 10. CERCLA requires that the PRP pay natural resources damages in Year 0 sufficient to cover those $10 million of costs in Year 10. Because of the inherent time value of money when invested, as well as inflation, an amount less than $10 million invested in Year 0 will yield CERCLA's required $10 million at the time restoration costs are actively incurred in Year 10. However, it is not

possible to know exactly how much should be collected from a liable PRP in Year 0 if one does not know in Year 0 exactly how much restoration costs will be in Year 10 (*i.e.*, if the $10 million figure proves to be wrong). Moreover, even if the Year 10 future restoration costs can be properly estimated in Year 0, the dollars collected from the PRP in Year 0 will not cover the Year 10 costs if the interest rate ("discount rate") applied to the Year 0 dollars is incorrect.

So, two related uncertainties arise as a result of the need to collect and invest natural resources damages judgments in the present, in order to pay for restoration costs in the future. First, one must take into account the reality that the value of a particular natural resource, and the cost of a restoration project, may rise over time. In ascertaining the measure of damages in Year 0, the public trustee must try to predict what the *future* Year 10 cost of restoration will be. An error of estimation in the present, when damages are paid by PRPs, will produce insufficient revenue to pay the cost of restoration in the future. Second, a mistake made in predicting the discount rate over time will also produce insufficient funds when the time arrives to restore the damaged natural resources. The higher the discount rate selected in Year 0, the smaller the present value of the funds that must be collected from the PRP in Year 0 to pay for restoration costs in Year 10. If the discount rate between Year 0 and Year 10 proves to be less than the rate selected in Year 0, there will not be enough funds to pay for the restoration in Year 10. The situation is compounded when the cost of future Year 10 restoration is underestimated in Year 0.

5. DEFENSES

CERCLA is extremely unsympathetic to traditional defenses to liability. Instead of using defenses applicable to common law tort actions, parties facing CERCLA liability must (1) negate the elements of the plaintiff's case described above; (2) assert one of the four statutory defenses to CERCLA liability set out in § 107(b); or (3) rely on one of the few non-§ 107(b) defenses that are available.

We have already considered the numerous elements of the CERCLA plaintiff's case (consistency with the NCP, PRP status of defendant, causation, etc.) and defendants' potential responses. Negating the plaintiff's case is likely to be extremely difficult. We turn our attention now to the statutory and non-statutory defenses.

a.   SECTION 107(B) DEFENSES

Reread section 107(b). In order for a defendant successfully to employ a § 107(b) defense, there must be proof that the "damages resulting [from a release]" were "caused solely" by some other source—an "act of God," or "an act of war," or "an act or omission of a third party" with whom the defendant does not have a "contractual relationship." The SARA Amendments of 1986 added a definition of "contractual relationship" which was intended to exclude from liability innocent landowners or buyers. CERCLA § 101(35)(A). All four of these defenses share the common requirement that the damages be caused *solely* by events having nothing to do with the defendant. *G.J. Leasing Co. v. Union Elec. Co.*, 854 F.Supp. 539, 566–67 (S.D. Ill. 1994). Conversely, if the defendant in any conceivable way contributed to the release or amount of damages incurred, then the § 107(b) defense is not available. *See United States v. Mottolo*, 26 F.3d 261 (1st Cir. 1994). The defenses will fail if the PRP had any role, no matter how attenuated, in the hazardous waste problem for which clean-up costs have been incurred. *See State of New York v. Shore Realty Corp.*, 759 F.2d 1032, 1048–49 (2d Cir. 1985).

i.   Acts of God and Acts of War

The CERCLA definition of an "act of God" is "an unanticipated natural disaster or other natural phenomenon * * * the effects of which could not have been prevented or avoided by the exercise of due care. * * * *" § 107(b)(1). The operative words here are "unanticipated" and "could not have been * * * avoided by * * * due care." Courts have construed these terms to defeat act of God claims involving winds, heavy rains or floods when the defendant should have exercised due care in preparing for the catastrophic but foreseeable event. *See United States v. Poly–Carb, Inc.*, 951 F.Supp. 1518 (D. Nev. 1996) (windstorm); *United States v. M/V Santa Clara I*, 887 F. Supp. 825 (D. S.C. 1995) (storm); *State of Colorado v. Idarado Mining Co.*, 707 F.Supp. 1227, 1236 (D. Colo. 1989) (floodwaters), *rev'd on other grounds*, 916 F.2d 1486 (10th Cir. 1990). Section 107(b) permits the defense only if the release of hazardous substances has been caused "solely" by the act of God. If other factors causally contribute to the release, such as omissions or lack of "due care" by the defendant, then the defense must fail. *See, e.g., United States v. Barrier Industries, Inc.*, 991 F.Supp. 678, 679–80 (S.D. N.Y. 1998); *United States v. Alcan Aluminum Corp.*, 892 F.Supp. 648, 658 (M.D. Pa. 1995).

As with the act of God defense, courts have narrowed the "act of war" defense of § 107(b)(2). The defense has been by companies that contaminated a site because of wartime contracts that required large production of a hazardous substance. Their claim is that spillage and leaks were the inevitable consequences of producing such enormous volumes of a substance. These arguments have been wholly unsuccessful. An "act of war" requires the use of force by one government against another, or the wartime destruction of private property so as to harm the enemy, neither of which is present when there is simply a contractual relationship between the United States and the defendant. *See United States v. Shell Oil*, 841 F.Supp. 962 (C.D. Cal. 1993), *aff'd,* 292 F.3d 1045 (9th Cir. 2002).

ii.   Third Party Defense

Section § 107(b)(3) provides that if the release or threatened release was solely caused not by the defendant, but some other party whose "act or omission" did not occur "in connection with a contractual relationship," then the defendant may escape liability if two other conditions are met—the defendant exercised "due care" with respect to the hazardous substance concerned, and "took precautions against foreseeable acts or omissions of any such third party. * * *" This defense is really limited to cases where an unrelated third party or total outsider dumped the contaminant on, or in, the defendant's property. *United States v. Poly–Carb. Inc.*, 951 F.Supp. 1518, 1530 (D. Nev. 1996) (no liability if release by vandals); *United States v. Stringfellow*, 661 F.Supp. 1053, 1061 (C.D. Cal. 1987). The defense can be easily defeated if the defendant has some contractual relationship with the party causing the release, *Chatham Steel Corp. v. Brown*, 858 F.Supp. 1130, 1154–55 (N.D. Fla. 1994), or fails to satisfy the "due care" or "took precautions" requirements of § 107(b)(3). *State of North Carolina ex rel. Howes v. W.R. Peele, Sr. Trust*, 876 F.Supp. 733, 745–46 (E.D. N.C. 1995).

In effect, then, there are four elements to the defense. The Defendant must show: (1) that the release was caused *solely* by the third party (which, as we have seen, is a nearly impossible standard to meet); (2) that third party's act or omission did not occur "in connection with a contractual relationship;" (3) that the defendant exercised "due care" with respect to the hazardous substance; and (4) that the defendant "took precautions against foreseeable acts or omissions" of third parties.

Absence of a Contractual Relationship. Much of the litigation surrounding the so-called "third party defense" has focused on the kinds of legal relationships between defendant and dumper that arguably fall within the "in connection with a contractual relationship" language. Many cases extended the notion of a contractual relationship to include not only agreements where the contractor did the dumping according to the defendant's instructions, *Shapiro v. Alexanderson*, 743 F.Supp. 268, 271 (S.D. N.Y. 1990), but also to virtually any legal relationship between defendant and dumper, no matter how casual or disconnected to waste disposal activities. *United States v. Monsanto Co.*, 858 F.2d 160 (4th Cir. 1988) (landlord-tenant); *Chatham Steel Corp. v. Brown*, 858 F.Supp. 1130, 1154–55 (N.D. Fla. 1994) (battery seller-recycler). Other courts have taken a closer look at the text of § 107(b)(3) and have concluded that a defendant should be precluded from raising the defense only if the contract between the defendant and dumper-third party is connected with the handling of hazardous substances. This result stems from the "in connection with" language. This phrase seems to require that there be a linkage between the release and the contract. *See, e.g., Shapiro v. Alexanderson*, 743 F.Supp. 268, 271 (S.D. N.Y. 1990); *Westwood Pharmaceuticals, Inc. v. National Fuel Gas Dist. Corp.*, 964 F.2d 85 (2d Cir. 1992); *American Nat. Bank and Trust Co. v. Harcos Chemicals, Inc.*, 997 F.Supp. 994, 1001 (N.D. Ill. 1998); *Reichhold Chemicals, Inc. v. Textron, Inc.*, 888 F.Supp. 1116 (N.D. Fla. 1995).[71] Thinking back to Congress' apparent intent in creating and limiting this defense, which is the better approach? Would a narrow reading of "contractual relationship" create an unacceptable loophole?

Exercise of Due Care. The "due care" inquiry tends to focus on whether the defendant had knowledge of the contamination and release, and if so,

71.   *See* M.A. Meehan, *Towards Defining the Contractual Relationship Exception to CERCLA's Third Party Defense*, 5 Vill. Envtl. L.J. 237 (1994); J.B. Ruhl, *The Third–Party Defense to Hazardous Waste Liability: Narrowing the Contractual Relationships Exception*, 29 S. Tex. L. Rev. 291 (1987).

what steps it took to limit harm. If the defendant had no awareness of the potential for release, it may be excused for failure to exercise due care. *United States v. A & N Cleaners and Launderers, Inc.*, 788 F.Supp. 1317 (S.D. N.Y. 1992). But if the property owner has notice of the potential threat, and chooses to take no action, such a party has failed to exercise due care. *Idylwoods Assocs. v. Mader Capital, Inc.*, 915 F.Supp. 1290 (W.D. N.Y. 1996) (defendant failed to take corrective steps after learning of barrels of PCB-contaminated waste on the land); *State of North Carolina ex rel. Howes v. W.R. Peele, Sr. Trust*, 876 F.Supp. 733, 745–46 (E.D. N.C. 1995) (defendant who owned facility remained idle while hazardous waste was leaking). On the other hand, due care is present when a new owner made aware of the problem takes affirmative steps to notify affected parties, monitor, and prevent the condition from worsening. *State of New York v. Lashins Arcade Co.* 91 F.3d 353 (2d Cir. 1996).

Precautions. As with the "due care" element of a third party defense, the "taking precautions" requirement asks if the defendant knew or should have known of the activity creating the threat of a release. *See, e.g., Lincoln Properties, Inc. v. Higgins*, 823 F.Supp. 1528 (E.D. Cal. 1992) (defendant may use defense when no awareness of dumping, and no further precautions were warranted). In contract to the due care condition, here courts tend to concentrate on whether the defendant should and could have taken precautionary steps before the release (or its discovery) to prevent the discharge of hazardous substances. *United States v. A & N Cleaners & Launderers, Inc.*, 854 F.Supp. 229, 243 (S.D. N.Y. 1994) (failure to make inquiry forecloses third party defense). The critical element is whether the waste disposal acts of third parties were foreseeable. If so, the defendant must take precautions against these acts. *United States v. Rohm & Haas Co.*, 939 F.Supp. 1142 (D. N.J. 1996); *Foster v. United States*, 922 F.Supp. 642 (D. D.C. 1996). Failure to take reasonable precautions against the foreseeable consequence of a pre-existing condition (*e.g.,* cracked sewer pipes) voids the third party defense when a third party actually triggers the release. (*e.g.,* pours hazardous substances into the pipes). *Westfarm Assocs. v. Washington Suburban Sanitary Com'n*, 66 F.3d 669 (4th Cir. 1995).

iii.   The Innocent Purchaser

Prior to 1986, real estate deeds, land contracts, and other instruments transferring title were deemed "contractual relationships" that prevented the use of the third party defense by an unsuspecting buyer of previously contaminated property. SARA changed this result in 1986 by adding § 101(35), which provides that such purchasers are not in contractual relationships for purposes of the third party defense when:

(1) the "facility" on which there is a hazardous substance was acquired *after* disposal of the substance. If disposal occurs during ownership, or while the purchase is being consummated, the defense is inapplicable. *United States v. Monsanto Co.*, 858 F.2d 160, 168–69 n.14 (4th Cir. 1988).[72]

---

72.   The innocent owner defense would "hardly ever be available" if "disposal" included

(2) at the time of acquisition the defendant "did not know and had no reason to know that any hazardous substance * * * was disposed of on, in, or at" the newly acquired property.[73] Actual knowledge of discharge of hazardous waste on the property defeats the defense. *United States v. Broderick Investment Co.*, 862 F.Supp. 272 (D. Colo. 1994); *Western Properties Service Corp. v. Shell Oil Co.*, 358 F.3d 678 (9th Cir. 2004) (determining innocent landowner defense was not available when landowner had knowledge of hazardous waste at time of purchase), *rev'd on other grounds*, 548 F.3d 774 (9th Cir. 2008). If a tenant had knowledge of the environmental contamination of a neighboring property when it took possession of a site, the tenant cannot raise the innocent landowner defense. *Clear Lake Properties v. Rockwell Int. Corp.*, 959 F.Supp. 763 (S.D. Tex. 1997). Knowledge at the time of purchase is also equivalent to a failure to exercise the "due care" standard of the third party defense—a buyer cannot remain idle after being informed of the presence of hazardous substances on the property. *Kerr–McGee Chemical Corp. v. Lefton Iron & Metal Co.*, 14 F.3d 321 (7th Cir. 1994); *Idylwoods Assoc. v. Mader Capital, Inc*, 915 F.Supp. 1290, 1302 (W.D. N.Y. 1996).

The "innocent buyer" or "innocent landowner" can then avoid liability if the other third party defense requirements, discussed above, are satisfied—

(3) release caused solely by someone other than the buyer,

(4) due care and

(5) adequate precautions taken by the buyer.

See, e.g., Mathews v. Dow Chemical Co., 947 F.Supp. 1517 (D. Colo. 1996) (due care satisfied by making reasonable environmental inspection); *Kerr–McGee Chem. Corp. v. Lefton Iron & Metal Co.*, 14 F.3d 321 (7th Cir. 1994) (failure to take precautions to prevent damage from hazardous substances known to be present on site precludes innocent buyer defense). It is, in other words, a narrow defense, but it provides a roadmap for the would-be purchaser to avoid CERCLA liability.

As a practical matter, the essence of the innocent land owner defense—or at least the aspect that a purchaser is in the best position to influence—is that the buyer had no reason to know that any hazardous substance had contaminated the property. To establish "no reason to know," § 101(35)(B) requires that "all appropriate inquiry [be made] into the previous ownership and uses of the property consistent with good commercial and customary practice. * * * "[74] These provisions in effect require

---

passive leaking. *ABB Industrial Systems, Inc. v. Prime Technology, Inc.*, 120 F.3d 351, 358 (2d Cir. 1997).

73. Section 101(35)(A)(ii–iii) also excepts from the definition of "contractual relationship" situations where (1) the defendant is a government entity which acquired the facility through escheat, involuntary transfer, or eminent domain, or (2) the defendant acquired the facility by inheritance or bequest.

74. The statute also requires that certain factors be taken into account in determining whether "all appropriate inquiry" has been made: (1) specialized knowledge by the landowner; (2) the relationship of the purchase price to the value of the uncontaminated property if uncontaminated; (3) commonly known information about the property; and (4) the obviousness of the presence of the contamination and the ability to detect it by inspection.

prudent buyers to undertake some pre-purchase environmental assessment of the property. To engage in such an environmental investigation is to satisfy both the "all appropriate inquiry" standard of the innocent land-owner defense, and the "due care" requirement of the third party defense. *American Risk v. City of Centerline,* 69 F. Supp. 2d 944 (E.D. Mich. 1999). Failure to make inquiries or to engage in an investigation of the site (and of the previous owner's activities that could create a hazardous waste problem) usually makes the innocent landowner defense unavailable. *Foster v. United States*, 922 F.Supp. 642 (D. D.C. 1996); *United States v. A & N Cleaners and Launderers, Inc.*, 854 F.Supp. 229, 243 (S.D. N.Y. 1994); *Acme Printing Ink Co. v. Menard, Inc.*, 870 F.Supp. 1465, 1480–81 (E.D. Wis. 1994).

Although CERCLA does not flesh out what exactly constitutes "all appropriate inquiry," both courts and the EPA have provided some guidance. Judicial interpretation of the legislative history of the innocent landowner defense reveals a three tier system: commercial transactions are held to the strictest standard; private transactions for personal or residential use are afforded more leniency; inheritances and bequests are given the most leniency. *In re Hemingway Transport, Inc.*, 993 F.2d 915, 933 (1st Cir. 1993); *United States v. Pacific Hide & Fur Depot, Inc.*, 716 F.Supp. 1341, 1348 (D. Idaho 1989). EPA innocent purchaser guidance states that two other important variables are known prior uses of the property (was it used as a residence or a waste disposal site?), and date of purchase (was it bought in 1950 or 1980?). EPA Guidance on Landowner Liability (June 6, 1989) at 11–12. Much of the pressure to undertake investigations of property comes from lenders, not surprisingly, who don't want their security to become worthless overnight. Consequently, lenders and private industrial standards organizations have reached a general consensus (with EPA acquiescence) on a tiered set of investigations ("Phase I," "Phase II," etc.) depending on the above factors.

With the enactment of the Brownfields Amendments, Congress provided clarity on the requirements to invoke the three main defenses: (1) Innocent Landowner, (2) Bona Fide Prospective Purchaser (BFPP), and (3) Contiguous Property Owner (CPO); the latter two are the result of the 2002 Amendments. All three defenses have this common element: a binding obligation to conduct an "all appropriate inquiry" before purchasing property. Failure to follow either standard will result in a failure to raise a CERCLA defense or contribution action. *See McDonald v. Sun Oil Co.,* 423 F. Supp. 2d 1114 (D. Or. 2006) (finding owners who purchased mercury mine did not do an all appropriate inquiry when they failed to conduct tests to determine other potential contamination in calcine tailings).

All Appropriate Inquiry Modification

Previously there were no standards as to what constituted an "all appropriate inquiry," evidence of a prospective purchaser's due diligence in determining the previous ownership, uses, and environmental conditions of a property. Now purchasers have two avenues to comply: (1) follow EPA's November 1, 2006 "All Appropriate Inquiries Final Rule," or (2) the standards set forth in the ASTM E1527–05 Phase I Environmental Site Assessment Process.

- **EPA's All Appropriate Inquiries:** EPA defines them as the process of evaluating a property's environmental conditions and assessing potential liability for any contamination. These inquiries must be conducted or updated within one year prior to the date of acquisition of a property. If the inquiries are conducted more than 180 days prior to the acquisition date, certain aspects of the inquiries must be updated.

- **ASTM E1527–05 Standard:** refers to those promulgated by the American Society for Testing and Materials, an organization that develops technical standards for materials, services, systems, and products. This standard qualifies as "generally accepted good commercial and customary standards and practices" in making an all appropriate inquiry. See CERCLA § 101(35)(B)(i)(I).

ALL APPROPRIATE INQUIRIES STANDARD	
Effective Nov. 1, 2006, a property purchaser must comply with **either** "Standards and Practices for All Appropriate Inquires" ("AAI") (*40 CFR Part 312*) or ASTM's revised Phase I environmental site assessment standard (ASTM E 1527–05) to show **due care** as required under CERCLA liability exemptions. EPA defines AAI as the "process of evaluating a property's environmental conditions and assessing potential liability for any contamination." **Ensure AAI is performed prior to purchase of any urban land.**	
"Standards and Practices for All Appropriate Inquiries" under CERCLA § 101(35)(B)(iii):	Inquiry must be conducted/supervised by a qualified environmental professional and include the following: • interviews with past and present owner, operators and occupants • reviews of historical sources of information; searches for environmental cleanup liens; • reviews of federal, state, tribal and local government records; • visual inspections of the facility and adjoining properties; • specialized knowledge or experience on the part of the prospective buyer/owner; • assessments of any specialized knowledge or experience of the prospective landowner (or grantee); • assessment of the relationship of the purchase price to the fair market value of the property, if it was not contaminated; • commonly known or reasonably ascertainable information; and • degree of obviousness of presence/likely presence of contamination at the property and the ability to detect it.

Phase I environmental site assessment standard (ASTM E 1527–05) (ASTM E 1527–05) Per EPA policy, following the American Society for Testing and Materials would suffice as meeting the AAI requirement. ASTM is an organization that develops technical standards for materials, services, systems, and products.	EXAMPLES: • Perform onsite visit (view present conditions, hazardous substances/petroleum products usage; evaluate any likely environmentally hazardous site history. • Evaluate risks of contamination or leakage from contiguous properties • Interviews persons knowledgeable of property history (past/present owners, site managers, tenants, neighbors). • Examine city/county planning files to check prior land usage and permits granted • Conduct file searches with health and environmental agencies having oversight of water quality/soil contamination issues • Examine historic aerial photography of the vicinity. • Examine current USGS maps to determine drainage patters and topography • Examine chain-of-title for Environmental Liens and/or Activity and Land Use Limitations (AULs).

Bona Fide Prospective Purchaser

For the first time since CERCLA's enactment, purchasers with knowledge that the site is, or may be, contaminated may avoid CERCLA's wide-ranging liability in specific circumstances. Key is the requirement that the purchaser buys the property *after* January 11, 2002, the date of the Brownfield Amendments. CERCLA § 101(40). The BFOO defense looks at a purchaser's status and conduct. Buyers using the BFPP defense must show that the disposal of hazardous substances at the facility occurred prior to the acquisition of the facility, they made all appropriate inquiries, and they are not potentially liable or affiliated with any PRP. See CERCLA § 101(40)(A), (B), and (H).

BFPP vs. Innocent Landowner Defense

An innocent landowner is a person who buys or acquires property without discovery or knowledge that the property is contaminated. A BFPP is one who knows the property is contaminated but buys it anyway—after January 11, 2002, the date of the Brownfield Amendments' passage. However, in either case, both the innocent landowner and the BFPP must have conducted an all appropriate inquiry and acquired the property *after* the disposal of hazardous waste or substances occurred at the facility. See CERCLA § 101(35)(A) and CERCLA § 101(40)(A). The BFPP defense was meant to be an additional defense, not to change or take the place of the Innocent Landowner

> defense. *City of Wichita v. Trustee of the Apco Oil Corp. Liquidating Trust,* 306 F. Supp. 2d 104 (D. Kan. 2003) (holding that neither the 2002 amendments nor the legislative history suggests that Congress intended to change the innocent landowner defense).

After acquisition of a property, the purchaser must meet all five remaining compliance requirements, the same as Contiguous Property Owners. Buyers who do not meet all of the requirements will fail in their attempt to assert the bona fide purchaser defense. *AMCAL Multi–Housing, Inc. v. Pacific Clay Products*, 457 F. Supp. 2d 1016 (C.D. Cal. 2006) (explaining that simply performing due diligence environmental investigations and cleanup under "the oversight" of various governmental agencies not sufficient).

A NOTE ON THE BFPP WINDFALL LIEN

BFPPs who bought property at which the EPA had previously incurred cleanup costs may be subject to a "windfall lien" for the increase in the fair market value (FMV) attributable to the U.S. government's cleanup efforts. CERCLA § 107(r). The lien approach prevents the prospective purchaser from profiting from the government's cleanup, which improved the property's value. The lien attaches until a prospective purchaser resells the property. Thus, if the government expends $2 million in cleanup costs, and the prospective purchaser resells the property for $3 million, the $1 million reflects the FMV increase, and the government may only recover $1 million from the prospective purchaser. Likewise, it limits the government from reaping a windfall if the prospective purchaser makes improvements upon the property independent of the government cleanup or because of other real estate factors. In July 2003, the EPA issued an "Interim Enforcement Discretion Policy Considering 'Windfall Liens' Under Section 107(r) of CERCLA." This memorandum listed such factors as the likelihood of recouping cleanup costs from liable parties and whether a BFPP would reap a significant windfall in EPA's determination to perfect a windfall lien.

Even if the EPA may perfect a windfall lien based on these factors, the EPA may elect not to do so in certain circumstances, for instance when the BFPP is going to use the property for public purposes, such as for a park. The EPA may issue a comfort or status letter where EPA will generally not pursue a windfall lien.

Continuing Obligations for BFPPs and CPOs

These defenses share the same following requirements to be eligible for CERCLA liability exemptions:

1) Reasonably prevent continuing or threatened releases and limit hazardous substances exposure. CERCLA § 101(40)(D) and CERCLA § 107(q)(1)(A)(iii).

---

2) Compliance, assistance and access for response actions or natural resource restoration. CERCLA § 101(40)(E) and CERCLA § 107(q)(1)(A)(iv).

3) Compliance with land use restrictions and institutional controls for facility cleanup. CERCLA § 101(40)(F) and CERCLA § 107(q)(1)(A)(v).

4) Compliance with EPA requests for information or subpoena. CERCLA § 101(40)(G) and CERCLA § 107(q)(1)(A)(vi).

5) Provide all legally required notices regarding the discovery or release of any hazardous substances at the facility. CERCLA § 101(40)(C) and CERCLA § 107 (q) (1)(A)(viii).

Contiguous Property Owner

The Contiguous Property Owner (CPO) defense is much more like the BFPP defense, in that it requires CPOs to make all appropriate inquiries, not be affiliated with any PRPs, and meet continuing compliance requirements (see box). CERCLA § 107(q)(1)(A)(ii) and (viii). Note that Congress has expressly excluded the requirement that a CPO perform a groundwater investigation or remediation as part of making "all appropriate inquiries." CERCLA § 107(q)(1)(D). Congress has explicitly recognized that CPOs are not to be presumed to be PRPs, defining them as "not considered to be an owner or operator." CERCLA § 107(q)(1).

To qualify for this defense, the CPO must own property that is or may be contaminated by hazardous substance release from adjacent or contiguous property, which the CPO does not own. A CPO may not have caused, contributed, or consented to the hazardous substance contamination. CERCLA § 107(q)(1)(A)(i). What happens if a CPO bought property knowing that it is contaminated? A CPO may invoke the BFPP exemption, so long as the owner meets those criteria. CERCLA § 107(q)(1)(C). The CPO defense does not preclude use of any other defenses available under the Superfund law. CERCLA § 107(q)(2)(A).

CERCLA Exemptions	Must meet these standards by preponderance of the evidence:
Third–Party Defense **CERCLA § 101(35)(A)**	**Third-party defense:** 3rd party: *solely* caused hazardous substance release/threatened release; is not owner's employee or agent; their acts/omissions did not occur in connection with any contractual relationship to current owner. Owner must exercise due care with respect to the hazardous substances and took precautions against third party's foreseeable acts or omissions.

Innocent Purchaser / Landowner Defense **CERCLA § 107(b)(3)**	Innocent Purchaser/Landowner: if contractual relationship existed (PRP) sold property to current owner), must show: - **Before acquisition:** *All* Hazardous waste disposals occurred. - **At time of acquisitions:** (1) No knowledge/reason to know of contamination. (2) Did not know / had no reason to know that any potentially/actually released hazardous substance was disposed of/on property. (3) Performed **all appropriate inquires** into previous property ownership and uses. - **After acquisition:** (1) Comply with & provide assistance/access to those conducting response actions or natural resource restoration. (2) Comply with land use regulations established for facility cleanup. (3) Do not impede any institutional control employed for the cleanup. (4) Exercise due care with respect to hazardous substances, taking reasonable steps to stop releases, prevent future ones, and limit exposure or any releases.
Contiguous Property Owner **CERCLA § 107(b)(3)**	**Before acquisition:** (1) Does not cause, contribute, or consent to release or threatened release of hazardous substances; (2) Makes all appropriate inquires into previous ownership/uses of facility *and* did not know/have reason to know the property was/could be contaminated by adjacent or surrounding properties; (3) Buyer not "affiliated" with any PRPs. **After acquisition:** (1) Take reasonable steps to prevent continuing/threatened releases and prevent/limit exposure to hazardous substances. (2) Fully comply with and provides assistance/access to EPA/others to conduct response actions or natural resource restoration. (3) Comply with land use restrictions established for facility cleanup and do not impede any institutional control employed for the cleanup. 4) Comply with EPA requests for information or subpoena. 5) Provides all legally required notices for discovery/release of any hazardous substances at the facility.

Bona Fide Prospective Purchaser (BFPP) **CERCLA § 101(40)** **Brownfield Amendment**	**Before acquisition:** (1) All hazardous substances disposed at the facility occurred before facility acquisitions. (2) Buyer made all appropriate inquires into previous ownership/uses using generally accepted practices. (3) Buyer not "affiliated" with any PRP. **After acquisition:** Same as Contiguous Property Owner requirements above.
Act of War **CERCLA § 107(b)(1)**	Requires use of force by one government against another or wartime destruction of private property to defeat the enemy.
Act of God **CERCLA § 107(b)(2)**	(1) Unanticipated grave natural disaster or other natural phenomenon. (2) Even exercise of due care could not prevent its effects (i.e., hazardous substance release into the environment).

NOTES AND QUESTIONS

1. Should the act of God defense be available when a pollution release occurs because of a fire caused by a lightning strike? *See Wagner Seed Co. v. Daggett*, 800 F.2d 310 (2d Cir. 1986).

2. Can you think of a plausible act of war situation in the U.S.? Would a release due to terrorism fall within this defense?

3. How do the "taking precautions" requirements affect the liability of lessors of property to industrial, commercial, or waste management concerns?

4. Suppose you have a client who wants to buy property that is currently occupied by a waste treatment operation. How risky is such a purchase?

5. Purchaser wishes to buy property from seller, but is concerned that it may be contaminated with hazardous substances. Purchaser hires an attorney who suggests that "all appropriate inquiry" be made to ensure an innocent purchaser defense if contamination is later discovered. Purchaser conducts a soil investigation with a bulldozer and backhoe which not only reveals the presence of contamination, but also causes the spread of contaminants. Should the innocent purchaser defense be available? *See United States v. CDMG Realty Co.*, 96 F.3d 706, 711 (3d Cir. 1996).

b. OTHER DEFENSES

In addition to § 107(b) defenses, a PRP can raise a number of other statutory and non-statutory defenses to avoid or minimize liability. These include: statute of limitations; equitable defenses; and indemnity or hold-harmless agreements.

i. *Statute of Limitations*

Section 113(g) establishes the limitations period for bringing a cost recovery action. A cost recovery action for a removal action must be filed within *three* years after "completion of the removal action," while an "initial action" must be filed within *six* years after "an initiation of physical on-site construction of [a] remedial action." § 113(g)(2). *See, e.g., United States v. Ambroid Co.*, 34 F. Supp. 2d 86 (D. Mass. 1999) (closing by EPA of a site subject to a removal action is evidence of completion of action, which starts the running of CERCLA's three-year limitations period for recovery of cleanup costs); *United States v. Findett Corp.*, 75 F. Supp. 2d 982 (E.D. Mo. 1999) (to be an "initial action" for remedial treatment action, the case need not result in the entry of a declaratory judgment); *RSR Corporation v. Commercial Metals Co.*, 496 F.3d 552 (6th Cir. 2007) (applying CERCLA's three year statute of limitations from "date of ... judicially approved settlement with respect to such costs or damages" for contribution actions when responsible party, who was part of a consent decree in the government's initial cost-recovery action, sought contribution from a party not part of the consent decree).

An important threshold issue is whether the clean-up action is characterized as a removal or remedial action. The general rule is that the investigation and study of clean-ups is "removal" action, even when a party is developing and testing—but not implementing—the contamination source control remedy. *Kelley ex rel. State of Michigan v. E.I. Dupont de Nemours*, 786 F.Supp. 1268 (E.D. Mich. 1992), *aff'd*, 17 F.3d 836, 840 (6th Cir. 1994). "Remedial" actions are response actions conducted in accordance with a Record of Decision over an extended period of time. *Advanced Micro Devices, Inc. v. National Semiconductor Corp.*, 38 F. Supp. 2d 802 (N.D. Cal. 1999); *United States v. Akzo Nobel Coatings, Inc.*, 990 F.Supp. 897, 904 (E.D. Mich. 1998). For remedial actions, the pertinent statute of limitations question is when "physical on-site construction" occurs. An event often must meet several criteria to be considered the initiation of physical on-site construction: (1) there is some "physical" action; (2) that physical action happens on the site; (3) the action is part of the remedial action; (4) the action constitutes "initiation" of the remedial action; and (5) the action plays a critical role in implementation of the permanent remedy. *See State of California v. Hyampom Lumber Co.*, 903 F.Supp. 1389, 1393–94 (E.D. Cal. 1995).[75]

ii. Equitable Defenses

Most courts read § 107(a) literally when it states that CERCLA liability is "subject only to the defenses" of § 107(b). *California ex rel. Dept. of Toxic v. Neville Chem.*, 358 F.3d 661 (9th Cir. 2004) (determining that the three defenses to CERCLA liability expressly listed in § 107(b) are the only defenses available; traditional equitable defenses are unavailable). This means that while equitable considerations such as estoppel, laches, unclean hands, and caveat emptor may have a role in apportionment of liability in a

---

75. When natural resources damages are sought, § 113(g)(1) requires that suit be filed within three years of "after the latter of the following: (A) The date of the discovery of the loss.... (B) The date on which regulations are promulgated under § 301(c)." *See California v. Montrose Chemical Corp.*, 104 F.3d 1507 (9th Cir. 1997) (limitations period for § 301(c) regulations began on March 20, 1987).

contribution action, they will not be considered in actions that determine whether a party is liable as a PRP in the first place. *United States v. Rohm & Haas Co.*, 939 F.Supp. 1142 (D. N.J. 1996); *United States v. Martell*, 887 F.Supp. 1183 (N.D. Ind. 1995); *Transportation Leasing Co. v. State of California*, 861 F.Supp. 931, 940–41 (C.D. Cal. 1993). Equitable defenses are particularly unsuccessful when asserted against the government. *O'Neil v. Picillo*, 682 F.Supp. 706, 726–27 (D.R.I. 1988), *aff'd*, 883 F.2d 176 (1st Cir. 1989). There are some rare decisions that presume equitable defenses are available in private cost recovery actions. *Folino v. Hampden Color & Chemical Co.*, 832 F.Supp. 757 (D.Vt. 1993); *Mardan Corp. v. C.G.C. Music, Ltd.*, 600 F.Supp. 1049, 1057–58 (D. Ariz. 1984). *But see Velsicol Chem. Corp. v. Enenco, Inc.*, 9 F.3d 524, 530 (6th Cir. 1993) (laches not available in private cost recovery action).

iii. Indemnity and Hold Harmless Agreements

If a person or company wishes to minimize the risk of financial liability in connection with a property sale, it is common to enter into an indemnification or hold harmless agreement with the other party to the transaction. Such risk allocation schemes do not constitute a defense in an EPA enforcement action as against a non-party to the agreement, *Smithkline Beecham Corp. v. Rohm & Haas Co.*, 89 F.3d 154 (3d Cir. 1996) (parties to an indemnification or hold harmless contract remain jointly and severally liable to the government), but they do permit the parties to allocate environmental responsibility among themselves. In § 107(e), CERCLA specifically recognizes the enforceability of indemnification and hold harmless agreements among responsible parties. *See Joslyn Manufacturing Co. v. Koppers Co., Inc.*, 40 F.3d 750 (5th Cir. 1994); *Olin Corp. v. Consolidated Aluminum Corp.*, 5 F.3d 10 (2d Cir. 1993); *Stearns & Foster Bedding Co. v. Fraklin Holding Corp.*, 947 F.Supp. 790 (D.N.J. 1996).

The two issues that arise with respect to such agreements are whether the language of the agreement is broad enough to cover CERCLA liability, and whether a party may contract to indemnify or hold harmless another for environmental liability even though CERCLA was not in existence at the time of contracting. An "as is" or "all claims" clause, or a narrowly written clause, may not be sufficient to include CERCLA liability. *FINA, Inc. v. ARCO*, 200 F.3d 266 (5th Cir. 2000). But CERCLA liability is encompassed by language that evinces a strong intent to cover all liability arising in connection with occupancy or use of the property (*e.g.,* "Party A should indemnify and hold harmless Party B against all claims, actions, demands, losses, or liabilities arising from the use or operation of the land."). *See Velsicol Chemical Corp. v. Reilly Industries,* 67 F. Supp. 2d 893 (E.D. Tenn. 1999). A party may also contract with another with respect to allocation of environmental liability even if the contract arose pre-CERCLA, so long as the language is sufficiently broad to suggest an intent to cover all possible liability claims. *Kerr–McGee Chem. Corp. v. Lefton Iron & Metal Co.*, 14 F.3d 321, 327 (7th Cir. 1994).

NOTES AND QUESTIONS

1.   The EPA brings a § 107(a) suit against a PRP seeking reimbursement of response costs already incurred at a Superfund site. Much of these costs have been from monitoring wells that have been drilled into the site by the EPA to sample the extent of the underground contamination. The PRP files a cross-motion for a preliminary injunction directing the EPA to cease installation of the wells, and to encase existing wells, alleging that the drill holes for the wells have exacerbated existing environmental damage, and will cause further irreparable harm to the environment. Should the PRP's request for equitable relief be granted if the allegations appear to be true? *See United States v. Princeton Gamma–Tech, Inc.*, 31 F.3d 138, 141–46 (3d Cir. 1994), *overruled sub nom. Clinton County Com'rs v. U.S. E.P.A.*, 116 F.3d 1018 (3d Cir. 1997).

2.   *Bankruptcy.* Claims that arise before the debtor files bankruptcy may sometimes be discharged under federal bankruptcy law. CERCLA is silent on the question of *when* an economic claim under CERCLA (*e.g.,* liability under § 107) arises for purposes of bankruptcy. In some jurisdictions, a CERCLA action becomes a claim under bankruptcy law when the release of hazardous materials occurs. *See, e.g., Ekotek Site PRP Comm. v. Self*, 932 F.Supp. 1328 (D. Utah 1996). This result permits discharge of a debtor prior to when the plaintiff may be able to identify the debtor as a PRP. Other courts that have considered the question of when a CERCLA claim arises for discharge purposes have decided that the critical time is when the claimant (usually a purchaser) can "tie the bankruptcy debtor to a known release of a hazardous substance which this potential claimant knows will lead to CERCLA response costs." *In re Chicago, Milwaukee, St. P. & Pac. R.R.*, 974 F.2d 775, 786 (7th Cir. 1992). This standard asks if sufficient information existed, had the claimant-purchaser sought it out, to give the claimant constructive knowledge that it possessed a CERCLA claim during the bankruptcy. *AM Int'l, Inc. v. Datacard Corp., DBS, Inc.*, 106 F.3d 1342, 1347–48 (7th Cir. 1997).

3.   Should an EPA administrative order under § 106 demanding clean-up action be considered a claim dischargable in bankruptcy?

E.   COST–RECOVERY ACTIONS AND APPORTIONMENT OF LIABILITY

CERCLA allows both government entities (the Federal Government, the states, and Indian tribes) and private parties to initiate clean-up actions with or without prior EPA approval. We now turn to the features of the actions that the government and private parties may initiate to recover response costs and (in the case of the government) to require PRPs to take response actions themselves. Not only are several types of civil action available to CERCLA plaintiffs, but they raise thorny issues of statutory interpretation, complex case management, and environmental policy.

1.   GOVERNMENT COST–RECOVERY AND ENFORCEMENT ACTIONS

When a government (federal, state, or tribal) takes the lead in responding to a release or threatened release of a hazardous substance, it may choose among several courses of action. As described above in subchapter C, the EPA may investigate and then clean up the contaminated site. In such a case, § 104(a) permits EPA to spend Superfund money as long as the response actions are consistent with the NCP. After the EPA has incurred response costs, it may recover those costs from PRPs found liable under § 107(a).[76] In several ways (and for obvious reasons) CERCLA requires governments to make only the basic (*i.e.,* the easiest) case for CERCLA liability. It can take advantage of the low standard of liability, the range of PRPs, the relaxed thresholds for liability,the full range of recoverable costs, and the extremely limited defenses to liability. Therefore, with the Superfund at its back and a ready ability to impose liability on others, it is not surprising that most Superfund litigation is initiated by the EPA. Indeed, theEPA and PRPs will often resolve liability issues by settlement *in advance* of using Superfund money, because the PRPs' liability is all but assured.

In addition to cost recovery under section 107, section 106 authorizes the United States (but not states, tribes, or private parties) to "secure such relief as may be necessary" from a court "as the public interest and equities of a case may require," or to "take other action * * * including * * * issuing such [administrative] orders as may be necessary to protect public health and welfare and the environment" when (a) there may be an imminent and substantial endangerment, (b) because of an actual or threatened release of a hazardous substance. In other words, when the situation warrants, the EPA can proceed directly against a responsible party by court injunction or administrative order.

a. JUDICIAL RELIEF

Section 106 adds considerably to EPA's bargaining power in cost-recovery actions or threatened cost-recovery actions. While actions under § 107 and § 106 are similar in many ways, there are also important differences:

ACTIONS UNDER § 106 AND § 107 COMPARED	
DIFFERENCES	
Authority to bring § 106 action	A § 106 action may be initiated only by the federal government, not states, *New York v. Shore Realty Corp.*, 759 F.2d 1032, 1049–50 (2d Cir. 1985), not cities, *Mayor and Council v. Klockner & Klockner*, 811 F. Supp. 1039 (D.N.J. 1993), and not private parties. *Cadillac Fairview/California, Inc. v. Dow Chemical Co.*, 840 F.2d 691, 697 (9th Cir. 1988). A § 107 action is available to federal and state governments, Indian tribes, and certain private parties.
Who pays?	Under § 106, "responsible" parties pay directly for the clean up.

---

76. The elements of governments' cause of action for response costs were, in essence, the subject of subchapter D.

Speed of clean-up	§ 106 can bring about a clean-up much more quickly, because it avoids the procedural hurdles of § 104.
National Priorities List	A site subject to § 106 need not be on the NPL; remedial action under § 104 is limited to sites on the NPL.
Triggers	§ 107 becomes relevant when there is a release/threatened release that causes the incurrence of response costs; § 106 is triggered when there is also an imminent and substantial endangerment because of a release/threatened release.
Defenses	While equitable defenses are generally unavailable in a § 107 context, they are available under § 106(a), which provides that courts should grant such relief "as the public interest and the equities of the case" require.
SIMILARITIES	
Liable parties	Both §§ 106 and 107 apply to persons qualifying as PRPs under § 107(a).
Standard of Liability	Most courts interpret § 106(a) as imposing the same standard of liability as is applicable for § 107(a), *i.e.,* strict liability. *United States v. Price*, 577 F. Supp. 1103, 1113 (D.N.J. 1983); *United States v. Outboard Marine*, 556 F. Supp. 54 (D. Ill. 1982).
Defenses	Although § 106 does not acknowledge any defenses, § 106(b)(2)(C) & (D) authorize parties who must remediate a site under § 106 to seek reimbursement from the Superfund, provided that they are not otherwise liable for response costs under § 107. One can construe this proviso as making available to § 106 defendants all the statutory defenses available under § 107(b).

The key element of proof in section 106 actions is the requirement of "may be an imminent and substantial endangerment to the public health or welfare or the environment." In the leading case of *United States v. Conservation Chemical Co.*, 619 F.Supp. 162 (W.D. Mo. 1985), virtually every one of the words in that phrase were broadly construed so as to encompass non-emergency situations when there is only the potential threat of harm. According to the court, the word "imminent" does not require proof that harm will occur "tomorrow," only that factors are present now giving rise to future endangerment. "Substantial" does not require quantification of the endangerment, merely reasonable cause for concern that someone or something may be exposed to a risk of harm. "Endangerment" does not require quantitative proof of actual harm, just a threatened or potential harm (the language of § 106 is triggered when there "may" be endangerment). Also, § 106 relief is available when *either* "the public health" *or* "welfare" *or* "the environment" is endangered.

Section 106 in some ways parallels RCRA § 7003, which authorizes the federal government to act when hazardous waste contamination produces an "imminent and substantial endangerment to health and the environment." But there are important differences. RCRA § 7003 has primary applicability to emergencies at active sites; § 106 includes emergency and non-emergency situations at both active and inactive sites. RCRA § 7003 is triggered when there is endangerment to public health or the environment; § 106 also protects "public welfare." RCRA § 7003 requires that the endangerment arise from the handling or storage of solid or hazardous waste; § 106 requires endangerment from a "release or threatened release of a hazardous substance." On the other hand, RCRA § 7003 covers the petroleum wastes excluded from CERCLA. Moreover, RCRA § 7003 is enforceable by private parties (and states) through RCRA's more generous citizen suit provision (§ 7002).

b. ADMINISTRATIVE ORDERS

Section 106(a) permits the President (through the EPA) to "issue such orders as may be necessary" to clean up a contaminated site. This administrative mechanism has several advantages over the judicial route. A "unilateral" order is much quicker, and it permits EPA to control the nature of the remedy imposed. Pre-enforcement judicial review of these orders is precluded by § 113(h), and if a challenge to the order is mounted after the clean-up is complete, courts must defer to the order unless it is arbitrary or capricious or illegal. § 113(j).

An administrative order usually results from one of two scenarios. EPA may notify the responsible party of its decision to require the clean-up of a site where the site is usually under the control of the responsible party (*e.g.*, as owner). The responsible party then contacts the EPA and the two begin to negotiate an order that will be acceptable to both. Based on these negotiations, the EPA issues a § 106 consent order that is binding on the responsible party. Alternatively, the responsible party may choose to resist such an order, and not negotiate.[77] In that case, EPA marshals evidence, compiles an administrative record, and then issues a unilateral order directing the responsible party to remediate the site. The recalcitrant party receives no hearing (only notice), and is denied the right to pre-enforcement judicial review by § 113(h). *Solid State Circuits, Inc. v. United States EPA*, 812 F.2d 383 (8th Cir. 1987); *Wagner Seed v. Daggett*, 800 F.2d 310 (2d Cir. 1986).

While judicial review is available when EPA moves to enforce its order, a recalcitrant party who is in fact liable under § 107 may be fined up to $25,000 per day of noncompliance. § 106(b)(1). If the noncompliance is "without sufficient cause," it may also be subject to punitive damages in an amount up to three times the EPA's clean-up costs. § 107(c)(3). "Sufficient cause" has been subject to considerable judicial debate. Some courts assume

---

77. One reason why a responsible party may be inclined to resist an EPA § 106 order is that such orders may require the party to clean up all hazardous substances at the site, including those that were not the result of that party's disposal practices. *Employers Insurance of Wausau v. Clinton*, 848 F.Supp. 1359 (N.D. Ill. 1994).

that sufficient cause exists if the responsible party has an *objectively* reasonable basis for believing the order is invalid. *Solid State Circuits, Inc. v. United States EPA*, 812 F.2d 383, 391 (8th Cir. 1987). Others permit a more *subjective* good faith belief by the responsible party that the order is invalid. *Aminoil, Inc. v. United States*, 646 F.Supp. 294, 299 (C.D. Cal. 1986); *United States v. Reilly Tar & Chemical Corp.*, 606 F.Supp. 412 (D. Minn. 1985).[78] Thus, if a responsible party believes that it should not be liable for clean-up of a site, the more prudent course of action is either to comply with the order and sue to recover the costs from the Superfund (§ 106(b)(2)),[79] or to bring a private cost recovery action against third parties (§ 107(a)(4)(B)). Unfortunately, recovery under either option is not guaranteed; moreover, the allegedly "innocent" responsible party will surely have to incur substantial litigation and/or clean-up expenses in order to eventually enjoy vindication.

PROBLEM

Although it is agreed that an EPA decision to seek injunctive relief, and not an administrative order, is subject to the liability standards of § 107, there is no consensus about whether the eventual remediation plan (to be carried out by the liable party) should be formulated by the court issuing the injunction or by EPA. Relevant statutory language includes:

- § 106(a)—"the * * * court * * * shall * * * grant such relief as the public interest and the equities of the case may require. * * * "

- § 121(a)—"Selection of remedial action. The [EPA] shall select appropriate remedial actions determined to be necessary * * * which are in accordance with [§ 121] and * * * the [NCP]."

- 113(j)(2)—"In considering objections raised in any judicial action * * * the court shall uphold the [EPA's] decision in selecting the response action unless * * * the decision was arbitrary and capricious. * * * "

What argument can be made that courts are to determine the appropriate remedy when EPA opts for injunctive relief under § 106? *See United States v. Ottati & Goss, Inc.*, 900 F.2d 429 (1st Cir. 1990). What arguments can be made that the EPA should make the selection of remedies when injunctive relief is sought under § 106? *See United States v. Akzo Coatings of America, Inc.*, 949 F.2d 1409, 1425 (6th Cir. 1991).

---

78. Inability to pay punitive damages does not constitute "sufficient cause." *United States v. Parsons*, 723 F.Supp. 757, 763–64 (N.D. Ga. 1989).

79. If the clean-up is unsuccessful (*i.e.*, hazardous substances remain), then it may be alleged that there is noncompliance with an administrative order, and reimbursement from the Superfund will be precluded. *Employers Insurance of Wausau v. Clinton*, 848 F.Supp. 1359 (N.D. Ill. 1994).

2.   Settlements and Consent Decrees

Although much of this chapter has been devoted to litigation remedies, the reality is that most CERCLA enforcement is accomplished through negotiation and settlement, a practice that was encouraged and regularized by SARA in section 122. Settlements are often memorialized in a consent decree, an order of the court, agreed to by all parties, which sets out in greater or lesser detail the remedy selected and the allocation of liability. There are incentives and disincentives for both the government (EPA) and private parties to avoid litigation. EPA has only a certain amount of congressionally-appropriated enforcement funding, and the Superfund monies are likewise limited. EPA does not have enough personnel to oversee the work of government-hired clean-up contractors at every NPL site. It is preferable for the EPA to shift the costs of CERCLA compliance to the PRPs, and to have responsible parties (and their contractors) do the clean-up work, after these parties have conceded their liability in a settlement. It is in that spirit that § 122(a) encourages settlements that are in the public interest and consistent with the NCP.

For their part, PRPs do not want to face the prospect of extended § 107 litigation or preemptory § 106 orders. Like EPA, private parties wish to reduce their costs, and PRPs who do not settle may be saddled with tens of millions of dollars in litigation expenses and liability costs. CERCLA adds a further, critical incentive to settlement: PRPs who settle are protected against additional, future liability, and they may seek contribution against non-settling PRPs. § 113(f)(2); *United States v. Colorado & Eastern Railroad Co.*, 50 F.3d 1530 (10th Cir. 1995); *In re Tutu Water Wells CERCLA Litigation*, 326 F.3d 201 (3d Cir. 2003) (upholding approval of consent decree over objections of non-settling parties); *City of Rialto v. West Coast Loading Corp.*, 581 F.3d 865 (9th Cir. 2009) (holding operator lacked standing to challenge validity of administrative orders issued against third parties). Moreover, since settling PRPs are themselves free of further contribution responsibility, if the settlement does not recover a percentage of the total clean-up cost attributable to the settling PRPs, those PRPs who did not settle will eventually have to pay more than their fair share of the cost.

The road to settlement often begins when the EPA determines that a site is contaminated with hazardous substances. The next step is to collect data on possible levels and sources of the contamination and to try to identify the individuals or companies who are PRPs. EPA then estimates the cost of remediating the site, and puts together an initial list of PRPs, together with an assessment of their financial wherewithal. CERCLA provides EPA with two sources of authority for collecting pertinent information: section 104(e) permits the EPA to seek information about all environmental matters, as well as about "the ability of a person to pay for or perform a clean-up," and section 122(e)(3)(B) gives EPA the power to issue subpoenas in order to implement the settlement provisions of § 122. Indeed, it is often the receipt of a "general notice" or "104(e) letter" that first notifies a PRP of its impending liability. The letter tells the recipients about the site, lists the other PRPs that have been identified, and warns of the potential liability for response costs. It states that EPA prefers to negotiate with all the PRPs as a single entity, so the letter also asks them to form a steering committee, which can begin settlement discussions on behalf of the entire group of PRPs. A number of actions may follow:

- The PRPs create subgroups in order to facilitate negotiations with EPA. There are typically two types at a major site—one or a few "major parties" who contributed most of the hazardous waste and many "de minimis parties" who contributed only a small volume.

- EPA may try to encourage settlement by preparing a "nonbinding preliminary allocation of responsibility" (NBAR) which offers an estimate of the relative liability of each PRP. § 122(e)(3).

- The EPA may already have incurred response costs with respect to the site, in which case it may use the threat of future § 107 liability to encourage a settlement. EPA can have the PRPs repay the Superfund according to their financial ability to pay. *United States v. Bay Area Battery*, 895 F.Supp. 1524 (N.D. Fla. 1995).

- EPA may employ the "special notice" procedures found in § 122(e), which permit PRPs to fast track the settlement process by making a proposal within 60 days to perform or finance a government clean-up. During this negotiation-settlement time period, a moratorium is imposed both on EPA response actions under § 104(a) and on unilateral administrative orders under § 106.

- A PRP, or a sub-group of PRPs, may decide not to settle (typically because they believe that the proposed settlement imposes a disproportionate burden). When this happens, the non-settlors face lawsuits both from the EPA (§ 107 liability) and the settling PRPs (§ 113 contribution). Lawsuits filed by non-settlors challenging the procedural and substantive components of the settlement inevitably fail. *See, e.g., United States v. Cannons Engineering Corp.*, 899 F.2d 79 (1st Cir. 1990).

POST–LITIGATION SETTLEMENT

Settlement can take place *after* litigation, sometimes even after settlement and litigation. Take the case of the Stringfellow Superfund site in California. The Stringfellow Acid Pits industrial waste facility is where 35 million gallons of hazardous substances were dumped into unlined ponds before 1972. It was the first location in California to be identified as a CERCLA Superfund site.

The property was first subject to a cleanup pursuant to a 1992 consent decree, under which the approximately 20 private generators of industrial waste agreed to remediate the site. Since it was a superfund site, the United States also incurred cleanup costs. The

PRPs have spent $90 million there, while the United States has incurred $80 million in costs. In 1993, a federal court found California liable as well for the cleanup at Stringfellow, because of its negligence in investigating, choosing, and designing the facility. In 1998, the federal court found the United States and California to be liable, along with the 20 private defendants. This 1998 order held that California was subject to counterclaims under CERCLA § 107(a) for cost recovery, and under § 113 for contribution.

In early 1999, after the consent decree and all this extensive litigation, it was announced that there was a proposed settlement between California and some 17 private PRPs that would finally end litigation over the cleanup of Stringfellow. The settlement has two conditions precedent to its execution: (1) the United States must agree to forbear from seeking to execute on a prior judgment regarding its past costs; and (2) California must secure sufficient monies from its insurance carriers to fulfill its financial obligations under CERCLA. After hundreds of millions of dollars spent on cleaning up the site, and after exhaustive CERCLA litigation, a settlement might be at hand that would end the uncertainty and adversarial relationship between the parties.

a. MAJOR PARTY SETTLEMENTS AND CONSENT DECREES

Before EPA can begin negotiations with the major contributors to a site, it first must cull those that had only a *de minimis* role. For those parties, CERCLA encourages specialized and flexible *"de minimis* settlements" under § 122(g). EPA then engages in settlement negotiations with the major parties, in which the ultimate goal is for all of them to sign a consent decree embodying the proposed settlement terms. For those who choose to opt out of a settlement/consent decree, the alternative is to face an EPA unilateral order or an EPA-lead clean-up. Moreover, non-settlors ("recalcitrants") are also subject to contribution claims by settling PRPs. *State of New York v. Solvent Chemical Co.*, 984 F.Supp. 160, 167 (W.D. N.Y. 1997), but the non-settlors do have standing to challenge the consent decree. *City of Bangor v. Citizens Commc'n Co.,* 532 F.3d 70 (1st Cir. 2008). The proposed consent judgment is filed with the appropriate federal district court, where if approved, it is entered as a final judgment. § 122(d)(1).

The settling PRPs typically pay for and/or perform the RI/FS and all remaining remedial activities at the site. Most important, they agree to an allocation of responsibility among themselves. EPA or a professional facilitator may act as a mediator in order to achieve some consensus, often using the NBAR as a starting point. The usual measure of apportioning liability is according to harm, *United States v. Cannons Engineering Corp.*, 899 F.2d 79, 87 (1st Cir. 1990), which is itself often measured primarily by the volume of waste attributable to each PRP. *United States v. Davis*, 11 F.Supp.2d 183, 190 (D.R.I. 1998); *United States v. Union Elec. Co.*, 934 F.Supp. 324, 329–30 (E.D.M. 1996) (liability should be based on volume rather than toxicity), *aff'd*, 132 F.3d 422 (8th Cir. 1997); *City of Detroit v. Simon*, 247 F.3d 619 (6th Cir. 2001) (determining PRP responsible for future costs only to the extent necessary to reach industrial cleanup levels). If the apportionment of liability seems substantively unfair, a reviewing court will reject a proposed consent decree. *United States v. Allied Signal, Inc.*, 62 F. Supp. 2d 713 (N.D.N.Y. 1999) (proposed consent decree unfair where municipalities were responsible for a majority of waste at site, but their liability would be less than cost of capping one acre of 74 acre site); *United States v. Davis,* 261 F.3d 1 (1st Cir. 2001) (upholding allocation of PRPs' liability because it was rationally and evenhandedly applied).

When the PRPs and EPA reach agreement CERCLA rewards them with several benefits. EPA signs a "covenant not to sue" settling PRPs for future liability, § 122(f)(1), though it is subject to a "reopener" for conditions unknown at the time of remediation completion or that endanger human health or the environment. § 122(f)(6). EPA may provide contribution protection to settling PRPs, largely immunizing them from contribution actions filed by non-settling PRPs. §§ 113(f)(2) & 122(h)(4). Another CERCLA provision, § 122(b)(1), permits EPA to agree to pay from the Superfund all remediation costs attributable to "orphan shares," that is, hazardous substances dumped on the site by bankrupt or unknown parties. Otherwise, the settling parties have to pay their pro rata percentage of the clean-up costs of the orphan share.

THE PERIL OF NON–SETTLORS

CERCLA intends that non-settlors have no contribution rights against settlors regarding matters addressed in the settlement. When the government reaches a settlement, it does not bear the risk that it settled for too little with one party, because under the Uniform Contribution Among Tortfeasors Act (UCATA), it may still pursue the non-settling parties for the remainder. *United States v. Cannons Engineering Corp.*, 899 F.2d 79, 92 (1st Cir. 1990) (when a party settles with the government, the non-settling party's liability is reduced only by the amount of the settlements); *State of New York v. Solvent Chemical Co., Inc.*, 984 F.Supp. 160, 168 (W.D. N.Y. 1997).

If a settlor brings a contribution action against non-settlors, it may do so, and the claim would be governed not by the UCATA, but by the Uniform Comparative Fault Act, which reduces a non-settlor's liability by the amount of the settlor's equitable share of the obligation, as determined by a trial on liability. *United States v. Gen Corp.*, 935 F.Supp. 928, 932–35 (N.D. Ohio 1996); *United States v. SCA Services of Indiana*, 827 F.Supp. 526, 533–36 (N.D. Ind. 1993). *See* Christopher Man, *The Constitutional Rights of Nonsettling Potentially Responsible Parties in the Allocation of CERCLA Liability*, 27 ENVTL. L. 375 (1997). Moreover,

> most courts have held that non-settlors should not be entitled to intervene when EPA and the settling parties seek to have a court approve the consent decree. *See, e.g., United States v. ABC Industries,* 153 F.R.D. 603, 608 (W.D. Mich. 1993); *Arizona v. Motorola, Inc.,* 139 F.R.D. 141, 146–47 (D. Ariz. 1991). *Contra United States v. Aerojet General Corp.,* 606 F.3d 1142 (9th Cir. 2010); *United States v. AlbertInv. Co., Inc.,* 585 F.3d 1386 (10th Cir. 2009) (allowing intervention of non-settling railroad company to protect its right to contribution); *United States v. Union Elec. Co.,* 64 F.3d 1152, 1166–67 (8th Cir. 1995) (nonsettlors have protectable interest under § 113(i) in ensuring that their contribution claim is not extinguished). *See* J.F. Mahoney, *Allowing Intervention by Non–Settling PRPs: Not the "Environmentally Correct" Decision, but One that is Unavoidable,* 14 Pace Envtl. L. Rev. 733 (1997).

b. *DE MINIMIS* SETTLEMENTS

Even before the EPA attempts to negotiate with major parties, it seeks to reach agreement with "de minimis" PRPs, those whose contribution to the site is minimal and for whom joint and several liability would be least fair. Section 122(g) urges the EPA to settle promptly with generators whose actions have produced small amounts of hazardous substances at the site.[80] Although the statute speaks of minimal contribution both with respect to quantity and toxicity, § 122(g)(1)(13), the courts have generally permitted volume to be the sole determinant. *United States v. Cannons Engineering Corp.,* 899 F.2d 79, 88 (1st Cir. 1990); *United States v. Wallace,* 893 F.Supp. 627, 633 (N.D. Tex. 1995). The rule-of-thumb is that any PRP who contributed less than 1% of total volume is a de minimis party.

There are several advantages to a de minimis settlement. As with major party settlements, de minimis settlements provide settling parties with government covenants not to sue, § 122(f) and (g)(2), and contribution protection from potential suits by other PRPs. §§ 113(f)(2) and 122(g)(4) and (h)(4). Unlike major party settlements, de minimis settlements do *not* contain "reopeners" allowing EPA to pursue settlors if conditions are discovered that were unknown at the time of settlement,[81] giving them true finality to the matter. De minimis settlements also reduce transaction costs, both for the government and the PRP, because such settlements occur relatively early in the negotiation process and do not need to be entered as a consent decree. In the 1990s, the EPA has reached de minimis settlements with over 10,000 parties.

---

80. Section 122(g)(1)(B) also authorizes EPA to enter into de minimis settlements with the owners of a contaminated site if the owners are not responsible in any way for the presence of hazardous wastes there.

81. Reopeners are still available if a PRP should not have been classified as a de minimis party, or if there are serious cost overruns in the clean-up.

Since the federal government largely loses its ability to revisit de minimis settlements, it requires that three conditions be met before it agrees to the settlement. First, it demands that PRPs provide it with all information relevant to the site, as well as an assurance that they will be cooperative with respect to all response activities at the site, whether carried out by EPA or the PRPs. Second, EPA will require that the settlors pay an amount equal to their share of the clean-up costs. Third, in exchange for the ability to settle without the normal reopeners, the EPA demands a "premium" payment in addition to the pro rata share. The premium, which ranges from 60% to 100% of actual costs, is intended to compensate EPA for the risks associated with possible cost overruns for a not-yet-selected remedy, EPA's potential inability to recover response costs from the Superfund or other responsible parties, and uncertainties about the nature of future response actions.

For PRPs whose contribution to a site is tiny, EPA has decided that it is appropriate to offer "de micromis" settlements so as to resolve their liability with virtually no transaction costs. To qualify for this special type of de minimis settlement, the parties must be responsible for an extraordinarily small percentage of the waste at a site (0.001% by volume). The de micromis settlement is similar to a de minimis settlement except that EPA does not demand a "premium" payment. A de micromis PRP must pay only its percentage share of the clean-up cost, and then it is immunized from both EPA and other PRP litigation. *Kalamazoo River Study Group v. Rockwell Int'l Corp.*, 274 F.3d 1043 (6th Cir. 2001) (finding manufacturer responsible for less than one-tenth of one percent of PCBs in river not accountable for response costs).

3.   CASE STUDY: LEADVILLE

About 100 miles southwest of Denver lies the city of Leadville. Unfortunately, the city has gained fame for less than ideal reasons. Since 1860, mining has been a major industry in the small Colorado town. In fact, Leadville is where some millionaires got their start. Mining in Leadville resulted in a number of family fortunes, including those of Marshall Field, Charles Dow, James Brown (husband of an unsinkable Molly) and Solomon Guggenheim. Both state and congressional legislatures encouraged the mining of the area through direct funding and legislative promotion. Leadville produced and supported mineral processing of lead, copper, silver, gold, and zinc.

Figure 6.5–Miner's cabin in the California Gulch, 1980's[82]

Leadville mining was concentrated in the California Gulch area, drained by the Arkansas River. Mine tailings surrounded California Gulch. When the California Gulch Mines shut down in the latter part of the 19th Century, the tailings, along with their high concentrations of heavy metals, remained in place. When the abandoned mines drained excess waters, primarily through the Yak Tunnel in California Gulch, the already polluted waters picked up more contaminants from the tailings piles, and spread toxic substances to the Arkansas River.

---

82. Source: Colorado Historical Society.

Figure 6.6–California Gulch Area[83]

Trouble began in 1982, when dead fish began floating down the Arkansas River. The death of fish was linked to the mines and the mine waters upstream from Leadville. The mines had shut down after 120 years of operation, but had left behind waste, mine tailings and slag that had polluted the surface waters.

Figure 6.7–Mine Tailings Site

The State of Colorado decided to conduct a blood lead level study for the Leadville area. In order to test the entire town, the state sent out what was labeled the "brown envelope letter." This letter requested that each resident allow the EPA to come to the property and test their soil and water; the letter also stated that failure to permit this sampling would result in the EPA investigating the recipient as a PRP. At this point, local outrage against the EPA began.

The investigations found high concentrations of lead, iron, manganese, cadmium, and zinc in the waters. Concern had mounted regarding immediate cleanup as a result of studies demonstrating that varied levels of lead in the human blood stream could be linked to learning deficits and lead poisoning. One area of particular concern was that the mining slag had been used in the asphalt to pave virtually all of the town's roads. The lead had been spread in thin layers on the streets of Leadville.

About a year later, in 1983, the Colorado Department of Public Health and Environment (CDPHE) initiated an action under CERCLA for "natural

83.   Source: Colorado Historical Society.

resources damage." The PRP Defendants in the case, mining and natural resources companies, denied the claims and filed a counterclaim against the United States and other third parties. CDPHE amended its complaint to include claims for reimbursement of costs already incurred, and those likely to be incurred in response to the release or threat of release of hazardous substances at the Yak Tunnel, California Gulch and for portions of the Arkansas River. CDPHE alleged strict liability and common law negligence claims against various PRPs for cleanup costs and other damages resulting from the contamination discharges.

The EPA joined with the CDPHE in concluding that a cleanup was mandated because of the health risks associated with the polluted runoff and lead deposits throughout Leadville. But the local community resisted. It was an unexpected reaction. Normally, the EPA is summoned by the community to clean up a site, and is praised for doing so. In Leadville, the EPA was hated. The community felt that the lead in the environment was not a problem. After all, many long time residents had lived to a ripe old age in Leadville without any health problems or complications from the lead. The community did not seem to care when the spring thaw came, and the flow of the Arkansas River was a rusty orange-red color instead of the bluish clear it should be. The runoff was being tainted by the iron and lead mine tailings, resulting in the red coloring, but the community was more concerned about federal intermeddling in local matters.

Figure 6.8–Mine Tailings Around Leadville

In 1986, the EPA became the lead agency, when the federal and state proceedings were combined. The EPA prepared to bring a § 107 action against all responsible parties. There were a total of 13 parties listed as defendants in the EPA's August 6, 1986 action. Of them, eight were either orphan shares or resulted in de minimis settlements. The remaining parties were: Resurrection Mining Co.; Asarco; Res–Asarco; Denver & Rio Grande Western Railroad (D & RG); and Hecla Mining Co.

In the beginning, the parties did not cooperate. Each PRP turned the blame onto the others. Each claimed the cause was from a different source, not under the control of that PRP. Some said it was the tailings, others alleged it was the slag, and others even blamed the smelters.

Figure 6.9–American Mining & Smelting Co.[84]

When trial time began approaching rapidly, something happened. The PRPs began working together and themes of "settlement" began to be heard. It is thought that this change of heart was a result of a leak about the strength of the case the EPA had against the defendants. The prevailing wisdom among the PRPs was that the evidence was so strong, that settlement was preferred over an EPA cleanup followed by certain § 107 liability. Prior to trial, consent decrees were reached with D & RG, Hecla, Resurrection, and Asarco. These decrees were somewhat unique because the Record of Decision (ROD), guiding cleanup and apportionment process, had yet to be completed.

The final decree of May 17, 1994 manifests a major party settlement resolving the cleanup responsibilities of Resurrection, Asarco, Res–Asarco, and the United States. The site is in excess of 16 square miles. Of this area, some will be cleaned up by some of the PRPs, another portion will be remediated by the EPA, and the remaining cleanup will be enforced through complaints against specific PRPs.

The EPA determined that each individual defendant's work area would be defined to correspond with the impacts attributable to each defendant's smelting, milling, or mining-related activities at the site. EPA began by settling with Asarco, Resurrection, and Res–Asarco. The PRPs are committed to perform cleanup activities in their work areas, but are released from

---

84. Source: Leadville: Colorado's Magic City, Blair.

liability in other areas of the site in which they may have had some contribution. However, the liability they may have avoided by their settlement is off-set by their agreeing to accept responsibility for orphan shares. Because they had minimal involvement in the contamination of the site, Hecla and D & RG will have to satisfy more limited responsibilities, and are protected from contribution claims by other PRPs.

Despite the settlement, there remained mixed community feelings towards the EPA. New residents of Leadville were concerned for the health of their children and wanted both the cleanup and continued investigations. Locals and long time residents believed the EPA was over-reacting; they were not worried about the lead and assumed that there was no risk. They were also outraged because they felt the studies conducted by the EPA never proved that lead in its natural state (not in paint, water or exhausts) was harmful when ingested. Blood levels seemed to confirm their suspicions. Children's blood levels in Leadville were at acceptable levels, and were even better than the levels at other mining towns.

Thirteen years after the final decree with the major PRPS, the cleanup effort was still not complete, due in large part to ongoing battles over agreements to continue monitoring and operating expensive cleanup efforts. Steve Lipsher, *"Leadville Cleanup Hits Snags,"* The Denver Post, Oct. 9, 2007, at 23. Finally, in 2008, 25 years after the EPA filed suit against the PRPs, a $138.5 million settlement was reached with the mining companies for cleanup and damages at the California Gulch Superfund site. The money will be used by Colorado for remediation, restoration and improvement projects at the site, and will allow the United States to recover virtually all of its past response costs for the period of time prior to the settlement's allocation of liability at the site. Mark Jaffe, *"Leadville Superfund Site Settlement Reached,"* The Denver Post, July 2, 2008, at 2B.

4.   Case Study: Lowry Landfill

The Lowry Landfill is a sprawling 500–acre site located 15 miles from downtown Denver. It once served as part of the Lowry Bombing Range during World War II for armament and bombing training, but its place in American history may come from its notoriety as one of the nation's largest Superfund sites. What follows is a case study on the ensuing CERCLA contribution actions.

The city and county of Denver operated the landfill from 1965 to 1980, until it turned management over to a private contractor. The landfill took in household and municipal solid waste and industrial liquid waste, among them industrial-strength degreasers, paint, pesticides, hospital and veterinary waste, metal-plating waste, petroleum products, and sewage sludge.

Over several decades, landfill operators poured liquid wastes in 78 unlined clay soil trenches spanning 200 acres. Into these trenches, they piled 25 to 60 feet of municipal solid wastes such as soil, tires, and household refuse to absorb the liquid wastes, much of it toxic. This method of mixing liquid and solid wastes was called "co-disposal" and was common practice at the time. In total, the landfill accepted an estimated 138 million gallons of industrial wastes, some of which were sprayed directly onto the soil.

The 1970s revealed the environmental mess caused by the landfill's disposal methods. Local residents reported odors and fires erupting in the landfill and complained about disposal practices, although the landfill complied with then-existing environmental regulations. The complaints prompted the EPA and the Colorado Department of Public Health and Environment (CDPHE) to investigate the landfill's groundwater, surface water, sediment, air quality, and soil gas. The EPA declared the landfill a Superfund site in 1983 and placed it on the National Priorities List (NPL). Investigations revealed that hazardous waste had seeped into the soil and groundwater. Gases from buried waste also bubbled to the surface and contaminated air spaces in subsurface soil.

Lowry Landfill's designation as a Superfund site started a chain of lawsuits and finger-pointing. Beginning in the mid-1980s, the EPA sent out notices to more than 600 PRPs—arrangers, transporters, and generators who had contributed to landfill waste. The EPA sought to recover costs to study the contamination and remediate the site, along with other environmental damages at the facility. Estimates for cleanup costs ranged from $50 million to $4.5 billion.

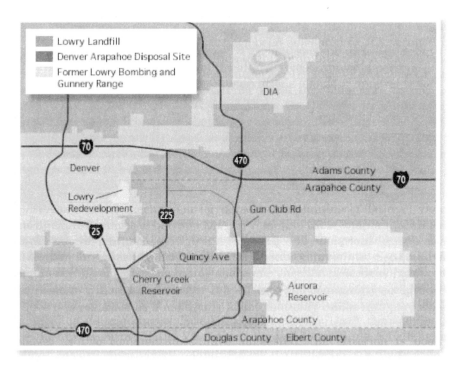

The PRPs constituted a diverse lot. They ranged from the historic Lowenstein Theater, which sent a mere 3 gallons of asbestos to the landfill, to the Adolph Coors Company, which generated almost 20 million gallons of sludge, solvents, and pesticides. In between were such PRPs as the cities of Littleton and Englewood, which operated a joint wastewater treatment plant and disposed of 2.9 million gallons of low toxicity, metal-laden, domestic sewage sludge (i.e., biodegradable "biosolids"), suitable for beneficial, agricultural reuse. Under the EPA's "mixture rule," the cities' sludge qualified as CERCLA hazardous waste—even though only one-quarter of one percent contained heavy metals—as the non-segregable metals were mixed in with the cities' waste stream. For Littleton and Englewood, the irony was that the EPA and CDPHE had previously approved their sludge disposal at Lowry, and the EPA had given the cities an award for beneficial reuse of its sludge. Under CERCLA's joint and several liability scheme, the Lowenstein Theater and the cities of Littleton and Englewood were just as liable for cleanup costs as the Adolph Coors Company and other major waste generators.

With such a large and diverse group of PRPs, the EPA had to establish a way to apportion the cleanup costs. The EPA recommended that the PRPs select steering committees to represent their respective interests. Several were devised to represent industrial PRPs, municipal PRPs, and small generator PRPs.

In 1990, the landfill stopped accepting waste to allow environmental investigators to continue without interference. A four foot thick layer of soil was placed over the main landfill site as part of the containment plan to prevent contamination off-site. The EPA also ordered the 34 major PRPs (in terms of the largest volume waste transporters or generators) to develop a site-wide plan to address the contamination and begin the cleanup phase.

In 1991, Denver sued almost 40 PRPs, including Waste Management of Colorado, Inc., its private contractor, as a current operator, and Chemical Waste Management, Inc., as a transporter in a CERCLA contribution action. Waste Management of Colorado, Inc. and Chemical Waste Management, Inc. later aligned themselves with Denver and settled with 119 *de minimus* contributors and other PRPs, such as the cities of Littleton and Englewood. The settlements resulted in payments in excess of tens of millions of dollars to assist in investigation, cleanup, and long-term monitoring costs, in exchange for certain prophylactic concessions on liability and damages. Many of the settlement agreements at Lowry were sealed, with a continuing confidentiality order governing the details of the settlements.

The ensuing CERCLA contribution action against non-settlers was acrimonious and bitter. *See City and County of Denver v. Adolph Coors Co.,* 829 F.Supp. 340 (D. Colo 1993). Plaintiffs had 40 attorneys working for them, answering more than 7,000 separate discovery requests from 82 counsel of record for the defendants. Waste Management of Colorado, Inc. and Chemical Waste Management, Inc. answered another 1,014 discovery requests on behalf of indemnified settlers. Lawsuits against insurance companies that refused to provide environmental damage coverage to PRPs clogged the court system.

The court actively sought to move the parties towards settlement, in line with CERCLA's twin goals of achieving prompt cleanup of hazardous waste sites and imposing cleanup costs on those responsible for the contamination. The court imposed a detailed case management order, reducing the number of parties to the lawsuit by dismissing all cross and third-party claims without prejudice, streamlining discovery and limiting depositions by the parties. The court also scheduled settlement conferences to facilitate negotiations. By the eve of trial in May of 1993, the parties had reached settlement agreements—16 months since the lawsuit was first filed, and almost ten years after the EPA declared the Lowry Landfill a Superfund site.

In 2005, two bits of good news emerged. First, Denver entered into a consent order with the EPA and agreed to pay $13.9 million to reimburse the federal government for money spent on the Lowry Landfill. The settlement resolved three years of litigation. Second, the EPA reported that initial clean-up at the site was nearly complete. The EPA's second Five-Year Review of the site was completed in February, 2007. While there was much progress in the clean-up, three new issues were identified, including the discovery of nitrate and 1,4-dioxane in surface and groundwater samples.

Chemical from Superfund site in water

The probable carcinogen 1,4-dioxane has been found in groundwater and surface water north of the Lowry Landfill Superfund site, leaving regulators to speculate about its origin and officials working to remove it.

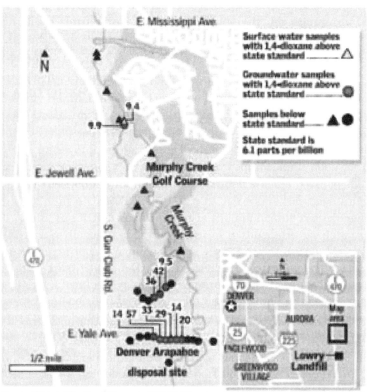

Source: City and County of Denver and Waste Management   The Denver Post

The chemical 1,4-dioxane, used to stabilize industrial solvents, has been shown to cause cancer in lab animals at high concentrations. Jeremy P. Meyer, "Officials Puzzled by How Lowry Toxin Got in Water," THE DENVER POST, January 29, 2007, at 1B. Concentration levels in the wells have ranged from undetectable to 42 parts per billion. The standard for 1,4-dioxane in surface and groundwater is 6.1 parts per billion.

The reason behind the chemical's presence in surface and groundwater is unknown. Federal regulators believe that it is leftover from when treated wastewater was pumped into the ground, rather than being sent to the wastewater treatment facility as it is now. Another theory is that there might be a leak in one of the barriers put in place to contain landfill pollution.

Whatever the reason for the new findings, its important to understand that while there might be successes in various cleanup projects at the site, long-term remediation, including environmental remedy maintenance, will likely continue for more than 30 years.[85]

NOTE ON BROWNFIELDS

"Brownfields," as defined by EPA, are "abandoned, idled, or under used industrial and commercial sites where expansion or redevelopment is complicated by real or perceived environmental contamination that can add cost, time or uncertainty to a redevelopment project." There are an estimated 400,000 contaminated brownfield sites in the United States, that could cost as much as $650 billion to clean up. In part because of fear of CERCLA liability, many contaminated sites within urban areas sit idle and undeveloped, although their location might otherwise make them attractive to investors. Instead, developers go to rural suburban sites ("greenfields") where there has been no contamination and no risk of CERCLA liability. To respond to this unintended side-effect of CERCLA, in January 1995, EPA announced reforms designed to loosen the grip of CERCLA and encourage brownfields' redevelopment.[86]

---

85. Case Study Sources:

1. http://www.epa.gov/region8/superfund/co/lowry/index.html

2. *Compass Ins. Co. v. City of Littleton*, 984 P.2d 606 (Colo. 1999)

3. http://www.epa.gov/region8/superfund/co/lowry/LowryFactSheet16_3_31_04.pdf

4. Daniel E. Muse et. al., *A Municipal Landfill Superfund Response Cost and Contribution Action—The City's Perspective,* 27 UrbLaw 129 (1995)—available on Westlaw

5. *City & County of Denver v. Adolph Coors Co.,* 829 F.Supp. 340 (D. Colo. 1993).

6. http://www.epa.gov/region8/compliance/report05.html

7. http://www.epa.gov/region8/superfund/co/lowry/1035745.pdf

8. http://yosemite.epa.gov/opa/admpress.nsf/20ed1dfa1751192c8525735900400c30/2clc7076d9d4c945852570d900462bdd!OpenDocument

9. http://www.cdphe.state.co.us/hm/rplowry.htm#review

10. http://www.lowry landfillinfo.com/maps/htm

11. Jeremy P. Meyer, "Officials Puzzled by How Lowry Toxin Got in Water," *The Denver Post*, January 29, 2007, at 1B

86. *See generally* William Buzbee, *Brownfields, Environmental Federalism, and Institutional Determinism*, 21 Wm. & Mary Envtl. L. & Policy Rev. 1 (1997); Robert Abrams, *Superfund and the Evaluation of Brownfields*, 21 Wm. & Mary Envtl. & Policy Rev. 265 (1997); Stephen Johnson, *The Brownfields Action Agenda: A Model for Future Federal/State Cooperation in the Quest for Environmental Justice?,* 37 Santa Clara L. Rev. 85 (1996).

The brownfield legislation contains four elements. *See* 42 U.S.C. § 9628 (2002); Pub. L. No. 107–118 (2002). First, the legislation exempts certain small volume contributors and municipal solid waste contributors from CERCLA liability. In addition, it shifts court costs and attorneys fees to a private party if a private party loses a Superfund contribution action against de micromis or municipal solid waste exempt party. Second, it provides legislative authority for brownfield programs including grants up to $200 million per year for assessment and cleanup. Third, and possibly most importantly, it exempts certain contiguous property owners and prospective purchasers from Superfund liability, and clarifies the innocent landholders defense to CERCLA liability. Finally, the legislation supports State and Tribal response programs by preserving the Federal safety net, providing $50 million per year for State and Tribal response programs, and expanding activities available for funding.

Which elements of CERCLA remedy selection and liability are moderated by these elements of brownfields reform? Do they go too far, or not far enough, in addressing the brownfields problem?

5.   PRIVATE COST–RECOVERY ACTIONS

It is the rare situation that a Superfund site involves just one PRP. Usually, multiple parties were involved with the site over a long period of time. In cases where more than one private party has played a role in the site, and there has been a private expenditure of response costs (voluntarily or as a result of some government action), the party who has expended funds will seek to recover some or all of the costs from other PRPs. CERCLA offers two ways for a private party to initiate a cost recovery action. Section 107(a)(4)(B) provides that a PRP shall be liable for "any other necessary costs of response" that have been "incurred by any other person." This provision is similar (but not identical) to governmental cost recovery under § 107(a)(4)(A), discussed above in Subchapter D. Alternatively, CERCLA § 113(f)(1) authorizes "any person" who is liable or potentially liable under § 107—*i.e.,* a PRP—"seek contribution from any other person who is [similarly] liable or potentially liable under [§ 107(a)] during or following a civil action under [§§ 106 or 107(a)]." Private party cost recovery claims do not need prior governmental approval unless EPA has initiated RI/FS activities. *See* § 122(e)(6); *Richland–Lexington Airport Dist. v. Atlas Properties, Inc.,* 901 F.2d 1206 (4th Cir. 1990). These private party v. private party cases now comprise the bulk of CERCLA litigation.

A private party who is not a PRP (and thereby limited to a contribution claim) may bring a cost-recovery action under § 107(a)(4)(B) if four conditions are met:

(1) plaintiff is a "person,"

(2) defendant caused the plaintiff to incur response costs,

(3) plaintiff incurred necessary costs of response,"

(4) The costs were "consistent with the national contingency plan,"

We treat these requirements in order.

a. "ANY OTHER PERSON"

Section 107(a)(4)(B) makes a responsible party liable for response costs incurred by "any other person." Since § 107(a)(4)(A) already provides a cost recovery action for United States, states, and Indian tribes, a party able to bring a private cost recovery action under § 107(a)(4)(B) is anyone other than these three entities. One court has restricted the class of private parties further, by requiring that the plaintiff have a property interest in the contaminated site. *Pennsylvania Urban Development Corp. v. Golen*, 708 F.Supp. 669 (E.D. 1989). This ruling has not been widely followed—can you figure out why not?

b. CAUSATION

As noted previously, under CERCLA a plaintiff need not directly link acts of a PRP to environmental harm. *Dedham Water Co. v. Cumberland Farms Dairy, Inc.*, 889 F.2d 1146, 1154 (1st Cir. 1989). However, CERCLA does require some proof that a defendant caused the plaintiff to incur response costs. *New Jersey Turnpike Authority v. PPG Industries*, 197 F.3d 96, 105 (3d Cir. 1999); *Matter of Chicago, Milwaukee, St. Paul & Pac. R. Co.*, 78 F.3d 285, 289–90 (7th Cir. 1996); *American National Bank and Trust v. Harcos Chem. Inc.*, 997 F.Supp. 994, 1000 (N.D. Ill. 1998). *See also Memphis Zane May Assocs. v. IBC Mfg. Co.*, 952 F.Supp. 541 (W.D. Tenn. 1996).

c. "NECESSARY COSTS OF RESPONSE"

The costs recoverable by a private party are the same as those by a governmental party excepting natural resources damages. *M.R. v. Caribe General Electric Products, Inc.*, 31 F. Supp. 2d 226 (D.P.R. 1998) (costs for providing alternative drinking water as a result of another's pollution are recoverable response costs); *City of Toledo v. Beazer Materials and Services, Inc.*, 923 F.Supp. 1001 (N.D. Ohio 1996) (recoverable response costs included costs of monitoring, assessment, and evaluation of hazardous substances at the site). The question has arisen, however, whether the qualifier "necessary" operates as a real limitation on recoverable costs. Courts have held that it does. The plaintiff must establish that an actual and real threat exists prior to initiating a response action. *Southfund Partners III v. Sears, Roebuck & Co.*, 57 F. Supp. 2d 1369 (N.D. Ga. 1999) (where no costs were needed to make property safe for its current use as an *industrial* site, response costs incurred to remove low level contamination in order to prepare site for *residential* use were not "necessary"). While costs associated with voluntary remediation efforts are recoverable, the plaintiff bears the burden of proving that the voluntary effort was "necessary" at the time it was undertaken. *South Fund Partners III*, *supra* (costs were not "necessary" response costs because plaintiff conducted the remediation to improve the land's value, not to address a threat to health or the environment); *Syms v. Olin Corp.*, 408 F.3d 95 (2d Cir. 2005) (concluding physical maintenance activities, including patching roadways, mowing grass, and plowing snow, were not recoverable costs where landowner could not demonstrate that such maintenance was undertaken to facilitate clean-up).[87] Why impose this additional step on private claims? Is there any practical likelihood that a private party would risk serious money on an unnecessary clean-up? *See G.J. Leasing Co. Inc. v. Union Elec. Co.*, 54 F.3d 379, 386 (7th Cir. 1995).

One other important question has been whether attorney's fees are "necessary costs of response." In *KeyTronic Corp. v. United States*, 511 U.S. 809 (1994), the Supreme Court held that CERCLA did not authorize an award of attorney fees associated with bringing a cost recovery action. Nor were non-litigation fees incurred in negotiating a consent decree with EPA recoverable. The court concluded that such expenses did not constitute necessary costs of response because the activities primarily served to protect the plaintiff's interests regarding its own liability for the clean-up. *See also AM International, Inc. v. Datacard Corp.*, 106 F.3d 1342 (7th Cir. 1997); *Ekotek Site PRP Comm. v. Self*, 1 F. Supp. 2d 1282, 1294–95 (D. Utah 1998). The *KeyTronic* Court carved out a narrow exception for lawyers' work performed in identifying other PRPs. *KeyTronic*, 511 U.S. at 819; *Atlantic Richfield Co. v. American Airlines, Inc.*, 98 F.3d 564, 571 (10th Cir. 1996).

d.   "CONSISTENT WITH THE NATIONAL CONTINGENCY PLAN"

CERCLA makes consistency with the NCP a condition to a private cost recovery action. As we saw above in connection with governmental cost recovery, consistency requires compliance with both procedural rules (*e.g.*, site investigations and public comment opportunities), and substantive requirements (*e.g.*, remedy selection, degree of clean-up). You will also recall that governmental plaintiffs may obtain reimbursement for costs "not inconsistent with" the NCP, § 107(a)(4)(A), while § 107(a)(4)(B) permits private cost recovery only if "consistent with the NCP." The semantic difference between the two sections has been construed to mean that the PRP-defendant bears the burden of showing that the government's costs are "not consistent with" the NCP, while the private party seeking cost recovery from a PRP has the burden of showing that its costs are "consistent with" the NCP. *County Line Investment Co. v. Tinney*, 933 F.2d 1508, 1512 (10th Cir. 1991); *Tanglewood East Homeowners v. Charles–Thomas, Inc.*, 849 F.2d 1568, 1574–75 (5th Cir. 1988).

This burden can be substantial. Before the 1990 NCP, private parties were held to a "strict compliance" standard. *Alcan–Toyo America, Inc. v. Northern Illinois Gas Co.*, 904 F.Supp. 833 (N.D. Ill. 1995) (since the bulk of plaintiff's site investigation costs were incurred prior to the effective date of the 1990 NCP, the question of whether these costs were consistent with the NCP would be governed by the 1985 requirement of strict compliance). With the advent of the revised NCP in 1990, EPA began to require only "substantial compliance" with procedural requirements and a "CERCLA-quality clean-up" under the substantive standards. 40 C.F.R. § 300(c)(3)(I). Accordingly, private parties must decide whether the benefits of a potential cost recovery are worth (1) the cost of undertaking a RI/FS and going

---

87.   The question of whether a response measure is necessary is usually answered at the damages stage of a case. *Cadillac Fairview / California, Inc. v. Dow Chemical Co.*, 840 F.2d 691, 695 (9th Cir. 1988).

through a public comment process,[88] as well as (2) the burden of showing that the remedy selected is the least costly alternative that is still permissible with the NCP. Although "CERCLA-quality clean-up" assumes that private party remedial action will meet the NCP's substantive requirements (*i.e.*, protective of human health, a permanent, cost-effective solution, and one that attains ARARs), the "substantial compliance" term is meant to soften some of the NCP's procedural demands. *See Anschutz Mining Corp. v. NL Ind., Inc.*, 891 F.Supp. 492 (E.D.Mo. 1995); 55 Fed.Reg. at 8793 (March 8, 1990) (EPA demands only "substantial" compliance because it recognizes that to provide a list of rigid requirements might defeat cost recovery for meritorious clean-up actions that experienced a mere technical failure); *but see Young v. United States*, 394 F.3d 858 (10th Cir. 2005) (confirming that plaintiff's response actions were inconsistent with the NCP where they failed to incur expenses for CERCLA-quality cleanup).

6.   Cost–Recovery *vs.* Contribution Actions

The other way for a private party to shift some or all of the costs of a clean-up to other private parties is through a private contribution action. Under § 113(f)(1) a SARA addition, "any person may seek contribution from any other person who is liable or potentially liable under § 107(a) during or following any civil action under § 106 or § 107(a)." As a result, plaintiffs who already are or may be liable for clean-up costs may, instead, demand contribution under § 113. There are many similarities between a private cost recovery action under § 107 and a contribution action under § 113. The substantive elements and the defenses are the same. *Uniroyal Chemical Co., Inc. v. Deltech Corp.*, 160 F.3d 238, 242 (5th Cir. 1998) (elements); *United States v. Taylor*, 909 F.Supp. 355 (M.D. N.C. 1995) (defenses). Regardless of whether a plaintiff proceeds under § 107 or § 113, it may also seek a judicial determination that the defendants are liable in the future for some or all of the clean-up costs; it may obtain this declaration of future liability once it has commenced an investigation at the site, or after it has incurred recoverable response costs. § 113(g)(2). Some courts have even integrated cost recovery and contribution actions; they test the merits of the claim for cost recovery against § 107, and allocate response costs between plaintiff and defendant according to § 113. *See Amoco Oil Co. v. Borden, Inc.*, 889 F.2d 664, 672–73 (5th Cir. 1989).

However, cost recovery and contribution actions are not identical. For several reasons it may be important to establish whether the private party is proceeding under § 107 or § 113. First, under § 107, as we have seen, liability is generally joint and several. By contrast, in actions seeking contribution under § 113, liability is several only; the PRP is liable for its equitable *share* of all response costs. *See Niagara Mohawk Power v. Chevron*, 596 F.3d 112 (2d Cir. 2010); *Kalamazoo River Study Group v. Rockwell Intern.*, 3 F.Supp.2d 799, 805 (W.D.Mich 1998); *United States v. Conservation Chemical Co.*, 619 F.Supp. 162, 229 (W.D. Mo. 1985). Conse-

---

88.   *See Union Pacific Railroad Co. v. Reilly Industries, Inc.*, 981 F.Supp. 1229 (D. Minn. 1997) (failure to provide public comment regarding remedial action is substantial departure from NCP, precluding private cost recovery).

quently, in contribution actions the burden is on the *plaintiff* to establish the defendant's equitable share of response costs. *Adhesives Research, Inc. v. American Inks & Coatings Corp.*, 931 F.Supp. 1231, 1244 n.13 (M.D. Pa. 1996). In addition, the 1986 SARA amendments added a new six-year statute of limitations for § 107(a), but a three-year period for contribution claims. § 113(g)(2)(3). Also, while courts have turned away most non-statutory defenses in cost recovery actions, they are sometimes willing to acknowledge equitable defenses in contribution actions. *See e.g., Shapiro v. Alexanderson*, 741 F.Supp. 472, 478–79 (S.D. N.Y. 1990) (fraudulently obtained indemnification agreement). Thus, PRPs who themselves contributed to the contamination of a Superfund site wanted to seek § 107 cost recovery, as well as § 113 contribution. The following case decided whether this is permissible.

Following Congress's adoption of § 113(f) in 1986, courts began directing all contribution actions involving plaintiffs who were also PRPs to § 113(f), regardless of whether the actions took place *during* or *following* any civil actions under § 106 or § 107(a). This practice continued until 2004, when the United States Supreme Court held in *Cooper Industries v. Aviall Services,* 543 U.S. 157 (2004) that PRPs who voluntarily cleaned up sites no longer had a cause of action in contribution under § 113(f), absent a civil action under § 106 or § 107(a). The majority declined to discuss whether an alternative cause of action existed under § 107(a)(4)(B), or whether there existed an implied right of contribution available to PRPs who were not eligible for contribution actions under § 113(f). *Cooper Industries* created a great deal of unrest in the environmental world first, because it eliminated contribution actions for PRPs who voluntarily incurred cleanup costs under § 113(f), and second, because several court of appeal decisions had already done away with the right of PRPs to sue under § 107.

However, the questions left open by *Cooper Industries* did not remain unanswered for long—three years later, the Supreme Court granted certiorari to review an Eighth Circuit case which had acknowledged two separate theories of cost recovery for PRPs: (1) a direct right of cost recovery under the plain language of § 107(a)(4)(B), or (2) an implied right of contribution arising under § 107. *United States v. Atlantic Research Corp.*, 551 U.S. 128 (2007) thus became the leading case for issues regarding the recovery of clean-up costs under CERCLA.

United States v. Atlantic Research Corp.
551 U.S. 128 (2007)

■ JUSTICE THOMAS delivered the opinion of the Court.

Two provisions of the Comprehensive Environmental Response, Compensation, and Liability Act of 1980 (CERCLA) §§ 107(a) and 113(f)-allow private parties to recover expenses associated with cleaning up contaminated sites. 42 U.S.C. §§ 9607(a), 9613(f). In this case, we must decide a question left open in *Cooper Industries, Inc. v. Aviall Services, Inc.*, 543 U.S. 157 (2004): whether § 107(a) provides so-called potentially responsible parties (PRPs), 42 U.S.C. §§ 9607(a)(1)–(4), with a cause of action to recover costs from other PRPs. We hold that it does.

Courts have frequently grappled with whether and how PRPs may recoup CERCLA-related costs from other PRPs. The questions lie at the intersection of two statutory provisions—CERCLA §§ 107(a) and 113(f). Section 107(a) defines four categories of PRPs, 94 Stat. 2781, 42 U.S.C. §§ 9607(a)(1)–(4), and makes them liable for, among other things:

"(A) all costs of removal or remedial action incurred by the United States Government or a State or an Indian tribe not inconsistent with the national contingency plan; [and]

"(B) any other necessary costs of response incurred by any other person consistent with the national contingency plan." § 9607(a)(4)(A)–(B).

Enacted as part of the Superfund Amendments and Reauthorization Act of 1986 (SARA), 100 Stat. 1613, § 113(f) authorizes one PRP to sue another for contribution in certain circumstances. 42 U.S.C. § 9613(f).

Prior to the advent of § 113(f)'s express contribution right, some courts held that § 107(a)(4)(B) provided a cause of action for a private party to recover voluntarily incurred response costs and to seek contribution after having been sued. *Cooper Industries v. Aviall Services*, 543 U.S. 157 (2004). After SARA's enactment, however, some Courts of Appeals believed it necessary to "direc[t] traffic between" § 107(a) and § 113(f). As a result, many Courts of Appeals held that § 113(f) was the exclusive remedy for PRPs. But as courts prevented PRPs from suing under § 107(a), they expanded § 113(f) to allow PRPs to seek "contribution" even in the absence of a suit under § 106 or § 107(a).

In Cooper Industries, we held that a private party could seek contribution from other liable parties only after having been sued under § 106 or § 107(a). This narrower interpretation of § 113(f) caused several Courts of Appeals to reconsider whether PRPs have rights under § 107(a)(4)(B), an issue we declined to address in *Cooper Industries*. After revisiting the issue, some courts have permitted § 107(a) actions by PRPs. *See Consolidated Edison Co. of N.Y. v. UGI Utilities, Inc.*, 423 F.3d 90 (C.A.2 2005); *Metropolitan Water Reclamation Dist. of Greater Chicago v. North American Galvanizing & Coatings, Inc.*, 473 F.3d 824 (C.A.7 2007). However, at least one court continues to hold that § 113(f) provides the exclusive cause of action available to PRPs. *E.I. DuPont de Nemours & Co. v. United States*, 460 F.3d 515 (C.A.3 2006). Today, we resolve this issue.

In this case, respondent Atlantic Research leased property at the Shumaker Naval Ammunition Depot, a facility operated by the Department of Defense. At the site, Atlantic Research retrofitted rocket motors for petitioner United States. Using a high-pressure water spray, Atlantic Research removed pieces of propellant from the motors. It then burned the propellant pieces. Some of the resultant wastewater and burned fuel contaminated soil and groundwater at the site.

Atlantic Research cleaned the site at its own expense and then sought to recover some of its costs by suing the United States under both § 107(a) and § 113(f). After our decision in *Cooper Industries* foreclosed relief under § 113(f), Atlantic Research amended its complaint to seek relief under § 107(a) and federal common law. The United States moved to dismiss, arguing that § 107(a) does not allow PRPs (such as Atlantic Research) to recover costs. The District Court granted the motion to dismiss.

The Court of Appeals for the Eighth Circuit reversed ... The court reasoned that § 107(a)(4)(B) authorized suit by any person other than the persons permitted to sue under § 107(a)(4)(A). Accordingly, it held that § 107(a)(4)(B) provides a cause of action to Atlantic Research. To prevent perceived conflict between § 107(a)(4)(B) and § 113(f)(1), the Court of Appeals reasoned that PRPs that "have been subject to §§ 106 or 107 enforcement actions are still required to use § 113, thereby ensuring its continued vitality." We granted certiorari, and now affirm.

The parties' dispute centers on what "other person[s]" may sue under § 107(a)(4)(B). The Government argues that "any other person" refers to any person not identified as a PRP in §§ 107(a)(1)–(4). In other words, subparagraph (B) permits suit only by non-PRPs and thus bars Atlantic Research's claim. Atlantic Research counters that subparagraph (B) takes its cue from subparagraph (A), not the earlier paragraph (1)–(4). In accord with the Court of Appeals, Atlantic Research believes that subparagraph (B) provides a cause of action to anyone except the United States, a State, or an Indian tribe—the persons listed in subparagraph (A). We agree with Atlantic Research.

Statutes must "be read as a whole." *King v. St. Vincent's Hospital,* 502 U.S. 215 (1991). Applying that maxim, the language of subparagraph (B) can be understood only with reference to subparagraph (A). The provisions are adjacent and have remarkably similar structures. Each concerns certain costs that have been incurred by certain entities and that bear a specified relationship to the national contingency plan. Bolstering the structural link, the text also denotes a relationship between the two provisions. By using the phrase "other necessary costs," subparagraph (B) refers to and differentiates the relevant costs from those listed in subparagraph (A).

In light of the relationship between the subparagraph, it is natural to read the phrase "any other person" by referring to the immediately preceding subparagraph (A), which permits suit only by the United States, a State, or an Indian tribe. The phrase "any other person" therefore means any person other than those three. See 42 U.S.C. § 9601(21) (defining "person" to include the United States and the various States). Consequently, the plain language of subparagraph (B) authorizes cost-recovery actions by any private party, including PRPs. See Key Tronic, 511 U.S., at 818, 114 S.Ct. 1960 (stating in dictum that § 107 "impliedly authorizes private parties to recover cleanup costs from other PRP[s]" (emphasis added)).

The Government's interpretation makes little textual sense. In subparagraph (B), the phrase "any other necessary costs" and the phrase "any other person" both refer to antecedents—"costs" and "person[s]"—located in some previous statutory provision. Although "any other necessary costs" clearly references the costs in subparagraph (A), the Government would inexplicably interpret "any other person" to refer not to the persons listed in subparagraph (A) but to the persons listed as PRPs in paragraphs (1)–(4). Nothing in the text of § 107(a)(4)(B) suggests an intent to refer to antecedents located in two different statutory provisions. Reading the statute in the manner suggested by the Government would destroy the symmetry of §§ 107(a)(4)(A) and (B) and render subparagraph (B) internally confusing.

Moreover, the statute defines PRPs so broadly as to sweep in virtually all persons likely to incur cleanup costs. Hence, if PRPs do not qualify as "any other person" for purposes of § 107(a)(4)(B), it is unclear what private party would. The Government posits that § 107(a)(4)(B) authorizes relief for "innocent" private parties—for instance, a landowner whose land has been contaminated by another. But even parties not responsible for contamination may fall within the broad definitions of PRPs in §§ 107(a)(1)–(4). *See* 42 U.S.C. § 9607(a)(1) (listing "the owner and operator of a … facility" as a PRP); *see also United States v. Alcan Aluminum Corp.*, 315 F.3d 179, 184 (C.A.2 2003) ("CERCLA § 9607 is a strict liability statute"). The Government's reading of the text logically precludes all PRPs, innocent or not, from recovering cleanup costs. Accordingly, accepting the Government's interpretation would reduce the number of potential plaintiffs to almost zero, rendering § 107(a)(4)(B) a dead letter.

According to the Government, our interpretation suffers from the same infirmity because it causes the phrase "any other person" to duplicate work done by other text. In the Government's view, the phrase "any other necessary costs" "already precludes governmental entities from recovering under" § 107(a)(4)(B). Even assuming the Government is correct, it does not alter our conclusion. The phrase "any other person" performs a significant function simply by clarifying that subparagraph (B) excludes the persons enumerated in subparagraph (A). In any event, our hesitancy to construe statutes to render language superfluous does not require us to avoid surplusage at all costs. It is appropriate to tolerate a degree of surplusage rather than adopt a textually dubious construction that threatens to render the entire provision a nullity.

The Government also argues that our interpretation will create friction between § 107(a) and § 113(f), the very harm courts of appeals have previously tried to avoid. In particular, the Government maintains that our interpretation, by offering PRPs a choice between § 107(a) and § 113(f), effectively allows PRPs to circumvent § 113(f)'s shorter statute of limitations. *See* 42 U.S.C. §§ 9613(g)(2)–(3). Furthermore, the Government argues, PRPs will eschew equitable apportionment under § 113(f) in favor of joint and several liability under § 107(a). Finally, the Government contends that our interpretation eviscerates the settlement bar set forth in § 113(f)(2).

We have previously recognized that §§ 107(a) and 113(f) provide two "clearly distinct" remedies. *Cooper Industries*, 543 U.S., at 163, n. 3, 125 S.Ct. 577. "CERCLA provide[s] for a right to cost recovery in certain circumstances, § 107(a), and separate rights to contribution in other circumstances, §§ 113(f)(1), 113(f)(3)(B)." Id., at 163, 125 S.Ct. 577 (emphases added). The Government, however, uses the word "contribution" as if it were synonymous with any apportionment of expenses among PRPs. This imprecise usage confuses the complementary yet distinct nature of the rights established in §§ 107(a) and 113(f).

Section 113(f) explicitly grants PRPs a right to contribution. Contribution is defined as the "tortfeasor's right to collect from others responsible for the same tort after the tortfeasor has paid more than his or her proportionate share, the shares being determined as a percentage of fault." BLACK'S LAW DICTIONARY 353 (8th ed.1999). Nothing in § 113(f) suggests that Congress used the term "contribution" in anything other than this traditional sense. The statute authorizes a PRP to seek contribution "during or following" a suit under § 106 or § 107(a). 42 U.S.C. § 9613(f)(1).Thus, § 113(f)(1) permits suit before or after the establishment of common liability. In either case, a PRP's right to contribution under § 113(f)(1) is contingent upon an inequitable distribution of common liability among liable parties.

By contrast, § 107(a) permits recovery of cleanup costs but does not create a right to contribution. A private party may recover under § 107(a) without any establishment of liability to a third party. Moreover, § 107(a) permits a PRP to recover only the costs it has "incurred" in cleaning up a site. 42 U.S.C. § 9607(a)(4)(B). When a party pays to satisfy a settlement agreement or a court judgment, it does not incur its own costs of response. Rather, it reimburses other parties for costs that those parties incurred.

Accordingly, the remedies available in §§ 107(a) and 113(f) complement each other by providing causes of action "to persons in different procedural circumstances." *Consolidated Edison*, 423 F.3d, at 99. Section 113(f)(1) authorizes a contribution action to PRPs with common liability stemming from an action instituted under § 106 or § 107(a). And § 107(a) permits cost recovery (as distinct from contribution) by a private party that has itself incurred cleanup costs. Hence, a PRP that pays money to satisfy a settlement agreement or a court judgment may pursue § 113(f) contribution. But by reimbursing response costs paid by other parties, the PRP has not incurred its own costs of response and therefore cannot recover under § 107(a). As a result, though eligible to seek contribution under § 113(f)(1), the PRP cannot simultaneously seek to recover the same expenses under § 107(a). Thus, at least in the case of reimbursement, the PRP cannot choose the 6-year statute of limitations for cost-recovery actions over the shorter limitations period for § 113(f) contribution claims.

For similar reasons, a PRP could not avoid § 113(f)'s equitable distribution of reimbursement costs among PRPs by instead choosing to impose joint and several liability on another PRP in an action under § 107(a). The choice of remedies simply does not exist. In any event, a defendant PRP in such a § 107(a) suit could blunt any inequitable distribution of costs by filing a § 113(f) counterclaim. Resolution of a § 113(f) counter-claim would necessitate the equitable apportionment of costs among the liable parties, including the PRP that filed the § 107(a) action. 42 U.S.C. § 9613(f)(a) ("In resolving contribution claims, the court may allocate response costs among liable parties using such equitable factors as the court determines are appropriate").

Finally, permitting PRPs to seek recovery under § 107(a) will not eviscerate the settlement bar set forth in § 113(f)(2). That provision prohibits § 113(f) contribution claims against "[a] person who has resolved its liability to the United States or a State in an administrative or judicially approved settlement...." 42 U.S.C. § 9613(f)(2). The settlement bar does not by its terms protect against cost-recovery liability under § 107(a). For several reasons, we doubt this supposed loophole would discourage settlement. First, as stated above, a defendant PRP may trigger equitable apportionment by filing a § 113(f) counterclaim. A district court applying traditional rules of equity would undoubtedly consider any prior settlement as part of the liability calculus. Cf. Restatement (Second) of Torts § 886A(2), p. 337 (1977) ("No tortfeasor can be required to make contribution beyond his own equitable share of the liability"). Second, the settlement bar continues to provide significant protection from contribution suits by PRPs that have inequitably reimbursed the costs incurred by another party. Third, settlement carries the inherent benefit of finally resolving liability as to the United States or a State.

Because the plain terms of § 107(a)(4)(B) allow a PRP to recover costs from other PRPs, the statute provides Atlantic Research with a cause of action. We therefore affirm the judgment of the Court of Appeals. It is so ordered.

NOTES AND QUESTIONS

1.   At issue in *New York v. Solvent Chemical Co., Inc.,* 685 F.Supp.2d 357 (W.D. N.Y. 2010), was a question left open by the Supreme Court in *Atlantic Research*. In *Atlantic Research*, the Court stated "[w]e do not decide whether these compelled costs of response are recoverable under § 113(f), § 107(a) or both." 551 U.S. at 139, n.6. The *Solvent* case involved this very situation, and the District Judge held that under such circumstances costs were recoverable under both provisions. Is this result consistent with *Atlantic Research*?

2.   *Questions Answered.* Following *Cooper Industries* and *Atlantic Research,* it became clear that PRPs who voluntarily cleanup sites have a direct right of cost recovery under § 107(a)(4)(B), even if their liability has not been established in a civil action under § 106 or § 107(a). *United States v. Atlantic Research Corp.,* 551 U.S. 128, 127 S.Ct. 2331, 2338 (2007). What about PRPs who have not *voluntarily* cleaned up a site, but have incurred costs as a result of a judgment or settlement? *Atlantic Research* clarified that such PRPs may sue for contribution under § 113(f), and courts will have the authority to equitably allocate costs in such contribution actions.

3.   *Administrative Orders and Settlement Agreements.* Two factual scenarios not addressed in either *Cooper Industries* or *Atlantic Research* where PRPs may want to recover costs are (1) costs incurred as a result of a government administrative order, and (2) costs incurred as a result of a

settlement agreement. Although not expressly addressed, the Court's analysis suggests that PRPs in the above scenarios may only recover costs through an action under § 107(a)(4)(B). Jeffery M. Gaba's article, *United States v. Atlantic Research: The Supreme Court Almost Gets It Right* both explores the issues that the Court clarified and those it did not address in *Cooper Industries* and *Atlantic Research.*

Jeffrey M. Gaba, United States v. Atlantic Research: The Supreme Court Almost Gets It Right
37 ELR 10810 (2007)

* * *

IV. Clarity and Confusion following *Atlantic Research*

A. *What Is Clear: Voluntary Cleanups and Reimbursement*

A few basic points are clear following *Atlantic Research* and *Cooper Industries.* PRPs who voluntarily cleanup property have a direct right of cost recovery under § 107(a)(4)(B), and they may not sue in contribution under § 113(f). Their § 107 action is subject to the three- or six-year statutes of limitations specified in § 113(g)(2). Although their initial action may be based on joint and several liability, courts may equitably allocate costs if the defendant properly counterclaims under § 113(f)(1).

In contrast, PRPs who have reimbursed the government or other PRPs for previously incurred response costs following either a civil judgment or government settlement may sue for contribution under § 113(f)... In a § 113(f) contribution action, the court will have the authority to equitably allocate costs.

* * *

C. *What Is Wrong: Contribution Protection*

The most troubling part of the Court's analysis in *Atlantic Research* was its cavalier treatment of "contribution protection" As noted, Congress provided for contribution protection under § 113(f)(2) to encourage settlement by limiting the liability of settling parties. Prior to *Cooper Industries,* one reason that courts had limited PRPs to an action for contribution was to preserve this incentive; if PRPs can only sue for contribution, then "contribution protection" protects settling PRPs from *all* CERCLA claims by nonsettling PRPs. *See e.g. Sun Co., Inc. (R & M) v. Browning–Ferris, Inc.,* 124 F.3d 1187 (10th Cir. 1997); *In re Reading Co.,* 115 F.3d 1111 (3d Cir. 1997). With the resurrection of a distinct right of cost recovery in § 107(a)(4)(B), *Atlantic Research* also resurrected the issue of whether contribution protection would also bar § 107 claims by nonsettling parties.

In *Atlantic Research,* however, the Supreme Court, with virtually no analysis, indicated that the contribution protection under § 113(f)(2) would not preclude an action for cost recovery under § 107(a). The Court's entire treatment of this issue was its observation that § 113(f)(2) "does not by its terms protect against cost recovery liability under section 107"; it characterizes this as "supposed loophole." Although the Court "doubts" that its conclusion will "eviscerate" settlement incentives, the Court clearly underestimates the consequences of the loss of contribution protection.

The Court indicated that trial courts will "undoubtedly" take the settlement into account in allocating liability in any § 107 action. The Court may not have doubts, but in a trial in which parties are allowed to present evidence relating to equitable allocation, it is far from certain that a settling PRP can be assured that it will not be required to pay more than the amount specified in the government settlement. Settlement will thus not buy the certainty as to the settling party's liability than previously provided by contribution protection. Even if trial courts will generally limit liability based on past settlement agreements, there is another significant consequence of the loss of contribution protection. It is one thing to have a defense to liability through "contribution protection" and thus be able to avoid litigation through a motion for summary judgment. It is quite another to be subject to liability under § 107 and therefore be required to proceed through trial in the hopes of a final equitable allocation by the court.

This problem need not arise. In the years following the adoption of § 113(f)(2), a number of courts extended contribution protection to bar nonsettling PRPs from asserting a variety of claims against settling parties. *See, e.g., City and County of Denver v. Adolph Coors Co.,* 829 F. Supp 340 (D. Colo. 1993) (settlement bars "response costs" claim as well as claim for contribution.); *Dravo Corp. v. Zuber,* 804 F. Supp. 1182 (D. Neb. 1992) (contribution protection provided to de minimus party settlements under § 122(g)(5) bars "independent response cost claim" cost recovery by nonsettling party for costs incurred in response to administrative order.) *See also United States v. Cannons Eng'g Corp.,* 899 F.2d 79, 92 (1st Cir. 1990) (section 113(f)(2) also bars claims for indemnification by nonsettling parties). One court, addressing the argument that contribution protection should not bar a claim for "independent cost recovery," stated, the "words of the contribution bar such claims no matter what they are called." *Dravo Corp. v. Zuber,* F. Supp. At 1189.

...The Court, through its narrow "traditional" characterization of contribution, has made it more difficult to extend contribution protection to § 107 claims, but it is not a great stretch to say both that a § 107 cost recovery claim has sufficient characteristics of contribution to justify its bar under § 113(f)(2). *See e.g., United States v. ASARCO, Inc.,* 814 F. Supp. 951 (D. Colo. 1993); *Transtech Indus., Inc. v. A & Z Septic Clean,* 798 F. Supp. 1079 (D.N.J. 1992). In fact, the Court specifically stated that it did not reach the question of whether PRPs had an "implied right of contribution" under § 107. *Atlantic Research, 127 S. Ct. at 2339 n.8.* If such an implied right of contribution were found to exist, it would be no great stretch to conclude that the contribution bar precluded a § 107 contribution claim. The problem, of course, is the Court's identification of an express right of cost recovery under § 107 independent of any such implied right. Perhaps, the Court's preservation of the possibility of an implied right contribution is enough of an opening for future courts to conclude that contribution protection also bars § 107 claims.

Whatever the rationale, extension of contribution protection to PRP claims under § 107 would complete the return to those preexisting, happy days of a stable understanding of CERCLA liability.

4. At issue in *New York v. Solvent Chemical Co., Inc.,* No. 83–CV–1401–JTC, 2010 WL 376328 (W.D. N.Y. 2010) was one of the question left open by the Supreme Court in *Atlantic Research*, specifically, whether a PRP may sustain expenses pursuant to a consent decree following a suit under CERCLA §§ 106 or 107(a) such that the party does not incur costs voluntarily, but also does not reimburse the costs of another party. Regarding this issue, the Supreme Court stated "[w]e do not decide whether these compelled costs of response are recoverable under § 113(f), § 107(a) or both." 551 U.S. at 139, n.6. The *Solvent* case involved this very situation, and the District Judge held that under such circumstances costs were recoverable under both provisions. Subsequently, the Third Circuit clarified the "blurry relationship" between § 113(f) and § 107(a). *Agere Systems v. Advanced Environmental Tech. Corp.,* 602 F.3d 204, 218 (3d Cir. 2010). In *Agere* the court barred private claims under § 107(a) where the private plaintiff would otherwise be liable under CERCLA, but, by virtue of contribution protection, would be immune from a counterclaim under § 113(f). Which holding is most consistent with *Atlantic Research*?

7.   Apportionment of Liability

CERCLA § 113(f)(1) provides only very general direction on the crucial issue of apportioning costs among PRPs: "In resolving contribution claims, the court may allocate response costs among liable parties using such equitable factors as the court determines are appropriate." This language gives courts extremely broad latitude in adopting factors, weighting them, and balancing them among PRPs. *See, e.g., Kerr–McGee Chemical Corp. v. Lefton Iron & Metal Co.,* 14 F.3d 321 (7th Cir. 1994). Nevertheless, there are several recognized methods available to courts.

The commentary to The Restatement (Second) of Torts § 886A suggests a "pro rata" approach in actions for contribution tortfeasors. Under this methodology, it is easy to calculate a PRP's pro rata share in a CERCLA case: the total clean-up costs are simply divided by the number of present and solvent PRPs found to be jointly and severally liable. The pro rata method has the advantage of ease of calculation, but it has the obvious—and fatal—disadvantage of being inequitable if PRPs have different degrees of responsibility for the status of the site.

Many courts have turned to the so-called "Gore Factors," named after a failed amendment to CERCLA proposed by then-Congressman Al Gore:[89]

- the parties' ability to distinguish their contribution

---

[89]   It is interesting to consider whether it is appropriate to adopt a legal standard from an amendment that did not pass Congress. Why might this be *in*appropriate? Why do you think courts have adapted it?

- the quantity of the hazardous substance

- the toxicity of the hazardous substance

- the degree of involvement in generation, transportation, treatment, storage, or disposal of the hazardous substance

- the degree of care exercised by the parties

- the degree of cooperation by the parties with government officials.

See generally Gould, Inc. v. A & M Battery & Tire Service, 987 F.Supp. 353, 370 (M.D. Pa. 1997); *Control Data Corp. v. S.C.S.C. Corp.*, 53 F.3d 930 (8th Cir. 1995); *Kerr–McGee Chemical Corp. v. Lefton Iron & Metal Co.*, 14 F.3d 321, 326 (7th Cir. 1994). Most courts relying on the Gore factors have concluded that the "volume" and "toxicity" of the material shipped to the site is the most useful basis for making an allocation decision. And as between volume and toxicity, volume is by far the easiest to measure. *Boeing Co. v. Cascade Corp.*, 207 F.3d 1177 (9th Cir. 2000); *Bancamerica Commercial Corp. v. Mosher Steel of Kansas, Inc.*, 100 F.3d 792, 802 (10th Cir. 1996); *In re Bell Petroleum Services, Inc.*, 3 F.3d 889 (5th Cir. 1993); *Kamb v. U.S. Coast Guard*, 869 F.Supp. 793, 799 (N.D. Cal. 1994).

Even the Gore factors, however, are only the starting point for allocation methodologies. Most courts have assumed that § 113(f)(1) permits consideration of "any factor," including "the state of mind of the parties, their economic status, any contracts between them bearing on the subject, any traditional equitable defenses as mitigating factors and any other factors deemed appropriate to balance the equities in the totality of the circumstances." *United States v. Davis*, 31 F. Supp. 2d 45 (D.R.I. 1998); *see, e.g., Akzo Nobel Coatings, Inc. v. Aigner Corp.*, 197 F.3d 302, 305 (7th Cir. 1999) (expense of doing cleanup work better measure than toxicity). When a court uses such equitable factors, it is properly invoking "its moral as well as legal sense." *Id.*; *Friedland v. TIC–The Indus. Co.*, 566 F.3d 1203, 1207 (10th Cir. 2009) ("[P]ermitting a CERCLA contribution-action plaintiff to recoup more than the response costs he paid out of pocket flies in the face of CERCLA's mandate to apportion those costs equitably among liable parties."); *United States v. Shell Oil Co.*, 13 F. Supp. 2d 1018, 1030 (C.D. Cal. 1998).

PROBLEM ORPHAN SHARES

An orphan share describes the share of a responsible party which is insolvent, bankrupt, dissolved, or impossible to find. In the context of a CERCLA private party action under § 113(f) or § 107(a)(4)(B), an orphan share means that a plaintiff will not be able to assign a measure of responsibility to an otherwise responsible party. In theory, there are two ways to allocate orphan shares. First, the traditional tort law rule is that defendants are liable only for their own share. Restatement (Second) of Torts. § 886A. Under this approach, the plaintiff in a private cost recovery action bears the risk of loss. Second, under § 2(d) of the Uniform Comparative Fault Act (UCFA), a court can apportion orphan shares among the economically viable parties. The UCFA approach permits courts to reallocate any orphan shares among all identifiable and solvent PRPs.

Nothing in CERCLA requires either result; nor does CERCLA prohibit a court from allocating orphan shares to all liable parties. *United States v. Kramer*, 953 F.Supp. 592, 598 (D.N.J. 1997). Which approach is better, especially in light of the purposes of CERCLA? *See Browning–Ferris Ind. of Ill. v. Ter Maat*, 13 F.Supp.2d 756, 773 (N.D. Ill. 1998); *City of New York v. Exxon*, 697 F.Supp. 677, 683 n.9 (S.D. N.Y. 1988). If orphan shares are to be apportioned to the PRPs, should it be to both plaintiffs and defendants in a private cost recovery or contribution action, or just to defendants? *Charter Township of Oshtemo v. American Cyanamid Co.*, 898 F.Supp. 506, 509 (W.D. Mich. 1995). And if, as the UCFA provides, orphan shares are to be allocated among *all* viable parties, then how should these shares be apportioned among the PRPs? *Allied Corp. v. ACME Solvent Reclaiming, Inc.*, 771 F.Supp. 219, 223 (N.D. Ill. 1990).

INDEX

References are to Pages